Can dian Immi ation Policy for the 21st Century

Edited by
Charles M. Beach, Alan G. Green
and Jeffrey G. Reitz

 JOHN DEUTSCH INSTITUTE FOR THE STUDY OF
ECONOMIC POLICY, QUEEN'S UNIVERSITY

Published in cooperation with
McGill-Queen's University Press
Montreal & Kingston • London • Ithaca

ISBN: 0-88911-952-X (bound)   ISBN: 0-88911-954-6 (pbk.)
© John Deutsch Institute for the Study of Economic Policy
Queen's University, Kingston, Ontario K7L 3N6
Telephone: (613) 533-2294   FAX: (613) 533-6025
Printed and bound in Canada

National Library of Canada Cataloguing in Publication

Main entry under title:

Canadian immigration policy for the 21st century / edited by
Charles M. Beach, Alan G. Green, Jeffrey G. Reitz.

Includes bibliographical references.
ISBN 0-88911-952-X (bound).--ISBN 0-88911-954-6 (pbk.)

1. Canada–Emigration and immigration–Government policy.
I. Beach, Charles M. II. Green, Alan G., 1932- III. Reitz, Jeffrey G.
IV. John Deutsch Institute for the Study of Economic Policy.

JV7233.C37 2003   325.71   C2003-904884-5

Table of Contents

iii

Section III:
Decentralization of Immigration Policy in Canada

Section IV:
International Labour Mobility and Policy Responses

Section VIII:
Wrap-Up Panel on Broad Labour Market Issues and Future Directions for Canadian Immigration Policy

Contributors

Preface

The papers and commentaries in this volume were originally presented at the John Deutsch Institute conference on "Canadian Immigration Policy for the 21st Century" held at Queen's University on October 18–19, 2002. The conference was organized by Charles Beach and Alan Green, both in the Department of Economics at Queen's, and Elizabeth Ruddick of Citizenship and Immigration Canada. The organizers also invited Jeffrey Reitz at the Munk Centre at the University of Toronto to organize papers for the Social Inclusion sessions of the conference. Funding for the conference came from the John Deutsch Institute, Citizenship and Immigration Canada, and the Western Research Network on Education and Training (whose funding originates from the Social Sciences and Humanities Research Council of Canada). The organizers thank the latter agencies for helping to make the conference possible.

The objective of the conference was to bring together researchers (in both universities and the public sector) and practitioners and policymakers in the immigration area to discuss the major issues on immigration policy in Canada. As noted in the Introduction, there have been substantial changes in the environment within which Canadian immigration operates, there has been an explosion of new research in the area which can inform immigration policy, and there have been a number of recent calls to re-examine the goals and current procedures affecting the immigration process in Canada. It seemed an opportune time to debate these issues. This volume is the product of the discussion from this conference.

The co-editors and organizers benefited from the assistance of a number of people in both the operation of the conference and the production of this volume. We especially wish to thank Sharon Sullivan of the

John Deutsch Institute for her assistance throughout the project, for her excellent job in the planning and managing of the conference, and for her exceptional editorial and development work in producing this volume. Mark Howes of the Queen's School of Policy Studies and Marilyn Banting provided excellent creative and editorial services for the volume. We also gratefully acknowledge the very helpful contributions of a large number of others who contributed to the project by providing advice or assistance and who served as discussants, chairs or manuscript reviewers: Naomi Alboim, Paul Anisef, Michael Baker, Dwayne Benjamin, Julian Betts, Barry Chiswick, Thomas Crossley, Craig Dougherty, George Frempong, David Gray, David Green, Thomas Jensen, Michael McCracken, Daniel Parent, Craig Riddell, Richard Roy, Robert Sweet, Christopher Worswick, and Xuelin Zhang. Finally, the co-editors especially wish to express their thanks to Elizabeth Ruddick for her excellent advice and help in molding the conference to blend researchers and policymakers towards an improved debate on Canada's immigration policy for the 21st century.

Charles M. Beach
Director
John Deutsch Institute

Alan G. Green
Queen's University

Jeffrey G. Reitz
University of Toronto

Introduction

Charles M. Beach, Alan G. Green and Jeffrey G. Reitz

Context of Immigration

This volume is based on a two-day John Deutsch Institute conference on "Canadian Immigration Policy for the 21st Century" organized by Charles Beach, Alan Green and Elizabeth Ruddick. It was held at Queen's University on October 18–19, 2002.

This is the second conference on immigration undertaken by the John Deutsch Institute. The first, also held at Queen's, was in 1988. It was a one-day meeting which was published as a "Policy Forum" under the title *The Role of Immigration in Canada's Future* (October 1988).

The context and environment within which the present conference and the earlier one occurred are very different. The 1988 meeting was set at the time of a rising tide of immigration which had gotten underway in the early 1980s following a decade of low annual levels of inflow. The latter was associated with the poor state of the Canadian economy; that is, severe inflation, high unemployment and slow productivity growth, which, like most of the rest of the world, were linked to changes in energy prices in the post-Organization of Petroleum Exporting Countries (OPEC) world. By 1984, annual immigration levels for this country had declined to approximately 83,000 immigrants — the lowest levels since the early 1960s, also a period of slow growth and high unemployment. In both cases, the government adjusted the total inflow to what it perceived as the "absorptive capacity" of the economy (i.e., any higher levels might well adversely affect the employment opportunities and nominal wages of the Canadian population).

The current conference is set in a very different world. The past decade has witnessed a sharp increase in the levels of immigration. At present, the annual inflow is over 200,000 a year. In fact, between 1981 and 2001, the cumulative inflow has amounted to about 3.6 million new immigrants. At the same time, the rate of natural increase in Canada's population has fallen to historically low levels. As a result of low fertility and high gross immigration rates, immigration now accounts for 60% of total population growth. Within ten years this could rise to 100%. Immigration has become the central dynamic in both population and labour force growth in Canada.

At the same time, federal and provincial governments have been down-sizing their programs (other than health), and the approach of governments has shifted away from direct support programs and towards creating incentives for individual initiative.

Between this and the last conference the government has set an explicit annual targeted inflow of 1% of the population (approximately 300,000 immigrants a year). The adoption of this fixed target policy signalled a shift towards a longer-run view of how admission numbers should be managed. At the same time the selection process has become more focused on attracting young skilled workers to this country. The impacts that these changes have had on the Canadian economy are in the early stages of investigation. Some of this new work is included in this volume.

The external environment has also changed. The post-September 11, 2001 (9/11) world is one concerned with border security and more careful monitoring of inflow of personnel. There is an ongoing shift of immigrants from traditional source countries such as the United Kingdom, the United States, and western Europe towards arrivals from Asia, Latin America, and Africa. And there is increasing international competition for skilled labour for both permanent and short-term employment.

Another major difference between this and the last conference is the way the government relates the level of inflow to short-run economic conditions in Canada. As mentioned above, it had been the practice of the government since the early years of the last century to adjust the inflow to short-run economic conditions — the famous absorptive capacity model. This approach was abandoned in the late 1980s. Since then, the government has set levels independently of short-run economic conditions, essentially ignoring the level of unemployment or the growth rate in setting total levels. This became particularly important in the early 1990s when the country faced high unemployment rates and slow growth, but continued to admit immigrants in the range of 200,000 or more a year. This has created a new set of problems of immigrant adjustment, integration, and fiscal stresses, some of which are addressed in this volume.

Despite the very different context within which these two conferences were set, the range of problems addressed are remarkably similar. The current conference, as in the first, was concerned with the aging of the population, the shortage of skilled workers and the composition of the inflow between economic immigrants and family relatives, plus the ongoing role Canada should play in relieving the plight of refugees. The new topics include questions about the annual levels of immigration; that is, is 1% of the population the optimal level of inflow? Should we be concerned whether over 80% of all arrivals head for just three cities — Toronto, Montreal, and Vancouver? Should we be concerned about the declining diversity in the composition of arrivals? Finally, how has post-9/11, with all its security implications, affected who should and who should not be admitted?

Major Issues Facing Immigration Policy

Several major issues face immigration policy in Canada at the beginning of the twenty-first century. Clearly, they are informed by the environments inside and outside the country, and they are very much interrelated.

First, Canada needs to review the goals and objectives of current immigration policy. As indicated, the environment of immigration to Canada has changed over the last 20 years. Large numbers of immigrants are settling predominantly in the three largest cities in Canada, with about half of the total arrivals living in and around Toronto. The speed and success of labour market integration of more recent immigrants have slipped compared to that of earlier arrival cohorts and compared to immigrants in the United States. Poverty rates among immigrant households within five years of arrival have increased dramatically since 1980 and are related to immigrant origins. Critiques of Canadian immigration policy (e.g., Daniel Stoffman's *Who Gets In: What's Wrong with Canada's Immigration Program — and How to Fix It*, 2002) have received high-profile coverage in the media. A lot is expected of immigration to meet several alternative goals — demographic, economic, social, humanitarian, and security. Indeed, as Alan Green's paper argues, perhaps too much is expected and immigration cannot be viewed as a silver bullet to satisfy all these objectives. It is thus worth having a public debate on the relative priorities we wish to set among these objectives of immigration policy, for these priorities will inform how we target and structure Canadian immigration policy. For example, a shift in emphasis from economic to social objectives for immigration will imply the need for closer cooperation between different levels of government with responsibility for community, education, housing, and social support systems.

Second, immigration policy has to address the issues of setting overall numerical targets and the selection criteria for admitting immigrants. One of the earliest classic studies of immigration in Canada was Mabel Timlin's book entitled *Does Canada Need More People?* (1951) and the debate is still ongoing on what is the appropriate total level of annual immigration and what should it depend upon. A more recent study by the Economic Council of Canada, *Economic and Social Impacts of Immigration* (1991), proposed a long-run target rate of 1% of population (or about 300,000 per year in current figures). How should such long-run targets be formulated and what consultation process should be involved? Also, for a given long-run target, should allowance be made for deviations from targets based on, say, short-run economic conditions and absorptive capacity — at either national or regional levels?

Immigrants arrive under different classes representing different program objectives. The three broad classes are: Family Class immigrants who enter on the basis of family relationships; Independent Class immigrants selected on the basis of a point system that reflects occupational skills, experience and likely adaptability to Canadian society; and Convention Refugee Class immigrants who are admitted on the basis of Canadian laws governing refugee admissions and likely adaptability to the Canadian environment. These are generally called family (reunification) class, economic class, and refugee class immigrants. Major concerns of immigration policy, then, are the *relative* numbers of immigrants to be admitted under these different classes, and the rules and procedures governing each of these admission classes. These do not exist in a vacuum, but are informed by overall goals and priorities, by actual economic success and rate of integration to Canadian society of the different immigrant groups, and by political and regional concerns. Within the point system, there has been considerable interest in the questions of appropriate selection criteria and the relative weights to attach to the specific criteria for economic immigrants such as education, age, occupational skills, knowledge of languages such as English or French, and likelihood of business success. What roles should be given to provinces in reaching such decisions? What rules and procedures should be applied to the selection of temporary immigrants, and who should have input into these decisions? Procedures should also ensure the integrity and security of Canadian borders in a post-9/11 environment. The success of the immigration program owes much to effective management, particularly of selection criteria. A number of the conference papers and discussions refer to these policy issues.

A third set of issues for immigration policy involves analyzing the adjustment process of recent immigrants to Canada and promoting the effective integration of permanent immigrants into the Canadian labour market and society. Good policy needs to be informed by up-to-date evidence and research. The period since the late 1980s has, in fact, seen a remarkable explosion and maturation of research on immigration issues in both Canada and the United States — see, for example, the major sets of studies in Smith and Edmonston (1997) and Borjas (2000) for the United States and the recent set of overviews for Canada in *Canadian Issues* (April 2003). The research is fostered by valuable new datasets and by the setting up of four dedicated research centres and programs focused on immigration related matters (i.e., the Metropolis project). It has also expanded to look at impacts of immigration and recent immigrant experience well beyond the labour market. Journal articles on all aspects of the immigration process, rare before 1980, are now part of the academic landscape. Many of the papers at this conference attest to this broadening range of inquiry. Such research helps to identify problems in the immigrant adjustment process, and to provide better understanding of the likely consequences of policy alternatives and of current rules and procedures.

The main involvement of federal policymakers in promoting the effective integration of permanent immigrants in Canada has largely been with settlement programs. These are directed mainly at smoothing the initial settlement process, and include counselling and language instruction. The objective has been to reduce the costs of settlement and help overcome early hurdles in the settlement process, and hence foster integration into the economy and society. A number of papers at the conference addressed various aspects of the immigrant adjustment process under the general headings of labour market adjustment and social integration, but clearly the two are linked. A number of significant issues and trends regarding the successful integration of immigrants go well beyond the initial settlement process. Much attention was devoted at the conference to the declining labour market performance of immigrants; the social welfare costs of immigration; difficulties in recognition of foreign educational and professional credentials; social exclusion or discrimination against immigrants or visible minorities in various sectors such as employment, education, housing and public services; and regional impacts and inter-governmental aspects of the uneven dispersion of immigrants across the country. Probably the most important of these issues in the short to intermediate term is the declining labour market performance of immigrants. Dealing with the above sets of issues will involve federal departments well beyond Citizenship and Immigration Canada as well as joint arrangements with provincial and even municipal levels of government.

Overview of the Studies in this Volume

Session one at the conference set out the above concerns in a broader context. In "The Global Context of Immigration", for example, Janice Stein outlines three factors that are central to shaping global population movement. First, are the economic and social consequences of a widening gap in ages between developed and less-developed countries — the "demographic divide". Second, is the impact that access to the newest technology will have on the growth in income inequality both within and between countries. Finally, as the demographic divide interacts with widening income inequality, ever greater pressure will be placed on countries like Canada to take in more immigrants. How we react to these pressures either by welcoming and including these new immigrants in the wider society or by marginalizing them will say much about how this country will evolve in the decades ahead. In the same section, Alfred MacLeod stresses the importance of placing immigration in a ten-year term planning time frame. The challenges facing policymakers in setting longer run immigration policy include such areas as globalization and competitiveness, security issues in light of 9/11, diversity versus a limited number of source countries, levels, and the role of immigration in solving the aging population problem. What emerges from this longer term view of formulating immigration policy is not only the need to involve more areas of the government in the decision-making process but also a need to expand the research agenda in this important area of public policy. Finally, Alan Green in "What is the Role of Immigration in Canada's Future?" takes a

Introduction

sceptical view on whether immigration alone is capable of solving the aging problem, future skill shortages and regional income inequality. For example, immigration adds to the growth of the labour force and so offsets rising dependency rates, but within politically tolerable limits it cannot change the basic age structure of the population. Its role in solving skill shortages is also limited. A better solution might be to expand the domestic education levels. Finally, we have little evidence that people can be moved to regions that are at odds with their personal preferences. Immigration on its own is simply no "silver bullet" in resolving the countries diverse social and economic problems.

In section two, Roderic Beaujot tackles the question of the impact of immigration on Canadian demographics in "Effect of Immigration on Demographic Structure". This study sets out in some detail the various characteristics of past and current immigration and shows how dramatically its role has changed over the decades. For example, Beaujot shows that periods of high immigration are associated with periods of high emigration. In fact, over the long run, immigration has just offset emigration, leaving little room for net immigration to contribute to population change. Statistically, results show that the growth of the labour force did not slow until after the mid-1980s unlike total population growth that began to slow down much earlier. In addition, immigrants are more concentrated in large cities than are their native counterparts (i.e., 60% of the foreign-born live in Montreal, Toronto, and Vancouver compared to only 27% of the native-born population). In terms of socio-cultural composition of population resulting from immigration, Beaujot argues that "Canada is becoming a multi-ethnic society where 'pluralism' rather than 'visible' minorities is the more appropriate term".

In "Occupational Mobility of Immigrant Men: Evidence from Longitudinal Data for Australia, Canada and the United States", Marc Frenette, Vincent Hildebrand, James McDonald and Chris Worswick analyze the occupational outcomes for three immigrant-receiving countries during the 1980s and 1990s. One of the goals of the paper is to examine whether the immigrants to these market-oriented economies faced similar adjustment experiences. Their cross-section results show that, with some exceptions, the occupational distributions for native- and foreign-born workers are generally similar. Differences that existed in the early years of settlement tended to disappear over time. The authors also use a first-order Markov transition model to examine the probability of workers moving between occupations over time for Australia and the United States. In general, the results suggest that, for recent immigrant arrivals, the probability of occupational switching was greater than it was for comparable native American workers and this difference decreased with years since migration. In the Australian case, the transition probabilities were about the same for native- and foreign-born workers right from the start.

In "Immigration and Capital Accumulation in Canada: A Long-Run Perspective", Stuart Wilson examines the effect of changing immigration on the rate of investment in Canada over the twentieth century. The author finds that a positive relationship exists between immigration and per capita fixed investment in the early years of that century. However, this relationship is reversed during the last third of the century. He ascribes this reversal to a relative decline in the human capital level of recent immigrants. The decline in human capital content then lowers the productivity of labour and so slows the growth in per capita investment. He supports this result through the application of time series analysis. This research confirms other work showing that it takes a much longer period of time for newly arrived immigrants to converge on the incomes of similarly positioned domestic workers than it did for earlier immigrant arrivals. The author contends that this decline in the productivity of recent immigrants may be due to a switch in immigration policy from an economic focus to one concerned more with humanitarian factors (i.e., family reunion, refugee movements, etc.). His solution to this problem is to invest more resources in the education and training of recent immigrants.

In the last few years provincial governments, following the earlier lead of Quebec, have become much more active in the formulation of immigration policy and its effect on their particular region. Section three reviews some of these experiences. For example, Gerald Clément sets out the initiatives that Manitoba has undertaken to attract immigrants to this province during the last few years. Gilles Grenier describes the unique features of immigration to Quebec. In particular, he points out the value of protecting linguistic duality. The evidence he provides suggests that the percentage of the immigrant population who speak French at home has increased over time. In terms of the influence of language and culture on migration decisions, the paper by James McDonald, "Location Choice of New Immigrants to Canada: The Role of Ethnic Networks", finds that these factors exert a powerful influence on the initial location of new immigrants. Ethnic networks provide a powerful incentive to new immigrants on where they might first locate. Information supplied by these prior migrants is invaluable as the more recent arrivals put down roots in their new home. These findings raise interesting questions about how successful the proposed government program to spread immigrants more evenly across regions will work.

Section four examined international labour mobility and policy responses. The first paper by John McHale considers "Canadian Immigration Policy in Comparative Perspective". He begins with an analytical assessment of a skill-focused immigration policy within a model of immigration surplus. He examines the concept of skill shortage and argues against using occupational shortages as a basis for a permanent immigration policy. He develops a framework for considering a skill-based optimal immigration policy, and evaluates recent immigration policy reforms both in Canada and elsewhere in terms of the design principles emerging from his model and finds that Canada's recently reformed system compares quite well. However, he notes that Canada's temporary immigration policy is rather cumbersome and would benefit from learning what other countries are doing in attracting skilled temporary workers. Looking at recent estimates of the number of Canadian-born workers in the United States, he finds a marked increase in the "brain drain" to the United States in contrast to the findings of a number of other studies.

Alice and Masao Nakamura and Erwin Diewert examine how overall labour productivity in the economy is affected by immigrants arriving with different skill levels and different market treatment of these skill levels in "The Potential Impacts of Immigration on Productivity in Canada". This is motivated by concerns about immigrants from origins other than the United States and United Kingdom experiencing lower average earnings than native-born workers in Canada. The authors develop an index number framework for considering how different sorts of immigrant inflows could be expected to affect traditional and new concepts of productivity growth.

Some expect Canadian immigration policy to offset the effects of a "brain drain" — the emigration of highly-skilled Canadians to other countries — but specific patterns of emigration have been difficult to pinpoint. David Card looks at "Canadian Emigration to the United States" by examining Canadian-born workers living in the United States from the US censuses over the period 1980 to 2000. Canadians living in the US have long been better educated than those remaining back in Canada. However, this pattern of selective emigration may have intensified in recent years due to two major factors: "the decline in Canadian average incomes relative to those in the United States, reflected in the fall of the Canadian dollar; and the sharp rise in relative wages of highly educated young workers in the United States".

Session five of the conference looked at Canadian data sources available for immigration research in Canada. Michael Abbott, in "The IMDB: A User's Overview of the Immigration Database", provides summary information on Statistics Canada's and Citizenship and Immigration Canada's longitudinal administrative database on landed immigrants in Canada going back to 1980. He discusses the main strengths and limitations of the IMDB from the perspective of an empirical researcher on immigration issues. The IMDB is uniquely suitable for empirically evaluating the effects of various worker and landing characteristics on immigrants' post-landing outcomes. Martha Justus and Jessie-Lynn MacDonald talk about the new "Longitudinal Survey of Immigrants to Canada" (LSIC) currently being set up by Statistics Canada. Its objective is to examine how new immigrants adjust to life in Canada over time and what factors help or hinder the integration process. Here, in contrast to the IMDB, workers' human capital characteristics can change over time. The first wave of interviews occurred April 2001 to March 2002 and focused on immigrants who came to Canada between October 2000 and September 2001. Douglas Norris of Statistics Canada provides information on "New Household Surveys on Immigration" available to researchers in Canada. The 2001 census, though not a new survey, does contain several relevant innovations for immigration researchers. It will allow one to distinguish between permanent and non-permanent residents and to identify second-generation Canadians and what has been happening to them. He also discusses three new or recent household surveys that provide useful information on immigrants in Canada. The Ethnic Diversity Survey looks at ethnic origin and ancestry. The Canadian Community Health Survey focuses on health indicators and health-related trends. Both surveys contain large samples of immigrants. Finally, the ongoing Survey of Labour and Income Dynamics (SLID) provides longitudinal information over a six-year panel on details of labour, employment, and income for both immigrant and non-immigrant households.

Session six of the conference looked at the changing immigrant experience in the labour market and labour market integration issues. Bert Waslander examines "The Falling Earnings of New Immigrant Men in Canada's Large Cities". Focusing on the eight largest metropolitan areas in Canada between 1980 and 1995, he finds that part of the earnings decline is due to changes in unemployment and an increased sensitivity of earnings to the unemployment rate, to the returns to educational attainment and foreign work experience of new immigrants being low and indeed declining, and to the changing origin mix of new immigrants over that period.

Abdurrahman Aydemir looks at the "Effects of Business Cycles on the Labour Market Participation and Employment Rate Assimilation of Immigrants". His study identifies the separate effects of macroeconomic conditions at the time of entry into the Canadian labour market and at the time of the survey on labour market outcomes of immigrants, while also allowing for cohort effects using annual SCF cross-sections over the period 1979 to 1997. He finds that estimated cohort effects and labour market assimilation profiles are sensitive to the inclusion of controls for macroeconomic conditions, and "the deterioration in assimilation of recent immigrants is partly due to the adverse economic conditions they face when they enter the labour market and in subsequent years".

Finally, Stephan McBride and Arthur Sweetman look at "Immigrant and Non-Immigrant Earnings by Postsecondary Field of Study". Using the 20% file from Canadian censuses for 1986–96, the authors explore differences in earnings by 50 fields of study. They find large differences in the distribution of workers across fields of study between immigrants and non-immigrants. In general, the differences between high- and low-earning fields are not as large for immigrants as for Canadian-born workers. But field of study differences do not explain much of the earnings differences observed between immigrant and native-born workers in Canada.

Section seven on social inclusion examined social processes of inclusion and exclusion affecting the integration of immigrants and racial minorities. In recent decades, immigration has dramatically increased racial diversity of the Canadian population. Although there is evidence that many Canadians welcome racial diversity, there also is evidence that new immigrants and racial minorities experience significant disadvantages including racial barriers to economic mobility and social inclusion. The four papers in this section reflect some of the most important themes of social science research on this subject in Canada.

Prevailing inter-group attitudes are a critical aspect of race relations. Although there is positive evidence of general support for multiculturalism, and for the fairly expansionist immigration policies of recent years, minority opposition to immigration is still substantial, however, and reflects a degree of discomfort towards immigrants that could be quite significant. The psychological basis of attitudes towards immigrants and racial minorities is explored from both theoretical and policy perspectives in the paper by Esses, Hodson and Dovidio on "Public Attitudes Towards Immigrants and Immigration: Determinants and Policy Implications". The analysis focuses on beliefs about immigrants, such as whether immigrants compete with Canadians for jobs, whether they threaten "Canadian culture", and so on. Individual beliefs on these matters are linked to attitudes towards immigrants and immigration generally. Esses *et al.* show that both beliefs and attitudes towards immigration can be resistant to change because they are linked to basic personality characteristics. For persons with these characteristics, negative beliefs about immigrants are resistant to change simply by presenting information that challenges those beliefs.

The relation between attitudes and behaviour is variable, of course, and it is important to examine the status of immigrants and race relations in various institutional contexts. Within labour markets, the transferability of immigrant skills and their recognition by Canadian employers is critical. This is the primary basis for the emphasis in Canadian immigration policy on the selection of highly-skilled immigrants. In recent years, the under-representation of immigrants in emerging occupations of the "knowledge economy" has become a critical issue. Reitz explores these processes on an occupation-specific basis in "Occupational Dimensions of Immigrant Credential Assessment: Trends in Professional, Managerial and Other Occupations, 1970–1996". His findings confirm that university qualifications are significantly discounted in competition for the best-paid professional jobs. However, he also finds that the extent of discounting varies among occupations. Skill discounting is greater in managerial occupations than in professional occupations, and it is still greater outside knowledge occupations altogether. It appears that institutional procedures to evaluate education-based job qualifications are actually more rigorous in professionalized occupations, and that immigrants face their most significant challenges of inclusion in less professionalized sectors of the workforce where in fact educational levels have been rising most rapidly. This suggests that, while programs to address skill recognition must include the licensed professions, to be successful the programs must extend well beyond the professional domain.

In the broader community of any multicultural society, a key question is the social impact of ethnic community differentiation. If immigrant groups create communities that provide a degree of separation from the "mainstream" society, does this in any way hamper their successful integration within that society? The paper by Hou and Picot on "Visible-Minority Neighbourhood Enclaves and Labour Market Outcomes of Immigrants" takes a broad approach and examines how residence in a racial minority "enclave" within one of Canada's immigrant-intensive cities affects occupational success. They find that in most cases the relationship is small or statistically insignificant. But they also find certain instances, particularly within the black community, where negative effects of minority context do appear to be consequential for group members. This analysis points towards the need for new policy approaches to community relations in a multiracial society.

From the standpoint of the long-term integration of immigrant minorities, the situation of the second generation has particular importance. Kaspar in "Mental Health of Immigrant and Non-Immigrant Children in Canada: Results of the National Longitudinal Study of Children and Youth" examines the experiences of immigrant children using the National Longitudinal Survey of Children and Youth. The positive health status of immigrants and their children — the well-known "healthy immigrant" effect — is usually attributed to selection processes, including self-selection. However, Kaspar shows that the advantage of immigrant children may partly be the transitional nature of their circumstances. When parents become established and have secure employment, the advantage is reduced or even disappears. These findings potentially are of considerable significance in attempts to gauge the impact of growing immigrant poverty on the children of immigrants in the future.

Finally, section eight was a wrap-up panel discussion on the major immigration issues and concerns of several leading commentators. Naomi Alboim begins by noting that much of the conference has focused on skilled workers, but we also need to consider what kind of institutional change on the part of employers, educational institutions, professional regulatory bodies, and government policies and regulations may be required to make better use of the arriving immigrants' human capital. She also discussed the growing attention to the regionalization of immigration in Canada and the distinct role of cities in this process. Cities want a say in terms of immigration policy formation because of how the three largest cities in the country are impacted by the large ongoing inflows of immigrants, and they want compensation for the initial costs and support they are called upon to bear on behalf of the new arrivals. She feels that the immigration decision process should be a bottoms-up process where cities should be leading the initiative to attract and retain immigrants. This will require institutional change at the local level in promoting their communities abroad and advertising their sectoral and occupational needs, and in developing local bridging/settlement programs to help the new arrivals to re-enter the occupations for which these immigrants have been trained.

Barry Chiswick raises the question of analyzing what is the optimal size of population or rate of change of population growth, and why do these matter? A relevant factor here is the need to rethink dependency ratios with people living healthy active lives well beyond age 65. He also draws attention to the growing phenomenon of footloose people and an international labour market for high-skilled workers. The result is wages for high-skilled workers will become more equalized, contributing to growing earnings inequality within many countries. Canada will need to examine policies to retain such labour and prevent it from becoming a way station for skilled workers on their way to the United States. He also notes that the attraction of low-skilled foreign workers into selected occupations, for example, in home health care and agriculture, likely contributes to keeping down already relatively low wages in these jobs for low-skilled domestic workers.

Donald DeVoretz also draws attention to the growing role of non-permanent immigrants and the role that Canada plays in attracting skilled immigrants who, after a period of adjustment in Canada, then move on to the United States as their ultimate destination. He expresses concern about how Canadian immigration policies and practices will be affected by post-9/11 events in the US and growing pressures to harmonize immigration policies at the Canada-US border in order to protect trading markets. Yvan Turcotte raises the question of whether foreign credentials are undervalued in the Canadian market because they are often viewed as of lower quality; if so, then one might consider adding quality of education to the point system selection grid. He also wondered whether more weight in this grid should be given to demographic criteria not only for the principal applicant, but also for the spouse and presence and age of children. He remarks that maintaining an open immigration policy needs a social consciousness in support of it, and this would benefit from a more open and frequent consultative process regarding the role of immigration in Canada generally.

Craig Riddell reiterates Alan Green's concern that Canadian society seems to be expecting too much of immigration as meeting a broad set of economic objectives; if anything, it seems to be more of a component of social rather than economic policy. He argues for improved data to better inform research and policy in the area. He raises the important analytical and policy question of what is the appropriate counterfactual against which to compare the relative labour market outcomes of immigrants — the native-born population as a whole or the subgroup of recent labour market entrants among the native-born? In his own research, he finds that, despite the views of many others, immigrant credentials do appear to be valued in the Canadian labour market and that there is little evidence of a decreased valuation of immigrant credentials since 1980. Direct measures of literacy skills on the earnings of immigrants and native-born also appear to have similar effects. He concludes that the sources of the lower return to the measured human capital of immigrants are more complex than the simple lower-quality-of-foreign-education stories would imply.

References

Beach, C.M. and A.G. Green, eds. (1988), *Policy Forum on the Role of Immigration in Canada's Future* (Kingston: John Deutsch Institute, Queen's University).

Borjas, G.J. (2000), *Issues in the Economics of Immigration* (Chicago: University of Chicago Press).

Canadian Issues / Thèmes Canadiens (2003), Special dedicated issue on "Immigration: Opportunities and Challenges" (April edition).

Economic Council of Canada (1991), *Economic and Social Impacts of Immigration* (Ottawa: Supply and Services Canada).

Smith, J.P. and B. Edmonston, eds. (1997), *The New Dimensions: Economic, Demographic, and Fiscal Effects of Immigration* (Washington, DC: National Academy Press).

Stoffman, D. (2002), *Who Gets In: What's Wrong with Canada's Immigration Program — and How to Fix It* (Toronto: Macfarlane, Walter and Ross).

Timlin, M.F. (1951), *Does Canada Need More People?* (Toronto: Oxford University Press).

Section I

International Context and Immigration Policy Goals

Introductory Remark

Alfred MacLeod

Introduction

A ten-year time frame provides an interesting context for considering the issues around immigration. These issues are becoming increasingly important for everyone at Citizenship and Immigration Canada. Although this context is selective, it gives a sense of direction — where we think our program may be headed, what we consider to be the challenges and, as a result, an agenda for the program directions.

Context

Globalization

There is a well-established debate on the impact of globalization on state power and how the market and the state compete for relevance in the nation-state. In the world of immigration we have to look beyond our own borders and have always been influenced by events taking place outside our country. Immigration to Canada has always been global. If we go from the global to the national we can establish that, in the context of the major strategic issues facing Canada and Canadians, immigration is certainly critical and there is a fundamental need for state-generated interventions. Now what informs those interventions may well go far beyond our national borders, but clearly there is still a role and a relevance for national government policies in establishing priorities and actions in the area of immigration.

Managing Immigration

In the world of immigration, countries have choices. In Canada we have made a definite choice: we want to have an immigration program that is open on a universal basis and, at the same time, controllable. Other countries make different choices, but they end up with essentially the same outcome: people arrive. When individuals in Western European countries talk about their immigration policies they say, "Well we hope to have immigration policies, what we have right now are asylum policies."

What we find is that countries that have decided to have open and managed immigration programs end up with far better results than countries that try to be overly restrictive. These countries end up with the same or even greater numbers of people arriving at their doorstep. This leads back to the idea of globalization with increasingly more people on the move, and the challenges that national governments face in regulating these movements in an orderly and controlled way. This becomes the policy challenge.

Fundamental Policy Changes

In the context of immigration and citizenship policy, there are three fundamental changes that we need to deal with in converting research into action, and in responding to the expectations of the public and the various constituencies with a direct interest in immigration.

The first is *policy horizons are lengthening*. Increasingly we see the need to look beyond one or two years to multi-year planning models. Perhaps the most obvious example of this is how we look at levels — the number of individuals that Canada will accept in its various categories annually. It is necessary to look beyond one, two or even three years and even to look beyond our own department to reach out to other constituencies to

Alfred MacLeod

help us understand *what the needs are and what the capacities are within Canada.*

The second fundamental change is to understand that *immigration is situated within broader strategic frameworks.* Over the last few years, there have been a number of people telling us that immigration is increasingly becoming an important part of their business. This includes, for example, Industry Canada, Human Resources Development Canada, and the Department of Foreign Affairs and International Trade. Immigration is now seen as an integral part of a larger and more strategic approach to critical issues facing us on both economic and social levels.

The third change is the *challenge for immigration to look beyond itself and to work with its constituents and to be very clear on who these constituents are.* Fundamentally, the constituents are the Canadian public, and the ultimate challenge is to ensure that what we do and how we do it maintains the confidence of the people and that we are seen to have legitimacy in what we do. But far beyond that there is a mass of constituents, a mass of interested parties who have financial, humanitarian, and personal interests in the way we conduct our business and in where we conduct our business.

Future Directions

This sets the context for our policies and programs. I will now review the critical challenges or areas which we need to understand better as we look at managing where we will go over the next ten years.

Critical Challenges

1. *Globalization and international competitiveness.*

- *Volume versus competitiveness*
  If 120 million people are on the move, this causes incredible pressures on the systems and the programs in place to process all these people and to facilitate their movement or, occasionally, to interrupt their movement from one place to another. This also speaks to the nature of

how Canada competes or positions itself with the rest of the world in attracting skilled workers. It also speaks to the notion of where immigrants come from.

- *Diversity versus a limited number of source countries*
Canada's immigration policy and many of the changes introduced in the 1960s took place when Canada's system of welcoming immigrants from around the world was built on diversity. From the 1960s until today, we went from a model that was based largely on Western Europe to a model that in the 1970s and in the 1980s became relatively more diverse, until today where three countries — India, Pakistan, and China — are closing in on 40% and moving towards 50% of the flow. Is that a problem? Or an opportunity? It is an open question. We have a system that essentially responds to demand and as a result there is no surprise that those three countries are the primary source of immigrants to Canada.

- *Diversity versus levels*
What does this mean for the diversity principle? There was a recent article in *The Toronto Star* by Alan Thompson which set out the issue in a fairly clear context. Citizenship and Immigration Canada have roughly 1,400 people working overseas. On an annual basis, we set immigration levels between 200,000 and 250,000 people; right now people are coming to Canada from almost every country in the world. If we chose to, we could ask 1,400 people to relocate in Beijing, and from Beijing we could on an annual basis meet all of our targets on immigration. That would be one way of achieving certain efficiencies. It also raises certain issues around diversity, the source of the immigration flow, and the impact of this strategy on Canada.

2. *Demographics (aging population and the effects on immigration policy).*

About six months ago immigration opportunists were quite ready to jump on the bandwagon when Statistics Canada released its first wave from the latest census. It is not surprising that six months after that we have had another forum asking for people to take a second look at the connection between immigration, population growth, and aging. It is important to have our facts right. What are we talking about? What is this phenomenon of aging and how is it affecting many policy areas across the government? Is there a role for immigration within that dynamic and if there is, what is the role? We could conclude at this point that if it is seen to be a problem, immigration likely will be a piece of the solution. Not just the only solution, because we need to know and understand more about the issues.

3. *Social inclusion and combatting discrimination.*

Immigration has worked for Canada because there has been essentially a reciprocal arrangement where Canada has opened its doors and welcomed people, people who have come here have worked incredibly hard to establish themselves, to actualize the dreams and the aspirations and it has been a success. How do we ensure that this formula continues to work for Canada? How do we continue to ensure that Canadians feel enriched both economically and culturally by receiving people from all over the world? How do we ensure that throughout the world Canada is seen as a welcoming place that admits immigrants and allows them to apply their skills?

Before joining the department, I spent a few years doing research on public opinions. One of my last assignments was in Toronto where, for different federal departments sponsoring the research, we did two sets of focus groups, 12 individuals from the general population, but designed to be representative of Toronto. Every time, I got the same comment from public servants about the composition of our groups, which varied from six to eight visible minorities out of the 12 individuals. I checked back with our office to find out how the recruitment of the groups matched the Statistics Canada data. And the evidence was there. Toronto was in the room. So this represents an issue that does not speak to the critical issues around poverty and integration. It does not speak to whether you know the second generation is establishing itself or whether we are actually exploiting the potential and the talent that immigrants bring with them when they arrive in Canada. It speaks to issues around peace, comfort, and acceptance by the host community and we have to be able to talk about those things.

4. *Immigration as an instrument of foreign policy.*

- *Perception of Canada's role in the world has evolved*
  If Canada's foreign policy is based on the Pearsonian model coming out of the 1960s, which is very much based on a Western European view of how Canada should position itself in the world, and how it should try to strike a middle way between its former colonial masters and its economic guardians to the south:
  - What does it mean when 50% of the population of Toronto is born outside Canada?
  - What does it mean when 50% of Toronto is visible minority?
  - What does it mean when the world and Canada go far beyond Western Europe?
  - What are the implications for the resonance of foreign policy?
  - How do we connect and how do we remain relevant to people who will have potentially very different expectations of Canada's foreign policy as it responds to conflicts throughout the world?

  We need only to look around us now to realize that the dynamic of how Canada reacts to Iraq is very different than it would have been 20 years ago.

- *Impact of immigration on trade*
  - What is the impact of immigration on our ability to expand our trade?
  - What are the direct costs and benefits?
  - Are we becoming a northern tiger, as some people suggest, as a result of our multi-ethnic, multicultural population with its links to countries all over the world?

5. *Migration and security.*

Post September 11, 2001, the focus has been on immigration and particularly the refugee determination system. Increasingly, there is a need for the government to respond to concerns over the security of our immigration program. This opens up a number of very important policy decisions and challenges for the government. They speak to issues in our backyard, and to questions of how we will align and deal with international affiliations that we have. *The Globe and Mail* reports on a Canadian citizen who was deported from the United States, and the Department of Foreign Affairs is desperately trying to identify where this Canadian citizen is. If we are to move towards a more integrated form of security and defence involving the United States, how do we then deal in a domestic context when situations like this arise?

6. *Immigration: a multilateral issue.*

Finally, not only does immigration cut across departments at the federal government level, it also cuts across jurisdictions domestically as witnessed by a recent meeting of provincial ministers of immigration in Winnipeg. I think what is noteworthy about this meeting is that there was an explicit statement that there is not just one immigration minister in Canada, there are several. Immigration ministers from provincial governments are increasingly vocal. The major issue for them is the concurrent responsibility for immigration. They recognize the need to take second looks and to prepare themselves to be active in the area of immigration beyond our national borders and with other governments.

From these challenges we can potentially derive a policy agenda by asking ourselves:

– How do we position Canada in the world through our immigration program?
– How do we use immigration as a policy tool for social and economic development?
– How do we ensure that what we do on behalf of Canadians is seen to benefit them, that they have confidence in the program?
– How do we work across jurisdictions to ensure that the benefits of immigration are attained?

Conclusion: Anticipation and the Role of Research

In the Department of Citizenship and Immigration, if we are looking at a ten-year time frame, we need to be able to anticipate. This speaks to the critical importance of research. Hence the importance of a conference like this one. Initial thinking and planning need to be done in order to get beyond the urgent issues of the day and to be able to deal with the important questions that we will confront in the future. We must be clear about what we know today and what we will need to know tomorrow in order to be successful in running an immigration program for Canada.

The Global Context of Immigration

Janice Gross Stein

This century is the century of mobility. People are moving in millions as never before — as immigrants, as refugees, and as most significantly in terms of numbers, as displaced persons. At the same time, the global and continental environment which sets the parameters for immigration is changing. I want to emphasize just three of many features which I think will be especially important both in shaping global immigration flows in the next decade and in shaping host policies. They are:

- the "global demographic divide",
- the demographic divide in a context of growing inequality, and
- enhanced security measures which create serious and targeted barriers to immigration.

Demographics: A Divided World

Among the most striking trends in the current global environment is the division of the world by age. To oversimplify, the population is aging in Europe, Japan, and China. In Canada and the United States, the aging demographic is moderated significantly by immigration. In the poorer countries, even though there have been significant successes in lowering the birth rate in some, population is still growing and will continue to grow as these societies move through the "demographic tunnel" (Peterson, 1999). The consequences of this "division by age" on global patterns of economic growth, governance, social inclusion, and security are potentially enormous. In both parts of this divided world, societies will look considerably different 50 years from now than they do today.

In the aging world, the "grey power" of older people will be an important political force, with a set of expectations from governments that range from enhanced pensions, to better health care and improved housing on a smaller scale. At the same time, the productive labour force in the economy will diminish. Today's ratio of working taxpayers to non-working pensioners in the developed world is 3:1. If the present trend continues in a linear way, in 30 years the ratio could fall to 1.5:1 (Peterson, 1999, p. 46).

Expectations will grow as the size of the productive labour force diminishes. In this environment, governments will face enhanced demands as the resource base to produce wealth diminishes. It is this expected demographic profile which is already leading policy planners to emphasize the importance of increased immigration of productive young people as one way out of the "demographic trap".

In the poorest countries, the majority of the population is under 15 years of age. The social impact of a young population is amplified by a growing pattern of global urbanization. Unless there is significant economic growth and opportunity for young people entering the labour market, a decade from now many societies will face significant social strain, increasing participation in black markets and criminal activity, limited access to the most basic social services of health care, sanitation, and education, alienation from government, and openness to participation in violence and networks of crime and terror as outlets for frustration and grievance. At the extreme, some states and governance will collapse under the stress, others will become attractive hosts for networks of terror and crime, and others will embrace authoritarian solutions to governance problems. The concept of global order will be hollowed out.

It is from these societies that there will be the strongest push to emigration. It hardly needs saying that there may not be a match between the global push to emigration and the global pull of immigration. If there is a serious disconnect, the social strains will intensify.

A Divided World in a Context of Growing Inequality

The "demographic divide" does not, however, inevitably result in this grim portrait of the future. Economic growth in these "young societies" which creates employment, builds social infrastructure, and distributes benefits can mitigate these social strains. The record of the past two decades, however, does not provide an encouraging platform on which to build the future.

The global knowledge-based economy has created significant wealth for those who are able to participate, directly and indirectly, in its processes. At the same time as the scope and pace of globalization have increased, however, income inequalities have grown, with serious consequences for the configuration of societies.

- By the end of the twentieth century, between-country inequalities had increased and were greater than they have been for two centuries.
- Two different patterns of within-country inequalities developed.
- Within the core group of technologically advanced countries, inequalities among households have remained stable or increased. Most countries, including Canada, have had relatively stable levels of inequality, while others — Britain, the United States, Australia, and New Zealand — have experienced a sharp rise in inequality in the last two decades.
- In the semi-periphery and periphery, inequalities have declined within many countries in Asia, but increased dramatically in China, Latin America, and throughout Africa. Market-led growth has gone in different directions in different countries, and a critical difference has been the mediating impact of the state.

The causes of marginalization and inequality are fiercely contested, but the consequences of growing inequality are clear. Growing numbers of young people in poor societies will have little opportunity for productive lives. Mass migration to societies experiencing dynamic growth, the safety valve of globalization one hundred years ago, will not be available as an escape in the next decade. If anything, current trends in European immigration policy point in the opposite direction.

The demographic divide interacts with patterns of growing inequality to create potentially malignant global consequences. Canada will not be able to isolate itself from these consequences.

Security and Barriers to Immigration

In the aftermath of September 11, 2001, governments around the world have stiffened barriers to immigration, particularly with respect to young men coming from the Middle East. Canada is no exception. We passed the Immigration and Refugee Protection Act (IRPA), effective June 28, 2002, which was further modified by the Anti-Terrorism Act and Bill C-55, the Public Safety Act, as well as the US-Canada Joint Statement on Cooperation on Border Security and Regional Migration Issues, and the Canada-US Smart Border Declaration. The emphasis is overwhelmingly on protecting Canada, controlling borders, and fighting threats created by international migration. In particular, the new Act has:

- increased and strengthened the powers of detention;
- expanded inadmissability categories on the basis of security and terrorism, categories which remain undefined in IRPA;
- restricted the right of immigration appeal on the grounds of security; and
- strengthened interdiction provisions without exempting humanitarian issues.

Immigration has now fallen within the broader envelope of security and is subject to ongoing pressures to harmonize policy with the United States, despite the fact that the hijackers were not immigrants, but visitors and "students" in the United States, admitted through special visas. Immigration policy — especially with respect to the Middle East — is increasingly seen in the context of security rather than economic growth or citizenship. There are deeply embedded contradictions within this policy envelope that will have to be fought out over the next few years.

Embedding Shared Citizenship

Canada must continue to be open to large numbers of immigrants if its society is to grow and flourish, but it must invest significantly to develop a shared understanding of citizenship and the reciprocal obligations of one citizen to another. More and more, Canada is becoming a microcosm of the world, a society rich in diversity whose members are networked through

Janice Gross Stein

complex webs of kinship and attachment to almost every society in the globe. This openness, diversity and set of connections are among Canada's most valuable assets.

If the true value of diversity and connectedness is to be realized, all Canadians must understand and internalize the values of Canadian society: the respect for diversity, the limits to disagreement, and the unconditional rejection of violence as an instrument to achieve social and political objectives. Government must also work hard to provide every opportunity for newcomers to realize their economic, social, and cultural dreams within Canada. Institutions must become more open, more flexible, and more accountable.

We are already seeing the escalating social and political tensions that have accompanied increased flows of immigration to Europe. These escalating tensions are not a necessary consequence of immigration, but, if they are to be avoided, they require public policy that speaks explicitly to the values and norms of "shared citizenship", the set of mutual and reciprocal obligations assumed by established citizens and new immigrants who would be citizens. Without this kind of policy, immigrants who are badly integrated, inadequately housed, segregated in poor neighbourhoods, condemned to an underground economy, and deprived of political voice can become breeding grounds for social discontent and political alienation. At worst, they can become fertile recruiting grounds for those who seek change through violence.

We can imagine two very different profiles of Canada a decade from now. I deliberately exaggerate the differences and draw two portraits at the poles of the spectrum. Where we are a decade from now is largely contingent on government policy.

In the first scenario, enlightened government policy works actively to attract a larger number of immigrants, but at the same time invests significantly in developing a shared understanding of citizenship, of the reciprocal obligations of one citizen to another, and of the limits to dissent. Government also works hard to make its institutions more open, more flexible, and more accountable. During the next decade, immigrants become full partners in Canadian society.

Or, immigrants to Canada are marginalized and live together in communities isolated from other Canadians. Significant gaps in income and education develop and grow. Although these kinds of conditions are difficult today to imagine in Toronto, Montreal, or Vancouver, they currently exist in Paris and Hamburg. Stereotyping increases and ethnic tension develops. Angry and fearful, immigrant communities in Canada's large cities become nodes in networks of illegal organizations, participants in black markets, and at worst, recruits for organizations committed to violence.

The consequences for Canada of these two different scenarios are not difficult to draw. Which future develops will largely be a consequence of government policy and broader patterns of social investment.

Reference

Peterson, P.G. (1999), "Gray Dawn: The Global Aging Crisis", *Foreign Affairs* 78(1), 42–55.

What is the Role of Immigration in Canada's Future?

Alan G. Green

Introduction

We are at a critical juncture in the history of immigration policy in this country. The voices of those opposed to current levels of immigration are being raised against those who see great benefits in maintaining, or even raising, the present levels of admission. The debate over the number of immigrants to be admitted is not unique to Canada. European countries are in even greater turmoil. For many, immigration is a whole new experience, since for almost two centuries most have been sending not receiving countries. With sharply declining birth rates, they find it imperative to import workers rather than send excess population overseas. The ascendancy of Le Pen in France and the rise of other extreme right-wing political parties is only the most recent manifestation of this problem over the admission of strangers. In Canada, there has been a spate of recent publications recommending a reduction in the level of inflow for both economic and security reasons (see Collacott, 2002; Francis, 2002; and Stoffman, 2002).

The United States is no exception to this debate. After almost two decades of admitting about one million documented immigrants a year, questions are being raised about the economic benefits of running at this level of admission. For example, George Borjas (1999), in his most recent book, *Heaven's Door*, suggests that this inflow be cut in half. His reasoning is straightforward. Research suggests that the average "quality" of immigrants admitted to the United States over the last three decades is lower than it was for those entering during the 1950s and 1960s. As a result, current immigration levels threaten to lower the pace of economic growth.

The current minister of immigration in Ottawa has taken a very different view towards immigration. In a recent policy statement Denis Coderre has pledged to admit over a million immigrants in the next decade. Indeed, the targeted number is equivalent to 1% of the population or a gross immigration of about 300,000 a year. Furthermore, this proposal has been made within the context of admitting this number annually regardless of the state of the current labour market in Canada. It is clear that this government, and the one that preceded it, have both adopted a strong pro-immigration position. Both Canada and the United States, therefore, have witnessed an upward trend in the level of admissions over the last 20 years.

Goals of Canadian Immigration Policy

It is here, with the parallel trends in admissions, that the similarity between Canada and the United States ends. Canada sees immigration as the solution to a wide range of current economic problems facing the country, while the United States focuses more on family reunification as the central goal of its immigration policy. Canadian goals are more demographic and economic. They include:

- The aging of the population; that is, an attempt to ease, through immigration, the fiscal burden associated with a rising share of non-working to working population.
- Responding, through immigration, to the need for additional skills (human capital), associated with the expansion of the knowledge economy.
- Promoting economic growth especially, at present, regional growth, by dispersing immigrants to small centres across Canada.

Alan G. Green

The question that arises, then, since the Canadian position on immigration seems to be out of step with other receiving countries (old and new), is "Can immigration solve these problems?" Or even more pointedly if the answer to this question is "no": "Do we need immigration at all?" These questions are not meant to downplay the contribution that immigration has played in shaping economic and social developments in this country in the past. They are raised to help us focus on just what role immigration might be expected to play over the next century. An attempt to answer such questions might also help us define more precisely what level of inflow would be viable in the future.

The Aging Population

The problem of an aging population first emerged in the early 1980s as the long-run consequences of the "Bust" in *Boom, Bust and Echo* (Foot, 2000) made its presence known. The newly elected Conservative government of the day was anxious to revive immigration levels after close to a decade of inflows that had fallen to levels not seen since the Great Depression. The taste for high levels of immigration had waned during the 1970s with the advent of stagflation and its accompanying high levels of unemployment and slow growth. The decade from 1974 to 1984 had been a sharp break from the quarter-century of rapid growth and high levels of immigration that Canada had enjoyed from the end of the war until the mid-1970s.

By the mid-1980s the full consequences of a steadily declining birth rate that had begun a decade or so earlier were finally being seen. Two effects of this decline in fertility were now evident. First, there was about to be a slowdown in the level of new domestic labour force entrants — a potential repeat of what had happened in the 1950s as a result of a similar drop in birth rates during the 1930s. Second, with declining youth dependency ratios, plus the fall in new domestic labour force entrants, older (i.e., over 65) dependency ratios were expected to rise in the years ahead. How, then, were the costs associated with this aging population to be covered and who was going to pay the bill? The answer given then, and repeated often since, was to lower the average of the population by accelerating the rate of immigration.

Another demographic problem was occurring at the same time. Quebec's rate of population growth was falling. Birth rates in the province which, in the 1950s had been the highest in Canada, had, by the 1980s, fallen to among the lowest in the country. Indeed these rates were well below replacement levels. The threat here was not just with the consequences of an aging population as bad as that may have been, but with maintaining the political and cultural viability of the province itself. The answer was similar to that for the aging problem — accelerate the rate of immigration into Quebec, and if possible focus this inflow from French-speaking countries. This goal was furthered by Quebec taking greater control over immigration destined to reside in the province. One way this was accomplished was to establish overseas offices to help attract immigrants to the province.

In an earlier conference volume *The Role of Immigration in Canada's Future* (Beach and Green, 1988), the noted French-Canadian demographer Jacques Henripin (1988) examined the consequences of such a plan, that is, to build up the population of Quebec through high levels of immigration. His conclusion was simple. The plan would not work! His reasoning was straightforward. At the level of immigration necessary to restore population growth to past rates, the effect would be to change the composition of that which its proposers sought to protect. By the early decades of the twenty-first century, he predicted that at these levels of inflow the foreign-born arrivals would dominate the population. For example, at levels of inflow that would eliminate the fertility deficit, the population of Montreal Island by mid twenty-first century would be 60% foreign-born. It was his contention that such inflows would have a profound effect on the cultural or ethnic or language composition of the host region/country. The newcomers, he suggests, may well not have the same attachment to such questions as independence as do many native-born Quebecers. Hence a low-fertility/high immigration strategy raises, at the very least, some disturbing questions about how the native-born population in Quebec (and for that matter in all of Canada), would respond to such an approach. One might recall the intemperate outburst of Jacques Parizeau on that fateful November night in 1995.

What about immigration as a solution to that other problem — the aging of the population? David Green and I (1999), drawing on research findings that, at politically acceptable levels, immigration has only a marginal effect on the host country's population age structure at least for modern economies. For example, at annual levels of inflow of 200,000 the ratio of those out of the labour force to those in the labour force is about 24%. When the annual inflow is increased to 500,000 a year, this ratio falls by only two percentage points to 22%. One of the reasons for this small decline in the ratio is that many immigrants, although in their twenties and thirties themselves, often sponsor older relatives (Green and Green, 1999).

Alan G. Green

In a study of Canada's demographic future (Canada. Health and Welfare, 1994), the authors come to similar conclusions. Under conditions of an annual inflow of 200,000 the study found that 22% of the population would be over the age of 65 by 2036. If the inflow was raised to 600,000 a year, the share of the population over 65 in 2036 would have fallen to 17%. This five-percentage point drop is not insignificant, but again it could only be achieved at levels of inflow that are clearly beyond a politically achievable level. Tom Kent (former deputy minister of manpower and immigration in the 1960s) suggested at the 1988 policy forum on immigration that future immigration policies be directed towards young immigrants. The latter would include orphans from the Third World, families with a number of young children, single mothers with children, etc. (Kent, 1988, p. 10). Even this approach, apparently, does not make a great difference to the age structure of the population. For example, recent work (the *Demographic Review 1994*) has found that, if one assumed 50% of the inflow entering the country was under 15 years of age, the drop in the percentage over 65 by 2036 would still only be five percentage points, that is, from 22 to 17%. However, although such a youth-oriented policy as advocated by Tom Kent would have only a limited impact on the age structure of the population, it would accelerate the growth of the labour force and hence aggregate savings rates (see the work of Stuart Wilson in this volume). In addition, a greater percentage of the immigrants entering the Canadian workforce would have been trained in this country and thus would integrate faster than migrants trained in their home countries.

Human Capital Expansion

One of the most highly publicized goals of immigration policy during the last three decades has been its role in adding to the stock of human capital; that is, augmenting the supply of skills available to employers. One of the main benefits of such a goal was seen as fostering intensive economic growth. Does it work this way? Not really. Over much of the twentieth century Canadian and American growth rates have, in the main, been very similar. In fact, for much of the last century Canadian growth rates have exceeded those of the United States (Green, 2000, p. 196), while the stock of human capital has grown much faster in the latter. Hence, simply expanding the growth of the labour force through immigration, is not a sufficient condition to insure strong economic growth.

Whether or not one is seeking to maximize the rate of growth of human capital there are important consequences in how this is accomplished. The import of highly skilled workers must be seen in the context of building the stock of human capital in the host country (see Green and Green, 1999, p. 442). Clearly immigration of such workers constitutes a substitute for the education of domestic workers. Thus, large inflows of skilled workers will have the effect of lowering the skill premia; that is, reducing the gap between the wages of skilled and unskilled workers. The lowering of this gap has important consequences for the decision-making process of Canadians interested in extending their education. In an imperfect world (i.e., one where innate ability is not evenly distributed) and where financing for advanced education is not equally available, the impact of lowering the skill premia is likely to discourage Canadians from seeking to acquire these skills. If the world were perfect (the reverse of the above conditions), this might not matter since the skill mix would remain unaltered even with immigration.

There are times, however, when immigration of skilled workers plays a critical role in the development of the economy. One of these times was in the 1960s. At that time the Canadian government was engaged in attempting to transform the economy from resource-based to an urban/industrial-based economy. The government recognized that there was a desperate shortage of skilled workers and a short fall in the whole educational structure, especially at the postsecondary level. The government was anxious to shift the focus of immigration from unskilled resource-directed workers to skilled workers. Immigrants were to be used as shock troops — to fill occupational gaps in the labour force. Recent research (Green and Green, 1998; and D. Green, 1999) has shown that this has worked, migrants tended to move towards expanding sectors faster than did native-born workers and out of declining sectors faster as well. To effect this change, immigration policy, first in 1962 and then with the introduction of the point system in 1967, changed the orientation from a country-of-origin-based policy to a universal admission approach based not on where the prospect immigrant was born but on the migrant's skill in relation to the demand for such skills within Canada.

This change towards a skill-based policy was driven by the realization, beginning in the late 1950s, that the Canadian economy was being driven more from the secondary manufacturing and service sectors than from the traditional resource industries. This structural shift required, therefore, a more sophisticated (i.e., better trained) labour force. Unfortunately, the Canadian labour was not adequately equipped to handle these new

Alan G. Green

demands. This problem was carefully presented in a Senate report on manpower and employment released in 1961.

An important conclusion to the study states:

> we emphasize(d) the structural changes that have taken place in the economy (since the end of the war); shifts between industries, the effects of evolving technology, the changing nature and rising level of skill demanded of workers, and above all the need for rapid adjustment which these changes have imposed on the labour force. (Canada, 1961, p. 57)

It was probably not an accident that a year after this report was published Canada shifted to a universal skills-based immigration policy. The interesting question is whether this shift, towards focusing on skills, was meant to be a temporary policy (i.e., until Canada got "on its feet" in terms of an educational infrastructure) or a permanent orientation in this direction. In essence, was this new policy meant to follow the old prescription of alternating large inflows targeted at specific economic goals followed by periods of virtual shut down in the face of domestic labour market conditions (Green and Green, 1999, p. 426) where the shut down would occur when the domestic educational infrastructure was finally in place?

Therefore the question today is whether immigration is still the most economically efficient means to fill skill gaps in the labour force. Clearly we can all think of situations where the answer to this question is "yes"; for example, a shortage of welders in the Alberta oil fields or a shortage of computer programmers in Kanata. On a broader level of skill acquisition the case is less clear. Besides the problem of credentialization, there is the question of the morality of transferring the best and the brightest from developing countries to meet our needs in Canada.

Three other problems are inherent in relying on imported skilled workers. First, it takes time for new entrants to adjust to the competitive conditions in the labour markets of a modern urban economy (see studies on the assimilation problem, e.g., Abbott and Beach, 1993). Second, it takes time to identify a skill shortage and to find someone qualified to fill the need — move the prospective immigrant to Canada. The search and moving time, including all the paperwork necessary prior to getting an entry visa, may well exceed the time needed to train a domestic worker to do the job, especially if the training time is less than two years; that is, about the average time to train students in a college of technology. One example of this approach, although over a longer training time, is the initiative of the

Ontario government to expand the number of students taking computer science courses. The government provided funds to allow participating universities to double their output of such students. Finally, it may not always be the case that the stated occupation of the new migrant is the occupation actually followed. Hence, the gap goes unfilled. Recall our earlier statement that large inflows of skilled immigrants may well distort the decision-making process of prospective labour force entrants; for example, dissuade them from seeking advanced training. This suggests that immigration policy can not be treated in isolation.

Regional Needs

One of the contributions of immigration is to spur economic growth. There is evidence that this was the case during the opening years of the last century (Green and Sparks, 1999). One way it has this effect is by increasing the size of the market, generating economies of large scale production. The effect of the latter is to increase real per capita income. This type of response has regional as well as national consequences. However, recent studies can find little direct link between population growth and an increase in the standard of living in mature economies (Economic Council of Canada, 1991).

It seems surprising, on the surface at least, that the current minister of immigration is proposing to disperse immigrants to the smaller centres across Canada. The policy implies that one, or both, of the following conditions hold. First, that the marginal cost (increased congestion on the highways, greater levels of pollution, access to public goods, etc.) of adding an additional person to the main urban receiving centres is rising faster than the marginal benefits (e.g., economies of scale, benefits of diversity, etc.) from a larger population, and so immigrants should be dispersed to the smaller centres and diverted from the major cities. Second, that the smaller centres lack the range of human skills necessary to promote growth in these areas, and immigration is the answer to this problem. The questions that need answering are whether immigration adds to the first problem, that is, marginal costs of increased population are rising faster than the marginal benefits, and second, can we close the income gap between the poor regions/smaller communities and the larger cities by dispersing immigrants to the former?

We have a natural experiment within the country to examine the success of attempting to steer immigrants to a new region. In 1925 the government passed the Railways Act. This Act allowed the two major railway companies (CN and CP) to search for and transport to Canadian farm workers and prospective farmers from Central and Eastern Europe who were willing to settle on the Prairies. By the late 1920s over 70% of those admitted declared that their intended destination was the Prairies and their intended occupation was farming. In a recent study by Byron Lew (2000) on the implications of this policy, he found that by 1931 few of the immigrants from these regions in Europe still resided in the west. The majority had drifted south, moved to the cities or went home. Indeed, the defection from the western farms was so great that inspectors had to be sent to the farms to check if the immigrants were still in residence. This does not mean that the policy was a complete failure. There were several short-run benefits from having additional workers available during at the harvest season. However, there were apparently few long-run benefits to emerge from this policy.

What about the current proposal to steer immigrants to smaller centres and lower income regions? First, most migration is from low to high income regions. Hence, deliberately sending immigrants in the reverse direction will clearly meet with some resistence. As in the case of the 1925 Railways Act, the stay in such regions will not last long as the new immigrants follow their native-born counterparts to the big cities. Second, the attempt, as has been suggested, to require new migrants to remain in these rural communities for three to five years (and if they don't, to deport them) would seem to run against the basic tents of freedom of movement guaranteed to all Canadian citizens, including landed immigrants. Hence, the government will be forced to enter into a contract with prospective immigrants that they will indeed stay in the centres to which they are directed. The question, then, is: Who is likely to sign such a contract? Clearly, only those migrants who are marginal to the review process for landed immigrant status. Immigrants with sufficient points to enter directly will not sign up for direction to rural areas. Hence, the plan will send low-skilled marginal migrants to the periphery and the best and the brightest will head for the cities. It is difficult to see how this arrangement will narrow the income gap between the lower income regions and the cities. Using immigration policy to solve congestion in the major cities and skill deficiencies in the smaller communities seems doomed to failure. History provides some interesting lessons in attempting to institute a plan to steer immigrants in non-market-determined directions.

We do not need to dip into deep history to see this point. The topic of dispersing immigrants away from the larger cities was examined almost three decades ago as part of the general review of immigration policy. In presenting a summary of this study on February 3, 1975, before the House, Robert Andras, then minister of immigration and manpower, said that

> few means exist at present to steer immigrants against prevailing population currents, and these are limited in their effectiveness. It would be an exercise in futility to attempt to direct people towards destinations where adequate employment opportunities and their accompanying social amenities were lacking. Canadian immigration policy has generally avoided measures to compel immigrants to settle and remain in any particular place ... however imaginatively the current techniques to induce more broadly distributed settlement are applied, it must be frankly recognized that the apparent irresistible attraction of major cities for migrants ... will persist in the years immediately ahead. (Andras, 1975, p. 6)

What was true then would seem to be true today. Directed or steered immigration is not the solution to eliminating regional income inequality.

Conclusion

The central conclusion of this paper, then, is that the goal of immigration policy in the twenty-first century is likely to be very different from what it was in the last century. For much of the twentieth century immigration was an important element of economic policy. Immigrants filled the west at the turn of the last century, filled the demographic gaps of the 1950s, and, in the 1960s, helped the country adjust quickly to a more sophisticated economy. These economic rationales, I would suggest, have largely disappeared. We have no empty lands, the major structural changes have taken place, and we now have an educational infrastructure in place that can meet our needs for skilled workers. The rationale for admitting immigrants in the future will be more social and humanitarian than economic. This does not mean that immigration will not continue to have an impact on the economy, only that, in framing future immigration policy, economic determinants are likely to play a much smaller role. In fact these are the same type of considerations that have dominated US immigration policy since the early 1920s. Family reunification and refugee policy have dominated immigration policy debates in the United States for the last 80 years.

Alan G. Green

As we enter the twenty-first century, then, the question we should be asking ourselves is "What type of society do we wish to build in Canada"? One of the great gifts brought to us by the new immigrants is diversity in our way of life. We need to address the question as to the extent of diversity we desire and the speed with which we wish to achieve this goal. One thing is certain: we have come a long way from the goals of immigration policy set out by Mackenzie King in his famous statement before the House in 1947. King put economic and demographic concerns at the core of immigration policy for the postwar period, and he put out of consideration any de-Europeanization of the population with his statement that "[the] people of Canada did not wish, as a result of mass immigration, to make a fundamental alteration in the character of our population" (quoted in Green and Green, 1999, p. 430). We have come a long way since then.

What does this shift in emphasis in policy direction suggest about the levels of immigration (we take as given the concept of a universal policy of admission based on an individual's personal characteristics, not on the prospective immigrant's place of birth)? The first thing it suggests is that setting the level of immigration at 1% of the population, or any other arbitrary level to satisfy presumed economic needs is out of step with the reality of the current role of immigration. As we outlined above, immigration, at any politically acceptable level, will not solve problems like the aging of the population or regional inequality. It is also the case that we now have the educational facilities to meet our domestic needs for skilled workers in all but extreme circumstances. Immigration is not the panacea for all our problems.

This new view of the role of immigration means that we will have to rethink how immigration policy is drafted. In the past, immigration policy, with the exception of its role within the National Policy (that trio of policies embracing western settlement, railway building and tariffs that dominated Canadian economic policy in the late nineteenth and early twentieth centuries), has been largely designed independently of other key economic and social policies. The shift towards a more social, humanitarian approach will reduce even further the role of the point system in assessing who will and who will not be admitted. Hence, closer attention will have to be paid to the impact that immigration plays on such social policies as unemployment, welfare, local education needs, etc. This will be particularly critical if the government continues with its policy of setting annual target levels independent of short-run economic conditions.

This shift in policy orientation in no way suggests an end to immigration. Immigrants have played, and will continue to play, an important role in the evolution of this country. However, this shift in emphasis opens the door for discussion about the appropriate level of immigration. The shift to a social/humanitarian base means that the current policy posture of using immigrants to solve economic problems is no longer valid.

As a contribution to this debate over levels, I would like to suggest a formula first set out almost 40 years ago by a leading American labour economist, Melvin Reder (1963). In the early 1960s the United States was in the midst of reviewing its immigration policy (ultimately revised in 1965). As mentioned earlier, the Quota Act of 1924 had set a limit on the number of immigrants that could be admitted in any one year. With the abandonment of this policy new guidelines were being sought to determine the "optimal" level of annual inflow. Reder came up with the following formula. Immigration levels should be allowed to rise until the new entrants threatened to lower the following ratio:

$$\frac{\text{per family income of the lowest decile of native families}}{\text{per family income of median of family income.}}$$

(Reder, 1963, p. 230)

At the very least, this formula provides us with an objective measure around which to debate the sensitive issue of how many immigrants are to be admitted over a period of time.

An examination of the long-run evolution of Canadian immigration policy suggests that, in this case, the past is not a prologue to the future. We are long past the time when a fundamental re-evaluation of the current goals of immigration policy is needed.

References

Abbott, M. and C. Beach (1993), "Immigrant Earnings Differential and Birth-Year Effects for Men in the Post-War Canadian Economy", *Canadian Journal of Economics* 26 (August), 505–525.

Andras, R. (1975), "Highlights from the Green Paper on Immigration and Population", tabled in the House of Commons, February 3.

Beach, C.M. and A.G. Green, eds. (1988), *The Role of Immigration in Canada's Future* (Kingston, ON: John Deutsch Institute, Queen's University).

Borjas, G.J. (1999), *Heaven's Door: Immigration Policy and the American Economy* (Princeton, NJ: Princeton University Press).

Canada (1961), *Report of the Special Committee of the Senate on Manpower and Immigration* (Ottawa: Supply and Services Canada).

Canada. Health and Welfare (1994), *Canada's Future: A Report of the Demographic Review Committee* (Ottawa: Supply and Services Canada).

Collacott, M. (2002), *Canada's Immigration Policy: The Need for Reform*, Occasional Paper No. 64 (Vancouver: Fraser Institute).

Economic Council of Canada (1991), *New Faces in the Crowd: Economic and Social Impact of Immigration* (Ottawa: Supply and Services Canada).

Foot, D. (2000), *Boom, Bust and Echo* (Toronto: Macfarlane, Walter and Ross).

Francis, D. (2002), *Immigration: The Economic Case* (Toronto: Key Porter Books).

Great Britain. Office of Population Censuses and Surveys (various years), *Demographic Review: A Report on Population in Great Britain, 1994* (London: HMSO).

Green, A.G. and D. Green (1998), "Structural Change and the Mobility of Immigrants: Canada, 1921–1961". Paper prepared for the Conference on Regions in Canadian Growth, Queen's University, Kingston.

_____ (1999), "The Economic Goals of Canada's Immigration Policy", *Canadian Public Policy/Analyse de Politiques* 25(4), 425–451.

Green, A.G. and G.R. Sparks (1999), "Population Growth and the Dynamics of Canadian Development: A Multivariate Time Series Approach", *Explorations in Economic History* 36, 56–76.

Green, A.G. (2000), "Twentieth Century Canadian Economic History", in R. Gallman and S. Engerman (eds.), *The Cambridge Economic History of the United States, Vol. III* (Cambridge: Cambridge University Press), ch. 3.

Green, D. (1999), "Immigrant Occupational Attainment: Assimilation and Adjustment over Time", *Journal of Labor Economics* 17(1), 49–79.

Henripin, J. (1988), "Panel Discussion on Canadian Immigration Objectives: Levels, Composition and Directions", in Beach and Green (eds.), *Policy Forum on the Role of Immigration in Canada's Future*, 94–95.

Kent, T. (1988), "Immigration Issues: A Personal Perspective", in Beach and Green (eds.), *Policy Forum on the Role of Immigration in Canada's Future*, 9–11.

Lew, B. (2000), "European Immigration to Canada During the 1920s: The Impact of United States Quotas and Canadian Restrictions" (Peterborough: Department of Economics, Trent University), unpublished paper.

Reder, M. (1963), "The Economic Consequences of Increased Immigration", *Review of Economics and Statistics* 35 (August), 221–230.

Stoffman, D. (2002), *Who Gets In? What's Wrong with Canada's Immigration Program and How to Fix It* (Toronto: Macfarlane, Walter and Ross).

Section II

Role of Immigration in Meeting Demographic, Occupational and Capital Market Needs

Effect of Immigration on Demographic Structure

Roderic Beaujot

Demography is defined as the study of population states and processes. The states refer to size, distribution over space, and composition of the population. The processes are fertility, mortality, migration, and other changes in state. The main purpose here is to study how immigration affects demographic structure in terms of the size, distribution, and composition of the population. Size may be further affected by the relative fertility and mortality of immigrants. Distribution is affected by the initial place of arrival, and by the internal migration of immigrants. The factors of composition that are considered are age, ethnicity, language, education, labour force status, and income. For the most part, the analyses are based on past trends, but projections are also useful when considering population size, age structure, and labour force. The paper will end with some thoughts that seek to put migration in an interpretive context.

Deborah Matthews and Jianye Liu are gratefully acknowledged.

Population Size and Growth

The impact of immigration on past population size and growth can be examined from three different perspectives: the direct impact of migration on population growth, the impact of children born to immigrants, and the proportion of people in Canada who are foreign-born.

Annual population estimates provide a summary measure of the *direct impact* of immigration on population growth. This measure includes only arrivals and departures, or the first generation of immigrants. Over the century 1901 to 2001, the total immigration of some 12.8 million persons and emigration of some 6.1 million produced a net gain of 6.7 million, representing a quarter of the population growth over the period (Table 1). The contribution of net international migration to population growth has varied considerably over history, reaching a peak in the 1901–11 decade when it accounted for 44.1%. Over the period 1951–91, net migration accounted for 25% of population growth. However, the 1991–2001 period shows close to 60% of population growth is due to net migration. On an annual basis, since 1994, net migration has comprised a larger proportion of total population growth than natural increase (Bélanger, 2002, p. 10).

As natural increase slows down, and especially after it becomes negative, the measures of the contribution of net immigration to population growth lose some of their intuitive value. Rather than comparing natural increase and net migration, it may be best to compare immigrants and births as additions to the population. For instance, over the period 1991–2001, immigration accounted for 59.7% of population growth, but the average annual immigration was 220,900, while average births were 367,900, that is immigrants amounted to 38% of the total additions to the population.

It should also be noted that we are not counting here the temporary residents, that is persons who have a student or work visa to stay in Canada for a limited period, and persons seeking refugee status whose cases have not been determined by the courts. Estimating those who are in Canada for at least one year, the number of non-permanent residents increased from about 85,000 in 1982 to 225,000 in 1990, and 288,000 in 2001 (Michalowski, 1993, p. 64; Statistics Canada, 2002a, p. 74). Their numbers are therefore slightly higher than one year's immigration.

The direct impact of immigration and emigration can also be appreciated through a comparison to the base population. In particular, it is useful to compute the average annual levels per one-hundred people in the Canadian population (Table 1). In the period around the turn of the

Roderic Beaujot

Table 1: Immigration, Emigration, and Contribution to Population Growth, Canada, 1851–2001

	Population (at end of period)	Immigration	Average Immigration (% of population)	Emigration	Contribution to Population Growth %
1851	2,523,000				
1851–61	3,230,000	352,000	1.22	170,000	23.0
1861–71	3,689,000	260,000	0.75	410,000	−32.6
1871–81	4,325,000	350,000	0.87	404,000	−8.5
1881–91	4,833,000	680,000	1.49	826,000	−28.7
1891–1901	5,371,000	250,000	0.49	380,000	−24.2
1901–11	7,207,000	1,550,000	2.46	740,000	44.1
1911–21	8,788,000	1,400,000	1.75	1,089,000	19.7
1921–31	10,376,700	1,200,000	1.25	970,000	14.5
1931–41	11,506,700	149,000	0.14	241,000	−8.1
1941–51	14,009,400	548,000	0.43	379,000	7.9
1951–61	18,238,200	1,543,000	0.96	463,000	25.5
1961–71	21,962,082	1,429,000	0.71	707,000	21.7
1971–81	24,820,382	1,429,000	0.61	636,000	28.6
1981–91	28,030,864	1,381,000	0.52	490,000	27.7
1991–2001	31,081,887	2,229,125	0.75	407,180	59.7

Sources: Beaujot and Rappak (1988, p. 27); Statistics Canada (2002a, pp. 18–19).

century there was an average of 2.46 annual arrivals per 100 population. The period of the 1950s had levels very close to 1% of the receiving population. Decades since 1971 have seen annual arrivals in the order of 0.52 to 0.75% of base population, and departures in the order of 0.13 to 0.27% of the base population. The averages for the period 1971–2001 show immigration amounting to 0.63% of base population, and emigration amounting to 0.20%, for a net migration of 0.43% of base population.

The second approach for estimating the demographic impact of immigration includes the impact of *births to immigrants* on population growth. Applying birth and death rates observed over the 1951–81 period to the 1951 population, the population would have changed from 14 million in 1951 to 20.4 million in 1981 (Le Bras, 1988, p. 9). Since the 1981 population was 24.3 million, this implies that 38% of the actual growth was a function of immigration and births to these immigrants over the period 1951–81.

Adopting the same method of using past vital rates to determine the population size without international migration, Duchesne (1993) reports the surprising finding that over the period 1871–1991 there is very little difference in ultimate population size with or without migration. This is because it took a long time to compensate for the departures towards the United States of the period 1871–95. Using the "counter-factual" scenario of no international migration over the period 1951–2001, Denton, Feaver and Spencer (2001) arrive at a 2001 population of 22.2 million. This implies that 51.5% of the growth from 14 million to 31.1 million, over the period 1951–2001, was due to the direct plus indirect effect of international migration.

The indirect impact of immigration is affected by the *relative vital rages* of the foreign-born and Canadian-born populations. Various analyses conclude that the foreign-born have a slight advantage in health and mortality (e.g., Chen, Ng and Wilkins, 1996; Trovato, 1996; Choinière, 1993). This advantage appears to decline over time, pointing to selection factors. Immigrant fertility was lower than the Canadian average in the past, but above that average in the 1991 census (Maxim, 1996; Beaujot, 1997; Bélanger and Dumas, 1998). At the 1961 and 1971 censuses, in each age group, the foreign-born had a lower number of children ever born than the Canadian-born population (Ram and George, 1990). In 1981, this pattern applied to age groups 30 and over. In 1991 the foreign-born at age groups 30–44 had higher fertility, but the differences remain minor. The study of fertility differentials show that persons born in other than Canada, Europe, and North America have a higher probability of having a third child

Roderic Beaujot

(Bélanger, and Dumas, 1998, p. 57). Data from Quebec over the period 1976–95 indicate strong differences in fertility, with an average of 1.5 births per woman for the Canadian-born and 2.5 for the foreign-born (Tossou, 2002, p. 114).

The third approach to studying the impact of immigration on the population is to consider the *proportion of foreign-born* in the census data (e.g. Badets and Chui, 1994). This figure has increased slowly from 15 to 18% over the censuses from 1951 to 2001. The second generation, that is persons whose parents are foreign-born, have not been captured in the censuses since 1971. That census found that 33.8% of persons were either foreign-born or had at least one foreign-born parent (Kalbach and McVey, 1979, p. 179). Using data on births and deaths, Edmonston (1996) calculates that over the period 1951–91 about 35% of the Canadian population has been first or second generation, while about half have been in the first three generations. The 2001 census included the "birthplace of parents" question for persons aged 15 and over, showing that 16% are Canadian-born with at least one foreign-born parent.

Immigration and Future Population Growth

In the projections based on the 1996 census, the medium fertility assumption of 1.48 births per woman, with zero international migration produces a population that reaches a peak of 31.5 million in 2018, then begins to decline (Loh and George, 2001). In the medium projection used in the Statistics Canada (2001a) projections, that is fertility of 1.48, immigration of 225,000 per year, emigration of 66,000 per year, and life expectancy reaching 82, the population reaches a peak of 37.1 million in 2040, before beginning a slow decline to 36.9 million in 2051. That is, compared to zero immigration, an immigration of 225,000 delays population decline by 22 years, and produces a 2040 population that is 27% higher.

Table 2 sets out the assumptions that have been used in Statistics Canada population projections following the various censuses. The low assumption following the 1996 census uses a fertility of 1.3 and an immigration of 180,000, while the high assumptions is based on a fertility of 1.8 and immigration of 270,000. Natural increase becomes negative by 2016 in the low projection, 2026 in the medium projection, and 2036 in the high projection. Population decline starts after 2030 in the low projection,

Table 2: Assumptions Underlying Statistics Canada Projections from 1971 to 1996 Censuses

Projection	Total Fertility Rate			Immigration			Life Expectancy M/F		
	L	M	H	L	M	H	H	M	L
1971 census	1.8	2.2	2.6	120,000	. . .	160,000		70.2/ 78.3	
1976 census	1.7	. . .	2.1	125,000	150,000	175,000		70.2/ 78.3	
1981 census	1.4	1.66	2.2	100,000	. . .	150,000		74.9/ 81.6	
1986 census	1.2	1.67	2.1	140,000	. . .	200,000		77.2/ 84.0	
1991 census	1.5	1.7	1.9	150,000	250,000	330,000	81.0/ 86.0	78.5/ 84.0	77.0/ 83.0
1996 census	1.3	1.48	1.8	180,000	225,000	270,000	81.5/ 85.0	80.0/ 84.0	78.5/ 83.0

Source:1. Statistics Canada (1974, pp. 26, 59; 1979, pp. 21, 29; 1985, pp. 27, 41; 1990, pp. 12, 26; 1994, p. 59; 2001a, p. 57).
2. Statistics Canada, Demography Division, special tabulations.

after 2040 in the medium projection, and there is continued growth in the high projection.

Without reviewing all other projections here, it is worth observing that in the 18th Actuarial Report on the Canada Pension Plan, the fertility rate is set at 1.64, life expectancy at 81 by 2025, and net migration of 0.50% of population (Office of the Chief Actuary, 2001, pp. 14, 18). With these assumptions, the population of Canada less Quebec is still growing in 2050, having increased 38.8% since 2001.

In their projections to 2046, Denton, Feaver and Spencer (2000) use medium assumptions of 1.55 for fertility, 225,000 for immigration, 0.19 for emigration and life expectancy of 82.9 in 2046. These assumptions show continued growth through the projection period, bringing the 2046 population to 37.7 million, or a growth of 21.5% since 2001.

Unless fertility were to return to higher levels, immigration will likely continue to be more important than the natural increase, and population growth will be slower than it has been in the past, with prospects for decline under low assumptions. For instance, over the period 1951–2001 the population of Canada more than doubled, while the high, medium, and low projections based on the 1996 census anticipate a total growth of 39.7, 19, and 4.2% respectively over the period 2001–2051 (Statistics Canada, 2001a, p. 61). The impact of immigration will clearly become larger as natural increase declines and eventually becomes negative. Nonetheless, in the medium projection, after natural increase becomes negative and all of the growth is due to immigration, births still comprise 59.3% of the additions to the population (births plus immigrants) in the period 2025–2030 (Statistics Canada, 2001a, p. 118).

Following a United Nations (2000) study, the concept of replacement migration is useful for summarizing the impact of immigration on future population. That is, how could migration bring forms of replacement that would keep the population more similar to what it has been in the past. The first definition of replacement migration is the number of immigrants necessary to avoid long-term population decline, in the context of below replacement fertility. Ryder (1997) uses the concept of replacement migration in the sense of the level of migration that would achieve the same ultimate population size as we would achieve if fertility were at replacement levels. Using the vital rates of the early 1990s, Ryder places the replacement net migration figure at 167,225, which might be translated into an immigration of 215,000. With a continuation of recent levels of fertility, the projections that we have reviewed suggest than an annual immigration slightly above 225,000 per year would prevent population decline in the foreseeable future.

Age Structure

The impact of immigration on the age structure can be appreciated by comparing the median age of immigrants at arrival to that of the Canadian population. The median age of immigrants was relatively stable, averaging 25 years for each year between 1956 and 1976, then increasing to 27 years in 1981–86, 28 years in 1986–90 and 30 years in 1994–99 (Beaujot, Shiel and Schoel, 1989; Beaujot and Hou, 1993; CIC, 1997, p. 40; 1999, p. 40;

Bélanger, 2001, p. 53). The median age of the entire Canadian population has changed much more, increasing from 26.3 in 1961 to 37.6 in 2001. In effect, the median age of arriving immigrants was about one to two years younger than that of the receiving population in 1961, compared to seven to eight years younger by 2000. Both immigrant arrivals and the receiving population have been aging, but arrivals remain younger on average. However, the overall impact is rather small given that immigrant arrivals represent a small part of the total population. Clearly, other demographic phenomenon, including the movement of the baby boom through the age structure, lower fertility, and mortality reductions at older ages, have a larger impact on the age structure than the arrival of immigrants.

Other measures confirm that immigration has a rather small impact on the age structure. For instance, simulating population change as a function only of births and deaths after 1951 produces a 1981 population with an average age that is only 0.5 years older than the actual average observed in that year. Stated differently, the 1951–81 immigration would have reduced the average age of the 1981 population by a half year (Le Bras, 1988, p. 12). As another example, with zero international migration over the period 1951 to 2001, the median age in 2001 is only 0.8 years older than the actual figure for that year (Denton, Feaver and Spencer, 2001).

Similar results are obtained with projections into the future. The Statistics Canada (1990) population projections based on the 1986 census produce a median age in 2036 that is almost two years younger under high immigration than under zero immigration. This means that the arrival of 200,000 immigrants per year for 50 years would have only reduced the average age by two years. In comparison, the median age of the Canadian population increased by 2.3 years between 1996 and 2001.

Other analyses confirm that immigration slightly reduces the average age. For instance, Li and Wu (2001) obtain the result that as long as the fertility of the foreign-born is higher than 34% of that of the Canadian-born, immigration would have a slowing effect on aging.

The projections based on the 1996 census indicate that the proportion of those 65 and over reaches 25.4% in 2051 with an immigration of 225,000 per year, compared to 29.8% with zero international migration, and a 2001 figure of 13.0% (Loh and George, 2001). Denton, Feaver and Spencer (2001) show the effects of three immigration assumptions to 2051: (i) the standard case with immigration of 225,000, (ii) immigration 50% higher, and (iii) double the standard case. The median age in 2051 is 46.5 in the standard case, 45.1 with immigration 50% higher, and 44.2 with immigration of 450,000 per year. Thus, an extra 225,000 immigrants per year for 50 years reduces the median age by 2.3 years, and reduces the percent aged 65 and over by three percentage points (from 25.9 to 22.9%).

Using the assumptions underlying the projections from the 1991 census, George, Loh and Verma (1997) compare the impact of the various alternative fertility, mortality, and immigration assumptions on various parts of the population. For the total population, the alternative immigration assumptions have the largest impact for the first 40 years, but after that a difference of 0.4 between high and low fertility has a greater impact than a difference of 180,000 immigrants. Clearly, the alternate fertility assumptions have the largest impact on the growth of the population aged 0 to 14. For the growth of the population aged 65 and over, alternate life expectancies have the largest impact, and fertility has no impact over the projection period. For the population aged 15 to 64, the alternate immigration assumptions have the largest impact, and the mortality assumptions have the lowest impact.

An alternative definition of the United Nations (2000) concept of replacement migration seeks to maintain the relative size of the population aged 15–64 to that aged 65 and over. As recognized by the authors of the report, this scenario leads to absurd results, sometimes assuming that the whole world move to one country to prevent an increase in the proportion aged 65+ compared to that aged 15–64 (Coleman, 2000). This is the strong sense of "replacement migration", with migrants eventually replacing the original population (Lachapelle, 2001). As indicated by various projections, including those from Denton, Feaver and Spencer (1997), there is not a demographic solution to aging.

It is probably for the study of aging that population projections play their most useful role. Table 3 gathers data on the ratio of population aged 20–64 to the population aged 65 and over. In 1951, this ratio was close to seven persons of working ages per person at retirement ages, it has declined to under five, and will be about 2.5 in 2050. Even an immigration of 500,000 per year brings the ratio to 2.7 in 2036.

Labour Force

In "One Hundred Years of Labour Force", Crompton and Vickers (2000) show that the periods of most rapid labour force growth were those of high immigration, especially the decades of 1901–11 and 1951–61. In addition,

Table 3: Ratio of Population Aged 20–64 to Population Aged 65+, Canada, 1950–2100

Historical data			
1951	6.97		
1976	6.49		
2001	4.86		
Statistics Canada medium projection (from 1971 census)			
2001	5.35		
Statistics Canada projections in 2001	*2026*	*2051*	
Low (Projection 1)	3.04	2.42	
Medium (Projection 2)	3.04	2.45	
High (Projection 3)	3.05	2.51	
Projected in CPP for (year)	*2000*	*2050*	*2100*
Reported 0 (1964)	6.22	5.61	
Report 6 (1977)	5.62	3.47	
Report 12 (1988)	4.83	2.48	2.32
Report 17 (1999)	4.92	2.39	2.17
Report 18 (2000)	4.90	2.36	2.23*
Projected with alternate immigration levels (year)	*2016*	*2036*	
Zero immigration	3.36	1.79	
100,000	3.54	2.02	
200,000	3.70	2.22	
300,000	3.86	2.40	
400,000	4.00	2.59	
500,000	4.15	2.70	

Note: * in 2075.
Source: 1. Statistics Canada (2001a, pp. 183–185); Denton, Feaver and Spencer (1997, pp. 39, 41).
2. Office of the Chief Actuary (2001, p. 18).

Roderic Beaujot

the period 1955–90 experienced an increase in women's labour force participation, from 20% of women aged 25 and over working, to a level of 56% in 1990. Consequently, the labour force grew rapidly in the postwar era. The period 1966–86 included the entry of the baby boom into labour force ages, the rising participation of women, and the substantial level of immigration. The rate of growth of this period was unmatched by any other western industrialized economy (Foot, 1987).

Both for growth and for aging, trends in the labour force and in the whole population have been rather different. While the rate of growth of the entire population had been slowing down since 1951–56, the labour force population continued to grow rapidly into the early 1980s. In the period 1966 to 1981, the labour force was growing at close to 3% per year, while the growth has been 1.2% per year in 1991–2001 (Statistics Canada, 2001b). For aging, while the whole population had been aging for over a century, the average age of the labour force did not increase until 1986 when the baby boom was completely at labour force ages.

In their "what if" scenario with no immigration since 1951, Denton, Feaver and Spencer (2001) show that the labour force would have been almost 30% smaller in 2001 if there had been no migration. On the other hand, the median age of the labour force would only have been 0.4 years older than its actual 2001 average age of 38.9 years.

Turning to projections, the low assumptions from Statistics Canada (2001a) anticipates that the population aged 18–64 would reach a peak of 21.9 million in 2016, then slowly decline to 18.9 million in 2051. In the medium projection, this population increases by 11.5% between 2001 and 2021, then declines by 4.0% to 2051. In the high projection, the total growth over the period 2001–2051 is 22.0%. Thus, in all scenarios labour force growth is likely to be markedly slower than it has been in the past, and the low assumptions imply declines after 2016. However, the medium projection would anticipate only a very minor decline, and the total in 2051 would be higher than that of 2001. In this medium projection, it is not inconceivable that there would be no decline, if women's participation continues to increase, and if the participation for persons ages 60 and over stops declining.

It is also noteworthy that youth population, defined as ages 18–24, corresponding to labour force entry, increases under all scenarios from 2001 to 2011, then declines in absolute size under all scenarios, at least for a ten-year period (Statistics Canada, 2001a, p. 74). Another useful comparison is between the population at ages 15–24 and 55–64, corresponding to typical ages for labour force entry and exit. At the time of release of the age and sex profile from the 2001 census, many commentators spoke of an imminent labour shortage, and the prime minister made a case for higher immigration. Yet, in 2001 there were 1.4 persons aged 15–24 for every person aged 55–64. While the relative size of the persons at ages for labour force entry will continue to decline, according to the medium projection this ratio will nonetheless be 1.2 in 2006. In 2011, when the leading edge of the baby boom will be in retirement ages, the ratio of persons 15–24 to 55–64 will be 1.02, but the ratio will be 0.82 in 2031 when all of the baby boom will be over 65 years of age. Thus, until 2011, the numbers of people at ages for labour force entry will remain higher than those at ages for labour force exit, but in the more distant future all scenarios show more people at ages for labour force exit than at ages for entry.

In their projections of population and labour force to 2046, Denton, Feaver and Spencer (2000) show the labour force starting to decline after 2016 under the medium assumptions (fertility at 1.55 and immigration at 225,000). However, the decline to 2046 is only by 364,000 people, 2.1% over 30 years, which could be made up with slight increases in participation. The low assumptions, fertility at 1.25 and immigration at 175,000, show the labour force starting to decline after 2011, with a decline of 12.7% over the next 35 years. Compared to an immigration of 225,000, annual immigration that is 50% higher increases the size of the labour force in 2051 by 18.5%, while double the immigration increases the size by 36.9% (Denton, Feaver and Spencer, 2001). However, doubling the immigration level only reduces the median age of the labour force in 2051 by 0.4 years compared to an average age of 40.9 years in the standard case.

A third meaning of replacement migration would seek to use migration to maintain the size of the labour force. If the objective is to prevent the labour force from declining, it is useful to appreciate that there are other factors that can be manipulated. McDonald and Kippen (2001) have outlined scenarios where, besides immigration, other factors are considered, in particular the participation rate in the labour force (including ages at entry and departure, and women's participation) and the level of fertility. In their results for Canada, along with the United States, New Zealand, Australia, and Singapore, decreases in labour supply can be avoided through continuation of the present fertility, immigration and labour force participation rates. These results are similar to those obtained by Denton and colleagues shown above, where the standard assumptions show very little labour force decline after 2016, which could be made up through higher participation. Compared to the other 16 countries studied by McDonald and Kippen (2001), Canada and Australia are seen as having

Roderic Beaujot

"moderate fertility, high immigration and low labour force participation". With current immigration, their results show the labour force rising only slowly but not declining. Compared to this standard assumption, the current fertility and labour force participation rates, but with zero immigration, would bring declines in labour supply after about 2015. Increased labour force participation rates, moving men's rates at ages 35+ towards their rates in 1970 and moving women's rates at ages 25+ towards Swedish rates, would lead to large increases in labour supply (25% increase from 2000 to 2030). A return to fertility of 1.8 would bring growth of the labour force after 2025, compared to holding fertility and migration constant.

The 2001 annual report to Parliament observes that 70% of labour force growth is due to immigration (CIC, 2001, p. 2). This figure is derived by looking at the change in the size of the labour force between two censuses, used as a denominator, compared to the number of labour force participants who had arrived in the previous five years. That is, of the change in the size of the labour force, what percentage is due to immigration? When the labour force is growing slowly, this figure is not very meaningful. For instance, if the labour force grew from 10,000,000 to 10,000,001 but one member of the labour force was an immigrant of the past five years, then 100% of the labour force growth would be due to the arrival of that one person. It would seem more appropriate to look at the relative size of the internal and external sources of entry into the labour force. The size of cohorts turning say 20 these days is about 408,000, while immigration is about 210,000. Of course, neither group would be completely in the labour force. If we estimate that 90% of those coming to labour force ages will be in the labour force at some point, and that 90% of immigrants aged 15–64 will also be in the labour force, then we would have 507,000 additions to the labour force, of which 72% would be due to internal recruitment and only 28% due to immigration.

That is, while immigration is an important source of recruitment to the labour force, some have exaggerated this importance. For instance, based on projections using zero immigration, Baxter is quoted as saying that "if we didn't have immigration, we'd stop regenerating our labour force in about four years" (Hutchinson, 2002, p. 32). This implies that there is little regeneration associated with the numbers of people leaving Canadian schools to enter the labour force. It is absurd to say that our labour force will not be renewed unless we have immigration! Clearly, immigration is an important source of recruitment, but there are other avenues. Depending excessively on immigration can also undermine other sources of recruitment, both in terms of appropriate educational investments and population groups that have lower labour force participation. For instance, demographers in Sweden are convinced that, by avoiding the solution of guest workers, the country was pushed to adopt family-friendly policies that encouraged women's participation (Hoem and Hoem, 1997).

In the Canadian case, the average hours worked per week is 37.9 for employed men and 32.3 for women. Applied to the 45% female in the labour force, increasing women's average hours to that of men would be comparable to a 6.6% increase in the size of the labour force. At ages 25 and over, the employment rate is 69.1 for men and 55.8 for women. Reducing that difference by half would be equivalent to a 4.4% increase in the labour force. If the aim of replacement migration is to prevent the labour force from declining, various means can be used, including having a continued annual immigration of some 225,000 per year, with very slight increases in participation.

Geographic Distribution

Given its uneven distribution over space, immigration has an impact on the geographic distribution of Canada's population. As immigration becomes the principle component of population change, there are increased regional inequalities in demographic growth. The subsequent re-migration of the foreign-born population accentuates this regional inequality. Rather than being a national phenomenon, immigration especially benefits population growth in a limited number of provinces and metropolitan areas.

Over the four decades 1956–96, the two provinces of Ontario and British Columbia have consistently had a percentage of immigrant arrivals that exceeded their percentage of the Canadian population (Denton, Feaver and Spencer, 1997, p. 42). What is more, except for Manitoba and Alberta in 1976–86, Ontario and British Columbia are the only provinces to have more immigrants than their share of the population over the period 1956–96.

The regional integration of immigrants follows especially on economic questions and the links established between sending and receiving areas. In their theoretical syntheses, Massey et al. (1994) propose that globalization creates both migrant populations following on economic displacements, and employment opportunities in large cities. With efficient means of communication, migratory exchanges are perpetuated between places of origin and destination. As a consequence, recent immigrants are concentrated in the large cities.

Considering five Canadian regions, in comparison to the Canadian-born population, immigrants are more concentrated in Ontario and British Columbia, and less concentrated in the Atlantic region and Quebec (Table 4). For instance, in 1996 Quebec represented 27.1% of the Canadian-born population but 13.4% of the foreign-born. In comparison, Ontario had 33.5% of the Canadian-born but 54.8% of the foreign-born. Among Canadian-born, the largest province exceeds the second by 24%, but foreign-born are four times as numerous as in Quebec.

The geographic impact is even more visible at the level of census metropolitan areas. While postwar immigration has largely been a metropolitan phenomenon, the Review of Demography (1989) more correctly concluded that this has involved the metropolitan areas west of the Quebec-Ontario border, plus Montreal. East of this border, the highest proportion of immigrants is in Halifax, but this is still under half of the national average (Statistics Canada, 1997). Even Winnipeg, Oshawa, Ottawa-Hull, Thunder Bay, Regina, Saskatoon and Sudbury have a smaller proportion of immigrants than the national average of 17.4% foreign-born in the 1996 census. In these distributions, it is especially Toronto and Vancouver that stand out, with 41 and 35% foreign-born respectively by 1996. In the Canadian-born population, Montreal retains its historical position as the largest Canadian city, but the immigrant population of Toronto is three times that of Montreal. In addition, immigrants to Quebec are highly concentrated in Montreal, amounting to 88% of Quebec's foreign-born in 1996.

In terms of total numbers, the three metropolitan areas of Toronto, Montreal, and Vancouver stand out, with 60.2% of the foreign-born compared to 26.8% of the Canadian-born population (Table 5). The concentration is even more uneven when considering recent immigrants. A fifth of the 1996 populations of Toronto and Vancouver consists of immigrants who have arrived since 1981 (Statistics Canada, 1997, p. 5). Over the immigrant arrival cohorts, Toronto and Vancouver have increased their share of immigrants, while this share is stable for Montreal, it has declined slightly for the total of other metropolitan areas, and significantly for the non-metropolitan areas. Consequently, the non-metropolitan population comprises 43% of the Canadian-born population but only 6.5% of immigrant arrivals of the period 1991–96.

More generally, the metropolitan destination of immigrants is pushing the urbanization trend. The metropolitan areas as a whole have been

Table 4: Regional Distribution of Canadian-Born and Immigrants by Arrival Cohorts, Censuses of 1971 to 1996, Canada (Percent)

	1971	1981	1991	1996
Canadian-born				
Atlantic	10.3	10.9	9.9	9.5
Quebec	30.7	28.9	27.5	27.1
Ontario	33.2	32.2	33.4	33.5
Prairies	16.5	17.8	17.7	17.7
British Columbia	9.3	10.3	11.1	11.8
Total	100.0	100.0	100.0	100.0
Immigrants 1961–70				
Atlantic	2.1	2.1	1.8	1.9
Quebec	18.0	16.0	14.2	13.9
Ontario	55.5	55.5	57.4	57.1
Prairies	11.3	11.3	10.5	10.4
British Columbia	13.0	15.1	15.9	16.6
Total	100.0	100.0	100.0	100.0
Immigrants 1971–80				
Atlantic	--	2.4	1.9	1.9
Quebec	--	14.1	13.6	13.3
Ontario	--	51.6	52.5	52.5
Prairies	--	15.1	14.3	13.7
British Columbia	--	16.8	17.6	18.5
Total	--	100.0	100.0	100.0
Immigrants 1981–91				
Atlantic	--	--	1.3	1.3
Quebec	--	--	15.8	14.4
Ontario	--	--	54.0	54.9
Prairies	--	--	13.1	12.3
British Columbia	--	--	15.7	17.0
Total	--	--	100.0	100.0
Immigrants 1991–96				
Atlantic	--	--	- -	1.1
Quebec	--	--	- -	14.5
Ontario	--	--	- -	54.2
Prairies	--	--	- -	9.3
British Columbia	--	--	- -	20.8
Total	--	--	- -	100.0

Note: Total includes the Territories.
Sources: Beaujot and Rappak (1990, p. 113); 1991 Census: 93–316, Tables 3 and 6; 1996 Census: N03–0411.1VT.

Roderic Beaujot

Table 5: Distribution of Canadian-Born and Immigrants by Arrival Cohorts, by Metropolitan Areas, Canada, 1991 and 1996 (Percent)

	Can-Born	Before 1961	1961–70	1971–80	1981–91	1991–96
			- 1991 -			
Toronto	10.2	25.1	35.4	36.5	39.4	--
Montreal	11.3	9.5	12.8	11.7	14.0	--
Vancouver	4.8	8.4	9.8	12.6	12.9	--
Sub-total	26.3	43.0	58.0	60.8	66.3	--
Other CMA	28.0	30.3	26.0	25.8	24.5	--
Other	45.6	26.6	16.0	13.4	9.2	--
Total	100.0	100.0	100.0	100.0	100.0	--
			- 1996 -			
Toronto	10.4	25.1	34.2	36.2	40.0	42.4
Montreal	11.4	9.4	12.4	11.6	12.8	12.9
Vancouver	5.0	8.1	10.0	13.0	13.7	18.3
Sub-total	26.8	42.6	56.6	60.8	66.5	73.6
Other CMA	30.1	30.2	26.8	24.9	23.9	19.8
Other	43.0	27.1	16.6	14.3	9.7	6.5
Total	100.0	100.0	100.0	100.0	100.0	100.0

Notes: CMA: census metropolitan areas. In 1996 the Canadian-born includes the non-permanent residents.
Sources: Special tabulations based on 1991 public use sample. 1996 Census: N03–0411.1VT and Population by age group, sex and marital status.

increasing through immigration but declining as a result of net internal migration. In a study of metropolitan areas of various sizes over the period 1976 to 1996, Gilbert, Bélanger and Ledent (2001) find that the growth of the largest metropolitan areas is largely due to immigration, while that of non-metropolitan regions is due mostly to internal migration. Over the 25 metropolitan areas of the 1996 census, the net internal migration of the 1991–96 period represents a net departure of 156,000 persons, while 971,000 immigrants had arrived in the five years that preceded the census (Table 6). Internal migration was positive in ten of the metropolitan areas, but except in Victoria recent immigrants are more numerous than net internal migrants. In eight metropolitan areas the immigrant arrivals are insufficient to compensate for the net departure by internal migration. However, in the remaining seven cities (Edmonton, Halifax, London, Montreal, Sherbrooke, St. Catharines-Niagara, and Toronto) there is a negative net internal migration of 167,485 persons but a net international arrival of 627,265 persons over the period 1991–96. Migration statistics for 2000–2001 indicate that these patterns have since continued. That is, there was positive net migration into the three largest metropolitan areas, but the internal migration indicates more people leaving than arriving (Statistics Canada, 2002b, p. 6). Not only is immigration pushing the urbanization trend, but in most of the largest cities it is helping to compensate for the net departure through internal migration.

The 2001 census has highlighted four large urban regions which together comprise just over half of Canada's population: the extended Golden Horseshoe from Oshawa to Kitchener in Southern Ontario with 6.7 million people or 22% of the country's population, Montreal and adjacent region with a population of 3.7 million or 12% of the country, British Columbia's lower mainland and southern Vancouver Island with 2.7 million people or 9% of the country, and the Calgary-Edmonton corridor, with 2.2 million people and 7% of the country. Compared to the total country which grew by 4% over the period 1996–2001, these four regions grew by 7.6%. Those provinces that did not include one of these urban regions either declined in population or increased by less than 1% in the five-year period.

Not only is the distribution of the immigrant population rather different from that of the Canadian-born, but the subsequent internal migration of the foreign-born tends to accentuate these differences, in favour of Ontario and British Columbia (Table 4). It is in the initial years after arrival that immigrants are most mobile; after 15 years of residence, their mobility is less than that of the Canadian-born population (Ram and Shin, 1999). The

Roderic Beaujot

Table 6: Immigrants of the 1991–96 Period and Net International Migration of the Period 1991–96, by Metropolitan Area, Canada

	Immigrants of 1991–96	*Net Internal Migration*
Total CMA	971,040	−156,425
Calgary	33,775	9,275
Chicoutimi-Jonquière	285	−4,060
Edmonton	27,270	−23,615
Halifax	4,850	−3,730
Hamilton	17,940	820
Kitchener	12,600	1,480
London	11,770	−3,440
Montreal	134,535	−47,880
Oshawa	3,785	13,005
Ottawa-Hull	38,040	1,695
Quebec	5,175	1,670
Regina	2,675	−4,520
Saskatoon	3,555	−3,960
Sherbrooke	2,095	−1,225
St. Catharines-Niagara	5,715	−190
St. John's	895	−3,950
Saint John	245	−1,520
Sudbury	745	−2,400
Thunder Bay	945	−3,585
Toronto	441,030	−87,405
Trois-Rivières	470	730
Vancouver	189,660	12,095
Victoria	6,250	9,715
Windsor	10,655	1,545
Winnipeg	16,080	−16,975

Source: 1996 Census: N03–0411.1VT; Statistics Canada (1998).

foreign-born are most likely to leave the Atlantic region as well as Manitoba, Saskatchewan, and Quebec, while they are least likely to leave Ontario (Edmonston, 1996). The provinces that receive disproportionate numbers of immigrants are less likely to see their departures for other provinces (Bélanger, 1993; Edmonston, 2002). That is, there is no evidence of an increased dispersion of immigrants over time (Edmonston, 1996).

Population distribution is thus different from other characteristics that distinguish immigrants. On most characteristics, the impact of immigration in terms of the differences that they represent, lessens over time (Beaujot, 1999). For instance, their fertility and mortality comes to resemble that of the Canadian-born, as do their economic characteristics. Even the visibility of minorities lessens over time, as styles of dress and speech become more similar with a longer length of residence. However, on geographic distribution, where immigration accentuates the uneven distribution of the population, the subsequent re-migration of immigrants tends to accentuate the largest areas of initial destination.

Given that immigrants are likely to settle mostly in metropolitan areas and to follow the pathways established by earlier cohorts, immigration will probably continue to accentuate the inequalities in Canada's regional population distribution. While there are efficiencies associated with more concentration of population, this also means that immigration cannot be seen as a means of demographic redistribution towards areas that have smaller populations. In an article on the social and political implications of recent immigration trends, Simmons (1997) expresses concern that those provinces that do not include large metropolitan areas will see a decline in their relative population share and associated political and economic correlates.

Socio-Cultural Composition

The main elements of socio-cultural composition to be considered are place of birth, visible-minority status and language. Generalizing about minorities in various countries, Lacroix (1991) makes the interesting observation that all societies have minorities and need to balance assimilation and the respect for differences. The uniqueness of Canada does not come from the presence of minorities and the dynamics of their integration, but from the fact that immigration plays a predominant role in such questions.

Figure 1 illustrates the changing composition of the immigrant stream over the period 1946-2001. Until 1970 more than half of arrivals were from Europe. Since 1979 the Asian component has been the largest. The proportion from Asia, Latin America, and Africa combined increased from 8% in 1961 to 65% in 1980 and has since increased to about 80% of total arrivals.

The term visible minorities is increasingly used to refer to the population of non-European origin. In view of employment equity programs, the visible-minority population is defined as persons who are neither white, caucasian nor Aboriginal. In effect, it is largely the population that originates directly or indirectly from Asia, Latin America, and Africa.

At the 1981 census, the visible-minority population was estimated at 1,130,000 persons (4.7% of the total population), of which 85% were of foreign birth (Samuel, 1987). In 1991, this population numbered 2,715,000 or 9.7% of the total population. Among persons with visible-minority status aged 15 and over in 1991, close to two-thirds had arrived since 1971, and 35% since 1981 (Kelly, 1995). The 1996 census enumerated 3.2 million persons with visible-minority status, including slightly more than 30% of

Figure 1: Place of Birth of Immigrants, 1946–2001, Canada

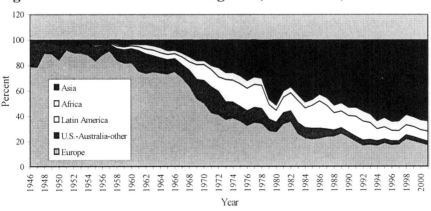

Notes: For 1997–2001, estimates were made based on published data for other regions.

Sources: Special tabulations from Employment and Immigration, Immigration Statistics, Citizenship and Immigration Statistics, and Facts and Figures from 1946–2001.

Toronto and Vancouver, and 74% of the 1991–96 immigrants (Chard and Renaud, 1999). Based on slightly lower mortality and slightly higher fertility than the national average, and with a continuation of immigration trends, it is projected that the visible-minority population would increase to about seven million in 2016, or close to 20% of the Canadian population (Dai and George, 1996). These projections are based on broad definitions to capture any element of non-caucasian origin. In particular, all children born from mixed parentage including caucasian and visible minorities are classified as visible minority. Thus, the projections are based on strong ethnic retention, while the very meaning of visible-minority status may change considerably over a 20-year period. It can be argued that Canada is becoming a multi-ethnic society where "pluralism" rather than "visible minorities" is the more appropriate term.

Turning to language, significant numbers do not know English or French at the time of arrival, but over time the majority come to associate with one or the other of the official languages. At the time of arrival, 30% of immigrants of the 1969–77 period, and more than 40% of those of the 1978–2001 period did not know either of the official languages (Thomas, 1992; CIC, 2002). In the 1991–96 cohort, only a quarter of immigrants were using an official language at home in 1996, and more than 10% knew neither of these languages (Table 7).

In order to highlight this tendency for immigrants to associate with the official languages, the concept of "predominant language" combines the responses on language spoken at home and knowledge of official languages. Persons who speak English or French at home were assigned this language as their predominant language. Persons speaking "other" languages at home were also assigned to English or French predominant language if they could speak "only" that language among the official languages. In effect, this measures which one among the official languages is a given person's predominant language.

Outside Quebec, the results are simple: immigration contributes to the English language, and there is less French among immigrants than in the Canadian-born population (Table 8). In Quebec, the foreign-born are clearly less French (41%) than the Canadian-born population (88.5%). In spite of the minority status of English in Quebec, immigrant cohorts before 1965 are more English than French. For the cohorts arriving since 1980, about 45% are French-predominant language, with 25% English, and the remaining 30% cannot be classified in either language. Other research finds that French is stronger for younger immigrants and for those who did not know English at the time of arrival (Veltman, 1988; Paillé, 1989).

Table 7: Knowledge and Use of Official Languages, by Sex, for Canadian-Born and Various Immigrant Cohorts, Canada, 1996 (Percent)

| | Know an Official Language | | | | Do not Know an Official Language | |
| | Spoken at Home | | Not Spoken at Home | | | |
	Male	Female	Male	Female	Male	Female
Canadian-born	97.1	97.2	2.5	2.4	0.4	0.4
Immigrants	55.1	54.7	39.6	36.7	5.3	8.6
Before 1951	83.1	84.3	15.9	13.9	1.0	1.9
1951–65	72.3	70.0	24.7	24.7	3.0	5.3
1966–75	69.1	68.0	27.6	25.7	3.3	6.3
1976–80	56.9	56.3	38.1	35.5	5.0	8.2
1981–85	47.5	47.6	46.1	40.9	6.4	11.5
1986–90	37.1	38.8	56.4	50.6	6.5	10.5
1991–96	27.5	28.3	62.3	57.3	10.2	14.4

Source: Census of Canada (1996). Public Use Micro-data File of Individuals.

Quebec also receives a greater proportion of immigrants who know neither of the official languages, and persons of third languages retain these longer. This longer retention is probably related to the larger potential for ethnic separateness provided by French-English tensions in Quebec. In addition, as we have seen, immigration is concentrated in the one metropolitan area of Montreal, and the city of Montreal in particular (Paillé, 1991). This concentration presents a difficulty for linguistic integration. For instance, in given localities, the French mother tongue children can be in a minority, even in French schools. It is found that immigrant students in French schools which have a high concentration of non-French ethnic origin are less positively oriented to learning French (McAndrew *et al.*, 2000). On the other hand, immigrants of third languages are more oriented to French than are non-immigrants of either English or third languages (Castonguay, 1992).

Table 8: Predominant Language for Canadian-Born and Various Immigrant Cohorts, Quebec and Rest of Canada, 1996 (Percent)

	Quebec			Rest of Canada		
	English	French	Other	English	French	Other
Canadian-born	9.3	88.5	2.2	95.8	3.3	0.9
Immigrants	31.9	41.0	27.1	90.6	0.6	8.9
Before 1951	69.0	20.8	10.2	98.1	0.2	1.7
1951–65	42.9	32.3	24.8	95.0	0.3	4.7
1966–75	34.3	42.6	23.1	93.5	0.5	6.0
1976–80	23.1	49.1	27.7	90.5	0.5	9.0
1981–85	23.4	45.0	31.6	87.5	0.6	11.9
1986–90	24.7	43.5	31.7	87.5	0.5	11.9
1991–96	26.3	43.7	30.0	83.8	0.7	15.4

Notes: The predominant language is determined on the bases of language spoken at home and knowledge of official languages. Those who speak one national language at home are assigned this predominant language. Those who do not speak English or French at home are assigned that predominant language if they know only English or French among the official languages. The "other" category comprises those who speak both English and French at home, plus those who speak neither language at home and know both or neither of the official languages.

Source: Census of Canada, 1996. Public Use Micro-data File of Individuals.

The general linguistic trends in Canada involve decreases in the official language minorities, that is English in Quebec and French in the rest of Canada. For the rest of Canada, immigration contributes to the trend as there is less French among immigrants than in the native-born population. In Quebec, immigration enhances the English minority because there is more English among immigrants than in the native-born, and a sizeable proportion of third-language migrants continue to transfer to the English

Roderic Beaujot

language. The immigrants to Quebec who are most likely to associate with the French language are those who were selected on the basis of prior knowledge of French, and children who arrive early enough to be schooled in French.

Immigration therefore plays an important role in Canada's changing linguistic distribution. Although the distribution by languages changes only slowly, immigration is the main element producing an increase in the relative size of the English language in comparison to the French language (Lachapelle, 1988a). While language policy in Quebec has promoted a greater association of immigrants to the French language, this is partly at the expense of departures of English and other linguistic groups. Therefore, it is at the expense of a lower total weight of Quebec in the population of Canada. Lachapelle (1988b) has put it well: it is hard to envisage scenarios that would both sustain the weight of Quebec in the Canadian total and increase the proportion of French in Quebec. The rest of Canada does not have such a problem: more of its international arrivals are English to start with, other immigrants retain their languages less, and almost all transfers favour English.

Socio-Economic Status

Immigration can also affect the characteristics of the population in terms of education, labour force status and income. These are best analyzed in regard to entry cohorts, which are here also separated by birthplace groups.

On *education*, the relative advantage of immigrants compared to the Canadian-born was highest in the immediate postwar period, when the Canadian educational system was poorly developed. Even for the 1961–69 arrivals, 23.1% of persons aged 25–64 had some university education in 1971, compared to 10.5% of the Canadian population.

Measured in terms of average years of education, Table 9 shows that immigrant men of given immigration cohort and age groups always have more average education than their Canadian-born counterparts. However, for women the differences are smaller and there are some comparisons, especially among women aged 45 and over for recent cohorts, where the Canadian-born have more education. Among the immigrant cohorts since 1975 or 1980, those from Europe and the United States typically have more

Table 9: Average Years of Education by Ten-year Age Group and Sex, Separately for Canadian-Born, Foreign-Born, by Arrival Cohort, and Place of Birth of Foreign-Born, Canada, 1996

	Female						Male					
	15–24	25–34	35–44	45–54	55–64	Total	15–24	25–34	35–44	45–54	55–64	Total
Canadian-born	12.5	13.7	13.1	12.3	10.9	12.7	12.0	13.4	13.1	12.5	10.8	12.6
Immigrants	12.8	13.7	13.2	12.5	10.7	12.6	12.5	13.9	13.6	13.3	11.9	13.1
Before 1951				12.9	11.1	12.1				13.4	11.8	12.6
1951–65	14.8	14.3	13.5	12.0	10.5	11.6	14.0	13.9	13.8	12.8	11.3	12.3
1966–75	13.7	14.2	12.9	12.8	11.5	12.9	13.4	13.8	13.4	13.4	12.7	13.4
1976–80	12.8	14.1	12.9	12.9	10.9	13.1	13.4	13.9	13.3	13.6	12.3	13.4
1981–85	12.8	13.3	13.3	12.6	10.1	12.8	12.5	13.8	13.7	13.9	12.5	13.3
1986–90	12.5	13.2	13.3	12.6	9.7	12.8	12.2	13.5	13.7	13.7	11.7	13.2
1991–94	12.3	13.7	13.4	12.2	9.5	12.8	12.1	14.4	13.9	13.3	11.3	13.2
Europe and US	12.9	14.0	13.3	13.5	10.6	12.4	12.6	13.7	13.5	13.0	11.5	12.8
Before 1951				12.9	11.1	12.1				13.4	11.9	12.7
1951–65	14.5	14.2	13.4	11.9	10.3	11.5	13.9	14.6	13.7	12.8	11.1	12.2
1966–75	13.6	13.9	12.3	12.3	10.9	12.4	13.3	15.0	12.8	12.8	12.0	12.8
1976–80	12.8	14.1	13.1	13.1	11.1	13.1	12.4	13.9	13.4	13.4	12.3	13.4
1981–85	12.1	13.7	14.2	13.6	12.0	13.6	11.9	13.4	14.1	14.5	13.0	13.7
1986–90	12.5	13.6	13.8	13.2	10.9	13.2	12.3	13.3	13.7	13.7	11.9	13.2
1991–94	12.3	14.8	14.4	13.9	12.0	14.1	12.3	13.6	14.4	14.4	13.1	13.9
Other	12.7	13.5	13.1	12.4	10.8	12.8	12.5	13.8	13.7	13.8	12.7	13.4
Before 1951				12.8	10.7	12.0				15.0	10.7	11.4
1951–65	15.2	14.9	14.2	13.1	12.0	12.9	14.2	14.1	14.3	13.7	12.8	13.4
1966–75	13.8	14.8	13.6	13.5	12.4	13.6	13.6	14.3	14.1	14.3	13.9	14.3
1976–80	12.8	14.1	12.9	12.7	10.8	13.0	12.5	13.9	13.3	13.7	12.4	13.5
1981–85	12.8	13.2	12.7	11.9	9.4	12.5	12.3	13.5	13.5	13.3	12.0	13.2
1986–90	12.6	13.1	13.1	12.4	9.4	12.6	12.0	13.3	13.7	13.7	11.7	13.2
1991–94	12.2	13.3	13.1	11.8	9.1	12.5	12.0	13.8	13.8	13.1	11.1	13.0

Source: Census of Canada, 1996. Public Use Micro-data File of Individuals.

Roderic Beaujot

education. For the older cohorts, the immigrants from other than Europe and the United States typically have more average education.

In the 1986 census, *labour force participation* at given ages was higher for immigrants than for the Canadian-born (Beaujot, 1991, p. 129). In the 1996 census, labour force participation is now slightly higher for Canadian-born than for immigrants (Table 10). There are significant differences by immigration cohort, with participation typically higher than that of the Canadian-born for cohorts arriving before 1980 or 1985. For the cohorts arriving since 1986, all but one of the ten-year age and sex groups has lower labour force participation than that of the Canadian-born. Labour force participation is typically higher for immigrants born in Europe and the United States, especially for men and for women arriving since 1980.

Table 11 shows two age-adjusted measures of *average income*. Total income relates to all persons who indicated a positive income in 1995. Employment income is based on persons aged 15–64 who worked full-time for at least 40 weeks in 1995.

In earlier censuses, immigrants as a whole were very close to the national average (Beaujot, Basavarajappa and Verma, 1988). In the 1996 census, the averages for total immigrants are 6 to 14% below the Canadian-born in average income. There are marked differences by arrival cohort and place of origin. Groups that arrived before 1975 largely have average incomes higher than that of the Canadian-born population, while the more recent immigrant cohorts have a disadvantage. Another change takes place over these same cohorts: the average income of immigrants from Europe and the United States moves from being less than to being more than that of immigrants from other continents. In the post-1976 cohorts there is a strong disadvantage for immigrants who are not from Europe and the United States, that is, the largely visible minorities. For persons admitted in the period 1981–90, the disadvantage at the time of the 1996 census is in the range of 25 to 35% for men and 15 to 25% for women. For arrivals in the last five years before the census, those from Europe and the United States have a disadvantage of some 20 to 35%, while those from other continents have a disadvantage of 40 to 50%.

Similar conclusions are reached by looking at the proportions with low-income status or who are unemployed. For the 1980s, Hou and Picot (2002) find that the propensities of low income were quite similar for the immigrants in comparison to the Canadian-born, but by 1999 the rates of low income were 33% higher in the foreign-born. Immigrants who had been in Canada less than five years already had low-income levels that were 1.29 times the rate of the Canadian-born in 1981, but this increased to 2.18 times

Table 10: Labour Force Participation Rate by Ten-year Age Group and Sex, Separately for Canadian-Born, Foreign-Born, by Arrival Cohort, and Place of Birth of Foreign-Born, Canada, 1996

	Female						Male					
	15–24	25–34	35–44	45–54	55–64	Total	15–24	25–34	35–44	45–54	55–64	Total
Canadian-born	61.3	79.4	80.3	74.0	39.0	70.0	64.2	92.4	92.5	89.0	59.8	81.9
Immigrants	51.6	72.9	75.7	74.5	42.3	66.2	53.6	88.6	90.7	90.0	67.6	81.5
Before 1951				77.7	42.4	61.2				89.0	64.3	76.6
1951–65		82.1	82.9	73.7	40.0	60.0		93.7	94.1	91.6	64.3	79.4
1966–75	81.7	81.1	81.5	78.4	51.5	74.6	79.6	92.4	92.5	91.5	76.5	88.3
1976–80	65.8	78.7	77.1	77.3	51.8	73.6	71.7	91.3	92.7	91.3	75.5	87.3
1981–85	54.8	74.5	76.0	76.7	42.7	69.5	57.7	90.1	91.6	91.1	69.5	83.1
1986–90	47.3	69.7	73.0	69.9	34.5	64.0	47.8	87.3	89.6	86.0	64.5	78.3
1991–94	42.3	66.1	65.1	56.5	24.1	56.4	44.1	83.8	84.6	79.6	43.2	71.7
Europe and US	61.2	77.6	79.3	75.1	41.6	67.1	63.0	92.5	93.4	91.7	67.9	83.9
Before 1951				77.8	43.1	61.8				89.0	64.5	77.2
1951–65		81.6	83.1	73.3	38.7	59.3		93.4	93.9	91.7	64.0	79.4
1966–75	83.1	81.3	80.3	75.6	46.5	72.0	80.6	93.3	93.1	91.6	74.7	88.1
1976–80	70.7	81.8	76.8	76.5	51.7	74.2	72.8	93.9	94.3	92.9	77.3	88.6
1981–85	59.2	77.2	78.6	80.0	56.6	73.6	63.3	93.1	92.9	93.3	79.6	85.6
1986–90	51.1	73.4	76.2	80.5	42.6	69.6	53.8	92.6	94.0	90.6	73.9	84.5
1991–94	53.3	70.9	73.5	69.1	33.0	66.5	54.5	89.0	91.8	93.1	78.5	83.1
Other	48.2	70.4	73.1	73.8	43.8	65.4	50.0	86.5	88.6	87.6	66.8	79.3
Before 1951				75.0	30.0	50.0				87.5	61.9	66.0
1951–65		84.8	81.5	77.6	50.4	65.9		94.7	95.8	90.5	66.6	80.0
1966–75	80.3	80.8	82.8	81.9	59.6	78.2	78.4	91.0	91.8	91.5	79.2	88.6
1976–80	62.8	77.0	77.2	78.0	51.9	73.3	71.0	90.0	91.8	90.2	74.1	86.6
1981–85	52.3	73.5	74.6	74.4	38.0	67.4	54.4	89.2	91.0	89.3	61.3	81.8
1986–90	46.1	68.3	71.7	67.0	32.7	62.0	45.8	85.6	87.7	84.4	62.7	76.2
1991–94	40.3	64.7	62.8	53.6	22.8	53.9	42.0	82.3	82.6	76.4	38.2	68.9

Source: Census of Canada, 1996. Public Use Micro-data File of Individuals.

Roderic Beaujot

Table 11: Indexes of Total Income and Employment Income, by Sex, Place of Birth, and Arrival Cohorts, Adjusted for Age, Canada, 1996

| | Total Income | | Employment Income | |
	Men	Women	Men	Women
Canadian-born	1.00	1.00	1.00	1.00
Immigrants	0.92	0.94	0.86	0.87
Before 1951	1.14	1.15	1.02	1.03
1951–65	1.08	1.09	1.03	0.99
1966–75	1.03	1.10	0.97	1.01
1976–80	0.92	0.96	0.87	0.90
1981–85	0.86	0.89	0.83	0.84
1986–90	0.70	0.75	0.70	0.74
1991–94	0.56	0.59	0.57	0.59
Europe and US	1.04	1.01	0.95	0.91
Before 1951	1.13	1.15	1.02	1.04
1951–65	1.08	1.07	1.02	0.97
1966–75	1.04	1.09	0.97	0.99
1976–80	1.06	1.00	0.98	0.90
1981–85	1.03	1.01	0.95	0.89
1986–90	0.89	0.83	0.83	0.75
1991–94	0.81	0.69	0.77	0.64
Other	0.78	0.86	0.77	0.83
Before 1951	1.49	1.14	--	--
1951–65	1.17	1.22	1.11	1.11
1966–75	1.00	1.12	0.96	1.05
1976–80	0.84	0.94	0.81	0.90
1981–85	0.76	0.85	0.75	0.82
1986–90	0.64	0.72	0.65	0.73
1991–94	0.51	0.56	0.51	0.58

Notes: -- fewer than 50 cases.
Adjustments for age (using ten-year age group of Canadian men and women as the standards), ages 15+ are used for total income and ages 15–64 for employment income. Employment income (wages and salaries plus self-employed income) is measured for those working full-time at least 40 weeks in 1995. Only persons with positive total income are used to calculate income.

Source: Census of Canada, 1996. Public Use Micro-data File of Individuals.

in 1989 and 2.93 times in 1999. Following male unemployment over the period 1982 to 1993, McDonald and Worswick (1997) find higher unemployment for the recent immigrants who had arrived in the period 1971–80, but not for those of the 1956–70 arrival cohorts. Especially during periods of recession, like the early 1980s and early 1990s, unemployment was significantly higher for the 1971–80 arrival cohorts. These same differences applied when considering only persons with university education.

The comparison of the 1961 and 1971 censuses had shown a very encouraging outcome for postwar immigrants (the 1946–60 cohort). In the majority of age-sex groups, the average income in 1961 was lower than that of the Canadian-born, but by 1971 these groups had largely exceeded the averages of Canadian-born counterparts (Richmond and Kalbach, 1980). Few similar transitions occurred over the 1971 to 1991 censuses (Beaujot and Rappak, 1990, p. 139; Beaujot, 1999, p. 111). In the vast majority of comparisons, a given immigrant cohort was either above or below the average of the Canadian-born population at each census. The transitions that did occur were as follows: the 1961–69 cohort had lower average incomes than the Canadian-born in 1971 but exceeded this average in 1981, and women of the 1970–74 cohort made a similar transition by the time of the 1986 censuses.

Table 11 shows no further transitions in the 1996 census for persons arriving since 1975. It would appear that the immigrant cohorts since 1975 may not reach the average income of persons born in Canada, in spite of their educational advantage. The situation is more positive for immigrants from Europe and the United States until 1985, whose average total income exceeds that of the Canadian-born. For the majority of recent immigrants, that is, those who are not from Europe and the United States, and who would largely be visible minorities, the four most recent cohorts show serious disadvantages. On the other hand, in the cohorts that preceded 1965, these immigrants from the "other continents" have an average income that is typically superior to the average for immigrants from Europe and the United States.

Further analyses based on the 1991 census indicate the importance of region of residence and socio-cultural characteristics. In particular, the disadvantage of recent cohorts, especially those of non-European origin, applies more to residents of metropolitan areas (Beaujot, 1997). Except for the most recent arrivals, the minority of immigrants who were living in non-metropolitan areas had average incomes that compared favourably to the Canadian-born in the same areas. Other results show that the advantages

Roderic Beaujot

of immigrants of European origin applies to the British but not to the Italian. At the same time, the disadvantage of non-European immigrants does not apply to Chinese arrivals of the 1961–80 period. Also, immigrants who speak one of the national languages at home have average levels of income that compare favourably to that of the Canadian-born.

Various analyses have highlighted the economic disadvantages of immigrants of the early 1990s, in spite of the increase in the relative size of the economic class and their high levels of education. Between 1990 and 2000, the proportion arriving as skilled workers increased while family and refugee classes declined. The principal applicants of the economic class comprised 23% of immigrants arriving in 2000, but 43% of the immigrants who were intending to join the labour force (Ruddick, 2001). Among the principal applicants of the economic class, the vast majority have university education and know at least one of the official languages. One year after landing, the employment earnings of these principal applicants were above the Canadian average for landing years 1980 to 1988, but below this average for 1989–97. Despite the high average education of the 1991–96 immigration cohort, at the time of the 1996 census, they were less likely to be employed, had relatively high unemployment rates, and had significant risks of low-income status (Thompson, 2002).

Other analyses of the 1986, 1991, and 1996 censuses show a trend towards lower rates of employment and earnings relative to the Canadian-born population. Looking at successive cohorts of immigrants, Reitz (2001) finds in particular that the increased education of the Canadian-born population has reduced the relative advantage of immigrants. In addition, over time, the increased returns to education are stronger for Canadian-born than for immigrants (see Boyd and Thomas, 2001). In particular, the proportion of immigrants aged 20–64 who are employed has declined, especially for men who have been in Canada 0–5 years (Reitz, 2001, p. 32). Among persons who are employed, at ages 20–64, immigrant men who had been in Canada less than 25 years, and women who had been in Canada less than 15 years, had average 1995 incomes that were below that of the Canadian-born of the corresponding gender (ibid., p. 35). In addition, from census to census the trends are downward, with the more recent censuses showing immigrants with given length of residence having lower relative income. A decomposition analysis indicates that, for most comparisons, a significant proportion of the increased disadvantage of more recent cohorts can be attributed to change in the relative immigrant education level, and change in the relative value of immigrant education in the labour market.

There are also differences across origin groups; for instance, for men with 6–10 years of residence in Canada, white immigrants in the 1996 census had a 5.7% disadvantage, compared to 33.0% for black immigrants, 22.6% for Chinese, 23% for South Asian, and 29.1% for Filipino. The average disadvantages for women in the same category of length of residence was 13.7% for white, 19.6% for black, 5.9% for Chinese, 22.6% for South Asian and 8.5% for Filipino immigrants (ibid., p. 36). Looking at immigrants with bachelor degrees or higher among persons who had come to Canada between 1980 and 1994, who were aged 20 or older at the time of arrival, and who were aged 25–54 at the 1996 census, Boyd (2001) finds that men who came from refugee-producing countries had high unemployment, were in low-skilled occupations, and had low earnings, in spite of their educational credentials.

Reitz (2001) discusses three possible sources of changes in immigrant relative socio-economic status: changes in the skills that immigrants bring, changes in the treatment received by immigrants within the labour market, and changes in the structure of the labour market itself. Compared to the 1960s, the skills of immigrants have increasingly been defined by academic degrees rather than technical training. Racial discrimination could be the reason for the increased discounting of immigrant skills, but this explanation seems inadequate since white immigrants are also affected, although to a lesser degree. The changed structure of the labour market towards a service economy may undermine the value of educational credentials obtained abroad, and may accentuate the negatives associated with lack of "Canadian experience" and Canadian references.

In summary, while the average level of education of immigrants has been increasing, this increase has not been as strong as that of the younger cohorts of internal entrants to the labour force. The cohort differences by labour force participation and average income clearly show that the strong negative differential at the time of arrival is reduced over time (Badets and Howatson-Leo, 1999). However, especially with regard to the average income of immigrants who are not from Europe and the United States, the disadvantage of the more recent cohorts are not being reduced as quickly. Counter to earlier cohorts, it is unlikely that more recent immigrant cohorts will come to match the average incomes of the Canadian-born, in spite of having more average years of education.

Nonetheless, two positive observations can be made. One is that immigrants who finish their education in Canada receive stronger economic value for this education (De Silva, 1997; Hum and Simpson, 1999). Second, while immigrants themselves often have economic disadvantages, the second generation has shown very strong levels of economic adaptation. Based on data for persons aged 25–64 in 1994, Boyd and Grieco (1998) find that second-generation men and women have positive outcomes in terms of education and occupational achievement.

An Interpretive Context

On both empirical and theoretical grounds, it is harder to make generalizations about migration than about the other demographic processes of mortality and fertility. Empirically, the main generalization about international migration to Canada seems to be that if immigration is going up, it will eventually come down, and if immigration is going down it will eventually come back up. Another empirical generalization seems to be that higher levels of immigration are linked with higher levels of emigration (Beaujot and Rappak, 1989; Michalowski, 1991). When there is more movement, it will occur in all directions, including onward moves to subsequent destinations, or returns to the place of origin. Looking at emigration from Canada, especially to the United States, and immigration to Canada, Zhao, Drew and Murray (2000) entitle their study "Knowledge Workers on the Move". In effect, another generalization is that persons with higher socio-economic status are more prone to migrate, because they have more opportunities. There is also more proneness to move in young adult ages, or at times of life course transitions.

While it is very difficult to theorize about migration because there are many potential factors at stake, it is useful to start with what might be called a natural tendency not to move. At the international level, it is noteworthy that 97.7% of the world population is living in their country of birth (Simmons, 2002). Staying represents integration with family and friends (Goldscheider, 1971). Questions of integration are consistent with the observation that people who have moved once are more likely to move again, and that return migration is a common phenomenon. The importance of social integration is also consistent with chain migration, that is, people who know each other follow from a given place of origin to a given destination. It could further be proposed that life course and social factors are more important in determining whether or not people move, while economic factors are more important in choosing the place of destination. People move especially at stages of the life course that involve disruptions,

Effect of Immigration on Demographic Structure

such as leaving home, finishing school, finding a job, starting or terminating a relationship, or retirement. Whether or not people move would also be a function of how comfortable or integrated they are in a given location. Once people are prone to move, economic factors, or more broadly the push and pull factors, determine the place of destination. When people are settled, especially when there is a two-income family with children, a higher salary at a different location will not be attractive. But when looking for a first job, a higher salary may prompt people to move, especially if they see other opportunities at the place of destination.

Thus, at the micro level, we theorize that social and life-course questions associated with extent of integration in family and community are more responsible for whether or not people move, and economic questions are more responsible for the choice of destination when people do migrate. At the macro level, there would be movement towards locations where there is greater potential to become integrated in both economic and social terms. Besides these push and pull factors, there are barriers as represented by information, communication, transportation and distance.

For international migration, the factors to consider include the opportunities for social and economic integration at places of origin and destination, along with links and barriers between countries, including policy barriers. Clearly, levels of immigration are a function of things happening within Canada and others happening outside the country, along with the links and barriers across countries, both in the short and longer terms (Simmons, 2002).

In *The Age of Migration*, Castles and Miller (1998) argue that international migration is a constant in human history and that population movements accompany demographic growth, technological change, as well as political conflict and warfare. In terms of population growth, the second phase of the demographic transition clearly involves much growth, with associated out-migration pressure. Castles and Miller also link the high levels of movement to the greater inequality across countries, and to transnational networks and cultural interchange.

These evolving aspects of immigration can also be related to globalization (Simmons, 2002). There is increased communication and information in a global village, with cultures becoming more homogenized. Globalization means more trade but also more movement of people, and more diversity, including both winners and losers. In their theoretical synthesis, Massey *et al.* (1994) propose that globalization creates both mobile populations following on various economic displacements, and demand for labour in the largest cities. With communication links, family and other networks, migratory exchanges are perpetuated between places of origin and destination (Boyd, 1989; Fawcett, 1989).

Freer trade brings various types of linkages between countries, including those of migration. In North America, the free trade agreements would enhance development in Mexico. This development would increase emigration pressure in the short and medium term, and reduce this pressure in the long run (Zlotnik, 1996). However, given the historical links between Mexico and the United States, this migration pressure is expected to have less effect on Canada.

Beyond North America, the demographic transition, especially the population pressures associated with the phase of rapid population growth, produces emigration pressure. Given this out-migration pressure, the medium term will show no shortage of a potential pool of people who want to come to Canada, and these outside pressures are probably increasing (Golini, 1996; United Nations, 1995). Development itself, which is clearly associated with the demographic transition, brings various displacements as economic change undermines various traditional forms of livelihood, especially in rural areas. Emigration pressure started in northern Europe over a century ago, later it was from eastern Europe, and in the postwar period from southern Europe. As these populations entered the third phase of the demographic transition, along with stable urban economies with high standards of living, the out migration pressure was lessened. The development, displacement, and out migration pressure from Third World countries is now dominant in world patterns.

Turning from the things happening outside, to Canada as a receiving country, the conclusions regarding determinants of immigration have largely been based on broad factors of political economy. In view of the geographic size of the country, and the need to control the resources that were present, immigration has often been seen as necessary if not essential (Sullivan, 1992). While arguments concerning family reunification and humanitarian attitudes to refugees have their importance, the economic argument has tended to be dominant in Canada's openness to immigration (Employment and Immigration, 1989; Simmons, 1999).

While the factors that have been analyzed from within Canada have been especially economic and demographic, a case can be made that they should be seen in social and political terms. Immigration is favourable to economic growth, but it is not a major factor (Economic Council of Canada, 1991; Green and Green, 1999). Immigration can sustain demographic growth, but it can only slightly reduce the pace of population aging.

In particular, the fact that unemployment is one of the better predictors of immigration can probably be mostly interpreted in social and political terms (Veugelers and Klassen, 1994a, 1994b; Foot, 1994; Simmons, 1994). In spite of the research to the effect that immigration contributes little to unemployment, there is a social and political tendency to be less favourable to immigration when economic conditions are more difficult (Palmer, 1996, 1999). That is, when the social mood is more favourable, there is a tendency to see immigration positively, especially in terms of increasing the cultural richness of Canada, contact with a broader pluralistic world, and being generous to the disadvantaged. When the climate is less favourable, there is a sense that we should first look after ourselves, or a felt need to retrench, to reduce the pace of change. Some theorists have seen natural tendencies towards opening and closing over intervals of time (Klapp, 1978).

Politically, the orientation has often been to follow the social climate, and thus not to deviate excessively from public opinion. Nonetheless, it is interesting to observe that the Conservative government continued its orientation of "planned controlled growth" through the recession of the early 1990s. The party was on record as having judged it a mistake on the part of the Liberal government to have reduced immigration in the recession of the early 1980s. In addition, in the early 1990s the governing party was at an all-time low in political opinion, having alienated various groups from the west who wanted more say in government, and from Quebec seeking a renewed constitution. It may be that the party sought the support of interest groups surrounding immigration, both multicultural groups and business interests, as a means to make public opinion inroads in these difficult political times (Foot, 1994).

If this interpretation is correct, to the effect that receptivity to immigration is mostly a function of social and political climate, then predictions of changes in trends are particularly difficult. We can be quite confident that the medium term will show continued out-migration pressure from various countries of emigration, and globalization brings more information and exchange, but the receptivity of countries of immigration is more difficult to predict.

References

Badets, J. and L. Howatson-Leo (1999), "Recent Immigrants in the Workforce", *Canadian Social Trends* 52, 16–22.

Badets, J. and T.W.L. Chui (1994), *Canada's Changing Immigrant Population*, Cat. No. 96–311 (Ottawa: Statistics Canada).

Beaujot, R. (1991), *Population Change in Canada: The Challenges of Policy Adaptation* (Toronto: Oxford University Press).

_____ (1997), "Comportements démographiques et statut socio-économique des immigrants canadiens", in J.L. Rallu, Y. Courbage and V. Piché (eds.), *Old and New Minorities* (Monrouge: Editions John Libbey Eurotext), 147–164.

_____ (1999), "Immigration and Demographic Structures", in S.S. Halli and L. Driedger (eds.), *Immigrant Canada: Demographic, Economic and Social Challenges* (Toronto: University of Toronto Press), 93–115.

Beaujot, R. and F. Hou (1993), "Projecting the Visible Minority Population of Canada: The Immigration Component" (Ottawa: Statistics Canada Employment Equity Data Program).

Beaujot, R. and D. Matthews (2000), "Immigration and the Future of Canada's Population", Discussion Paper 2000–1 (London: Population Studies Centre, University of Western Ontario).

Beaujot, R. and J.P. Rappak (1988), "The Role of Immigration in Changing Socio-demographic Structures", Report for Review of Demography (Ottawa: Health and Welfare).

_____ (1989), "The Link Between Immigration and Emigration in Canada, 1945–1986", *Canadian Studies in Population* 16(2), 201–216.

_____ (1990), "The Evolution of Immigrant Cohorts", in S.S. Halli *et al.* (eds.), *Ethnic Demography* (Ottawa: Carleton University Press), 111–139.

Beaujot, R., K.G. Basavarajappa and R. Verma (1988), *Income of Immigrants in Canada*, Cat. No. 91–527 (Ottawa: Statistics Canada).

Beaujot, R., S. Shiel and L. Schoel (1989), "Immigration and the Population of Canada". Report prepared for Immigration Policy Branch, Employment and Immigration.

Bélanger, A. (1993), "La migration interprovinciale des personnes nées à l'étranger, Canada, 1981–1986", *Cahiers Québécois de Démographie* 22(1), 153–178.

_____ (2001), *Report on the Demographic Situation in Canada 2000*, Cat. No. 91–209 (Ottawa: Statistics Canada).

_____ (2002), *Report on the Demographic Situation in Canada 2001*, Cat. No. 91–209 (Ottawa: Statistics Canada).

Bélanger, A. and J. Dumas (1998), *Report on the Demographic Situation in Canada 1997*, Cat. No. 91–209 (Ottawa: Statistics Canada).

Boyd, M. (1989), "Family and Personal Networks in International Migration: Recent Developments and New Agendas", *International Migration Review* 23(3), 638–670.

_____ (2001), "High Skill Workers and Refugees: Blurring the Line or Maintaining Difference", *Demographic Futures in the Context of Globalization: Public Policy Issues* (Ottawa: Federation of Canadian Demographers), 85–93.

Boyd, M. and E.M. Grieco (1998), "Triumphant Transitions: Socioeconomic Achievements of the Second Generation in Canada", *International Migration Review* 32(4), 853–876.

Boyd, M. and D. Thomas (2001), "Match or Mismatch? The Employment of Immigrant Engineers in Canada's Labor Force", *Population Research and Policy Review* 20, 107–133.

Canada. Citizenship and Immigration Canada (CIC) (1997), *Citizenship and Immigration Statistics 1994* (Ottawa: Citizenship and Immigration Canada).

_____ (1999), *Citizenship and Immigration Statistics 1996* (Ottawa: Citizenship and Immigration Canada).

_____ (2001), *Pursuing Canada's Commitment to Immigration: The Immigration Plan for 2002* (Ottawa: Citizenship and Immigration Canada).

_____ (2002), *Facts and Figures 2001: Immigration Overview* (Ottawa: Citizenship and Immigration Canada).

Canada. Employment and Immigration (1989), *Immigration to Canada: Economic Impacts* (Ottawa: Employment and Immigration).

Castles, S. and M. Miller (1998), *The Age of Migration: International Population Movements in the Modern World* (Houndmills: MacMillan).

Castonguay, C. (1992), "L'orientation linguistique des allophones à Montréal", *Cahiers québécois de démographie* 21(2), 95–118.

Chard, J. and V. Renaud (1999), "Visible Minorities in Toronto, Vancouver and Montreal", *Canadian Social Trends* 54, 20–25.

Chen, J., E. Ng and R. Wilkins (1996), "The Health of Canada's Immigrants in 1994–95", *Health Reports* 7(4), 33–45.

Choinière, R. (1993), "Les inégalitiés socio-économiques et culturelles de la mortalité à Montréal à la fin des années 1989", *Cahiers Québécois de Démographie* 22(2), 339–361.

Coleman, D. (2000), "Who's Afraid of Low Support Ratios? A UK Response to the UN Population Division Report on 'Replacement Migration' ", draft paper for October 2000 meeting of Expert Group at United Nations, October.

Crompton, S. and M. Vickers (2000), "One Hundred Years of Labour Force", *Canadian Social Trends* 57, 2–13.

Dai, S.Y. and M.V. George (1996), *Projections of Visible Minority Population Groups, Canada, Provinces and Regions, 1991-2016*, Cat. No. 91–541 (Ottawa: Statistics Canada).

Denton, F., C. Feaver and B. Spencer (1997), "Immigration, Labour Force and the Age Structure of the Population", QSEP Research Report No. 335 (Hamilton: McMaster University).

_____ (2000), "Projections of the Population and Labour Force to 2046: Canada", QSEP Research Report No. 347 (Hamilton: McMaster University).

_____ (2001), "Alternative Pasts, Possible Futures: A "what if" Study of the Effects of Fertility on the Canadian Population and Labour Force". Paper presented at the meetings of the Federation of Canadian Demographers, Ottawa, December.

De Silva, A. (1997), "Earnings of Immigrant Classes in the Early 1980s in Canada: A Reexamination", *Canadian Public Policy/Analyse de Politiques* 23(2), 179–202.

Duchesne, L. (1993), "Evolution de la population au Québec et au Canada depuis un siècle et demi en l'absence de migrations", *Cahiers Québécois de Démographie* 22(1), 1–22.

Economic Council of Canada (1991), *Economic and Social Impacts of Immigration* (Ottawa: Economic Council of Canada).

Edmonston, B. (1996), "Interprovincial Migration of Canadian Immigrants". Paper presented at the meetings of the Population Association of America, New Orleans, May.

_____ (2002), "Interprovincial Migration of Canadian Immigrants". Paper presented at the meetings of the Canadian Population Society, Toronto, June.

Fawcett, J.M. (1989), "Networks, Linkages and Migration Systems", *International Migration Review* 23(3), 671–680.

Foot, D.K. (1987), "Population Aging and the Canadian Labour Force", Discussion Paper No. 87.A.5 (Montreal: Institute for Research on Public Policy).

_____ (1994), "Canada's Unemployment-Immigration Linkage: Demographic, Economic and Political Influences", *Canadian Journal of Sociology* 19(4), 513–524.

George, M.V., S. Loh and R. Verma (1997), "Impact of Varying the Component Assumptions of Projected Total Population and Age Structure in Canada", *Canadian Studies in Population* 24(1), 67–86.

Gilbert, S., A. Bélanger and J. Ledent (2001), "Immigration, migration interne et croissance urbaine au Canada pour le période de 1976 à 1996". Paper presented at the meetings of the Association des Demographes du Québec, May, Sherbrooke.

Goldscheider, C. (1971), *Population, Modernization and Social Structure* (Boston: Little, Brown and Company).

Golini, A. (1996), "International Population Movements: Imbalances and Integration", in B. Colombo, P. Demeny and M.F. Perutz (eds.), *Resources and Population: Natural, Institutional, and Demographic Dimensions of Development* (Oxford: Oxford University Press), 287–301.

Green, A. and D. Green (1999), "The Economic Goals of Canada's Immigration Policy: Past and Present", *Canadian Public Policy/Analyse de Politiques* 25(4), 425–451.

Hoem, B. and J.M. Hoem (1997), "Sweden's Family Policies and Roller-Coaster Fertility", Stockholm Research Reports in Demography No. 115.

Hou, F. and G. Picot (2002), "Do Changes in Low-income Rates among Immigrants Account for Rising Low-income in Canada?" Paper presented at the meetings of the Canadian Population Society, Toronto, May.

Hum, D. and W. Simpson (1999), "Wage Opportunities for Visible Minorities in Canada", *Canadian Public Policy/Analyse de Politiques* 25(3), 379–394.

Hutchinson, M. (2002), "Baby Boom Bust", *Aboriginal Times* 6(5), 30–33.

Kalbach, W.E. and W.W. McVey (1979), *The Demographic Bases of Canadian Society* (Toronto: McGraw-Hill).

Kelly, K. (1995), "Visible Minorities: Diverse Group", *Canadian Social Trends* 37, 2–8.

Klapp, O. (1978), *Opening and Closing: Strategies for Information Adaptation in Society* (Cambridge: Cambridge University Press).

Lachapelle, R. (1988a), *L'immigration et le caractère ethnolinguistique du Canada et du Québec*, Documents de Recherche No.15 (Statistics Canada: Direction des études analytiques).

_____ (1988b), "Quelques tendances démolinguistiques au Canada et au Québec", *L'Action Nationale* 78, 329–343.

_____ (2001), "La notion de migration de remplacment: sa portée, ses limites et ses prolongements". Paper presented at meetings of the Association des Démographes du Québec, Sherbrooke, May.

Lacroix, J.-M. (1991), "Le pluriethnisme canadien: au delà de la fusion et de la confusion", *Revue internationale d'études canadiennes* 3, 153–170.

Le Bras, H. (1988), "The Demographic Impact of Post-War Migration in Selected OECD Countries", Working Party on Migration (Paris: OECD).

Li, N. and Z. Wu (2001), "Migration and Aging of Canada". Paper presented at the meetings of the Canadian Population Society, Quebec City, May.

Loh, S. and M.V. George (2001), "Projected Population Size and Age Structure of Canada's Population with and without International Immigration". Paper presented at the meetings of the Canadian Population Society, Laval University, May.

Massey, D. *et al.* (1994), "International Migration Theory: The North American Case", *Population and Development Review* 20(4), 699–751.

Maxim, P.S. (1996), "Estimating Fertility Differentials Between Immigrant and Nonimmigrant Women in Canada". Paper presented at the meetings of the Canadian Population Society, St. Catherines, June.

McAndrew, M., M. Jodoin, M. Pagé and J. Rossell (2000), "L'aptitude au francais des élèves montréalais d'origine immigrée: impact de la densité ethnique de l'école, du taux de fancisation associé à la langue maternelle et de l'ancienneté d'implantation", *Cahiers Québécois de Démographie* 29(1), 89–117.

McDonald, J. and C. Worswick (1997), "Unemployment Incidence of Immigrant Men in Canada", *Canadian Public Policy/Analyse de Politiques* 23(4), 353–373.

McDonald, P. and R. Kippen (2001), "Labor Supply Prospects in 16 Developed Countries: 2000–2050", *Population and Development Review* 27(1), 1–32.

Michalowski, M. (1991), "Foreign-Born Canadian Emigrants and their Character-istics, 1981–1986", *International Migration Review* 25(1), 28–59.

_____ (1993), "Redefining the Concept of Immigration in Canada", *Canadian Studies in Population* 20(1), 59–84.

Office of the Chief Actuary (2001), *Actuarial Report (18ᵗʰ) on the Canada Pension Plan* (Ottawa: Office of the Chief Actuary).

Paillé, M. (1989), "Aménagement linguistique et population au Québec", *Journal of Canadian Studies* 23, 54–69.

_____ (1991), "Choix linguistiques des immigrants dans les trois provinces canadiennes les plus populeuses", *Revue internationale d'études canadiennes* 3, 185–194.

Palmer, D. (1996), "Determinants of Canadian Attitudes Toward Immigration: More than just Racism?" *Canadian Journal of Behavioural Science* 28(3), 180–192.

_____ (1999), "Canadian Attitudes and Perceptions Regarding Immigration: Relations with Regional per Capita Immigration and Other Contextual Factors". Paper submitted to Citizenship and Immigration Canada.

Ram, B. and M.V. George (1990), "Immigrant Fertility Patterns in Canada, 1961–1986", *International Migration* 28(4), 413–426.

Ram, B. and E. Shin (1999), "Internal Migration of Immigrants", in S.S. Halli and L. Driedger (eds.), *Immigrant Canada: Demographic, Economic and Social Challenges* (Toronto: University of Toronto Press), 148–162.

Reitz, J. (2001), "Immigrant Success and Changing National Institutions: Recent Trends in Canada, a U.S. Comparison, and Policy Options". Paper prepared for Weatherhead Centre for International Relations and Department of Sociology, Harvard University, February.

Review of Demography and its Implications for Economic and Social Policy (1989), *Charting Canada's Future* (Ottawa: Health and Welfare).

Richmond, A. and W. Kalbach (1980), *Factors in the Adjustment of Immigrants and their Descendants* (Ottawa: Statistics Canada).

Ruddick, E. (2001), "Trends in International Labour Flows to Canada", *Demographic Futures in the Context of Globalization: Public Policy Issues* (Ottawa: Federation of Canadian Demographers), 67–84.

Ryder, N. (1997), "Migration and Population Replacement", *Canadian Studies in Population* 24(1), 1–26.

Samuel, T.J. (1987), "Visible Minorities in Canada", *Contributions to Demography* (Edmonton: Population Research Laboratory).

Simmons, A. (1994), "Commentary", *Canadian Journal of Sociology* 19(4), 513–540.

_____ (1997), "Canadian Immigration and Nation Building: Social and Political Implications of Recent Trends", in R. Hébert and R. Théberge, *Re(Defining) Canada: A Prospective Look at our Country in the 21ˢᵗ Century* (Winnipeg: Presses Universitaires de Saint-Boniface), 43–70.

_____ (1999), "Immigration Policy: Imagined Futures", in S.S. Halli and L. Driedger (eds.), *Immigrant Canada: Demographic, Economic and Social Challenges* (Toronto: University of Toronto Press), 21–50.

_____ (2002), "Mondialisation et migration internationale: tendances, interrogations et modèles théoriques", *Cahiers Québécois de Démographie* 31, 7–33.

Statistics Canada (1974), *Population Projections for Canada and the Provinces and Territories, 1972–2001*, Cat. No. 91–514 (Ottawa: Statistics Canada).

_____ (1979), *Population Projections for Canada and the Provinces and Territories, 1976–2001*, Cat. No. 91–520 (Ottawa: Statistics Canada).

_____ (1985), *Population Projections for Canada and the Provinces and Territories, 1984–2006*, Cat. No. 91–520 (Ottawa: Statistics Canada).

_____ (1990), *Population Projections for Canada and the Provinces and Territories, 1989–2011*, Cat. No. 91–520 (Ottawa: Statistics Canada).

_____ (1994), *Demographic Projections for Canada, Provinces and Territories, 1993–2016*, Cat. No. 91–520 (Ottawa: Statistics Canada).

_____ (1997), *The Daily*, November 4.

_____ (1998), *The Daily*, April 14.

_____ (2001a), *Demographic Projections for Canada, Provinces and Territories, 2000–2026*, Cat. No. 91–520 (Ottawa: Statistics Canada).

_____ (2001b), *Historical Labour Force Statistics*, Cat. No. 71–201 (Ottawa: Statistics Canada).

_____ (2002a), *Annual Demographic Statistics 2001*, Cat No. 91–213 (Ottawa: Statistics Canada).

_____ (2002b), "Migration", *The Daily*, September 26, 6–7.

Sullivan, T.A. (1992), "The Changing Demographic Characteristics and Impact of Immigrants in Canada", in B.R. Chiswick (eds.), *Immigration, Language and Ethnicity: Canada and the United States* (Washington: American Enterprise), 119–144.

Thomas, D. (1992), "The Social Integration of Immigrants in Canada", in S. Globerman (ed.), *The Immigration Dilemma* (Vancouver: The Fraser Institute), 211–260.

Thompson, E. (2002), "The 1990s have been Difficult for Recent Immigrants in the Canadian Labour Market", *Quarterly Labour Market and Income Review* 3(1), 21–25.

Tossou, A. (2002), "Fécondité différentielle des immigrants et des natifs: Québec, 1976–1996", *Cahiers Québécois de démographie* 31, 95–122.

Trovato, F. (1996), "Marital Status and Mortality among Immigrants in Canada". Paper presented at the meetings of the Canadian Population Society, St. Catharines, June.

United Nations (1995), *Population and Development: Programme of Action Adopted at the International Conference on Population and Development, Cairo, 5–13 September 1994*, New York: United Nations Ser.A\149.

_____ (2000), *Replacement Migration: Is it a Solution to Declining and Aging Populations?* (United Nations: Population Division).

Veltman, C. (1988), *L'impact de l'immigration internationale sur l'équilibre linguistique à Montréal*, Report for Review of Demography, Health and Welfare (Ottawa).

Veugelers, J.W.P. and T.R. Klassen (1994a), "Continuity and Change in Canada's Unemployment-Immigration Linkage (1946–1993)", *Canadian Journal of Sociology* 19(3), 351–370.

_____ (1994b), "Response", *Canadian Journal of Sociology* 19(4), 535–540.

Zhao, J., D. Drew and T.S. Murray (2000), "Knowledge Workers on the Move", *Perspectives on Labour and Income* 12(2), 32–46.

Zlotnik, H. (1996), "Policies and Migration Trends in the North American System", in A. Simmons (ed.), *International Migration, Refugee Flows and Human Rights in North America: The Impact of Trade and Restructure* (New York: Center for Migration Studies), 81–103.

Occupational Mobility of Immigrant Men: Evidence from Longitudinal Data for Australia, Canada and the United States

Marc Frenette, Vincent Hildebrand,
James Ted McDonald and Christopher Worswick

Introduction

The labour market adaptation of immigrants has been the focus of considerable policy debate in traditional immigrant-receiving countries such as Australia, Canada, and the United States. Since these countries continue to accept large numbers of immigrants each year, determining the extent to which recent immigrants have been successful in adjusting to their new labour market is crucial for the design of future immigration policy. The primary measures of labour market success are based on employment earnings — specifically, how immigrants' earnings compare with the earnings of the native-born, and the extent to which immigrants' earnings increase as the time spent in the new country increases.[1] However, an

---

[1]Chiswick (1978) was the first to carry out an analysis of this kind. Recent work includes Beggs and Chapman (1988) and McDonald and Worswick (1999) using Australian data; Borjas (1985), LaLonde and Topel (1991), Borjas (1995), Chiswick and Miller (1995) and Duleep and Regets (1997) using US data; and

important dimension of successful labour market adjustment for immigrants is the ability to find a job suited to the immigrant's skills.

While an extensive literature exists on the earnings performance of immigrants, only a few studies have analyzed the occupational outcomes of immigrants. Richmond and Kalbach (1980) employ the 1971 Canadian census and find that immigrants in Canada were relatively overrepresented in professional and semi-professional occupations as well as service and manufacturing occupations. However, they note that these immigrant/native-born differences in occupational distribution are in general small. Boyd (1985) using the 1973 Job Mobility Survey of Canada reaches a similar conclusion in terms of the magnitude of immigrant/native-born differences in occupational outcomes. Borjas (1992) uses the 1940, 1960, 1970 and 1980 US census files and analyzes occupational distributions of immigrants across time. He finds that in the 1970 census, recent immigrants were more likely to be in professional and managerial occupations than were the native-born, but that this difference diminished and became negative for more recent immigrant arrival cohorts by the time of the 1980 US census.

An important recent study was carried out by Green (1999). Combining micro data from the 1981, 1986 and 1991 Canadian census files. He estimates a multinomial logit model of occupational outcomes for immigrant and Canadian-born men. In addition, Green employs special tabulations from immigrant landing records carried out by Citizenship and Immigration Canada. These contain information on immigrants' intended occupations at the time of landing in Canada broken down by sex, age at landing, and country of birth. Green finds immigrants to be overrepresented in professional and machining occupations and underrepresented in the less skilled primary and processing occupations. He also finds evidence of differences across immigrant arrival cohorts consistent with a movement away from skilled occupations. Finally, Green concludes that immigrants appear to be more occupationally mobile than the Canadian-born. However, much of the mobility occurs in the period between the 1986 and 1991 census and since it occurs for both recent cohorts and earlier cohorts, he

---

Baker and Benjamin (1994), Bloom, Grenier and Gunderson (1995), McDonald and Worswick (1998) and Grant (1999) using Canadian data.

suggests that it may be due to the generally strong labour market conditions over the period.[2]

Our analysis extends this area of research in two directions. The multinomial approach to occupational outcomes employed by Green (1999) is replicated on survey data for Canada as well as being estimated for American and Australian data over the period 1984 to 1996. This allows for a characterization of the net flows of immigrants in terms of the proportions in each occupational category and in the not working category. In addition, the data for each of the three countries have a longitudinal element allowing for the estimation of Markov transition models. Using these models it is possible to estimate the probabilities of staying in the current occupation as well as the probabilities of switching into another occupation (or into the not working state) for each occupational state and for each country. The current paper includes the results of this analysis for the United States and for Australia. We are currently in the process of completing that part of the analysis for Canada.

Our motivation for carrying out the analysis for three of the main immigrant-receiving countries has two parts. First, the labour market settlement process of new immigrants is likely to have many common factors for immigrants arriving in these three developed, market-oriented economies. Therefore, our hope is that the analysis will help us to identify common experiences that immigrants in general will face when adjusting to a new labour market. Second, institutional differences in the labour market setting across the three countries may lead to differences in occupational mobility of immigrants (relative to the native-born) across the three countries. This second part of the analysis is at this point under-developed but is expected to be extended in the next iteration of the paper.

---

[2]Two other recent studies should be noted. Chiswick and Miller (2002) employ longitudinal data on a recent cohort of immigrants to Australia and analyze their occupational mobility over the first three and a half years of residence in Australia. Also, Bauer and Zimmermann (1999) analyze occupational mobility of immigrants to Germany.

The Data and Estimation Sample

The American data used in the estimation come from the Survey of Income and Program Participation (SIPP) for the years 1984, 1988, 1990, 1991, 1992, 1993, and 1996. The SIPP contains detailed demographic information as well as income, labour supply, and program-participation information. Each SIPP panel contains information on the individual at four-month intervals over a period of up to 32 months. Therefore, the years listed above represent the years for the first wave of the panel. In the cross-sectional estimation we employ the information from the first cross-section of each of the panels. The SIPP data for the years 1988, 1990, 1991, 1992, and 1993 also contain retrospective information on past jobs and their occupations. Therefore, information is available on the job the person held at the time of the first interview as well as the answers to questions related to the job the person held prior to the current job. Therefore, it is possible to define a fixed window of time (two years in our case) and determine whether the person switched jobs over that time period and whether that job switch involved a change in occupation. It is also possible to infer from the questions whether the person only held one job over the two-year window and in that case whether the person was not working at the beginning of the window (in other words, whether the person entered the window not working, found a job over the period and was still working in that job at the end of the two-year window).

The Canadian data used in the estimation came from the 1988 Labour Market Activity Survey (LMAS) and the 1993 and 1996 panels of the Survey of Labour and Income Dynamics. Both these surveys were developed and administered by Statistics Canada and are longitudinal in nature. The LMAS data covered the period 1988–90, the first SLID panel covered the period 1993–98 and the second SLID panel began in 1996 and was on-going at the time of commencement of this project. We employ the first three years (1996–98). The cross-sectional analysis of occupational outcomes employs the first survey year of each of the three Canadian surveys (1988, 1993, and 1996).

The Australian data used in the estimation are taken from the Labour Mobility Survey (LMS) of the Australian Bureau of Statistics for the years 1984, 1987, 1989, 1991, 1992, 1994, and 1996. These surveys were single cross-sections that give information on labour market status, occupation and demographic variables such as education, gender, immigrant status, and year of arrival in Australia. The sample frame differs from the American and Canadian surveys in that each LMS is a representative sample of all Australians who held a job either at the time of the survey or in the 12 months preceding the survey. However, an appealing feature of the data is that each respondent was asked about jobs held over the previous 12 months. From the answers to these questions it is possible to identify whether a person changed jobs over the previous 12 months and the occupation of the previous job if applicable. Therefore, we can identify occupational mobility over the 12-month period using the LMS. The cross-sectional model of occupational outcomes employs the survey period occupational status for each of the LMS years. The longitudinal estimation of the occupational models employs both the current occupational information and the retrospective occupational information for each of the survey years of the LMS.

For each country, the sample used contains men between the ages of 21 and 60 at the time of the survey. Sample means of selected variables are presented in Table 1 for each country and separately for immigrants and the native-born. For each country the data are pooled over the available survey years (as described above). Occupations are generated based on the person's main job. For Australia and the United States, the survey asks for information related to the person's main job at the time of the survey. For the case of Canada, information on more than one job is available and the main job was chosen by selecting the job with the highest number of hours in the month of December. Occupations are grouped into three broad categories with all other individuals grouped into the not working state. The managerial/professional grouping includes managers, engineers, social scientists, teachers, health occupations, and the arts. The white collar grouping includes clerical, sales, and service occupations. The blue collar grouping includes processing, machining, construction, farming, primary, transportation, and other occupations.

For the case of the United States, immigrants are more likely than the native-born to be in blue collar occupations and less likely to be in managerial or professional occupations, although the differences are small in each case. For the Canadian case, immigrants are less likely to be in blue collar occupations than are the native-born; however, in general the occupational distributions of immigrants and the native-born are similar. Immigrants in Australia are less likely (relative to the native-born) to be in managerial or professional occupations as well as white collar occupations and more likely to be in blue collar occupations.

Table 1: Sample Means of Key Variables

Variable	Australia		Canada		United States	
	FB	NB	FB	NB	FB	NB
Occupations						
Man./prof.	0.2532	0.2730	0.2497	0.2448	0.1948	0.2278
White collar	0.1736	0.2081	0.1888	0.1815	0.2469	0.2446
Blue collar	0.4975	0.4559	0.3298	0.3664	0.3957	0.3812
Not working	0.0757	0.0629	0.2316	0.2074	0.1625	0.1463
Education						
High school	0.4400	0.4661	0.5240	0.5878	0.5388	0.4823
Post sec.	0.4024	0.4133	0.2528	0.2510	0.1749	0.2412
University	0.1575	0.1206	0.2231	0.1612	0.2863	0.2765
Sample size	34,905	83,205	3,959	33,401	7,180	65,674

Notes: 1. FB denotes immigrants, NB denotes the native-born.
2. The American data are from the Survey of Income and Program Participation (SIPP) for the years 1984, 1988, 1990, 1991, 1992, 1993, and 1996.
3. The Canadian data are from the 1988 Labour Market Activity Survey (LMAS) and the 1993 and 1996 panels of the Survey of Labour and Income Dynamics.
4. The Australian data are from the Labour Mobility Survey (LMS) of the Australian Bureau of Statistics for the years 1984, 1987, 1989, 1991, 1992, 1994, and 1996.
5. The relevant weights for each set of surveys were employed in generating these means.
6. Individuals who had not held a job in the previous 12 months were not interviewed in the Australian surveys.

Estimating Procedures

For the first part of the analysis, we employ a multinomial logit model of occupational outcomes with controls similar to those used by Green (1999). The value of a particular occupational choice is represented by:

M. Frenette, V. Hildebrand, J.T. McDonald and C. Worswick

$$I_{itl}^{j} = x_{itl}\beta_{j} + \alpha_{j}FB_{i} + \delta_{j}YSM_{it} + \gamma_{j}(YSM_{it})^{2} +$$

$$\sum_{l=1}^{L-1}(\alpha_{jl} + \delta_{jl}YSM_{it})C_{il} + \varepsilon_{itl}^{j}$$

(1)

where j indexes the alternative, l indexes the entry cohort of the immigrant, t indexes the survey year, i indexes the individual, x_{itl} is a vector of person-specific characteristics, FB_{i} is an immigrant dummy variable, YSM_{it} is the number of years-since-migration for immigrants and equals zero for the native-born; and C_{il} is a dummy variable for immigrants in cohort l for $l=1$, ..., $L-1$; β_{j} is a parameter vector specific to alternative j, α_{j}, δ_{j}, γ_{j} and α_{jl}, and δ_{jl} are parameters for $l=1$, ..., $L-1$; ε_{itl}^{j} is an error term.

The notation chosen follows that of Green (1999) as closely as possible. Green estimated the model separately using three Canadian census files. Instead, we employ three surveys for Canada and seven surveys for Australia and for the United States. We estimate the models separately for each country. However, in the separate estimation for each country we pool across the surveys. The parametric specification employed allows us to exploit the rich information on each cohort across time while employing a parsimonious specification. This specification allows for cohort effects that vary by years-since-migration (through linear YSM interactions with the cohort variables). The default cohort, denoted by L, has both a linear and quadratic YSM effect. The other cohorts have linear deviations from this common quadratic YSM profile.

In the second stage of the analysis, Markov transition models of occupational outcomes are estimated. The probability of being in a particular occupation in period t is allowed to depend on the occupational state of the person in period $t-1$. The estimation procedure involves the estimation of a separate multinomial logit model for each occupational state in period $t-1$. In each case, the parameterization of the index functions associated with each occupational outcome for period t (given an outcome in period $t-1$) is based on equation (1).

Estimation Results

Cross-sectional Model of Occupational Outcomes

At each stage of the analysis of this paper, a large number of parameter estimates are generated for each index of the relevant multinomial choice model of occupational outcomes. Rather than present all of these estimates, we have used them to generate predicted differences in probabilities of being in each of the four occupational states (managerial/professional, white collar, blue collar and not working). Using these probabilities, we generated predicted differences in the probabilities between a native-born man and an immigrant man based on the default set of characteristics for each value for the immigrant cohort variables and each value of years-since-migration. These predicted differences are presented graphically.

The first set of results relate to the first-stage analysis based only on cross-sectional information on occupational outcomes. Figures 1 to 4 contain differences in predicted probabilities of being in a particular occupation (for each of the four occupational groupings) between immigrants and the native-born for each of the three countries. Immigrants in Australia are more likely to be blue collar workers than are the Australian-born with this difference ranging from as high as 10% for a relatively recent immigrant to as low as 5% for earlier immigrants. The differences are far less pronounced for both Canada and the United States. In the Canadian case, recent cohorts have had very similar probabilities of being blue collar workers to those of the native-born. A similar pattern is true of the United States where the immigrant probabilities of being blue collar workers are either equal to that of the native-born or are somewhat higher (with a maximum of five percentage points difference).

Figure 2 contains the equivalent relationships but for the case of white collar workers. Recent immigrants to the United States and Canada have similar probabilities of being white collar workers to their native-born counterparts. For both countries there is some evidence of assimilation towards higher probabilities of being in white collar jobs (relative to the native-born comparison groups) with this effect being larger for the case of Canada. For the case of Australia, immigrants have 5 to 10% lower probabilities than native-born Australians of being in a white collar occupation and the difference is largest for recent immigrants. For the 1971–80 cohort of immigrants, there is evidence of assimilation towards

Figure 1: Blue Collar Occupations, Cross-Sectional Estimates

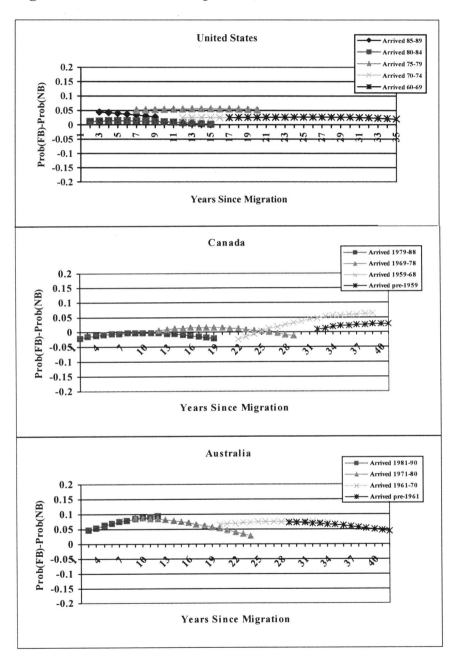

Figure 2: White Collar Occupations, Cross-Sectional Estimates

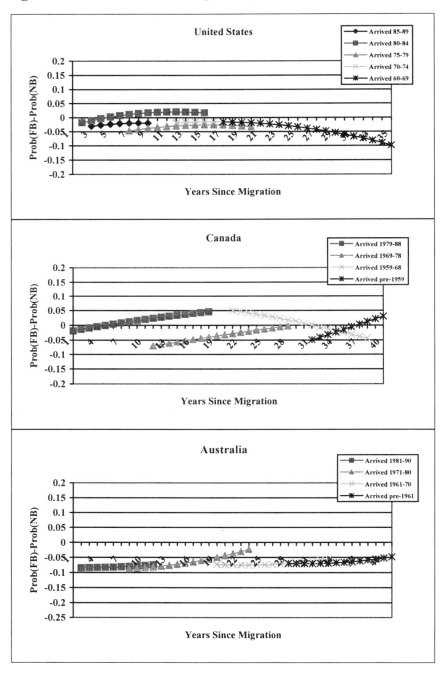

M. Frenette, V. Hildebrand, J.T. McDonald and C. Worswick

the native-born probability of being in a white collar job with years-since-migration. However, the effect is not pronounced and the other cohorts do not appear to experience any change in their probability of being white collar relative to that of the Australian-born.

In Figure 3, the same relationships are presented for the case of professional and managerial occupations. For all three countries, a common pattern is present of new immigrants generally having 5 to 10% lower probabilities of being in the professional/managerial occupations (relative to the native-born) but with these differences declining with more years-since-migration. The fastest catch-up appears to occur in the United States where the difference appears to converge to near zero by around ten years of residence for most cohorts.[3] The slowest rate of catch-up applies to Australia where the difference remains small but negative after 40 years of residence.

Figure 4 contains the predicted differences in probability of being in the not working group between immigrants and the native-born. The general patterns are similar for all three countries. New immigrants have a 6 to 13% higher probability of being in the not working group than do otherwise similar native-born men with the difference being largest for the case of Canada. In all three countries, the effect of more years-since-migration is to reduce this difference indicating an assimilation towards the not working probabilities of the native-born.

In summary, the predicted occupational distributions of immigrants and the native-born are generally similar in all three countries with the following exceptions. Australian immigrants are 5 to 10% more likely to be in blue collar jobs and 5 to 10% less likely to be in white collar jobs than are their native-born counterparts. Also, recent immigrants to the United States and Canada are less likely to be in managerial and professional occupations than are the native-born at the time of arrival. However, this difference diminishes with years-since-migration leading to very similar probabilities of being in these occupations after roughly 15 years of residence in Canada. Finally, for all three countries, recent immigrants are at least 6% more likely to be in the not working category shortly after arrival relative to their native-born counterparts. Time spent in the new country is associated with a decline in this difference leading to a convergence to similar probabilities of being the not working category by

---

[3]The 1975–79 cohort is the exception.

Figure 3: Professional/Managerial Occupations
Cross-Sectional Estimates

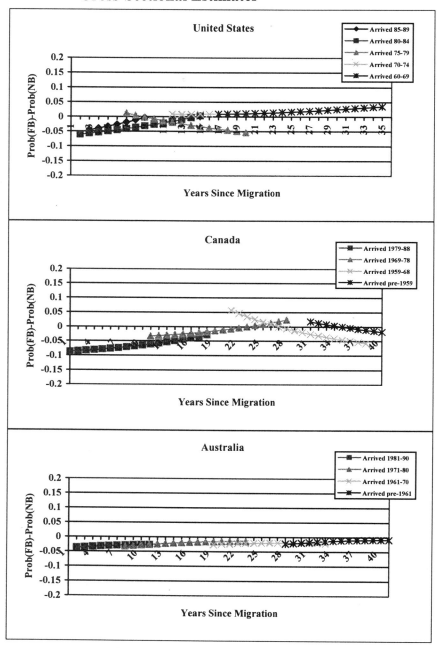

M. Frenette, V. Hildebrand, J.T. McDonald and C. Worswick

Figure 4: Not Working, Cross-Sectional Estimates

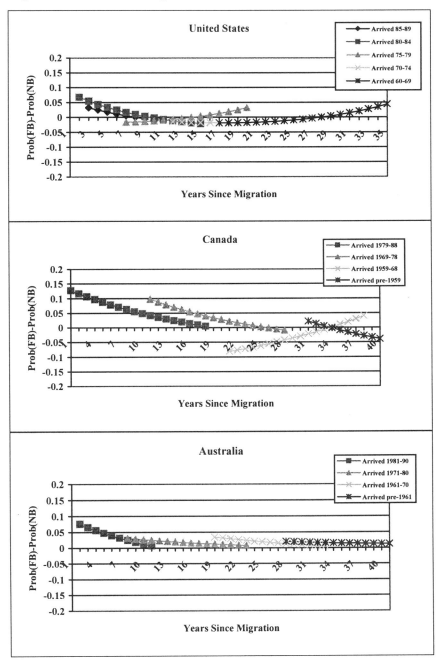

seven years for the United States, 20 years for Canada and ten years for Australia.

Longitudinal Models of Occupational Mobility

As noted above, a weakness of the existing literature on the occupational mobility of immigrants is the scarcity of longitudinal datasets suitable for this type of analysis. The datasets employed in this study are longitudinal in nature and allow for the estimation of models with history dependence. The next stage of the analysis involves the estimation of a first-order Markov transition model between the following four states: (i) blue collar occupations, (ii) white collar occupations, (iii) professional/managerial occupations and (iv) not working. The approach is similar to the one employed by Jones and Riddell (1999) in their analysis of the transition between labour force states. The same estimation is employed here to analyze the transition probabilities for workers of moving between different occupations and the not working state.

Figures 5 through 8 present predicted probabilities of being in each of the four occupation/working states conditional on having been in a blue collar occupation the previous period. For the American analysis, a two-year window is employed so that the probability being modelled relates to any changes in the state that may occur over a two-year period. For the Australian results, the dataset restricted us to using a one-year window. Therefore, care should be taken when comparing across countries since the time period is twice as long for the United States.[4] A person is considered to have moved from one occupation to another if that person held a job in a blue collar occupation in their first job over the two-year window and if they also held a new job in an occupation other than a blue collar occupation at some point later in the two-year window. A transition from blue collar to not working occurs if the person only had one job over the period, it was a blue collar job, and the person ended up without a job at the end of the two-year window. The definitions have purposefully been chosen so as to reduce the number of movements into and out of the not working state in order to maximize our likelihood of observing movement

---

[4]The two-year window was chosen for the United States (rather than a one-year window) in order to increase our chances of observing transitions between occupations.

Figure 5: Markov Transition Models
Blue Collar in Last Job — Blue Collar in New Job

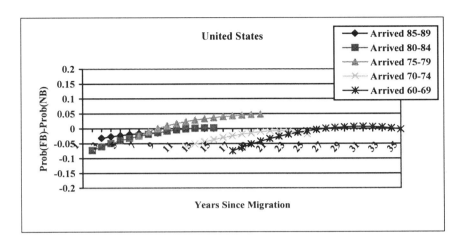

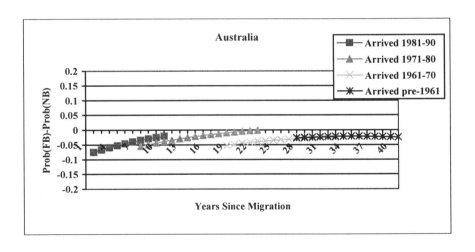

Figure 6: Markov Transition Models
Blue Collar in Last Job — White Collar in New Job

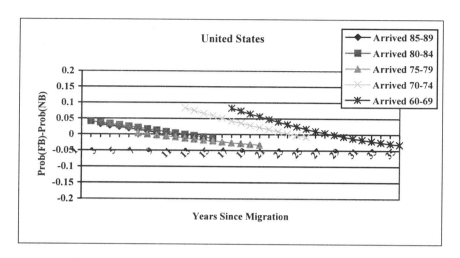

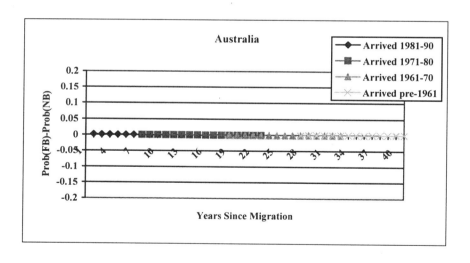

M. Frenette, V. Hildebrand, J.T. McDonald and C. Worswick

Figure 7: Markov Transition Models
Blue Collar in Last Job — Prof./Manag. in New Job

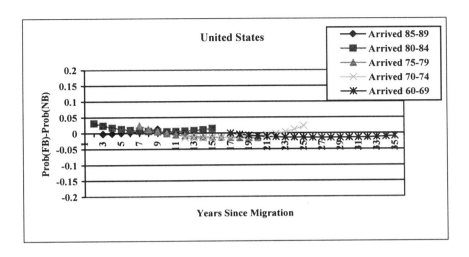

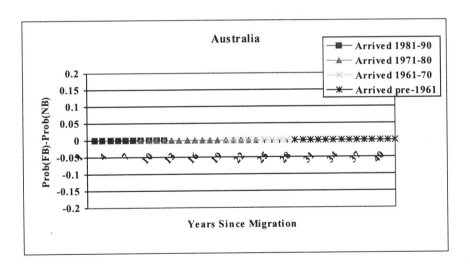

Figure 8: Markov Transition Models
Blue Collar in Last Job — Not Working

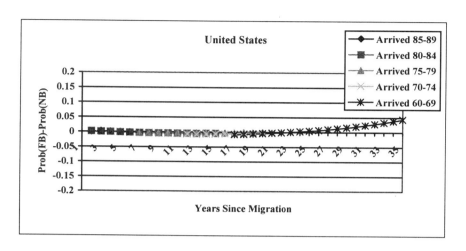

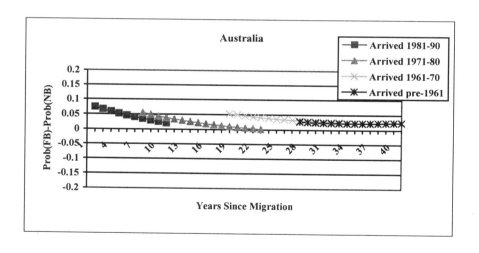

between occupations. However, it does mean that our estimates of movements into and out of not working may appear artificially small.

The figures for the United States indicate that new immigrants with blue collar jobs have higher rates of exiting out of those jobs than do American-born persons with blue collar jobs and higher rates of exiting into both white collar jobs and to a lesser extent professional/managerial jobs. Also, the probability of exiting out of a blue collar job into the not working category is virtually identical to that of the American-born with blue collar jobs.

The Australian figures are generally consistent with less occupational mobility. For immigrants in blue collar jobs, their probabilities of exiting these jobs and entering either white collar jobs or professional/managerial jobs is virtually identical to the equivalent probabilities for Australian-born men at all values of years-since-migration. The only immigrant/non-immigrant differences apparent can be summarized as lower probabilities of remaining in a blue collar job at low values of YSM and a higher probability of exiting from a blue collar job into the not working state than is the case for Australian-born men with blue collar jobs.

Figures 9 to 12 capture the same relationships as Figures 5 to 8 but for the case where the initial job was in a white collar occupation. For the United States, evidence is found that is consistent with a higher rate of exit into blue collar jobs from white collar jobs for recent immigrants and this difference is found to diminish with YSM.[5] There is also evidence of cohort differences implying that more recent cohorts are less likely to make this transition than were earlier cohorts at the same number of YSM. An opposite relationship is found in terms of probabilities of staying in white collar jobs. Recent immigrants to the United States are less likely to stay in white collar jobs than are the American-born, but this difference quickly diminishes and virtually no difference exists over the range of 17 to 30 YSM. The immigrant probability of exiting a white collar occupation and entering a professional/managerial job is very close to that of the American-born for close to the entire YSM range of Figure 11. Also, the probability of exiting a white collar job and entering the not working category is initially higher for recent immigrants than for the American-born and this effect diminishes with time in the United States leading to basically no difference in the probabilities after 15 years of residence.

---

[5]With the exception of the earliest cohort which shows an increase at very high levels of YSM.

Figure 9: Markov Transition Models
White Collar in Last Job — Blue Collar in New Job

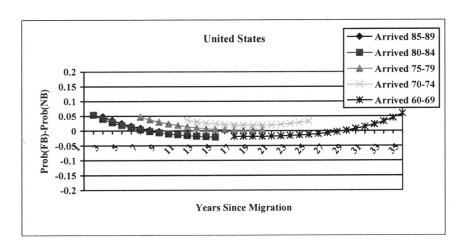

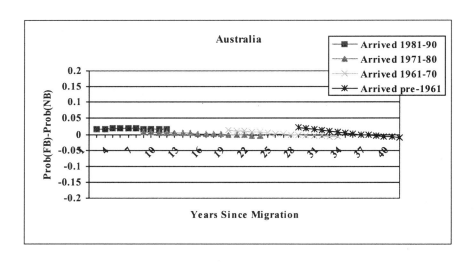

Figure 10: Markov Transition Models
White Collar in Last Job — White Collar in New Job

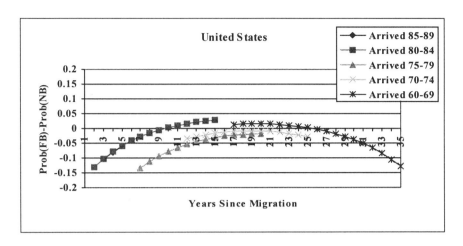

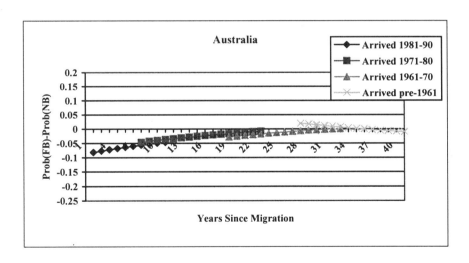

Figure 11: Markov Transition Models
White Collar in Last Job — Prof./Manag. in New Job

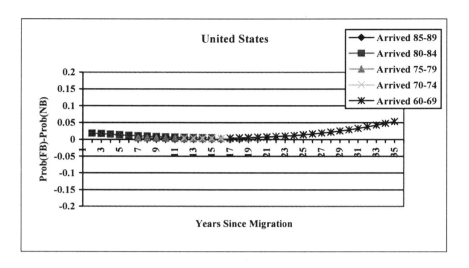

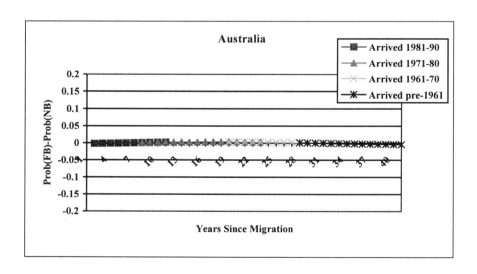

Figure 12: Markov Transition Models
White Collar in Last Job — Not Working

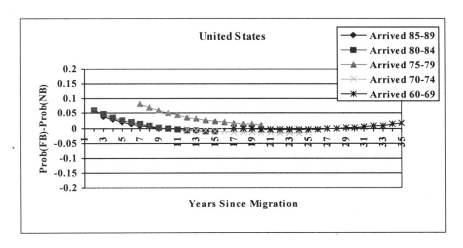

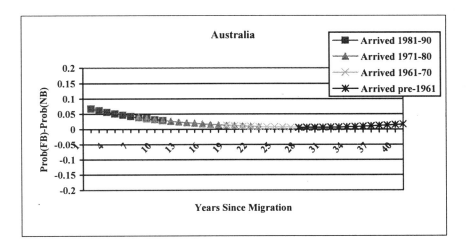

The figures for Australia indicate that immigrants in white collar jobs have probabilities of switching into the other occupational states that are generally very similar to those of the Australian-born. However, as was found for the United States, recent immigrants in Australia are less likely to remain in the white collar state shortly after arrival compared with the Australian-born men. This difference is less than 10% and shrinks with time in Australia, implying virtually no difference after 15 years in the country. Also similar to what was found for the United States, recent immigrants to Australia are more likely to exit white collar jobs and enter the not working group recently after arrival in Australia than are the Australian-born, but this difference also shrinks with time in Australia.

Figures 13 to 16 replicate the analysis described above but for the case of the initial job being in one of the professional or managerial occupations. For the United States, recent immigrants with professional or managerial jobs are more likely to exit into white collar jobs than are the American-born and are less likely to remain in the professional or managerial occupations than are the American-born. In each case, these differences diminish with years of residence in the United States, indicating virtually no differences between immigrants with YSM above 20 and the American-born.

For the case of Australia, probabilities of switching from professional or managerial jobs into either blue collar or white collar jobs are equal to those of the Australian-born. As was found for the United States, the probability of remaining in the professional or managerial occupation grouping is less than that of the native-born in the first years after migration. However, this difference is larger in the Australian case and diminishes quickly with YSM leading to only a small difference after nine years of residence in Australia. Almost the mirror image of this relationship is found in terms of transitions from the professional or managerial occupations to the not working category. Recent immigrants are more likely to experience this transition than are the Australian-born, however, this difference drops quickly with YSM until only a small positive difference exists after nine years of residence in Australia. These results indicate that immigrants in the professional or managerial occupations are no more likely to switch occupations than are the Australian-born in those occupations. However, they are more likely to switch into the not working category as part of the adjustment to the new labour market in the first years after migration.

In summary, the transition estimates for Australia and the United States reveal a number of patterns that add to the understanding of occupational

Figure 13: Markov Transition Models
Prof./Manag. in Last Job — Blue Collar in New Job

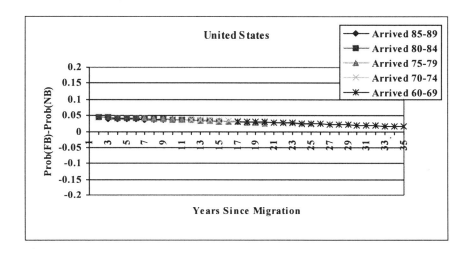

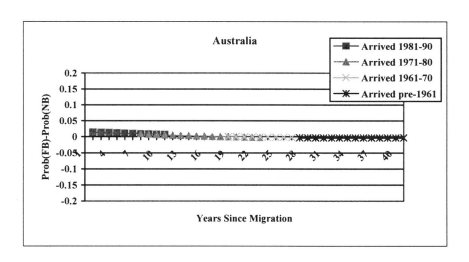

Figure 14: Markov Transition Models
Prof./Manag. in Last Job — White Collar in New Job

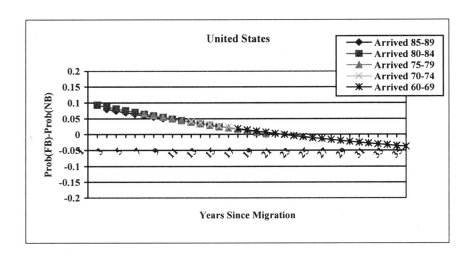

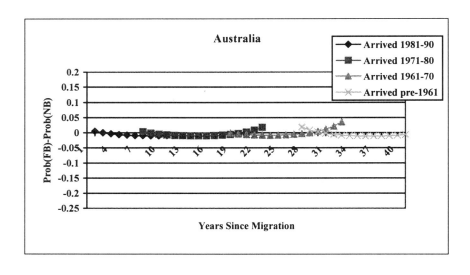

Figure 15: Markov Transition Models
Prof./Manag. in Last Job — Prof./Manag. in New Job

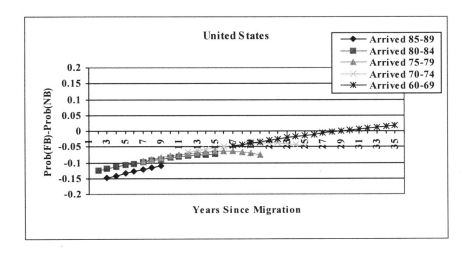

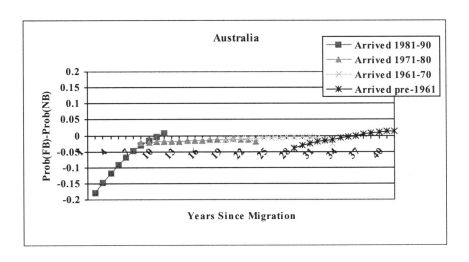

Figure 16: Markov Transition Models
Prof./Manag. in Last Job — Not Working

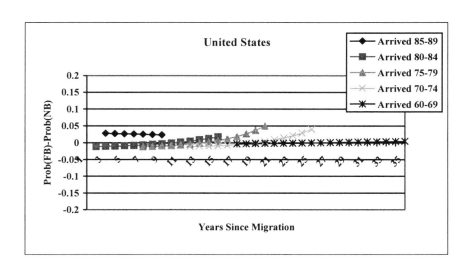

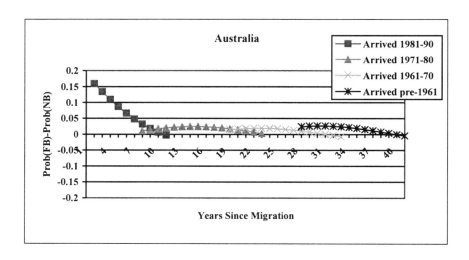

mobility of immigrants gained from the first stage, cross-sectional analysis. In general, immigrants in the United States are more likely to switch from one occupational grouping to another than are the American-born. These differences are largest for immigrants who have recently arrived in the United States and diminish with YSM leading to a convergence to no immigrant/native-born differences in transition probabilities in virtually all cases. For the case of Australia, occupation to occupation transitions are generally very similar between immigrants and the native-born.

Transitions out of an occupation and into the not working state are generally more common for recent immigrants than for the native-born in both Australia and the United States. However, this effect diminishes with YSM leading to a convergence to the native-born probabilities over time. This behaviour is consistent with a number of possibilities. It may be that recent immigrants benefit more from job search while not employed than do the native-born, and periods spent in the not working state may be part of the post-migration investment process for recent immigrants. It may also be that recent immigrants are exiting from the labour force in order to spend time in education and training programs. An exploration of these different possibilities is left for the next iteration of this paper.

Finally, the results from the transition model for the United States is consistent with a higher degree of occupational mobility than is indicated from the cross-sectional model. In particular, high probabilities (relative to the native-born) have been estimated for occupational switches between blue collar and white collar occupations, between white collar and blue collar occupations, and between the professional or managerial occupations and white collar occupations. In each case, these differences are present for recent immigrants, but the magnitude diminishes to near zero with time in the United States. These relationships indicate that immigrants may experience a high frequency of occupational switches relative to the American-born shortly after arrival with many of these occupational switches, in effect, "canceling each other out". This indicates that occupational mobility (at least for the United States) may be an important part of the immigrant labour market adjustment process and that longitudinal data are required in order to fully document the nature of the differences in occupational mobility between immigrants and the American-born.

Conclusions

The occupational outcomes of immigrant and the native-born men have been analyzed using data from Australia, Canada, and the United States. The results are consistent with immigrants having similar occupational distributions to the native-born in each country with a number of exceptions.

First, immigrants to Australia appear to be overrepresented in the blue collar occupations and underrepresented in the white collar occupations. While some variability in these relationships is present, they do not appear to change in a clear fashion across immigrant arrival cohorts or for different values of years-since-migration (YSM).

Second, immigrants to Canada and the United States (and to a lesser extent Australia), appear to be underrepresented initially in the professional or managerial occupations. These differences tend to diminish with YSM and converge to being close to the native-born probabilities with time in the new country. These patterns coincide with an over-representation of recent immigrants in the not working category over similar values of YSM. The results are consistent with recent immigrants whose intended occupations fall into the professional or managerial grouping needing to invest time in the not working state (perhaps involved in job search or education) in order to secure an appropriate job. However, the magnitude of the not working immigrant/native-born difference is larger for each country than the magnitude of the immigrant/native-born difference in probability of being in the professional or managerial occupational grouping. Therefore, it is likely that spells in the not working category are an important part of the labour market adjustment process of immigrants irrespective of their intended occupation.

Third, results from transition models of occupational outcomes that exploit the longitudinal nature of the data for Australia and the United States were estimated. The results indicate that occupational switching is more common for recent immigrants to the United States than it is for the American-born but that this difference diminishes to near zero with more time in the United States. These relationships are particularly pronounced for the following cases: (i) blue collar to white collar switches, (ii) white collar to blue collar switches, and (iii) professional/managerial to white collar switches. In addition, for both the United States and Australia, movements into the not working state appear to be an important part of the adjustment process to the new labour market for recent immigrants.

For the case of Australia, probabilities of occupation to occupation switches are very similar to those of the Australian-born. This stands in contrast to the results found for the United States. One possibility is that institutional differences in the labour markets of the two countries may explain these differences in behaviour. An exploration of this possibility is left for future work.

Finally, in virtually all cases, immigrant/native-born differences in behaviour appear at low values of YSM and shrink to near zero within the first 20 years that the immigrants spend in the new country. Therefore, the occupational mobility of immigrants has important differences from that of the native-born in the first years after arrival. However, the general pattern is one of convergence to native-born patterns with time in the new country.

References

Baker, M. and D. Benjamin (1994), "The Performance of Immigrants in the Canadian Labour Market", *Journal of Labor Economics* 12, 369–405.

Bauer, T. and K.F. Zimmermann (1999), "Occupational Mobility of Ethnic Migrants", IZA Discussion Paper No. 58, September.

Beggs, J.J. and B.J. Chapman (1988), "Immigrant Wage Adjustment in Australia: Cross Section and Time-Series Estimates", *Economic Record* 64(186), 161–167.

Bloom, D.E., G. Grenier and M. Gunderson (1995), "The Changing Labour Market Position of Canadian Immigrants", *Canadian Journal of Economics* 28(4), 987–1005.

Borjas, G.J. (1985), "Assimilation, Change in Cohort Quality, and the Earnings of Immigrants", *Journal of Labor Economics* 3, 463–489.

_____ (1992), "National Origins and the Skills of Immigrants in the Postwar Period", in G.J. Borjas and R.B. Freeman (eds.), *Immigration and the Workforce* (Chicago: University of Chicago Press), 17–47.

_____ (1995), "Assimilation and Changes in Cohort Quality Revisited: What Happened to Immigrant Earnings in the 1980s?" *Journal of Labor Economics* 13, 201–245.

Boyd, M. (1985), "Immigration and Occupational Attainment in Canada", in M. Boyd, J. Goyder, F.E. Jones, H.A. McRoberts, P.C. Pineo and J. Porter (eds.), *Ascription and Achievement: Studies in Mobility and Status Attainment in Canada* (Ottawa: Carleton University Press), 383–445.

Chiswick, B.R. (1978), "The Effect of Americanization on the Earnings of Foreign-Born Men", *Journal of Political Economy* 86, 897–921.

Chiswick, B.R. and P.W. Miller (1995), "The Endogeneity Between Language and Earnings: International Analyses", *Journal of Labor Economics* 13(2), 246–288.

_____ (2002), "Longitudinal Analysis of the Occupational Mobility of Immigrants". Paper presented at the Canadian Employment Research Forum's Conference on Immigration, Calgary, June.

Duleep, H.O. and M.C. Regets (1997), "Measuring Immigrant Wage Growth Using Matched CPS Files", *Demography* 34(2), 239–249.

Grant, M.L. (1999), "Evidence of New Immigrant Assimilation in Canada", *Canadian Journal of Economics* 32(4), 930–955.

Green, D.A. (1999), "Immigrant Occupational Attainment: Assimilation and Mobility Over Time", *Journal of Labor Economics* 17(1), 49–79.

Jones, S.R.G. and W.C. Riddell (1999), "The Measurement of Unemployment: An Empirical Approach", *Econometrica* 67(1), 147–161.

LaLonde, R. and R. Topel (1991), "Immigrants in the American Labor Market: Quality, Assimilation, and Distributional Effects", *AEA Papers and Proceedings*, 297–302.

McDonald, J.T. and C. Worswick (1998), "The Earnings of Immigrant Men in Canada: Job Tenure, Cohort and Macroeconomic Conditions", *Industrial and Labor Relations Review* 51(3), 465–482.

_____ (1999), "The Earnings of Immigrant Men in Australia: Assimilation, Cohort Effects and Macroeconomic Conditions", *The Economic Record* 75(228), 49–62.

Richmond, A.H. and W.E. Kalbach (1980), *Factors in the Adjustment of Immigrants and their Descendants* (Ottawa: Statistics Canada).

Immigration and Capital Accumulation in Canada: A Long-Run Perspective

Stuart J. Wilson

Introduction

Canada has experienced tremendous change over the twentieth century, growing from a small country of 5.4 million residents of primarily European descent, to a country with more than 30 million residents with a rich multicultural background. The prospects for Canada at the dawn of the twentieth century appeared limitless as the west was being settled, a transcontinental economy was developing, and Canada was in the middle of an investment boom. At the end of the twentieth century, Canada was ranked the best country in the world in which to live, according to the United Nations Human Development Index.

Immigrants from all over the world come to Canada. Annual immigration levels have exceeded 200,000 in the 1990s. However, over the last decade, evidence has shown that recent immigrants are performing poorly

The author thanks Maximillian Schmeiser for research assistance in compiling the data series used herein, and thanks seminar participants and Charles Beach and Alan Green for comments. None other than the author can be held accountable for errors or oversights.

in the Canadian labour market, while at the same time, the rate of investment has declined. Is there a link between these two developments? What impact do immigrants have on domestic investment? The purpose of this paper is to examine the relationship between immigration and investment in Canada over the twentieth century.

Immigration policy at the beginning of the twentieth century focused on attracting wealthy migrants from the United States and the United Kingdom, and experienced farmers to help settle the west. In the latter half of the century, immigration policy became more accommodating of humanitarian concerns and goals. Immigrants now come from all regions of the world, most notably from Asia, Africa, and Latin America. There has recently surfaced an increasing amount of evidence pointing to the relatively poor performance of recent immigrants in the North American labour market. An article by Baker and Benjamin (1994) showed that a recent decline in immigrant labour market performance has been the result of a fundamental change in the countries of origin and skills of immigrants.

A consequence of declining immigrant labour market performance is a fall in the rate of investment, according to standard growth models. A slowdown in labour force productivity due to a slowdown in human capital would lower the returns to physical capital, decrease the incentives for investment, and result in a decline in the growth rate of the stock of physical capital. By extension, economic growth stalls with the decline in human capital growth and in physical capital accumulation. Has the rate of investment decreased in step with the deteriorating relative performance of recent immigrants in the Canadian labour market? Canada has tried to reduce the number of unskilled migrants with the establishment of a points system that rewards education, language, and intended occupation. Canada has also recently focused more attention on attracting business immigrants, those with enough wealth to start their own businesses in Canada, or with enough wealth to invest in Canadian businesses.

The paper will examine the effect of changing immigration patterns on the rate of investment over the twentieth century. The evidence presented here suggests that the rate of investment in physical capital has slowed with a coincident decline in the effectiveness of immigrant human capital in the domestic labour market. This finding is consistent with the recent diminishing returns literature examining the poor labour market performance of recent immigrants. The policy implications of this finding are similar to those in the diminishing returns literature. Unless the human capital of recent immigrants can be improved, we should expect the rate of investment in Canada to remain relatively low. However, it appears unlikely that improving the success of immigrants in the Canadian labour market can be accomplished by reverting to the policies of the past which favoured immigrants from preferred regions of the world, namely the United States, the United Kingdom, and northwestern Europe. Instead, policy should focus on improving the human capital of recent immigrants upon arrival, to improve their potential for success in the Canadian labour market and business environment, and by doing so, improve the incentives for investment in Canada, and improve economic growth.

The paper proceeds as follows: the next section provides an overview of immigration, immigration policy, and some key economic indicators for Canada in the twentieth century; section three presents a theoretical framework to set up the discussion of the empirical model and model results in the following section, for the purpose of examining the long-run relationship between investment and immigration in the twentieth century; the final section concludes the analysis.

Immigration in the Twentieth Century

In 1901, the Canadian population amounted to 5.4 million. By 1911, the population had risen to 7.2 million. Annual immigration levels averaged 164,000 in the first decade of the twentieth century, and peaked at 400,000 in 1912, just before the outbreak of World War I. Vast quantities of capital flowed into Canada from foreign investors. Immigrants also brought capital funds into Canada. The country experienced a massive immigration and investment boom. The rate of gross investment as a proportion of gross national product rose from 15% in 1896 to 33% in 1912. A transcontinental economy was being developed, with growth across all sectors, fuelled by capital and labour inflows.

Canada continues to be a prime destination for immigrants. In the late 1990s, Canada was declared the best country to live according to the United Nations Human Development Index rankings. Many immigrants believed the standard of living in Canada was second to none (Ley, 2000, p. 25). Immigration has averaged over 200,000 annually since 1986. However, the investment rate has fallen in the last two decades of the twentieth century. There has been a considerable amount of research pointing to a decline in the effective human capital of immigrants based on earnings data. Is this decline also reflected in the investment data? What effect have changes in immigration and policy had on the rate of capital accumulation? This section provides an overview of immigration patterns, policy, and economic developments for Canada over the twentieth century.

Immigration policy over the twentieth century may be evenly split into two different regimes. During the first half of the twentieth century, immigration policy was very selective. Canada wanted migrants from the United States and Britain, and northwestern Europe. Immigration policy discriminated against migrants from other regions of the world. In the second half of the twentieth century, Canada began admitting more migrants on humanitarian grounds. Past immigrants to Canada were permitted to sponsor more family class immigrants, and Canada opened its doors to refugees, no longer splitting the world into preferred and non-preferred sources of immigrants. Immigration policy during the second half of the twentieth century was more humanitarian and less discriminating.

Each of these two periods may be divided again into two due to changes in economic conditions within each half-century. Table 1 presents a set of selected statistics for Canada over the 1897–1929, 1930–50, 1951–85, and 1986–2001 periods. The first period corresponds to the Wheat Boom Era in Canadian economic history, the second to a period of disruption that includes the Great Depression and World War II. The third period corresponds to the postwar boom period, and the fourth period corresponds to a period when Canadian immigration policy focused more on long-term goals, and on attracting migrants with investment capital to spur a slowing economy. An overview of each subperiod will now be provided, with a focus on immigration policy, income growth, and the rate of investment.

Massive Immigration during the Wheat Boom Era (1897–1929)

After three decades of slow economic growth and the experience of net emigration, the pattern of Canadian development was dramatically altered around 1897. The new Liberal prime minister, Wilfrid Laurier, installed Clifford Sifton, a Manitoba politician, as minister of the interior. Sifton was determined to see a massive inflow of settlers into the Canadian west and developed the Immigration Branch to carry out this vision. Canada was actively promoted and advertised as a new promised land of prosperity, and immigrants were recruited from the United States and Britain. Sifton also wanted experienced farmers with capital. As the years passed, recruitment

Table 1: Selected Canadian Statistics

Statistic	1897–1929	1930–1950	1951–1985	1986–2001
Immigrant arrivals (period total, thousands)	4,622	755	4,974	3,201
Immigrant arrivals (annual average)	140,050	20,269	135,111	200,086
Immigrant arrivals/ population (annual average, in %)	1.92	0.30	0.73	0.69
Gross domestic capital formation/GNP (the gross investment rate, annual average)	20.41	13.54	22.62	20.56
Real per capita income growth (annual average)	2.69	1.82	2.62	1.76

campaigns were expanded to eastern Europe, to the Ukraine, Germany, and Russia — to regions populated by hard-working farmers who knew the rigors of farming — to continue the pace of western settlement.

The surge in population growth at the beginning of the twentieth century has been credited primarily to the emergence of the wheat economy in Canada. The western provinces were rapidly settled during this period. The increase in prairie homesteading has been attributed to a variety of factors, including the rise in the international price of wheat, the introduction of dry-farming techniques and the reduction of transportation costs due to rail expansion (Norrie, 1975; Marr and Percy, 1978; and Borins, 1982). It has been shown that the feasible region of cultivation expanded after 1896 due to the construction of rail lines and an increase in wheat yields (Lewis, 1981). New and improved equipment also enabled farmers to cultivate larger crop acreage (Ward, 1994). Settlers rushed to the Canadian Prairies once the economic incentives appeared after 1896 for successful farming. Canada was developing a wheat economy, and would dominate the international market for wheat in the 1920s.

Immigrants, however, did not move to Canada only to farm. Many immigrants settled in the cities and many found occupations in industry and transportation. Green and Green (1993) showed that British migrants were arriving to settle across the country and in various occupations. This period was one of extensive growth in various sectors of the Canadian economy and also marked the development of advanced manufacturing, for example, a modern iron and steel industry (Green and Urquhart, 1994).

The data in Table 1 show that an average of 140,000 immigrants arrived annually over the 1897–1929 period, at an average annual rate of 1.9% of the population. The Canadian population doubled, from 5 million in 1896, to ten million in 1929. During this population boom, gross investment rose from 15% of gross national product (GNP) in 1896 to a high of 33% in 1912; the rate of gross investment averaged over 20% for the period as a whole. Strong rates of investment and labour force growth led to strong growth in real income. On a per capita basis, real incomes grew by 2.7% annually, a marked increase from the last three decades of the nineteenth century when real incomes grew by 1% per year. This period of strong performance ended abruptly with the onset of the Great Depression.

Closed Doors: The Period of Disruption (1930–1950)

After a period of strong growth, both in economic prosperity and in population, Canada closed its doors to the world, with the exception of wealthy British and American immigrants, and wealthy farmers. Western settlement had contributed greatly to Canadian development, but with depressed international commodity prices and drought conditions, nominal incomes on the prairies fell by 70%, and nominal incomes fell by 45% for the country as a whole from 1929 to 1933. Even if European migrants came, they would be hard-pressed to find work, as the unemployment rate averaged over 12% from 1929 to 1937, and migrants from Europe had higher unemployment rates than others in the Canadian labour market (Green, 2000, pp. 216–222).

Immigration dropped from over a hundred thousand in 1930 to a low of 11 thousand in 1935. During the course of the Depression, Canada even deported unemployed troublemakers to their countries of origin (Norrie, Owram and Emery, 2002, p. 337). Immigration increased by a few thousand per year after 1935, but then fell again during the Second World War, to a low of seven and a half thousand in 1942. During the 1930–50 period, the average annual flow of immigrants amounted to 20 thousand, an annual rate of 0.3% of the population. Canada was a net exporter of capital during this period, and the rate of investment fell to an annual average of 13.5% of GNP. Real per capita income grew at an average annual rate of 1.8%, but almost all of the growth over this period occurred during the war (Green, 2000, p. 214).

Canada continued its policy of restricting immigration in the first two years following World War II (Knowles, 2000). Canada then slowly opened its doors to displaced Europeans beginning in 1947. As a result of shortages, firms applied to immigration authorities for immigrant labour, and immigration agents looked for workers amongst the refugees and the displaced in European camps. In 1948, the US liberalized policy and became a favoured destination for immigrants. As a result, Canada also liberalized its policy to maintain immigration levels and to fill labour shortages. The primary sources of immigrants shifted from the United States and northwestern Europe, to central, eastern and southern Europe. However, with structural change, as a result of the transition from a wartime to peacetime economy, per capita incomes fell by 0.18% per year over 1944 to 1950.

The Post-War Boom and Accommodating Immigration (1951–1985)

The postwar boom began in the 1950s. The performance of the Canadian economy and the flow of immigrants over the next few decades mirrored the Canadian economy of the Wheat Boom Era. Canada opened its doors to immigrants from Europe to fill needs in the labour market in light of the availability of labour in Europe following the war. Immigration restrictions gradually eased during the 1950s as the search for labour expanded to the non-preferred regions of Europe (Green and Green, 1995, p. 1011). Canada also admitted many immigrants on humanitarian grounds, and family class immigration increased.

The search for migrants expanded to Asia, Africa, and other parts of the world with the elimination of discriminatory immigration policy in 1962. No longer would there be any favoured source of immigrants, but a set of favoured immigrant characteristics. The points system was established in 1967 to screen skilled and educated independent migrants. The changes to the independent migrant category were used to increase the skill and education level of immigrants and to reduce the number of unskilled migrants entering Canada. The composition of immigrants by source quickly shifted away from Europe, to poor and developing nations in Asia, Africa, the Caribbean, and South America. In 1966, 87% of immigrants were of European descent, whereas in 1970, 50% were from Asia.)

Immigration policy for this period as a whole can be viewed as increasingly accommodating and humanitarian. Canada opened its doors to displaced Europeans and refugees, placed an emphasis on family class immigration, and removed discriminatory barriers. Canadian immigration policy accommodated labour market demands during the postwar boom. The annual average immigrant flow was 135 thousand, at a rate of 0.7% of the population. During the postwar boom period, the average rate of gross investment rose to 22% of GNP, and real per capita incomes grew at an average rate of 2.6% per year.

The Focus on Economic Migrants since 1985

With another review of immigration policy by the new Conservative government in 1985, a significant change occurred. Immigration would become more of a long-term economic policy and demographic tool in Canada, as a means to stimulate population growth and counter the effect of low fertility rates. Immigration levels were to be increased, with a stronger focus on increasing the number of economic migrants, although again not at the expense of family class and refugee immigration. In the category of economic migrants, the investor class was added to stimulate the arrival of migrants with considerable assets who could contribute investment funds to Canadian enterprise.

The economic migrant category includes skilled workers and the business class. Skilled workers are admitted on the basis of the points system, and their skills, education, and ability to speak English or French hold much weight in the determination of admissibility. For admission in 1993, potential immigrants must have scored 67 points out of a total of 100 (Green and Green, 1999, p. 433). The business class consists of three categories, the entrepreneur, the self-employed, and the investor. The entrepreneur is admitted on the basis of having business experience, a net worth of at least $300,000, and the intention of actively controlling a Canadian business within three years of obtaining permanent residency. The self-employed migrant must start or buy, and run a business that makes a contribution to the Canadian economy. The investor is required to place at least $400,000 of capital in trust with participating provinces, and the provinces then use these funds to help create domestic jobs. Business class immigrants are also subject to a points system, but the cut-off for admission is relatively low. Admission has been granted to immigrants with a score of 25 out of a maximum of 87 points (CIC, 1999). Many business immigrants have been admitted without the ability to speak in either of the Canadian official languages, and without post-secondary education (CIC, 1998).

The record of the business immigrant program, based on the official statistics, suggests the program has been a huge success in attracting immigrants and capital to Canada. From 1986 to 2000, 41,500 principal applicants arrived as entrepreneurs, 12,847 as self-employed, and 19,239 were admitted as investors. The investor program led to an inflow of $5.76 billion of funds for investment in Canada, 12% in 2000. The entrepreneur program in 2000 had 1,184 immigrant entrepreneurs contributing a total of $184 million to domestic investment, and creating 1,832 full-time and 918 part-time jobs, the majority of which were in British Columbia and Ontario (CIC, 2001).

Other research portrays a gloomy picture as to the long-run economic contribution of many business immigrants to Canada. Ley (2000) presented evidence that much immigrant investment in Vancouver was directed into real estate, contributing to the boom in house prices in the late 1980s and 1990s. Many immigrants were unable to find appropriate employment and faced downward mobility, took early retirement, or returned to their home countries to work. Despite high levels of home ownership, the majority of recent immigrants also reported incomes below the low-income cut-offs (Ley, 2000, p. 32).

It has been suggested that the government was poorly prepared for the flood of business migration. A substantial amount of investment funds entered Canada with immigrants, but was allocated in a new, poorly regulated and mismanaged environment. Many business immigrants were "reluctant exiles", from Hong Kong and Taiwan, establishing residency in Canada as a result of political instability, more specifically uncertain future relations with China. Immigrant investment was not always directed to profitable manufacturing and value-added ventures, but more often into real estate. In light of the harsher taxation and regulatory environment in Canada, of the poor incomes of recent immigrants, and of improving political conditions in East Asia with the turnover of Hong Kong in 1997, the rate of business migration has fallen, and along with it, the quantity of immigrant investment funds to Canada (see Ley, 2000; Skeldon, 1994).

Table 1 shows that the level of immigrant arrivals increased to an average of 200,000 per year, when economic performance declined. The rate of investment fell to an average of 20.6% of GNP, and real per capita income growth slowed to an average of 1.76% per year. This remarkable increase in immigration levels did not translate into a higher investment rate and stronger economic growth in the aggregate.

In the first half of the twentieth century, immigration policy was selective. New immigrants were predominantly from the United States and Britain, and were young adult males. The rate of investment rose when the rate of immigration increased in the years before and after World War I. When wartime and depressed conditions arose and the rate of domestic investment fell, the Canadian borders closed except to the very wealthy. In the second half of the twentieth century, immigration policy was more humanitarian and accommodating. Canada opened its doors to more family class migrants and refugees, and the search for immigrants expanded to southern and eastern Europe, and later to Asia, Africa, and Latin America. After 1985, economic migrants were recruited as a means of increasing domestic investment, and creating jobs. Unfortunately, this did not translate into higher rates of investment. Figure 1 shows the pattern of immigration to Canada, and shows the ratio of investment to income in Canada since 1897.

Figure 1: Rate of Immigration and Gross Investment as a Proportion of GNP, Canada, 1897–2001

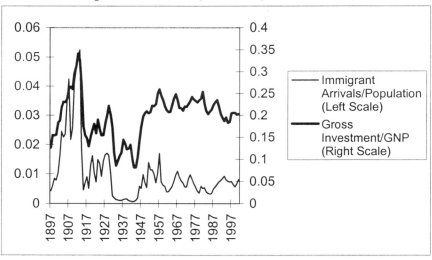

Source: See Appendix.

When immigration policy became less restrictive following the Second World War, the Canadian economy grew strongly and real per capita incomes grew at a rate similar to that of the Wheat Boom Era. Since 1988, however, immigration levels have increased while the rate of investment has declined. There has been a fundamental change in immigration policy and the characteristics of immigrants over the last half-century. Has there also been a fundamental change in the relationship between immigration and investment?

A Simple Theoretical Framework

Recent work has shown that the recent decline in the earnings of recent immigrants relative to natives and past immigrant cohorts has been the result of a change in the countries of origin and skills of immigrants to Canada. Chiswick and Miller (1992) found that immigrants who arrive from non-English-speaking countries are at a disadvantage upon arrival and accordingly suffer a larger earnings gap relative to natives than immigrants from English-speaking countries. Bloom and Gunderson (1991), Abbott and Beach (1993), Coulson and DeVoretz (1993), Baker and Benjamin (1994), and Worswick (1996) all find evidence of a relative decline in the earnings of recent immigrants relative to natives and past immigrant cohorts, low rates of assimilation, and poor returns to education received outside Canada. The decline in immigrant earnings relative to both natives and earlier immigrant cohorts suggests a decline in the relative human capital of recent immigrants in the North American labour market. A decline in the relative human capital of immigrants has consequences not only for growth, but also for investment in physical capital. This section provides a theoretical framework for discussing the relationship between immigration, investment and growth.[1]

---

[1]Interested readers can refer to the models of Romer (1986), Lucas (1988), and Rebelo (1991), those presented in Barro and Sala-i-Martin (1995), Jones (1995), Romer (1996), and Li (2002), and extensions of the Diamond overlapping generations model presented in Huggett (1996), Rios-Rull (2001), and Wilson (2003).

Production in a One-Sector Economy

Consider a one-sector standard neoclassical constant returns-to-scale production function incorporating human capital:

(1) $Y_t = F(K_t, N_t) = K_t^a (A_t H_t N_t)^{1-\alpha}$.

In this context, Y denotes output, K denotes the stock of physical capital, N denotes the population size, H denotes human capital per capita (a weighted average of human capital in the aggregate), and A is an exogenous scale parameter, denoting labour-augmenting technology. This production function can be re-written, with L denoting effective labour, and equal to the population size times human capital and labour-augmenting technology:

(2) $L_t = A_t H_t N_t$;

(3) $Y_t = F(K_t, L_t) = K_t^a L_t^{1-\alpha}$.

Given this production function, the returns to the inputs to production are as follows, per unit of physical capital, K (the real interest rate, r, plus depreciation, δ), and per unit of effective labour, L (wage rate, w):

(4) $r_t + \delta_t = F_1(K_t, L_t) = \alpha K_t^{\alpha-1} L_t^{1-\alpha} = \alpha (L_t / K_t)^{1-\alpha}$;

(5) $w_t = F_2(K_t, L_t) = (1 - \alpha)(K_t / L_t)^{\alpha}$.

With perfectly competitive markets, workers will receive their marginal products based on their effective labour (i.e., the product of their human capital, and labour-augmenting technology). Assuming competitive markets and an infinitely elastic supply of capital in a small open economy, when new workers offer their labour services, physical capital will also be offered in a manner so as to keep the interest rate constant. As a result, the capital-to-effective labour ratio, K/L, remains constant.

New immigrants with a relatively lower value of human capital compared to natives will be equipped for production with a smaller amount of physical capital than natives, will receive lower wages (although the immigrant will receive the same wage rate per effective labour unit supplied), and will supply less output than natives in the economy.

Stuart J. Wilson

Illustrative Example

As an illustration, assume that a native and an immigrant worker compete in the same one-sector economy, using the same technology, and both receive their marginal products. Assuming that the immigrant has a lower value of human capital than natives in the labour market, and normalizing N to 1 for both natives and immigrants, the following characterizes production, the return to physical capital, and total wages received:

(6) $Y_i = K_i^\alpha (AH_i)^{1-\alpha}$;

(7) $r_i = \alpha(AH_i / K_i)^{1-\alpha} - \delta$;

(8) $w_i N_i = (1 - \alpha)K_i^\alpha (AH_i)^{1-\alpha}$;

with $i = R$ for natives and I for immigrants. For the real return to capital to be constant in the economy, $r_R = r_I$, so that the following must hold:

(9) $\alpha(AH_R / K_R)^{1-\alpha} = \alpha(AH_I / K_I)^{1-\alpha}$.

As such, it must hold that if $H_R > H_I$ (i.e., a native holds more human capital), then $K_R > K_I$ (i.e., the capital stock associated with a native in production will be greater than that associated with an immigrant). Consequently, given (8), total wages received by immigrants will be lower than those received by natives, and the output attributed to immigrants will also be lower than that attributed to natives. At an aggregate level, an inflow of immigrants with relatively less human capital will lower the level of per capita earnings, and per capita capital stock. This will also occur if immigrants have higher unemployment rates and lower labour force participation rates than natives and past immigrants (note that individuals who are not working at any point in time are assigned a value for H of 0).

Growth

The consequences of a decline in human capital growth can also be examined in a dynamic setting. Standard neoclassical growth models predict that a fall in the growth of human capital will also reduce the rate of growth of physical capital and income in the aggregate, and will also lower the ratio of investment to income.

Consider an economy with production once again described by equation (1). Assuming a small open economy, with an infinitely elastic supply of capital, the capital stock adjusts to maintain a constant real interest rate, and a constant ratio of physical capital to labour efficiency units (K/L) in the long run. Since the capital-labour (K/L) ratio remains constant, physical capital, K, grows at the rate of growth in L.[2] By extension, from equation (3), output, Y, also grows at the rate of growth of L. Growth in labour efficiency is the sum of growth in exogenous labour-augmenting technology, growth in per capita human capital and growth in population. Therefore, the rates of growth in labour-augmenting technology, per capita human capital, and population determine the rates of growth of physical capital and output. Isolating the effect of human capital growth, any decrease in the rate of growth in human capital as a result of immigration will result in a relative decline in the earnings of recent immigrants, a decline in the growth of income, and a decline in the growth of physical capital.

In the steady state, the ratio of physical capital to output will also remain constant (as a consequence of a constant interest rate and perfectly elastic supply of capital), and the ratio of gross investment to income will be a function of the capital-output ratio, and the growth rates of the population (n), labour-augmenting technology (a) and human capital (h), and the rate of depreciation of physical capital (δ):

$$(10) \quad \frac{I}{Y} = \frac{K}{Y} \times (n + \alpha + h + \delta).$$

It follows from equation (10), that if there is a slowdown in the growth of human capital as a result of changes in the effectiveness of recent immigrants in the domestic labour market, all else being equal, the ratio of investment to income will fall.

On a per capita basis in the aggregate (following (1) and dividing through by N or following (6) by normalizing N to 1), production is described by:

---

[2]Wilson (2003) used this framework of a small open economy, to examine the impact of the massive inflow of immigrants to Canada at the beginning of the twentieth century, on savings and investment.

(11) $Y = K^{\alpha}(AH)^{1-\alpha}$,

where Y now denotes per capita output, K now denotes per capita physical capital stock, and A and H are as before. In the steady state, per capita output and per capita physical capital grow at the rate of per capita labour efficiency (the sum of growth in exogenous labour-augmenting technological change and growth in human capital) in the long run. The rates of growth in human capital and in technological change determine the rate of growth of physical capital and output on a per capita basis. Isolating the effect of human capital growth, any decrease in the rate of growth in human capital as a result of a change in the characteristics of immigrants will result in a decrease in per capita income and per capita physical capital.

In summary, given the small open economy setting, long-run changes in the growth of per capita income and investment are primarily driven by changes in the growth of labour-augmenting technological change and by changes in the growth of human capital. If recent immigrants have a lower value of human capital in the domestic labour market (including the effect of higher unemployment rates and lower labour force participation rates), compared to natives and past immigrants, not only will this reflect in lower relative wages, but in smaller capital requirements and investment to equip these immigrants for production, and slower per capita investment and income growth in the aggregate. The following section attempts to empirically determine the relationship between immigration, investment, and income on a per capita basis for Canada over the twentieth century.

Empirical Analysis

Over the twentieth century, Canadian immigration policy changed from a highly selective policy to one that was more accommodating and humanitarian. The primary sources of immigrants have also shifted from the United States, the United Kingdom, and northwestern Europe, to Asia, Africa, and Latin America. Has the relationship between immigration and investment changed as a result of the change in the characteristics of immigrants? This relationship will be examined using the vector-autoregressive framework, allowing for long-run equilibrium relationships between co-integrated variables.

The vector-autoregressive (VAR) framework has been used in recent work to examine the relationship between demographic change and investment in Canada. Green and Sparks (1999) looked at the relationships between income, exports, investment, and population in a VAR framework using Canadian data over 1870 to 1939. Looking more closely at the period leading up to the First World War, they found that population innovations due to massive immigration were a significant factor in explaining the dramatic increase in investment in Canada at the beginning of the twentieth century. Wilson (2000) examined the Canadian economy since 1870 and showed that population changes were also significant determinants of savings using a VAR model with co-integrated processes. The VAR modelling framework was also used in Wilson (2001a) to examine the relationships between the real and financial sectors of the economy, along with immigration, for Canada from 1870 to 1967. In that study, the results showed a strong influence of immigration patterns on both investment and savings.

Data

The variables of interest for this investigation are: (i) real income per capita, denoted y, which will be equal to the natural logarithm of GNP divided by the GNP deflator and the population size; (ii) real investment per capita, denoted i, equal to the natural logarithm of gross domestic capital formation divided by the GNP deflator and the population size; and (iii) im, equal to the natural logarithm of the ratio of immigrant arrivals to the total population. In this study, two subperiods will be examined, the first from 1897 to 1950 when immigration policy was selective, and the second from 1951 to 2001, when policy was more accommodating and humanitarian.[3]

Given the theoretical background outlined in the previous section, in the small open-economy setting with an infinitely elastic supply of capital, it is changes in human capital and labour-augmenting technological progress that drive movements in physical capital (and thus investment) and movements in output per capita. Since it is difficult to quantify human capital, although some have used the level of schooling as a proxy for human capital at the aggregate level in panel data, the rate of immigration

---

[3]See the Appendix for more information on the data series.

Stuart J. Wilson

will be used to examine changes in the human capital stock of immigrants relative to natives on a per capita basis.[4] By extension, measuring technological progress is also difficult, and considering that in econometric investigations, there is considerable feedback between income and investment and other variables in partial equilibrium models, changes in income per capita can be an indicator of changes in labour-augmenting technology and human capital in the aggregate.[5]

Modelling Framework

Since many economic time-series are non-stationary (for example, income and investment), econometric investigations require that the time-series of interest be transformed into stationary series, usually by taking first differences of the logarithmic forms of the original series to examine growth rates (e.g., the growth rates of income and of investment). With this transformation, the long-run relationships between non-stationary variables could not be examined (e.g., the long-run income elasticity of investment), in the fear of mistaking a spurious regression between two trending variables for a stable long-run relationship.[6]

The first step in proceeding with this empirical investigation is to determine whether or not the series of interest in this study are non-stationary in their logarithmic forms. The standard Augmented Dickey-Fuller Tests were conducted for this purpose.[7] The test results are presented in Table 2. All series in levels appear to be non-stationary, while all series in first differences appear to be stationary. However, the long-run relationships

---

[4]See Li (2002) for the use of schooling as a proxy for human capital in international panel regressions.

[5]See McLean (1994), Taylor and Williamson (1994), Wilson (2000, 2001a) for results indicating feedback from income growth to savings and investment rates, and from per capita income to per capita savings and investment.

[6]See Davidson and MacKinnon (1993, pp. 669–673) or Charemza and Deadman (1992, pp. 124–127) for further discussion of spurious regressions.

[7]See Davidson and MacKinnon (1993, pp. 700–715) or Charemza and Deadman (1992, pp. 130–136) for further discussion of procedures used to test for stationarity.

Table 2: Augmented Dickey-Fuller Test Statistics

ADF (3) Test Statistics for	1897–1950	1951–2001
y	−2.73	−1.36
i	−2.66	−2.53
im	−2.56	−2.70
Δy	**−4.37**	**−3.67**
Δi	**−3.70**	**−4.36**
Δim	<u>−3.45</u>	**−3.87**

Notes: Test statistics in bold are significant at the 0.05 significance level, and statistics that are underlined are significant at the 0.10 significance level. The critical values for significance levels of 0.10 and 0.05 are −3.18 and −3.50 respectively, for a sample size of 50 (Fuller, 1976). Three lags were required to remove serial correlation in all the test regressions. An insignificant test statistic indicates that the null hypothesis of non-stationarity cannot be rejected at the given significance level.

between the non-stationary variables of interest may be explored due to recent developments in econometrics, namely co-integration analysis.

The introduction of co-integration analysis in the 1980s by Granger and Engle has been viewed as one of the most important contributions to time-series econometrics.[8] If a long-run relationship exists between non-stationary variables, then deviations from this long-run relationship are stationary. In such a case, these variables are co-integrated. There are several methods used to test for co-integrated variables. One approach, pioneered by Johansen and Juselius, uses the maximum likelihood technique to identify long-run equilibrium relationships between non-

---

[8]See Granger (1981) and Engle and Granger (1987).

stationary variables, and uses the vector-autoregressive framework.[9] The VAR framework is applied to the full-system estimation model with the variables in levels:

$$(12) \quad z_t = \sum_{i=1}^{k} \Pi_i z_{t-i} + \varepsilon_t ,$$

where z_t is an $n \times 1$ matrix of the n variables of interest in the system of equations. The model is then reparametrized, to account for the non-stationarity of the variables in levels, as follows:

$$(13) \quad \Delta z_t = \sum_{i=1}^{k-1} \Gamma_i \Delta z_{t-i} + \Pi z_{t-k} + \varepsilon_t , \quad \varepsilon_t \sim Niid(0,\Omega) .$$

All of the first-differenced variables (Δz) are stationary. If there exist co-integrating relationships between the variables in z, then the matrix Π will determine the extent of co-integration. If Π is a null-matrix, then there exists no stationary long-run relationships amongst the variables in z. If Π is non-zero, then Πz_{t-k} is stationary, and the rank, r, of the matrix will indicate the number of co-integrating relationships between variables. Π is then unpacked as $\Pi = \alpha\beta^T$, where β is an $n \times r$ matrix of parameters denoting the r co-integrating relationships amongst the n variables in z, and α is an $n \times r$ matrix of parameters denoting the speed of adjustment of a dependent variable towards a long-run equilibrium (co-integrating) relationship. It is in this framework that the long-run relationship between per capita income, investment and immigration will be examined.

Equation (13) will be used in the subsequent analysis, where $z = [y \; i \; im]^T$, and $\Pi=\alpha\beta^T$. In this context, β is a $3 \times r$ matrix of parameters denoting the r co-integrating relationships amongst variables in z, and α is a $3 \times r$ matrix of parameters denoting the speed of adjustment of a dependent variable towards a long-run equilibrium (co-integrating) relationship. The unrestricted VAR analysis indicated that a value of k set to three for equation (13) generated satisfactory residuals for both sample periods. Tests were then conducted to identify the rank of the matrix Π. The

---

[9]See Johansen (1988), Johansen and Juselius (1994), and Juselius (1991) for further explanation of the empirical framework.

Johansen L-max rank test results, presented in Table 3 suggested that there exists only one co-integrating relationship among the variables in z.[10]

The unrestricted VAR results also suggested that income was weakly exogenous for the 1897–1950 period, meaning that, for this sample, the income variable was not affected by disturbances in the long-run equilibrium relationships.[11] The multivariate model for this sample was reduced to the following to reflect the weak exogeneity of y:

$$(14) \; \Delta v_t = \Gamma_0 \Delta x_t + \sum_{i=1}^{k-1} \Gamma_i \Delta z_{t-i} + \Pi z_{t-k} + \varepsilon_t \, , \; \varepsilon_t \sim Niid(0, \Omega) \, ,$$

with $v = [i \; im]^T$, $x = [y]^T$, and $\Pi = \alpha \beta^T$. Now, β is a 3×1 matrix of parameters representing the co-integrating relationship among the variables in z, and α is a 2×1 matrix of parameters denoting the speed of adjustment of the dependent variables in v, towards the long-run equilibrium relationship between i, im, and y.

Long-Run Equilibrium Relationships

The parameter estimates that describe the long-run stationary equilibrium relationship for each sample are presented in Table 4. These relationships are:

$$(15) \quad (1897 - 1950) \quad \hat{\beta}^T z_{t-3} = i_{t-3} - 0.237 im_{t-3} - 1.104 y_{t-3} \; ;$$

$$(16) \quad (1951 - 2001) \quad \hat{\beta}^T z_{t-3} = i_{t-3} + 0.203 im_{t-3} - 0.847 y_{t-3} \; .$$

---

[10] The Johansen L-max test procedure is described in Juselius (1991).

[11] Growth in income per capita, Δy, was not affected by deviations in the long-run co-integrating relationship described by βz. This is suggested by the insignificant value for α corresponding to the estimated equation for Δy in the full system. The χ^2 (1) test statistic for the null hypothesis of weak exogeneity of y was 0.04, for the 1897–1950 sample (the 95% critical value is 3.84). Please refer to Juselius (1991) for further discussion of the test for weak exogeneity.

Stuart J. Wilson

Table 3: Johansen Rank Test (L-max Test)

L-max Test	1897–1950	1951–2001	90% Critical Value
H_0: $r = 0$ (no co-integrating relationships)	15.25	23.10	13.39
H_0: $r = 1$ (at most one co-integrating relationships)	6.06	3.76	10.60

Notes: The Johansen Rank Test is used to identify the rank of the matrix Π. The rank of this matrix indicates the number of co-integrating relationships among the variables included in the study. Interested readers may refer to Juselius (1991) for further explanation of the test procedure.

Table 4: Estimates for β

Variable	1897–1950	1951–2001
i	1.00	1.00
im	–0.237 (0.024)	0.203 (0.052)
y	–1.104 (0.095)	–0.847 (0.046)

Notes: Standard errors are in parentheses. Standard errors are not available for the parameter associated with i, which is scaled and restricted to 1.

These relationships can be re-written as follows to focus on investment and its relationship with immigration and income, although it must be highlighted that a direction of causation cannot be established in this estimation framework:

(17) $(1897 - 1950)$ $\quad i_{t-3} = 0.237 im_{t-3} + 1.104 y_{t-3}$;

(18) $(1951 - 2001)$ $\quad i_{t-3} = - 0.203 im_{t-3} + 0.847 y_{t-3}$.

The results for the first sample suggest that, in the long run, both increases in the rate of immigration and in income coincided with increases in investment. In the first half of the twentieth century, when immigration policy was selective and discriminating, an increase in the immigration rate coincided with an increase in per capita investment. The income elasticity of investment was greater than one during this period when the Canadian economy was growing strongly, diversifying, and becoming modern. The west was settled, and towns, cities, and railroads were built, and the social infrastructure requirements were massive to go along with massive immigration. At the beginning of the century, young males had a much higher rate of immigration than any other demographic group. As a consequence, the labour force grew faster than the population as a whole, and in per capita terms, investment also grew at a high rate.

In the second half of the twentieth century, the relationship between investment and immigration was dramatically altered. Increases in the immigration rate coincided with decreases in per capita investment, all else being equal. Immigration policy during this period was more accommodating and humanitarian in nature. Canada opened its doors to family class immigrants, refugees, and immigrants from the previously non-preferred regions of the world. The long-run income elasticity of investment also fell below unity, suggesting that per capita investment was less responsive to increases in per capita incomes in the second half of the twentieth century.[12] One explanation of this result is the general decline in labour productivity since the 1970s: in an environment with lower labour productivity growth, the ratio of investment to income declines.[13] Another explanation is the increase in government deficits in Canada since the 1970s. Even though Canada is a small open economy, domestic investment demand may not have been fully satiated by foreign sources, since many of the industrialized nations also experienced increases in government deficits, and international sources of investment capital also declined. Government deficit financing may have crowded out investment. The complete estimation results with additional test statistics are presented in Appendix Tables A1 and A2.

---

[12]A simple likelihood ratio test under the hypothesis that the income elasticity of investment is unity, yields a test statistic of 8.59, with a p-value of 0.03.

[13]See Wilson (2001b) for a discussion of the effect of changes in productivity on savings and investment in an overlapping generations framework.

Stuart J. Wilson

Discussion

Over the twentieth century, Canada had essentially two different immigration policy regimes. Early twentieth-century immigration policy focused on recruiting US and UK migrants, the wealthy, and hearty farmers. Canada was not accepting of the "huddled masses" of the poor at the beginning of the twentieth century. Immigration policy before the post-war period was discriminatory and prejudicial. In the second half of the last century, Canadian immigration policy became more humanitarian and less discriminatory. Canada allowed more family class immigration, accepted refugees, and recruited workers from all regions of the world. The econometric results suggest that the fundamental relationship between investment and immigration changed over the last century as well. In the first half of the twentieth century, increases in investment coincided with increases in immigration on a per capita basis. In the second half of the century, increases in per capita investment coincided with decreases in immigration. This finding may have several explanations.

First, these results are consistent with the findings of a recent decline in relative immigrant earnings. Bloom and Gunderson (1991), Abbott and Beach (1993), Coulson and DeVoretz (1993), Baker and Benjamin (1994), and Worswick (1996) all pointed out the lower wage rates of immigrants relative to natives, and falling entry earnings and rates of assimilation across successive cohorts. This literature suggests that the change in the primary source countries and favouring of refugee and family immigrant classes have resulted in an increase in immigrants with fewer skills or skills of lesser value, fewer professionals, and immigrants whose foreign education is not as highly valued or even recognized in North America. It was perhaps much easier to find work in the boom years of the Canadian economy in the early twentieth century, and in face of less strict labour force regulations, including those affecting the integration of professionals with foreign credentials. In this case, recent immigrants have a lower realized value of human capital relative to those already in the Canadian labour force, and investment per capita falls following the theoretical framework provided in the previous section.

Second, this result may be due to a shift towards a higher proportion of immigrants who do not enter the labour force upon arrival. Figure 2 shows that the age and gender distribution of immigrants has dramatically shifted from the beginning to the end of the twentieth century. Immigration at the beginning of the twentieth century was concentrated among working-age males with high labour-force participation rates, whereas today, immigra-

Figure 2: Average Immigration Rates by Age, Cohort and Gender, 1901–1911 and 1991–2001

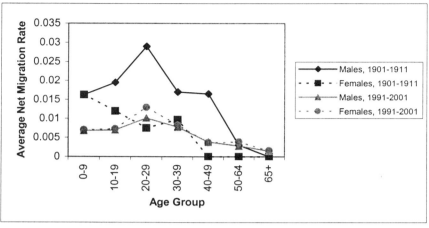

Source: 1901–1911 estimates are from Wilson (2003), 1991–2001 estimates are from CANSIM Table 051–0011 (immigration estimates) and Table 051–0001 (population estimates).

tion is more evenly balanced across age and gender groups. At the beginning of the twentieth century, immigrants between the ages of 15 and 25 entered the labour force, while today, these immigrants are more likely to go to school. Canada accepted a larger proportion of family class immigrants and refugees in the second half of the twentieth century, and some of these may not enter the Canadian workforce. When employment prospects fell dramatically in the 1930s, so too did immigration levels, unlike the Canadian experience after the 1970s. Gunderson (1998) stated that when the employment situation in Canada deteriorated in the 1980s and early 1990s, immigrants, the less-educated, and women who spoke neither English nor French were more severely affected. It was during this period, starting in the mid-1980s, that immigration policies began to focus more on long-term goals and immigration levels dramatically increased, especially during the recession of the early 1990s. If many immigrants come to Canada and either do not work, or face barriers to employment, investment per capita will fall with the inflow of non-working immigrants. This explanation is also consistent with the theoretical model presented in the previous section, where immigrants who do not work, or cannot find

Stuart J. Wilson

work appropriate to their skills in the Canadian labour market, cause the weighted average of human capital of the population to decline.

Third, as the Canadian economy industrialized and prepared for a massive inflow of immigrants to settle the west at the beginning of the twentieth century, investment requirements were massive as railways, towns and cities were built. Green and Urquhart (1976) stressed the significance of population-sensitive investment at the dawn of the twentieth century for immigrant-receiving New World nations. The opportunities that were present for population-sensitive investment in the beginning of the twentieth century were very different from those of today. It is possible that the relatively large positive coefficient on immigration in equation (17) for the 1897–1950 period is partially due to the effect of large population-sensitive investment in social infrastructure that disappeared with the end of western settlement.

In the beginning of the twentieth century during the immigration and investment boom, the balance of payments data indicate that migrants brought much wealth with them. Field (1914, p. 183) estimated that over 1902–1914, 891 thousand US emigrants brought $850 per person to Canada, 974 thousand British emigrants brought $150 per person to Canada, and 656 thousand emigrants from continental Europe brought $15 per person. After 1985, corresponding to the increased attention to economic migrants and increased immigration levels, the balance of payments data show that immigrant wealth again increased dramatically as a proportion of gross national product. Figure 3 shows the ratio of immigrant wealth (immigrant receipts in the balance-of-payments accounts) to gross national product over the twentieth century for Canada. As part of the business immigrant program, immigrants were being recruited as a means of increasing domestic investment, and in order to create jobs, and the average immigrant was much wealthier after 1985, as shown in Figure 4. Yet, the pattern of investment after 1985 does not mirror the pattern in the wealth of immigrants coming to Canada. It would appear that in the latter half of the twentieth century, immigrants have not transferred all foreign wealth to be used in Canada for investment in productive physical capital. The available balance of payments data do not distinguish between wealth brought into Canada for domestic use, or wealth left in foreign countries that "become" Canadian-owned foreign assets. This data series has yet to be fully explored, and this is left for future research.

What can policymakers do to address the issue of a coincident decline in relative immigrant earnings, and economic growth and investment? Canada does not have the same opportunities it had at the beginning of the

Figure 3: Rate of Immigration and Immigrant Wealth as a Proportion of GNP, Canada, 1897–2001

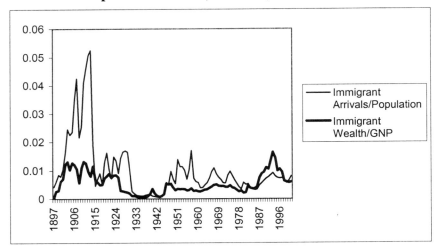

Source: See Appendix.

Figure 4: Real Wealth per Immigrant Arrival

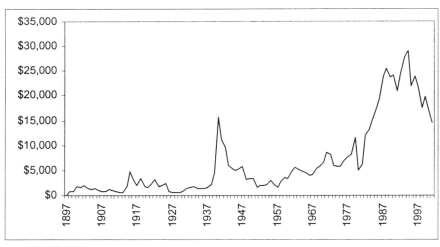

Source: See Appendix.

Stuart J. Wilson

twentieth century, when it could attract massive amounts of immigrants and capital during a time of tremendous settlement, and development. Nor does it seem possible today to attract the majority of migrants from the wealthy nations of northwestern Europe, the United States, and the United Kingdom, without reducing the level of immigration to almost nil. The findings presented in this article support the call for better education and training programs for recent immigrants. It may not be that recent immigrants possess poor human capital in general, but that they are less suited to the Canadian labour market or to the Canadian way of doing business, or that they face labour market rigidities with respect to foreign professional credentials. With more resources devoted to improving the skills of recent immigrants and improving their performance in the Canadian labour market, the incentives for investment will improve, as will the prospects for economic growth.

Conclusion

Immigration policy in Canada during the twentieth century has shifted from selective and discriminating policy, to accommodating and humanitarian policy. At the beginning of the twentieth century, Canada courted migrants from the United States and the United Kingdom, as well as hearty farmers. By the end of the twentieth century, Canada had eliminated discriminating between immigrants by country of origin, and admitted refugees and allowed more immigration for the purpose of family reunification. The majority of immigrants these days come from non-English-speaking countries.

There has been much research documenting the decline in the labour market success of recent immigrants. Recent immigrants to North America have lower wage rates than natives, and slower rates of assimilation than earlier immigrant cohorts. It appears that recent immigrants have human capital of lesser value in the Canadian labour market. This paper presents results obtained using a vector-autoregressive modelling framework with co-integrated processes, which supports this view. The rate of physical capital accumulation has declined in the latter half of the twentieth century, at the same time as the decline in the effectiveness of immigrant human capital in the domestic labour market. Even the recent focus on business immigration has not led to an increased rate of investment in per capita terms.

What are the policy options for the twenty-first century? It appears highly unlikely that Canada can repeat the immigration experience of the first half of the twentieth century. The opportunities for economic development then were certainly much different than those of today. Canada cannot expect to attract massive amounts of migrants from the United States, the United Kingdom, and northwestern Europe. Labour no longer flows from the Old World to the New World. Labour now flows from Latin America and the Caribbean, from Asia and Africa, and from the Third World to the industrialized nations. It appears that immigrants are poorly prepared for the Canadian labour market and business environment. Policy should focus on improving the prospects of immigrants through education and training, and help improve the assimilation of immigrants into Canadian society. By doing so, the incentives for investment will increase, and the goal of stronger economic growth will be achieved.

References

Abbott, M.G. and C.M. Beach (1993), "Immigrant Earnings Differentials and Birth-year Effects for Men in Canada: Postwar-1972", *Canadian Journal of Economics* 26, 505–524.

Baker, M. and D. Benjamin (1994), "The Performance of Immigrants in the Canadian Labor Market", *Journal of Labor Economics* 12, 369–405.

Barro, R. and X. Sala-i-Martin (1995), *Economic Growth* (New York: McGraw-Hill).

Bloom, D. and M. Gunderson (1991), "An Analysis of the Earnings of Canadian Immigrants", in J. Abowd and R. Freeman (eds.), *Immigration, Trade and the Labor Market* (Chicago: University of Chicago Press).

Borins, S. (1982), "Western Canadian Homesteading in Time and Space", *Canadian Journal of Economics* 15, 18–27.

Canada. Citizenship and Immigration Canada (CIC) (1998), *Facts and Figures 1997: Immigration Overview* (Ottawa: Citizenship and Immigration Canada).

Charemza, W.W. and D.F. Deadman (1992), *New Directions in Econometric Practice* (Vermont: Edward Elgar Publishing Limited).

Chiswick, B.R. and P.W. Miller (1992), "Language in the Labor Market: The Immigrant Experience in Canada and the US", in B. Chiswick (ed.), *Immigration, Language and Ethnicity: Canada and the United States* (Washington, DC: American Enterprise Institute).

_____ (1999), *Immigrant Services* (Ottawa: Citizenship and Immigration Canada).

_____ (2001), *Business Immigration Statistics 2000* (Ottawa: Citizenship and Immigration Canada).

Coulson, R.G. and D.J. DeVoretz (1993), "Human Capital Content of Canadian Immigrants: 1967–1987", *Canadian Public Policy/Analyse de Politiques* 19, 357–366.

Davidson, R. and J.G. MacKinnon (1993), *Estimation and Inference in Econometrics* (New York: Oxford University Press).

Engle, R.F. and C.W.J. Granger (1987), "Co-integration and Error-Correction: Representation, Estimation and Testing", *Econometrica* 55, 251–276.

Field, F.W. (1914), *Capital Investments in Canada*, 3d ed. (Toronto: The Monetary Times of Canada).

Fuller, W. (1976), *Introduction to Statistical Time Series* (New York: John Wiley).

Granger, C.W.J. (1981), "Some Properties of Time Series Data and their Use in Econometric Model Specification", *Journal of Econometrics* 16, 121–130.

Green, A.G. (2000), "Twentieth Century Canadian Economic History", in S. Engerman and R. Gallman (eds.), *Cambridge Economic History of the United States* (Cambridge: Cambridge University Press).

Green, A.G. and D.A. Green (1993), "Balanced Growth and the Geographic Distribution of European Immigrant Arrivals to Canada, 1900–1912", *Explorations in Economic History* 30, 31–59.

_____ (1995), "Canadian Immigration Policy: The Effectiveness of the Point System and Other Instruments", *Canadian Journal of Economics* 28, 1006–1041.

_____ (1999), "The Economic Goals of Canada's Immigration Policy: Past and Present", *Canadian Public Policy/Analyse de Politiques* 25, 425–451.

Green, A.G. and G.R. Sparks (1999), "Population Growth and the Dynamics of Canadian Development: A Multivariate Time Series Approach", *Explorations in Economic History* 36, 56–71.

Green, A.G. and M.C. Urquhart (1976), "Factor and Commodity Flows in the International Economy of 1870–1914: A Multi-Country View", *Journal of Economic History* 36, 217–252.

_____ (1994), "New Estimates of Output Growth in Canada: Measurement and Interpretation", in D. McCalla and M. Huberman (eds.), *Perspectives on Canadian Economic History* (Toronto: Copp Clark Longman Ltd.).

Gunderson, M. (1998), *Women and the Canadian Labour Market: Transitions Toward the Future*, Cat. No. 96–321–MPE No. 2 (Toronto and Ottawa: Statistics Canada and ITP Nelson).

Huggett, M. (1996), "Wealth Distribution in Life-Cycle Economies", *Journal of Monetary Economics* 38, 469–494.

Johansen, S. (1988), "Statistical Analysis of Cointegration Vectors", *Journal of Economic Dynamics and Control* 12, 231–254.

Johansen, S. and K. Juselius (1994), "Identification of the Long-Run and Short-Run Structure: An Application to the ISLM Model", *Journal of Econometrics* 63, 7–36.

Jones, C. (1995), "Time Series Tests of Endogenous Growth Models", *Quarterly Journal of Economics* 110, 495–525.

Juselius, K. (1991), *CATS in RATS: A Manual to Cointegration Analysis* (Copenhagen: Institute of Economics, University of Copenhagen).

Knowles, V. (2000), *Forging Our Legacy: Canadian Citizenship and Immigration, 1900–1977*, Public Works and Government Services Canada. Available at <http://www.cic.gc.ca/english/department/legacy>.

Lewis, F. (1981), "Farm Settlement on the Canadian Prairies, 1898 to 1911", *Journal of Economic History* 41(3), 517–535.

Ley, D. (2000), "Seeking *Homo Economicus*: The Strange Story of Canada's Business Immigration Program", RIIM Working Paper Series No. 00–02 (Vancouver: Vancouver Centre of Excellence).

Li, D. (2002), "Is the AK Model Still Alive?" *Canadian Journal of Economics* 35(1), 92–114.

Lucas, R. Jr. (1988), "On the Mechanics of Economic Development", *Journal of Monetary Economics* 22, 3–42.

Marr, W. and M. Percy (1978), "The Government and the Rate of Prairie Settlement", *Canadian Journal of Economics* 11, 757–767.

McLean, I. (1994), "Saving in Settler Economies: Australian and North American Comparisons", *Explorations in Economic History* 31, 432–452.

Norrie, K. (1975), "The Rate of Settlement of the Canadian Prairies, 1870–1911", *Journal of Economic History* 25, 410–427.

Norrie, K., D. Owram and J.C.H. Emery (2002), *A History of the Canadian Economy*, 3d ed. (Toronto: Nelson).

Rebelo, S. (1991), "Long-Run Policy Analysis and Long-Run Growth", *Journal of Political Economy* 99, 500–521.

Rios-Rull, J.V. (2001), "Population Changes and Capital Accumulation: The Aging of the Baby Boom", *The B.E. Journals in Macroeconomics*, Number 1, Article 7 (May).

Romer, D. (1996), *Advanced Macroeconomics* (New York: McGraw-Hill).

Romer, P. (1986), "Increasing Returns and Long-Run Growth", *Journal of Political Economy* 94, 1002–1037.

Skeldon, R., ed. (1994), *Reluctant Exiles: Migration from Hong Kong and the New Overseas Chinese* (Armond, NY: M.E. Sharpe).

Taylor, A.M. and J.G. Williamson (1994), "Capital Flows to the New World as an Intergenerational Transfer", *Journal of Political Economy* 102, 348–371.

Urquhart, M.C. (1988), "Canadian Economic Growth, 1870–1980", Discussion Paper No. 734 (Kingston: Institute for Economic Research, Queen's University).

_____ (1993), *Gross National Product, Canada 1870–1926: The Derivation of the Estimates* (Kingston: McGill-Queen's University Press).

Ward, T. (1994), "The Origins of the Canadian Wheat Boom, 1880–1910", *Canadian Journal of Economics* 27, 865–883.

Wilson, S.J. (2000), "The Savings Rate Debate: Does the Dependency Hypothesis Hold for Australia and Canada?" *Australian Economic History Review* 40(2), 199–218.

_____ (2001a), "Financial Intermediation, Capital Accumulation and Economic Growth: Evidence from Canada", Department of Economics Discussion Paper No. 87, University of Regina. Available at <http://www.econ.uregina.ca/papers>.

_____ (2001b), "The Decline in Savings: Should We Be Surprised?" Department of Economics Discussion Paper No. 100, University of Regina. Available at <http://www.econ.uregina.ca/papers>.

_____ (2003), "A Dynamic General Equilibrium Analysis of Migration and Capital Formation: The Case of Canada", *Review of Economic Dynamics* 6, 455–481.

Worswick, C. (1996), "Immigrant Families in the Canadian Labour Market", *Canadian Public Policy/Analyse de Politiques* 22(4), 378–396.

Appendix: Data Sources

The data was taken from Urquhart (1993), the electronic edition of Historical Statistics of Canada (http://www.statcan.ca/english/freepub/11-516-XIE/sectiona/toc.htm), and E-Stat/CANSIM II from Statistics Canada. The number of immigrant arrivals and the population figures are from Historical Statistics of Canada (HSC) from 1890 to 1976, and from CANSIM II series v391099 and v466668 from 1976 to 2001. The resulting series were spliced in 1976 by taking the average of the two component series in 1976. Investment figures are for gross domestic capital formation, taken from Urquhart (1993) from 1890 to 1926, and HSC from 1926 to 1976, and from CANSIM II series v646944 and v646946 (business and government capital investment) from 1976 to 2001. In 1926 and 1976, the resulting series was spliced by taking averages of the overlapping series. The GNP series was constructed using data from Urquhart (1993) for 1890 to 1926, HSC for 1926 to 1976, and from CANSIM II series v647785 for 1976 to 2001. Immigrant wealth was constructed using the immigrant receipts series, from Urquhart (1993) from 1890 to 1926 and CANSIM II series v113736 from 1926 to 2001. This series includes the total of cash and claims brought at the time of immigration, plus any amounts to be transferred later, including foreign securities or real estate. Relevant series were converted into real dollars by using the GNP deflator (1981=100) from Urquhart (1988) from 1890 to 1981, then using the GDP implicit chain price index, CANSIM II series v3860248 (1997=100, renormalized so that 1981=100) from 1981 to 2001.

Appendix Table A1: Estimation Results for the 1897–1950 Sample

Regressor \ Regressand Or Statistic \	Δi	Δim
Δi_{t-1}	0.353 (2.491)	0.937 (1.545)
Δi_{t-2}	0.026 (0.202)	0.487 (0.868)
Δim_{t-1}	0.012 (0.256)	−0.199 (−0.965)
Δim_{t-2}	0.062 (1.399)	−0.224 (−1.172)
Δy_t	1.382 (7.501)	1.702 (2.156)
Δy_{t-1}	0.196 (0.821)	0.347 (0.340)
Δy_{t-2}	−0.565 (−2.667)	−0.776 (−0.851)
$\hat{\beta} z_{t-3}$ (estimate for α)	−0.513 (−4.141)	−1.536 (−2.892)
Constant	−0.754 (−4.098)	−2.308 (−2.926)
R^2	0.732	0.297
Test for normality – χ^2 (2)	0.012	0.677
Test for ARCH – χ^2 (3)	2.227	0.487
	Joint Tests	*p-value*
Joint tests for autocorrelation		
L-B (26) – χ^2 (42)	43.808	0.39
LM(1) – χ^2 (4)	1.542	0.82
LM(4) – χ^2 (4)	0.090	1
Joint test for normality – χ^2 (4)	0.380	0.98

Note: *t*-values in parentheses. $\hat{\beta}^T z_{t-3} = i_{t-3} - 0.237 im_{t-3} - 1.104 y_{t-3}$.

Appendix Table A2: Estimation Results for the 1951–2001 Sample

Regressor \ Regressand Or Statistic \	Δi	Δim	Δy
Δi_{t-1}	0.122 (0.632)	1.519 (1.907)	−0.106 (−1.305)
Δi_{t-2}	0.210 (1.093)	1.441 (1.821)	0.176 (2.182)
Δim_{t-1}	0.037 (1.205)	0.082 (0.648)	0.003 (0.245)
Δim_{t-2}	0.024 (0.850)	−0.075 (−0.632)	0.003 (0.258)
Δy_{t-1}	0.583 (1.211)	2.344 (1.178)	0.399 (1.965)
Δy_{t-2}	−0.045 (−0.099)	−4.459 (−2.353)	−0.263 (−1.358)
$\hat{\beta}z_{t-3}$ (estimate for α)	−0.355 (−3.890)	−1.117 (−2.967)	−0.108 (−2.823)
Constant	−0.393 (−3.876)	−1.262 (−3.011)	−0.103 (−2.413)
R^2	0.355	0.421	0.250
Test for normality − χ^2 (2)	2.048	0.976	1.355
Test for ARCH − χ^2 (3)	3.801	3.200	1.677

	Joint Tests	p-value
Joint tests for autocorrelation		
L-B (12) − χ^2 (87)	82.377	0.62
LM(1) − χ^2 (9)	11.750	0.23
LM(4) − χ^2 (9)	13.777	0.13
Joint test for normality − χ^2 (6)	4.711	0.58

Note: t-values in parentheses. $\hat{\beta}^T z_{t-3} = i_{t-3} + 0.203 im_{t-3} - 0.847 y_{t-3}$.

Summary of Discussion

Jeffrey Reitz notes that in the conventional economics literature the term "quality of immigrants" is used as a short-hand to refer to relative earnings of immigrants. But this is a very unhelpful and inappropriate term to use because others in the media or elsewhere may interpret declining quality of immigrants to mean declining quality of immigrants themselves as individuals, and emphasis on quantity leads to policy efforts to improve immigrant quality by selecting immigrants more carefully to ensure they have more human capital skills. This terminology reflects a theoretical perspective that is rather limited because the performance of immigrants in the labour market is determined by several sets of circumstances. One is the characteristics of immigrants themselves, a second set is the way in which they relate within the economic institutions of society, and the third is the characteristics of the institutions themselves. By focusing only on the first of these, we limit the range of policy options that can be considered. This is especially dramatic if one looks at this in a comparative context relative to the United States and Australia where, although the relative earnings of immigrants are also declining, they are declining less rapidly than in Canada. So from this point of view, you might say that the quality of immigrants is declining less rapidly in the United States and Australia, but in fact the educational level of immigrants has been rising in Canada and falling in the United States. The educational level of immigrants has been rising in Australia, but not as rapidly as in Canada. This suggests not focusing attention entirely on the characteristics of immigrants themselves. Indeed, from the point of view of immigrants looking at alternative destinations, they might just as easily say that Canada is a declining quality destination because their earnings experience in Canada is relatively more negative than in the United States or Australia. Citizenship and Immigration Canada has improved the selection process of immigrants, yet we know that the relative earnings of immigrants continue to decline. So Reitz believes that we have to address the issue of the economic performance of immigrants in a more complete fashion than simply referring to it as declining quality of immigrants.

Barry Chiswick makes the point that immigrant relative earnings at various points in time in the destination country are a function of the transferability of skills. If your immigrant pool is largely from Britain and the United States, the arrivals are going to have highly transferable skills. But if they are from various other parts of the world, their skills are likely to be much less transferable. This has an important impact on the time path of immigrant earnings. What he found in the United States, given the change in the transferability of skills with the change in source countries, is that immigrant earnings upon arrival relative to natives have declined, other things being the same. But if you evaluate immigrant earnings 15 years after arrival, you find that their earnings ratio relative to native earnings has not changed over time. So in terms of discussing declining immigrant relative earnings, it is very important to consider the point in time after arrival at which you evaluate it.

A second point made by Barry Chiswick is that one needs to be clear in how wealth is defined in comparative wealth-holding studies. Does the definition of wealth include pension wealth (which native workers may have a longer working career in Canada in which to accumulate it) or assets held abroad (of which immigrants may have more)?

A third speaker noted that, when comparing immigration before and after some date such as 1950, it is important to consider how Canada's own labour market and its professions started to introduce requirements that removed the ability of many immigrants to fully participate in the labour market. For example, a medical doctor immigrating prior to 1950 simply registered with the local medical association and was given a licence to practise, and this applied to most professions. Now we live in a society where credential-based requirements define employment admission into professions. This may now be hurting us as a society. The quality of the immigrants may be higher because we are selecting them that way. Unfortunately, when they get here, we now say to them that their capacity to contribute to the economy is significantly less because of the road-blocks to foreign credential recognition.

Section III

Decentralization of Immigration Policy in Canada

Location Choice of New Immigrants to Canada: The Role of Ethnic Networks

James Ted McDonald

Introduction

As the Canadian government's large-scale immigration program continues apace (over 229,000 immigrants entered Canada in 2000), expanding our understanding of the social and economic experiences of immigrants, as well as the social and economic effects of immigration on the native-born population, becomes vitally important for the evaluation and formation of government policy. Although an extensive literature has developed on many dimensions of immigrants and immigration, one area that remains relatively underdeveloped is also one of far-reaching importance: Where in Canada do new immigrants choose to settle? Immigrants' location decisions directly affect their subsequent social and economic assimilation because of local employment opportunities, access to settlement and language programs, support from the local ethnic community, and so on. Immigrants' location decisions also directly affect the welfare of the domestic

I would like to thank Jeff Borland, Chris Worswick, and seminar participants at the University of Tasmania and Australian Bureau of Statistics for helpful comments and discussions, and Susan Munn for excellent research assistance.

population, both positively through stimuli to the local economy provided by new immigration (particularly if immigrants have investment capital or skills in short supply) and negatively through increased strain on urban infrastructure, and increased use of health services and social/income support programs.

The negative effects of immigration have gained greater media attention because of the distinct settlement patterns of recent immigrants, and the popular perception that immigrants to Canada live primarily in Canada's largest cities is confirmed by Canadian census data. In 1996, over 60% of overseas-born people were located in Toronto, Montreal, and Vancouver, compared with approximately 27% of the native-born Canadian population. Although in 1996 only 17.2% of the Canadian population was born outside Canada, 41.6% of people living in the Toronto census metropolitan area (CMA) and 35% of people living in the Vancouver CMA were born outside Canada. Further, the continued growth in population of Canada's major cities is being driven primarily by new immigration. Over the period 1996–2001, Toronto CMA gained 445,000 new immigrants (or 19 per 1,000 of population) and this added 2% per year to Toronto's population. Over the same period, 180,000 new immigrants settled in Vancouver and 126,000 new immigrants settled in Montreal (CIC, 2000). One question that arises is whether increasing concentrations of immigrants in particular areas become a magnet for further immigration to those areas, thereby increasing the rate of population growth in areas already experiencing significant population increases.

The focus of this paper is on the determinants of the initial location decision of recent immigrants to Canada. Particular attention is given to the role of "ethnic networks" in this location decision. The ethnic network — the concentration of people in the same geographic area who are of similar ethnic background, culture, and language — can be an important source of financial or personal support, information and guidance, and social mores. I restrict attention to new immigrants since, as Borjas (1999) suggests, the fixed costs of moving normally associated with geographic mobility are less of a factor for new immigrants since they are a self-selected sample of people who have already chosen to bear the fixed costs of moving to Canada.[1] Further, the decision about where to locate in Canada is almost entirely at the discretion of the individual migrant since there are few

---

[1]Day and Winer (2001) find moving costs to be one of the most important determinants of interprovincial mobility flows.

legislative restrictions on this decision. The recognition that immigration can spur economic growth and meet skill shortages is one reason why policies have been developed to encourage immigration into particular areas, for example, through immigrant investor programs (Green and Green, 1995, p. 443) and through provincial nominees agreements between the federal government and some Canadian provinces.[2] However, the proportion of the total immigrant intake falling under these categories is very small. In a similar vein, sponsors of immigrants migrating to Canada under the "family" category must guarantee to provide financial support to the new migrant (if needed) for up to ten years after migration. This increases the likelihood that new immigrants will choose to locate in relatively close geographic proximity to their sponsors, but there is no requirement to do so. Sponsors must sign an "undertaking" with the Government of Canada, but sponsored immigrants are not excluded from accessing government assistance nor are there any institutional restrictions on their geographic mobility.[3]

The plan of the paper is as follows. After a review of previous work and a discussion of econometric methodology, I outline the data sources, sample selection, and creation of the measures of ethnic networks. I then present results from the estimation of a model of location choice and the predicted geographic distribution of recent immigrants under a range of alternative hypothetical assumptions about the geographic distribution of immigrants already in Canada. I conclude with implications for economic policy and directions for further research.

---

[2]In fact, the immigrant investor program does not require that the investor physically settle in a particular province, only that his or her investment capital is invested in the province.

[3]According to CIC (1997), sponsors who fail to support those accepted into Canada as sponsored immigrants may lose their right to sponsor additional immigrants, and may be expected to pay back any financial assistance collected by the sponsored relative. Limitations on sponsored immigrants are limited to the possibility that sponsors' income may be considered in assessing an immigrant's eligibility for government financial assistance.

Literature and Methodology

Geographic Mobility and Ethnic Networks

There is an extensive empirical literature in Canada on the determinants of geographic mobility, including recent work by Osberg, Gordon and Lin (1994), Finnie (2000) and Day and Winer (2001). (See Day and Winer, 1994, for a review of earlier work.) In general, studies of geographic mobility (typically interprovincial mobility) find that the major determinants of mobility are differences in labour market characteristics across regions, for example, differences in earnings and employment prospects, and moving costs. Differences in the public policy environment across provinces, reflected in parameters of Employment Insurance (EI) and social assistance schemes, direct and indirect tax rates, and direct spending by governments on health and education, are typically found to have only small effects on interprovincial mobility.[4]

Econometric literature specifically on the geographic mobility of immigrants in Canada is more limited. Lin (1998) uses the Labour Market Activity Survey of Statistics Canada to compare the interprovincial mobility of foreign-born and native-born Canadians. He finds that while immigrants are relatively less likely to move provinces, this difference is due to distributional and compositional differences between immigrants and native-born Canadians rather than structural differences in the determinants of mobility. Newbold (1996) uses the 1986 Canadian census to examine interprovincial migration of immigrants to Canada, and finds that after controlling for personal and ecological effects, country-of-birth explains relatively little of the observed differences in mobility between immigrants and the native-born. However, Newbold's study is noteworthy because he includes a variable for what he terms cultural similarity — the proportional share of the 1981 provincial population that belongs to an immigrant's ethnic group — and finds it is positively correlated with interprovincial migration.

The principal focus of the current study is on the role that local ethnic networks may have in influencing the initial location decision of new

---

[4]An exception is Finnie (2000) who finds that receipt of employment insurance and social assistance significantly increases the probability that an individual changes provinces.

immigrants. Ethnic networks refer to the externalities, both positive and negative, that arise from living in proximity to people of similar culture, ethnicity or language.[5] Intuition suggests that for immigrants considering where to live in Canada, the fact that certain areas already have relatively high concentrations of immigrants from the same country of origin may make those areas more attractive destinations. Local ethnic communities can provide an important support system for new immigrants through, for example, the provision of information about social-assistance programs and employment opportunities, or through the provision of direct financial assistance and support. More generally, the ethnic network can provide a sense of community and security to immigrants moving to a new and unfamiliar country. In addition, large communities of immigrants may imply greater availability of services directly tailored to new immigrants, for example, English-language courses and immigrant adjustment programs offered by federal, provincial, and local governments.[6] The role of ethnic networks in immigrant location decisions has been a feature of some US research, for example, Bartel (1989), Dunlevy (1991), Zavodny (1999) and Funkhouser (2000). A common result of these papers is that the presence of other foreign-born people is an important determinant of the location decision of immigrants. Zavodny, for example, finds that the fraction of a state's population that is foreign-born is the primary determinant of location choice of new immigrants, and this is true for immigrant groups disaggregated by both country of origin and admission category.

One question that follows directly from this idea is whether ethnic networks assist or inhibit social and economic assimilation of recent immigrants. Though not analyzed in this paper, the links between ethnic networks and other dimensions of economic behaviour of immigrants have

---

[5]The concept of network effects is much broader than the specific role of local ethnic network effects considered in this paper. See, for example, Montgomery (1991) and Benabou (1996). Borjas (1992, 1995) develops the idea of ethnic capital in which higher ethnic group average earnings and stronger networks based on ethnicity will drive differences in educational attainment, earnings, and intergenerational mobility.

[6]This discussion suggests some testable hypotheses that will be explored later in the paper. For example, it seems reasonable to expect that ethnic networks will be most important for those recent immigrants most likely to rely on them — for example, immigrants without English- or French-language skills, or immigrants with low levels of human capital.

been the subject of a growing body of research. This includes links between ethnic networks and educational attainment (Borjas, 1995; Cardak and McDonald, 2001), and between ethnic networks and welfare participation (Borjas, 1999; Bertrand, Luttmer and Mullainathan, 2000; Dodson, 2001). There is also an important literature that has focused on the effects of immigrant location choices on the mobility patterns of the native-born population or immigrants already resident in the United States. See, for example, Frey (1996), Borjas (1998), and Funkhouser (2000).

Empirical Framework

The theoretical starting point for most analyses of geographic mobility is the notion that individuals compare the (expected) utility that they would receive across all of the regions to which they potentially could settle. For individuals already resident in Canada, this choice set would also include the option to stay where they are, that is, not move regions. Utility is typically specified to be a function of a variety of factors that differ across regions and may be individual-specific, including earnings and employment opportunities, generosity of welfare and other social assistance, cost of living, level of amenities, climate, financial and psychic moving costs, and so on. The impact of many of these attributes on the mobility decision will be strongly correlated with personal characteristics of the potential mover, for example, moving costs will be higher for married couples and families with children. To control for these factors, I include a set of individual-specific demographic characteristics typically found to be significant determinants of interprovincial mobility in the literature: age (which enters as a quadratic), education level, marital status, and presence of children in the household.

Language fluency is likely to be a crucial determinant of location choice, and while language fluency at time of migration would be the ideal measure to use, this information is unavailable. Three alternative measures of language fluency are available in the census files: fluency in one or both of Canada's official languages as of the census date, the language normally spoken at home, and the respondent's self-identified "mother tongue". It is likely that language fluency at census date is endogenous to the mobility decision, for example, if an immigrant moves to a particular area that has easy access to English-language programs. As well, language skills at the census date will reflect up to four years already spent in Canada. The second option, mother tongue, will be highly correlated with controls for country of origin and may have little to do with language fluency. For this reason, I control for language fluency using dummy variables reflecting whether the language normally spoken at home is French or English. Although these controls might also suffer from endogeneity bias, the fact that the census question relates to the language *normally* used implies a closer relationship to pre-immigration language use, particularly since the focus of the paper is on recent immigrants.[7]

The key question of interest in this paper is the importance of ethnic network effects on location choice of immigrants, and in the next section I detail the construction of alternative measures of ethnic network concentration to gauge these effects. However, while the focus of this paper is on ethnic network effects rather than the determinants of mobility per se, it is still necessary to control for all potentially important (and possibly unobserved) determinants of utility that may affect location choice. Failing to control for unobserved effects may give rise to a finding of significant ethnic network effects when none in fact exist.[8] For this reason, I adopt the approach of assuming time-invariant region-specific characteristics (such as urban infrastructure and climate) are reflected in a set of region dummy variables, and that time-varying region-specific characteristics (such as economic conditions, changes in cost of living or changes in the availability of government settlement programs) are captured by a time dummy variable interacted with each of the regions.[9] Similarly, it is also important to be able to distinguish local ethnic network effects from ethnic group unobserved heterogeneity that affects location choice. To control for unobserved time-invariant characteristics important to location choice and

---

[7]When "mother tongue" is used instead of language spoken at home, the results are broadly similar to those reported later in the paper, although coefficient estimates are in magnitude and have lower t-statistics.

[8]See also the discussion of the "reflection problem" in identifying endogenous social effects in Manski (1993).

[9]In the empirical analysis I experiment with additional interaction terms to allow for changes over time in a region's characteristics to have differential effects on different groups of people in the sample. For example, including a time dummy variable interacted with region dummy variables and education levels allows for changed economic conditions across regions over time to affect people with a university degree differently from people with less than high school education. None of these interactions affected the main results.

specific to country of origin, I include a full set of dummy variables for region of origin interacted with dummy variables for the Canadian regions. (The identification of network effects when both ethnic group and region dummy variables are included is also discussed in the next section.)

I estimate the model using a Conditional Logit specification (McFadden, 1973) given by:

$$(1) \quad \Pr(y_{ij} = 1 / z_{ij}) = F(\alpha_i + z_{ij}\beta)$$

where $F(.)$ is the Logistic distribution. The dependent variable y_{ij} is a binary indicator variable that takes the value 1 if person i chooses to reside in region j and zero otherwise. The vector $z_{ij} = [x_{ij} \ w_i]$ is a set of explanatory variables that includes attributes of the choice x_{ij} (ethnic concentration measures in the current context), and attributes of the individual w_i (demographic and other controls). Each variable in w_i is interacted with a set of Canadian region dummy variables in the estimating equation.[10]

Data Sources and Specification of Network Effects

The data are drawn from the public use files of the Statistics Canada census files for 1991 and 1996. In order to focus on the initial location decisions of new immigrants, I focus on two groups of immigrants. The first group consists of those people in the 1991 census born outside Canada who arrived in Canada within the five-year period 1986–91. The second group consists of those people in the 1996 census born outside Canada who arrived in Canada within the five-year period 1991–96. The census files report year of landed residency rather than year of arrival in Canada, so I define recent arrivals to be those individuals who were granted residency status in Canada in the five years preceding the census and who reported

---

[10]Omitting the attribute of the choice x_{ij} means (1) is equivalent to a multinomial Logit model.

James Ted McDonald

living outside Canada five years before the census date.[11] In order to exclude those people whose initial location decision reflected choice of educational facility, I restrict the sample to include only adults aged between 25 and 64. For this paper, I also restrict the sample to men.

A number of metropolitan areas are identified in the public use census files. However, given the trade-off between the level of disaggregation and intraregional sample size as well as anecdotal evidence that immigrants tend to concentrate in Canada's three largest cities — Toronto, Vancouver, and Montreal — I define the following distinct regions in the analysis: Montreal, rest of Quebec, Toronto, rest of Ontario, Prairies (Manitoba and Saskatchewan), Alberta, Vancouver, rest of British Columbia. Region-of-birth categories for immigrants living in the Atlantic provinces and Canadian territories are too broadly defined to be useful, so I omit from the sample individuals living in these areas of Canada.[12]

Measures of ethnic networks are computed using characteristics of the Canadian population inferred from the most recent Canadian census prior to the five-year migration window of each arrival group. Thus, for the recent arrivals in the 1991 census, I compute network concentration statistics from the 1986 census. For the recent arrivals in the 1996 census, I use the 1991 census. In defining distinct regions of origin outside Canada, consistency is required across all three census files. Given this limitation, it is possible to define 16 distinct regions of birth outside Canada that are consistent across the three census surveys. These regions include seven for Europe: UK and Ireland, French-speaking parts of Europe, other western European countries, Mediterranean countries, Poland, Slavic countries, and other European countries (a heterogeneous mix of Scandinavian countries, Turkey, and the former Czechoslovakia); four for Asia: Middle Eastern and western Asian countries, South Asian countries, China and Hong Kong, and South East Asian countries; and five for the rest of the world: African

---

[11]One weakness of this approach is that since some of the recent immigrants may have already been in Canada for up to four years prior to the census date, current region of residence may reflect internal mobility after moving to Canada. I experiment with more restricted definitions of recent immigrants in the empirical analysis.

[12]Even if disaggregated data on country of origin were available, small sample sizes for many cells would make estimation difficult. Only 1.4% of the sample of recent immigrants in each census year reside in Atlantic Canada and the Canadian territories.

countries, the Caribbean, South and Central America, the United States and other regions.[13]

It is possible to proxy for network effects in a variety of ways and I will focus on three similar methods that have been used in the literature. The first involves computing the share of a particular ethnic group that lives in each region of Canada (see Bartel, 1989; and Borjas, 1999). This measures how dispersed a particular ethnic group is across Canada and is computed as:

$$(2) \quad A_{ij} = P_{ij} / \sum_{j} P_{ij}$$

where i indexes the country/area of origin, and j indexes the Canadian region of residence. P_{ij} is the number of adults from country/area i living in region of Canada j. A second method involves computing, for each country/area of birth and for each of the eight defined regions of residence in Canada, the proportion of the total adult population residing in that Canadian region that was born in the particular country/area (see Borjas, 1999; and Bertrand, Luttmer and Mullainathan, 2000). This measure is computed as:

$$(3) \quad B_{ij} = P_{ij} / \sum_{j} P_{ij}$$

Note that the index i includes the subgroup of the total population that was born in Canada. Bertrand, Luttmer and Mullainathan (2000) also compute a variation of this measure in which the proportion of a region's population that is from a particular country/area of origin is scaled by dividing by that ethnic group's share of the total Canadian population. That is, they compute a relative concentration measure given by:

$$(4) \quad R_{ij} = B_{ij} / \left[\sum_{j} P_{ij} / \sum_{i} \sum_{j} P_{ij} \right]$$

---

[13]The reported categories for region of birth are markedly different in the 1981 census compared to later census years, and this precludes inclusion of recent immigrants in the 1986 census in the current analysis.

James Ted McDonald

or

$$(5) \quad R_{ij} = \left[P_{ij} \Big/ \sum_i P_{ij} \right] \Big/ \left[\sum_j P_{ij} \Big/ \sum_i \sum_j P_{ij} \right].$$

The expression for R_{ij} is closely related to the expression for A_{ij} in equation (1). In fact, multiplying R_{ij} by the proportion of the total Canadian population resident in Canadian region j yields the expression for A_{ij}:

$$(6) \quad \begin{aligned} R_{ij} & \bullet \left[\sum_i P_{ij} \Big/ \sum_i \sum_j P_{ij} \right] \\ & = \left[P_{ij} \Big/ \sum_i P_{ij} \right] \Big/ \left[\sum_j P_{ij} \Big/ \sum_i \sum_j P_{ij} \right] \bullet \left[\sum_i P_{ij} \Big/ \sum_i \sum_j P_{ij} \right] \\ & = P_{ij} \Big/ \sum_j P_{ij} = A_{ij}. \end{aligned}$$

R_{ij} has the convenient property that if immigrants from a particular country/area are equally distributed across the Canadian regions, each of the R_{ij} values for group i is equal to 1. I focus on this measure as the main proxy for network effects, although I investigate the sensitivity of the results to the alternative measures A_{ij} and B_{ij}. All of the network measures are computed using the full adult sample from the most recent census file prior to the arrival of the immigrant group in Canada.

The network effects are identified in the presence of the ethnic group fixed effects and region-time interactions through changes between the census years in the intraregional ethnic group specific concentration measure. Thus, if the distribution of immigrants across Canadian regions did not change between the two census years, it would not be possible to disentangle network effects from the unobserved fixed effects.[14] In addition, allowing for a single magnitude of effect of ethnic networks for all immigrants irrespective of demographic characteristics may be overly

---

[14]Differences between 1986 and 1991 will arise for two reasons: the location decisions of the immigrants arriving between 1986 and 1991, and the interregional movements of both immigrants and native-born Canadians during the period.

restrictive. To this end, I allow for more flexible specifications in which interactions of the network variable with education level, language fluency, and broad region of origin also enter as regressors. *A priori*, if immigrants are choosing where to live, at least in part because of potential support from Canadian residents of similar background, culture, and language, the effects should be weaker for immigrants who can assimilate more easily, for example, individuals from English-speaking backgrounds or individuals with tertiary educational qualifications. I test these conjectures in the next section.

Econometric Results

To provide some context for the econometric analysis, I first present some descriptive statistics on the characteristics of recent immigrants and their geographic distribution in Canada. Table 1 reports the distribution of immigrant men by region of origin for three groups: recent immigrants in the 1991 census, recent immigrants in the 1996 census (these two groups compose the estimating sample), and all other immigrants in the pooled census files. Sample means of the regional distribution and demographic controls for the same three groups are reported in Table 2. For illustration, I also include sample means for native-born men aged 25–64. All means are weighted to reflect the population.

It is clear from Table 1 that there have been pronounced shifts over time in the composition of immigrant inflows by region of origin, mainly from European immigrants to immigrants from Asia. For example, the proportion of recent immigrants from Asia is over 50% in the 1991 census and over 60% in the 1996 census, compared to around 25% for other immigrants. There is also some volatility in the regional composition of recent immigrants across the two census years, reflecting events such as the war in the former Yugoslavia in the early 1990s.

Table 2 illustrates substantial differences in the choice of region of residence between recent immigrants and native-born men, with over 70% of recent immigrants residing in Canada's three largest cities (over 40% in Toronto alone) compared to 29% of native-born men. Recent immigrants are also more likely than other immigrants to be residents of Toronto and

Table 1: Region of Origin of Recent Immigrant Men

Variable	Arrived 1986–91 (1991 Census)	Arrived 1991–96 (1996 Census)	All Other Immigrants
UK and Ireland	0.038	0.031	0.151
French-speaking	0.009	0.017	0.014
Mediterranean	0.036	0.009	0.172
Eastern European/Slavic	0.027	0.088	0.037
Poland	0.085	0.025	0.029
Western Europe	0.018	0.014	0.106
Other Europe	0.031	0.028	0.044
Middle East and Western Asia	0.104	0.065	0.035
Southern Asia	0.111	0.157	0.066
South-East Asia	0.146	0.169	0.082
China and Hong Kong	0.172	0.232	0.065
Caribbean	0.029	0.028	0.040
South/Central America	0.089	0.051	0.065
Africa	0.085	0.068	0.046
United States	0.017	0.014	0.042
Other regions	0.002	0.003	0.003
Sample Size	5,205	5,140	77,238

Table 2: Sample Means of Immigrant and Native-Born Men Aged 25–64 Years

Variable	Arrived 1986–91 (1991 Census)	Arrived 1991–96 (1996 Census)	All Other Immigrants	All Native-Born Men
Age	37.3	39.1	45.0	41.2
Married	0.745	0.760	0.755	0.611
At least one child at home	0.309	0.327	0.297	0.304
University degree	0.392	0.446	0.319	0.247
Other postsecondary	0.257	0.217	0.313	0.322
High school only	0.135	0.131	0.099	0.139
Some secondary school	0.122	0.125	0.143	0.201
Primary school only	0.094	0.081	0.126	0.090
Language spoken at home				
English	0.240	0.184	0.588	0.685
French	0.039	0.039	0.047	0.306
Other	0.724	0.778	0.368	0.013
Mother tongue				
English	0.154	0.118	0.316	0.627
French	0.025	0.029	0.032	0.327
Other	0.822	0.854	0.653	0.050
Region of residence				
Toronto	0.429	0.404	0.355	0.104
Montreal	0.149	0.123	0.123	0.130
Vancouver	0.138	0.223	0.112	0.054
Rest of Quebec	0.013	0.016	0.017	0.188
Rest of Ontario	0.138	0.109	0.208	0.257
Prairies	0.035	0.029	0.038	0.086
Alberta	0.080	0.072	0.089	0.108
Rest of BC	0.019	0.025	0.057	0.073
Percent of pooled census file dataset	1.3	1.3	19.8	77.6
Sample size	5,205	5,140	77,238	60,390

Vancouver. In terms of demographic characteristics, recent immigrants are more likely to be younger and have a university degree compared with other immigrants and native-born men. They are also substantially more likely to speak a language other than French or English at home, and to identify their mother tongue as a language other than French or English.

Since the magnitude of the coefficients obtained from estimation of the conditional Logit do not have a simple interpretation, I present estimation results in two parts. First, I report the levels of significance of the network effects and their directions of effect, and I examine the sensitivity of the results to alternative specifications and parameterizations of the network variables. Second, I examine the magnitudes of the network effects for various groups of recent immigrants, and conduct some simulations of location choice under a variety of alternative (hypothetical) population structures.

For brevity, Table 3a contains coefficient estimates of the network effects only, for three alternative specifications. In the first column, relative concentration (RC) is included on its own as the control for ethnic networks. This assumes that ethnic networks affect the location decisions of immigrants from all regions of the world similarly, regardless of language or education. The coefficient has a positive sign but is not significant at conventional levels. In the second column, RC is interacted with indicator variables for whether the person has a university degree, and if the person's language normally used at home is neither French nor English. Both interactions are highly significant. If the person's language spoken at home is not French or English, that person is significantly more likely to settle in a region of Canada with a relatively higher concentration of people from that person's country or region of origin. That is, after controlling for demographic characteristics (including language), ethnic group fixed effects, region fixed effects and macroeconomic conditions, there is evidence that the location decisions of earlier immigrants exert a significant influence on the location decisions of the immigrants who follow. However, this is only true for recent immigrants who speak neither English nor French.

In contrast, the coefficient on the interaction of RC and a dummy variable for university degree is negative and highly significant. This implies that highly educated new immigrants are more likely to settle in a region with a relatively lower concentration of people from their country or region of origin, *ceteris paribus*. Further, this result is not simply reflecting improved economic opportunities for university graduates in areas with low immigrant concentrations. Including a set of year-region

Table 3a: Selected Econometric Results: Networks Effects [a,b]

Variable	(1)	(2)	(3)	(4)
Relative concentration (RC)	0.162 (0.137)	0.072 (0.148)		
RC*(other home language)[c]		0.229*** (0.061)		
RC*(university degree)		−0.183*** (0.035)	−0.174*** (0.035)	−0.153*** (0.035)
RC*(European born)			−0.725** (0.314)	
RC*(UK or US born)			−0.102 (1.217)	
RC*(Asia or Africa born)			0.075 (0.165)	
RC*(other home language) *(European born)			0.582*** (0.122)	0.590*** (0.123)
RC*(other home language) *(Asia or Africa born)			0.352*** (0.064)	0.391*** (0.0062)
Log likelihood	−14022.7	−14000	−13985	−13505[d]
Pseudo R2	0.296	0.297	0.298	0.300

Notes: [a] White's heteroskedastic-consistent standard errors in parentheses.
[b] * denotes significance at the 10% level, ** at the 5% level, *** at the 1% level.
[c] language normally spoken at home is neither French nor English.
[d] Log-likelihood values are not directly comparable since the underlying sample size for the specification estimated in column (4) is smaller due to the exclusion of immigrants from "other Europe".

James Ted McDonald

dummy variables interacted with a dummy variable for university degree leaves these network effects almost unchanged.[15]

In column 3, I allow for network effects by language also to differ by broad area of origin: (i) Asia and Africa, (ii) continental Europe, and (iii) English-speaking regions.[16] Consider first immigrants without a university degree. The location decisions of immigrants from English-speaking regions are not affected by network concentrations, as expected. Immigrants from Asia or Africa who speak a language other than English or French at home are more likely to reside in a location if the concentration of people from the same country or region is larger, but this is not the case for immigrants who speak English or French at home. For immigrants from continental Europe, the pattern is more complex. While the coefficient on relative concentration for immigrants who do not speak English or French at home is positive and significant, the coefficient on the network effect for all European-born immigrants is negative and significant. However, this latter result appears to be driven by the inclusion of the aggregate "other Europe" as a homogeneous ethnic group. Omitting people from "other Europe" from the sample leaves the coefficient on relative concentration for other-language immigrants from Europe almost unchanged (0.615 with a standard error of 0.127), while the coefficient on relative concentration for all European immigrants is reduced to insignificance (−0.480 with a standard error of 0.482).[17] Column 4 summarizes this by omitting "other Europe" from the sample as well as dropping other insignificant terms. As can be seen, the main results are qualitatively the same as in column 3. Finally, the coefficient on relative concentration interacted with university degree continues to be negative and significant, indicating that the

---

[15]When more flexible specifications are estimated, significant university effects are also found separately for immigrants from both English-speaking and non-English-speaking backgrounds. However, the effect appears to be limited to university education. An interaction of the network variable with a dummy variable for other postsecondary education was not significant.

[16]Identification of network effects is driven by variations in relative concentration of immigrants across immigrant groups within each broad area.

[17]To check whether other results are being driven by other particular groups of immigrants, I re-estimated the models after sequentially dropping immigrants from each of the countries/areas of origin available in the data. The results are not sensitive to the exclusion of any particular group of immigrants.

magnitude of the positive network effect is significantly less for other-language immigrants with degrees, and negative for English- or French-language immigrants with degrees. Allowing additional interactions of this term with broad area of origin yields no new insights. As before, the university effect appears to be present for immigrants from each broad area of origin, including immigrants from predominantly English-speaking countries.[18]

Results for the other potential determinants of location mobility from the preferred specification (reported in the last column of Table 3a) are contained in Appendix Table A1. Due to the large number of coefficient estimates obtained from the conditional Logit, I report instead p-values from a series of Wald tests on groups of estimated coefficients. (Recall that choice-invariant regressors are interacted with a set of N-1 region dummy variables. A joint test of these terms is a test of whether the individual attribute has any significant effect on the location choice of the individual.) Results of these tests indicate that age, university education, presence of children, and language spoken at home are all significant determinants of immigrants' location choice. In addition, region fixed effects are highly significant, as are the interactions of region fixed effects with a year dummy variable for 1996. Finally, the country/region of origin fixed effects are also highly significant determinants of location choice, both in total and for each country/region of origin.

Table 3b presents results from sensitivity checks based on the two alternative specifications of the network effects discussed in the previous section. While the magnitudes of the coefficient estimates differ because of differences in the mean value of the particular measure of network effects used, in both cases the sets of results are qualitatively very similar to those reported in Table 3a. The only difference is that in specifications (1) and (5) with the single network variable, this term is now significant and positively signed.

In the first part of the econometric results, evidence was found that ethnic networks exert a statistically significant influence on recent immigrants' location decisions. However, as the results do not have a

---

[18]Since recent immigrants may have been in Canada up to five years prior to the survey, location choice as of the survey date may reflect internal migration. To control for this possibility, I restricted the sample to immigrants gaining residency within two years of the census date. Results based on this subsample are qualitatively the same as those reported in the text.

Table 3b: Alternative Measures of Networks Effects [a,b]

Variable	% of Population[d]				% of Ethnic Group[e]			
	(1)	(2)	(3)	(4)	(5)	(6)	(7)	(8)
Concentration (C)	0.137** (0.060)	0.039 (0.069)			0.024** (0.010)	0.023** (0.011)		
C*(university degree)		−0.110*** (0.025)	−0.107*** (0.025)	−0.096*** (0.025)		−0.019*** (0.003)	−0.018*** (0.003)	−0.015*** (0.003)
C*(other home language)[c]		0.186*** (0.039)				0.011*** (0.005)		
C*(European born)			0.019 (0.235)				−0.040* (0.024)	
C*(UK/US/Caribbean born)			−0.031 (0.173)				−0.065 (0.064)	
C*(Asia/Africa born)			−0.018 (0.085)				0.018 (0.012)	
C*(European born) *(other home language)			0.209*** (0.052)	0.219*** (0.051)			0.038*** (0.007)	0.043*** (0.007)
C*(Asia/Africa born) *(other home language)			0.266*** (0.051)	0.282*** (0.043)			0.024*** (0.005)	0.031*** (0.005)
Log likelihood	−14020.8	−13995.9	−13987.8	−13506.3[f]	−14020.6	−14000.2	−13982.8	−13982.8[f]
Pseudo R2	0.296	0.297	0.298	0.299	0.296	0.297	0.298	0.300

Notes: [a] White's heteroskedastic-consistent standard errors in parentheses.
[b] * denotes significance at the 10% level, ** at the 5% level, *** at the 1% level.
[c] language normally spoken at home is neither French nor English.
[d] "% of Population" is the percentage of the population of a Canadian region that belong to a particular ethnic group.
[e] "% of Ethnic Group" is the percentage of the ethnic group that reside in a particular Canadian region.
[f] Log-likelihood values are not directly comparable since the underlying sample size for the specifications estimated in columns (4) and (8) is smaller due to the exclusion of immigrants from "other Europe".

straightforward economic interpretation, they give no insight into whether this influence is economically significant. To investigate this issue, I use the regression results to predict the probability that a recent immigrant with a given set of characteristics will settle in each of the eight Canadian regions that I have defined. I then simulate what the probabilities would have been under a range of alternative hypothetical assumptions. Results of this simulation exercise are reported in Tables 4a to 4e and are discussed below. For exposition purposes, I use an individual with the following set of characteristics as my "base case": age 30, single, no children at home, and a high school education. The main conclusions of the simulations are not sensitive to choice of base case. The predictions are based on the preferred estimation results reported in the final column of Table 3a and in Appendix Table A1.

In the top panel and the first column of Table 4a, I present the predicted location choice of a base-case individual from China (the largest single group of immigrants in the data) who speaks a language other than English or French at home, and using the true relative concentrations of Chinese already resident in Canada as of the 1986 census. It is clearly evident that this base-case immigrant is far more likely to settle in Toronto (49.6% probability) and Vancouver (28.2% probability) than anywhere else in Canada. Column 2 contains the predicted location choices of the same immigrant but under the hypothetical assumption that immigrants from China already resident in Canada are dispersed according to the same distributional pattern as that of native-born Canadians. Column 3 assumes a uniform distributional pattern in which Chinese immigrants already resident in Canada are assumed to be equally likely to reside in each of Canada's regions. In comparison to column 1, recent Chinese immigrants would be much less likely to settle in Vancouver (7.4% compared to 28.2%) and more likely to settle in most other regions of Canada if Chinese immigrants already resident in Canada were not so concentrated in Vancouver. In particular, they would be more likely to settle in Ontario (outside Toronto), Montreal, the Prairies, and Alberta. However, regardless of the distributional assumption, close to 50% of recent Chinese immigrants would still choose to reside in Toronto.

The second and third panels of Table 4a repeat this analysis for two other groups of immigrants from Asia: immigrants from South-East Asian countries and immigrants from the Middle East. Immigrants from South-East Asia are predicted to be more evenly distributed across regions of Canada than immigrants from China, but are still relatively concentrated in Toronto and Vancouver. Alternative hypothetical distributions of South-

Table 4a: Predicted Location Choices, Immigrants from Asia

(language other than English or French spoken at home)

	Actual 1986 Distribution	1986 Native-Born Distribution	Equal Distribution
China/HongKong			
Montreal	.057	.122	.128
Rest of Quebec	.002	.005	.005
Toronto	.496	.473	.460
Rest of Ontario	.050	.163	.116
Prairies	.024	.044	.054
Alberta	.086	.112	.131
Vancouver	.282	.074	.099
Rest of BC	.004	.007	.009
South-East Asia			
Montreal	.106	.125	.126
Rest of Quebec	.006	.009	.009
Toronto	.425	.394	.379
Rest of Ontario	.076	.130	.104
Prairies	.075	.076	.084
Alberta	.098	.098	.105
Vancouver	.206	.159	.184
Rest of BC	.008	.009	.010
Middle East			
Montreal	.364	.240	.276
Rest of Quebec	.007	.013	.014
Toronto	.325	.244	.260
Rest of Ontario	.208	.399	.311
Prairies	.012	.017	.023
Alberta	.049	.054	.070
Vancouver	.033	.029	.042
Rest of BC	.002	.003	.004

Notes: Predictions are generated using a base case: man aged 30 who is single with no children at home and with a high school education. Coefficient estimates underlying the predictions are from the preferred specification reported in the final column of Table 3a and in the Appendix Table A1.

Table 4b: Predicted Location Choices, Immigrants from Europe
(language other than English or French spoken at home)

	Actual 1986 Distribution	1986 Native-Born Distribution	Equal Distribution
Poland			
Montreal	.053	.052	.067
Rest of Quebec	.003	.006	.007
Toronto	.450	.278	.321
Rest of Ontario	.312	.533	.398
Prairies	.038	.023	.037
Alberta	.091	.065	.097
Vancouver	.046	.036	.064
Rest of BC	.007	.005	.010
Mediterranean			
Montreal	.059	.052	.066
Rest of Quebec	.002	.006	.006
Toronto	.612	.275	.316
Rest of Ontario	.220	.528	.391
Prairies	.022	.034	.053
Alberta	.044	.064	.095
Vancouver	.038	.036	.063
Rest of BC	.004	.005	.009
Eastern Europe			
Montreal	.119	.149	.176
Rest of Quebec	.019	.039	.042
Toronto	.463	.275	.295
Rest of Ontario	.227	.388	.269
Prairies	.038	.030	.044
Alberta	.082	.082	.114
Vancouver	.048	.034	.056
Rest of BC	.003	.003	.004

Notes: Predictions are generated using a base case: man aged 30 who is single with no children at home and with a high school education. Coefficient estimates underlying the predictions are from the preferred specification reported in the final column of Table 3a and in the Appendix Table A1.

James Ted McDonald

East Asian immigrants already in Canada suggest new immigrants would be less likely to settle in Vancouver and more likely to settle in Ontario outside Toronto. Similarly for recent immigrants from the Middle East, a more even distribution of Middle Eastern immigrants already resident in Canada would see recent immigrants more likely to settle in Ontario and less likely to settle in Montreal and Toronto.

Table 4b presents a similar set of results but for recent immigrants from selected areas of Europe. Although the predicted distribution of location choice differs somewhat across the groups, for each it is the case that a more even distribution of immigrant residents from that group makes recent immigrants substantially more likely to settle in the rest of Ontario rather than Toronto. For example, if immigrants from Poland already resident in Canada were distributed across Canadian regions similarly to native-born Canadians, the probability a recent Polish immigrant resides in Toronto falls from 45% to 28%, and the probability the immigrant resides in the rest of Ontario increases from 31% to 53%.[19]

Tables 4c to 4e use simulations to examine the effect that language, education, and period of migration have on the location decisions of recent immigrants. In Table 4c I present the results of simulations for two groups of immigrants from regions — namely, Africa and Southern Asia — where the predominant language is a language other than English or French but with significant proportions of recent immigrants whose usual language at home is English. (The vast majority of immigrants from continental Europe and the other regions of Asia speak a language other than English or French at home.) From the top panel of Table 4c, recent immigrants from Africa who speak a language other than French or English at home are most likely to settle in Toronto (38%) or Montreal (28%). In contrast, African immigrants who speak English at home are much less likely to settle in Montreal (9%), and more likely to settle in every other region of Canada except Quebec. Not surprisingly, immigrants who speak French at home are overwhelmingly likely to settle in Montreal. Similar results are obtained for recent immigrants from Southern Asia, although the magnitude of the changes is smaller.

---

[19]Though not reported in the tables, the predicted location choice of recent immigrants from the United Kingdom and the United States are broadly similar to the population concentrations of native-born English-speaking Canadians. Immigrants from the United Kingdom and United States are less likely to settle in the Prairie provinces, and are marginally more likely to settle in BC outside Vancouver, Toronto, and the rest of Ontario.

Table 4c: Predicted Location Choices: Effect of Language Normally Spoken at Home

| | Other Language Spoken at Home | | | English Spoken at Home | French Spoken at Home |
	Actual Distribution	Native-Born Distribution	Equal Distribution	Actual Distribution	Actual Distribution
Africa					
Montreal	.278	.195	.216	.088	.774
Rest of Quebec	.010	.016	.017	.003	.101
Toronto	.380	.297	.307	.487	.043
Rest of Ontario	.165	.334	.259	.198	.058
Prairies	.037	.047	.060	.042	.002
Alberta	.076	.070	.086	.092	.012
Vancouver	.047	.032	.044	.073	.005
Rest of BC	.007	.009	.012	.017	.004
Southern Asia					
Montreal	.130	.193	.206	.073	n/a
Rest of Quebec	.002	.004	.004	.001	
Toronto	.553	.428	.427	.595	
Rest of Ontario	.096	.211	.158	.106	
Prairies	.019	.025	.031	.019	
Alberta	.063	.070	.083	.078	
Vancouver	.117	.053	.071	.102	
Rest of BC	.020	.016	.021	.026	

Notes: Predictions are generated using a base case: man aged 30 who is single with no children at home and with a high school education. Coefficient estimates underlying the predictions are from the preferred specification reported in the final column of Table 3a and in the Appendix Table A1.

James Ted McDonald

Table 4d: Predicted Location Choices: Effect of Tertiary Education

	High School Education			University Degree		
	Actual Distribution	Native-Born Distribution	Equal Distribution	Actual Distribution	Native-Born Distribution	Equal Distribution
China/HongKong						
Montreal	.057	.122	.128	.071	.114	.116
Rest of Quebec	.002	.005	.005	.002	.004	.004
Toronto	.496	.473	.460	.528	.526	.512
Rest of Ontario	.050	.163	.116	.049	.100	.081
Prairies	.024	.044	.054	.032	.046	.052
Alberta	.086	.112	.131	.078	.093	.101
Vancouver	.282	.074	.099	.237	.111	.129
Rest of BC	.004	.007	.009	.004	.005	.006

Table 4e: Predicted Location Choices: 1991 Compared to 1996

	Arrived 1986–91 1986 Distribution	Arrived 1991–96 1991 Distribution	Arrived 1991–96 1986 Distribution
China/HongKong			
Montreal	.057	.045	.045
Rest of Quebec	.002	.002	.002
Toronto	.496	.446	.425
Rest of Ontario	.050	.044	.045
Prairies	.024	.021	.021
Alberta	.086	.075	.080
Vancouver	.282	.360	.375
Rest of BC	.004	.006	.006

Notes: Predictions are generated using a base case: man aged 30 who is single with no children at home and with a high school education. Coefficient estimates underlying the predictions are from the preferred specification reported in the final column of Table 3a and in the Appendix Table A1.

Since the determinants of location choice are significantly different for recent immigrants with a university degree, it is useful to examine the magnitude of these differences. For illustration purposes, I focus on recent immigrants from China, although the tenor of the results is similar for other ethnic groups. The right panel of Table 4d presents the same set of simulations as before but for recent Chinese immigrants with university degrees. For ease of comparison, the left panel of Table 4d repeats the top panel of Table 4a (recent Chinese immigrants with high school education). Comparing predicted location distribution based on the actual distribution of Chinese immigrants already in Canada, it can be seen that recent immigrants with a university degree are relatively more likely to settle in Toronto and Montreal and less likely to settle in Vancouver. However, a more evenly distributed population of Chinese immigrants already in Canada would have a smaller effect on the location decisions of recent Chinese with degrees.

The final set of simulations is presented in Table 4e and illustrates predicted changes in the location decisions of recent immigrants in 1996 compared to 1991 (again for recent Chinese immigrants). Comparing columns 1 and 2, it can be seen that Chinese immigrants arriving in Canada in the period 1991–96 are around eight percentage points more likely to settle in Vancouver than comparable Chinese immigrants arriving in Canada in 1986–91, and less likely to settle in almost every other region of Canada. This change is not due to changing location patterns of immigrant Chinese already resident in Canada. From column 3, if the composition of settled immigrants in 1991 was the same as in 1986, the estimated shift to Vancouver would have been even larger. In additional regressions not reported here, I attempted to parameterize changing macroeconomic conditions between 1986 and 1991 that might explain the shift. Using census data, I constructed a series of unemployment rates and average earnings decomposed by region, education level, and broad age group and included them as additional regressors. However, they were uniformly insignificant and had no impact on the estimated year-region interaction terms.

Extension: The Importance of Immigrant Visa Class

One potentially important source of omitted variable bias is that the Canadian census files do not record the visa category in which immigrants were accepted into Canada. Immigrants migrate to Canada in one of three broad categories — family, independent, and refugee — and the composition of immigrant inflows has changed somewhat over the sample period. From Citizenship and Immigration Canada (CIC) aggregate data on immigrant intakes (CIC, 1996), the proportion of immigrants entering as refugees declined from 18.2% in the 1986–90 period to 15.5% in the 1991–96 period. As long as changes over time in the aggregate figures are due to a changing mix of immigrants by country of origin and not changes in composition within country of origin, then any effects on location choice of changing composition of visa class will be captured by the ethnic group dummy variables. However, it is evident from Figures 1 and 2 that this is not the case — within a number of particular countries or areas of origin there have been substantial compositional changes by visa class.

The most striking example is for immigrants from Poland. Almost 80% of immigrants from Poland who became permanent residents in 1989 were admitted as refugees, while less than 5% of new Polish immigrants in 1994 were refugees. If visa category is an important determinant of location choice of new immigrants, then the significant ethnic network effects identified earlier may in fact be reflecting the changing mix over time of immigrants by visa category. While it is not possible to examine this issue precisely due to data limitations, some insight can be gained by combining immigrant flows data from Citizenship and Immigration Canada with the census data. I proceed as follows. First, I compute the proportion of immigrants who were refugees for each year from 1986 to 1996 for each of the 16 regions of the world identified earlier in the paper. Since year of residency is available in the census data, I assign the relevant refugee proportion to each observation in the dataset. (Note that this variable is an individual-specific characteristic that is invariant to location choice.) Finally, I re-estimate conditional Logit specifications that include controls for visa composition.[20]

Before presenting the results, it is important to mention two caveats about the immigration data. First, the refugee statistics are generated from immigrant flows for men and women together, since data are not reported

---

[20]I do not include controls for the proportion of immigrants admitted to Canada in other visa categories, on the assumption that refugee status is the key demarcation by visa class likely to affect mobility. It might be expected that refugees will have different determinants of location choice than economic or family migrants since the decision to migrate to Canada is presumably based more on safety from persecution than economic factors.

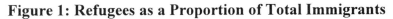

Figure 1: Refugees as a Proportion of Total Immigrants

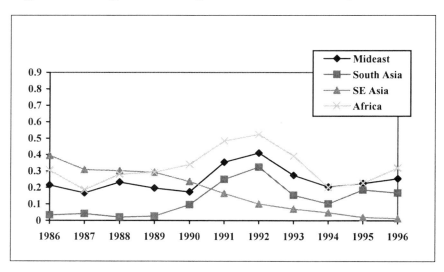

Figure 2: Refugees as a Proportion of Total Immigrants

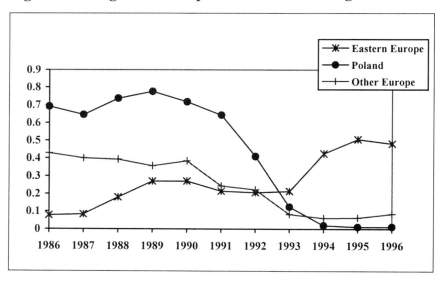

Source: Author's calculations based on data contained in *Citizenship and Immigration Statistics*, an annual report published by Citizenship and Immigration Canada.

disaggregated by country of origin and gender. Second, the country of origin reported in the immigration statistics is the country of last permanent residence rather than country of birth as in the census data. Thus, the matching of composition data to census micro-data is not exact.

Results are reported in Table 5 and are based on the same specifications as in Table 3a but with the addition of a term reflecting the interaction of ethnic density and the visa class composition variable. Each regression also includes the same set of demographic controls as before, plus a full set of interactions of the regional dummy variables with the visa class composition variable, and each of these terms further interacted with a dummy variable for a language other than English or French spoken at home. It can be seen from Table 5 that the inclusion of the visa category controls does not alter the significance of the ethnic network variables, although the interaction of visa category and ethnic density is negative and significant. This implies that the higher the proportion of immigrants from a country/area that are refugees, the weaker is the attraction of ethnic networks. However, since the average proportion of refugees is around 0.16 (with a maximum of 0.77), the magnitude of the reduction is generally relatively small. Further, for no group of immigrants speaking a language other than English or French at home is the net effect negative. Although the results imply a negative ethnic network effect for immigrants speaking French or English at home, most of the immigrants of these language groups are from countries or areas of the world with only small numbers of refugees (which again implies a small effect).

Discussion and Conclusions

As Canada's ambitious immigration program continues, the settlement pattern of immigrants is an increasingly important issue in assessing the benefits and costs of immigration policy. The key result of this paper is that ethnic networks do play a significant role in affecting the location choice of recent immigrants to Canada, even after controlling for a range of observed and unobserved factors. This implies first that the geographic distribution of future immigrants will continue to reflect a strong urban bias because of the current concentration of immigrants in Canada's three major cities, in particular Toronto. Second, the results imply that government policy designed to encourage immigration to other areas of Canada may

Table 5: Selected Econometric Results, Controls for Visa Category[a,b]

Variable	(1)	(2)	(3)
Relative concentration (RC)	−0.014 (0.165)		
RC*(other home language)[c]	0.323*** (0.069)		
RC*(university degree)	−0.182*** (0.035)	−0.174*** (0.035)	−0.155*** (0.035)
RC*(European born)		−0.695** (0.341)	
RC*(UK or US born)		0.010 (1.221)	
RC*(Asia or Africa born)		−0.055 (0.182)	
RC*(other home language) *(European born)		0.612*** (0.126)	0.617*** (0.127)
RC*(other home language) *(Asia or Africa born)		0.458*** (0.070)	0.482*** (0.068)
RC*(% refugees)	−0.614** (0.254)	−0.528** (0.258)	−0.627** (0.258)
Log likelihood	−13986.1	−13970.1	−13491.6[d]
Pseudo R2	0.298	0.299	0.300

Notes: [a] White's heteroskedastic-consistent standard errors in parentheses.
[b] * denotes significance at the 10% level, ** at the 5% level, *** at the 1% level.
[c] language normally spoken at home is neither French nor English.
[d] Log-likelihood values are not directly comparable since the underlying sample size for the specification estimated in column (3) is smaller due to the exclusion of immigrants from "other Europe".

have a positive spillover effect for future immigration. However, simulations show that even with radically different population distributions that would not be observed in practice, Canada's major cities will continue to attract the lion's share of new immigrants.

The current project has some obvious extensions. First, it would be interesting to examine the role of ethnic networks in affecting internal migration of immigrants and native-born Canadians. One focus of this future work could be on the location decisions of new entrants to the labour market since they are also a group of individuals for whom mobility costs should be relatively low. Specifically it would be of interest to see whether new labour market entrants show a similar tendency to locate in Canada's major cities.

References

Bartel, A. (1989), "Where Do the New U.S. Immigrants Live? *Journal of Labor Economics* 7(4), 371–391.

Benabou, R. (1996), "Equity and Efficiency in Human Capital Investment: The Local Connection", *Review of Economic Studies* 63, 237–264.

Bertrand, M., E. Luttmer and S. Mullainathan (2000), "Network Effects and Welfare Cultures", *The Quarterly Journal of Economics* 115, 1019–1055.

Borjas, G.J. (1992), "Ethnic Capital and Intergenerational Mobility", *The Quarterly Journal of Economics* 107, 123–150.

_____ (1995), "Ethnicity, Neighborhoods, and Human-Capital Externalities", *American Economic Review* 85, 365–390.

_____ (1998), "To Ghetto or Not to Ghetto: Ethnicity and Residential Segregation", *Journal of Urban Economics* 44, 228–253.

_____ (1999), "Immigration and Welfare Magnets", *Journal of Labor Economics* 17(4), 607–637.

Canada. Citizenship and Immigration Canada (CIC) (1996), *Citizenship and Immigration Statistics*, Cat. No. C+I-371-10-99. [Also issues for 1986–1995] (Ottawa: Citizenship and Immigration Canada).

_____ (1997), *Fact Sheet 7: Sponsorship*, Cat. No. C+I-134-06-97 (Ottawa: Citizenship and Immigration Canada).

_____ (2000), *Facts and Figures: Immigration Overview*, Cat. No. C+I-291-08-01E (Ottawa: Citizenship and Immigration Canada).

Cardak, B. and J.T. McDonald (2001), "Neighborhood Effects, Preference Heterogeneity and Immigrant Educational Attainment", Working Paper No. 2001–03 (Hobart: Department of Economics, University of Tasmania).

Day, K. and S. Winer (1994), "Internal Migration and Public Policy", in A. Maslove (ed.), *Issues in the Taxation of Individuals* (Toronto: University of Toronto Press).

_____ (2001), "Policy-Induced Migration in Canada: An Empirical Study", Working Paper No. 2001–08 (Ottawa: Carleton University).

Dodson, M. (2001), "Welfare Generosity and Location Choices Among New United States Immigrants", *International Review of Law and Economics* 21, 47–67.

Dunlevy, J. (1991), "On the Settlement Patterns of Recent Caribbean and Latin Immigrants to the United States", *Growth and Change* 22, 54–67.

Finnie, R. (2000), "Who Moves? A Panel Logit Model Analysis of Inter-Provincial Migration in Canada", Research Paper No. 142 (Ottawa: Analytical Studies Branch, Statistics Canada).

Frey, W.H. (1996), "Immigration, Domestic Migration and Demographic Balkanization in America: New Evidence for the 1990s", *Population and Development Review* 22(4), 741–763.

Funkhouser, E. (2000), "Changes in the Geographic Concentration and Location of Residence of Immigrants", *International Migration Review* 34(2), 489–510.

Green, A. and D. Green (1995), "Canadian Immigration Policy: The Effectiveness of the Point System and Other Instruments", *Canadian Journal of Economics* 28(4b), 1006–1041.

Lin, Z. (1998), "Foreign-Born vs Native-Born Canadians: A Comparison of their Inter-Provincial Labour Mobility", Research Paper No. 114 (Ottawa: Analytical Studies Branch, Statistics Canada).

Manski, C.F. (1993), "Identification of Endogenous Social Effects: The Reflection Problem", *Review of Economic Studies* 60, 531–542.

McFadden, D. (1973), "Conditional Logit Analysis of Qualitative Choice Behavior", in P. Zarembka (ed.), *Frontiers in Econometrics* (New York: Academic Press).

Montgomery, J. (1991), "Social Networks and Labor-Market Outcomes: Toward an Economic Analysis", *American Economic Review* 81, 1408–1418.

Newbold, K. (1996), "Internal Migration of the Foreign-Born in Canada", *International Migration Review* 30(3), 728–747.

Osberg, L., D. Gordon and Z. Lin (1994), "Interregional Migration and Inter-industry Labour Mobility in Canada: A Simultaneous Approach", *Canadian Journal of Economics* 27(1), 58–79.

Zavodny, M. (1999), "Determinants of Recent Immigrants' Locational Choices", *International Migration Review* 33(4), 1014–1030.

Appendix Table A1: Selected Econometrics Results: Demographic Variables

(Wald test p-values of the null hypothesis that the variable does not affect location choice across the specified regions of Canada)

Variable Group	No Effect Across All Regions	No Effect Across English-Speaking Regions	No Effect Across Regions Other Than Tor., Van., Mtl.
Married	.380	.432	.638
Kids	.034	.112	.182
Less than high school	.085	.031	.095
Postsecondary	.238	.290	.356
University	.001	.000	.671
Age-squared	.374	.421	.175
Age and age-squared	.000	.000	.003
French spoken at home	.000	.022	.000
Language other than French/English at home	.000	.000	.000
Region fixed effects	.000	.003	.002
Region fixed effects in 1996	.000	.000	.010
Country/area of birth[a]	.000	.000	.000

Notes: [a] the significance of the set of ethnic group-specific regional dummy variables is tested separately for each ethnic group. In each case, the regional dummy variables are highly significant.

The Manitoba Experience

Gerald L. Clément

I will discuss here the how and why Manitoba became significantly involved in the area of immigration policy. I will try to provide an overview of the historical events that allowed Manitoba to go forward in this area, to outline what impacts bilateral agreements have had on the degree of centralization, and to underline the importance of partnerships in addressing immigration policy directions, achieving levels objectives, and ensuring retention and settlement in urban and rural localities.

In an area of shared jurisdiction, outlined in the Canadian constitution, the fact that immigration ministers have met for the first time since 1895 speaks to some of the concerns that provinces have. Manitoba recognized that the 1978 Immigration Act gave us an opportunity that the previous Act did not. It allowed us to have formal agreements with the Government of Canada so that we could actually put some muscle behind some of the objectives that we had set out. In the early 1980s the Government of Manitoba and the Government of Canada signed a bilateral agreement and at that time it was quite modest. It was to look at the special needs of certain refugees and to ensure that there would be a coordinated program to facilitate their entry into Canada.

Well, we learned quickly that the program needed to expand into other areas and it had implications in terms of the social impact on those individuals who had come to Canada. From that point on Manitoba recognized that it had to be prepared for the admission of immigrants. To better prepare oneself, you have to be organized internally. In 1990 the

Government of Manitoba collected all of the services that had been defined to address the needs of the immigrant population, both those coming from abroad and those interprovincially, and put them together under one department. It sounds like a simple situation, but in many provinces, immigration is handled by Departments of Education or Social Services. In Manitoba the benefits of putting the general responsibility for immigration under one department were clear. In 1996, after a couple of years of serious discussion and a lot of arm wrestling, a first framework agreement was established between the Government of Canada and the Province of Manitoba. This outlined our objectives, our directions, our priorities, and also paved the way for other agreements, which we negotiated a couple of years later. The agreement is important because it allowed Manitoba to have some control over the levels of immigration. As far back as 1984, Manitoba has been requesting a proportional share of immigration equivalent to the proportional share of the province's population within Canada. That level is 4%. Is our absorptive capacity 4%? We believe so. We believe that our economy can and does integrate a large number of skilled immigrants. The economy has, at least in the last five years, been leading Canada in terms of employment participation.

Toronto, Vancouver, and Montreal receive all the publicity. A good marketing approach is necessary to promote other cities. Manitoba was one of the first to create a Website. It was one of the first steps. However, in terms of the results of the number of people who were selecting to come to Manitoba, it did not have any impact. So we took the next approach, which was to negotiate again with the federal government for the opportunity to recruit, select, and nominate individuals who were destined to our labour market or whose entry to Manitoba would have a positive impact on our economy.

Prior to 1998 I think the category "provincial nominee" would have been something that people would not really know. Since that time, however, I think ministers in at least eight provinces now have provincial nominee agreements. We have all recognized that it is an effective tool. It is important because we can identify criteria that reflect the needs of our communities, the needs of our cities, the needs of our various economic sectors. It allows for involvement by individuals who know the province, who know the regions where people are going to be settling. It allows for families, friends, others who have first knowledge of the individuals who are perhaps wanting to come to the province to allow for a form of sponsorship. Though it is not a family reunification or humanitarian program, we certainly do look, as part of our criteria, at what is the possible attachment

Gerald L. Clément

to Manitoba and what are the opportunities for a successful integration there. By providing the opportunity for a provincial nominee program, we, of course, needed to invest in the infrastructure within the province — the resources to be able to deal with the kinds of applications that we anticipated. We started very modestly. We said, if we could attract 200 families, with the principal applicant selected on the basis of specific economic criteria and the families that would join them, that we could possibly attract (assuming a family with a spouse and a child) 600 arrivals — at a time when immigration levels were about 3,000. Well beyond our wildest expectations, the program took off, and within six months we had received a significant number of very qualified applications. We therefore negotiated with our federal counterparts to increase those levels to the point where today, just four years after the program was initiated, we will be approving or nominating 1,000 principal applicants for this year. There is the potential of almost doubling the current level of immigration to our province, which has now gone up to 5,000 immigrants per year.

There is no doubt that a program like this comes with its own challenges. Certainly, at a time when our federal counterparts introduced a new Act, with new tighter regulations for the skilled worker program, we naturally had to deal with the whole issue of whether the individuals being nominated actually wanted to come to Manitoba or were using our program as a way to enter Canada apart from the worker skill requirements. We have ensured that we evaluate how individuals are doing after arrival. We follow up, and for that component of the provincial nominee population that arrived in the 1990s and the year 2000 we found that a 90% retention rate was achieved and that 94% of the principal applicants were employed, either in the area that they had indicated they would be working in or in areas related to their expertise. These are very encouraging signs. Perhaps because of the size of the program, we were able to monitor and to work with those who come to Manitoba to some of the more rural areas, finding ways to assist them.

The other thing that we did was to ensure that we would have the tools to help people settle. We negotiated with the federal government a settlement agreement which meant that the federal government was ready to devolve the responsibilities for settlement services to the provinces. Manitoba felt that, in order to ensure that individuals destined to our province received the services that were properly available in the regions where they would be living, the province made modifications to the federal programs in order to have them available specifically in the areas where immigrants had settled.

In terms of partnerships, I think one of the keys to our success has been an openness to partnerships with a number of communities. Ted MacDonald's presentation was quite accurate in saying that communities, be they ethnic communities or geographic communities are an important dimension of the immigrant integration process. Rural communities have been very supportive and have been open to involvement in the settlement process and in assisting individuals to find employment.

We also had some challenges with regard to the francophone community in Manitoba. We have a well-developed francophone community with a lot of infrastructure, but regrettably the level of francophone immigration to minority communities has been limited. This was underlined by the Commissioner for Official Languages.

We are also working with a number of groups and communities that are hoping to expand their membership through immigration.

Immigration Policy in Canada: A Quebec Perspective

Gilles Grenier

Most of the time, the discussion of immigration issues and policies in Canada is done in an overall national context, sometimes with mention of regional dimensions, but usually with very little attention being paid to the special nature of the Quebec society. The purpose of this comment is to show a Quebec perspective on immigration.

I will start with a quotation from the Office of the Commissioner of Official Languages, which is the official agency whose goal is to promote bilingualism in Canada, especially in the field of federal government services, but in other areas as well:

> Linguistic duality is a value that is central to the Canadian identity and as such the government can no longer side step the issue. (Office of the Commissioner of Official Languages, 2002, p. 7)

This quotation reflects an ambiguity. While the commissioner, Dyane Adam, believes that linguistic duality is a central Canadian value, she seems to think that the government does not care enough about it. That may reflect the feeling of many Canadians as well, who do not put linguistic duality as one of the most important Canadian values. I will argue that in the field of immigration policy, very little attention has been paid by the federal government to linguistic duality. This is why the Quebec government had to step in to correct the situation.

Immigration policy in Canada has not contributed to maintaining linguistic duality. The large majority of immigrants who have come to Canada have joined English Canada. Historically, of all immigrants who have adopted one of the two official languages in Canada, more than 90% have chosen English. The proportion of recent immigrants who have chosen French is higher than that of older immigrants, but it is still smaller than the proportion speaking French among the Canadian-born population. In the past, French Canadians did not care much about immigration. They had very high fertility and could reproduce themselves without relying on immigration. Things have now changed, and immigration is necessary to maintain a French presence in Canada.

The rest of my comment will cover three points: history of immigration in Quebec, evolution of language attributes of immigrants in Quebec, and economic performance of immigrants in Quebec.

We do not know who were the first Europeans to come to Canada, but according to the history books, Canada was discovered by Jacques Cartier in 1534 and Champlain founded Quebec City in 1608. During the French Regime there were about 10,000 immigrants who came from France. With the French Canadian high fertility rate, that number had multiplied to about 70,000 people at the time of the Conquest and to more than six million today. After the Conquest, there were almost no French-speaking immigrants coming to Canada for about 200 years.

The British took over in 1760 and they tried to bring immigrants of their own. Actually, it could be argued that much of the immigration policy in Canada for a very long time was a deliberate attempt to make the British a majority and the French a minority. That was not easy but eventually the British succeeded. The American Revolution brought about 10,000 Loyalists to Canada. These settled mainly in Upper Canada, now Ontario. There were also Loyalists who went to the Maritimes. Those Loyalists increased substantially the British presence. Following the rebellion of 1837–38, the Durham report recommended that the French Canadians be assimilated into the English language and culture. To that effect, the Union Act in 1840 amalgamated the two provinces of Canada allowing the British to become the majority. But the French Canadians were not assimilated. In 1867, Confederation occurred and Quebec became a province. Immigration was made the responsibility of the federal government. One of the goals was to develop western Canada.

Immigrants came in large numbers, in various waves during the nineteenth and twentieth centuries. Those immigrants were initially British, but later they arrived from several European countries, such as Germany and the Ukraine. The immigrants, while keeping part of their cultural background, adopted the English language. That was also true for immigrants who settled in Quebec, from many cultural backgrounds. The French Canadians and the Quebec government were more or less left out of that immigration process.

It is only in the 1960s that French Canadians became concerned about immigration. With the Quiet Revolution, Quebec society modernized rapidly, and fertility rates started to go down. There was a concern that most immigrants in Quebec, even those who were culturally close to the French Canadians, such as the Italians, were absorbing the English language. The survival of the French Canadian community was at stake and immigration was seen as a policy tool that should be used to maintain the presence of a French-speaking population. The Quebec Department of Immigration was created in 1968. A major landmark was the so-called Cullen-Couture Agreement (from the names of the federal and Quebec ministers of immigration respectively) in 1978. Quebec had its own point system for the admission of independent immigrants, with more emphasis on being able to speak French. Another very important landmark was the well-known Bill 101 in 1978, which regulated language use. The children of immigrants were required to go to French schools, which had a very important impact on the language behaviour of immigrants afterwards. In 1991, Quebec was given the sole responsibility of independent immigrants while the family class and refugee class still remained under the control of the federal government.

François Vaillancourt provided an economic rationale for having Quebec take care of its own immigration policy (Vaillancourt, 1988). He argued that differences in tastes for the composition of immigration, in particular with respect to language, justify the intervention of the Quebec government. However, the presence of externalities, such as the possibility for immigrants to move between provinces, justifies that the Quebec policies be coordinated with those of the federal government. Another study on language and immigration was done recently for the Commissioner of Official Languages by Jack Jedwab (2002). This study recommends that linguistic duality be considered in immigration policy, not only in Quebec, but in other provinces as well, in order to maintain the vitality of the French communities in those provinces. Following this recommendation, the federal policy was changed recently to favour immigrants who know both official languages.

I now move to the second point of my comment, which is about the language attributes of immigrants in Quebec. A major goal of immigration policy in Quebec was to induce more immigrants to choose French. There are Canadian data on various language attributes of the population: mother tongue, language used at home, and knowledge of official and non-official languages. I will focus here on the language used at home, which I think is the best available indicator of the way immigrants integrate or assimilate to their new society. Note that in Quebec, unlike the rest of Canada, immigrants have two directions: French or English. Figure 1 shows the language use of cohorts of immigrants at various points in time after their arrival. The data come from the 1971, 1981, 1986, 1991, and 1996 censuses. The languages under consideration are respectively English, French, and other languages (in most cases, the languages spoken in the immigrants' home countries).[1] The cohorts are shown along the horizontal axis, with each bar representing a successive census.

The first panel of the figure shows the use of English. For those who have arrived before the early 1970s, the use of English increases through time, reflecting the assimilation of those cohorts to the English-speaking community. But the use of English decreases for recent cohorts. This shows that fewer immigrants are assimilating to English. However, this may also reflect the fact that some English-speaking immigrants leave Quebec shortly after they arrive.

The second panel of the figure shows the same for the use of French. Contrary to English, the use of French increases through time as we move from the old to the recent cohorts. This is probably the result of the immigration policy and the language legislation. The third panel of the figure shows the same for the use of other languages, that is, immigrants who still use the language of their country of origin. We note that recent cohorts tend to use their language of origin more for a given number of years in Canada. This is related partly to the countries of origin of the recent immigrants, who come in larger number from Asia, Africa, and Latin America. Those immigrants keep their languages longer than earlier immigrants.

From this figure it appears that the use of English as the language of the home has declined in favour of French as was the intention of the policy, but also in favour of the maintenance of the language of origin of immigrants. It should be mentioned, however, that the anglophones in

---

[1]Language use data are complicated by the fact that some people report using equally several languages at home. For the assumptions that I made to produce this figure, see Grenier (2001).

Figure 1: Proportion of Quebec Immigrant Cohorts Speaking Various Languages at Home, Working Population, Aged 25 to 64, 1971 to 1996

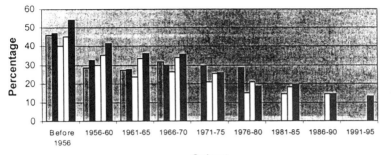

English

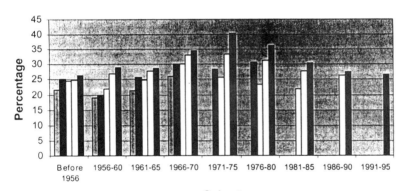

French

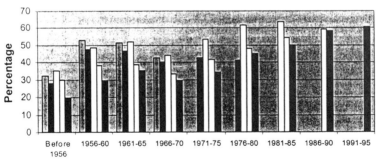

Other languages

| ▦ 1971 | ■ 1981 | ☐ 1986 | ☐ 1991 | ■ 1996 |

Quebec still assimilate more immigrants than their proportion in the population. Therefore, immigration is still the factor that contributes to the growth of the anglophone population in Quebec. The major factor that contributes to its decline is emigration to other Canadian provinces and elsewhere in the world. The use of French has made important progress, but many immigrants prefer to keep their language rather than switch to French or English. Some immigrants, when faced with the pressure to use French rather than English, have decided to do neither, that is, to keep using their mother tongue at home.

The last point of my comment pertains to the economic performance of immigrants in Quebec, in relation to their language choices. I will summarize the results of a recent study that I have done with data on earnings, immigration, language use and other characteristics from the five Canadian censuses of 1971, 1981, 1986, 1991, and 1996 (Grenier, 2001). The relative earnings of recent immigrants in Quebec have declined, as they have done elsewhere in Canada, but perhaps a bit less in Quebec. This may be due to the fact that immigration levels have increased less in Quebec than in the rest of Canada in the early 1990s, at the same time as the Canadian economy was going through a recession. The relative earnings of French speakers have improved through time, but without catching up completely with those of English speakers. Actually, the progress of francophones took place mainly in the 1970s and early 1980s, relative earnings having levelled off since then. The above is true for both Canadian-born and immigrant workers.

As noted earlier, recent immigrants have tended to integrate into the French language more than earlier ones. The results of my research show that there were no costs to doing that. In other words, recent immigrants speaking French at home have done well economically, as well as those speaking English. This was not the case in the past, as immigrants who spoke English did much better than those who spoke French. However, a matter of concern is that immigrants who did not assimilate to one of the official languages, that is, those speaking another language at home, have not done very well.

To summarize and conclude, the purpose of my comment was to show that many immigration issues are different in Quebec than in the rest of Canada. Most of the Canadian research has ignored the particular situation of Quebec. Let us hope that more research will be done on the Quebec case. In my view, linguistic duality is a Canadian value that we should try to maintain and protect because it is part of the social structure of Canada. Until recently, the Canadian immigration policy has not contributed to preserving linguistic duality, but things have changed. The Quebec government has made interventions to promote the use of French, and the federal government has acted recently in the same direction.

References

Grenier, G. (2001), "Immigration, langues et performance économique: le Québec et l'Ontario entre 1970 et 1995", *L 'Actualité économique* 77(3), 305–338.

Jedwab, J. (2002), *Immigration and the Vitality of Canada's Official Language Communities: Policy, Demography and Identity* (Ottawa: Office of the Commissioner of Official Languages).

Office of the Commissioner of Official Languages (2002), *Annual Report, 2001-2002* (Ottawa: Supply and Services Canada).

Vaillancourt, F. (1988), "The Views of Immigration from Quebec — Quebec 's Immigration Policy: An Economic Assessment of its Rationale and Impact ", in C.M. Beach and A.G. Green (eds.), *The Role of Immigration in Canada's Future* (Kingston: John Deutsch Institute for the Study of Economic Policy, Queen 's University).

Comments

Samuel Laryea

First, I would like to say a few remarks about Ted McDonald's paper, which examines the location choice of new immigrants to Canada. It is an excellent piece of work and the results are consistent with other results in the literature, especially in the United States and Australia. See, for example, Bartel (1989) and Chiswick, Lee and Miller (2002). The paper examines the determinants of the initial location choice of new immigrants to Canada, with particular emphasis on the role of ethnic networks in this location decision. The author employs data from both the census (i.e., 1991 and 1996) and Citizenship and Immigration Canada's (CIC) administrative data sources. Using a Logistic methodological framework, the author concludes that ethnic networks do play a significant role in affecting the location decisions of recent immigrants to Canada, even after controlling for other personal and demographic characteristics.

I have two comments on the paper. First, the author cites various measures of ethnic concentration in the paper, and it would be instructive to discuss the pros and cons of some of these measures. The reasons he opted for one particular measure of ethnic concentration as opposed to the other measures need to be discussed. For example, in the paper by Chiswick, Lee and Miller, they also used a measure called the "G Index" initially introduced by geographers as a measure of ethnic concentration. Second, in examining the role of visa class vis-à-vis the locational choices of new immigrants, the author employs administrative data from CIC which is not disaggregated by gender. Since the study pertains to only men, using disaggregated data for both men and women is bound to introduce some measurement errors in the estimations, which were correctly alluded to in the paper. The Immigration Database (IMDB) would be better in calculating the proportion of the refugees in the immigrant flow to overcome this problem. Finally, although the initial location patterns of new immigrants is important for policy formulation purposes, their subsequent internal migration patterns are also worth exploring. This will be a useful extension of the current study.

Let me now turn attention to Gilles Grenier's paper, which articulates a Quebec viewpoint on immigration policy in Canada. My comments will touch on some policy dilemmas as well as dispersion issues, which complement the theme of this session. Since the 1990s, the Government of Quebec has tried to settle immigrants outside Montreal, under a policy dubbed the "Regionalization of Quebec" (CIC, 2001). This policy could pose some policy dilemmas which the paper should address. As you are aware, since 1991 Quebec has controlled the skilled component (i.e., the independent class) of its immigration flows. This follows from the Cullen-Couture Agreement concluded in 1978. However, the federal government still controls the family class and the refugee components. To the best of my knowledge, there are no mandatory requirements for family class immigrants or refugees to settle outside Montreal. This could create externalities which would require cooperation and coordination between the federal government and the province of Quebec, if the regionalization plan is to achieve its goals. The recently published longitudinal study of approximately 290 immigrant families in Quebec by Jean Renaud also addresses important settlement issues which should be mentioned in the paper.

Finally, I focus remarks on the broader issue of immigrant dispersal in the light of recent proposals by Minister Coderre to locate a proportion of future immigrants outside the three largest cities. First, the government should focus on what I call second-tier cities. This is a more achievable goal, compared to settling new immigrants in rural areas and saying to them "be fruitful and multiply". This is because the rural areas often lack the good employment opportunities and the necessary ethnic support networks that are imperative for successful integration. In fact, my own research on this issue (Laryea, 2002) suggests that immigrants' earnings convergence in some smaller and medium-sized cities is much faster than in Montreal, Toronto or Vancouver, the traditional cities of choice for most immigrants. So there is a case to be made here for second-tier cities. Finally, the availability of timely labour market information to immigrants could facilitate their integration into these second-tier cities. This information should be made available to the immigrants before they arrive in Canada. If they are not aware that life could be better in other parts of Canada, apart from

Montreal, Vancouver, and Toronto, they are not going to move to these areas. Thus, the aggressive marketing of second-tier or other cities would be important to the success of any future immigrant dispersal policy.

References

Bartel, A. (1989), "Where do the New U.S. Immigrants Live?" *Journal of Labour Economics* 7(4), 371–391.

Canada. Citizenship and Immigration Canada (CIC) (2001), "Towards a More Balanced Geographic Distribution of Immigrants", Strategic Research and Review, Special Study, May.

Chiswick, B.R., Y.L. Lee and P.W. Miller (2002), "The Determinants of the Geographic Concentration among Immigrants: Application to Australia", Discussion Paper No. 462 (Bonn: Institute for the Study of Labour, IZA).

Laryea, S.A. (2002), "Does City-Size Matter? Immigrants' Earnings Performance in Selected Canadian Cities". Paper prepared for the seventh International Metropolis Conference, Oslo, September 9–13.

Renaud, J. *et al.* (2001), Ils sont maintenant d'ici. *Les dix premiéres années au Québec des immigrants admis en 1989.* Les Publications du Québec, Etudes, recherches et statistiques Numéro 4, MRCI.

Summary of Discussion

Naomi Alboim makes the point that we really have to talk about the role of cities since immigration is an urban phenomenon. Communities are fine, but she would look forward to the day when a Federal-Provincial Ministers' Meeting also has some representation from some of the major cities so they can directly influence policy at that table as well as play an important role in terms of on-the-ground provision of services to effectively settle people.

Someone else raised the question that, because most immigrants come from large urban centres, we seem to believe they are inclined to settle in the larger centres. Is there any data to support this? Ted McDonald responded that, from available Canadian data, we do not know much about the circumstances from which immigrants left their country of origin, except perhaps their visa category. The best we could do at this stage would seem to be to correlate out-migration rates of the various countries of origin with their demographic and other characteristics.

Yvan Turcotte points out that, while one of the reasons why Quebec decided to take part in immigration management was to help maintain the French language in Quebec, it was not the sole or even the principal reason. Quebec decided more or less 40 years ago that they would use immigration as a tool for collective development of society by shaping the intake of immigrants received, not just to attract French-speaking people, but also to reflect humanitarian concerns, for example. In fact, we receive almost as many people who speak English as people who speak French. So, management of immigration can be seen as a global tool for achieving a variety of goals that reflect the variety of needs and values of Quebec society.

Louis Grignon notes that employment and job availability are very important for the settlement decision of immigrants, especially being able to work at a job for which one is qualified. In most Canadian provinces there are problems with immigrants having difficulties getting their credentials recognized. This would seem to offer an opportunity for provinces that do not receive the share of immigrants they would wish to be very proactive in working with professional regulatory bodies (which operate strictly at the provincial level) to do something about this. Gerry Clément was very happy this question had been raised, for only two weeks before the Manitoba minister for labour and immigration put out a call to action on this issue of the recognition of foreign credentials. Manitoba has job-placement programs for immigrants to help people get jobs in their field of expertise. But what was missing and is still missing today is a coordinated approach that allows those individuals to have their credentials recognized. So this call to action is a government saying it is time to move to work out solutions to this problem. Yes, the regulatory bodies fall under provincial controls, but there are also various federal departments with a role to play here as well, as we are not just talking about the evaluation of a document, but we are also talking about issuing a licence, bridging gaps, and training.

Section IV

International Labour Mobility and Policy Responses

Canadian Immigration Policy in Comparative Perspective

John McHale

Introduction

In June of 2002, a major reform of Canadian immigration policy came into effect under the Immigration and Refugee Protection Act and its related regulations. A central element of the new policy is a revised approach to skill-based immigration, with a shift away from a focus on occupational shortages and towards human capital indicators of long-term earnings potential as the basis for acceptance under the points system. Factors that indicate lifetime productivity and adaptability in the Canadian labour market — educational attainment, facility with the official languages, experience in a wide range of skilled occupations, a formal job offer, etc. — are now the determining factors for which economic migrants are accepted.

Thanks to Ajay Agrawal, Charles Beach, Julian Betts, Marc Busch, Richard Roy, and Mihkel Tombak for very helpful comments. Thanks also to Tonya Hood for her invaluable help with file recovery, and to Charles Beach, Alan Green, and Elizabeth Ruddick for organizing the conference. Of course, I bear sole responsibility for all remaining errors in the paper.

Part of the background to this reform is a new competitiveness-driven determination among industrialized countries to attract and retain internationally mobile talent. Most visibly, the United States dramatically increased the cap on its long-stay professional visas (H-1B) in 1998 and again in 2000 under intense lobbying pressure from technology industries. The United Kingdom has greatly expanded its issuance of work permits since the mid-1990s, and has recently introduced on a pilot basis a points-based system for attracting high-earning professionals. In the mid-1990s, Australia successfully introduced new long-stay temporary visas aimed at the highly skilled; and has recently been increasing the share of the skill stream in its points-based system for permanent migration. In mid-2000, Germany introduced its Green Card program to attract information technology professionals on a temporary basis; and in the summer of 2002 signed into law a points/earnings-based system of permanent migration. Policies aimed at attracting skilled workers have also been introduced in Denmark, France, Ireland, Netherlands, New Zealand, and Norway (see, e.g., McLaughlan and Salt, 2002). Although the bursting of the tech bubble and events of September 11, 2001 have undoubtedly slowed this reform momentum,[1] continuing skill-biased technical change, aging populations and education system deficiencies in science and computing should ensure the re-emergence of the reform momentum before long.

How well is Canada positioned to compete for and benefit from the world's mobile skilled workers? To help answer this question, I consider in this paper some principles that should guide the design of immigration policy from a narrow economic perspective. I assume that the goal is to maximize the "immigration surplus" — the value of the immigrant's product less the wage and net fiscal costs — accruing to domestic residents from immigration, while recognizing, of course, that this is just one factor that politicians and electorates must consider when setting immigration policy. I then compare Canada's policies for permanent and temporary economic immigration with the resulting design principles, and also compare these policies to those being adopted by Canada's competitors in the market for mobile talent.

---

[1]For example, the United Kingdom has recently taken all information technology occupations off its list of occupations for expedited processing, and approved petitions for H-1B visas were just 60,500 for the first nine months of Fiscal Year 2002 compared to 130,700 for the same period in FY 2001.

The development of the principles occupies the next section through to the fourth. In the second section, I adopt an immigration surplus maximizing perspective to look at the relative benefits of skilled- and unskilled-focused immigration policies. I first look at a basic model with constant returns to scale over skilled and unskilled workers and competitive wage-setting. In this model, an immigration policy that replicates the current factor mix yields no net gains, extreme factor specialized immigration policies trump diversified immigrant pools, and (with constant elasticity of substitution between skilled and unskilled workers) the relative productivity of skilled workers is surprisingly irrelevant to the optimal immigration policy. I then show how extending the model to include features such as a progressive fiscal system, specialized skills, and knowledge spillovers, can strengthen the case for the skill-focused extreme.

Notwithstanding the less than overwhelming case for the skilled alternative, the third and fourth sections take as given that the government wants to pursue a skill-focused policy and examines basic design issues. In the first of these sections, I look at the broad choice between an approach based on occupational shortages and one based on predicted long-term earnings. After a review of various, concepts of "shortage", the basic finding is that occupational shortages are a poor basis for a *permanent* migration policy in an economy with ever-shifting labour demands and supplies, though shortage considerations might be relevant in the design of a *temporary* migration system.

The fourth section then turns to the design of an alternative human-capital-based points system for permanent migration. The key underlying assumptions are that the *ex ante* attractiveness of an immigrant rises with their predicted long-term earnings, and that there is an earnings cut-off below which migrants should not be admitted. The first step is to show how an estimated earnings regression based on observed human capital characteristics and a chosen earnings cut-off can provide a foundation for a simple points system. The second step is then to show how the earnings regression should be specified (and thus the sources of points chosen) to minimize the errors in predicted earnings and thereby maximize the average quality of the applicant pool.

In the fifth section, I review Canada's recent immigration policy in light of the discussion of optimal design, and also compare the Canadian policy with that of its competitors in the market for mobile talent. I then take a brief detour to consider how Canada has been doing in the competition for its own mobile workers, and present some suggestive evidence that there has been a surge in US-bound emigration in recent years, possibly facilitated by immigration policy changes under NAFTA. The final section concludes with a summary of the main findings.

Why Immigration? Why Skilled?

As a prelude to the later discussion of immigration policy design, I briefly review in this section some of the insights that economics offers on the gains from immigration. I examine the gains from immigration generally, and also the relative merits of a skills-focused immigration policy. Throughout the discussion I take the economic well-being of "those already present" (or simply "natives") as the basis of policy concern. Of course, policymakers may also be concerned with the welfare of the immigrants themselves and indeed the welfare of the populations "left behind" in the origin countries.[2] Policymakers are also likely to be concerned with non-economic determinants of well-being such as reuniting families and allowing escape from persecution, although these factors will not be considered here. For the most part, I also have little to say about the distributional effects of immigration. Thus I make no pretense that this is an *all-things-considered* analysis of immigration policy, but rather offer a narrow analysis of the economic surplus due to immigration that leaves out much of what politicians and electorates must consider.

In looking at this *immigration surplus,* I first assume the economy is: (i) closed to international trade; (ii) has constant returns-to-scale production technology with no spillovers; (iii) has competitive markets (so that all factors receive the value of their marginal products); and (iv) has no fiscal system. I then relax each of these assumptions in reverse order to see the likely implications for immigration policy. To focus more clearly on the choice between skilled and unskilled immigrants, I also assume that skilled and unskilled workers are the only factors of production.

---

[2]As when immigration policies lead to the loss of badly needed doctors in aids-ravaged countries, for example.

Classic Gains from Immigration

Figure 1 reproduces the classic depiction of the gains from immigration of a given skill-type i [i = skilled (s), unskilled (u)].[3] It is noteworthy that an immigrant will only yield a net gain for natives if they are paid less than the value they add to the economy. Thus, in a competitive labour market a single immigrant yields no net gain. Admitting multiple immigrants does yield a net gain, however, with the gain rising (approximately) with the square of the number of immigrants. Taking a linear approximation marginal value product (or labour demand) curve at the pre-immigration wage level, we can calculate the aggregate gain from immigration of skill-type i by,

$$(1) \quad G_i \approx \frac{1}{2} \varepsilon_i \frac{w_{i,0}}{F_{i,0}} N_i^2 ,$$

where G_i is the net gain in native incomes from immigration, ε_i is the wage elasticity with respect to the number of workers, $w_{i,0}$ is the pre-immigration wage of factor-type i, $F_{i,0}$ is the pre-immigration number of workers, and N_i is the number of immigrants.[4]

What is the source of this gain? Although there is strictly no temporal dimension to this framework, a useful way to interpret the diagram is to see the gain as arising as additional immigrants drive down the wage for "previous" immigrants. Take, for example, an arbitrarily chosen "first" immigrant. The diagram shows that the wage that immigrant is paid after all N_i have immigrated is less than their value as measured by the marginal value product curve. Thus there is a surplus available for distribution to

---

[3]See Bhagwati and Rodriguez (1976); Grubel and Scott (1966); Johnson (1967); and Borjas (1995).

[4]Equation (1) is simply a formula for the area of the triangle formed based on a linear approximation to the labour demand curve at the initial wage-employment combination and the number of immigrants.

Figure 1: The Classic Immigration Surplus

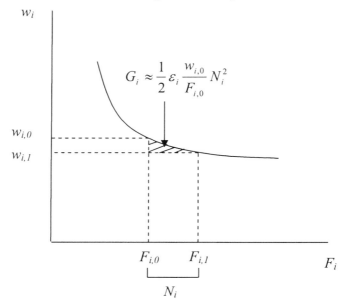

$$G_i \approx \frac{1}{2}\varepsilon_i \frac{w_{i,0}}{F_{i,0}} N_i^2$$

natives. The greater the number of immigrants the more the wage is driven down and the larger is this surplus.[5]

From the viewpoint of an economically based immigration policy, this model has three rather surprising implications: a "balanced" inflow of skilled and unskilled workers yields no surplus gain; immigration policies

---

[5]Of course, there is also a distributional effect, with income transferred from skilled to unskilled natives as the skilled wage is bid down. There is a large empirical literature that attempts to measure the effect of immigration on wages (see Borjas, 1994; Friedberg and Hunt, 1995, for surveys). There are three main types of studies: area studies that compare wages across labour markets receiving different numbers of immigrants; natural experiments that look for immigration changes that are independent of developments in local labour markets; and calibration studies that estimate how relative factor supplies affect relative wages for different skill groups and then calculate how immigration with a given skill mix affects relative wages. Advocates of the latter method argue that the first two types of study fail to account for native outflows in response to immigrant inflows. The first two types of studies tend to find small wage effects (see Altonji and Card, 1991; Card, 1990). The third type of study tends to find larger wage effects (see Borjas, Freeman and Katz, 1996).

John McHale

with "extreme" factor mixes — all skilled or all unskilled — are preferred to more diversified factor mixes; and, at least for an economy with a CES production function employing skilled and unskilled workers, relative factor productivities play no part in determining which extreme policy is better. I discuss each of these surprises in turn.

First, the constant returns-to-scale assumption implies that a balanced immigrant inflow — i.e., an immigrant inflow that has the same skill proportions as the domestic factor mix — has no effect on factor incomes. Thus, simply scaling up the economy through immigration yields no overall gain or distributional effect. If an economy's labour force is 60% skilled, allowing in 600 skilled workers followed by 400 unskilled workers has no effect on the incomes of the initial residents. The lack of an overall gain in economic surplus may strike some as puzzling, since the skilled immigration by itself yields a gain, and, given this skilled immigration has occurred, the unskilled immigration yields a further gain. The solution to this puzzle is that part of the unskilled immigration surplus gain is received by the earlier skilled immigrants. When we subtract off this gain to earlier immigrants the net effect of the two inflows is zero.

A second surprising implication of this model is that, for a given overall level of immigration, an extreme policy of either all skilled or all unskilled will yield a larger gain than a diversified inflow of skilled and unskilled (see Borjas, 1995, for details). The intuitive reason is that the gain from immigrants of a given skill level rises with the *square* of the number of immigrants of that level. Thus, if it makes sense for the first few immigrants to be skilled, there is an even stronger (surplus-based) case for the next immigrant to be skilled. And so on until all the available immigration slots are filled by skilled immigrants.[6]

But which extreme form of immigration policy is best? Suppose that the aggregate production function takes the constant elasticity of substitution form,

$$(2) \quad Y = \left[(A_s F_x)^\rho + (A_u F_u)^\rho \right]^{\frac{1}{\rho}},$$

---

[6]It is possible that the total gains are equal at each of the extreme immigrant mixes. In this case the choice between the extremes is arbitrary, but each of the extremes will produce bigger gains than any more balanced mix.

where Y is output, A_s/A_u is a measure of the relative productivity of skilled and unskilled workers, and ρ is less than or equal to one. The elasticity of substitution between skilled and unskilled workers is then $1/(1-\rho)$. One might expect that the best form of immigration policy will depend on the relative productivities, the relative factor supplies, and the ease of substitutability between the two factors. Using equation (1) to compare the gain from an all-skilled policy, G_s, with the gain from an all-unskilled policy, G_u, yields the following condition for the superiority of the skilled alternative:

$$
(3) \quad
G_s > G_u \quad iff \quad \varepsilon_s \frac{w_{s,0}}{F_{s,0}} > \varepsilon \frac{w_{u,0}}{F_{u,0}}
$$

$$
\Rightarrow \quad \frac{w_{s,0}}{w_{u,0}} > \frac{\varepsilon_s}{\varepsilon_u} \frac{F_{s,0}}{F_{u,0}} .
$$

For the constant elasticity of substitution case,

$$
(4) \quad \frac{w_{s,0}}{w_{u,0}} = \left(\frac{A_s}{A_u}\right)^{\rho} \left(\frac{F_{s,0}}{F_{u,0}}\right)^{\rho-1} ,
$$

and

$$
(5) \quad \frac{\varepsilon_s}{\varepsilon_u} = \left(\frac{A_s}{A_u}\right)^{\rho} \left(\frac{F_{s,0}}{F_{u,0}}\right)^{\rho} .
$$

Substituting equations (4) and (5) into equation (3) reveals that a necessary and sufficient condition for the all-skilled alternative to yield a larger surplus gain is simply that *there are fewer skilled workers than there are unskilled workers.* Strikingly, relative productivity has no bearing on a surplus-based choice between these extreme immigration policies for this commonly used and reasonably flexible production function.

John McHale

Extensions

This brief review of the classic gains from immigration has certainly not yielded a presumption in favour of a skill-focused immigration policy. Indeed, in a highly developed human capital rich economy, the foregoing analysis suggests, if anything, the superiority of augmenting scarce less-skilled resources. This classic treatment also alerts us to the key requirement for an immigration gain: the immigrants must be paid less than the value they add. I turn now to some extensions to the classic model that bear on this surplus. These extensions generally strengthen the case for the skill-focused alternative.

Fiscal effects. The classic model did not allow for a fiscal system. Suppose instead that the country has a progressive fiscal system such that skilled workers are net contributors, paying more in taxes than they receive in government benefits. Figure 2 shows the market for skilled workers, with each worker facing a net tax rate t_s. There is now a fiscal surplus rectangle in addition to the standard immigration surplus triangle. In contrast to the classic case, even a single skilled immigrant will yield a net benefit. This fiscal surplus triangle does not measure the impact of immigration on the government's budget, since revenues and expenditures are also affected by changes in factor prices and by any induced changes in tax and benefit policies. It does, however, measure the aggregate effect on natives through the fiscal channel for any post-immigration fiscal regime.[7]

Heterogeneity/non-competitive wage-setting. The classic model treats all skilled workers as homogenous with a wage determined competitively in the labour market. In reality skills are heterogeneous and skilled workers are imperfect substitutes for one another. For concreteness, suppose that a particular skilled immigrant has some special skills that are uniquely

---

[7]The fiscal effect chapters in National Research Council (1997) give detailed estimates of the long- and short-run effects of immigration to the United States, finding, for example, that the average long-term net fiscal impact of a college-educated immigrant is almost $200,000 (1996 dollars). Storesletten (2000) examines whether a selective immigration policy could solve the fiscal problems associated with an aging US population. Using a calibrated general equilibrium model, he estimates that a policy of admitting 1.6 million high-skilled immigrants aged between 40 and 44 per year would allow the United States to avoid future benefit cuts and tax increases.

Figure 2: The Fiscal Surplus

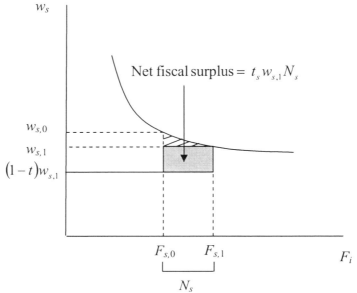

matched to a particular firm. If the worker does not work for this firm he or she will receive the going competitive wage for general skills. Denoting the value of this worker to the firm as V and the competitive wage as $\overline{w}$, and assuming that the surplus on the labour contract is split equally between the firm and immigrant worker, the value of the skilled immigrant to the firm is $V - w = (1/2)(V - \overline{w})$. Moreover, if we assume that the competitive wage (based on general skills) is proportional to V, the size of the surplus to the firm rises with the overall skill level (V) of the immigrant. That is, the gain to the domestic economy will tend to rise with the skill level of the immigrant.

Spillovers. The classic model assumed that employers and employees appropriate the full value of the employment relationship. In other words the private value of the immigrant product is equal to the social value of that product. It is possible that some of the value spills over to others in the economy as the immigrant passes on knowledge about foreign markets, technologies, etc. To the extent that skilled workers have more knowledge to impart, the existence of such spillovers increases the *relative* social value to natives of this group. This again improves the case for the skill-focused policy alternative.

Open economy effects. The analysis thus far has assumed that the economy is closed to international trade. Allowing for an open economy can dramatically change how immigration affects the economy. The impact of immigration, however, is quite model-dependent (see Trefler, 1997, for an excellent review of immigration effects in a variety of trade models). Here I only consider the effects of immigration in the context of a Heckscher-Ohlin trade model with common technologies and full factor price equalization.[8] The fact of full factor price equalization immediately alters us to the fact that the wage-reduction mechanism that is at the core of the classic model cannot be operating. Thus, immigration has no effect on native incomes. The famous Rybczynski Theorem, however, shows that immigration will affect the *output structure* of the economy if it affects relative factor endowments. Skilled immigration will cause skill-intensive sectors (such as information technology) to expand and less skill-intensive sectors (such as agriculture) to contract. To the extent that it is considered desirable to expand skill-intensive sectors beyond their free market levels — possibly because of spillover effects or a combination of greater learning opportunities and capital market imperfections — policymakers might pursue skilled immigration as a means of shifting the resource allocation of the economy, even in the absence of any immediate income gains to natives.[9]

---

[8]In a provocative recent paper, Davis and Weinstein (2002) use a Ricardian trade model to examine the impact of balanced flows of factors to an economy (they focus on the United States) with a superior CRS technology. To the extent that the resulting increased size of the economy leads to a worsening of its terms of trade, the balanced inflow of productive factors leads to lower welfare (see also Trefler, 1997). They argue that the United States has been made *worse off* due to its openness to foreign capital and workers. On the sending side, a balanced outflow of factors will lead to an improvement in welfare provided it is large enough for its terms of trade to change. A welfare loss to the sending country could re-emerge if the factor outflows are unbalanced (say all skilled workers) or if there are economies of scale.

[9]Another possible benefit of immigration for an open economy is that immigrants can reduce the barriers to international trade. Immigrants' knowledge of foreign markets can help in the search for trading partners and in the communication of customization requirements. Immigrants who are members of cross-national networks can also act as "reputational intermediaries", using their long-term relationships with firms and individuals in their original- and new-home

Designing a Skill-Focused Immigration Policy I: Shortage Occupations or Human Capital?

As a prelude to the discussion of a points system I design in the next part, I briefly consider in this section two competing orientations for a skill-focused immigration policy: a *shortage occupation approach* based on acute labour market needs; and a *human capital approach* based on long-term earnings potential. In designing a skill-focused policy, should the government focus on attracting skills that are currently in short supply in the domestic labour market? Or should it try to attract immigrants with human capital characteristics (education level, language skills, etc.) that predict long-run labour market success?

In considering the shortage approach it is useful to distinguish three distinct degrees of shortage. A *pure* shortage exists when the wage is set too low to clear the labour market in a particular occupation. The economist's instinctive question is: What is stopping market forces from pushing the wage upwards? Looking beyond the obvious government wage controls, Arrow and Capron provide a possible answer in their classic paper on the market for scientists and engineers: "The interaction of rising demand with price movements that do not instantaneously equate supply and demand provides a plausible interpretation of the recent [engineer-scientist shortage]" (1959, p. 203).

Although the Arrow and Capron explanation shows how shortages might persist in markets without a government imposed wage ceiling, what sometimes passes for a labour market shortage can be less than the pure form of disequilibrium they describe. It is well-known, for example, that monopsony power in a labour market can lead to a *quasi*-shortage. The sole employer would like to hire more workers at the going wage, hence the apparent shortage; but is unwilling to raise the wage for everyone to attract more employees. Such monopsony power is thought to be important in markets for health-care workers dominated by a large hospital or government run health-care system (Staiger, Spetz and Phibbs, 1999).

Casual observations about labour market shortages often refer to a phenomenon that would not normally be labelled as a shortage by an economist at all. These *pseudo*-shortages are typically situations where

---

countries to facilitate contracting where legal contracting is difficult. (See Rauch, 2001, for a survey of the search and contract facilitating roles of immigrants.)

John McHale

labour demand is rising faster than labour supply and the wage is being forced up. Unlike the Arrow and Capron situation, the labour market is clearing, but the skill in question is becoming more expensive. It is no surprise that such wage rises can lead to calls by employers — replete with claims of damaging shortages — to ease the cost pressure with selective immigration of the in-demand workers. A good example is the rising demand for software developers during the recent high-tech boom.

Do any of these degrees of "shortage" provide a rationale for an occupation-targeted immigration policy? Applying the type of surplus calculation that I used earlier, we see that the going wage is below the marginal value product in the case of a pure shortage. Thus allowing even a single immigrant in the relevant "shortage occupation" will yield an immigrant surplus. Such a shortage-driven policy is a poor basis for a policy on *permanent* migration, however, as the occupations in short supply today may not be the occupations in short supply next year or a few years from now.

In contrast to the likely temporary nature of the pure occupational shortages, the monopsony-caused quasi-shortages are likely to endure. Employers will argue that they are constantly looking to hire more workers, but cannot find qualified workers to take the jobs. In the case of nurses, for example, there can be an almost permanent crisis as positions go unfilled and qualified nurses choose to leave the field citing pay and conditions. Hiring skilled foreign nurses at the going wage is certainly surplus enhancing, and may meet muted opposition from the domestic workers who had partly borne the burden of understaffing with heavier workloads. The question here is whether an ongoing use of "emergency" immigration acts as an impediment to the long-run workings of the relevant skill markets, especially when lower earnings limit investments in these skills.

The final case of rising costs — pseudo-shortages — is probably the most common reason for targeting workers in particular occupations. To the extent that rising wages go together with high wages, the analysis from the last section is relevant. Although we saw there that the classic immi-gration surplus argument does not in general provide a reason for targeting more highly paid workers, various extensions relating to fiscal effects, knowledge spillovers and heterogeneous skills, do. But again it is question-able whether a policy targeting occupations that have recently had rising wages is a good basis for a permanent immigration policy. The obvious alternative is to base a skill-focused immigration policy on various human capital characteristics — which certainly can include current occupation — that help predict long-term earnings.

I examine the design of such a human-capital-based policy in the next section. But before leaving the topic of specific skill shortages, it is worth asking if a shortage occupation approach provides a good basis for a *temporary* skilled migration policy. The standard form of such a policy is to require that the applicant has a job offer (often it will be the employer who applies for the work permit), and to conduct a labour market test to ensure no adverse effect on domestic workers. In the context of the classic immigration surplus model the idea of such a labour market test seems quite self-defeating — in that model there will *only* be a surplus gain when competing domestic workers are harmed. In practice it may be possible to formally pass the test when wages are rising. But the test can be a costly bureaucratic barrier for employers and a source of delay for workers. This makes the labour market test ill-suited for a policy aimed at filling temporary shortages or helping to match supply with rising demand. An alternative basis for a skill-focused temporary migration is to maintain an "occupations in demand" list that allows for fast approvals of work permit requests, or to provide automatic approval for applicants with wage offers over a given threshold. I now turn to examine how a variant of an earnings cut-off can also be a key component of a human-capital-based approach to skill-focused permanent immigration policy.

Designing a Skill-Focused Immigration Policy II: Points System Design

In this section, I take it as given that the government wants to pursue a skills-focused immigration policy. My goal is to see how human capital theory can underpin the design of such a policy. The analysis proceeds in two steps. I first show how the immigration authority can use the combination of an estimated immigrant earnings function and a chosen earnings cut-off to develop a simple points system. I then consider how the variables to be included in the earnings function — and thus the points categories — should be chosen so as to minimize earnings prediction errors and maximize the *ex post* average quality of the immigrant pool for any given earnings cut-off.

Human Capital-Based Earnings Functions and a Points System

Putting aside the numerous provisos discussed in the previous sections, I now take it as given that a potential immigrant's net value to the economy rises with their earning power *(w)*, and that there is a cut-off earnings level *(w*)* below which the immigrant's net value is expected to be negative. The central problem that the immigration authority faces in designing an immigration system that selects the right applicants is that it does not know what post-immigration earnings will be, and thus, which applicants should be accepted. To predict earnings, the immigration authority can estimate an earnings function using earnings and skill data on past immigrants and (possibly) native-born workers. Suppose, for example, that the following earnings function is estimated using ordinary least squares,

(6) $\ln w = \beta_0 + \beta_1 Schooling + \beta_2 Experience + u$,

where u is a normally distributed disturbance term with variance given by σ^2. Noting that the log of the predicted wage is equal to predicted value of the log wage plus half the estimated variance of the regression ($\hat{\sigma}^2$), we obtain an expression for the log of the predicted wage,

(6') $\ln \hat{w} = \dfrac{\hat{\sigma}^2}{2} + \hat{\beta}_0 + \hat{\beta}_1 Schooling + \hat{\beta}_2 Experience$.

Together with the cut-off predicted earnings level, $w*$, this estimated equation provides an obvious basis for a simple points system. If we arbitrarily choose the 100 points as the cut-off, say, we can easily calculate the points that should be given per year of schooling and per year of experience from the coefficient of the right-hand-side of a rearranged equation (6')

$$(6")$$

$$\left(\frac{100}{\ln w* - \frac{\hat{\sigma}^2}{2} - \hat{\beta}_0}\right)(\ln w* - \hat{\beta}_0) = \left(\frac{100\hat{\beta}_1}{\ln w* - \frac{\hat{\sigma}^2}{2} - \hat{\beta}_0}\right)Schooling$$

$$+ \left(\frac{100\hat{\beta}_2}{\ln w* - \frac{\hat{\sigma}^2}{2} - \hat{\beta}_0}\right)Experience.$$

All applicants with combinations of schooling and experience that yield at least 100 points have predicted earnings at or above the cut-off level and should be admitted (see Figure 3).

A drawback with this simple points system is that it does not allow for rising earnings with length of time in the country — that is, it does not allow for economic assimilation. One approach to remedying this defect is to set a cut-off for the present discounted value of earnings rather than the

Figure 3: Who Gets In? A Simple Points System

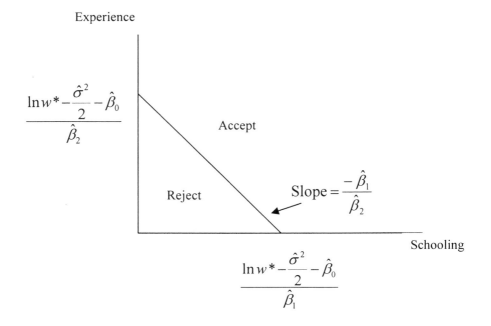

John McHale

level of initial earnings and adding a "years since migration" (YSM) variable to the earnings regression.[10] Equation (7) provides an example of such a minimally extended estimated earnings function,

$$(7) \quad \ln \hat{w} = \frac{\hat{\sigma}^2}{2} + \hat{\beta}_0 + \hat{\beta}_1 Schooling + \hat{\beta}_2 Experience + \hat{\beta}_3 YSM.$$

With a $T+1$ year horizon $(0, 1, \ldots T)$, a discount rate δ applied to future earnings, and a cut-off present discounted value of Z^*, the point allocations are now given by the relevant coefficients on the right hand side of equation (8).

$$(8)$$

$$
\left(\frac{100}{\ln Z^* - \dfrac{\hat{\sigma}^2}{2} - \hat{\beta}_0 - \ln(1 + e^{\hat{\beta}_3 - \delta} + \ldots + e^{(\hat{\beta}_3 - \delta)T})} \right) \left(\ln Z^* - \frac{\hat{\sigma}^2}{2} - \hat{\beta}_0 - \ln(1 + e^{\hat{\beta}_3 - \delta} + \ldots + e^{(\hat{\beta}_3 - \delta)T}) \right)
$$

$$
= \left(\frac{100\hat{\beta}_1}{\ln Z^* - \dfrac{\hat{\sigma}^2}{2} - \hat{\beta}_0 - \ln(1 + e^{\hat{\beta}_3 - \delta} + \ldots + e^{(\hat{\beta}_3 - \delta)T})} \right) Schooling
$$

$$
+ \left(\frac{100\hat{\beta}_2}{\ln Z^* - \dfrac{\hat{\sigma}^2}{2} - \hat{\beta}_0 - \ln(1 + e^{\hat{\beta}_3 - \delta} + \ldots + e^{(\hat{\beta}_3 - \delta)T})} \right) Experience.
$$

All else being equal, a larger coefficient on the *YSM* variable in equation (8) will raise the number of points given for both schooling and experience.[11] In effect, the immigration authority is anticipating how earnings will rise with time in the country, and adjusting the points given accordingly.

---

[10]The *YSM* variable could also be interacted with the other human capital variables to allow the return to human capital to vary with time spent in the country.

[11]The relative number of points for schooling and experience is unchanged, however. This is not necessarily true once we allow the returns to school and experience to change with *YSM.*

Points for What?

Specifying the earnings function. The foregoing analysis shows how an earnings function can be used as the basis for a points system. But it does not tell us *which* variables should be included in the earnings function, and what the sources of points should be. To answer this question note that a more fully specified earnings function will typically produce an immigrant pool with a higher average quality *for* any given projected earnings cut-off. To see this intuitively, suppose that years of schooling is the only variable in the earnings function. Some of the people who will qualify based on their schooling will turn out to have earnings that are below the cut-off earnings level, while some of the people who are rejected based on their lack of schooling would have had earnings above this level. That is, there will be mistakes due to earning projection errors: acceptances of some applicants that should be rejected and rejections of some applicants that should be accepted.

Now suppose that experience is added to the earnings function. One likely reason for why those who qualify based on schooling alone turn out to have low earnings is that they lack experience. On the other hand, a likely reason for why those who do not qualify based on schooling alone would have had high earnings if they had been admitted is their substantial experience. Thus, adding experience to the earnings function (and thus the points system) can reduce both types of projection errors and consequently lead to an immigrant pool with a higher *ex post* average quality.[12] Other

---

[12]This discussion glides over some of the difficulties in minimizing projection errors. Projection errors have various causes: biased parameter estimates due to specification errors; mismeasured values for the explanatory variables used for the prediction; sampling variation in the parameter estimates; and random variation in earnings. I assume that the first two of these sources of error are not present; that is, unbiased estimates of the parameter values are available as are accurate measures of potential immigrant's schooling, experience, etc. The third and fourth sources of error are assumed to be present, however. Adding extra variables to the regression model will tend to increase the variance of the parameter estimates but reduce the variance of the regression. Thus, adding variables to the regression involves a trade-off from the viewpoint of minimizing prediction errors. (I make the strong assumption that there is negligible multicollinearity between the explanatory variables. If multicollinearity is present, the parameter estimates will be biased unless the regression model is correctly specified. This will obviously complicate the task of specifying the earnings regression as the additional trade-off between

John McHale

direct measures of human capital — language skills or occupation — can be similarly added to further minimize mistakes.

For what other human capital characteristics should someone get points? The immigration authority will do better in its selection exercise if it recognizes its comparative disadvantage in identifying immigrant skill. But who knows better? The obvious candidates are the potential immigrants themselves, as well as those who have an independent interest in their capabilities. Therefore, the points system can be improved by understanding the process by which people select to emigrate, and by piggybacking on the related selection efforts of others who are better informed.

Self-selection. Borjas (1987) has shown that the quality of immigrants with given observable human capital characteristics (schooling, experience, etc.) depends partly on the degree of earnings inequality in the origin country relative to earnings inequality in the destination country.[13] A highly skilled Brazilian may be able to do quite well in highly unequal Brazil relative to how they do in Canada with its progressive tax structure and generous public benefits. It is less-skilled Brazilians that find Canada relatively more attractive. The lower returns to skill available in India will, in contrast, make Canada a relatively more attractive destination for highly skilled Indians, whose rewards at home are limited by a more compressed income distribution. This suggests that country of origin could be included among the explanatory variables in the earnings regression.[14]

Of course, such country-specific points raise the specter of origin-based discrimination. Canada and Australia, for example, now look back in embarrassment at how they operated blatantly discriminatory policies up to as recently as the 1960s (Canada) and 1970s (Australia). Yet although explicit country-specific criteria are now frowned upon, discrimination can

---

parameter bias and the parameter estimate sampling variation must be considered. In general, allowing for multicollinearity — and thus the risk of omitted variable bias — should lead us to a more inclusive specification of the earnings regression.)

[13]Knowledge of the origin country can also be useful in predicting earnings when the quality/transferability of schooling or experience differs across countries (see, e.g., Friedberg, 2000).

[14]A less overtly discriminatory alternative is to give points based on origin-country characteristics rather than directly for the countries. Possible characteristics include measures of income inequality and per capita income.

come in more subtle ways, as when limited resources allocated to deal with processing backlogs for particular countries, when country caps are placed on visa availability,[15] or when language skill requirements are used as a barrier to people with dissimilar cultural backgrounds.

Selection by others. Policymakers have tools other than country-specific discrimination for distinguishing the quality of applicants with identical observable human capital characteristics. One important tool is to rely on the selection efforts of others who have better knowledge of the applicant. Does the applicant have *a formal job offer?* If yes, then the employer is likely to have identified certain skill traits. What are the applicant's *earnings in their home country?* Home-country employers will have to pay more to attract and keep more skilled workers. As an example, the recently introduced pilot for a points-based skilled migrant program in the United Kingdom gives points based on origin-country earnings. (Interestingly, the point allocations are country specific, introducing a possible avenue for country-of-origin-based discrimination.) Does the applicant have a *highly educated spouse?* It is well-known that that the better educated tend to match together, which sometimes goes under the rather impersonal heading of "positive assortive mating" (see, e.g., Becker, 1973). Has the individual ever been *admitted to an educational institution* in the country? This can be an indicator of the quality/compatibility of their education, and can also allow the immigration authority to free ride on educational institutions' selection processes.

To sum up, human capital theory suggests various variables that should be included in the underlying earnings regression for the points system. Some of the variables relate directly to observable measures of human capital accumulation. But additional variables are suggested by both the process by which an individual selects to emigrate, and the related selection problems faced by the immigration authority and other actors interested in the quality of applicant — potential employers, past employers, spouse, etc. The better the final earnings regression is at predicting future earnings, the higher the *ex post* average earnings will be for any given earnings cut-off.

---

[15]For example, the US limits each country to 7% of available employment preference visas. This is a binding constraint on large countries such as India.

Comparing Skill-Focused Immigration Policies

In what has been called the most significant change in Canadian immigration policy in 25 years, the Immigration and Refugee Protection Act came into effect on June 28, 2002. Table 1 summarizes the changes to the points system for permanent skilled immigration as a result of the legislation and associated regulations. The table reveals a fundamental shift in the focus of the skill stream. Shortage-occupation-related points have been eliminated,[16] and the emphasis has shifted to observed attributes that indicate flexible skill sets for an economy with ever-shifting skill demands.

Before turning to a comparison of Canadian skilled immigration policy with the policies of other countries, I first briefly consider how well the new points system has been designed in light of the discussion in the previous section. Of course, it is not possible to say much in the absence of a well-specified immigrant earnings function; however, the list of variables for which points are allocated is broadly consistent with an earnings prediction framework. The vast empirical literature on earnings functions that has followed Mincer (1958) has shown the explanatory power of education, experience, and language skills — all of which are emphasized in the new system. Our discussions of selection effects and relative quality of foreign-acquired education and experience also broadly support the granting of points for a formal jobs offer, spousal education, post-secondary education (applicant or spouse) in Canada, and past work experience (applicant or spouse) in Canada.[17]

Some of the design features are harder to understand, however. For example, providing the full available ten points for age to anyone between

---

[16]To be classed as a skilled worker, an applicant must still be in an occupation listed as either Skilled type 0 Manager Occupation or Skill levels A or B on the National Occupations List.

[17]The new Canadian system also has the advantage of a relatively unified design. In contrast, the Australian points system consists of a number of different programs, each aimed at a particular type of applicant — applicants with family in Australia, applicants being sponsored by an Australian employer, applicants with Australian postsecondary qualifications, etc. The Canadian system also gives special credit for these applicant characteristics, but does so more compactly under the adaptability/job offer points factors.

Table 1: New and Old Skilled Worker Points-Based Selection Grids

New System		Maximum Points
Education		25
Language		24
First	16	
Second	8	
Experience		21
Age		10
Arranged employment		10
Adaptability		10
Spouse's education	3–5	
1-year auth. work in Canada	5	
2-years postsecondary study in Canada	5	
Points received under arranged employment	5	
Family relationship in Canada	5	
Total		100
Initial Pass Mark		75

Old System		Maximum Points
Education/training factor (occupation-specific)		18
Education		16
Language		15
First	9	
Second	6	
Occupation (based on General Occupations List)		10
Age		10
Arranged employment		10
Work experience		8
Relative in Canada		5
Demographic Factor	(subject to change)	8
Total		100
Pass Mark		70

John McHale

21 and 49, with two points lost for every year below 21 or over 49, seems a rather more blunt instrument than we would expect based on an estimated earnings function. Given the cost of state pension and health-care entitlements for retirees, it is unlikely that someone in their late forties yields that same discounted benefit as someone in their early twenties. Other examples of dubious design features include the credit for bilingualism, which has the hallmark of politics rather than economics, and the curious requirement of substantial years of full-time study for those targeted as skilled tradespersons, whose skill training is presumably gotten primarily on the job. Although the large credit given for education is consistent with the human capital approach, the way points are credited across different levels of education achievement are also unlikely to find much basis in a human-capital-based earnings regression. The greatest number of points for the university educated is granted to someone with a master's or a PhD (25), followed by someone with two or more bachelor's degrees (22), and then someone with a two-year university degree (20). Thus, someone with a single four-year bachelor's degree curiously gets the same education-based points as someone with a two-year degree.

The initial pass mark in the new points system has been set at 75. Although it is at the discretion of the immigration minister to change this cut-off, this initial cut-off seems high given the substantial numbers that have been entering Canada in the skill stream in recent years and when judged by the kind of people who will now be excluded. For example, a 22-year-old applicant (10 points), with a four-year computer science degree (20 points), one year's experience (15 points), high proficiency in English but no proficiency in French (16 points) would score only 61 points. Even with a formal job offer or maximum adaptability points based on a Canadian education/experience and a university-educated spouse, this applicant would score only 73 points and be rejected.[18]

Although one can quibble with the design of the new points system, Canada has (with Australia) pioneered the development of skill-focused immigration in recent decades. More recently, however, Canada has faced increasing competition in the market for internationally mobile skill.

---

[18]On the other hand, the fact that the cut would be made by a 45 year-old (10 points), with a two-year degree (20 points), four years experience (21 points), high proficiency in English and moderate proficiency in French (24 points), and no formal job offer or adaptability points (0 points), hints that the problem lies with the relative point allocations as well with the rather stringent cut-off.

Table 2 provides a broad overview of skill- focused permanent immigration policies in Canada and four "competitor" countries.[19] Australia revamped its points system in 1999, and has been increasing the absolute number and relative share of skilled workers. Under the shadow of an aging population and massive unfunded social insurance liabilities, the Schroder government in Germany pushed through an immigration reform bill with a points-based system for permanent skilled immigration — in spite of Germany's structural unemployment problem and a looming election. The United Kingdom introduced its Highly Skilled Migrant Programme (HSMP) in early 2002 on a pilot basis as its (tentative) effort to compete for skilled workers. Finally, in the early 1990s the United States increased the number of employment preference permanent immigration visas, though permanent immigration policy still retains a family unification focus.

These reforms contain a number of innovative design elements that should be of interest to Canadian policymakers. Efforts to incorporate information on earnings where applicants have job offers and also information on past earnings are interesting in the context of the discussion of predicting wages in the earlier section. The proposed German policy will use direct cut-offs for certain highly skilled workers with job offers, with a Canadian-style points system being used for skilled workers without job offers. In contrast, the UK system gives points for past earnings.[20]

The new German and UK system also emphasize speed. Processing backlogs for applicants to the Canadian skill-based points system, especially for high-volume countries such as China and India, can hold up applications for years. Approval time and bureaucratic ease are important instruments in competition for the most sought-after workers. A positive element of the new law that should diminish the significance of slow processing is that the ambiguity which had previously existed on the per-missability of applying for permanent status while working in Canada under a temporary work visa has been removed under the new rules. Status change is now clearly allowed, allowing the most sought-after workers to

---

[19]Much of this competition is quite recent indeed: Germany's program was only signed into law in June of 2002 and scheduled to begin operating in 2003; and the UK' s Highly Skilled Migrant Programme (HSMP) went into effect on a pilot basis at the beginning of 2002.

[20]Poorer countries, which tend to pay lower wages at given skill levels, receive the available points at lower pound sterling earnings level than richer countries.

come on a temporary visa and work while waiting for their permanent residency application to be processed.

Canada's policy seems less well competitively positioned for attracting *temporary* skilled migrants (see Table 3). Canada's system of Employment Authorizations, with its requirement for a labour market test or "validation" by Human Resources Development Canada (HRDC) to ensure that the job opening could not be filled by a domestic worker, is an impediment to fast moving recruitment in a competitive talent market. In contrast, Australia has shifted the focus of its long-stay temporary employment visas from showing an absence of harm to domestic workers to showing positive effects on such factors as trade and competitiveness. Employers can also pre-qualify for a fixed or even unlimited number of imported workers in advance. The German "Green Card" program for information technology (IT) professionals has placed great stress on speed and un-bureaucratic procedures to give it a competitive edge despite the less widespread knowledge of the German language. The system also incorporates earning thresholds for job offers, with sufficiently high earnings compensating for the absence of high-level formal qualifications. The UK's work permit program, though requiring a labour market test in general, has made exceptions for a range of "shortage occupations", predominantly in engineering, IT, and health care. Applicants in these occupations can be processed quite quickly. Of potentially most concern to Canada, the US government responded to intensive lobbying by high-tech industries in the late 1990s by dramatically increasing the availability of H-lB visas for professional workers.[21] H-lB employers are not subject to a labour market test by the Department of Labor, but must "attest" that the worker is being offered the prevailing wage and thus is not adversely affecting domestic workers.

How should Canada respond to increased competition? If the government really believes in the benefits of skill-focused immigration, the most obvious shortcoming in current policy is on the temporary migration side. Though it would undoubtedly encounter political opposition, consideration

---

[21]The H-1B visa was introduced with an annual cap of 65,000 in the early 1990s. The cap first became binding in September of the 1997 fiscal year. The cap bound even earlier (May) of the following year, spurring industry lobbying efforts to pass legislation to expand the cap. Legislation passed in 1998 expanded the cap to 115,000 for 1999 and 2000, 107,500 for 2001, before returning to 65,000 in 2002. But as IT skill shortages continued to get worse, legislation passed to relax the caps still further: 195,000 for 2001 to 2003, before returning to 65,000 in 2004.

Table 2: Skilled-Focused Permanent Migration Programs in Selected Countries

	Canada	Australia	Germany	UK	US
Program	*Independent skilled workers program*	*Skill migration (multiple programs[a])*	*New immigration law (not scheduled to go into effect until 2003)*	*Highly skilled migrant program[b] (introduced on pilot basis in January 2002)*	*Employment-based Preferences (permanent residency)*
Number (% of total) 1995 2000	81,000 (38%) 118,000 (52%)	24,100 (29%) 44,730 (56%)	… …	… …	85,300 107,000
Cap	No	No	No	No	Yes (140,000)
Points system	Yes	Yes[c]	Yes	Yes	No
Labour market test	No	No	No	No	Yes (with exceptions)
Selection criteria	Age, language, education, experience, job offer, adaptability	Age, language, education, occupation,[d] experience	(i) Highly skilled professionals with job offers: qualifications and earnings; (ii) workers without job offers: points system	past earnings[e], education, experience, prof. achievement	Job offer (certification from the Department of Labor of no adverse impact on domestic workers required in most cases[f])
Leading recipient countries in 2000	China (23%) India (10%) Pakistan (8%) Korea (4%)	UK (15%) S. Africa (14%) India (10%) Indonesia (9%)	Not applicable	Not applicable	India (15%) China (13%) Philip. (10%) Canada (7%)

John McHale

Notes to Table 2:

a Included programs (number in 2000/01): employer nominations (7,510); business skills (7,360), distinguished talents (230); skilled independent (22,380); skilled Australia sponsored (7,200); and 1 November onshore (60).

b This program is not strictly designed for permanent migration. Initial acceptance is for a period of one year. The applicant can then apply to have the visa extended for further three years. At the end of the four years, a migrant wishing to remain in the United Kingdom permanently can apply for permanent residence or "settlement". This route to permanent residency is also available to work permit holders, so the difference between the two programs as a means to permanent residency should not be exaggerated. A key difference, however, is that those entering under the HSMP are not tied to a particular employer.

c A new points system was introduced in July 1999. A new category for skilled independent overseas students was added in July 2001. Applicants with Australian qualifications that apply within six months of completing their studies are exempt from the work experience requirement. No points test applies to the employer nomination stream, though candidates must meet basic requirements.

d Occupation must be on the Skilled Occupations List (SOL).

e Points based on past earnings are country-specific, with poorer countries tending to receive more points for a given level of pound sterling earnings. For example, someone from Canada would need to have earned £250,000 to receive the maximum 50 points in this category, whereas someone from India would need to have earned £90,000.

f There are five preference categories: (E1) priority workers (28.6%), certification not required; (E2) professionals holding advanced degrees (28.6%), certification required; (E3) professional holding bachelor's degrees and other workers (28.6%), certification required; (E4) special immigrants (7.1%); and (E5) employment creation investors (7.1%), must invest between $0.5 million and $1 million depending on geographic area and create at least ten full-time jobs.

Table 3: Skilled-Focused Temporary Migration Programs in Selected Countries

	Canada	Australia	Germany	UK	US
Program	*Employment authorization — temporary residents*	*Temporary (long stay) business entry*	*IT specialists temporary relief program ("Green Card")[a]*	*Work permits*	*H-1B — Specialty professional workers*
Number (2000/01)	86,225[b]	40,493[c]	8,000[d]	82,437[e]	201,079[f]
Job offer required	Yes	Yes	Yes	Yes	Yes
Cap	No	No	Yes (20,000 total)	No	Yes (195,000 per year)[g]
Labour market test	Yes (validation required by HRDC; exception for software developers)	No (but employers must show that the temporary entrant will provide a "benefit to Australia")[h]	Yes (employment agency checks EU worker available and qualifications / remuneration)	Yes (waived for "shortage occupations")	No (but employers must "attest" to no adverse affect on US workers)
Tied to employer	Yes	Yes	No[i]	Yes[j]	Yes
Length of visa (max.)	3 years	4 years	3 years	5 years	3 years
Renewable	Yes	Yes	Yes (5 year max.)	Yes (10 year max.)	Yes (6 year max.)
Spousal employment	No[k]	Yes	Yes (after 1 year)	Yes	No
Possibility of permanent settlement	Yes (under new law)	Yes	No (but possible under new law)	Yes (after four years)	Yes[l]

Notes to Table 3:

a Program was introduced in August 2000 to relieve perceived shortages in the IT sector. Germany also operates a much larger work permit system (333,381 in 2000). The aim of the "Green Card" system was to make the recruitment of IT professionals easier through un-bureaucratic, rapid and transparent procedures (McLaughlan and Salt, 2002).

b Number is for 2000. The stock of temporary workers with employment authorizations on December 31, 2000 was 88,962 (Citizenship and Immigration Canada, 2001).

c Number is for 2000/01 and includes 3,411 independent executives establishing businesses in Austrlia. In addition, 3,438 visas were issued to medical practitioners and their dependents and 1,738 visas were issued to people joining educational and research institutions. The estimated stock of long stay business entrants as of June 30, 2001 was 56,000. The median duration of stay of visa holders as of that data was just under six months.

d Number is for the period from August 2000 to June 2001.

e Includes only out-of-country work permit approvals (McLaughlan and Salt, 2002).

f Number is for Fiscal Year 2001 (which begins in October 2000). A further 130,127 petitions were approved for continuing employment (INS 2002).

g Renewals do not count towards the cap.

h The benefit can come in various ways: create or maintain employment; expand trade; develop links with international markets; or improve competitiveness. Emphasis is on positive effects rather than the absence of harm.

i Switching employers is possible without further labour market test. Five-year limit applies to combined employments.

j Employees switching employers must have new employer apply for a new permit.

k Spouses can apply for employment authorization on their own merit. Under the Spousal Employment Authorization Program, spouses of workers in engineering, management, technical and skilled grades can receive an authorization without a labour market test (McLaughlan and Salt, 2002).

l Visa holders can apply for permanent residency while they are in H-1B status. Extensions to H-1B status are possible in one-year increments for those whose visa expires when an application for permanent residency has been pending for more than one year (McLaughlan and Salt, 2002).

should be given to eliminating the labour market test. This test could be replaced with an Australian-styled focus on positive benefits (with fast-turnaround) or possibly set a German-styled direct earnings threshold above which validation is automatic.[22]

Canada's Brain Drain: A Reality after all?

The government's policy challenge is not only to decide whether and how Canada should best compete for internationally mobile talent, but also how best to retain its own skilled workers. A reform such as the expansion of the H-IB program in the United States threatens Canada's long-standing policy-related advantage in the immigration market, and threatens to worsen any southbound "brain drain".

A recent paper by Ross Finnie (2001) provides a clear statement of an apparent emerging consensus about the seriousness of the Canadian brain drain problem, and what should be done about it (see also Helliwell,1999; and Zhao, Drew and Murray, 2000, for useful reviews of the available data). Finnie's argument can be summarized in four propositions: (i) the brain drain is not quantitatively large; (ii) it is concentrated in certain skilled occupations such as doctors and R&D workers; (iii) broadly based tax reductions are a very blunt instrument for stemming the brain drain given the numbers involved; and (iv) more targeted approaches that allow competitive remuneration for the affected groups is a more efficient response.

I focus here on the first of Finnie's propositions — that the overall numbers leaving are small. Figure 4 shows the growing importance of the CUFTA/NAFTA related immigration reforms as measured by the annual numbers of visas granted to Canadians. The TN visa under NAFTA gives skilled Canadians with a US job offer relatively easy access to the US labour market. Provided that their occupation is on a rather extensive list of accepted professions and they meet a minimal educational standard for

---

[22]As temporary employer-specific migration can be a way station on the way to permanent migration — especially now that the new immigration law has cleared up the ambiguity about status change — more efficient temporary recruitment can improve the applicant pool for permanent migration as well.

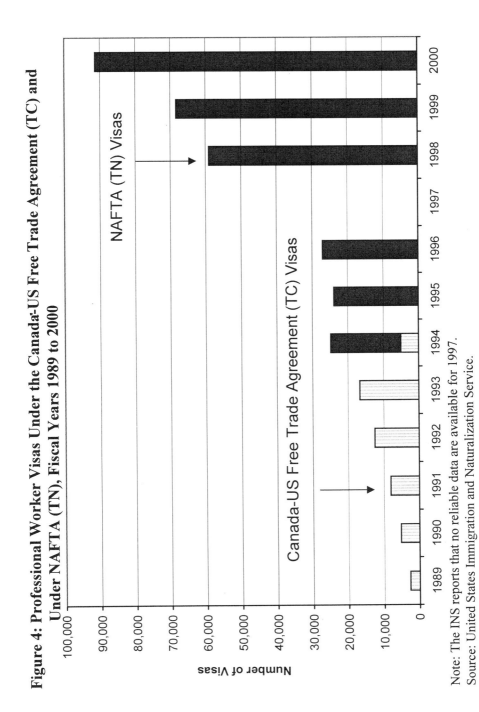

Figure 4: Professional Worker Visas Under the Canada-US Free Trade Agreement (TC) and Under NAFTA (TN), Fiscal Years 1989 to 2000

NAFTA (TN) Visas

Canada-US Free Trade Agreement (TC) Visas

Number of Visas

Note: The INS reports that no reliable data are available for 1997.
Source: United States Immigration and Naturalization Service.

their occupation (most often a bachelor's degree), the TN visa can be applied for at the border. Although it is valid for only one year it can be renewed indefinitely. Its great advantage is that it avoids the cumbersome labour market test of employment preference visas and even the employer attestation required for the H-IB visa. The figure shows a surge in TN visa grants in fiscal years 1998, 1999, and 2000. (More recent data are not yet available from the Immigration and Naturalization Service.)

A number of analysts have downplayed the importance of this surge in NAFTA visas, pointing, for example, to the fact that many of the visas may be used for very short stays. The reason that the TN numbers are not viewed as a cause for concern, however, is that they have not been confirmed in other datasets that are thought to give better measures of the stock of Canadian-born living in the United States. John Helliwell (1999), for example, has argued that the annual March supplement to the *Current Population Survey* in the United States gives a better measure of that stock. This survey includes all those who are resident in the United States for six months or more. Using this survey, Helliwell showed how the size of the Canadian-born population had continued its century-long downward trend through most of the 1990s.

Figure 5 shows US census estimates of the size of the Canadian-born population in the United States up to March 2002. Focusing on the period outside Helliwell's window (i.e., 1998–2002), there is some evidence of a surge in outflows in the late 1990s, leading to a significant increase in the size of this population over the course of the decade as a whole. The estimated number of Canadian-born in the United States was around 600,000 in 1998 — but had risen to over 740,000 in 2001, before falling back to 715,000 as the US economy soured in 2002. For the component of this population aged between 25 and 64 (about 65% of the total), roughly half have a university degree or better, suggesting substantial missing skill. Of course, these figures must be treated with caution as yearly estimates of population groups are subject to sampling error. However, much more reliable evidence from the 1-in-6 sample from the 1990 and 2000 decennial censuses also shows a reversal of the decade's long shrinkage in the size of this population during the 1990s, with an increase from roughly 740,000 at the time of the 1990 census to 821,000 at the time of the 2000 census. This increase, and its consistency with the late-decade surge in NAFTA-related visas, is a warning that Canada might have been losing reasonably large numbers to the United States in the late 1990s after all.

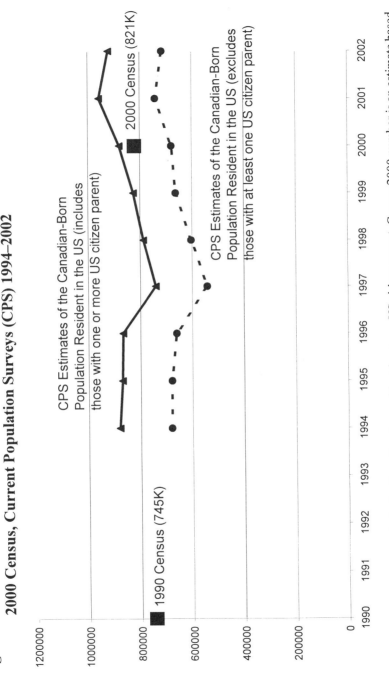

Figure 5: US Census Bureau Estimates of the US Resident Canadian-Born Population, 1990 Census, 2000 Census, Current Population Surveys (CPS) 1994–2002

Notes: Census numbers exclude the Canadian-born with at least one US citizen parent. Census 2000 number is an estimate based on a 1-in-6 sample.

Summary and Conclusions

As the paper has ranged over a number of issues related to skill-focused immigration policy in Canada and elsewhere, I try in this final section to summarize the main points and tie the pieces together. The paper posed a number of questions: What degree of skill focus is best from the standpoint of maximizing aggregate economic surplus given some allowable number of immigrants? Assuming that a skill-focused immigration policy is best, should the immigration policy be based on targeting particular occupations with apparent shortages or on predictions of long-term earnings potential? Assuming that a policy based on long-term earnings potential is best, how should a human capital-based points system be designed? In light of this "optimal design", how well does the recent reform of Canada's points system for skilled immigration compare? How do Canada's policies for skills-based permanent and temporary migration compare with policies in other countries following recent efforts by a number of countries to explicitly reform their immigration policies to compete for world's best talent? And how has Canada done recently in the international competition for its own domestically grown talent?

The paper began with a review of what I called the classic model of the immigration surplus based on constant returns to scale and competitive factor markets. A skill-focused immigration policy for an already human capital rich economy does not fare particularly well in this model. One surprising result that emerged for the case of a constant elasticity of substitution between skilled and unskilled workers is that the relative productivity of skilled workers has no bearing on the relative desirability of a skill-focused policy. Thus, the recent observed skill-biased technical change (see Acemoglu, 2002) does not strengthen the case for a skill-focused policy in this model. But various extensions to the classic model — a progressive fiscal system, specialized skills, and knowledge spillovers — do strengthen the case for selectively admitting skilled workers as a means of maximizing economic surplus.

Despite remaining doubts about the superiority of a skill-focused policy, the paper assumed such a policy is pursued and considered some basic design issues. After reviewing different concepts of shortage, I argued against occupational shortages as a basis for a permanent migration policy. The design of an alternative system based on predictions of long-term earnings was then considered in two steps. First, I showed how the combination of a human-capital-based earnings regression and a chosen earnings cut-off provides a consistent basis for a points system. Second, I argued that the earnings regression (and consequent points system) should be specified to minimize prediction errors and thus maximize the average quality of the applicant pool for any given chosen earnings cut-off.

The paper then turned to compare recent Canadian skilled immigration policy reforms both with the design principles that emerge in the third and fourth sections and also with policy reforms in other countries. I find that the broad direction of the reforms to Canada's points system for permanent skilled migration is consistent with the design principles. Although some of the details are puzzling (not least the high points cut-off), the new system is clearly designed to predict Canadian labour market success, utilizing both observable correlates of earning potential and the related selection decisions of interested other parties. A brief review of the immigration reforms in a number of Canada's OECD partners showed that the country is facing significantly greater competition in the market for mobile talent. Even though the United Kingdom and Germany have recently introduced or proposed policies for Canadian-style points systems with some interesting design features, Canada's reformed system compares quite well, though some competitor's policies might be better along such dimensions as using direct information on future and past earnings and on speed of processing.

The same positive assessment cannot be given for Canada's temporary migration policy. Although Canada does attract a substantial number of temporary workers, its system for selecting such workers — notably the rather cumbersome requirements for labour market validations — is probably a factor driving skilled migrants to other destinations. Here the government could learn from what other countries are doing. Examples of possible lessons include: employer attestations rather than labour market validations (US H-1B program); lists of shortage occupations that do not require labour market tests (UK Work Permits); employer-specific rather than employee-specific approvals (Australian Long-Stay Temporary Business Visas); and wage offer requirements rather than labour market test requirements (German Green Cards).

The last section took a very brief detour to consider how well Canada has been doing in the international competition for its domestically trained skilled workers. Here the paper questioned the emerging conventional wisdom that the "brain drain" to the United States is quantitatively small. Recent estimates of the size of the Canadian-born population in the United States are consistent with NAFTA-facilitated surge in emigration, though the size of the outflow should not be exaggerated. Although recent terrorism-related fears and the strong cyclical performance of the Canadian economy have probably eased outflow pressures considerably, Canadians cannot afford to be complacent about the country's capacity to attract and retain the most sought-after and mobile talent.

References

Acemoglu, D. (2002), "Technical Change, Inequality, and the Labor Market", *Journal of Economic Literature* 40(2), 7–72.

Altonji, J. and D. Card (1991), "The Effects of Immigration on the Labor Market Outcomes of Less Skilled Natives", in J. Abowd and R. Freeman (eds.), *Immigration, Trade, and the Labor Market* (Chicago: University of Chicago Press).

Arrow, K. and W. Capron (1959), "Dynamic Shortages and Price Rises: The Engineer-Scientist Case", *The Quarterly Journal of Economics* 73(2), 292–308.

Becker, G. (1973), "A Theory of Marriage: Part I", *Journal of Political Economy* 81(4), 813–846.

Bhagwati, J. and C. Rodriguez (1976), "Welfare-Theoretical Analysis of the Brain-Drain", *Journal of Development Economics* 2, 195–221.

Borjas, G. (1987), "Self-Selection and the Earnings of Immigrants", *The American Economic Review* 77, 531–553.

_____ (1994), "The Economics of Immigration", *Journal of Economic Literature* 32(4), 1667–1717.

_____ (1995), "The Economic Benefits of Immigration", *Journal of Economic Perspectives* 19(2), 3–22.

Borjas, G., R. Freeman and L. Katz (1996), "Searching for the Effect of Immigration in the Labor Market", *The American Economic Review* (Papers and Proceedings), 246–251.

Canada. Citizenship and Immigration Canada (2001), *Facts and Figures 2001: Immigration Overview* (Ottawa: Citizenship and Immigration Canada).

Card, D. (1990), "The Impact of the Mariel Boatlift on the Miami Labor Market", *Industrial Labor Relations Review* 43(2), 245–257.

Davis, D. and D. Weinstein (2002), "Technological Superiority and the Losses from Migration", NBER Working Paper No. 8971 (Cambridge, MA: National Bureau of Economic Research). Available at <http://www.nber.org/papers/w8971>.

Finnie, R. (2001), "The Brain Drain: Myth and Reality, What It Is and What Should be Done", *Choices* 7(6) (Institute for Research in Public Policy), 3–29.

Friedberg, R. (2000), "You Can't Take it with You? Immigrant Assimilation and the Portability of Human Capital", *Journal of Labor Economics* 18(2), 221–251.

Friedberg, R. and J. Hunt (1995), "The Impact of Immigrants on Host Country Wages, Employment, and Growth", *Journal of Economic Perspectives* 9(2), 23–44.

Green, A. and D. Green (1999), "The Economic Goals of Canada's Immigration Policy: Past and Present", *Canadian Public Policy/Analyse de Politiques* 25(4), 425–451.

Grubel, H. and A. Scott (1966), "The International Flow of Human Capital", *American Economic Review* 56(1/2), 268–274.

Helliwell, J. (1999), "Checking the Brain Drain: Evidence and Implications", *Policy Options* (Institute for Research in Public Policy), September, 6–17.

Johnson, H. (1967), "Some Economic Aspects of the Brain Drain", *Pakistan Development Review* 7, 379–411.

McLaughlan, G. and J. Salt (2002), *Migration Policies Towards Highly Skilled Foreign Workers*, Report to the United Kingdom Home Office. Available at <http://www.homeoffice.gov.uk/rds/pdfs2/migrationpolicies.pdf>.

Mincer, J. (1958), "Investment in Human Capital and Personal Income Distribution", *Journal of Political Economy* 66(4), 281–302.

National Research Council (1997), *The New Americans: Economic, Demographic, and Fiscal Effects of Immigration* (Washington, DC: The National Academy Press).

Rauch, J. (2001), "Business and Social Networks in International Trade", *Journal of Economic Literature* 39(4), 1177–1203.

Staiger, D., J. Spetz and C. Phibbs (1999), "Is there Monopsony in the Labor Market? Evidence from a Natural Experiment", NBER Working Paper No. 7258 (Cambridge, MA: National Bureau of Economic Research). Available at <http://www.nber.org/papers/w7258>.

Storesletten, K. (2000), "Sustaining Fiscal Policy through Immigration", *Journal of Political Economy* 108(2), 300–323.

Trefler, D. (1997), "Immigrants and Natives in General Equilibrium Trade Models", NBER Working Paper No. 6209 (Cambridge, MA: National Bureau of Economic Research). Available at <http://www.nber.org/papers/w6209>.

Zhou, J., D. Drew and T.S. Murray (2000), "Brain Drain and Brain Gain: The Migration of Knowledge Workers from and to Canada", *Education Quarterly Review* 6(3), 8–35.

The Potential Impacts of Immigration on Productivity in Canada

Alice Nakamura, Masao Nakamura
and W. Erwin Diewert

Introduction

Immigration has been an important source of population and labour force growth for Canada. Beaujot (2000) finds that over the period of 1901 to 1996, the total immigration of some 12 million persons and the estimated emigration of some six million produced a net population gain of six million. This represents a fifth of Canada's population growth over that period. By historical standards, immigration levels have been especially high in more recent years. For the 1951–91 period, net migration accounted

This research was funded by grants from the Social Sciences and Humanities Research Council of Canada (SSHRC). The authors thank Logan McLeod of Statistics Canada for carrying out computations with the master 1991 and 1996 Census of Canada data files. We also thank Susanto Basu, Charles Beach, Kevin Lang and Emi Nakamura for comments, and Julian Betts, Peter Kuhn and Arthur Sweetman for comments on an earlier workshop version. All opinions and any errors of fact or interpretation are the sole responsibility of the authors. The corresponding author is Alice Nakamura.

for about a quarter of population growth, and this proportion rose to 51% for the years 1991 to 1996.[1]

In many respects, Canadians seem to prefer immigrants who mirror their own behaviour patterns. Certainly some past immigration policies reflect this preference (see Green, 1995). However, when it comes to workforce qualifications and performance, the hopes and fears for where immigration will lead the nation stem from expectations that immigrants will do differently than the incumbent population. Earlier waves of immigrants to Canada achieved higher average earnings than the Canadian-born. It is widely believed that this is because they contributed skills and knowledge in scarce supply and were unusually hard working. Many Canadians would like the immigration program to continue to make this sort of contribution to Canadian economic development.

We show that more recent immigrants from the United States and United Kingdom have continued to enjoy relatively high earnings compared with the Canadian-born. However, more recent immigrants born outside the United States and United Kingdom seem not to have done as well on average. Moreover, the proportion of immigrants born outside the US and UK has risen over time, so their experiences have come to dominate the overall immigrant results.[2] Some Canadians fear that the lower earnings of more recent immigrants mean that they are less desirable to employers because their skills or work habits are less well-suited for Canada. There are fears that these newer immigrants will pull down the productivity of the nation, with productivity being viewed as an important long-run determinant of the standard of living. We present, and probe the implications of, empirical facts and alternative measures of labour input and productivity growth that are relevant to assessing these concerns.

Using 1991 and 1996 Canadian census data, we replicate and extend findings of others on the earnings outcomes of more recent immigrants to Canada.

---

[1]Information on the immigrant population and the Canadian immigration program can be found in Citizenship and Immigration Canada (1994, 2000, 2001) and in Informetrica (2000).

[2]Other studies include Baker and Benjamin (1994), Beach and Worswick (1994), Grant (1999), Li (2001), Nakamura and Nakamura (1992), and Nakamura *et al.* (1999).

We then explore how influxes of workers who do better, or worse, on average than the Canadian-born would be expected to affect the productivity growth of the nation. We show that the answer depends, in part at least, on the formula adopted for measuring productivity growth. The choice of a formula depends, in turn, on the concept of the true productivity growth that is embraced. A framework is developed for assessing the potential labour and total factor productivity growth effects of immigration.

Earnings of Immigrant vs. Canadian-Born Workers

In this section, we examine earnings and other employment outcomes for immigrant and Canadian-born workers. Our analysis is limited to those 25 to 64 years of age in the designated census year. We also restricted our immigrant data samples to those who were at least 15 at the time of immigration.[3] The immigrant data samples were divided into two place-of-birth categories: the United States or United Kingdom, and elsewhere. (We sometimes refer to these groups as "US/UK born" and "born elsewhere", respectively.) We also divided the immigrant data samples into three periods of immigration categories: (i) those who came before 1971, (ii) those who came in 1971–81, and (iii) those who came in 1981–90. We examine the average annual earnings of the Canadian-born and immigrant workers, and the averages for their hours of work in the census reference week, their weeks of work in the previous calendar year, and their estimated hourly and weekly rates of pay.[4]

---

[3]Kossoudji (1989) finds it is important to exclude, or separately examine, those who immigrated before age 15 in studies of the workplace assimilation of immigrants. Schaafsma and Sweetman (2001) also find that age at immigration seems to have substantial effects on the relative earnings of visible-minority immigrants.

[4]The census reference week is the week prior to when the designated census was conducted. Those immigrants included in the 1991 Census of Canada are persons who applied for and were approved for immigration, who came, and who were still alive and living in Canada as of when the 1991 census was taken. We did not include in this study those who reported that they were in Canada on a temporary basis or illegally.

Table 1 shows the country of birth composition of Canada's foreign-born population. We see that as of the 1991 Census of Canada, the proportion born in the United States or United Kingdom was 29.6% for those who came before 1971, 20.0% for those who came in 1971–80, and 9.8% for those who came in 1981–91. The Anglo-American inflow had dwindled by 1981–91 to less than the inflow from other parts of the world such as Asia.

The next eight tables document the employment outcomes for different immigrant groups and the Canadian-born.

The figures in Table 2 are for workers in all industries. These figures show that, in general, the US/UK born immigrants who came before 1981 as well as those who came in 1981–90 had higher average earnings than the Canadian-born.[5] We also see that the average earnings of the immigrants born elsewhere who came in 1981–90 (column 5) were considerably lower than for the Canadian-born.[6]

Is it a problem that more recent immigrants born in countries other than the US and UK have lower average earnings than the Canadian-born? There are many aspects of that question that go beyond the scope of this paper. Here we confine our attention to the question of whether the lower average wages for some groups of immigrants might be an indication that they are dragging down the productivity of the nation. From this perspective, a key issue is whether the lower average wages reflect the reality that, in comparison with their Canadian-born counterparts, the work effort or qualifications of these immigrants provide lower average productive value to employers.

There is no direct evidence in the Census of Canada for 1991 or 1996 on work effort. However, there is information on the worker occupation, years of schooling, and certain personal attributes, including sex and visible-minority status that may be useful for assessing the potential

---

[5]The exception is that women born in the United States/United Kingdom who came in 1981–90 had lower earnings for the year than the Canadian-born women, although their average hourly wage rate was higher. These US/UK born women earned less for the year because they worked fewer weeks in 1990 and fewer hours per week.

[6]In our forthcoming monograph (listed in the references as Nakamura et al., 2003) we demonstrate that the findings based on the group mean value patterns presented in this paper are unchanged when multivariate methods are used.

Table 1: Percentage Distributions of Foreign-Born by Country of Birth for Three Periods of Immigration

| Country of Birth | Period of Immigration | | |
	Before 1971	1971–80	1981–91
United States (US)	5.4	6.7	4.3
Europe			
United Kingdom (UK)	24.2	13.3	5.5
Federal Republic of Germany	7.2	1.6	1.3
Italy	15.3	2.8	0.7
Portugal	3.0	6.2	2.7
Poland	4.6	1.1	6.3
USSR	3.9	0.8	0.9
Other Europe	23.8	9.9	7.1
Asia			
Middle East and Western Asia	0.9	3.0	8.1
Southern Asia	1.6	8.4	9.1
Hong Kong	0.6	4.0	7.8
Peoples' Republic of China	1.9	4.0	5.8
Philippines	0.5	4.6	5.4
Viet Nam	0.0	4.5	5.5
Other East/South East Asia	0.8	4.9	6.3
Africa	1.6	5.9	6.1
Central and South America, Caribbean and Bermuda	4.0	16.8	16.2
Other	0.6	1.4	1.0
Total	100.0	100.0	100.0

Source: Based on the 1991 Census Public Use Sample data for individuals, available from Statistics Canada.

Table 2: Mean Values for All Industries

	US/UK Born			Born Elsewhere	
	Native-Born	Came before 1981	Came in 1981–90	Came before 1981	Came in 1981–90
Men 25–64 who worked in 1990					
Annual earnings ($)	35,275	47,456	42,727	35,935	24,524
Weekly earnings ($)	791	1,010	995	814	605
Hourly earnings ($)	17.64	22.53	22.98	18.11	13.27
Weeks of work in 1990	46	48	47	46	42
Hours of work per week	38	38	40	36	34
Sample size	133,864	4,153	639	16,102	6,739
Women 25–64 who worked in 1990					
Annual earnings ($)	21,010	23,818	20,116	21,440	15,813
Weekly earnings ($)	503	534	508	511	422
Hourly earnings ($)	14.33	15.37	16.11	14.26	10.78
Weeks of work in 1990	44	45	41	44	40
Hours of work per week	29	28	27	30	27
Sample size	111,764	3,832	732	12,000	5,672

Source: Based on the 1991 Census Public Use Sample data for individuals, available from Statistics Canada.

productivity relevance of the lower wage rates of more recent immigrants born outside the United States and United Kingdom.

The main patterns of interest in Table 2 for workers in all industries show up as well for each of the 11 major industry groups. This can be seen, for example, for the finance, real estate and business services industries in Table 3; for the manufacturing industries in Table 4; and for the retail trade industries in Table 5.

The 1991 census data reveal that, in high-earning and low-earning industries alike, the immigrants born in the US or UK had higher average annual earnings and hourly wage rates than the Canadian-born, with the

Alice Nakamura, Masao Nakamura and W. Erwin Diewert

Table 3: Finance, Real Estate and Business Services Industries Mean Values

	US/UK Born			Born Elsewhere	
	Native-Born	Came before 1981	Came in 1981–90	Came before 1981	Came in 1981–90
Men 25–64 who worked in 1990					
Annual earnings ($)	44,209	53,243	52,189	43,113	29,486
Weekly earnings ($)	943	1,117	1,133	979	656
Hourly earnings ($)	21.96	27.91	24.35	21.49	16.12
Weeks of work in 1990	47	48	47	48	44
Hours of work per week	39	39	40	37	36
Sample size	13,867	650	115	1,547	861
Women 25–64 who worked in 1990					
Annual earnings ($)	23,245	27,212	23,125	25,739	20,271
Weekly earnings ($)	532	589	647	569	499
Hourly earnings ($)	14.92	17.15	14.01	17.18	13.17
Weeks of work in 1990	45	46	41	46	42
Hours of work per week	30	30	27	32	29
Sample size	15,903	610	127	1,403	909

Source: Based on the 1991 Census Public Use Sample data for individuals, available from Statistics Canada.

Table 4: Manufacturing Industries Mean Values

	US/UK Born			Born Elsewhere	
	Native-Born	Came before 1981	Came in 1981–90	Came before 1981	Came in 1981–90
Men 25–64 who worked in 1990					
Annual earnings ($)	35,757	47,746	44,402	35,811	24,199
Weekly earnings ($)	782	985	977	803	587
Hourly earnings ($)	16.83	21.73	20.49	17.38	12.18
Weeks of work in 1990	47	49	48	47	43
Hours of work per week	36	37	39	35	32
Sample size	25,320	872	134	4,237	1,722
Women 25–64 who worked in 1990					
Annual earnings ($)	21,280	26,240	23,362	18,975	14,924
Weekly earnings ($)	516	563	498	461	406
Hourly earnings ($)	11.85	13.32	11.66	10.41	8.68
Weeks of work in 1990	44	46	45	44	40
Hours of work per week	30	32	30	29	28
Sample size	9,827	286	59	2,342	1,137

Source: Based on the 1991 Census Public Use Sample data for individuals, available from Statistics Canada.

Alice Nakamura, Masao Nakamura and W. Erwin Diewert

Table 5: Retail Trade Industries Mean Values

	US/UK Born			Born Elsewhere	
	Native-Born	Came before 1981	Came in 1981–90	Came before 1981	Came in 1981–90
Men 25–64 who worked in 1990					
Annual earnings ($)	28,979	35,319	34,898	30,347	20,874
Weekly earnings ($)	631	724	755	649	550
Hourly earnings ($)	14.04	16.17	16.75	14.20	11.67
Weeks of work in 1990	47	49	46	48	41
Hours of work per week	39	39	36	40	36
Sample size	11,810	242	46	1,392	688
Women 25–64 who worked in 1990					
Annual earnings ($)	15,077	15,632	15,646	17,812	13,354
Weekly earnings ($)	375	376	437	439	351
Hourly earnings ($)	10.59	11.79	11.37	13.29	8.51
Weeks of work in 1990	43	45	39	45	39
Hours of work per week	27	25	25	30	29
Sample size	13,073	444	77	1,325	597

Source: Based on the 1991 Census Public Use Sample data for individuals, available from Statistics Canada.

exception sometimes of the women who came in 1981–90. On the other hand, the men and women who were born elsewhere and came in 1981–90 consistently had average earnings below their Canadian-born counterparts. Thus, the higher earnings of the US or UK born immigrants and the lower earnings of the more recent immigrants born outside the United States and United Kingdom seem to be an economy-wide phenomena.

Differences in earnings are often thought to reflect differences in schooling. Certainly, more schooling can often raise the productive value of a worker to employers.

The mean values for years of schooling for the different groups of workers are shown in Table 6 for all industries as well as for the three industry groups for which earnings results were shown in Tables 3 through 5. We see that male workers had more schooling than the corresponding groups of female workers, and their earnings averages are consistently higher. Both male and female workers in the high-earnings finance, real estate and business services industry group generally had more schooling than those in manufacturing or retail trade. Schooling differences appear to be part of the explanation as well for the higher earnings of the US/UK born immigrants.

However, the immigrants born outside the US and UK who came in 1981–90 typically have more years of schooling than the Canadian-born workers. Yet these immigrants were found to have the *lowest* earnings averages.

Some observers have suggested that the reason immigrants born in countries other than the United States or United Kingdom have done less well in the Canadian labour market is that many belong to visible minorities. The suggestion is that they suffer from discrimination (see Li, 2001; Reitz, 2001; Beck, Reitz and Weiner, 2002). Table 7 shows that by 1981–90, visible minorities comprised 70 to 80% of the immigrants born outside the US and UK who worked. If we rank the immigrant columns in this table by how high the percent is of those belonging to visible minorities, going from the lowest to the highest, column 2 for the US/UK born who came before 1981 gets a rank of 1, column 3 for the US/UK born who came in 1981–91 gets a rank of 2, column 4 for those born elsewhere who came before 1981 gets a rank of 3, and a rank of 4 goes to those born elsewhere who came in 1981–90. For the men, this is the same ordering that results from ranking by the average annual earnings, going from highest to lowest. This pattern is less clear for women, but the column 5 average earnings figures for those born outside the United States and United Kingdom who came in 1981–90 are always the lowest. The pattern for men, at least, could be a symptom of labour market discrimination against visible minorities.

Table 6: Average Years of Schooling

| | US/UK Born | | | Born Elsewhere | |
	Native-Born	Came before 1981	Came in 1981–90	Came before 1981	Came in 1981–90
Men 25–64 who worked in 1990					
All	12.7	14.6	15.2	12.1	13.6
Finance, real estate and business services	15.5	14.9	15.6	14.8	15.5
Manufacturing	12.2	14.0	14.8	11.4	12.7
Retail trade	12.3	13.7	14.1	12.0	13.5
Women 25–64 who worked in 1990					
All	13.0	13.9	14.5	11.9	13.3
Finance, real estate and business services	13.3	13.9	14.3	13.9	14.6
Manufacturing	12.0	13.1	14.1	9.5	11.7
Retail trade	12.0	12.7	13.6	11.6	13.4

Source: Based on the 1991 Census Public Use Sample data for individuals, available from Statistics Canada.

Table 7: Percentage Belonging to a Visible Minority: Men and Women 25–64 Who Worked in 1990

| | US/UK Born | | | Born Elsewhere | |
	Native-Born	Came before 1981	Came in 1981–90	Came before 1981	Came in 1981–90
All men	1.2	1.9	6.9	39.8	71.3
Men in finance, real estate and business services	1.9	2.2	11.3	53.0	78.3
Men in manufacturing	0.8	1.9	4.5	39.1	72.0
Men in retail trade	1.2	2.1	10.9	47.0	79.7
All women	1.3	2.0	4.6	48.3	73.3
Women in finance, real estate and business services	1.5	2.1	4.7	59.2	79.5
Women in manufacturing	1.2	2.8	10.2	41.8	73.0
Women in retail trade	1.2	1.6	2.6	41.9	74.9

Source: Based on the 1991 Census Public Use Sample data for individuals, available from Statistics Canada.

The Potential Impacts of Immigration on Productivity in Canada

It is true, as can be seen from Table 7, that high proportions of the immigrants born elsewhere and who came in 1981–91 belong to visible minorities.[7]

However, Table 8 reveals that when we divide the immigrants into those belonging to a visible minority and those who do not, the earnings averages for the non-minority immigrants are still lower by a considerable amount for those born outside the US and UK who came in 1981–91.[8] Moreover, the average years of schooling of the non-minority immigrants born elsewhere who came in 1981–91 are higher than for the native-born.[9]

These results for the more recent non-minority immigrants born outside the United States and United Kingdom suggest that something other than, or in addition to, discrimination is responsible for the relatively low earnings of the more recent immigrants born elsewhere. Lacking convincing evidence of what that something else might be, in the following section where we introduce alternative measures of productivity growth we simply note that understanding the causes of the observed immigrant earnings

---

[7]In the 1991 census, persons were classified as to whether they belonged to a *visible minority* in Canada primarily by their responses on the ethnic origin question. However, the classification process also made use of responses on place of birth, mother tongue, and religion. The definition of visible minorities used in deciding on this classification process was developed by the Interdepartmental Working Groups on Employment Equity Data. Ten visible-minority subclassifications were also established (Black, South Asian, Chinese, Korean, Japanese, South East Asian, Filipino, Other Pacific Islanders, West Asian and Arab, and Latin American). However, we made no use of these subclassifications in the reported empirical work.

[8]We first presented this part of our results in Nakamura *et al.* (1999).

[9]In contrast, the corresponding visible-minority immigrants have somewhat less schooling on average than their native-born counterparts. This may explain why Baker and Benjamin find that "the immigrant advantage in this dimension has been declining over time — most dramatically, between 1981 and 1986" (1994, p. 376). The mean values for years of schooling that Baker and Benjamin report for native-born Canadians are 11.01 years for the 1971 census, 12.82 years for the 1981 census, and 13.76 years for the 1986 census. The corresponding values that they report for Canadian immigrants who arrived in the five years prior to each of the censuses are 12.51, 14.21 and 14.50, with visible minorities making up large portions of these more recent groups.

Table 8: All Industries Mean Values, Men and Women 25–64 Who Worked in 1990

	US/UK Born			Born Elsewhere	
	Native-Born	Came before 1981	Came in 1981–90	Came before 1981	Came in 1981–90
Annual earnings (1990$), men					
Non-minority	35,287	47,566	43,624	36,056	28,041
Minority	34,266	41,741	30,597	35,752	23,105
Years of schooling, men					
Non-minority	12.7	14.6	15.2	11.0	13.6
Minority	14.1	14.7	14.8	13.8	13.6
Sample size, men					
Non-minority	133,321	4,074	595	9,700	1,937
Minority	1,543	79	44	6,402	4,802
Annual earnings (1990$), women					
Non-minority	20,978	23,786	20,100	20,265	16,223
Minority	23,566	25,361	20,459	22,696	15,663
Years of schooling, women					
Non-minority	13.0	13.9	14.5	10.7	13.7
Minority	13.8	14.7	14.1	13.1	13.2
Sample size, women					
Non-minority	110,351	3,755	698	6,201	1,516
Minority	1,413	77	34	5,799	4,156

Source: Based on the 1991 Census Public Use Sample data for individuals, available from Statistics Canada.

patterns is relevant for assessing the impact of immigration on national productivity.

Tables 1 through 8 are based on Public Use Sample data from the 1991 Census of Canada. This data source can be obtained and used by anyone: a potentially important advantage in an emotionally charged area of policy choice. Moreover, the qualitative results we have presented hold when multivariate methods are used with the Public Use Sample data and other aspects of human capital are accounted for as well, including knowledge of English or French (see Nakamura *et al.*, 2003). However, one problem with these results could be that to protect the privacy of individuals, the Public Use Sample only contains records for a sample of the individuals covered in the master census files. Hence, the number of observations in some immigrant groups is small. Also, only partial information is provided for some variables. Of special relevance for this study, earnings are top-coded in the Public Use Sample data, meaning that all those in a region with incomes above a specified top-code value have their incomes reported as equal to that value.[10]

In Table 9 we compare key aspects of our 1991 Public Use Sample results with the results from special tabulations prepared by Statistics Canada for us and based on the master 1991 and 1996 census data files. The 1996 census results shown in Table 9 also allow us to check what happened in 1991–95 to those immigrants who arrived in 1981–90 and before, and to observe the situation of the immigrants who came in 1991–95.

Table 9 consists of three panels for men and three for women: one for annual earnings, one for years of schooling, and one giving the sample sizes. To facilitate comparisons, in the top two rows of each panel we again show the relevant annual earnings averages from Table 8. The next two rows are based on the special Statistics Canada tabulations from the master 1991 census data. The first of these rows is for non-minority workers while the second is for the visible-minority workers. The last two rows in each panel are based on the special Statistics Canada tabulations from the master 1996 census data file. Again, the first of these is for non-minority workers while the second is for those who belong to a visible minority.

The Table 9 results from the master file computations fully confirm the Table 8 Public Use Sample results. Moreover, the 1996 census figures reveal a further earnings drop relative to the native-born for those born elsewhere who came in 1991–95. This is despite the fact that, for those who do not belong to a visible minority, there is a rise in their average years

---

[10]The top-code amount differs from region to region depending on the population size of the demographic group and its employment rate and earnings distribution. Lower values are used in smaller places like the Atlantic provinces and for groups, like married women, that have lower percentages of higher earning workers.

Table 9: All Industries Mean Values: 1991 Public Use Sample Data versus 1991 and 1996 Full Census Data

		US/UK Born			Born Elsewhere		
	Canadian-Born	Came Before 1981	Came in 1981–90	Came in 1992–95	Came before 1981	Came in 1981–90	Came in 1992–95
Annual earnings, men 25–64							
1991 Public Use Sample[a]							
Non-minority	35,287	47,566	43,624		36,056	28,041	
Minority	34,266	41,741	30,597		35,752	23,105	
1991 Census Data[b]							
Non-minority	36,842	50,350	44,669		40,151	30,373	
Minority	36,462	42,447	31,906		38,566	24,639	
1996 Census Data[b]							
Non-minority	40,704	54,837	50,274	48,378	42,937	35,421	28,132
Minority	37,109	38,822	36,403	30,305	41,808	28,169	20,843
Years of schooling, men 25–64							
1991 Public Use Sample[a]							
Non-minority	12.7	14.6	15.2		11.0	13.6	
Minority	14.1	14.7	14.8		13.8	13.6	
1991 Census Data[b]							
Non-minority	12.7	14.2	14.7		11.3	13.3	
Minority	13.7	14.4	14.3		13.5	13.2	
1996 Census Data[b]							
Non-minority	13.2	14.5	14.7	15.1	11.8	13.4	14.4
Minority	14.1	14.5	14.5	14.5	13.7	13.3	13.6

Table 9 continued

Sample size, men 25–64

1991 Public Use Sample[a]						
Non-minority	133,321	4,074	595		9,700	1,937
Minority	1,543	79	44		6,402	4,802
1991 Census Data[b]						
Non-minority	1,037,571	30,299	5,256		66,944	14,795
Minority	11,439	601	313		43,707	36,352
1996 Census Data[b]						
Non-minority	1,003,028	23,421	5,493	1,640	49,118	18,834 · 7,581
Minority	11,458	363	297	101	36,505	42,043 · 22,272

Annual earnings, women 25–64

1991 Public Use Sample[a]						
Non-minority	20,978	23,786	20,100		20,265	16,223
Minority	23,455	25,361	20,459		22,696	15,663
1991 Census Data[b]						
Non-minority	22,220	25,737	21,559		22,421	17,956
Minority	25,214	25,254	20,383		24,645	17,061
1996 Census Data[b]						
Non-minority	25,901	30,083	26,956	24,030	25,646	22,325 · 16,478
Minority	27,884	31,998	24,121	19,636	28,589	20,943 · 14,950

Table 9 continued

	Years of schooling, women 25–64						
1991 Public Use Sample[a]							
Non-minority	13.0	13.9	14.5		10.7	13.7	
Minority	13.8	14.7	14.1		13.1	13.2	
1991 Census Data[b]							
Non-minority	13.1	13.8	14.3		10.9	13.2	
Minority	13.8	14.0	14.2		12.9	12.6	
1996 Census Data[b]							
Non-minority	13.5	14.0	14.4	14.8	11.5	13.4	14.3
Minority	14.3	14.4	14.3	14.8	13.2	13.0	13.2
Sample size, women 25–64							
1991 Public Use Sample[a]							
Non-minority	110,351	3,755	698	1,543	6,201	1,516	
Minority	1,413	77	34	101	5,799	4,156	
1991 Census Data[b]							
Non-minority	855,034	27,925	5,507		43,509	11,278	
Minority	9,905	536	278		38,542	31,178	
1996 Census Data[b]							
Non-minority	862,023	22,437	5,938		34,022	14,637	
Minority	10,132	331	337		33,078	36,153	

Notes: [a] Masao Nakamura carried out the computations for these portions as well as for Tables 1–8 using the 1991 Public Use Sample data. [b] Logan McLeod of Statistics Canada carried out the computations for these portions using the master 1991 and 1996 census data files.

of schooling in moving from the pre-1981 arrival group to the 1981–90 one
and then to the 1991–95 one.

Immigration and Labour Productivity

> Productivity is commonly defined as a ratio of a volume measure
> of output to a volume measure of input use.
> (Paul Schreyer, 2001)

In the previous section we found that, on average, immigrants born in
the United States or United Kingdom have higher annual and hourly
earnings than Canadian-born workers. We found too that more recent
immigrants born in countries other than the US or UK have tended to have
lower average annual earnings and hourly wages than Canadian-born
workers. How might immigrant influxes of these sorts affect Canadian
productivity? We examine the definitions for alternative measures of labour
and multi-factor productivity growth, and then consider how the values of
these would be affected by immigrant inflows of specific sorts.

Productivity Growth: The 1–1 Case

A ratio of output quantity to input quantity is how productivity is usually
defined.

For a production process with a single output and a single input (the
1–1 case), there is no need to decide how to add up the quantities of
different output goods or of different input factors to construct aggregates
for total output quantity and total input quantity. Thus, it is easy to define
a measure of productivity in the 1–1 case. We denote the quantity for the
single output good by y^t the quantity for the single input factor by x^t.[11]

---

[11]We use the term production scenario to refer to a production unit in a
given time period. The production unit could be a plant or firm or a conglomerate
of producers such as an industry or nation. When productivity comparisons are
made for the same production unit over time, then the superscript t is used to denote
time. When comparisons are made over multiple production units for the same time

Total factor productivity (TFP) for a 1–1 process can be defined and measured by the ratio of the observed period t output and input quantities:

$$(1) \quad a^t = y^t / x^t \; TFP^t, \qquad \qquad for \; t = 1, \dots, T.$$

The coefficient a^t in (1) is referred to in the engineering and production management literatures as an output-input coefficient.[12]

For the 1–1 case, total factor productivity growth (TFPG) from period s to t can be represented equivalently as the ratio of the output-input coefficients for the two time periods, or as the ratio of the period t and period s rates of transformation of input into output, or as the growth rate of output divided by the growth rate of input, with the growth rate of a variable represented as the ratio of the period t and period s values of the variable. Thus we have:

$$(2) \quad a^t / a^s = (y^t / x^t) / (y^s / x^s) = (y^t / y^s) / (x^t / x^s) = TFPG^{s,t}.$$

For the 1–1 process, we say that productivity growth is positive when (a^t / a^s) is greater than 1.[13] The Statistics Canada productivity measurement

---

period, the superscript denotes the production unit. With panel data, separate superscripts for time and the production unit are often used.

[12]By itself, an output-input coefficient is no more abstract than, say, speed measured as distance travelled per some unit measure of time. This is true as well of the ratio of the quantity for a single output to the quantity of any one input for a multiple input production process. In contrast, in the economics literature when a^t is specified to be an exogenous shift term in a production function obeying certain assumptions, this is an abstract concept. See Diewert and Nakamura (2003).

[13]TFP^t and $TFPG^{s,t}$ are summary statistics for a production process. These summary measures can be shown, under certain conditions, to equal parameters in producer behavioural relationships, as specified in economic theory. However, the measures can still be computed whether or not the assumptions enabling a structural, economic theory interpretation are true. See Diewert and Nakamura (2003).

program focuses on productivity growth rather than productivity levels, and so do we.[14]

Notice that we can represent the growth in output as the product of productivity growth and input growth terms. We have:

$$(3) \quad \frac{y^t}{y^s} = \left(\frac{a^t}{a^s}\right)\left(\frac{x^t}{x^s}\right) = TFPG^{s,t}\left(\frac{x^t}{x^s}\right).$$

The appeal of getting more output growth for any given rate of input growth is the reason for public and government interest in productivity growth.

Productivity growth can happen because of the adoption of a new production technology; that is, it can happen because of technical progress. Or it can happen because the period s technology is operated in period t at a more efficient level, allowing the production unit to reap the benefits of increasing returns to scale. Immigration can have both technical progress and returns-to-scale effects. From only the observed input and output data, we cannot usually determine the relative contributions of technical progress and returns to scale. However, the aspects of immigration and other policy measures that might result in productivity gains from returns to scale versus technical progress are different. Hence, it is useful to recognize that $TFPG^{s,t}$ is affected by both.

Productivity Growth Measurement with Multiple Inputs

Of course, many production processes yield joint outputs, and virtually all involve multiple inputs. Certainly nations have many outputs and inputs. With multiple inputs and outputs, productivity growth is measured as a ratio of an index for total output quantity growth divided by an index for the growth in the quantity of one, some, or all of the input factors used in producing the output.

---

[14]A good procedural reference for the Statistics Canada productivity measurement program is the Statistics Canada monograph by Baldwin *et al.* (2001) (especially the first chapter by Baldwin, Harchauoui, Hosein and Maynard and Appendix 1 by Harchauoui, Kaci and Maynard).

For general M output, N input production processes just as for 1–1 ones, there are two main ways in which increases in productivity growth can occur: technical progress and growth with increasing returns to scale. People who move to Canada from other countries bring with them knowledge that may enable technical progress. Also, if a production unit enjoys increasing returns to scale, then as the scale of operation rises, so does productivity.

Some of the suggested sources of increasing returns to scale for producers include:

- *The Laws of Physics.* The three-dimensional nature of space and the physics laws governing things such as friction can lead to economies of scale.[15]
- *The Law of Large Numbers.* These efficiencies result from the laws of probability theory and the mathematics of risk and insurance. For example, a large bank will not require as high a proportion of cash reserves to meet random demands as a small bank.[16] In a similar vein, a large property insurance company whose risks are geographically diversified faces a smaller probability of bankruptcy than a small insurance company.
- *The Existence of Fixed Costs.* Efficiencies can result from averaging or amortizing fixed costs (a kind of indivisibility) over higher output levels. For example, before a machine can yield a benefit from its operation, an operator may need to be transported from another location,[17] and the machine may also require a warming up period. These

---

[15]For example, Marshall (1920, p. 290) noted that: "A ship's carrying power varies as the cube of her dimensions, while the resistance offered by the water increases only a little faster than the square of her dimensions; so that a large ship requires less coal in proportion to its tonnage than a small one. It also requires less labour, especially that of navigation: while to passengers it offers greater safety and comfort, more choice of company and better professional attendance."

[16]This application of probability theory to the determination of adequate bank reserves dates back to Edgeworth (1888, p. 122). He also applied his statistical reasoning to the inventory stocking problem faced by a restaurant or club and noted that optimal inventory stocks are proportional to the square root of anticipated demand (1888, p. 124).

[17]This example of a fixed cost is due to Adam Smith (1963, p. 7).

The Potential Impacts of Immigration on Productivity in Canada

are examples of costs whose effects become relatively smaller the greater the scale of operation.

- *Indivisibilities and Bulk Purchasing Opportunities.* Most labour and capital inputs can only be acquired in certain amounts.[18]
- *Specialization of Factor Usage.* Adam Smith (1963, p. 14) long ago pointed out that, as the scale of an establishment grows due to the growth of markets for its outputs, the possibility of using specialized labour inputs also grows. A worker who is able to concentrate on one or a few tasks may become more proficient. Larger scale also enables more dedicated use of other factors including plant and office space.

If increasing returns to scale are a reality for enough businesses and if immigration permits Canadian businesses to grow in size, this could be a means by which immigration helps to boost productivity.

For a general M output, N input production process (an M-N process), an index for multi-factor productivity growth from period s to t can be defined as

$$(4) \quad MFPG^{s,t} = Q^{s,t} / Q^{*s,t} \; ,$$

where the numerator, $Q^{s,t}$, is some sort of an index for the growth of the total output quantity, and the denominator, $Q^{*s,t}$, is an index for the growth of the quantity of the specified inputs.

Different names are used for the productivity growth measure given in (4) depending on whether one, some, or all of the input factors for the production process are accounted for in the input quantity growth index in the denominator, and depending on the type or types of inputs included. When only one input factor is taken into account, this is a single factor productivity growth index: an SFPG index. When some, or all, input factors are accounted for, the productivity growth index is a multi, or a total, factor productivity growth index: an MFPG or TFPG index. When only labour

---

[18]Bulk purchasing means that the supplying firm may be able to achieve internal economies of scale and thus can offer lower selling prices.

inputs are included in $Q^{*s,t}$, then (4) is a labour productivity growth index: what we will denote as an LPG index.[19]

Statistics Canada produces both single and multi-factor labour productivity growth indexes as well as a variety of MFPG indexes that incorporate comprehensive sets of inputs and are intended to approximate, and will be referred to hereafter as, TFPG indexes. Both the labour productivity growth indexes and also the MFPG indexes approximating TFPG measures have as their numerator an index for the growth of total output for the nation, though there are some differences in the specification of these output indexes. The various productivity growth indexes differ primarily because of their denominators — they incorporate different input quantity indexes.

A formula must be chosen for the output quantity index, $Q^{s,t}$, in the numerator of (4) and for the input quantity index, $Q^{*s,t}$, in the denominator. These formulas specify how the amounts for the different output goods and for the designated input factors are added up.

The amounts of the output goods $m=1,...,M$ that are produced in period t ($t=1,...,T$) are denoted by $y_1^t,...,y_M^t$, and the corresponding unit prices by $p_1^t,...,p_M^t$. An output quantity index for the growth in volume for total output can be represented as

$$(5)\quad Q^{s,t} = \frac{\sum_{m=1}^{M} p_m y_m^t}{\sum_{m=1}^{M} p_m y_m^s},$$

where the p_m are weights. When period s prices are used as the weights — that is, when we set $p_m = p_m^s$ for $m=1,...,M$ — then (5) is the formula for the well-known Laspeyres output quantity index, $Q_L^{s,t}$. A Laspeyres output index evaluates the growth in output from period s to t using period s prices. Alternatively, when period t prices are used as the weights in (5) — that is, when we set $p_m = p_m^t$ for $m=1,...,M$ — then this is the formula for

---

[19]Labour productivity growth indexes are often thought of as SFPG measures because they only take account of labour and ignore the other factors of production, but actually they are MFPG measures when the quantities of different types of labour (e.g., Canadian-born versus immigrant) are included as separate factors with their appropriate weights.

the Paasche output quantity index, , $Q_P^{s,t}$. This index evaluates the output growth from period s to t using period t prices. The Fisher output quantity index is defined as the square root of the product of the Laspeyres and Paasche quantity indexes: $Q_F^{s,t} = (Q_L^{s,t} Q_P^{s,t})^{1/2}$. Statistics Canada uses Fisher type indexes to produce measures of the growth of the output of the nation.

Turning to the input side, the quantities and prices of the input factors used in producing the M outputs are denoted by $x_1^t, \ldots, x_N^t$ and $w_1^t, \ldots, w_N^t$, respectively. An input quantity index can be specified for the growth in total volume for any selected subset of the N factors of production. An input quantity index for NS of the input factors ($\leq N$) can be defined as

(6) $\qquad Q^{*s,t} = \dfrac{\sum_{n=1}^{NS} w_n x_n^t}{\sum_{n=1}^{NS} w_n x_n^s}$.

In (6), the w_n are weights. Suppose price weights are used in (6). If we set $w_n = w_n^s$ for $n=1,\ldots,NS$, then (6) is a Laspeyres input quantity growth index. Alternatively, if we set $w_n = w_n^t$, then (6) is a Paasche input quantity growth index. The square root of the product of these is a Fisher input quantity index.

When Laspeyres, Paasche or Fisher indexes are used for the output and input quantity indexes, then (4) is a Laspeyres, Paasche or Fisher productivity growth index, respectively. Fisher indexes have been found to be especially desirable and are used by Statistics Canada because of that.[20] However, the points we wish to make involving price weighted indexes can be illustrated using Laspeyres, Paasche or Fisher indexes. We will use Laspeyres-type indexes for expositional convenience. (The interested reader could replicate our analysis for a Paasche-type index. The results for

---

[20]The relative merits of these different index number formulas, and of other functional forms that have been proposed, are examined in the index number literature. See Diewert (1987, 1992a, 1992b and 1998) and Diewert and Nakamura (2003). However, the choice among alternative price weighted measures is not our focus in this paper.

Alice Nakamura, Masao Nakamura and W. Erwin Diewert

the preferred Fisher index could then be obtained by taking the square root of the product of the Laspeyres and Paasche indexes.)

Our primary concern here is with the choice between a wage weighted representation for the quantity of labour versus a labour aggregate formed by simply adding the hours of work for the different types of workers. This choice will systematically affect the measured impacts of influxes of immigrants of different types on labour productivity growth. (Similar conclusions hold for TFPG indexes and for MFPG indexes that incorporate a labour input.)

The traditional labour productivity growth measure incorporates an input quantity index that includes only labour inputs, with the weights all set equal to 1.[21] The Laspeyres (L) form of the traditional (TR) labour productivity growth index can be represented as

$$(7) \quad LPG_{TR,L}^{s,t} = \frac{Q_L^{s,t}}{H^t / H^s} = \frac{\left(\sum_{m=1}^{M} p_m^s y_m^t\right) / H^t}{\left(\sum_{m=1}^{M} p_m^s y_m^s\right) / H^s},$$

where $H^t = \sum_{n=1}^{NS} X_n^t$ for $t=1,...,T$.

A traditional labour productivity growth index can be interpreted as the growth rate of output per hour of work, measured in constant dollars.[22] From a household welfare perspective, this measure has obvious relevance (see Basu and Fernald, 1997). However, from a producer perspective, the hours of work of different types of workers usually have different costs and provide different sorts of labour services.

In a 1967 paper, Jorgenson and Griliches presented what they termed a "constant quality index" for labour, with workers differentiated by their educational attainment. Subsequently, Gollop and Jorgenson (1980)

---

[21]Both Statistics Canada and the US Bureau of Labor Statistics (BLS) previously relied on measures of labour input of this basic sort in their productivity measurement programs. See Baldwin *et al.* (2001) for details.

[22]If a Laspeyres index is used for the output quantity index, as specified in (7), then the output for periods *t* and *s* is evaluated using period *s* prices whereas if a Paasche output quantity index is used, then the output for period *s* and *t* is evaluated using actual period *t* prices. If a Fisher index is used, this is equivalent to deflating the dollar values using a Fisher output price index.

produced constant quality indexes of labour input for 51 industrial sectors of the US economy. They compiled data on the hours of labour input for each industry by age, sex, educational attainment, class of employment, and occupation of the workers and then computed weighted aggregates of the hours of work data utilizing the associated hourly wages.[23]

The US Bureau of Labor Statistics (BLS) accepted the need to allow for different types of workers in measuring labour input and began producing new wage-weighted labour aggregates and using these in their labour and MFPG/TFPG productivity measurement programs. Statistics Canada now also produces wage-weighted labour aggregates.

The term "quality adjusted" as used by Griliches, Jorgenson and others in the productivity measurement literature is problematical, especially if applied in an analysis of immigrant versus native-born workers.[24] In common parlance, a poor quality worker is someone who performs their particular job poorly. Thus it is possible, for instance, for a childcare worker, who is low paid but performing a job where the parents of the children cared for have preferences for how it is carried out, to be "high quality" and for a highly paid professional, such as a surgeon who makes frequent mistakes that harm his or her patients, to be "poor quality". On the other hand, when wages are used as a metric for worker quality, then all the surgeons are classified as high quality and all the childcare workers are classified as low quality. This terminology problem is easily remedied by referring to the new labour aggregates as what they really are: wage-weighted labour aggregates.

Semantic issues aside, the deeper question that lies at the heart of inquiries into the impacts of specific sorts of immigration flows on the productivity of the nation is: What do we mean by the quantity of labour? We address this question by first posing an easier one: What do we mean by the quantity of coal? Lumps of coal are easier to size up than workers, and yet, with coal too, we face the issue of whether to use a simple sum of the quantities of different types or a price-weighted aggregate.

---

[23]This work was extended and updated by Jorgenson in collaboration with Fraumeni. See the papers in Jorgenson's 1995 collected works and also the 1987 book by Jorgenson, Gollop and Fraumeni.

[24]Statistics Canada has tried to use the term "composition adjusted" rather than quality adjusted, but others keep reasserting the "quality adjusted" terminology. There might be more receptivity to calling these aggregates "wage weighted" rather than just composition adjusted.

Alice Nakamura, Masao Nakamura and W. Erwin Diewert

Coal is often sold by the ton and in other units of weight that can be converted to ton equivalents. We could measure the total in tons. However, there are different types of coal that produce different amounts of heat and release different amounts of pollutants. The coal types that produce more heat and less pollution are more valuable to producers and also scarcer, leading to higher prices. Since coal is sold in competitive international markets and there are established procedures for grading coal, economic theory arguments suggest that the prices of different types should reflect their relative use values to producers. If so, then if we weight the quantities for the different types by their per ton prices, the sum will be a measure of the productive use value of the coal that was used. One desirable property this aggregate will have is that a pure mix change in the quantities for the different types of coal — that is, a change in the quantities of the different types that leaves the price weighted sum unchanged — should also leave unchanged the total productive use value of the whole amount. In addition, by construction, the total amount spent on coal will be unchanged.

The decision of whether to use a simple measure of the total tons of coal of all sorts or a price-weighted one rests on whether we want to measure the change in output with respect to the change in weight for this input, without regard to the mix of the types of coal, or with respect to the change in the productive use value of the coal, or perhaps a measure of expenditure on coal. It is a choice, and one with implications for what is meant by the words "productivity growth".

Similar issues must be confronted in deciding how to aggregate the quantities of different types of labour, though there is more uncertainty involved in determining and certifying the productive use values of different types of workers, especially for workers who have acquired some of their education and work experience in other countries.

Examples with Just Two Types of Labour

To illustrate some implications of using a traditional labour productivity growth index versus a new style LPG measure incorporating a wage-weighted labour aggregate, we will suppose there are just two time periods, s and t with period s coming first, and that there are just two sorts of labour: Canadian-born (C) and immigrant (I). The hours of work and hourly wage for these two types of workers are denoted for the Canadian-born by x_C^t and w_C^t and for the immigrants by x_I^t and w_I^t. For this simplistic case, the traditional measure of the labour input for any given time period, say t, is

(8) $H^t = x_C^t + x_I^t$.

The new wage-weighted measure of the labour input for any given time period t is

(9) $w_C x_C^t + w_I x_I^t$,

where w_C and w_I are wage weights of some sort. In what follows, we will take the wage weights to be for period s, making (9) a Laspeyres-type wage-weighted labour aggregate.

To focus attention on the issues at hand, we make the further simplifying assumption that there is just one output and that we know the quantities of this output that were produced by the Canadian-born workers, y_C^t, and by the immigrant workers, y_I^t. The output of the Canadian-born and immigrant workers is sold for the same price.

For this production situation, the traditional labour productivity growth index is given by

(10)
$$LPG_{TR}^{s,t} = \frac{\left(y_C^t + y_I^t\right) / \left(y_C^s + y_I^s\right)}{\left(x_C^t + x_I^t\right) / \left(x_C^s + x_I^s\right)}$$
$$= \frac{\left(a_C^t x_C^t + a_I^t x_I^t\right) / \left(a_C^s x_C^s + a_I^s x_I^s\right)}{\left(x_C^t + x_I^t\right) / \left(x_C^s + x_I^s\right)},$$

where, $a_C^t = y_C^t / x_C^t, a_C^s = y_C^s / x_C^s, a_I^t = y_I^t / x_I^t$ and $a_I^s = y_I^s / x_I^s$ are the output-input coefficients for the Canadian-born and the immigrant workers, respectively.

The new style (N) Laspeyres-type LPG index for this production situation is given by

(11) $LPG_{N,L}^{s,t} = \dfrac{\left(a_C^t x_C^t + a_I^t x_I^t\right) / \left(a_C^s x_C^s + a_I^s x_I^s\right)}{\left(w_C^s x_C^t + w_I^s x_I^t\right) / \left(w_C^s x_C^s + w_I^s x_I^s\right)}.$

Notice that the numerator of (11) is the same as for the traditional LPG index in (10). In the denominator, period s wage weights are used because this is the Laspeyres form of the new style LPG index.

To consider the trade-offs involved in using the traditional LPG index given in (10) instead of a new style LPG index like the one given in (11), we must specify our concept of the "quantity of labour". In this paper, we take a producer perspective and define the true quantity of labour by its productive use value to employers. This means that we take as the true definition of labour productivity growth the growth in total output divided by the growth in the productive use value of the work time. The implications of these choices will be illustrated by example. We examine the consequences of using a traditional versus a new style LPG index to measure labour productivity growth in a variety of hypothetical cases and under two alternative scenarios concerning the extent to which the wages of Canadian-born and immigrant workers mirror the productive value of their work.

In Scenario I, we assume that the wage rates of workers of different types accurately reflect the relative productive value of their work time. Under this assumption, formulas (9) and (11) give the Laspeyres approximations of what, in scenario I, we will treat as the true value for the quantity of labour and the true LPG value. Better approximations to "the truth" could be obtained by using Fisher approximations, obtained as the square root of the product of the Laspeyres and Paasche approximations, but we ignore this from here on so as to focus attention on the consequences of using wage-weighted labour aggregates. More specifically, the question we ask for this scenario is: What happens if we use a traditional LPG measure?

Case 1. Suppose the Canadian-born and immigrant workers get paid the same wage rates and have the same rates of production, which may change over time. In this case, the traditional labour productivity growth index, $LPG_{TR}^{s,t}$ given in (10), and also the new style LPG index, given in (11), both reduce to

$$(12) \quad LPG_{TR}^{s,t} = LPG_{N,L}^{s,t} = \frac{a^t}{a^s}.$$

Thus, when the Canadian-born and the immigrant workers are equally productive and earn the same wages, the same correct answers will result from using a traditional or a new style measure of labour productivity growth.

Case 2. Next, suppose the Canadian-born and immigrant workers earn different wages and suppose their wages mirror their true productivity.[25] Now the new style and traditional LPG measures will not give the same answers.

In this case, an influx of immigrants like those born in the United States or United Kingdom who have higher earnings on average than their Canadian-born counterparts will cause the traditional labour input measure to rise less than the true one, and the traditional LPG index will overestimate the labour productivity growth compared with the results from a new style LPG measure. Similarly, given an influx of immigrants with lower wage rates and lower per hour rates of production, a traditional LPG measure will tend to overestimate the immigrant addition to labour services and will underestimate the resulting labour productivity growth.

Of course, the direct evidence on immigrant earnings shows only that their earnings are lower on average. This could be because the immigrants have lower productivity on their jobs compared with Canadian-born, or it could be that the immigrant workers are paid smaller shares of their full productive value compared with the Canadian-born workers. For instance, the newer immigrants might only be able to get temporary jobs, with temporary workers being paid less for the same work than those hired on a continuing basis. Also, newer immigrants usually have less information about the Canadian labour market than Canadian-born workers, and Canadian employers tend to have less good information about the credentials of immigrant workers, with their information deficit being more severe for immigrants from countries with which Canadian employers are less familiar.

---

[25]In studies that use the new "constant quality" labour aggregates, there is often an implicit or explicit acceptance of the proposition that the productive value to the employer of an added dollar of expenditure on each of the types of workers is the same. Economists have worked out conditions under which this would be expected to be true. For example, this would be expected when the markets for labour are perfectly competitive and employers have perfect information about worker productive attributes. Also, pay for performance compensation arrangements, including piece rate pay and straight commission pay, equalize, on an ongoing basis, the productive value to the employer of different workers, regardless of their type.

In Scenario II, the hourly wages of workers are assumed to represent differing fractions of what they produce: say, γ_C^t for the Canadian-born workers and γ_I^t for the immigrant workers.

Now the Laspeyres approximation of the total true productive use value of the work time of the Canadian-born and immigrant workers for any given period t is

$$(13) \qquad (w_C / \gamma_C) x_C^t + (w_I / \gamma_I) x_I^t = a_C x_C^t + a_I x_I^t$$

where w_C and w_I are the observed wage rates, γ_C and γ_I are the proportions of their productive contributions that the workers of each type capture as wages, and x_C^t and x_I^t are the period t hours of work for the Canadian-born and immigrant workers for $t=1,...,T$. If period s wages and payout proportions are used in computing the aggregate, as in (12), this will be a Laspeyres-type aggregate. (Note that for Laspeyres-type aggregates, we will also have period s output-input coefficients on the right-hand side of (13) whereas we would have period t output-input coefficients here if this were a Paasche-type aggregate.) The Laspeyres-type (L) wage capture adjusted (WC) labour productivity growth is now given by

$$(14) \qquad
\begin{aligned}
LPG_{WC,L}^{s,t} &= \frac{\left(a_C^t x_C^t + a_I^t x_I^t\right) / \left(a_C^s x_C^s + a_I^s x_I^s\right)}{\left(a_C^s x_C^t + a_I^s x_I^t\right) / \left(a_C^s x_C^s + a_I^s x_I^s\right)} \\
&= \frac{\left(a_C^t x_C^t + a_I^t x_I^t\right)}{\left(a_C^s x_C^t + a_I^s x_I^t\right)} .
\end{aligned}$$

If a new style wage-weighted LPG index is used, what it will show can be seen from the following:

$$(15) \qquad
\begin{aligned}
LPG_{N,L}^{s,t} &= \frac{\left(a_C^t x_C^t + a_I^t x_I^t\right) / \left(a_C^s x_C^s + a_I^s x_I^s\right)}{\left(w_C^s x_C^t + w_I^s x_I^t\right) / \left(w_C^s x_C^s + w_I^s x_I^s\right)} \\
&= \frac{\left(a_C^t x_C^t + a_I^t x_I^t\right) / \left(a_C^s x_C^s + a_I^s x_I^s\right)}{\left(\gamma_C^s a_C^s x_C^t + \gamma_I^s a_I^s x_I^t\right) / \left(\gamma_C^s a_C^s x_C^s + \gamma_I^s a_I^s x_I^s\right)} .
\end{aligned}$$

The traditional LPG index takes no account of the worker-type productivity differences. Moreover, now the new wage-adjusted LPG index will also give systematically biased estimates because it ignores the fact that the workers capture differing proportions in wages of their true productive values. These implications are illustrated in our final two example cases:

Case 3. Suppose that the Canadian-born and immigrant workers have differing rates of production per hour, and also the two types of workers capture different proportions of their productive values in wages.

If a traditional LPG measure is applied, the results will be the same as for Case 2 above.

Alternatively, if a new style wage-weighted LPG measure is used, it reduces to the following for this case:

$$(16) \quad LPG_{TR,L}^{s,t} = \frac{a_C^t x_C^t + a_I^t x_I^t}{a_C^s x_C^t + a_I^s x_I^t} \ .$$

This is the case where relative wage rates reflect true worker productivity without any discrimination effects, and the wage-weighted LPG gives the correct results. The only way the value of $LPG_{N,L}^{s,t}$ can be greater (less) than 1 in this case is through increases (decreases) in the rate of production for the Canadian-born or the immigrant workers or both.

Case 4. Suppose, finally, that the Canadian-born and immigrant workers have differing rates of production per hour and also capture differing proportions of their productive labour services in wages.

If a traditional LPG measure is used, the results will be just as for Case 2 above.

If a new style wage-weighted LPG measure is used, the results can be determined by comparing the second line of (15) with the second line of (14), which is now "the truth".

Suppose there is an influx of immigrants who are more productive (i.e., $a_I > a_C$). Suppose also that they have greater bargaining power because their skills are in short supply in the domestic economy and their hourly wage represents a higher share of the output produced. We see from (15) that with $\gamma_I > \gamma_C$, the contribution to labour services of an influx of more productive immigrants will be incorrectly assessed, though in the opposite way from the contribution of the Canadian-born workers. For this situation, we cannot say whether this will lead to too low or too high an estimate of LPG.

Now suppose instead that the immigrants are less productive than the Canadian-born on average (i.e., $a_I < a_C$) and have lower bargaining power (i.e., $\gamma_I < \gamma_C$). This is what many people believe is happening, on average, for the more recent immigrants. In this case, the relative contribution to the supply of productive services owing to an immigrant influx will tend to be underestimated by a new style labour aggregate and the new style LPG index will lead to an overestimate of the labour productivity growth, defined as the growth in output divided by the growth in the use value of the labour input.

The new wage-weighted LPG index no longer can be thought of as the ratio of the output growth rate to the rate of growth in productive labour services. However, it will probably give answers closer to "the truth" than the traditional LPG measure. Also, it will still be the case that $LPG_{N,L}^{s,t}$ gives the ratio of the growth rate in output to the rate of growth in constant dollar labour costs.

If we had empirical or *a priori* estimates of the extent of discrimination, then the effects of this could be corrected for in measuring labour productivity growth as the ratio of the growth in total output to the growth in the productive value of labour services.

Concluding Remarks

We have discussed alternative ways of representing the labour input in labour productivity growth measures. These alternatives have different implications for measured labour productivity growth in any period when immigrants enter the workforce in substantial numbers who have productivity attributes that differ on average from the incumbent Canadian workforce.

On balance, our analysis suggests that the use of a wage-weighted aggregate for the labour input of workers of different types rather than a simple sum of hours of work will be an improvement for considering the impact of immigrants on the productivity of the nation. Thus, we support the Statistics Canada move to this type of labour aggregates.

We demonstrate that the new wage-weighted measure of labour supply and the labour and total factor productivity indexes incorporating these measures provide a useful framework for addressing "what if" type questions as well as for incorporating available empirical information about immigrant versus Canadian-born worker productivity and wage bargaining differences.

References

Baker, M. and D. Benjamin (1994), "The Performance of Immigrants in the Canadian Labor Market", *Journal of Labor Economics* 12, 369–405.

Baldwin, J.R., D. Beckstead, N. Dhaliwal, R. Durand, V. Gaudreault, T.M. Harchauoui, J. Hosein, M. Kaci and J.-P. Maynard (2001), *Productivity Growth in Canada*, Cat. No. 15-204-XPE (Ottawa: Statistics Canada).

Baldwin, J.R., T. Harchauoui, J. Hosein and J.-P. Maynard (2001), "Chapter 1 – Productivity: Concepts and Trends", in Baldwin *et al.*, *Productivity Growth in Canada*, 13–24.

Basu, S. and J.G. Fernald (1997), "Returns to Scale in U.S. Production: Estimates and Implications", *Journal of Political Economy* 105(2), 249–283.

Beach, C.M. and C. Worswick (1994), "Is There a Double Negative Effect on the Earnings of Immigrant Women?" *Canadian Public Policy/Analyse de Politiques* 19, 36–53.

Beaujot, R. (2000), "Immigration and Canadian Demographics: State of the Research, Citizenship and Immigration Canada", Cat. No. MP22-16/2-2000E. At <www.cic.gc.ca>, May 1998.

Beck, J.H., J.G. Reitz and N. Weiner (2002), "Addressing Systemic Racial Discrimination in Employment: The Health Canada Case and Implications of Legislative Change", working paper.

Bureau of Labor Statistics (1993), *Labor Composition and U.S. Productivity Growth, 1948–90*, Bulletin 2426 (Washington, DC: U.S. Department of Labor, Government of the United States).

Citizenship and Immigration Canada (CIC) (1994), *Canada 2005: A Strategy for Citizenship and Immigration*. Background document (Ottawa: CIC).

_____ (2000), *The Economic Performance of Immigrants: Immigration Category Perspective, IMDB Profile Series*, December 1998, Citizenship and Immigration Canada, Cat. No. MP22-18/2-2000E. At <www.cic.gc.ca>.

_____ (2001), *Facts and Figures 2000: Immigration Overview*, Citizenship and Immigration Canada, Cat. No. MP43-333/2001E. At <www.cic.gc.ca>.

DeVoretz, D. (1995), *Diminishing Returns: The Economics of Canada's Recent Immigration Policy*, Policy Study 24, C.D. Howe Institute and The Laurier Institution.

Diewert, W.E. (1987), "Index Numbers", in J. Eatwell, M. Milgate and P. Newman (eds.), *The New Palgrave: A Dictionary of Economics*, Vol. 2 (London: Macmillan), 767–780, and reprinted as Chapter 5 in Diewert and Nakamura (1993), 71–104.

_____ (1992a), "The Measurement of Productivity", *Bulletin of Economic Research* 44(3), 163–198.

_____ (1992b), "Fisher Ideal Output, Input, and Productivity Indexes Revisited", *Journal of Productivity Analysis* 3, 211–248, and reprinted as Chapter 13 in Diewert and Nakamura (1993), 211–248.

_____ (1998), "Index Number Issues in the Consumer Price Index", *The Journal of Economic Perspectives* 12(1), 47–58.

Diewert, W.E. and A.O. Nakamura (1993), *Essays in Index Number Theory*, Vol. I (Amsterdam: North-Holland).

_____ (2003), "Index Number Concepts, Measures and Decompositions of Productivity Growth", *Journal of Productivity Analysis* 19(2/3), 127–159.

Duleep, H.O. and M.C. Regets (1992), "Some Evidence of the Effects of Admissions Criteria on Immigrant Assimilation", in B.R. Chiswick (ed.), *Immigration, Language and Ethnicity: Canada and the United States* (The AEI Press) (Monograph Series), Ch. 10, 410–439.

Duleep, H.O., M.C. Regets and S. Sanders (1999), *Skills, Investment, and Family Ties: A Study of Asian Immigrants* (Kalamazoo, MI: Upjohn Institute of Employment Research).

Edgeworth, F.Y. (1888), "The Mathematical Theory of Banking", *Journal of the Royal Statistical Society* 51, 113–127.

Gollop, F.M. and D.W. Jorgenson (1980), "U.S. Productivity Growth by Industry, 1947–1973", in J.W. Kendrick and B. Vaccura (eds.), *New Developments in Productivity Measurement and Analysis*, NBER Studies in Income and Wealth, Vol. 41 (Chicago, IL: University of Chicago Press), 17–136.

Grant, M.L. (1999), "Evidence of New Immigrant Assimilation in Canada", *Canadian Journal of Economics* 32(4), 930–955.

Green, A.G. (1995), "A Comparison of Canadian and US Immigration Policy in the Twentieth Century", in D. DeVoretz (ed.), *Diminishing Returns: The Economics of Canada's Recent Immigration Policy*, Policy Study 24 (Toronto: C.D. Howe Institute and the Laurier Institution), 31–64.

Harchauoui, T.M., M. Kaci and J.-P. Maynard (2001), "Appendix 1 — The Statistics Canada Productivity Program: Concepts and Methods", in Baldwin *et al.*, *Productivity Growth in Canada*, 143–176.

Informetrica (2000), *Recent Immigrants in Metropolitan Areas*, Citizenship and Immigration Canada, Cat. Nos. MP22-20/2-2000E, MP22-20/3-2000E, MP22-20/4-2000E. At <www.cic.gc.ca>.

Jorgenson, D.W. (1995), *Productivity*, Vols. 1 and 2 (Cambridge, MA: Harvard University Press).

Jorgenson, D.W. and Z. Griliches (1967), "The Explanation of Productivity Change", *Review of Economic Studies* 34(3), 249–280.

Jorgenson, D.W., F.M. Gollop and B.M. Fraumeni (1987), *Productivity and U.S. Economic Growth* (Cambridge, MA: Harvard University Press).

Kaci, M., J.-P. Maynard and W. Gu (2001), *The Changing Composition of the Canadian Workforce and Its Impact on Productivity*, June 19, 2001 draft, Microeconomic Analysis Division, Statistics Canada.

Kossoudji, S.A. (1989), "Immigrant Worker Assimilation: Is It a Labour Market Phenomenon?" *Journal of Human Resources*, 474–527.

La Londe, R. and R. Topel (1991), "Immigrants in the American Labor Market: Quality, Assimilation and Distributional Effects", *American Economic Review* 81(2), 297–302.

Li, P.S. (2001), "The Market Worth of Immigrants' Educational Credentials", *Canadian Public Policy/Analyse de Politiques* 27(1), 77–94.

Marshall, A. (1920), *Principles of Economics*, 8th ed. (first edition, 1890) (London: The Macmillan Co.).

Nakamura, A. and M. Nakamura (1992), "Wage Rates of Immigrant and Native Men in Canada and the U.S.", in B.R. Chiswick (ed.), *Immigration, Language and Ethnicity: Canada and the United States* (Washington, DC: American Enterprise Institute), 145–166.

Nakamura, A., M. Nakamura, C.J. Nicol and W.E. Diewert (1999), "Labour Market Outcomes and the Recruitment Information Needs of Immigrant and Other Job Seekers". Paper presented at "Shaping the Future: Qualification Recognition in the 21st Century", October 14, Toronto.

_____ (2003), *Immigrant Employment, Earnings and Expenditures: Patterns and Policy Implications* (Montreal and Kingston: McGill-Queen's University Press), forthcoming.

Picot, G., A. Heisz and A. Nakamura (2000), "Were 1990s Labour Markets Really Different?" *Policy Options* 21(6), 15–26.

Reitz, J. (2001), "Immigrant Skill Utilization in the Canadian Labour Market: Implications of Human Capital Research", *Journal of International Migration and Integration* 2(3), 347–378.

Schaafsma, J. and A. Sweetman (2001), "Immigrant Earnings: Age at Immigration Matters", *Canadian Journal of Economics* 34(4), 1066–1099.

Schreyer, P. (2001), *OECD Productivity Manual: A Guide to the Measurement of Industry-Level and Aggregate Productivity Growth*. Available for download in unabridged form at <http://www.oecd.org/catch_404/?404>; <http://www.oecd.org/subject/growth/prod-manual.pdf>.

Smith, A. (1963), *The Wealth of Nations*, Vol. 1 (first published in 1776), (Homewood, IL: Richard D. Irwin).

Summary of Discussion

David Green remarked that everybody seems to be getting on the band-waggon on the need to use immigration policy for acquiring more skills. But it is not always the case that, even if there is capital-skill complementarity, this means that more skill is better for everything. In particular, imagine a situation where there are two technologies in the economy — one uses high-skilled labour and capital and the other uses unskilled labour and capital — and you bring in more skilled labour. The capital will go over to the technology with the skilled labour, and actually result in reduced wages for the unskilled labour and reduced wages for the skilled labour. So it is not immediately obvious that bringing in skilled immigrants is going to do what most people believe it is going to do.

As a second point, David Green raised the moral issue that we do not like it when the United States takes our human capital, yet we are actively engaging in a policy to try to acquire human capital from other often less-wealthy countries than Canada. Yvan Turcotte responded that, when you select or attract people with human capital who come from a country where there is a surplus and where jobs are not available for all of the people with human capital — such as, say, Tunisia — there is no moral issue anymore because you are helping that country. Quebec indeed had representation from the Tunisian government which would like Quebec to take more of these well-educated young people because it helps to prevent social tensions there. David Green acknowledged this point if that were indeed the Canadian criterion for going out and attracting human capital. But it does not seem that that criterion is on the radar at the moment.

Jeffrey Reitz commented on the declining earnings of immigrants and that economic studies have not addressed the full dimensions of the decline.

The decline has occurred not only for recently arrived immigrants, but also for those who have been in the country for longer, and this is not due just to business-cycle effects. There is also a decline in the proportion of immigrants who have been able to get jobs. Looking just at the earnings of those who are employed misses a good part of the problem of the declining economic position of immigrants.

Jeffrey Reitz also raises a question about immigration policy and temporary immigrants, viz., whether temporary migrants stay or not. This is definitely an aspect of our temporary migration program that we need to look at closely. In the United States with their huge illegal population, this is a real problem. Their illegal population is being added to by the temporary migrants who came in large numbers to California during the dot-com boom, but only about half of them are leaving. One of the strengths of the Canadian immigration policy is the fact that we have a border with only one country, the United States. That has made it possible for us to avoid the substantial illegal population that the United States has. Nonetheless, the policy towards temporary migrants in Canada needs to be carefully thought through.

Barry Chiswick addressed the issue of why American and UK immigrants earn so much in Canada. He feels the reason for their high levels of earnings is very simple. If you can earn a lot in the United States, you are not going to move to Canada or stay in Canada unless you get high earnings in Canada. Whereas, if you are from Bangladesh, low earnings in Canada is a lot of money compared to what you could get in Bangladesh.

Louis Grignon was concerned about the waste in human capital of skilled immigrants who come here, but cannot get jobs that fit their skill and training because of problems in credential recognition and evaluation. Canadian institutions have not adapted to the reality of the new immigration. He feels we need to do something more to change these institutions in order to be able to better accommodate these new immigrants. One example of something that could be done — not minimizing the difficulties involved — would be to invite applicants to come here after being approved for positions or occupations. That way, they would better know what they are getting into when coming to Canada. He believes we have to find a way to crack this problem and have some regulatory bodies go abroad and approve these people where they are.

Canadian Emigration to the United States

David Card

Canada has always been a country of immigrants and emigrants. Figure 1, for example, shows decadal immigration and emigration rates from the 1850s to the 1990s.[1] During the second half of the nineteenth century, Canada actually lost more people than it gained from international migration. Over the twentieth century net migration was positive, but even since 1960 the emigration rate has remained at about one-third of the immigration rate. Many of those leaving Canada go to the United States. In 1940, roughly 10% of all immigrants in the United States — 1% of the total US population — were born in Canada. Today, because of the decline in emigration rates from Canada and the rapid rise in inflows from Mexico, Central America, and Asia, Canadians are a proportionally smaller group, accounting for only about 2% of all immigrants in the United States and less than 0.3% of the US population.

Flows of Canadians to the United States have long been a topic of interest on this side of the border.[2] Much of the concern among policy

---

[1] This figure is based on data in Zhao, Drew and Murray (2000, Table 6). The 1850s decade refers to the period from 1851 to 1861. Rates are expressed relative to the population at the beginning of the decade.

[2] For example, nearly every Canadian can identify a list of prominent expatriots living in the United States. Interest on the US side is negligible. The situation was brought to light in a 1987 article in *Spy Magazine*, "The Canadians

Figure 1: Canadian Immigration and Emigration Rates, 1981–1998

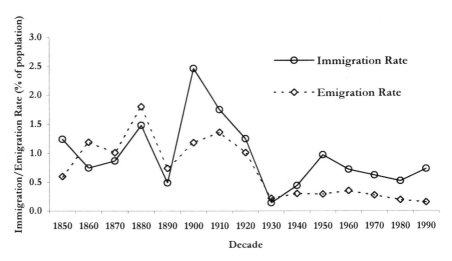

makers has been on the social cost of losing highly skilled workers to the United States — the so-called "brain drain".[3] From a broader perspective, however, the characteristics of Canadians in the United States, including their education, earnings, and even the success of their children, provide many insights into the Canadian economy.

This paper provides a brief overview of an ongoing research project with Thomas Lemieux that evaluates recent changes in the United States and Canadian labour markets, and the contribution of changing labour market incentives for immigration between the two countries. I will begin with an overview of historical patterns, starting with data from the 1940 US census. Then, I will present a simple framework for comparing wage structures in the two countries and describing changes over time in the

Among Us". The low profile of Canadians was attributed to the fact that "they act like us. They talk like us" and to the excessive politeness of Canadians.

[3]The first Special Study of the nascent Economic Council of Canada (Parai, 1965) addressed the issue of "brain drain". Zhao, Drew and Murray (2000) update Parai, and also frame skilled emigration in the context of overall imbalances of supply and demand for skilled workers in Canada.

David Card

relative wage structures on each side of the border. This framework highlights the effect of changes in the US labour market on the economic incentives for highly educated workers to move south.

Historical Perspectives

Tables 1 and 2 present some simple data showing an important historical fact: Canadian emigrants to the United States have always had above-average education levels relative to those who stayed home. The data in these tables are drawn from the US and Canadian censuses, and (for the most recent period) from pooled files of the March Current Population Survey (CPS). Looking first at men (Table 1), Canadians living in the United States in 1940 were about as likely as US natives to hold a university degree. This does not seem so remarkable until one looks at the situation in Canada, where only about 3% of men had a Bachelor of Arts (BA) or higher degree, according to published tabulations of the 1941 Canadian census.[4] By 1970, the fraction of Canadian immigrants with a university degree had risen above the level of the US-born, and currently Canadians living in the United States are 60% more likely to hold a degree than US natives, and about 2.7 times more likely than men in Canada. Even more striking is the relative frequency of advanced degrees (Master's of Arts (MAs), doctorates (PhDs), law and medical degrees). Currently, about 8% of Canadian immigrants in the United States have an advanced degree, compared to 3% of US men and just over 1% of Canadian men.

Similar conclusions hold for women, as shown in Table 2, although it took until 1990 for the education level of Canadian women living in the

---

[4]I am grateful to Thomas Lemieux for assistance with developing this estimate. The published tables only distinguish people with some postsecondary education (including a first degree), and those with an advanced degree. The fraction of men in these two categories was 5.1% and 1.5% respectively. Based on later data, I suspect that only 1/4 to 1/3 of those with any postsecondary education have a BA. This leads to an estimate of around 3% for the fraction with a BA or higher. The tabulations for women show 5.8% with some postsecondary education and 0.5% with an advanced degree, suggesting about 2% had a BA or higher.

Table 1: Percentages of Adult Men with a University Degree

	US Natives in US	*Canadians in US*	*Canadians in Canada*
1940	5.9	5.8	3.0 (est)
1970	14.4	15.0	--
1980	20.4	24.9	11.8
1990	22.7	33.3	--
2000	26.9	44.3	16.0
Addendum: percent with advanced degree			
2000	3.3	8.1	1.1

Notes: 1940–1990 data in columns 1 and 2 are from tabulations of the 1940–1990 US censuses; 2000 data are from combined samples from the 1995–2002 March Current Population Surveys. Data in column 3 is from tabulations of the 1981 and 1996 Canadian census; 1940 entry in this column is an estimate based on published tabulations of 1941 Canadian census.

Table 2: Percentages of Adult Women with a University Degree

	US Natives in US	*Canadians in US*	*Canadians in Canada*
1940	4.3	3.3	2.0 (est)
1970	9.1	7.6	--
1980	13.9	12.7	7.5
1990	19.0	22.7	--
2000	25.0	36.7	15.2
Addendum: percent with advanced degree			
2000	1.5	5.0	0.5

Notes: see notes to Table 1.

David Card

United States to surpass the rate of US women. As is true for men, Canadian immigrant women also have relatively high rates of holding an advanced degree: three times above the rate for US natives, and about ten times higher than the rate back home.

The data in Tables 1 and 2 point to three main conclusions. First, since at least 1940, Canadian emigrants have been more likely to come from the upper tail of the education distribution. Second, the degree of relative selectivity of the emigrant population seems to have accelerated in the 1980s and 1990s. Third, if anything, the degree of relative selectivity is currently a little higher for Canadian women living in the United States than for Canadian men, although historically it was the other way around.

An interesting observation about the selectivity of Canadian emigrants is that the flow of people across the border tends to accentuate, rather than narrow, the education gap between Canada and the United States. Although Canada has high education levels by world standards, there is still a substantial shortfall in educational attainment relative to the United States. This is illustrated in Table 3, using comparisons between the 1996 Canadian census and the 1995–2002 CPS. The gap is particularly large at the low end of the distribution: Canada has three times as many high school dropouts as the United States relative to its population.[5] Another difference between the countries is in the "some college" range. This group includes people with two- or three-year degrees awarded by community colleges, as well as those who attended a four-year college but never graduated. In Canada, it also includes a relatively large subgroup of people who completed apprenticeship and trade certificate programs, despite the fact that not all of them actually graduated from high school. Even including this group in the some college category, however, it is clear that the distribution of educational attainment in Canada is shifted to the left relative to the United States.

---

[5]See Parent (2001) for an interesting comparison of high school completion in the United States and Canada. Parent notes that high school completion rates continued to rise in the 1975–2000 period in Canada, but were stable in the United States, so the gap is closing rapidly.

Table 3: Comparisons of Current Educational Attainment in Canada and the United States

| | Men | | Women | |
	Canada	US	Canada	US
Dropout	32.2	9.8	28.0	9.1
High school	20.8	34.9	24.3	35.3
Some college	31.1*	28.4	32.5*	30.6
University or higher	16.0	26.9	15.2	25.0

Notes: Canadian data are from the 1996 Canadian census, and include only native-born Canadians age 21–64. US data are from pooled samples of the 1995–2002 March Current Population Surveys, and include only US-natives age 21–64.

* 25% of Canadian men with "some college" and 20% of Canadian women with "some college" lack a high school graduation certificate.

Returns to Emigration Circa 1980

To gain some insights into the economic incentives underlying the selective emigration patterns in Table 1 and 2, I will begin with the situation circa 1980. This choice of benchmark dates is driven by the fact that the 1981 census was the first to collect detailed information on educational attainment and weeks of work, making it easier to draw comparisons with US data. The late 1970s also represented a high point in the relative economic performance of Canada, so changes from that point may be especially salient in policy circles.[6]

---

[6]For example, real GDP per capita relative to the United States peaked in 1975, and remained at historically high levels until the mid-1980s. See Bank of Montreal (1999).

Figure 2a provides a simple framework for evaluating the relative economic gains to emigration for Canadian men in different age and education groups.[7] Specifically, the graph plots average log weekly earnings of Canadian men in the United States for each of 16 age/education groups (derived from the 1980 US census) against log weekly earnings of the same groups in Canada (derived from the 1981 Canadian census).[8] For reference purposes the graph also shows a 45 degree line. The points would fall on this line if Canadian men in the United States in a given age/ education group earned as much as similar men in Canada. In fact, all but one of the points are above the line, implying that for most age/education groups, average earnings of emigrants were higher than in Canada. The exception is the group with lowest average wages — young high school dropouts — who were actually earning higher average wages in Canada than in the United States in 1980–81.

The tendency of the points in Figure 2a to lie on a line with a slope greater than 1 implies that wage differentials across age/education groups were bigger in the United States than Canada as of the early 1980s.[9] Assuming for the moment that there are no differences in unobserved skill characteristics between emigrants and people who remain in Canada, wider pay differentials in the United States mean that more highly skilled Canadians have a bigger economic incentive to emigrate, even ignoring the different combination of taxes and social benefits in the two countries. The package of lower taxes and lower social benefits in the United States relative to Canada arguably reinforces this incentive.

The issue of unobserved skill differences between Canadians who leave and those who stay is complex, and ultimately difficult to resolve. Standard models of migrant selectivity suggest that conditional on observed characteristics, the gap in unobserved skill between movers and stayers will

---

[7]This framework is adapted from Card and Lemieux (1996).

[8]Earnings are expressed in 2000 US dollars using the 1980 exchange rate and changes in the United States and Canadian CPI since then. The age groups are 21–30, 31–40, 41–50, and 50–64. The education groups are less than high school, high school, some postsecondary, and BA or higher.

[9]The slope of a regression line fit to the points is 1.24 (standard error 0.07).

Figure 2a: Gains from Immigration for Canadian Men, 1980–1981

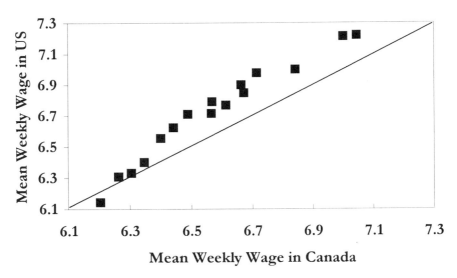

be larger for skill groups with lower observed skills.[10] To the extent this is true, the evidence in Figure 2a may actually understate the relative economic incentives for emigration of more highly skilled Canadians.

Figure 2b presents a parallel analysis for women. In contrast to men, the data for women suggest that wage differentials in the 1980s were compressed in the United States relative to Canada. In particular, Canadian women with a BA or higher education who lived in the United States earned lower average weekly wages than comparable women in Canada.[11]

---

[10]Suppose that mean log wages in Canada for a worker with observed skills m and unobserved skills v are given by $\log(w) = m + v$. Suppose that mean log wages in the United States for the same worker are $\alpha + \beta(m + v)$, where the coefficient β is greater than 1. Finally, suppose an individual emigrates if the expected difference in mean log wages exceeds a moving cost C. Then movers are those for whom $m+v > (C-\alpha)/(\beta-1)$. If C is constant this implies a higher expected value of unobserved skill for those who move with lower observed skills.

[11]The three highest wage groups in Figure 2b — all below the 45 degree line — are women with a university degree age 31–40, 41–50, and 51 and older.

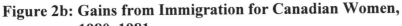

Figure 2b: Gains from Immigration for Canadian Women, 1980–1981

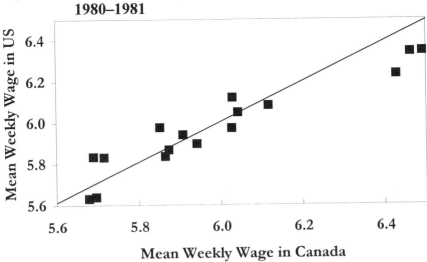

Mean Weekly Wage in Canada

It is interesting to speculate whether the contrast between men and women reflects the relatively low pay of teachers and nurses in the United States — occupations traditionally held by highly educated women — or whether it is driven by differences in the selection process underlying the emigration decisions of men and women.[12]

Changing Wage Structures in Canada and the United States and Implications for Emigration Incentives

How have incentives for emigration changed over the past two decades? One important factor is the rise in average real incomes in the United States

---

[12]Baker and Fortin (2000) show that in Canada these two occupations do not have particularly low wages. Mincer (1978) and Borjas and Bronars (1991) present models of family migration decision-making which suggests different patterns of selectivity bias among the observed wages of immigrant men and women. In future research it would be interesting to compare Canadian emigrants who moved alone, and with a spouse.

relative to Canada since the early 1980s. This change has meant that all workers can earn more in the United States than in Canada. A second factor is changes in the relative wage structures in the two countries. While relative wage gaps across skill groups have stayed roughly constant in Canada, they have expanded rapidly in the United States (see e.g., Autor and Katz, 1999).

Figure 3 illustrates the changing levels of real wages for different skill groups in Canada. As in Figures 2a and 2b, each point in the graph represents a specific age/education group. In Figure 3, however, I have plotted mean log weekly wages in 1996 for Canadian workers (in US dollars) against mean log weekly wages in 1981 (also in US dollars). The figure also shows the 45 degree line, and another line parallel to the 45 degree line but 25 log points lower. The figure makes two simple points. First, measured in US dollars, wages in Canada declined substantially between 1981 and 1996. Since inflation rates have not been too different in the two countries, the decline is equivalent to the fall in the value of the Canadian dollar. Second, although there are some differences in wage trends across age and education groups, these were relatively small compared to the overall decline in average wages. Both features are also evident in the evolution of wages for women in Canada over the same period.[13]

The situation in the US labour market was quite different. Figure 4 plots data for US men in different skill groups in 1980 and in 1994–2002. Notice first that, as in Canada, average real wages declined in the United States. However, the decline was bigger for workers at the bottom of the labour market, and smaller for those at the top, so on average wage differences between groups expanded in the United States. Second, the mean wages of younger college graduates (those under the age of 40) actually kept pace with inflation, and rose substantially relative to other workers. Indeed, the economic "return" to a university degree for younger men — measured by the wage gap between those with a BA and those with only a high school diploma — roughly doubled between 1980 and 2000 (see Card and DiNardo, 2002, Figures 7 and 8). Similar changes occurred

---

[13]In recent work, Thomas Lemieux, Craig Riddell and I have compared patterns of changing wage inequality in Canada using public use samples of the censuses, and using other data sources (Card, Lemieux and Riddell, 2003). We believe that the absence of a rise in inequality between skill groups is a general feature of the Canadian data, and not specific to the census.

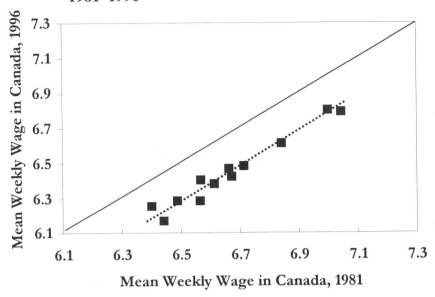

Figure 3: Evolution of Wage Structure: Canadian Men, 1981–1996

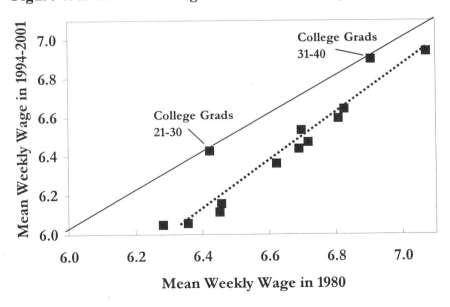

Figure 4: Evolution of Wage Structure: US Men, 1980–2001

Canadian Emigration to the United States   *305*

for women, although the overall decline in real wages was smaller for women, resulting in a roughly 15 percentage point closing of the gap between men and women (Card and DiNardo, 2002, Figure 12).

Putting the pieces together, the combination of declining average wages in Canada relative to the United States, widening wage inequality in the United States, and constant wage inequality in Canada imply that the economic incentives for emigration have increased for all Canadians, but especially for younger, highly educated Canadians. Figure 5a shows the same information as in Figure 2a, updated to the late 1990s. (The wider variability in the points in Figure 5a is attributable to the much smaller sample sizes in the 1995–2002 CPS than in the census. Each skill group only has 30 to 100 observations in the pooled CPS files.) Relative to the situation in 1980–81, the points lie on an even steeper line that is further above the 45 degree line. The points for the three highest wage groups (all with BA or higher education) are on average 40 log points above the 45 degree line, implying that Canadian emigrants in the United States with a college degree earned 40% more than similar workers back home in the late 1990s. By comparison, the same three groups had only a 15% average wage advantage in the United States in 1980–81.

As shown in Figure 5b, the situation for women is murkier, in part because of the very small cell sizes available from the CPS. Nevertheless, all the points are on or above the 45 degree line, and the relative disadvantage of highly educated emigrant women noted in Figure 2b has disappeared. While a complete analysis will have to await availability of data from the 2000 and 2001 censuses, it seems clear that the overall level of economic incentives for emigration, and the distribution of incentives across different education groups, have changed over the past two decades in a direction to magnify the "brain drain".

A Caveat on Selectivity

As I have noted earlier, comparisons such as those in Figures 2a/2b and 5a/5b rest on the assumption that unobserved skill characteristics (e.g., ambition) are not too different between emigrants and those who remain at home. Many analysts would agree than migrants are systematically different, and that comparisons between the earnings of Canadians in the

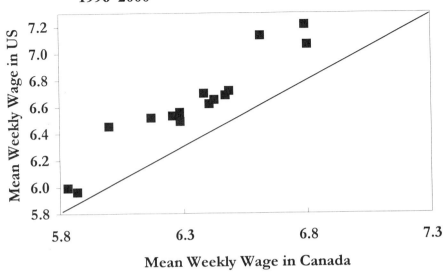

Figure 5a: Gains from Immigration for Canadian Men, 1996–2000

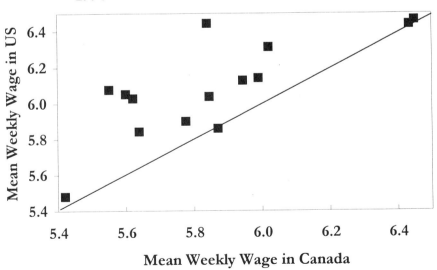

Figure 5b: Gains from Immigration for Canadian Women, 1996

United States and those in Canada reflect both differences in labour market opportunities in the two countries, and differences between movers and stayers. One way to evaluate the mover-stayer component is to compare Canadian emigrants in the United States to US natives with the same observed skills. If Canadian movers are really highly selected, one might expect them to stand out in the US labour market.

Figures 6a and 6b present an analysis along these lines. Figure 6a plots the average earnings of Canadian men in the United States in 1980 (in each of 16 age/education groups) against the average earnings of US natives in the same skill groups. Figure 6b conducts the same analysis for women. The information in these graphs is summarized in Table 4, along with comparable data for 1940 and the late 1990s. Looking at Figure 6a, it seems clear that Canadian men living in the United States tend to earn more than US natives, even controlling for age and education. As shown in Table 4, the average wage advantage of Canadian men, controlling for age and education, was 10.6% in 1980. For women, the data on Figure 6b suggest much smaller differentials between Canadian emigrants and US natives. This is confirmed in Table 4: on average, Canadian women in the United States earned only 3% more than similar US natives.

Interestingly, comparisons in 1980 represent a relative low point for the average wage differential of Canadians in the US labour market. In 1940, the adjusted gaps for both men and women were around 22%, and in the late 1990s the gaps were both about 15%. There are several possible explanations for this "U-shaped" pattern of Canadian differentials. One is that changing forces underlying emigration flows have led to changes in the unobserved skills of Canadians who leave, as well as changes in the observed skills. An alternative is that there are changing economic rewards to characteristics like ambition in the US labour market. Sorting out these alternatives will be an important challenge for future work.

Summary

The results of the analysis here point to five main conclusions. First, Canadian immigrants in the United States are relatively well educated. This has been true for at least the past 60 years. In earlier years, Canadian emigrants were better educated than other Canadians, but not too different

Figure 6a: Earnings of Canadian Men in US vs. Native Men, 1980

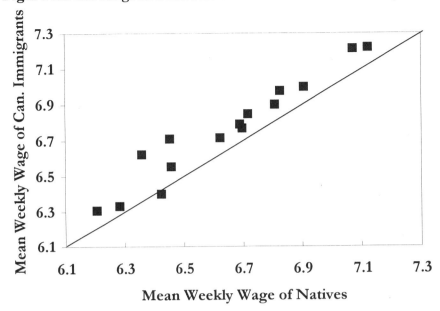

Figure 6b: Earnings of Canadian Women in US vs. Native Women, 1980

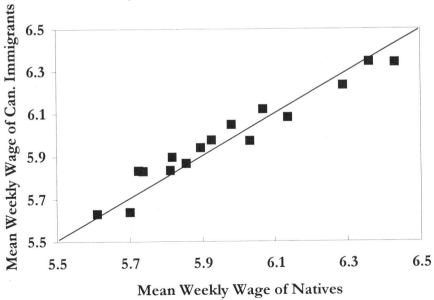

Table 4: Relative Wage Advantage of Canadian Immigrants in the United States

	Men		Women	
	Unadjusted	*Adjusted*	*Unadjusted*	*Adjusted*
1940	26.0	21.9	18.3	21.2
1980	17.5	10.6	4.6	3.0
2000	24.3	14.0	27.8	15.7

Notes: Entries represent percentage differences in average weekly wages of 21–64 year old Canadian immigrants and US natives. Unadjusted differences represent differences in mean log wages. Adjusted differences are from a regression model that also includes interactions of age and education dummies. 1940 data are from 1940 US census. 1980 data are from 1980 US census. 2000 data are from combined samples from the 1995–2002 March Current Population Surveys.

from US natives. Over the past couple of decades, however, with convergence in education levels between the two countries and a rise in the relative emigration rate of highly-educated Canadians, Canadians in the United States are now substantially more educated than US natives.

Second, outflows of relatively well-educated men and women from Canada accentuate the skill differences between the two countries. The migration process is not closing the skill gap between countries; it is actually contributing to a further widening of the existing gap between average education levels in the United States and Canada.

Third, over the 1980s and 1990s, important economic trends have intensified the economic incentives for Canadians to emigrate to the United States, particularly Canadians with at least a university education. The remarkable rise in the relative wages of younger college-educated workers in the United States has created economic incentives not just for Canadians but for people from all around the world to move to the United States. I suspect that Canadian concerns over the brain drain are echoed in many other countries.

David Card

Fourth, some of the difference between the earnings of Canadian emigrants in the United States and those back home are probably due to the selective nature of the migration process. Compared to US natives with similar observed skills, Canadian immigrants in the United States earn more. The wage advantage earned by Canadians in the United States declined between 1940 and 1980, and has risen since then, perhaps reflecting changes in the migration decision process, or changes in the rewards to the unobserved characteristics that emigrants have always taken with them.

Finally, comparisons between the United States and Canada provide an interesting perspective on the issue of skill shortages. Some Canadians have expressed concerns over an impending skill shortage, and the recent policy focus on the brain drain is partly motivated by a belief that emigration is contributing to a shortage of highly skilled workers. Looking at wages in the United States and Canada, however, there is no evidence of a shortage of educated workers in Canada. Indeed, while relative wages of highly educated workers have risen sharply in the United States since the early 1980s, they have remained constant in Canada. The market signal that might be expected to help remedy an impending skill shortage — a rise in the relative pay of better educated workers — has not yet occurred.

References

Autor, D. and L. Katz (1999), "Changes in the Wage Structure and Earnings Inequality", in O. Ashenfelter and D. Card (eds.), *Handbook of Labor Economics*, Volume 3A (Amsterdam: Elsevier).

Baker, M. and N. Fortin (2000), "Occupational Gender Composition and Wages in Canada: 1987–1988", CIRANO Working Paper No. 2000s-48 (Montreal: CIRANO).

Bank of Montreal (1999), "Trends in Canada-US Migration: Where's the Flood?" *Economic Analysis*, March 24 (Toronto: Bank of Montreal).

Borjas, G.L. and S.G. Bronars (1991), "Immigration and the Family", *Journal of Labor Economics* 9 (April), 123–148.

Card, D. and J.E. DiNardo (2002), "Skill Biased Technical Change and Rising Wage Inequality: Some Problems and Puzzles", *Journal of Labor Economics* 20 (October), 733–783.

Card, D. and T. Lemieux (1996), "Wage Dispersion, Returns to Skill, and Black-White Wage Differentials", *Journal of Econometrics* 74 (October), 319–361.

Card, D., T. Lemieux and W.C. Riddell (2003), "Unionization and Wage Inequality: A Comparative Study of the U.S., the U.K., and Canada", NBER Working Paper No. 9473 (Cambridge, MA: National Bureau of Economic Research).

Mincer, J. (1978), "Family Migration Decisions", *Journal of Political Economy* 86 (October), 749–773.

Parai, L. (1965), *Immigration and Emigration of Professional and Skilled Manpower During the Post-War Period*, Special Study No. 1. Prepared for the Economic Council of Canada (Ottawa: Queen's Printer).

Parent, D. (2001), "Return to a High School Diploma and the Decision to Drop Out: New Evidence from Canada", CIRANO Working Paper No. 2001s-09 (Montreal: CIRANO).

Zhao, J., D. Drew and T.S. Murray (2000), "Brain Drain and Brain Gain: The Migration of Knowledge Workers from and to Canada", *Education Quarterly Review* 6(3), 8–35.

Section V

Canadian Immigration Data Sources

The IMDB: A User's Overview of the Immigration Database

Michael G. Abbott

I have been asked to provide some summary information and observations on the IMDB, the Canadian Immigration Database. I do so not from the perspective of someone who has been involved in the development of this unique new database, but rather as someone who has some experience (in collaboration with Craig Dougherty of CIC) with using micro-level data from the IMDB for analytical purposes. After summarizing the nature and characteristics of the IMDB, I identify what I think are the main weaknesses and strengths of the IMDB as an individual-level database for empirical investigations of the post-landing outcomes of Canadian immigrants.

Nature and Characteristics of the IMDB

The IMDB is a longitudinal administrative database on the landed immigrant population in Canada. It has been compiled by Statistics Canada and Citizenship and Immigration Canada (CIC) from two administrative data

I thank Craig Dougherty of Citizenship and Immigration Canada for helpful comments.

sources: landing records compiled by CIC from immigration documents recorded at the time a landing visa is issued; and personal income tax records assembled from the annual personal income tax returns filed by individual immigrants (primarily the T1).

From an analytical perspective, the IMDB provides two types of information: landing record information; and personal income tax data. The landing record information on each immigrant taxfiler is *time-invariant* — what CIC calls "tombstone data". It is recorded as of the date of issue of the landing visa and does not subsequently change. It consists of information on immigrants' demographic characteristics at the time they are granted permanent residence in Canada such as place of origin, marital status, age and gender; information on the programs through which each individual is admitted to Canada, such as immigrant category, family status, and points at selection; and information on immigrants' human capital characteristics such as education, language ability, and intended occupation. In contrast to the landing record information, the personal income tax data on each immigrant taxfiler is *time varying*. It consists of limited information on immigrants' demographic characteristics at the end of each tax year, specifically province of residence, marital status, and detailed information on immigrants' incomes, government transfer payment receipts and personal income tax payments over the entire tax year.

With respect to coverage of the IMDB, the subject population consists of all landed immigrants who filed at least one income tax return since their arrival in Canada. The database is updated annually to include more recent immigrant landings and more recent longitudinal observations on all previous landings back to 1980. The IMDB database currently covers landing years and tax years from 1980 to 2000. The IMDB is broadly representative of the Canadian population of immigrant taxfilers who were landed as permanent residents over the period 1980–2000, as distinct from the population of all Canadian immigrants.

The structure of the IMDB is basically that of an individual-level panel database. At its most disaggregated level, the cross-sectional unit of analysis in the IMDB is the individual immigrant taxfiler. The time-series unit of analysis is the tax year, which coincides with the calendar year. Each IMDB observation, or micro-record, thus consists of immigration and tax data on a single immigrant taxfiler for a specific tax/calendar year. Individual immigrants are identified by a unique person-specific serial number and their landing year, defined as the year in which they were granted permanent resident status in Canada. For each immigrant taxfiler, individual observations are identified by the tax year to which the current income tax data pertain. Since an IMDB record does not exist for those years in which an immigrant taxfiler did not file an income tax return, the IMDB micro-database constitutes an unbalanced panel.

Weaknesses of the IMDB

What are the major limitations of the IMDB as a database for empirical analysis of Canadian immigrants' labour market outcomes and performance?

One major weakness of the IMDB is the paucity of data it contains on immigrants' current characteristics — specifically their current demographic, human capital, and job characteristics. Contemporaneous, or current-year, data in the IMDB are limited to the information reported on personal income tax returns (T1 General forms). Such information does not include data on many demographic and human capital characteristics of immigrants — e.g., education, training, work experience, job and firm tenure, and family circumstances. We therefore cannot measure in the IMDB how such immigrant characteristics change over time, for example, how immigrants' educational attainment, official language fluency, and occupational qualifications change after landing in Canada. Nor does the IMDB include information on immigrants' current labour force status (employment, unemployment, and labour force participation status) or their current job and employment characteristics such as current occupation, hours worked per week, weeks worked per year, union membership and coverage status, firm and establishment size, and so on — information that typically is available in many survey micro-datasets, both cross-sectional and longitudinal. Consequently, the IMDB does not permit one to control for many observable time-varying attributes when estimating the effects of immigrants' landing characteristics on their post-landing outcomes.

A second major limitation of the IMDB is that it does not incorporate information on Canadian-born taxfilers comparable to that provided on immigrant taxfilers. This means that the IMDB cannot be used to investigate, at least at the individual level, the labour market outcomes of foreign-born Canadian residents vis-à-vis those of native-born Canadians. The absence of comparable data on native-born taxfilers has several implications for what analysts can and cannot do with the IMDB micro-data. First, it is not possible to separately identify the three effects on immigrant outcomes on which much previous immigration research has focused, namely the *assimilation effect* (the effect of years of residence in the destination country), *entry cohort effects* (the effects of unobserved differences across successive entry cohorts of immigrants), and *period effects* (the effects of unobserved period-specific factors such as aggregate shocks and the business cycle). In micro-datasets that include native-born as well as foreign-born individuals, a conventional strategy for identifying these three effects is to assume that period effects are the same for immigrants and non-immigrants. But in the absence of individual-level data on native-born persons, this identification strategy is obviously not available. Consequently, using only IMDB micro-data on individual immigrants, it is not possible to separately identify all three of these effects.

The absence of comparable data on native-born (non-immigrant) taxfilers has implications for the measurement of assimilation and cohort effects on immigrant outcomes. First, the IMDB does not permit empirical investigation of assimilation and cohort effects *relative to native-born Canadians*, which is how they are conventionally defined in the economics literature on immigrant earnings and other labour market outcomes. Second, the IMDB measures the assimilation effect differently than do most survey micro-datasets. In particular, the IMDB measures the number of years that have elapsed since an immigrant was landed in Canada as a permanent resident, which is obviously not identical to the number of years since initial arrival in Canada for those immigrants who resided in Canada before they became landed permanent residents. The assimilation effect that can be estimated from IMDB data is therefore a *years-since-landing* effect as distinct from a *years-since-arrival* effect.

Some additional limitations of the IMDB stem from the fact that all its income and earnings data are obtained from personal income tax returns. First, the IMDB obviously excludes immigrants who do not file income tax returns. Second, the IMDB likely exhibits some degree of non-reporting and underreporting of incomes arising from tax avoidance and tax evasion, although in fairness it must be acknowledged that household survey data are also subject to unknown measurement errors in reporting incomes. Finally, the IMDB contains no information on immigrants' families or households. Since individual taxfilers are not linked to the families or households in which they reside, the IMDB provides no data on the characteristics and incomes of spouses and dependants or on the size and demographic composition of the family units in which individual immigrants live.

Strengths of the IMDB

In contrast to the paucity of data it provides on immigrants' contemporaneous demographic, human capital, and job characteristics, the IMDB furnishes an abundance of detailed data on immigrants' landing characteristics, that is, the initial characteristics of Canadian immigrants at the time they were landed in Canada as permanent residents. In fact, the richness of the landing information it provides is probably the paramount strength of the IMDB relative to the micro-data on Canadian immigrants available from censuses and household surveys. This landing information can be organized into three broad categories: demographic characteristics, human capital attributes, and administrative or programmatic information related to visa application and issuance processes.

Information on immigrants' *demographic characteristics* includes data on gender, age at landing, marital status at landing, mother tongue (native language), country of birth, country of last permanent residence, country of citizenship, and province of intended destination in Canada. Information on immigrants' *human capital characteristics* includes data on formal education at landing, occupational skills and qualifications, intended occupation of employment, and (self-assessed) fluency in English and French, Canada's two official languages. Finally, the *programmatic information* on immigrants includes data on year of landing, admission or visa category, principal applicant status, special program codes (live-in caregiver program, administrative review program, backlog clearance program), location of the visa-issuing office, and employment status at landing (whether the immigrant had arranged employment or was destined for employment in a designated occupation). Much of this programmatic information relates directly to the policy environment in which it is captured, and is virtually never available in Canadian census and household survey micro-datasets that distinguish between foreign-born and native-born residents. Table 1 presents just one of the classifications of visa category available in the IMDB — the so-called IMCAT classification — which groups immigrants according to the selection criteria under which they were granted permanent resident status in Canada.

A second major strength of the IMDB consists of the detailed information it contains on immigrants' incomes, both employment earnings and investment income. The IMDB provides data not only on each immigrant's total labour market earnings and investment income, but also on the

Table 1: The IMCAT Classification of Permanent Resident Visas in the IMDB

IMCAT Code	Description of IMCAT visa Category
1	Family Class
2	Entrepreneur, not special program, landed from abroad
3	Self-employed, not special program, landed from abroad
4	Skilled Worker, not special program, landed from abroad
5	Investor, not special program, landed from abroad
6	All economic immigrants granted permanent resident status through special programs and/or those who were processed within Canada
7	Assisted Relatives processed abroad, not special program
8	Assisted Relatives processed in Canada and/or through special programs
9	Retired Persons
10	Government-Sponsored Refugees
11	Privately Sponsored Refugees
12	Refugees Landed in Canada
13	Live-in Caregivers and/or Foreign Household Domestics
14	Administrative Review
15	Refugee Backlog Clearance and/or Refugee Clearance Dependent
16	Deferred Removal Order Class (DROC)

individual components of personal income. Table 2 displays some of the personal income components measured in the IMDB; it illustrates the detailed nature of the information on immigrant incomes available in the IMDB. Note in particular that the IMDB provides data not only on total self-employment earnings and total investment income, but also on their individual components.

Table 2: Components of Immigrants' Personal Incomes Measured in the IMDB

Annual *labour market earnings*: sum of/
- *Employment earnings* = all earnings from paid employment: sum of
  - T4 earnings (line 101 of T1 General)
  - Other employment income (line 104 of T1 General)
- *Self-employment earnings* = net income from self-employment: sum of
  - Limited partnership income
  - Net business income
  - Net professional income
  - Net commission income
  - Net farming income
  - Net fishing income

Annual *investment income*: sum of
- Dividend income
- Interest income
- Net capital gains income
- Net rental income

Annual *government transfer payment receipts*
- Social assistance payments
- Employment insurance benefits

A final, but by no means unimportant, advantage of the IMDB is its size. Since it includes a record for every income tax return filed by every landed immigrant over the period 1980–2000, the IMDB is capable of yielding very large analysis samples of micro-level data. This feature not only enhances statistical precision in estimating the effects of immigrant characteristics on post-landing outcomes, but is also likely to permit empirical investigation of detailed aspects of the immigrant selection system.

Concluding Observations

I conclude with some observations on what I think are the empirical research topics for which the IMDB is likely to prove most appropriate and useful. Not surprisingly, these topics are suggested by the IMDB's major strengths. Since it provides detailed information on immigrants' landing characteristics, much of it not available in other Canadian micro-datasets, the IMDB is uniquely suitable for investigating the effects of these characteristics on immigrants' post-landing outcomes. And given the abundance of data it contains on immigrants' personal incomes, the IMDB is likely to be invaluable for investigating the evolution and observed correlates of immigrants' personal income and its several components in the years following their landing in Canada as permanent residents. In short, I think the IMDB will prove most valuable in conducting empirical investigations into the effects of immigrants' landing characteristics — particularly the immigrant selection system — on the incidence, level and growth of their paid employment earnings, self-employment earnings, investment income (and its components), social assistance (welfare) benefits, and unemployment insurance benefits.

Let me end by acknowledging the debt of gratitude that all of us owe the individuals at Citizenship and Immigration Canada who are responsible for assembling the IMDB and making it available to members of the immigration research community. In addition to those such as Elizabeth Ruddick and Craig Dougherty, I would like to thank someone who has played an instrumental role in the development of the IMDB, Claude Langlois. Claude has been a driving force behind the IMDB from its inception over ten years ago. On behalf of all of us interested in Canadian immigration research, I extend a very big "thank you" to Claude Langlois.

Michael G. Abbott

Longitudinal Survey of Immigrants to Canada

Martha Justus and Jessie-Lynn MacDonald

We want to discuss the Longitudinal Survey of Immigrants to Canada, which is presently underway and will continue for the next few years. We want to look at why we are undertaking this work, some more specifics about the survey itself, and also what we hope to get out of it.

The basic objective of the Longitudinal Survey of Immigrants to Canada (LSIC) is to study how new immigrants adjust to life in Canada through time. It is pretty straightforward. The survey was designed to include representative samples of as many categories of immigrants by province as possible. We have all of the major immigrant categories covered and we will be able to draw conclusions for all the three major census metropolitan areas (CMAs): Toronto, Montreal, and Vancouver. In addition, Alberta and British Columbia have provided extra funding to increase their provincial samples.

This kind of study has not been done since the 1970s. There was a longitudinal survey at that time, and 20 years later seemed like a good time to look again. Things have obviously changed. We are not the only people looking at a longitudinal analysis of this kind. The Australians have completed one longitudinal survey and are now in the process of examining a second cohort. The New Zealanders are also conducting a longitudinal survey of immigrants, and the Americans are preparing to do so. The Israelis have undertaken similar kinds of studies, using similar instruments, but their program is significantly different, it is rather like comparing apples and oranges.

We want to use the survey to provide information on factors that can help or hinder the integration process for immigrants. Basically, we want to identify things that can be affected through policy levers. So the questionnaire is very detailed and has a policy thrust implicit in it. We also want to complement other policy research that is underway. There is the Immigration Database (IMDB). However, it talked about the change in human capital characteristics, for example, of immigrants through time. The longitudinal survey has been designed to complement that activity. The IMDB tells us about the immigrant outcomes; hopefully, LSIC will tell us about why those outcomes come about.

The pilot study was done in 1996–97 and was found to be a feasible way to collect information. Refusal rates were very low. This is very important because it is a very extensive interview; it takes approximately an hour and a half to complete. We also had many concerns about people moving and our being able to keep in touch with the survey participants. The mobility of immigrants did affect the response rates, but not as much as we anticipated. The sample frame was created in October 2000 through September 2001, so those are the people that we interviewed. The first wave was collected over the period of a year, April 2001 to March 2002. People were interviewed six months after their arrival in Canada. The second wave was to have taken place in October 2002, but we are roughly two months behind to start up the second wave. We have had delays in finalizing the application. But the methodological implications of this are not expected to be particularly great, so we are still very comfortable with the likely results. The third wave will go into the field between October 2004 and September 2005. That means the respondents will have been in the country for four years.

We are studying immigrants who came to Canada between October 2000 and September 2001. They must have landed from abroad, so people who were already in Canada are not in the sample. The latter category includes, in particular, asylum refugees, so the survey does not cover asylum refugees. Most of those people have been here for a few years and we think that their adaptation process is somewhat different, so they are not included in the survey group. The respondents must also be 15 years of age or older. That does not mean we will not have information about children. There are specific questions in the questionnaire to cover children under the age of 15.

Let me also say something about the survey design. We are conducting the interview at three points in time: after the immigrants have been here six months, two years, and four years. The majority of interviews for wave one were conducted face to face, using computer-assisted interviewing. The average household visit is about 90 minutes. While 75 minutes of that are dedicated to the core questionnaire, the other 15 minutes are for what we call entry and exit, which is just gathering household information and introducing the survey.

The unit of analysis is the individual immigrant and one person per family is being interviewed. This is a little bit different from the Australian survey because in the Australian survey the principal applicant is the one interviewed, and in ours it is just one person per household. Again, the respondent must be 15 years or older. We are interviewing in 15 different languages; English and French and 13 others. With this we are hoping to cover about 91–95% of the immigrant population. We are not conducting the interviews in the Northwest Territories, the Yukon or Nunavut because the costs of doing so are very high. We are tracing respondents if they move within Canada between the waves and will interview them where they are. We are also collecting information if they move to the United States but we are not interviewing at that point.

We ask a lot of questions in 75 minutes. It is very extensive. In wave one we asked about their reasons for coming to Canada which we do not have to follow up within wave two. We ask about their social interactions: Were they sponsored to come here? Did they have a host when they came? We ask about family and friends in Canada, as well as their knowledge and use of different services and resources. We ask about their language skills, their ability to communicate and get by in both English and French and also their acquisition of language skills. We ask about their housing. Because we want to track their mobility over time, we ask about all the locations in which they have lived. In wave one we wanted all the places that they have lived in since they arrived, and then in wave two we ask about all the locations since the wave one interview. We ask about the type of residence and whether they rent or own their home, the number of rooms in the home, and their approximate monthly costs. Education is a big module. A current topic of discussion is "recognition of foreign qualifications". We ask about barriers to education and training and their reasons for furthering or not furthering their training. We ask them questions about their spouse and children in this module.

In the employment module, again we ask about the recognition of foreign work experience. We ask about all their jobs, and in wave two we follow up with all the jobs since wave one.

In the health module, we ask about their current health status, their access to health care and health-care providers. How important is it that the health-care provider speaks the same language, is the same gender, or has the same cultural background as the individual? In wave two, we have expanded the module to ask questions about emotional health issues as well.

We ask about values and attitudes, how important is it to the respondent to maintain their ethnic or cultural ties and about adopting Canadian values or traditions. We ask them about their plans to take out Canadian citizenship. We ask them specific questions about their income structure, and about changes in their financial status. We ask them how they have felt about their settlement so far, and we will continue to ask those questions.

We are also going to try to do some event history analysis to examine combinations of activities around finding a job, around finding a house, around accessing training, and around similar important events. We also have what is affectionately known as the problem grid. This is a consistent problem grid for all activities, so we will be able to see if there are similarities or consistent difficulties.

The final thing that we want to note is what and how we plan to make information available. There will be a release of the first wave results in the StatsCan *Daily* or *le Quotidien* in June 2003. That does not mean the data will be available then. There is a great deal of information to be processed. We hope to complete an analytical publication that we are doing jointly with Statistics Canada for the Fall of 2003, but that will be largely a basic description, a profile kind of publication. We are also planning to have the information available through remote access. We have decided to do this instead of putting together a public use file because we felt that a public use file would probably be too limiting. We have a fairly extensive advisory committee, and we felt that there would be too much suppression of the survey results if we went that way. We are working with Statistics Canada to make arrangements so that the data are available through the regional data centres.

New Household Surveys on Immigration

Doug Norris

Introduction

This is an opportunity for me to discuss a number of new data sources. I will review, first, the census. Although not a new data source, a few things are being done a little differently for the 2001 census. There are also two new surveys: the Ethnic Diversity Survey and the Canadian Community Health Survey, which has just started rolling out. I will then cover some of the issues around using the data from the Survey of Labour and Income Dynamics. Finally, I will briefly mention several other surveys that might be of interest.

Census of Population

The census has long been an important data source for looking at immigration issues. Basic questions have covered place of birth, citizenship, and year of immigration. In recent years, the Canadian census has added the distinction of allowing us to differentiate between permanent residents and non-permanent residents. That is, people who are living in Canada on temporary visas are now included in the census and can be identified as such. As a result, for the last three censuses we have been able to analyze separately the data on permanent and non-permanent residents.

A question on birth place of parents was new in 2001. This will allow us to determine who are second-generation Canadians and to analyze what is happening to them. Although a similar question had been asked in the 1971 census, it was not continued in subsequent censuses. Its reintroduction is going to open up some new avenues for research.

The census has both strengths and weaknesses. It has a very large sample and has been done much the same way since 1981. Although individuals cannot be linked from one census to another, the fact that there is a census every five years means that one can trace cohorts over time and I believe this offers some real potential for research, particularly in areas such as immigration. Another strength of the census is the fact that it does have family and household data. These data, however, have not been used extensively in the past, mainly because they have not been available to use easily.

On the other hand, a weakness of the census is that it does not contain information on characteristics at time of landing (e.g., education, class of immigrant, etc.). This is the real strength of the Immigration Database (IMDB), and I believe there is substantial gain to be made by using the census and IMDB to complement one another.

Another new census initiative under consideration is in the area of dissemination. One of the things we were trying to do for the 2001 census is to create a hierarchal file that would allow for much easier and more detailed family and household analysis. In Canada, thus far, our census public use files have not been hierarchal. Although for confidentiality reasons we cannot produce a hierarchal public use file for 2001, if things work out, we hope to be able to put an unsuppressed data file into our new Research Data Centres to allow people to use the data. This should open up some new avenues of research.

The census results are rolled out in waves. Although we have not yet put out immigration data, the fact that immigration is an increasingly important component of population growth has resulted in the topic receiving considerable attention in the early releases on basic demographic change. The immigration data is scheduled for release in January 2003, but since the economic and education data will not be, the release will cover basic descriptive information on characteristics. In February we will release labour market data, in March, education data; and income in May. So, by summer 2003 all of the information should be out. Nevertheless, I expect that immigration data will figure in many of the releases beginning in January.

Ethnic Diversity Survey

In the area of household surveys, there are a number of new surveys. The Ethnic Diversity Survey is a new post-censal survey done following the 2001 census. That is, we drew the sample for this survey from the census. This gives us some real advantages in terms of stratifying the sample to find groups that ordinarily would be difficult to find through a regular population survey because the groups are too small (e.g., second generations of various origins). We stratified the sample first by generation. We also employed broad ethnic background, essentially British/French in one group, European in another, and non-Europeans in the last. Using that stratification we allocated the sample to get sufficient samples in each of the generations by ethnic group.

The sample size is quite large. It is about 40,000 of which probably 10,000 to 15,000 are immigrants. But it is the stratification that I think will bring interesting potential to obtaining information about groups that normally would not be able to be analyzed because of their small sample size. The survey was done this past summer and the data should be out late summer or early fall in 2003.

The survey looked at measuring the rather complex issue of ancestry, ethnic origin, and identity. It also included some information on the respondents' backgrounds, some more detailed language data, even more detailed than what we have in our census, family interaction, social networks, and civic participation. In fact, the survey touches on the area of social capital — a topic of current interest. I am not sure how to measure social capital, but some of the dimensions that people talk about are included in this survey.

Canadian Community Health Survey

Data from the new Canadian Community Health Survey have just been released and the micro-data should be coming out fairly soon. This survey was conducted in response to the growing interest in health and the need to develop health indicators. Following discussions between the various ministers of health on the health agenda, there is a set of health indicators that are produced regularly to monitor heath-related trends. This survey provides many of these indicators. It also has a very large sample, 132,000 in the first wave.

This survey was designed to provide data for each of the 136 health regions in the country. These data include basic information on health status, health behaviour, smoking, drinking, exercise, health utilization, and a number of other health-related topics.

The immigrant sample is also fairly large in this survey, about 20,000, which gives a good number to work with. A first paper on the health status of immigrants has been released in *Health Reports* and is available on Statistics Canada's Web site. However, there is certainly much more that can be done with the information received. The survey is done every two years so it will be updated on a fairly regular basis.

Survey of Labour and Income Dynamics

I would also like to provide a quick review of the Survey of Labour and Income Dynamics (SLID). This survey has been around since the early 1990s. It is a longitudinal survey over a six-year period and has a couple of panels going at any one time so there is a double sample if the data are examined cross-sectionally. It has an immigrant sample of around 3,500 to 4,000 in each of the panels. If both panels were used, the sample would be around 7,000, which is a fairly healthy representation of the immigrant population in which to look at the issues of labour and income.

Doug Norris

Other Surveys

Virtually every survey we do has a question that allows us to identify immigrants and generally the year of landing and country of origin. The problem is that in many surveys the sample size is not sufficient to allow for a very detailed analysis of immigrants. However, in some cases overall sample sizes have been increased or the sample of immigrants has been augmented.

I will touch on some of these sources of data. The General Social Survey (GSS) has been ongoing since the mid-1980s. However, in 1999, the sample size was increased from 10,000 to 25,000 and the increased sample size now results in a much higher sample of around 4,200 immigrants. The sample size of 10,000 was a little low for analysis, whereas a sample of 25,000 offers more potential. Some of the GSS surveys, although not all, have information on birth place of parents, which allows users to obtain second-generation information as well. Some of the topics covered over the last three or four years have been victimization, technology, and families. Social support and aging are also being studied. The 2003 GSS will actually come back to the topic of social capital and some of the dimensions such as social networks, social participation, trust, etc.

The Workplace and Employee Survey (WES) is a survey of establishments examining turnover, innovation and technology adoption, and other dimensions of the workplace. However, we also sample workers within the workplace and find data similar to the SLID survey, for instance. But this is about a 25,000–30,000 worker sample and the immigrant portion data is large enough to use effectively. It is possible to look at, for example, more detail about the kinds of firms in which immigrants work as compared to the native-born, for instance, regarding innovation technology adoption, things that are in addition to industry.

Another survey is the Youth in Transition Survey (YITS). The first panel was done in 2001. The sample had about 1,200 15-year-olds and measured their reading, writing, and mathematical abilities. This survey is also part of an international panel which allows some comparisons globally. Many countries have done a component of that survey, providing a unique opportunity for international comparisons.

The Department of Citizenship and Immigration has funded additional surveys of immigrants in the International Adult Literacy Survey, to be conducted next year, and the recently completed World Values Survey.

The Survey of Financial Security and the National Longitudinal Survey of Children and Youth are of interest from the perspective of immigration. However, analysis is very limited because of small sample sizes. Some work has been done on children of immigrants, but I would caution against using the surveys with the smaller sample sizes. Although small samples are a problem because of high sampling variability, the sampling variability gets even higher if the survey comes from the Labour Force Survey sampling frame. Since the Labour Force Survey is a very highly clustered survey sample, it is important to consider the effect that clustering will have in terms of the potential bias in the sample of immigrants in a survey that has come from the Labour Force Survey. It is not only the sample size, but is also the survey design, and care needs to be taken when the samples are small.

The future is bright for new areas of immigration-related research with the expanding new data sources.

Section VI

Labour Market Immigrant
Integration Issues

The Falling Earnings of New Immigrant Men in Canada's Large Cities

Bert Waslander

Introduction

The term "falling" quite accurately describes what has happened to earnings of new immigrant men. In 1980, a male immigrant who had landed in Canada in 1976, 1977 or 1978 — two to four years earlier — earned $25 thousand on average; by 1995, a male immigrant who landed two to four years earlier made only $13 thousand. The reasons for this dramatic change remain a matter of debate and research, to which this paper is intended as a contribution.

This paper inquires to what extent the decline in earnings of new immigrants is due to changes in the attributes of Canada's immigrants, and to what extent changes in the labour market are to blame. Canada experienced a severe recession in the first half of the 1990s, and it seems reasonable to suppose that new immigrants bore the brunt of this. Toronto, the destination of more than one-third of new immigrants, was particularly

Comments by Gilles Grenier at several stages of the work and by Louis Grignon at the conference are gratefully acknowledged. This paper expands on earlier work (Waslander, 2001) and benefits from comments made by Abdurrhaman Aydemir when that work was presented.

hard hit by this recession. From the late 1980s through to 1995, the level of immigration was kept at a high level of 250,000 or more, in contrast to efforts in earlier economic downturns to limit the number of new entrants. Thus, more new immigrants were competing for scarce jobs in the mid-1990s than in the mid-1980s when unemployment was also high.

Over a longer period there have been important changes in the characteristics of immigrants, such as in country of origin and immigration class. At the same time, the Canadian economy and labour force keep on evolving, presenting different challenges to the new immigrant. This paper aims to shed some light on the relative contributions of two sets of factors: changes in the state of labour markets, and changes in the relative attributes of immigrants.

I have chosen to focus on new immigrants and avoid the question of adjustment after entry. This leads me to use census micro-data files because new immigrants are a relative small part of Canada's population with only a very small number of observations in any survey other than the large census questionnaire. As censuses provide few observations of the labour market in time, this paper exploits geographic detail, that is, Canada's largest metropolitan areas, where the overwhelming majority of new immigrants settle. The variation in labour market conditions across cities and over time is used to identify its impact on the changing earnings of new immigrants. However, the paper does not address how the experience of new immigrants differed among cities; it tells only one story, about all new immigrants in the eight cities taken together.

A third feature of this paper — in addition to the focus on new immigrants and on large cities — is a focus on average earnings of all new immigrant prime-age men, including those with zero earnings. Perhaps more than Canadians generally, new immigrants are dependent on earnings to provide for their families. A sharp decline in annual earnings is a serious matter for new immigrants, and should be of concern to policymakers, whether it derives from changes in employment or in rates of pay.

It is common in the literature to analyze the employment and the wage rate separately, for various reasons. I focus on annual earnings of an age-gender group, including observations of zero earnings to explore the role of various factors. At a later stage, I turn to the standard approach of treating employment and the wage separately.

A fourth key aspect of the approach in this paper is an emphasis on measuring contributions to the change in the fortunes of new immigrants. Most studies use regression analysis to estimate models and identify significant factors. This paper takes the further step of showing how various estimated models account for the change in the fortunes of new immigrants. This is done in three different stages. First, I analyze how fixed coefficient models account for the change in average annual earnings of new immigrants and the Canadian-born. This decomposition attributes the change in wages entirely to changes in the values of independent variables, that is, the unemployment rate and characteristics of persons. Next, coefficients are allowed to change over time, and part of the change in earnings is then attributed to changes in the coefficients, such as the impact of the unemployment rate on wages. Finally, I analyze changes in employment and wages separately, using fixed-coefficient models.

The paper is structured as follows. The first section describes the phenomenon to be examined, along with changes in some key labour market indicators. This is followed by a review of the literature. The analysis section presents linear regressions of annual earnings for new immigrants and the Canadian-born, and the accounting for the change in earnings that is derived from this analysis. Fixed coefficient models are presented first, and models with coefficients varying over time next. Employment and the wage are then examined separately using fixed coefficient models, with the related accounting for change.

The Facts

The Data

The individual micro-data files of the 1981, 1986, 1991, and 1996 censuses form the factual basis for this paper. The focus is on the residents of Canada's eight largest metropolitan areas, also referred to as cities: Toronto, Montreal, Vancouver, Ottawa-Hull, Hamilton,[1] Winnipeg, Calgary, and Edmonton, and on two groups of men between the ages of 25 and 54: Canadian-born men and new immigrants. The latter are identified by year of immigration: two to four years prior to the year for which the census reports earnings. For instance, the 1996 census reports earnings for

---

[1]The 1986 census does not identify residents of Hamilton separately, but combines them with residents of St. Catharines-Niagara and Kitchener-Waterloo.

the year 1995, and new immigrants are persons who landed in 1991, 1992 or 1993.[2]

Earnings are the sum of wages and salaries and income from self-employment in the year prior to the census, deflated by the Consumer Price Index. Employment is measured by positive earnings for the year.[3]

There is a good deal of continuity in the definitions of variables and categories in the four census files. However, no visible minority indicator is present in the 1981 census file. I have constructed an indicator using information on ethnic identification.[4] Persons not in private households, non-permanent residents, and persons for whom information on age, year of immigration, labour force activity or hours per week is missing are excluded.

Earnings and Employment of New Immigrants and the Canadian-Born

Indicators of earnings and employment of new immigrant men show a dramatic decline between 1980 and 1995, in absolute terms and compared to Canadian-born men (Table 1).

---

[2]I would have liked to include also immigrants who landed in the year prior to that for which earnings are reported. This detail, however, is not available in the 1986 census file, and I have chosen to maintain a consistent definition of period since landing in order that changes in employment and earnings of new immigrants from census to census cannot be attributed to differences in length of stay.

[3]Some of the self-employed have negative earnings. These are included in the measure and analysis of earnings in this paper. However, they are ignored when earnings are split into employment and wages, as only positive wages can be analyzed using a semi-logarithmic model. Accordingly, measures of employment, hours, and the wage pertain to persons with positive wages only.

[4]A person included in the 1981 census micro-data file is considered to belong to visible minorities if his or her ethnic origin is African, Caribbean or Haitian (category 03) or Chinese (category 04), and also, for other single and multiple responses for ethnic origin (categories 17 and 22) if place of birth is Asia, Africa, South and Central America, including Caribbean, or Other (categories 30 to 33).

Bert Waslander

Table 1: Average Earnings (in 1995 dollars) and Employment, Men, 1980 and 1995

	New Immigrants			Canadian-Born		
	1980	*1995*	*Change (%)*	*1980*	*1995*	*Change (%)*
Men 15 and over						
Real earnings	24,875	13,321	−46	25,078	22,309	−11
Employment ratio	84%	67%	−20	80%	74%	−7
For those working						
Weekly pay	685	523	−24	743	719	−3
Weeks worked	43.6	39.9	−8	41.7	41.4	−1
Full-time jobs	90%	81%	−10	87%	83%	−5
Men 25–54						
Real earnings	32,219	17,438	−46	35,935	31,619	−12
Employment ratio	94%	80%	−14	95%	90%	−6
For those working						
Weekly pay	755	556	−26	847	796	−6
Weeks worked	46.3	41.7	−10	46.0	45.0	−2
Full-time jobs	96%	86%	−10	95%	93%	−3
Men 25–54 in eight CMAs						
Real earnings	31,256	16,651	−47	40,179	35,152	−13
Employment ratio	94%	79%	−16	95%	91%	−4
For those working						
Weekly pay	725	550	−24	906	849	−6
Weeks worked	46.4	41.5	−11	47.2	46.1	−2
Full-time jobs	96%	86%	−10	95%	92%	−3

	Ratio of New Immigrants to Canadian-Born		
	1980	*1995*	*Change*
Men 15 and over			
Real earnings	99%	60%	−40
Employment ratio	105%	91%	−14
For those working			
Weekly pay	92%	73%	−21
Weeks worked	104%	96%	−8
Full-time jobs	103%	97%	−6
Men 25–54			
Real earnings	90%	55%	−38
Employment ratio	99%	90%	−10
For those working			
Weekly pay	89%	70%	−22
Weeks worked	101%	93%	−8
Full-time jobs	101%	93%	−7
Men 25–54 in eight CMAs			
Real earnings	78%	47%	−39
Employment ratio	99%	88%	−12
For those working			
Weekly pay	80%	65%	−19
Weeks worked	98%	90%	−8
Full-time jobs	101%	93%	−7

Source: 1981 and 1996 census, micro-data files for individuals.

Every measure of earnings and employment declined both for the Canadian-born and for new immigrants. For the Canadian-born, the changes are non-trivial, and for new immigrants they are very large. Real earnings of new immigrants in 1995 were just over one-half of what they were in 1980. This is true for all men of 15 and over, for prime-age men, and for prime-age men in the eight largest metropolitan areas. For these same three groups of Canadian-born, real earnings declined by a little more than 10%.[5]

The decline in average earnings is due in roughly equal measure to changes in pay rates and in the amount of paid work. The weekly pay of new immigrants fell by about one-quarter. This may in part be due to changes in the number of hours worked, but the census does not give precise information about this. It only asks whether paid work was mainly full-time work, and the share of new immigrant men who answered positively fell by 10%.

For both new immigrants and the Canadian-born, all men in Canada and prime-age men in the eight largest cities experienced the same *percentage changes* in earnings, pay, and activity between 1980 and 1995. However, the *level* of earnings of new immigrants relative to the earnings of the Canadian-born varied markedly according to the age group and geography chosen. For instance, in 1980, new immigrant men in all of Canada earned approximately the same as Canadian-born men, an average of about $25 thousand. But new immigrant men of 25 to 54 years old in the large cities on average earned about $31 thousand, only 78% of the average earnings of their Canadian-born counterparts.

New immigrants are concentrated in the large cities. Among prime-age men, 83% of new immigrants lived in the eight largest cities in 1995, compared to 40% of the Canadian-born.[6] In the large cities, new immigrant men compete in the labour market with a subset of Canadian-born men who earn more and work somewhat more than Canadian-born men generally. This reality is reflected in the analysis in this paper, as it focuses on the eight cities.

---

[5]Outside the eight large cities, new immigrant men experienced a decline in annual earnings of 34%, mainly as a result of lower weekly earnings. Earlier immigrant prime-age men in the large cities (those who landed 20 years or more before the year in which earnings were recorded) saw their earnings and employment change in almost exactly the same way as the Canadian-born.

[6]In 1980 the shares were 76% and 37%.

Earnings of new immigrants fell relative to those of the Canadian-born in all eight cities (men aged 25 to 54, Figure 1). For the eight cities taken together, relative earnings of new immigrant men fell steadily over the four pre-census years. The relative employment ratio declined in 1990 and 1995, whereas relative weekly pay declined in 1985, recovered in 1990, and declined again in 1995 (Figure 1, top left).

Figure 1: Average Earnings, Employment Ratio and Weekly Earnings, Ratio of New Immigrants to Canadian-Born, Men 25–54 Years of Age, Eight Large Cities, 1980–1995

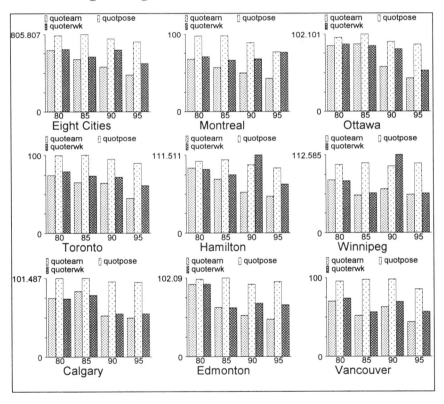

Source: 1981, 1986, 1991 and 1996 census, micro-data files for individuals. From left to right the three columns represent: real earnings (quotearn), the employment ratio (quotpose), and weekly earnings (quoterwk). Every column gives the ratio of the average value for new immigrants to the average value for the Canadian-born.

Falling Earnings of New Immigrant Men

While a decline in all three indicators occurred in almost every city, the rate of decline and the time path vary to some extent. For instance, weekly pay in Montreal is highest in 1995, and in Winnipeg the employment ratio is steady throughout while weekly pay peaks in 1990. The employment ratio does not fall very much in the western cities, except in Vancouver in 1995. Figure 1 indicates some diversity among the eight cities that this paper has aimed to exploit.

Labour Market Conditions in Canada's Large Cities

The four censuses from 1980 to 1995 reflect two business cycles of the Canadian economy, with 1980 and 1990 being cyclical peaks (1990 is somewhat past the peak), and 1985 and 1995 both being years of recovery from a cyclical trough two years earlier (Figures 2 and 3).

The unemployment rates and employment ratios of the country as a whole and the eight cities taken together show very much the same cyclical pattern (Figures 2 and 3). The rates converge over time. In the late 1970s, unemployment in the eight cities was one percentage point lower than the national rate; by 1995 the two were the same. By the same token, early in the period the employment ratio was three to four points higher in the large cities, while by the mid-1990s the difference had shrunk to one to two points. Thus, between 1980 and 1995, the large cities more or less lost their advantageous position of high-employment, low-unemployment areas. Here perhaps is one small part of the story of the declining fortunes of new immigrants, as they live mainly in the large cities. In fact, the large influx of new immigrants from the late 1980s to the mid-1990s may have contributed to the trend towards convergence of labour market conditions between Canada and its eight largest cities. This reality is reflected in the analysis in this paper, as it focuses on the eight cities.

Within this general pattern there are differences among the cities. In central Canada, Toronto was particularly hard-hit by the recession of the nineties (Figure 4). The unemployment rate in Canada's largest city, which customarily was two to four percentage points below the national rate, reached the same level as the national rate in 1993. By contrast, the western cities experienced a very severe recession in the 1980s and saw unemployment return to levels below the national average in the 1990s (Figure 5). Figures 4 and 5 indicate some diversity among the cities that this paper has aimed to exploit.

Figure 2: Unemployment Rate, Canada and Eight Large Cities

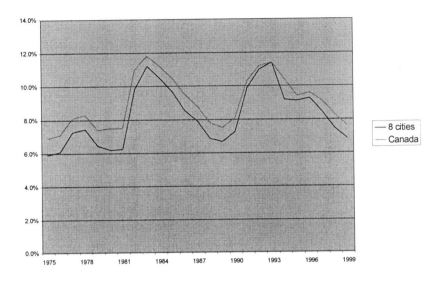

Figure 3: Employment Ratio, Canada and Eight Cities

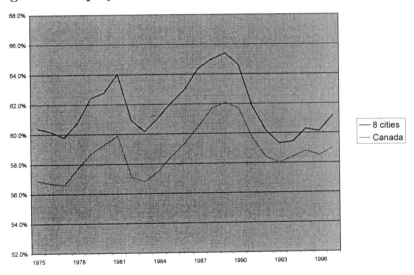

Figure 4: Unemployment Rate, Canada and Four Central Cities

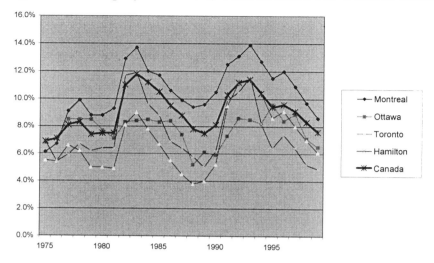

Figure 5: Unemployment Rate, Canada and Four Western Cities

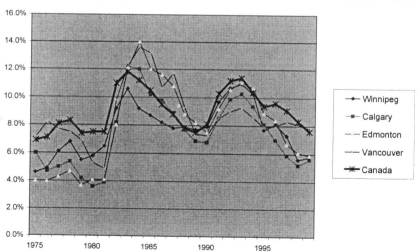

Bert Waslander

The Literature

The Wage

There have been more studies of the relative rates of pay of immigrants than of their labour force participation and employment. Most studies of pay rates consider earlier as well as recent immigrants and allow for an entry effect and adjustment according to length of stay in the host country. Broadly speaking this literature shows:[7]

- There is an entry effect and a catch-up in years after landing in the pay rates of immigrants. Historically both were modest. Successive immigrant cohorts have experienced lower earnings upon entry, and it is uncertain whether the catch-up rate has increased sufficiently to ensure that more recent immigrant cohorts will achieve parity with established Canadians.
- Studies examining changes during the 1970s and 1980s point to profound changes in the selection of immigrants: different world regions of birth and the rise of the family class (e.g., Bloom, Grenier and Gunderson, 1995).
- More recently, studies have focused on the extent of discrimination against immigrants and visible minorities, and on a lack of recognition of foreign credentials and work experience as contributing factors (e.g., de Silva, 1997; Li, 2001).
- Immigrant experience has been linked to rising inequality in pay rates in host countries (e.g., Reitz, 1998).
- The human capital model is not as strong a determinant of pay of immigrants upon entry and during adjustment as it is of host country residents generally (e.g., Chiswick, Cohen and Zach, 1997).

As regards human capital characteristics, Reitz (1998) has devoted a book to the thesis that education accounts for one-half of the differences in the earnings of new immigrants among major cities in the United States,

---

[7]This is a brief summary that does not do justice to the rich body of work. Many other aspects of the immigrant experience have been examined, including the role in the adjustment process of families (Baker and Benjamin, 1997) and of age at entry (Schaafsma and Sweetman, 2001).

Canada and Australia. Reitz also attributes an important role to inequality in rates of pay and segmentation of labour markets.

Inequality in the labour market has increased over the past two decades, and new labour market entrants in Canada have not fared as well as their predecessors, having a lower entry-level wage without much sign of a catch-up (Beaudry and Green, 2000). Recently, Green and Worswick (2002) brought this finding to bear on the experience of successive immigrant cohorts. They find that the decline in earnings of new labour market entrants generally between the early 1980s and mid-1990s accounts for about 40% of the decline in the earnings of new immigrants. As for the remainder, they find evidence of a large decline in the value of foreign experience in the Canadian labour market.

As regards the influence of the state of the labour market, it has been found that wages received by immigrants are sensitive to the unemployment rate shortly after landing. This effect wears off, and there is no long-term scarring effect (Chiswick and Miller, 2002, for the United States). Grant (1999) reports a break in the trend of deteriorating earnings of immigrants: the 1986–90 cohort of immigrant men had higher earnings than the previous cohort did five years earlier; immigrant men who landed during 1980–85 had a higher rate of increase in earnings between 1985 and 1990 than earlier cohorts with the same length of stay. Grant explores the role of labour market conditions but finds they did not play a major role.

McDonald and Worswick (1998) find that weekly earnings of adult male immigrants of prime labour force age who landed during the 1970s were influenced by the unemployment rate and the unemployment rate interacted with years in Canada. According to their equations, this group of immigrant men lost ground relative to the Canadian-born in the early 1990s when unemployment increased sharply.

Employment

As regards the employment experience of immigrants, Chiswick, Cohen and Zach (1997) find that the labour market status of immigrant men in the United States is more cyclically sensitive than that of the native-born. The prospects of immigrants are affected by the business cycle, but there is no long-term scarring effect of high employment at entry. They also find that employment status of immigrants is less strongly determined by human capital than for native-born men, and suggest that human capital from outside the United States does not transfer fully.

Aydemir (2002) specifically examined the role of labour market conditions. He found that there are significant negative cohort effects in labour force participation and employment of new immigrants after entry. These cohort effects become insignificant when the unemployment rate is added to the regressors. This suggests an important role for the state of the labour market in the deterioration of average earnings of all new immigrants.

To sum up, the literature about the changing experience of new immigrants has identified a number of factors. This literature has shown that changes in human capital attributes and changes in their value in the Canadian labour market have played a major role. New immigrants face stiffer competition from host-country labour market entrants, who in the case of Canada have much higher educational credentials than earlier cohorts. Macroeconomic conditions have also been examined, but not to the same extent. Current literature points to changes in the structure of wages, with more recent entrant cohorts earning less than earlier cohorts with the same human capital. This paper considers these three broad sets of factors jointly.

Regression Analysis and Accounting for Change

We now turn to the analysis of changes in annual earnings of new immigrants and the Canadian-born. Equations have been estimated separately for new immigrants and the Canadian-born, on the basis that these two groups are not subject to the same earnings-generation process. All new immigrants, in contrast to the Canadian-born, are relatively new entrants in the labour markets of the eight cities, for instance, and they obtained their education and work experience largely outside Canada.

To make explicit how the estimated models explain changes in earnings over time, estimation results are converted into an accounting of such changes. In the case of a model estimated over all four census years with coefficients that do not change in time, the contribution of each independent variable to the change in the average of the dependent variable is the change in the average of the independent variable multiplied by the estimated coefficient. In models estimated separately over different census years, both changes in independent variables and changes in coefficients contribute to the change in the dependent variable. The contribution of the change in a coefficient is evaluated using the average of the related independent variable.

A Model of Real Annual Earnings with Period and Location Effects

The model used is a standard human capital model of wages, augmented with a labour market indicator. In the literature, this model is used to estimate the wage offer as well as labour force participation or employment. The model is applied to real annual earnings, ignoring for the time being whether changes in earnings are the result of changes in the wage or in employment. As zero earnings are included among the observations, a linear model is estimated, using OLS.

Three human capital attributes are included:

- age is represented by three ten-year age groups, 25–34, 35–44, and 45–54;
- a single binary variable captures visible minority status; and
- there are five levels of educational attainment: elementary school only, some high school, a high school diploma, a college or trade diploma, and a university degree.

Visible minority status is included to represent the changing origins of new immigrants. It is intended not merely to represent race, but also differences in cultural background associated with country of origin. I chose this variable because it is available for the Canadian-born as well as for new immigrants.[8] The approach of this paper is to analyze the earnings of new immigrants and Canadian-born men in a parallel manner, using a general model.

The sample counts and observed shares of the various categories are presented in Table 2, for each of the years for which the four censuses report earnings. The greatest contrast between new immigrant and Canadian-

---

[8]I have estimated earnings equations for new immigrants with world region of birth and visible minority status as independent variables, and find that world region of birth is significant and reduces the coefficient of the visible minority variable. Thus, it is reasonable to interpret the visible minority status variable as indicating not only race but also world region of birth.

Table 2: Means of Independent Variables in Regressions, 1980 to 1995
(percent of all men 25–54 years old living in eight large cities)

	Canadian-Born Men				New Immigrants			
	1980	*1985*	*1990*	*1995*	*1980*	*1985*	*1990*	*1995*
Sample count	27,891	35,736	57,121	56,501	1,020	1,050	2,511	3,757
Visible minority share	0.5	1.3	1.9	2.0	50.5	58.2	73.4	76.8
Age 25–34	46.7	48.0	44.6	38.2	63.3	58.6	48.1	44.8
Age 35–44	28.7	31.3	34.0	36.8	27.1	31.7	38.4	37.5
Age 45–54	24.6	20.7	21.4	25.0	9.6	9.7	13.5	17.6
University degree	19.6	20.2	22.0	23.8	22.6	27.9	24.9	28.0
College/trade diploma	22.4	24.4	26.3	30.1	31.3	27.1	24.9	25.8
High school diploma	28.4	28.1	30.0	27.5	23.4	21.6	27.7	24.7
Some high school	19.1	20.4	17.2	15.2	11.9	14.0	13.8	14.4
Elementary school	10.4	6.9	4.6	3.4	10.8	9.3	8.7	7.0
Montreal	32.3	28.3	29.2	29.1	20.2	15.6	16.7	17.4
Ottawa	8.6	8.2	9.1	9.2	3.4	4.0	16.7	4.0
Toronto	22.2	22.6	23.7	23.6	39.3	44.2	54.8	48.9
Hamilton	4.8	9.9	4.9	4.8	39.3	5.6	2.3	1.9
Winnipeg	6.0	5.6	5.7	5.7	3.7	3.4	2.9	1.7
Calgary	7.0	6.5	7.2	7.5	7.5	6.9	3.6	4.2
Edmonton	7.3	7.8	7.8	7.4	9.0	6.2	2.9	2.8
Vancouver	11.6	7.8	12.4	12.6	13.5	14.1	12.6	19.2

Source: 1981, 1986, 1991 and 1996 census micro-data files and calculations by the author.

born men 25 to 54 years old lies in the share belonging to visible minorities. Only 0.5% of the Canadian-born belonged to this category in 1980, and by 1995 just 2%. Just over half of new immigrants were non-white in 1980, rising to three-quarters in 1995. New immigrants are younger than the Canadian-born, but showed a greater shift to older age groups. New immigrants have more university degrees in relation to their number than the Canadian-born and increased their lead in this regard, but overall, educational attainment of the Canadian-born improved more. Also shown in Table 2 are the distributions of both groups across the eight cities.

The distribution of new immigrants shifted remarkably from the Prairie cities to Toronto and Vancouver.

The three-year average unemployment rate (i.e., the average for the year in which earnings are recorded and the two previous years) for each city is used to describe labour market conditions. Averaging over three years means that the measure is sensitive to the duration of variations in unemployment, that is, the length of periods of growth and recessions, and that it includes the discouraged-worker effect of prolonged high unemployment.[9]

To this basic model are added fixed location effects and fixed period effects. These effects capture unobserved differences in the qualities of labour market participants and in labour market conditions among cities and in time, additional to cyclical variations reflected in the unemployment rate. If cohorts are tracked over time, as is the case in many studies, it is possible to distinguish period and cohort effects. In this paper, period and cohort effects coincide.[10]

Estimation results for the Canadian-born and new immigrants. As expected on the basis of the vast human capital literature, age and education are found to be major factors determining the level of earnings of the Canadian-born (Table 3).[11] Visible minority status also plays a role, with a negative effect of approximately six thousand dollars annually in all four

---

[9]I have also used the employment ratio, but found it to be less satisfactory than the unemployment rate. The employment ratio has a trend reflecting the increasing participation of women, and this makes the variable less useful as a measure of labour market tightness.

[10]The earnings equations in this paper are based on four sets of cross-sectional data, and do not describe the earnings profile of successive cohorts over their working lives.

[11]The t-values are based on OLS estimation. The assumption that residual errors are independent, an essential condition for validity of inference based on OLS, is questionable because the unemployment rate is an aggregate variable. Following Moulton (1990), one could assume that residual errors on observations associated with a single value for the unemployment rate are correlated. Using that approach, the standard errors would be nearly twice as large as those obtained in OLS estimation, and t-values would drop to approximately one-half the size reported in Table 2.

models. The unemployment rate is significant. An increase in the unemployment rate of 1% (100 basis points) reduces average annual earnings of the Canadian-born by $1,212, according to model (1) in Table 3.

The two workhorses of the human capital model, age and education, play a much smaller role in the equation for new immigrants, as indicated by the size of the coefficients and the related t-values.[12] As regards age, the new immigrant of around 40 years fares somewhat better than his counterpart who is ten years younger, but new immigrants around 50 years of age have virtually no such advantage. By contrast, a middle-aged Canadian-born earns $16 thousand per year more than someone 20 years younger, evidence of a high return to work experience in Canada. Clearly it is difficult to break into the Canadian labour market at middle age — work experience outside Canada is not highly valued. As regards education, a university education increases earnings of new immigrants by about one-half as much as for the Canadian-born, while lack of a high school diploma carries a major earnings penalty for the Canadian-born and a very small one for new immigrants. Visible minority status plays a more important role for new immigrants than the Canadian-born: it depresses yearly earnings by about $10 thousand per year.[13]

New immigrant earnings are more sensitive to the state of the labour market than the earnings of the Canadian-born, by approximately 50% in all four models.

Differences among the four models. The impacts of the human capital variables are more or less the same across the different models in Table 3, whether one examines the Canadian-born or new immigrants. This is not the case with the unemployment rate variable. Fixed city effects (model 2)

---

[12]As the sample for the Canadian-born (177,249) is 21 times as large as the new immigrant sample (8,338), an equivalent level of significance would be a t-value 4.5 times as large in the former equation. This follows from the fact that standard errors are inversely proportional to the square root of the size of the sample. After adjustment for sample size by scaling by a factor of 4.5, the equation for new immigrants has smaller t-values for age and education and larger t-values for city and period effects than the equation for the Canadian-born.

[13]The model has also been estimated jointly for new immigrants and the Canadian-born. The coefficients of the age and education variables, jointly, and of visible minority status were found to be significantly different at the 5% level from those for the Canadian-born.

Table 3: Regression Coefficients of Fixed Effects Models

	(1) Basic Model		(2) Basic Model Plus Fixed City Effects		(3) Basic Model Plus Fixed Period Effects		(4) Model (2) Plus Fixed Period Effects	
	Coefficient	T-value	Coefficient	T-value	Coefficient	T-value	Coefficient	T-value
Canadian-Born (N=177,249)								
Unemployment rate	-1.2	-49.8	-1.0	-33.4	-1.2	-37.4	-0.6	-9.2
Visible minority	-6.3	-12.6	-6.8	-13.7	-5.7	-11.5	-6.2	-12.5
Age (reference group: 25–34 years old)								
Age 35–44	12.1	85.0	12.1	85.5	12.4	87.5	12.5	88.1
Age 45–54	16.2	100.2	16.3	100.8	16.6	102.4	16.7	103.2
Education (reference group: high school diploma)								
University degree	17.8	101.1	17.7	100.3	17.9	101.9	17.8	101.5
College/trade diploma	3.2	19.1	3.1	18.6	3.4	20.2	3.3	19.9
Some high school	-6.2	-32.9	-6.2	-32.8	-6.4	-34.2	-6.4	-34.1
Elementary school	-15.9	-55.0	-15.6	-53.9	-16.7	-57.7	-16.5	-57.0
Fixed city effects (reference group: Montreal)								
Ottawa			-1.1	-4.2			0.7	2.1
Toronto			2.8	13.2			4.8	15.9
Hamilton			1.4	4.8			2.6	7.4
Winnipeg			-3.2	-10.8			-1.9	-5.7
Calgary			1.8	6.7			3.3	10.6
Edmonton			1.4	5.3			2.3	8.3
Vancouver			1.3	6.0			2.5	9.8
Fixed period effects (reference group: 1980)								
1995					-4.2	-18.9	-6.6	-22.8
1990					-3.2	-16.7	-3.5	-18.3
1985					1.0	4.3	-1.6	-5.0
Intercept	37.7	148.5	35.3	93.0	39.7	133.2	33.3	56.0
Rbar2	0.1658		0.1686		0.1712		0.1744	

... continued

Bert Waslander

Table 3: continued

	New Immigrants (N=8,338)							
Unemployment rate	-1.8	-22.4	-1.8	-18.6	-1.5	-12.9	-0.9	-4.8
Visible minority	-10.7	-22.7	-10.7	-22.4	-9.6	-20.1	-9.7	-20.1
Age (reference group: 25–34 years old)								
Age 35–44	2.4	5.2	2.4	5.2	3.0	6.5	3.0	6.4
Age 45–54	0.9	1.5	1.0	1.6	1.8	2.8	1.8	2.8
Education (reference group: high school diploma)								
University degree	9.3	15.5	9.3	15.6	9.3	15.6	9.3	15.7
College/trade diploma	3.9	6.6	3.9	6.5	3.7	6.3	3.7	6.3
Some high school	-0.3	-0.4	-0.3	-0.5	-0.3	-0.5	-0.4	-0.6
Elementary school	-2.3	-2.7	-2.3	-2.6	-2.8	-3.3	-2.7	-3.2
Fixed city effects (reference group: Montreal)								
Ottawa					-1.1	-1.3	1.9	1.4
Toronto					0.8	0.6	4.0	4.2
Hamilton					0.0	0.1	2.2	1.4
Winnipeg					-0.9	-1.4	0.2	0.1
Calgary					2.6	3.0	4.9	3.9
Edmonton					3.2	3.9	4.8	3.7
Vancouver					-0.8	-0.6	2.0	2.1
Fixed period effects (reference group: 1980)								
1995					-7.1	-8.4	-9.4	-9.0
1990					-4.9	-6.7	-4.9	-6.6
1985					-0.5	-0.6	-2.9	-2.6
Intercept	40.4	46.0	39.7	31.0	41.8	38.7	35.2	18.1
Rbar2		0.1511		0.1546		0.1663		0.1697

Source: 1981, 1986, 1991 and 1996 census micro-data file and calculations by the author. Each coefficient represents the change in real annual earnings, measured in thousands of dollars, that is associated with belonging to the category. The coefficient of the unemployment rate indicates the change in annual earnings, in thousands of dollars, associated with an increase in the unemployment rate of one percentage point (100 basis points).

and period effects (model 3) somewhat reduce the influence of the un-employment rate. However, in the presence of both city and period effects (model 4), the influence of the unemployment rate drops by one-half, both for the Canadian-born and for new immigrants. Both the location and period effects are more important in each other's presence (model 4) than by themselves.

The period effects are quite large, especially in model 4. Between 1980 and 1995, earnings of Canadian-born males dropped by $6.6 thousand, and earnings of new immigrants dropped by $9.4 thousand, even in the presence of controls for major human capital factors and for labour market conditions. The largest part of the declines occurred between 1990 and 1995 ($3.1 thousand for the Canadian-born, and $4.5 thousand for the new immigrant, with an increase in the gap of $1.4 thousand).

Analyzing the decline in earnings. Using the model with location and period effects, contributions to change in real earnings are measured by the change in the average value of the independent variables from 1980 to 1995, multiplied by their respective coefficients (Table 4).

Panel A of Table 4 gives the changes in the independent variables and their impact. As regards human capital, the most striking difference between the Canadian-born and new immigrants is the change in the share belonging to visible minorities, which for new immigrants increased from one-half to three-quarters, while for the Canadian-born it changed from 1% to 2%. New immigrants became older: the shares of the 35–44 and 45–54 age group increased substantially at the expense of the share of the 25–34 year group. The shift in the age distribution was much larger than for the Canadian-born, and it could have meant a large increase in earnings were it not for the fact that for new immigrants a higher age — more years of work experience in other countries — counts for little in the Canadian labour market.

As for education, the share of university graduates increased more among new immigrants than among those born in Canada, but the effect on average annual earnings of this change is muted compared to the effect of swelling of the ranks of university graduates among the Canadian-born. As regards the other levels of educational attainment, new immigrants have not kept pace with the Canadian-born. This had little effect on their average earnings. The Canadian-born, meanwhile, gained significantly from higher educational attainment below the university level. The drop of seven percentage points in the share with only elementary schooling stands out as the most important of all human capital changes of Canadian-born men,

Bert Waslander

Table 4: Change in Real Annual Earnings and in Contributing Factors, Canadian-Born and New Immigrant Men 25–54 Years Old Living in Eight Large Cities, 1980–1995 (percentage points or thousands of dollars), Fixed Effects Model

Panel A: Details	Canadian-Born		New Immigrants	
	Change in Rate/Share	Impact	Change in Rate/Share	Impact
Visible minority share	1.5	−0.09	26.3	−2.54
Age 35–44	8.1	1.01	10.5	0.32
Age 45–54	0.5	0.08	8.0	0.15
University degree	4.2	0.75	5.4	0.50
College/trade diploma	7.6	0.25	−5.5	−0.20
Some high school	−3.9	0.25	2.6	−0.01
Elementary school	−7.0	1.16	−3.8	0.10
Unemployment rate	3.5	−1.95	3.8	−3.46
Ottawa	0.5	0.00	0.6	0.01
Toronto	1.4	0.07	9.6	0.39
Hamilton	0.0	0.00	−1.4	−0.03
Winnipeg	−0.3	0.01	−2.1	0.00
Calgary	0.5	0.02	−3.3	−0.16
Edmonton	0.1	0.00	−6.2	−0.30
Vancouver	1.0	0.02	5.0	0.10

Panel B: Summary	Canadian-Born	New Immigrant	Difference NI-CB
Visible minority share	−0.1	−2.5	−2.4
Age	1.1	0.5	−0.6
Education	2.4	0.4	−2.0
Sum: Total human capital	3.4	−1.7	−5.1
Unemployment rate	−1.9	−3.5	−1.6
City effects	0.1	0.0	−0.1
Period effect	−6.6	−9.4	−2.8
Change in earnings (total)	−5.0	−14.6	−9.6

Source: Based on model 4 in Table 3, the change in the rate or shares in panel A are expressed in percentage points. The unemployment rate increased by 3.5 percentage points for the Canadian-born, and by 3.8 percentage points for new immigrants; the difference is a result of the way both groups are distributed over the eight cities. Impacts in panel A and all of panel B are measured in thousands of dollars in annual earnings. For instance, Toronto's share of new immigrants increased by 9.6 percentage points between 1980 and 1995. This resulted in an increase in average annual earnings of new immigrants of 0.39 x $1,000, i.e., $390. This increase was offset by the declining shares of Calgary and Edmonton, also cities with higher (given age, education and visible minority status) annual earnings of new immigrants than Montreal, the reference category.

Falling Earnings of New Immigrant Men

with a somewhat larger effect on earnings than the increase in years of work experience.

The change in the unemployment rate depressed the earnings of both groups. New immigrants were affected more seriously, both because of their changing distribution over the eight cities, and also because their earnings are more sensitive to changes in the unemployment rate.

The changing distribution of new immigrants and Canadian-born men over the eight cities had no material effect on average earnings, even though there are substantial differences in earnings levels among the cities over and beyond differences in human capital and labour market conditions allowed for by the model.[14]

Interestingly, the two equations jointly attribute the change in the earnings differential between new immigrants and the Canadian-born primarily to changes in human capital (Table 4, panel B, column 3). Increases in age and education of both groups have yielded greater gains in earnings for the Canadian-born, while the increase in the share of the population belonging to visible minorities worked strongly against new immigrants' earnings only. Compared to these changes, the period effect is modest, and the effect of changes in labour market conditions small.

The period effect is a general decline in earnings, affecting both new immigrants and the Canadian-born whose source is not made explicit. Both groups faced increasing competition in the labour market from women, who participated in ever larger numbers, with younger cohorts of women having better educational credentials than their male counterparts. As well, the large increase in educational attainment of the Canadian labour force, plus the increase in average work experience as the baby boom generation began to approach middle age, should have resulted in an increase in productivity

---

[14]The observations on which the model for new immigrants is estimated are dominated by the large cities, especially Toronto, and by the latter two censuses. Out of 8,338 observations on new immigrants, 3,213 or 39% pertain to Toronto in the years 1990 and 1995. To examine if this influences the findings unduly, I calculated change in earnings, estimated the equations and analyzed changes over time giving each city-census year combination equal weight. This resulted in a larger decline in earnings for both the Canadian-born ($5.5 thousand) and new immigrants ($15.6 thousand). The unemployment rate became somewhat more important, and changes in age assumed slightly more importance at the expense of educational attainment than in the estimates based on census sample counts presented in Table 3. Because the results of this fixed-weight estimation were quite similar to the results reported here, I did not pursue this further.

Bert Waslander

that did not come about. Indeed, the real weekly wage was lower in 1995 than in 1980. Thus, the existing relationship between the wage, education, and work experience was no longer viable. To explore how the wage structure changed, the next section explores how coefficients of the earnings equations changed over time.

A Model of Annual Real Earnings with Time-Dependent Coefficients

The method. The fixed coefficient model explored up to this point identified the role of changes in characteristics and labour market conditions in the story of falling earnings, and left a good part of the decline unexplained. To explore matters further, parameters are allowed to change over time, on the basis that processes that generate the earnings of the two groups of men may have changed over time. Thus, two broad sets of change factors are allowed for: changes in the values of independent variables, and the remainder, changes in the values of coefficients. In the well-known Oaxaca-Blinder procedure these components of change are called the "explained" and the "unexplained" parts of the change.[15]

I would prefer different terminology because I believe changes in values of coefficients convey meaningful information. However, caution is necessary, as the contributions of changes in individual coefficients to the change in the dependent variables depends on the choice of reference group for categorical variables, and on the way in which continuous variables are measured (Oaxaca and Ransom, 1999). While the decomposition yields a unique value for the total change related to changes in coefficients (the "unexplained" part of the change), the contributions of individual coefficients are not uniquely determined. Thus, the analysis results in different stories about what lies behind the observed changes, depending on the perspective chosen.

As reference groups I have chosen white, the youngest age group, and the lowest education level. This produces a story that revolves around changes in the discount in earnings experienced by visible minorities and in returns to work experience and education. For the state of the labour market I take the unemployment rate less 4%, a level commonly taken to

---

[15]See Morissette and Drolet (2000) for a recent description of the Oaxaca-Blinder method and related methods.

represent full employment. Rarely has the unemployment rate reached a lower value in any of the cities (Figures 4 and 5).[16]

Estimation results. Estimation was first performed on single-year, cross-sectional data. City effects were omitted since they cannot be included jointly with the unemployment rate in cross-section estimation. Estimated on 1980 and 1995, the model gives unsatisfactory results. The coefficient of the unemployment rate becomes smaller for both new immigrants and the Canadian-born, and the change is very large for new immigrants. The fit is also poor for new immigrants in 1995 (Table 5 left-hand panel). These estimates are based on cross-sectional variation only.

Better results are obtained for new immigrants when the first equation is estimated on two years of observations, 1985 and 1980, and the second set on 1995 and 1990 (Table 5 right-hand panel). The result of this estimation suggests new immigrants have become somewhat more sensitive to the state of the labour market.[17] Adding observations for 1985 and 1990 brings about a similar change in the results for the Canadian-born, but with a large change in the coefficient of the unemployment rate. This is contrary to an expected larger change for new immigrants as new labour market entrants.

---

[16]If the unemployment rate is defined as the deviation of the rate from its average (8.6%), changes in the coefficient of the unemployment rate over time contribute virtually nothing to the change in earnings of either the Canadian-born or new immigrants. If the observed unemployment rate is used as an independent variable, the change in the coefficient of the unemployment rate makes a large contribution to the change in earnings. This illustrates how measurement of continuous independent variables affects the decomposition of change due to changing coefficients. Scaling of the variable has no effect on the decomposition, but choice of the mean value does have an effect.

[17]Aydemir (2002) has shown that labour force participation and employment of new immigrants has become more sensitive to the unemployment rate in recent decades.

Bert Waslander

Table 5: Selected Results of Model (4) for Different Subperiods

	1980	1995	1980/85	1990/95
Canadian-born				
Coeff Ur	−12.8	−1.2	-96.7	-1.4
R2	0.1706	0.1631	0.1779	0.1678
New immigrants				
Coeff Ur	−2.4	−1.1	-1.6	-1.8
R2	0.1582	0.0817	0.1678	0.1353

Analyzing the decline in earnings. An Oaxaca-Blinder analysis[18] of changes based on this latter model is presented in Table 6. These results may be compared with the results of the model estimated on the four census years combined, in Tables 3 (coefficients of model 4) and 4 (analysis of change).

The human capital characteristics of both groups change in the same directions as with the earlier model, but not as much, because Table 6 reports the changes from the 1980s to the 1990s, whereas Table 3 gives the change from 1980 to 1995. The contributions of changes in human capital characteristics to the change in real earnings, accordingly, are similar to but smaller than those in the earlier analysis based on a model estimated over all census years (panel B of Tables 4 and 6).

---

[18] As the Oaxaca-Blinder method is commonplace in econometric analysis it is not described and documented here. In applying the method, I have taken the average of the two possible decompositions, since I have no preference for one set of coefficients over the other. The first column in Table 7 gives the change in the mean of each variable between the two periods, multiplied by the average of the two values of the related coefficients. The second column evaluates the changes in coefficients by multiplying by the average of the means of the related independent variable. Age and education are combined into a single measure, as the two variables are completely interacted.

Table 6: Changes in Independent Variables (in percentage points), Coefficients and Contributions to Change in Real Earnings from 1980/1985 to 1990/1995 (in thousands of dollars), Men 25–54 Years Old in Eight Large Cities, Oaxaca-Blinder Method

Panel A: Details	Canadian-Born			New Immigrants		
	Change in	Coeffs		Change in	Coeffs	
	Rate/Share	1980/85	1990/95	Rate/Share	1980/85	1990/95
Visible minority share	1.0	−6.2	−5.7	21.0	−9.4	−9.6
Age 35–44	5.2	13.5	11.9	8.5	4.6	2.5
Age 45–54	0.8	16.5	16.5	6.3	4.7	1.0
University degree	2.9	33.9	35.2	1.5	15.2	10.7
College/trade diploma	4.6	18.9	20.8	−3.8	8.6	5.6
High school diploma	0.5	16.6	17.0	3.4	4.2	2.1
Some high school	−3.7	11.0	10.1	1.2	3.3	1.9
Unemployment rate	−0.2	−1.0	−1.4	0.3	−1.6	−1.8

Panel B: Summary	Canadian-Born		New Immigrant		New Immigrant Relative to Canadian-Born	
	Char.	Valu.	Char.	Valu.	Char.	Valu.
Visible minority	−0.1	0.0	−2.0	−0.1	−1.9	−0.1
Age	0.8	−0.5	0.5	−1.2	−0.3	−0.7
Education	1.6	0.7	0.1	−2.7	−1.6	−3.4
Sum: Total human capital	2.4	0.2	−1.5	−4.0	−3.8	−4.2
Unemployment rate	0.3	−2.3	−0.6	−1.0	−0.8	1.4
Period effect	0.0	−2.1	0.0	−1.0	0.0	1.1
Total	2.6	−4.3	−2.0	−6.0	−4.7	−1.7
Change in average real earnings		−1.6		−8.0		−6.4

The coefficients of the human capital variables do not change very much over time in the case of the Canadian-born. The returns to work experience (the earnings premium for older age groups) declined somewhat, and the return to education increased. For the Canadian-born, the human capital part of the model appears to have been rather stable over the period 1980 to 1995.

For new immigrants the numbers make for a different story. The age premium for new immigrants declined considerably between the 1980s and the 1990s, and so did earnings premiums for all education beyond elementary school. Jointly these changes in the valuation of new immigrant attributes reduced new immigrant annual earnings by $3.9 thousand, one-half of the change in real annual earnings. This finding corresponds in a general way to the recent finding of Green and Worswick (2002) of a devaluation of foreign experience in the Canadian labour market. I find that the decline in the value of foreign educational credentials in the Canadian labour market contributed more to the earnings decline of new immigrants than the change in the valuation of foreign experience.

The effect of the change in the unemployment rate is very small, and this is a consequence of the choice of periods for comparison — the 1980s and the 1990s. The average unemployment rate (more precisely, the three-year average unemployment rate, averaged over the two pre-census years) did not increase very much between the two decades. In fact, for the Canadian-born the unemployment rate was lower in the 1990s than in the 1980s, given the distribution of these persons over the eight cities.

However, both new immigrant and Canadian-born men became more sensitive to the unemployment rate, the latter more so. This increasing sensitivity may be the result of increasing competition from women and from recent immigrants. Both groups were larger in number in the 1990s than in the 1980s. As well, the youngest age group has a weaker attachment to the labour force recently, because of greater enrolment and longer duration of postsecondary education. The earnings of new immigrant men have also become more sensitive to the unemployment rate, and continue to be more so than the earnings of Canadian-born men. New immigrants have been affected by the same factors as the Canadian-born, and probably more so, as they are new entrants. This latter point is not borne out by the estimation results, which indicate that the increase in sensitivity was greater for the Canadian-born than for new immigrants.

To sum up, the variable coefficients model adds two elements to the story of declining real earnings: men's earnings have become more sensitive to the state of the labour market, and new immigrants' educational credentials and work experience count for less than they used to. In the decomposition presented here — one of several possible stories[19] — part

---

[19]When visible minorities, age 45 to 54 and university degree are chosen as reference groups, a very different story emerges for new immigrants. Changes in the valuation of age and educational attainment *add* $2.5 thousand and $1.8 thousand to the earnings of new immigrants between 1980 and 1995, and there is

of the decline in earnings remains unexplained: the period effect of $2.1 thousand for the Canadian-born and $1 thousand for new immigrants. Thus, for the Canadian-born, the analysis does not explain the decline in earnings. Instead, it points out that human capital factors worked against the decline. For new immigrants, the analysis explains a large part of the decline that took place.[20]

Time Worked and the Weekly Wage

The data. This section reports separate findings for employment and pay rates, the two factors behind annual earnings. This is the approach generally taken in the labour market literature, for theoretical and methodological reasons. The employment decision depends, among other things, on the wage offered by employers and the reservation wage of the individual. Conflating employment and the wage into earnings hides this decision-making process. Further, inclusion of a large number of zero observations in the dependent variable (earnings) makes the assumption of independent, normally distributed residuals that underlies inference in OLS estimation untenable.

In this section, employment and the wage rate are examined separately using the same set of independent variables as in the analysis of earnings. Only a fixed coefficient model is used. While this further exploration falls

---

also a very large negative period effect of $9.4 thousand. The objective fact underlying either story is that earnings differentials associated with age and education have decreased. It is plausible to regard this as a drop in the returns to foreign work experience and education, as done in the main text, since that helps explain the decline. The alternative story presented in this footnote does not explain the decline and has therefore been rejected.

[20]As noted earlier, this analysis of change is based on successive snapshots of the earnings spectrum. It is quite different from the cohort-based perspective used by Beaudry and Green (2000) and Green and Worswick (2002). Our results are compatible with declining earnings for successive entry cohorts, and also with stable earnings for new entrants. If earnings of successive cohorts of new entrants were stable up to the 1980s and then started to decline, we would have seen increasing returns to age in the model used in this section. That we did not indicates that the decline in earnings of new entrants observed by Beaudry and Green was already occurring in 1980.

Bert Waslander

well short of the models used in the literature to analyze employment and the wage rate, it does help pinpoint the factors behind the changes in the experience of new immigrants somewhat more precisely. I expect to find that the state of the labour market affected employment more than the wage, and that the human capital factors affected the wage more than employment.

Annual earnings are the result of four factors: the employment ratio, the number of weeks worked by those who were employed, hours worked per week, and the real weekly wage. The product of the first three factors is a comprehensive measure of time worked. However, the census does not inquire about hours worked per week in the reference year, but only whether work was mainly full-time or part-time. By using this measure in the equation for weekly earnings it is possible to derive an estimate of average hours of part-time workers relative to full-time workers, and to calculate average hours worked per week as a percentage of full-time hours.[21]

This measure indicates that average hours per week worked by new immigrant men of prime labour force age declined by 4%. This change in time worked for pay comes on top of the decline in employment of 15.7% and the decline in weeks worked by employed persons of 10.6%. Expressing time worked in full-time equivalent (FTE) weeks per year, total time worked by new immigrants fell from 42.9 weeks to 31 FTE weeks, or by 26.7% (Table 10). Time worked by the Canadian-born was reduced by 7.6% (Table 7). Of the reduction in time worked for pay (including self-employment) by both groups, employment accounted for the largest share, followed by weeks worked and hours per week, in that order.

---

[21]The equation for the log of the weekly wage includes the same independent variables as the equations for annual earnings, plus a variable indicating the person worked mainly full-time during the year. The coefficient of the latter variable in the equation for new immigrants was 0.532, indicating that full-time workers were paid 70.2% more than part-time workers, or that part-time workers were paid 58.7% of what full-time workers received for a week's work. Assuming this difference in pay reflects only difference in hours worked, part-time hours averaged 58.7% of a full-time week. This means that in 1980, when 95.6% of employed new immigrants worked full-time, employed new immigrants on average worked 0.982 of a full-time week (0.956 x 1 + 0.044 x 0.587), and this fell to 0.942 (0.86 x 1 + 0.14 x 0.587) in 1995, a drop of 4% (Table 7). The same procedure was used to calculate hours per week for the Canadian-born.

Table 7: Time Worked, Men 25–54 Years Old in Eight Large Cities

	1980	1995	Change	(%)
Canadian-Born				
Employment ratio	94.7%	90.6%	−4.1	−4.3
Weeks worked (employed persons)	47.2	46.1	−1.1	−2.3
Weeks worked (all persons)	45.1	42.5	−2.6	−5.9
Full-time (share of employed persons)	95.7%	92.2%	−3.5	−3.7
Hours per week (percentage of full-time)	97.8%	95.9%	−1.8	−1.9
Time worked, all persons (FTE weeks)	44.1	40.8	−3.4	−7.6
New Immigrants				
Employment ratio	94.1%	79.3%	−14.8	−15.7
Weeks worked (employed persons)	46.4	41.5	−4.9	−10.6
Weeks worked (all persons)	43.7	32.9	−10.8	−24.6
Full-time (share of employed persons)	95.6%	86.0%	−9.6	−10.0
Hours per week (percentage of full-time)	98.2%	94.2%	−4.0	−4.0
Time worked, all persons (FTE weeks)	42.9	31.0	−11.9	−27.7

Method. The incidence of employment and of full-time work is analyzed using a logistic regression, and OLS is applied to weeks worked. In line with the human capital model, the weekly wage is examined in log form. The equations are estimated without fixed city effects, since in the employment equation for new immigrants, inclusion of such effects makes the unemployment rate insignificant.

As for the analysis of the change over time in the dependent variable, for fixed coefficient models estimated with OLS the contribution of each variable to the change is measured by the change in its average value multiplied by its coefficient. For non-linear equations (the logistic equations for employment and full-time work), following Even and McPherson (1990), the contributions are calculated based on the linear part of the regression equation, scaled so that these contributions sum to the change in the dependent variable.[22] The treatment of change in the wage is analogous. Contributions are calculated from the equation for the log wage, and then scaled to apply to the wage in 1995 dollars.

The change in time worked can be decomposed into contributions of its three components — employment, weeks, and hours. This is accomplished by adding the changes in the three components, each weighted by the product of the average values of the other two components. The contributions of the explanatory variables unemployment, age, etc. to the change in each of the three components are then derived from regression analysis in the same way as for earnings. Substituting these contributions into the equation for the change in total time worked gives an accounting of the change in comprehensive measure of the amount of paid work.

To state this formally, the change in time worked may be written as follows:

$$(1) \quad \Delta(e*w*h) = w*h*\Delta(e) + e*h*\Delta(w) + e*w*\Delta(h)$$

where Δ indicates the change from 1980 to 1995, e represents the average employment ratio, w represents weeks worked, and h an index of hours per week. Equation (1) is derived by differentiating total time worked with respect to time.

For e and h, the contribution of each independent variable is measured by

$$(2) \quad \textit{Effect } (X_i) = a*b_i*\Delta X_i$$

where a is a scalar such that $\sum_i a*b_i*\Delta X_i$ equals the change in the dependent variable.[23] By replacing $\Delta(e)$, $\Delta(w)$ and $\Delta(h)$ by the effects described in (2), a complete decomposition is obtained.

---

[22]The Even-McPherson method is the analog for logistic equations to the Oaxaca-Blinder decomposition for linear regression models. For a recent description and application of the Even-McPherson method, along with the Oaxaca-Blinder method, see Morissette and Drolet (2000).

[23]For the employment ratio and hours per week, a is the inverse of the logistic equation, and for weekly pay, a is the antilog.

Findings. The standard model with fixed period effects and without location effects gives credible results for new immigrants (Table 8). From the selected coefficients shown it is evident that older new immigrants (ages 45–54) are less likely to be employed than younger immigrants, and by a large margin, but if employed, are not significantly different with regard to number of weeks worked and hours per week.

Labour market conditions are a significant factor in all three equations for new immigrants. It is no surprise, therefore, that changes in the local unemployment rates account for about one-half of the reduction in time

Table 8: Employment Ratio and Weeks Worked, Men 25–54 Years Old in Eight Large Cities, Selected Estimates, Standard Model with Fixed Time Effects and Without Location Effects

	Employment Ratio (logit)		Weeks Worked by Employed		Worked Full-Time (logit)	
	Coefficient	t-value	Coefficient	t-value	Coefficient	t-value
Canadian-Born						
Unemployment rate	−10.517	−20.6	−26.188	−18.0	−6.398	−11.2
Visible minority	−0.530	−8.1	−1.391	−4.6	−0.540	−8.1
Age 35–44	0.067	3.0	2.512	39.7	0.553	22.3
Age 45–54	−0.062	−2.6	2.948	40.6	0.578	20.0
Period effect	−0.537	−14.8	−0.756	−7.6	−0.534	−13.2
Number of observations		177249		164269		164269
Log likelihood		−43272				−36191.33
R squared	(pseudo)	0.0679		0.0244	(pseudo)	0.0225
New Immigrants						
Unemployment rate	−15.862	−8.5	−69.337	−7.5	−14.024	−6.1
Visible minority	−0.531	−6.5	−1.391	−3.8	−0.425	−4.4
Age 35–44	−0.086	−1.2	0.739	2.1	0.110	1.2
Age 45–54	−0.422	−4.8	0.214	0.4	−0.085	−0.7
Period effect	−0.692	−4.4	−2.107	−3.3	−0.645	−3.4
Number of observations		8338		7151		7151
Log likelihood		−3190.9				−2208.93
R squared	(pseudo)	0.0648		0.0285	(pseudo)	0.0387

Bert Waslander

worked by new immigrants (Table 9).[24] The other half of the change remains unexplained, as the human capital factors had a modest effect only.

Changes in unemployment also account for about half of the change in time worked by Canadian-born men (Table 9). The age (work experience) variables had a more positive effect on the outcomes for the Canadian-born

Table 9: Contributions to Change in Time Worked from 1980 to 1995, Men 25–54 Years Old in Eight Large Cities (percentages of time worked in 1980)

Change in	Employment Ratio	Weeks Worked	Hours per Week	Total Time Worked
Due to	**Canadian-Born**			
Unemployment rate	–2.1	–1.9	–0.6	–4.6
Visible minority	0	0	0	–0.1
Age	0	0.5	0.1	0.6
Education	1.1	0.8	–1.5	2.1
Period effect	–3.1	–1.6	–1.8	–6.2
Time worked (FTE weeks)	–4.2	–2.2	–1.8	–8.2
	New Immigrants			
Unemployment rate	–6.1	–5.2	–1.5	–12.7
Visible minority	–1.4	–0.7	–0.3	–2.3
Age	–0.4	0.2	0	–0.2
Education	0.1	0.3	0	0.4
Period effect	–6.9	–4.1	–1.8	–12.7
Time worked (FTE weeks)	–14.6	–9.5	–3.5	–27.6

[24]The three components of the change in total time worked are shown with different values in Tables 7 and 9, both for the Canadian-born and for new immigrants. In Table 7, the last column gives percentage changes, and the total change in time worked is derived by taking the product of the three factors in 1980 and 1995, and calculating the percentage change. In Table 9, the change in total time worked is broken down into three additive components, following equation (1).

than for new immigrants. Middle-aged men are less likely to be employed than younger men, but they work more weeks and longer hours. Accordingly, age had a positive effect on the change in time worked between 1980 and 1995, and so did education. The human capital model works well in describing employment and amount of time worked for Canadian-born men.

According to these results, the deterioration in labour market conditions accounts for a larger part of the decline in time worked (about one-half) than of the decline in annual earnings. As shown in Table 3, the fixed coefficient model of annual earnings attributed less than 40% of the earnings decline of Canadian-born men to increasing unemployment, and one-quarter of the earnings decline of new immigrants.

As regards the weekly wage, the changes due to the reduction in hours worked are first removed, since these are included in total time worked. What remains is the change in the wage for a full-time week of work (Table 10). The unemployment rate once again proves to be the largest known source of change. It caused a larger absolute decline for new immigrants than for the Canadian-born.

The human capital variables have acted to push up the weekly wage, both for the Canadian-born and new immigrants, much more so for the former. But this positive force was overpowered by the deterioration in labour market conditions and a large unexplained further decline (the period effect). Evidently this equation does not really tell a complete story about the change in the weekly wage. For the Canadian-born, two forces were more or less in balance: gains in education and work experience pushed wages up, and higher unemployment pushed them down. The causes of the entire drop in the weekly wage thus remain unidentified. For new immigrants, unemployment and visible minority status combined to push the wage down, while education and work experience had only a very small effect in the opposite direction. These factors explain less than half the change that occurred.

Selection effects. To address the issue of selection, that is, the absence of observations of the wage for those who were not employed, I have estimated a Heckman two-step model of wage formation, using the same set of regressors as in the earlier models in both the wage and the employment equation. Included as selection variables in the equation for the probability of being employed were marital status (married vs. single), the presence of children, use of unemployment insurance and use of government transfers.

Table 10: Contributions to Change from 1980 to 1995 in Weekly Pay for Full-Time Work, Men 25–54 Years Old in Eight Cities

	Canadian-Born		New Immigrants	
Change in	*Dollars per Week*	*Percent of Total*	*Dollars per Week*	*Percent of Total*
Due to				
Unemployment rate	−$18.2	43.6%	−$43.3	27.9%
Visible minority	−$0.5	1.2%	−$27.7	17.9%
Age	$6.7	−16.2%	$3.3	−2.1%
Education	$13.6	−32.7%	$4.5	−2.9%
Period effect	−$43.4	104.1%	−$91.8	59.2%
Change FTE wage	−$41.7	100.0%	−$155.0	100.0%
	1980	*1995*	*1980*	*1995*
Weekly wage	$906	$849	$725	$550
Change		−$57.1		−$175.4

These variables were selected on the basis of a review of some recent literature.[25]

The results are striking. Marital status is of overwhelming importance in the employment equation, both for new immigrants and the Canadian-born. The inverse of Mill's ratio is significant in both equations for the log

---

[25]Hum and Simpson (1999) included city size, regional dummies, age and age squared, and family size in their probate equation for positive earnings, and excluded these variables from the wage offer equations. de Silva (1997) used receipt of unemployment insurance benefits and of social assistance and other government transfers as selection variables. de Silva and Dougherty (1996) used these same two variables and the incidence of income from self-employment in a probit equation for employment. These authors note a lack of uniformity in modelling employment selection. Family status variables and receipt of government transfer payments are fairly widely used.

of the weekly wage, and makes unemployment insignificant in the case of the Canadian-born, while reducing its role in the new immigrant equation by one-half. Hence, assuming that the selection model is correct, this indicates that the state of the labour market had an effect on the wage mainly through selection, that is, the employment decision, rather than directly. The direct contribution of unemployment to change in the wage, accordingly, would have been much smaller than shown in Table 10.[26]

Conclusion

This analysis used variation in space and time to measure the effect of changes in the state of the labour market and in the characteristics of new immigrants in the decline of the fortunes of new male immigrants. A basic human capital equation augmented with the unemployment rate was used to obtain an accounting for the change in annual real earnings of both new immigrant and Canadian-born men. Three different decompositions were presented. The first was based on a model of annual real earnings estimated over the entire period, with coefficients fixed in time, and fixed location and period effects. The second decomposition, also of annual real earnings, was derived from two equations, estimated over the 1980s and 1990s, without period and location effects. This accounting includes the effects of changes in coefficients as well as of changes in independent variables. The third decomposition presented separate accounting of changes in total time worked, subdivided into the three factors: employment, weeks worked and incidence of full-time work, and in weekly pay for full-time work.

In spite of the lack of robust results for the unemployment rate, it is evident that the decline in earnings of new immigrants is much greater than can be readily explained by changes in the unemployment rate. This is borne out by the large period effects in the fixed coefficient models. It is also readily demonstrated by comparing the 1980s and the 1990s: new immigrant earnings dropped by $8 thousand, while the average unemployment rate hardly changed at all. While estimation results suggest that the earnings of both Canadian-born and new immigrant men have become more sensitive to the unemployment rate, this too does not fully account for the decline in earnings of new immigrants.

---

[26]These results are available from the author on request.

Contrary to the findings regarding the unemployment rate, the effect of major human capital attributes on earnings and change in earnings was rather robust across different models. Educational attainment and work experience of both Canadian-born and new immigrant men increased, and this had a positive effect on their earnings. The effect was much stronger for the Canadian-born, while the changing ethnic make-up of new immigrants had a substantial negative effect on their earnings. Part of the decline in earnings of new immigrants can be attributed to a drop in the returns to foreign education and work experience. Interestingly, the human capital variables account for a large part of the increase of the earnings differential between new immigrants and the Canadian-born.

Part of the decline in earnings remains unexplained in most of our results, both for new immigrants and the Canadian-born. I would venture that this unexplained decline has more to do with changes in the Canadian labour market than with changes in new immigrants, whose most important attributes are present in the models presented in this paper. In further work it may be useful to unpack the notion of sensitivity of earnings to the unemployment rate. One could attempt to describe changes in the labour market — changing composition of the labour force, changes in immigration levels, changes in attachment to the labour force — and measure the effect of these phenomena on earnings of new immigrants and the Canadian-born. Refining the human capital variables might be another fruitful extension, as would be a cohort-oriented approach for the Canadian-born.

References

Aydemir, A. (2002), "Effects of Business Cycles on the Labour Market Assimilation of Immigrants". Paper presented at the CERF conference, Calgary.

Baker, M. and D. Benjamin (1997), "The Role of the Family in Immigrants' Labor-Market Activity: An Evaluation of Alternative Explanations", *American Economic Review* 87, 705–727.

Beaudry, P. and D. Green (2000), "Cohort Patterns in Canadian Earnings: Assessing the Role of Skill Premia in Equality Trends", *Canadian Journal of Economics* 33(4), 907–936.

Bloom, D.E., G. Grenier and M. Gunderson (1995), "The Changing Labor Market Position of Canadian Immigrants", *Canadian Journal of Economics* 27(4b), 987–1005.

Chiswick, B.R., Y. Cohen and T. Zach (1997), "The Labor Market Status of Immigrants: Effects of the Unemployment Rate at Arrival and Duration of Residence", *Industrial and Labor Relations Review* 50(2), 289–303.

Chiswick, B.R. and P.W. Miller (2002), "Immigrant Earnings: Language Skills, Linguistic Concentrations and the Business Cycle", *Journal of Population Economics* 15(1), 31–57.

de Silva, A. (1997), "Earnings of Immigrant Classes in the Early 1980s in Canada: A Reexamination", *Canadian Public Policy/Analyse de Politiques* 28(2), 179–202.

de Silva, A. with C. Dougherty (1996), "Discrimination against Visible Minority Men", Working Paper No. 96–6E (Ottawa: Citizenship and Immigration Canada).

Even, W.E. and D.A. MacPherson (1990), "Plant Size and the Decline of Unionism", *Economics Letters* 32, 393–398.

Grant, M.L. (1999), "Evidence of New Immigrant Assimilation in Canada", *Canadian Journal of Economics* 32(4), 930–955.

Green, D.A. and C. Worswick (2002), "The Earnings Assimilation of Immigrants and the Native-Born in Canada: An Investigation of the Importance of Labour Market Entry Cohort and Labour Market Conditions". Presented at the CERF conference, Calgary.

Hum, D. and W. Simpson (1999), "Wage Opportunities for Visible Minorities in Canada", *Canadian Public Policy/Analyse de Politiques* 25(3), 379–394.

Li, P.S. (2001), "The Market Worth of Immigrants' Educational Credentials", *Canadian Public Policy/Analyse de Politiques* 27(1), 23–38.

McDonald, J.T. and C. Worswick (1998), "The Earnings of Immigrant Men in Canada: Job Tenure, Cohort, and Macroeconomic Conditions", *Industrial and Labour Relations Review* 51(3), 465–482.

Morissette, R. and M. Drolet (2000), "Pension Coverage and Retirement Savings of Young and Prime-Age Workers in Canada: 1986–1997", SLID Research Paper, Cat. No. 75F0002MIE-00009 (Ottawa: Statistics Canada).

Moulton, B.R. (1990), "An Illustration of a Pitfall in Estimating the Effects of Aggregate Variables on Micro Units", *The Review of Economics and Statistics* 72(2), 334–338.

Oaxaca, R. and M.R. Ransom (1999), "Identification in Detailed Wage Decompositions", *The Review of Economics and Statistics* 81(1), 154–157.

Reitz, J.G. (1998), *Warmth of the Welcome: The Social Causes of Economic Success for Immigrants in Different Nations and Cities* (Boulder, CO: Westview Press).

Schaafsma, J. and A. Sweetman (2001), "Immigrant Earnings: Age at Immigration Matters", *Canadian Journal of Economics* 34(4), 1066–1099.

Waslander, B. (2001), "First Contact: The Falling Earnings of New Immigrant Men". Paper presented at the Statistics Canada Economic Conference on the Economy, Ottawa.

Effects of Business Cycles on the Labour Market Participation and Employment Rate Assimilation of Immigrants

Abdurrahman Aydemir

Introduction

Labour market success of immigrants is the subject of considerable re-search in the economics literature, receiving much attention in recent years with the reported decline in performance of recent immigrant cohorts. Identifying the factors that cause this deterioration is crucial from a policy perspective since different factors call for different policy prescriptions.

The immigration literature tries to explain differences in labour market outcomes of different immigrant arrival cohorts by differences in observ-able characteristics and by cohort effects. In standard earnings regression observed characteristics refer to such characteristics as schooling and

I would like to thank Charles Beach, Miles Corak, Chris Robinson, and Chris Worswick for helpful discussions. This paper also benefited from comments of participants at the 2002 CERF conference, John Deutsch Institute conference on immigration, and seminar participants at Statistics Canada and UWO. I am solely responsible for the remaining errors in the paper. The views presented in this paper belong to the author and do not represent the views of Statistics Canada.

experience, while cohort effects are generally interpreted as other un-observed "quality" differences. Accounting for the phase of the business cycle that immigrants face both at the time of arrival and during the survey year is important since this may affect their labour market prospects in the host country. If these macro conditions are not controlled for, one may conclude that there are significant cohort effects and interpret them as "quality" differences across cohorts, when in fact they are due to the business cycle.

The goal of this paper is to explore the role of macroeconomic conditions in determining the labour market success of immigrants. Allowing for cohort effects, both effects of macro conditions at the time of arrival and at the time of survey year are explored. Previous works in the literature, however, study either the effects of macro conditions at arrival by assuming away the cohort effects or the effects of macro conditions at the time of the survey allowing for cohort effects. In this second approach, cohort effects also embody the effects of macro conditions at the time of arrival, therefore, separate identification of the effects of macro conditions at entry is not possible.[1] This study identifies separate effects of all three factors simultaneously, that is cohort effects, effects of macro conditions at arrival, and effects of macro conditions in the survey year. The importance of controlling for macroeconomic conditions in interpreting cohort effects is discussed by exploring the sensitivity of the estimated cohort coefficients to the inclusion of controls for the business cycle.

Another difference from the previous literature is also in terms of how labour market assimilation is captured. Job market opportunities and the opportunity cost of not working as measured by wages vary by the phase of the business cycle. Therefore, macroeconomic conditions are likely to have an impact on labour force participation (LFP) decisions, as well as whether an immigrant will be able to secure a job conditional on participation and how good the fit will be between the job and the skills of the immigrant. Existing studies focus on the effects of macro conditions on assimilation of immigrants by exploring effects either on earnings or the incidence of employment (unemployment). For a new immigrant, however, the first challenge is to decide when to enter the labour force. First, this paper extends the previous literature by exploring the effects of macro conditions on LFP along with the employment outcome. Identifying difficulties

---

[1]The only exception to this is McDonald and Worswick (1998) which is discussed below.

Abdurrahman Aydemir

that immigrants may be facing at the LFP margin is important in determining the best policy to help them. Secondly, studies that focus on incidence of employment (unemployment) and earnings are examining a selected group of individuals, those who participate in the labour force and those who are successful enough to get a job and report positive earnings correspondingly. Therefore, it is important to understand the selection mechanism that shapes the pool of individuals that are in the labour force.

The literature addressing the effects of macro conditions on immigrant assimilation explores the impact of macro conditions at arrival and the impact of current (survey year) macro conditions. For the macro conditions at arrival, the question is: Does arriving during a worse economic environment shift an immigrant's assimilation profile down, causing a permanent disadvantage? On the other hand, different macro conditions at the survey year are thought to cause movements along this assimilation path. Therefore, for assessing the rate of assimilation, current macro conditions need to be taken into account since rate of assimilation is sensitive to between which points (i.e., survey years that may represent different macro conditions) it is measured. This sensitivity may be even more so for young immigrants since they are more likely to be affected by the business cycle. Chiswick, Cohen and Zach (1997) argue that employers have less information about the credentials and characteristics of new immigrants resulting in more mismatches between employers and employees which will lead to more separations. This may also lead to less firm-specific training and seniority among young immigrants and therefore they may be more affected by an economic downturn. As years of residence in the host country increases, however, immigrants are expected to become more insulated from the effects of business cycles.

Previous literature has uncovered several facts on the impact of macro conditions. Stewart and Hyclak (1984), using 1970 US census found that a higher annual growth rate in real gross national product (GNP) in the period of *entry* was associated with higher immigrant earnings among the foreign-born. Nakamura and Nakamura (1992), using 1980 US census and 1981 Canadian census, found that for both immigrants and the native-born a higher unemployment rate in the year of labour market *entry* was significantly associated with a lower current hourly wage. The results also showed that the effect of the unemployment rate at the time of *entry* is stronger for immigrants than for natives. Chiswick, Cohen and Zach (1997) use the Current Population Survey and show that poor labour market conditions at the time of *survey* have an adverse effect on employment probability and there is weak support for the hypothesis that immigrants are more cyclically sensitive to the current macroeconomic conditions than the native-born. However, poor macro conditions at the time of *entry* are found to have no adverse effect on employment opportunities or the incidence of unemployment among immigrants. Using 1990 US census, Chiswick and Miller (1999) find that earnings are lower among those who enter the US labour market in a period of high unemployment. By interacting the unemployment rate at labour market entry with duration in the United States, they test whether the effects of macro conditions at entry vary by duration of residence in the destination and they find that this effect is temporary. These studies test the effect of macro conditions at entry and at the survey year on employment and earnings, however, they do not allow for cohort effects.

Using 11 cross-sectional surveys of Survey of Consumer Finances (SCF), McDonald and Worswick (1997) find that immigrants from recent arrival cohorts have higher unemployment probabilities than similar non-immigrants in survey years corresponding to a recessionary period. However, this differential disappears as the number of years of residence increases. Using the same data, McDonald and Worswick (1998) report a significant impact of the current macroeconomic conditions (at the time of survey) on the earnings of immigrants. They also note that controlling for the unemployment rate at the time of entry to the labour market is found to have a negative but insignificant impact on earnings, but these results are not presented in the paper.

This paper shares a methodology similar to McDonald and Worswick (1998). Both studies allow for cohort effects and control for the effect of current macro conditions (at the time of survey). McDonald and Worswick use public-use files of SCFs where immigrant arrival cohorts can only be identified over an extended period, such as 1956 to 65. It is not possible to identify in which year over this period an immigrant has arrived. Therefore, in order to control for entry macro conditions either the average unemployment rate over this ten-year period or unemployment rate in a specific year within this period has to be used. Chiswick, Cohen and Zach (1997) discuss in their study that using an average unemployment rate over a period of three years after an immigrant's arrival is less appropriate as a measure of labour market conditions at entry than is the unemployment rate at the year of arrival. The macroeconomic environment can change substantially even over a three-year time frame. Therefore, in a rapidly changing macroeconomic environment, measures other than the unemployment rate at the year of arrival will be a poor measure of macro conditions at entry. McDonald and Worswick's (1998) finding that entry macro conditions

Abdurrahman Aydemir

have no significant impact may be partly because the measure used does not adequately reflect the conditions at entry. This paper uses master files of SCFs and is able to identify the year of immigration for immigrants consistently across all survey years. This provides a better measure of macro conditions at entry.

Secondly, McDonald and Worswick (1998) use survey years 1981–92 and the latest immigrant cohort they can identify using the public use files is the 1976–80 immigrant arrival cohort. In this study, immigrants who arrived until 1996 are identified using survey years covering 1979–97. This allows the studying of experiences of immigrant cohorts, including the recent arrival cohorts, over a longer period of time. The declining performance of recent immigrant cohorts has attracted a lot of attention and I address their performance relative to earlier cohorts and explore the role that macro economic conditions played in creating differences between recent and earlier immigrant cohorts.

Finally, McDonald and Worswick's (1998) focus is on earnings. I focus on LFP and employment outcomes. This allows an exploration of the impacts of macro conditions at different stages of transition to the labour market.

Given the reported decline in the performance of recent immigrants, the interesting questions in this context are whether the timing of immigration has a permanent effect (a "scarring effect" as it is sometimes called) on how well immigrants assimilate, and if a permanent effect exists, what are the appropriate policy tools to address the issue. In the Canadian context, before the early 1990s, the government cut the level of immigration during recessions when the "absorptive capacity" of the economy was believed to be low. The screening process was used to adjust the level and composition of immigrants. As an example, during 1983–85 all independent immigrants were required to have arranged employment in order to get admission. This resulted in a sharp decline in the number of individuals accepted under the independent class (see Table 2 for changes in class composition of immigrants over 1980 to 1998 which uses the Immigration Database, IMDB). Starting with the early 1990s recession and the following boom the Canadian government moved away from its time honoured pattern. The effect of macro conditions on immigrants is a concern for other immigrant-receiving countries as well, and several other countries have immigration policies tailored to take into account the stage of the business cycle. Australia changes the annual immigration quotas on the basis of the state of the economy. The United States may implicitly do so through administrative tightening of criteria for labour market visas, although this constitutes a small portion of total migration to the United States (Chiswick, Cohen and Zach, 1997). Israel, on the other hand, does not tie its immigration policies to the short-term labour market conditions. Given the different practices of major immigrant-receiving countries, it is interesting to compare relative performance of immigrant cohorts arriving over different phases of the business cycle.

The results show that cohort effects are very sensitive to the inclusion of controls for macroeconomic conditions. Without controls for macro-economic conditions there are significant negative cohort effects for the latter immigrant cohorts suggesting that they are doing worse than the earlier immigrant cohorts. Controlling for macro conditions and allowing the effects to vary between immigrants and native-born results in cohort effects becoming significantly smaller. This suggests that the deterioration in assimilation of recent immigrants documented in the previous literature is partly due to the adverse economic conditions.

Macro conditions at the time of entry to the labour market have adverse impacts on LFP and employment probability. A higher unemployment rate at the survey year has a stronger negative effect on both. With the inclusion of controls for macro conditions the significance and magnitude of the coefficient measuring assimilation (coefficient on *years since migration*) increases. Therefore, not only the estimated cohort effects but also the assimilation profiles are sensitive to the inclusion of controls for business cycles.

Data

The data used in this study comes from the Survey of Consumer Finances master files. The SCF was carried out in a two-week period in each April between 1980 to 1998. The individuals are a weighted sample of all individuals 15 years of age and older in Canada at the time of the survey. A set of sample weights are provided and used in the estimation to enable generalizations of results to the Canadian population. Immigrants are identified by their year of arrival in the master files. This makes it possible to identify immigrant cohorts by each year of arrival compared to the public use files where immigrants are identified as multi-year arrival cohorts over-lapping for arrival years after 1990. The SCF, however, does not provide information on visa category or country of origin for immigrants. The SCF yearly files are supplement to the April Labour Force Survey (LFS) where in addition to the questions asked in the LFS for the *reference week*, the SCF asks additional detailed income questions about the previous year (*reference year*). Therefore, for example, in the 1990 survey year, questions regarding the reference week refer to the activity in the week containing the 15th of April 1990, whereas questions for the reference year refer to 1989. Using SCF files it is possible to explore several dimensions of labour market activity, such as LFP, employment, and earnings.

I restrict the SCF sample to males who were between the ages of 25 and 55 in the survey year. The native-born sample is a 15% random sample of all non-immigrant men age 25 to 55 in the survey year. Immigrants are restricted to those whose age at migration was over 17. The former age restriction is intended to focus on men who are likely to have finished their education and are not yet at the mandatory retirement age. The latter restriction on age at migration is intended to focus on the effect of business cycles on immigrants who come in as adults and are less likely to have host-country specific education. The experiences of the immigrants who arrive at the host country at younger ages and the effects of the business cycles on them may be quite different, more like the effect of business cycles on Canadian-born. Also excluded are those immigrants whose year of arrival is the same as the reference year. These individuals spend less than one full year during the reference year in the host country after their arrival. Therefore, measures of LFP, earnings, and employment for the reference year refer to a shorter period of time for these individuals compared to others who arrived prior to the reference year.

Using samples of immigrant and Canadian-born individuals drawn from SCF datasets I study the role of macroeconomic conditions on LFP and employment. The study focuses on immigrants who arrived from 1966 to 1996. In the SCFs it is possible to identify immigrants who migrated prior to 1966, however, due to small sample sizes (especially in the later survey years) these immigrants are left out of the analysis. In existing literature, cohort definitions are dictated by the information available in the data on year of immigration. For example, public use files of SCF identifies only the multi-year period over which an immigrant has arrived, such as 1976 to 1980, which leads to a cohort definition of 1976–80. In the master files, exact year of immigration is identified. Cohorts in this paper are defined as the 1966–70, 1971–75, 1976–79, 1980–82, 1983–85, 1986–89, 1990–92, and 1993–96 cohort. These cohort definitions are motivated by important shifts in immigration policy regime, business-cycle dates, and the trends in the country of origin and class composition of immigrants over the years. Over the 1966–79 period, country of origin of immigrants shifted from

Western Europe to Eastern Europe and Asia. This was a result of the regulatory changes in immigration policy in early 1960s that abolished the policy that gave preference to British, French, and American citizens and set limits on immigrants from Asiatic countries. The cohorts that arrived after this period are defined by shorter periods reflecting the important changes in immigration policy and business-cycle dates. The 1980–82 cohort arrived during the early 1980s recession. The 1983–85 cohort arrived during a period when immigration under the skilled-worker category required an arranged employment (this restriction significantly altered the composition of immigrants by visa category). The 1986–89 cohort arrived during the following boom, while the 1990–92 cohort arrived during the 1990s recession. Finally, the 1993–96 cohort arrived at the start of the recovery following the severe recession of the early 1990s. Furthermore, 1990 marks the year when the immigration policy that tailored the immigration levels to the macro conditions was abandoned and this resulted in a significant increase in the level of immigration.[2]

The outcome variables are *LFP* and *Employed*. LFP is a dichotomous variable equal to one if the male respondent was in the labour force any time during the reference year, zero if he was not employed and did not look for work for the whole year. Employed is defined for only labour force participants. It is equal to one if respondent had positive earnings during the reference year; zero if he did not have any positive earnings.[3]

LFP is an indicator of the first stage of transition to the labour market, the labour force participation decision; employed is an indicator of success in finding a job given the respondent decides to participate in the labour force.[4]

---

[2]Sensitivity of results to alternative cohort definitions is explored. Two alternative specifications are estimated: first, a specification which defined cohorts as simple five-year arrival cohorts (1966–70,..., 1986–90,...) and a second, one where cohort definitions used in this paper for immigrants who arrived before 1980 is modified to allow for a more detailed cohort definition. Results are found to be robust to these alternative definitions.

[3]This measure of employment is compared below to the employment rate obtained from information on the number of weeks worked conditional on labour force participation.

[4]The literature that studies earnings outcomes of immigrants concentrates on these individuals who are labour force participants and report positive earnings.

Abdurrahman Aydemir

Analysis

This section first summarizes the trends in LFP and employment in Figures 1 and 2 over the 1979–97 period using the SCF data. Figure 1 presents the LFP rates for immigrants and Canadian-born which shows a downward trend for both groups over the sample period. The adverse effects of the early 1980s and 1990s recessions on participation rates are evident. The decline in LFP rates for immigrants during recessions is higher than that for the Canadian-born. Immigrants have slightly higher participation rates in the early 1980s relative to Canadian-born, however, after the 1990s recession this pattern reverses and immigrants have relatively lower participation rates. The gap remains between the two groups until the end of the sample period. Figure 2 presents the employment rates for labour force participants.[5] Employment rates are similar for both groups until the 1990s and again a drop in employment rates of immigrants relative to Canadian-born is observed starting with the 1990s recession. The gap closes between the two groups to some extent in the following boom. The effects of business cycles are evident on both groups with a fall in employment rates during recessions and a recovery after each recession. The sharp decline in performance of immigrants in the early 1990s recession in terms of both LFP and employment is especially notable.[6]

---

[5]Figure 2 presents the incidence of positive earnings (IPE) for labour force participants. In Figure 3, for the immigrants who are labour force participants the trend in IPE is compared to employment rates obtained using the information on number of weeks worked in the reference year. The two series are very close to each other. Employment rates using information on number of weeks worked is slightly higher since some individuals might have worked but reported negative earnings (such as those self-employed). In the rest of the paper the IPE for participants is referred to as employment rate.

[6]The early 1990s recession was very severe relative to previous ones. Bodman and Crosby (2000) give the number of quarters it takes the economy to surpass its previous peak after the contraction has ended. After the 1981–82 recession the recovery duration to previous peak was three quarters. After the 1990–91 recession the recovery duration to previous peak was nine quarters. The longest recovery period observed after a recession from 1947 to 1980 was that after the 1947–48 recession which took three quarters to reach the previous peak.

**Figure 1: Labour Force Participation (LFP) Rates,
Reference Year, Males 25–55, Canadian-Born
and Immigrants (year of immigration 1966–96)**

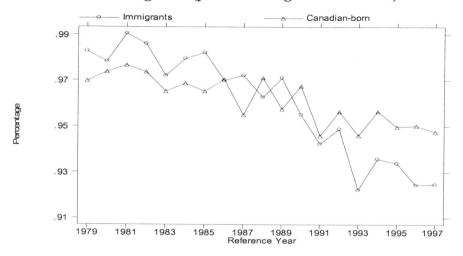

**Figure 2: Employment Rates (incidence of positive earnings for
labour force participants), Reference Year,
Male 25–55, Canadian-Born and Immigrants
(year of immigration 1966–96)**

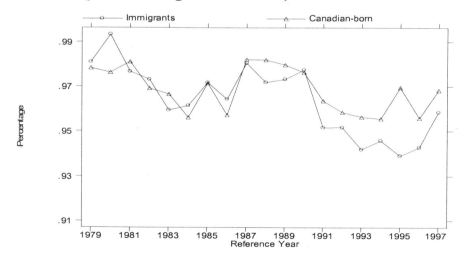

382   *Abdurrahman Aydemir*

Figure 3: Incidence of Positive Earnings (IPE) for Labour Force Participants and Employment Rate for Labour Force Participants, Reference Year, Male 25–55, Immigrants (year of immigration 1966–96)

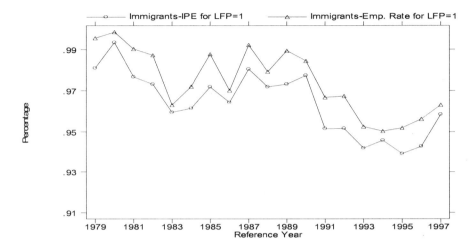

The deterioration in the performance of immigrants may be due to the differences in observed and unobserved characteristics of different immigrant cohorts. Also, the phase of the business cycle and the severity of the 1990s recession might have played a role in this outcome.

Table 1 shows that immigrant arrival cohorts prior to 1980 are older than Canadian-born in the survey year, whereas more recent immigrants are younger. More recent immigrant arrival cohorts have higher education than their predecessors and also relative to the native-born. For example, 61.3% of 1993–96 cohort has a postsecondary certificate/diploma, or a university degree, compared to only 38% of the native-born. Immigrants are over-represented in Ontario and British Columbia and the fraction of immigrants that choose to live in large urban areas increased with more recent arrival cohorts. There is also a shift in the mother tongue of immigrants from English and French to other mother tongues. This observation is consistent with the shift in the country of origin of immigrants from Western Europe

Table 1: Sample Means (%)
SCF Data

	Canadian-Born							*Immigrant Cohorts*			
		1966–70	1971–75	1976–79	1980–82	1983–85	1986–89	1990–92	1993–96
Education									
0–8 years	10.6	16.5	15.0	10.1	10.0	8.7	8.4	7.3	4.5
Some sec., no post-secondary	43.1	32.1	32.1	33.9	34.4	36.9	32.4	33.2	29.5
Some postsecondary	8.4	6.6	7.3	7.1	7.7	7.6	7.2	5.8	4.8
Postsec. certificate or diploma	21.9	19.5	20.4	23.6	22.9	19.9	28.6	25.8	28.1
University degree	16.1	25.3	25.3	25.2	25.1	26.9	23.5	27.9	33.2
Age	37.9	44.4	40.9	38.3	37.1	36.2	36.2	36.7	36.8
Region									
Atlantic	9.7	1.6	1.4	1.6	1.5	1.4	0.9	0.9	1.5
Quebec	29.1	14.3	13.3	16.9	19.5	23.1	15.2	20.5	17.9
Ontario	32.7	57.2	54.7	47.7	48.4	50.4	61.6	50.6	48.2
Prairies	17.4	10.4	13.7	18.5	17.8	13.7	9.3	9.6	9.5
British Columbia	11.1	16.7	16.8	15.3	15.9	11.4	13.0	18.5	22.9

Table 1: continued

	Canadian-Born	Immigrant Cohorts							
		1966–70	1971–75	1976–79	1980–82	1983–85	1986–89	1990–92	1993–96
Mother Tongue									
English	65.8	39.9	38.6	34.4	26.0	20.8	19.2	15.4	14.7
French	30.7	5.1	3.6	4.8	4.2	4.3	3.3	4.1	3.8
Other	3.5	55.0	57.8	60.9	69.8	74.9	77.5	80.5	81.5
Area Size									
Urban, >=500,000	40.6	72.3	76.6	76.7	79.7	83.6	85.1	87.3	86.1
U,100,000–499,999	16.0	13.8	11.5	10.8	9.3	8.7	8.3	7.5	7.7
U,30,000–99,999	9.3	3.8	3.3	3.5	3.8	2.3	2.7	1.8	2.3
U,2,500–29,999	4.2	1.7	1.5	1.4	1.5	1.0	0.7	0.6	0.4
U,<2,500	9.9	3.0	2.6	2.8	2.2	1.2	1.2	1.3	1.6
Rural	20.1	5.5	4.6	4.9	3.4	3.2	2.1	1.5	1.9

Notes: The Altantic region contains the following provinces: Prince Edward Island, Nova Scotia, New Brunswick, and Newfoundland. The Prairie region contains Manitoba, Saskatchewan, and Alberta.
Source: Author's compilation based on SCF Data, Statistics Canada (1980–1998).

Table 2: Distribution of Immigrants by Class (IMDB data, males, age at migration 25–55)

Landing Year	Family Class	Business Class	Skilled Worker	Assisted Relative	Refugee Class	Other
1980	20.6	4.8	33.9	13.1	27.6	0
1981	23.7	5.5	42.7	15.7	12.4	0
1982	22.9	6.3	39.3	12.0	19.4	0.1
1983	34.5	9.7	24.5	7.1	24.4	0.1
1984	37.2	8.2	18.8	10.0	25.3	0.6
1985	33.8	9.1	19.8	10.0	27.1	0.3
1986	27.5	8.2	19.3	6.7	26.2	12.0
1987	20.1	7.0	27.2	9.4	17.0	19.3
1988	16.6	10.0	37.5	12.9	22.0	1.1
1989	23.1	9.0	31.3	11.9	24.1	0.6
1990	25.9	7.4	27.4	11.7	21.6	5.9
1991	25.6	6.4	20.0	8.9	18.6	20.5
1992	27.1	9.4	14.3	7.5	18.6	23.1
1993	33.2	12.7	19.9	9.9	11.8	12.4
1994	31.5	12.8	26.6	14.4	11.1	3.5
1995	24.6	8.7	33.1	16.0	15.6	2.1
1996	19.5	8.0	39.9	14.4	14.3	3.9
1997	17.7	8.2	46.9	12.4	12.5	2.4
1998	18.4	7.3	49.2	9.5	13.6	2.0
1980–98	24.4	8.5	30.6	11.4	17.9	7.2

Abdurrahman Aydemir

to Asia and other non-European countries over this period.[7] In the next section, using a fixed-effects specification of the effects of macro conditions on immigrants' assimilation is explored along with the cohort effects.

Multivariate Analysis of LFP and Employment

Flexible form specification. The differences between immigrants and Canadian-born in Figures 1 and 2 could be caused by the differences in the observed characteristics. In order to identify the differences between the two groups holding observed characteristics constant, a binary choice model (BCM) is utilized. BCM is used to model differences in LFP and employment using a "flexible form" that imposes no particular functional form on the relationship between years-since migration and the probability of observed outcome. In this specification:

$$(1) \quad I_i(t) = X_i(t)\beta(t) + \sum_{j=1}^{J} \sum_{t=1}^{T} \delta^j(t)C_i^j Y(t) + u_i(t)$$

In the case when $I_i(t)$ refers to the LFP, individual i is in the labour force in period t if $I_i(t) \geq 0$, out of labour force otherwise. Probit estimation of above equation generates the probability that each individual i will be in the labour force in period t given his personal characteristics. The BCM is similarly defined for employment outcome. The vector X is the vector of characteristics of individual i at time t and controls for the following:

$X_i(t) = \{$education, region of residence, size of the centre of
residence, mother tongue, marital status, age$\}$

A different set of coefficients $\beta(t)$ is estimated for each survey year, allowing the effect of characteristics in X to be different in each survey year. For example, the effect of having a low level of education on

---

[7]There is no information in the SCFs on the country of birth except the information of whether or not an individual was born in Canada. Therefore, changes in the distribution of the country of birth over time cannot be addressed with these data.

probability of employment may be stronger during recessions if those with fewer skills are more adversely affected by an economic downturn.

The cohort effects for immigrants are captured by C_i^j dummies that identify each immigrant arrival cohort ($j=1,\ldots,J$). The interaction of C_i^j with survey year dummy variables $Y(t)$ gives a different estimate of cohort effects $\delta^j(t)$ for each survey year. $\delta^j(t)$ shifts the intercept of the index for immigrants in each cohort in each year allowing the differences between immigrants and native-born to be sensitive to the phase of the business cycle. Cohort effects in this context may be driven by differences across cohorts in terms of years of residence in the host country, macro conditions at the time of entry and survey year and differences in unobserved quality.

Results based on probit estimation of the model using specification (1) are presented in Table 3a for LFP and Table 3b for employment. Rather than presenting parameter estimates from 19 survey years, these tables present the estimates of differences in probability of observed outcome (such as LFP) between immigrant cohorts and the Canadian-born. For example, in Table 3a for the 1976–79 cohort in survey year 1982, a coefficient of 0.019 means that an immigrant from that cohort was 1.9% more likely to be a labour force participant compared to a Canadian-born, controlling for other observable characteristics. In this table each row for a given survey year gives the cross-sectional profile of immigrant cohorts and should be comparable to results from a single cross-sectional study. A column, on the other hand, shows the experience of a given cohort over years 1979 to 1997. Similar results are presented by McDonald and Worswick (1997) analyzing unemployment probabilities using SCF files from 1982 to 1993.[8]

Results from Table 3a show the difficulties experienced by recent immigrant cohorts. For immigrant cohorts that arrived before 1985 the differences between immigrants and Canadian-born which are significant are all positive (except for 1984 and 1988 for the 1976–79 cohort) whereas

---

[8]Note that there are some differences in selection of samples between this study and the study by McDonald and Worswick (1997). In this study individuals who are 25–55 in the survey year are studied and the sample of immigrants are restricted to those who were at least 18 when they arrived to Canada. Age at migration restriction does not exist in the McDonald and Worswick study and also they restrict their sample to those who were 24 to 53 in 1982, that is, they follow a birth cohort. Finally, the measure used by McDonald and Worswick refers to the reference week, whereas the measures used in this study refer to the reference year.

Table 3a: Differences in Labour Force Participation Rates between Immigrants and Canadian-Born by Arrival Cohort and Survey Year (probit estimates using flexible forms specification)

Survey Year	Sample Size	Immigrant Cohorts							
		1966–70	1971–75	1976–79	1980–82	1983–85	1986–89	1990–92	1993–96
1979	3876	0.004 (0.014)	-0.009 (0.018)	-0.002 (0.017)					
1980	1725	-0.029 (0.021)	-0.005 (0.014)	-0.042 (0.031)					
1981	3868	0.007 (0.010)	0.010 (0.010)	0.001 (0.016)	-0.058 (0.056)				
1982	4044	0.001 (0.014)	0.010 (0.012)	0.019*** (0.007)	-0.031 (0.023)				
1983	1699	0.022* (0.014)	-0.009 (0.023)	0.001 (0.026)	-0.021 (0.029)				
1984	3992	-0.001 (0.020)	-0.008 (0.023)	-0.062* (0.034)	-0.018 (0.031)	-0.095 (0.077)			
1985	3984	0.025*** (0.006)	0.005 (0.012)	-0.007 (0.019)	0.025*** (0.005)	0.008 (0.015)			
1986	3374	-0.001 (0.015)	0.006 (0.018)	-0.022 (0.029)	-0.029 (0.029)	-0.025 (0.032)			
1987	4587	0.015 (0.016)	0.021* (0.012)	0.007 (0.017)	0.008 (0.023)	0.004 (0.023)	0.007 (0.029)		
1988	3933	-0.014 (0.024)	-0.035 (0.034)	-0.081* (0.049)	0.013 (0.015)	-0.049 (0.049)	-0.163** (0.073)		
1989	4363	0.009 (0.017)	0.022* (0.013)	0.018 (0.18)	0.019 (0.016)	0.008 (0.022)	0.001 (0.028)		

1990	4592	−0.043 (0.029)	−0.052 (0.036)	−0.047 (0.053)	0.022* (0.013)	−0.063 (0.044)	−0.086** (0.043)		
1991	4493	0.018 (0.16)	0.021 (0.018)	0.034*** (0.012)	0.007 (0.022)	0.026 (0.017)	−0.001 (0.026)	−0.099 (0.072)	
1992	4178	0.001 (0.023)	0.005 (0.020)	−0.040 (0.050)	−0.070 (0.063)	−0.074 (0.059)	−0.041 (0.038)	−0.066 (0.056)	
1993	3974	−0.002 (0.031)	0.042*** (0.013)	0.039** (0.017)	0.019 (0.027)	−0.035 (0.055)	−0.005 (0.030)	−0.004 (0.033)	
1994	4549	−0.024 (0.028)	−0.016 (0.026)	0.025 (0.020)	−0.028 (0.031)	−0.025 (0.033)	−0.052* (0.030)	−0.104*** (0.036)	−0.183*** (0.065)
1995	3916	0.030* (0.018)	−0.032 (0.034)	−0.048 (0.040)	−0.082 (0.051)	−0.058 (0.048)	−0.051 (0.038)	−0.079* (0.043)	−0.078 (0.049)
1996	3972	0.029 (0.018)	0.032** (0.015)	0.019 (0.023)	0.008 (0.025)	0.017 (0.029)	0.011 (0.021)	0.006 (0.024)	−0.032 (0.034)
1997	4011	0.012 (0.024)	0.016 (0.022)	0.038** (0.019)	0.032 (0.019)	0.016 (0.032)	−0.017 (0.029)	−0.008 (0.029)	−0.064 (0.040)

Notes: 1. * indicates significance at the 10% level, ** and *** at the 5% and 1% levels respectively.
2. DF/dx is for discrete change of dummy variable from 0 to 1. To evaluate the marginal effect of a variable marginal effect of that variable is evaluated for each observation, and then mean over the sample of these marginal effects are found. Estimated standard errors are asymptotic standard errors computed using the delta method.
Source: Author's calculation based on SCF Data, Statistics Canada (1980–1998).

Abdurrahman Aydemir

Table 3b: Differences in Employment Rates between Immigrants and Canadian-Born by Arrival Cohort and Survey Year (probit estimates using flexible forms specification)

Survey Year	Sample Size	Immigrant Cohorts							
		1966–70	1971–75	1976–79	1980–82	1983–85	1986–89	1990–92	1993–96
1979	3763	0.007 (0.010)	0.017*** (0.007)	0.006 (0.011)					
1980	1685	0.013 (0.009)	0.010 (0.007)	0.002 (0.011)					
1981	3789	-0.009 (0.020)	-0.019 (0.021)	-0.032 (0.034)	-0.023 (0.033)				
1982	3949	0.016* (0.010)	-0.004 (0.016)	-0.020 (0.023)	-0.021 (0.022)				
1983	1643	-0.014 (0.024)	-0.053** (0.026)	0.018 (0.014)	-0.032 (0.030)				
1984	3865	-0.004 (0.018)	0.010 (0.018)	-0.052* (0.031)	-0.018 (0.028)	-0.195** (0.090)			
1985	3875	-0.013 (0.019)	-0.007 (0.017)	-0.025 (0.028)	-0.051 (0.036)	-0.033 (0.035)			
1986	3281	0.010 (0.017)	-0.003 (0.022)	0.012 (0.020)	0.004 (0.021)	-0.004 (0.027)			
1987	4415	0.019*** (0.007)	-0.009 (0.018)	0.019 (0.016)	-0.046 (0.027)	-0.020 (0.030)	-0.055 (0.081)		
1988	3803	0.004 (0.015)	-0.008 (0.018)	0.014 (0.012)	-0.028 (0.026)	0.001 (0.007)	-0.092 (0.062)		
1989	4209	-0.010 (0.026)	-0.018 (0.023)	0.007 (0.15)	0.002 (0.017)	0.018*** (0.006)	-0.001 (0.016)		

Effects of Business Cycles on Immigrant Assimilation

Table 3b: Continued

Year	N							
1990	4422	−0.025 (0.028)	−0.068 (0.052)	−0.063 (0.048)	0.012 (0.013)	0.023*** (0.006)	0.020** (0.008)	
1991	4280	−0.020 (0.37)	0.038*** (0.004)	0.014 (0.021)	0.012 (0.018)	−0.026 (0.037)	−0.043 (0.036)	−0.182** (0.090)
1992	3986	0.001 (0.029)	0.008 (0.021)	−0.040 (0.046)	0.043*** (0.006)	−0.016 (0.044)	−0.037 (0.037)	−0.073 (0.054)
1993	3758	0.020 (0.025)	0.008 (0.021)	0.024 (0.019)	0.015 (0.019)	−0.022 (0.049)	−0.061 (0.043)	−0.027 (0.036)
1994	4315	0.006 (0.020)	0.022* (0.013)	−0.051* (0.031)	−0.014 (0.025)	0.001 (0.025)	−0.019 (0.023)	−0.064** (0.031)
1995	3684	−0.021 (0.029)	0.015 (0.016)	−0.012 (0.028)	0.003 (0.027)	−0.063 (0.046)	−0.041 (0.029)	−0.032 (0.030)
1996	3757	0.012 (0.022)	−0.010 (0.030)	0.021 (0.018)	−0.046 (0.043)	−0.023 (0.039)	0.026* (0.014)	−0.030 (0.033)
1997	3750	−0.005 (0.029)	0.006 (0.024)	0.026** (0.013)	0.015 (0.019)	−0.001 (0.031)	0.011 (0.019)	0.003 (0.023)

Additional right-hand column:

Year	Value
1994	−0.079 (0.050)
1995	−0.135** (0.055)
1996	−0.089* (0.051)
1997	−0.026 (0.035)

Notes: 1. * indicates significance at the 10% level, ** and *** at the 5% and 1% levels respectively.
2. DF/dx is for discrete change of dummy variable from 0 to 1. To evaluate the marginal effect of a variable marginal effect of that variable is evaluated for each observation, and then mean over the sample of these marginal effects are found. Estimated standard errors are asymptotic standard errors computed using the delta method.

Source: Author's calculation based on SCF Data, Statistics Canada (1980–1998).

Abdurrahman Aydemir

for post-1985 cohorts all statistically significant differences between immigrants and Canadian-born are negative. These results show that immigrants arriving prior to 1985 have higher participation rates, whereas post-1985 cohorts have lower participation rates. For example, the 1986–89 cohort had a 16.3% lower participation rate in 1988 compared to the Canadian-born in the same year. The difference between pre-1985 and post-1985 may be due to the fact that earlier arrival cohorts have spent more time in the host country. However, when the experiences of 1976–79 and the 1986–89 cohorts in the first few years after arrival are compared to that of the latter arrival cohorts at similar points after their arrival there are still negative differences for the latter cohorts, but not for the earlier ones. These negative differentials become smaller over time. For the 1986–89 cohort, for example, 16.3% lower participation rate in 1988 falls to 8.6% in 1990 and no significant difference is observed for the rest of the period. Previous literature studies only the unemployment experience and earnings of immigrants. The differences found in this study among different immigrant cohorts in terms of labour force participation shows that problems with economic assimilation may start as early as the participation stage.

Another observation from Table 3a is that although for some survey years (such as 1993 and 1994) immigrants from earlier cohorts are doing better than later cohorts, this cannot be generalized to all survey years. Also, following a cohort across survey years shows that differences between a given immigrant cohort and Canadian-born can be different from one year to another. The 1976–79 cohort, for example, has 1.9% higher participation rate in 1982, but 6.2% lower in 1984. This may be due to higher sensitivity of immigrant outcomes to the changing macro conditions.

The next table, Table 3b, presents results for the probability of being employed for those in the labour force. Patterns similar to those in Table 3a are also seen here, suggesting that more recent immigrants are having harder times at the employment margin as well. For example, the 1983–85 cohort had 19.5% lower employment rate in 1984 and the 1990–92 cohort had 18.2% lower employment rate in 1991. Table 3b illustrates that the 1986–89 cohort never had a negative employment differential that is statistically significant over these survey years. On the contrary, they had 2% higher employment in 1990 and 2.6% higher employment in 1996. Judging from these figures one would conclude that this cohort is doing relatively well. The conclusion would be quite different if the same cohort's LFP experience is assessed using information in Table 3a. The same cohort had 16.3% lower participation rate in 1988 and 8.6% lower participation rate in 1990. These figures suggest a substantially lower rate of entry to the labour market, however, those who entered the labour market did relatively well. If only the most successful are entering the labour market then their employment rates and earnings rates can paint a favourable picture for the performance of that cohort. Yet, there may be substantial difficulties in the short term, preventing labour market participation in the first place.

Estimated differences between immigrants and native-born in Tables 3a and 3b control for observed characteristics in X of specification (1). The next section uses a fixed-effects specification commonly used in studies of immigrant economic assimilation and extends that framework to assess the role of business cycles.

Fixed effects specification. The immigration literature studying earnings assimilation uses a parametric specification, with assimilation being captured by years since migration and differences across cohorts captured by cohort dummies that allow for a separate intercept shift for each cohort. This conventional approach is called a fixed-effects model and the corresponding BCM is given by:

$$(2) \quad I_i(t) = X_i(t)\beta + \sum_{j=1}^{J} \delta_j C_i^j + \alpha_1 YSM_i + \alpha_2 YSM_i^2 + u_i$$

Specification (2) is estimated by merging data across all survey years and X refers to the following set of characteristics:

$X_i(t) = \{$education, region of residence, size of the centre of residence, mother tongue, marital status, age$\}$[9]

C^j is a cohort dummy equal to 1 for immigrants in cohort j, 0 otherwise. YSM is the number of years an immigrant spent in the host country. This model is extended to control for macro conditions by the following BCM:

---

[9]See Table A1 in Appendix for variable definitions used in multivariate analysis.

Abdurrahman Aydemir

$$(3) \quad I_i(t) = X_i(t)\beta + \sum_{j=1}^{J} \delta_j C_i^j + \alpha_1 YSM + \alpha_2 YSM_i^2$$
$$+ \phi_e U_i^e + \phi_s U_i^s + u_i$$

In specification (3) U^e refers to the national unemployment rate at entry and U^s refers to the unemployment rate at the survey year. Given significant differences in terms of labour market conditions across provinces, the survey year unemployment rate is captured at the provincial level using the information about the region of residence for individuals in each survey year. For the native-born U^e refers to the labour market conditions at the year of completion of schooling calculated as (survey year − years of schooling − 6).[10] For immigrants, it refers to the unemployment rate at the year of completion of schooling if the highest degree is obtained after arrival to the host country.[11] Otherwise, it refers to the unemployment rate at the year of immigration.[12] There is no information in the data about the province an individual first lived in or for how long after completion of schooling for the native-born and after arriving to the host country for immigrants. Therefore, the national unemployment rate is used to capture macro conditions at entry.

---

[10]This assumes no interruptions in the course of schooling for labour market or other reasons.

[11]For example, age 22 is assumed to be the age of completing university. If an individual's age at migration is 18 and he reports having a university degree, then this individual is assumed to have obtained the university degree after migrating to Canada. Year of entry to the labour market and U^e are calculated accordingly.

[12]In the analysis the immigrant sample is restricted to adults who were at least 18 years old at arrival. Most of this group will have finished their schooling by that time. The group that is most likely to get further education in the host country is the age group 18 to 22 at the time of migration. This group constitutes 4.8% of male immigrants and close to 50% of this group has high school or less education in survey year 1997. This indicates that by the time this group arrived in Canada they have most likely completed all their schooling in the source country. This is consistent with the findings of Hashmi (1987) which has shown that adult immigrants have on average very little post-immigration schooling.

Specification (3) restricts the effects of macro conditions at the time of entry and at the survey year to be the same for immigrants and native-born. The previous literature has evidence that immigrants can be more sensitive to the business cycle than natives. To allow for this possibility specification (3) is extended to include various interaction terms that lead to results in columns (3) to (8) of relevant tables.

Above, a cohort is defined as immigrants arriving over a number of years, such as 1986–89. Within a given cohort immigrants arrive at different years and face different labour market conditions. This variation of macro conditions at entry among immigrants within a given cohort allows for the separate identification of cohort effects and macro conditions at entry.[13, 14] The interpretation of cohort effects in this context is then the unobserved differences common to immigrants within a given cohort. The literature interprets these cohort effects as differences in "unobserved quality". This may be driven by changes to the immigration policy resulting in changes in source country and visa category distribution of immigrants, or by changing incentives to immigrate that affect unobserved quality of immigrants. A separate BCM is estimated for each of the outcomes of interest, that is LFP and employment and the results are presented in Tables 4a and 5a. Tables 4b and 5b present the estimated marginal effects correspondingly.[15]

---

[13]There is significant variation in labour market conditions at entry for both immigrants and native-born. Immigrants in the sample arrive over the 1966–96 period, whereas native-born could have finished their schooling over a period from the early 1940s to 1996.

[14]If cohorts were defined as single-year arrival cohorts, both the effects of unemployment at entry and cohort effects could still be identified if a common effect of macro conditions at entry is assumed for both immigrants and native-born. However, identification of the differential impact of entry macro conditions on immigrants is not possible in this case. In all other cohort definitions this identification is possible. The practice in the immigration literature has always been to define cohorts as multi-year arrival cohorts. This paper adopts the same approach in defining cohorts.

[15]Other control variables are used in estimation but are not presented in these tables for conciseness. Those include controls for region of residence, size of the centre of residence, education, age, marital status, and mother tongue.

Abdurrahman Aydemir

Table 4a: Labour Force Participation Outcome: Coefficient Estimates (probit models using fixed effects specification, 1979–97 SCF sample)

Variable	(1)	(2)	(3)	(4)	(5)	(6)	(7)	(8)
Coh6670	0.409 (0.12)***	0.303 (0.12)**	0.176 (0.18)	-0.084 (0.19)	0.369 (0.19)*	0.539 (0.16)***	-0.158 (0.33)	0.428 (0.19)**
Coh7175	0.258 (0.11)**	0.197 (0.11)*	0.130 (0.13)	-0.148 (0.16)	0.342 (0.17)**	0.407 (0.16)***	-0.168 (0.31)	0.368 (0.17)**
Coh7679	0.052 (0.11)	0.034 (0.11)	0.005 (0.12)	-0.297 (0.16)*	0.240 (0.16)	0.227 (0.16)	-0.292 (0.32)	0.237 (0.16)
Coh8082	-0.067 (0.11)	-0.054 (0.11)	-0.068 (0.11)	0.435 (0.20)**	0.178 (0.15)	0.130 (0.15)	-0.385 (0.32)	0.119 (0.15)
Coh8385	-0.215 (0.11)*	-0.150 (0.12)	-0.131 (0.12)	0.365 (0.20)*	0.147 (0.17)	-0.009 (0.16)	-0.520 (0.38)	0.055 (0.17)
Coh8689	-0.350 (0.09)***	-0.322 (0.09)***	-0.341 (0.10)***	0.149 (0.20)	-0.084 (0.16)	-0.128 (0.16)	-0.642 (0.33)*	-0.105 (0.16)
Coh9092	-0.491 (0.09)***	-0.424 (0.10)***	-0.435 (0.10)***	0.191 (0.27)	-0.185 (0.16)	-0.270 (0.15)*	-0.801 (0.35)***	-0.203 (0.16)
Coh9396	-0.709 (0.09)***	-0.643 (0.10)***	-0.647 (0.10)***	-0.740 (0.27)	-0.425 (0.15)***	-0.547 (0.14)***	-1.098 (0.37)***	-0.476 (0.15)***
Ysm	0.008 (0.01)	0.012 (0.01)	0.034 (0.03)	0.031 (0.03)	0.018 (0.03)	-0.008 (0.02)	0.058 (0.003)*	0.012 (0.03)
Ysmsq	-0.001 (0.0004)***	-0.001 (0.0004)***	-0.001 (0.0005)***	-0.001 (0.0005)***	-0.001 (0.0006)*	-0.0007 (0.0004)	-0.002 (0.0006)**	-0.001 (0.0006)*
Unempent	--	-0.019 (0.009)**	-0.018 (0.009)**	-0.018 (0.009)**	-0.024 (0.009)***	-0.046 (0.009)***	-0.026 (0.009)***	--
Unempsy	--	-0.039 (0.009)***	-0.039 (0.009)***	-0.039 (0.01)***	-0.042 (0.009)***	--	-0.042 (0.009)***	-0.040 (0.01)***
Ysm*unempent	--	--	-0.002 (0.002)	-0.002 (0.002)	-0.002 (0.002)	--	-0.006 (0.003)**	-0.002 (0.002)
M_unempent	--	--	--	0.043 (0.016)***	--	--	0.066 (0.03)**	--
M_unsy70	--	--	--	-0.056 (0.020)***	--	--	--	--
M_unsy80	--	--	--	-0.069 (0.030)**	--	--	--	--
M_unsy90	--	--	--	--	--	--	--	--
Unsy1t10	--	--	--	--	0.038 (0.009)***	0.036 (0.008)***	0.039 (0.009)***	0.036 (0.009)***
M_unsy1t10	--	--	--	--	-0.050 (0.013)***	-0.045 (0.01)***	-0.052 (0.013)***	-0.048 (0.01)***
Unen5	--	--	--	--	--	--	--	-0.189 (0.08)**
Unen4	--	--	--	--	--	--	--	-0.234 (0.07)***
Unen3	--	--	--	--	--	--	--	-0.129 (0.05)***
Unen2	--	--	--	--	--	--	--	-0.186 (0.04)***
Wald Chi2	1357.46	1411.88	1413.64	1445.83	1434.81	1417.34	1438.97	1442.01
No. of obs.	73130	73130	73130	73130	73130	73130	73130	73130

Notes: 1. * indicates significance at the 10% level, ** and *** at the 5% and 1% levels respectively.
2. Other control variables are used in estimation but not presented in these tables for conciseness. Those include controls for region of residence, size of the centre of residence, education, age, marital status, and mother tongue.

Table 4b: Labour Force Participation Outcome: Marginal Effects (probit models using fixed effects specification, 1979–97 SCF sample)

Variable	(1)	(2)	(3)	(4)	(5)	(6)	(7)	(8)
Coh6670	0.018 (0.004)	0.014 (0.005)	0.009 (0.008)	-0.005 (0.01)	0.015 (0.006)	0.020 (0.004)	-0.010 (0.02)	0.017 (0.006)
Coh7175	0.013 (0.005)	0.010 (0.005)	0.007 (0.007)	-0.010 (0.01)	0.015 (0.006)	0.018 (0.006)	-0.010 (0.02)	0.016 (0.006)
Coh7679	0.003 (0.006)	0.002 (0.006)	0.0003 (0.007)	-0.022 (0.01)	0.011 (0.006)	0.011 (0.006)	-0.020 (0.02)	0.011 (0.006)
Coh8082	-0.004 (0.007)	-0.003 (0.007)	-0.004 (0.007)	0.019 (0.007)	0.009 (0.006)	0.007 (0.007)	-0.030 (0.03)	0.006 (0.007)
Coh8385	-0.015 (0.009)	-0.010 (0.009)	-0.008 (0.009)	0.017 (0.007)	0.007 (0.007)	-0.0005 (0.009)	-0.042 (0.03)	0.003 (0.009)
Coh8689	-0.025 (0.009)	-0.022 (0.008)	-0.024 (0.009)	0.008 (0.01)	-0.005 (0.009)	-0.008 (0.01)	-0.050 (0.04)	-0.006 (0.01)
Coh9092	-0.044 (0.013)	-0.035 (0.012)	-0.036 (0.012)	0.010 (0.01)	-0.012 (0.011)	-0.019 (0.01)	-0.080 (0.06)	-0.013 (0.012)
Coh9396	-0.076 (0.017)	-0.064 (0.016)	-0.064 (0.017)	-0.005 (0.02)	-0.033 (0.016)	-0.048 (0.02)	-0.144 (0.09)	-0.038 (0.017)
Ysm	0.0005 (0.0007)	0.0007 (0.0007)	0.002 (0.002)	0.002 (0.002)	0.001 (0.001)	-0.0004 (0.0009)	0.003 (0.002)	0.0006 (0.001)
Ysmsq	-0.0001 (0.00003)	-0.0001 (0.00002)	-0.0001 (0.00003)	-0.0001 (0.00003)	-0.0001 (0.00003)	-0.0001 (0.00003)	-0.0001 (0.00003)	-0.0001 (0.00003)
Unempent	- -	-0.001 (0.0005)	-0.001 (0.0005)	-0.001 (0.0005)	-0.001 (0.0005)	- -	-0.001 (0.0005)	- -
Unempsy	- -	-0.002 (0.0006)	-0.002 (0.0005)	-0.002 (0.0006)	-0.002 (0.0006)	-0.003 (0.0006)	-0.002 (0.0006)	-0.002 (0.0006)
Ysm*unempent	- -	- -	-0.0001 (0.0001)	-0.0001 (0.0001)	-0.0001 (0.0001)	- -	-0.0003 (0.0002)	-0.0001 (0.0001)
M_unempent	- -	- -	- -	- -	- -	- -	- -	- -
M_unsy70	- -	- -	- -	0.002 (0.0009)	- -	- -	0.004 (0.002)	- -
M_unsy80	- -	- -	- -	-0.003 (0.001)	- -	- -	- -	- -
M_unsy90	- -	- -	- -	-0.004 (0.001)	- -	- -	- -	- -
Unsy1t10	- -	- -	- -	- -	0.002 (0.0005)	0.002 (0.0005)	0.002 (0.0005)	0.002 (0.0005)
M_unsy1t10	- -	- -	- -	- -	-0.003 (0.0007)	-0.003 (0.0007)	-0.003 (0.0007)	-0.003 (0.0007)
Unen5	- -	- -	- -	- -	- -	- -	- -	-0.011 (0.005)
Unen4	- -	- -	- -	- -	- -	- -	- -	-0.015 (0.005)
Unen3	- -	- -	- -	- -	- -	- -	- -	-0.007 (0.003)
Unen2	- -	- -	- -	- -	- -	- -	- -	-0.012 (0.003)

Notes: Average marginal effects for the following reference person: migrant, living in Ontario, size of centre of residence>500K, married, has some secondary education or postsecondary education but no postsecondary certificate or diploma, age between 30 and 34, mother tongue is neither French nor English. Average marginal effects are calculated using the estimated coefficients from Table 4a. Standard errors are calculated by delta method and presented in parenthesis.

Abdurrahman Aydemir

Table 5a: Employment Outcome (conditional on labour force participation) — Coefficient Estimates (probit models using fixed effects specification, 1979–97 SCF sample)

Variable	(1)	(2)	(3)	(4)	(5)	(6)	(7)	(8)
Coh6670	0.014 (0.11)	-0.132 (0.12)	-0.281 (0.17)*	-0.267 (0.20)	-0.241 (0.18)	-0.069 (0.14)	-0.241 (0.29)	-0.250 (0.19)
Coh7175	-0.114 (0.10)	-0.207 (0.11)*	-0.286 (0.12)**	-0.272 (0.16)*	-0.243 (0.15)	-0.172 (0.14)	-0.243 (0.27)	-0.252 (0.15)*
Coh7679	-0.167 (0.09)*	-0.207 (0.09)**	-0.240 (0.10)**	-0.229 (0.15)	-0.189 (0.14)	-0.194 (0.14)	-0.189 (0.27)	-0.196 (0.14)
Coh8082	-0.214 (0.09)**	-0.213 (0.09)**	-0.228 (0.09)**	0.037 (0.19)	-0.174 (0.13)	-0.214 (0.13)*	-0.174 (0.28)	-0.192 (0.13)
Coh8385	-0.252 (0.10)**	-0.204 (0.11)*	-0.181 (0.11)	0.083 (0.19)	-0.120 (0.15)	-0.256 (0.14)*	-0.120 (0.34)	-0.137 (0.15)
Coh8689	-0.394 (0.09)***	-0.365 (0.09)***	-0.387 (0.09)***	-0.124 (0.18)	-0.338 (0.14)**	-0.370 (0.14)***	-0.338 (0.28)	-0.357 (0.14)***
Coh9092	-0.535 (0.09)***	-0.461 (0.09)***	-0.472 (0.09)***	0.105 (0.28)	-0.424 (0.14)***	-0.494 (0.13)***	-0.424 (0.31)	-0.425 (0.14)***
Coh9396	-0.732 (0.09)***	-0.683 (0.09)***	-0.688 (0.10)***	-0.164 (0.27)	-0.639 (0.14)***	-0.739 (0.13)***	-0.640 (0.33)*	-0.655 (0.14)***
Ysm	0.028 (0.01)**	0.034 (0.01)***	0.061 (0.02)**	0.058 (0.02)**	0.057 (0.03)*	0.029 (0.01)**	0.057 (0.03)*	0.059 (0.03)**
Ysmsq	-0.001 (0.0004)***	-0.001 (0.0004)***	-0.001 (0.0005)***	-0.002 (0.0005)***	-0.002 (0.0005)***	-0.001 (0.0004)**	-0.002 (0.0006)**	-0.002 (0.0005)***
Unempent	--	-0.018 (0.009)*	-0.017 (0.009)*	-0.017 (0.009)*	-0.019 (0.009)**	--	-0.020 (0.01)**	--
Unempsy	--	-0.073 (0.01)***	-0.074 (0.01)***	-0.072 (0.01)***	-0.076 (0.01)***	-0.079 (0.01)***	-0.076 (0.01)***	-0.077 (0.01)***
Ysm*unempent	--	--	-0.003 (0.002)	-0.003 (0.002)	-0.002 (0.002)	--	-0.002 (0.002)	-0.003 (0.002)
M_unempent	--	--	--	0.0007 (0.02)	--	--	-0.000003 (0.03)	--
M_unsy70	--	--	--	-0.029 (0.02)	--	--	--	--
M_unsy80	--	--	--	-0.063 (0.03)**	--	--	--	--
M_unsy90	--	--	--	--	--	--	--	--
Unsy1t10	--	--	--	--	0.017 (0.008)**	0.015 (0.008)*	0.017 (0.008)**	0.017 (0.008)**
M_unsy1t10	--	--	--	--	-0.016 (0.01)	-0.012 (0.01)	-0.016 (0.01)	-0.016 (0.01)
Unen5	--	--	--	--	--	--	--	-0.120 (0.08)
Unen4	--	--	--	--	--	--	--	-0.085 (0.07)
Unen3	--	--	--	--	--	--	--	-0.045 (0.05)
Unen2	--	--	--	--	--	--	--	-0.016 (0.05)
Wald Chi2	463.02	505.52	508.49	548.27	520.28	509.81	520.89	517.30
No. of obs.	70229	70229	70229	70229	70229	70229	70229	70229

Notes: 1. * indicates significance at the 10% level, ** and *** at the 5% and 1% levels respectively.
2. Other control variables are used in estimation but not presented in these tables for conciseness. Those include controls for region of residence, size of the centre of residence, education, age, marital status, and mother tongue.

Table 5b: Employment Outcome (conditional on labour force participation) — Marginal Effects (probit models using fixed effects specification, 1979–97 SCF sample)

Variable	(1)	(2)	(3)	(4)	(5)	(6)	(7)	(8)
Coh6670	0.001 (0.007)	-0.009 (0.01)	-0.023 (0.02)	-0.021 (0.02)	-0.018 (0.02)	-0.005 (0.01)	-0.018 (0.03)	-0.019 (0.02)
Coh7175	-0.008 (0.008)	-0.015 (0.008)	-0.022 (0.01)	-0.021 (0.02)	-0.018 (0.01)	-0.012 (0.01)	-0.018 (0.02)	-0.019 (0.01)
Coh7679	-0.012 (0.008)	-0.015 (0.009)	-0.018 (0.009)	-0.017 (0.01)	-0.013 (0.01)	-0.014 (0.01)	-0.013 (0.02)	-0.014 (0.01)
Coh8082	-0.016 (0.009)	-0.016 (0.008)	-0.017 (0.009)	0.002 (0.01)	-0.012 (0.01)	-0.016 (0.01)	-0.012 (0.02)	-0.014 (0.01)
Coh8385	-0.020 (0.01)	-0.015 (0.01)	-0.013 (0.01)	0.005 (0.01)	-0.008 (0.01)	-0.020 (0.01)	-0.008 (0.02)	-0.009 (0.01)
Coh8689	-0.032 (0.01)	-0.028 (0.009)	-0.030 (0.01)	-0.008 (0.01)	-0.025 (0.01)	-0.028 (0.01)	-0.025 (0.03)	-0.027 (0.01)
Coh9092	-0.054 (0.01)	-0.042 (0.01)	-0.044 (0.01)	0.006 (0.02)	-0.037 (0.02)	-0.046 (0.02)	-0.037 (0.04)	-0.037 (0.02)
Coh9396	-0.086 (0.02)	-0.075 (0.02)	-0.076 (0.02)	-0.012 (0.02)	-0.067 (0.02)	-0.084 (0.02)	-0.066 (0.05)	-0.069 (0.02)
Ysm	0.002 (0.0008)	0.002 (0.0008)	0.004 (0.002)	0.004 (0.002)	0.004 (0.002)	0.002 (0.0009)	0.004 (0.002)	0.004 (0.002)
Ysmsq	-0.0001 (0.00003)	-0.0001 (0.00003)	-0.0001 (0.00003)	-0.0001 (0.00003)	-0.0001 (0.00003)	-0.0001 (0.00003)	-0.0001 (0.00003)	-0.0001 (0.00003)
Unempent	- -	-0.001 (0.0006)	-0.001 (0.0006)	-0.001 (0.0006)	-0.001 (0.0006)	- -	-0.001 (0.0006)	- -
Unempsy	- -	-0.005 (0.0008)	-0.005 (0.0008)	-0.005 (0.0009)	-0.005 (0.0008)	-0.005 (0.0008)	-0.005 (0.0008)	-0.005 (0.0008)
Ysm*unempent	- -	- -	-0.0002 (0.0001)	-0.0002 (0.0001)	-0.0002 (0.0001)	- -	-0.0002 (0.0002)	-0.0002 (0.0001)
M_unempent	- -	- -	- -	0.00005 (0.001)	- -	- -	-0.00001 (0.002)	- -
M_unsy70	- -	- -	- -	-0.002 (0.001)	- -	- -	- -	- -
M_unsy80	- -	- -	- -	-0.004 (0.002)	- -	- -	- -	- -
M_unsy90	- -	- -	- -		- -	- -	- -	- -
Unsy1t10	- -	- -	- -	- -	0.001 (0.0005)	0.001 (0.0005)	0.001 (0.0005)	0.001 (0.0005)
M_unsy1t10	- -	- -	- -	- -	-0.001 (0.0007)	-0.001 (0.0006)	-0.001 (0.0007)	-0.001 (0.0007)
Unen5	- -	- -	- -	- -	- -	- -	- -	-0.008 (0.006)
Unen4	- -	- -	- -	- -	- -	- -	- -	-0.006 (0.005)
Unen3	- -	- -	- -	- -	- -	- -	- -	-0.003 (0.003)
Unen2	- -	- -	- -	- -	- -	- -	- -	-0.001 (0.003)

Notes: Average marginal effects for the following reference person: migrant, living in Ontario, size of centre of residence>500K, married, has some secondary education or postsecondary education but no postsecondary certificate or diploma, age between 30 and 34, mother tongue is neither French nor English. Average marginal effects are calculated using the estimated coefficients from Table 5a. Standard errors are calculated by delta method and presented in parenthesis.

Abdurrahman Aydemir

For each of the outcome variables eight different specifications are estimated. The first specification is the fixed-effects specification (2) which controls for years since migration but does not control for macro conditions (column (1) in Tables 4 to 7); the second column is the specification (3) which, in addition, controls for macro conditions at entry and at the survey year but restricts the effects of macro conditions to be the same for immigrants and native-born. Next specification (column 3) allows for assimilation profiles of immigrants to be affected by the macro conditions at entry by including an interaction term of *YSM* with U^e. Following the earlier literature, column (4) introduces interaction terms of U^s with cohort dummies (McDonald and Worswick, 1998, allow for interaction terms for *cohort* × U^s and *cohort* × U^s × *ysm* in their analysis of earnings). A larger negative coefficient on the interaction term for more recent cohorts is interpreted as more recent immigrants being more sensitive to the current macro conditions. However, these interaction terms may be confounding the cohort quality (captured by cohort dummies) with effects of current macro conditions (U^s). For that reason, column (5) employs an alternative specification that replaces *cohort* × U^s interaction terms. This new specification has two variables: *unsy1t10* — capturing the effect of current macro conditions on a recent labour market entrant (product of U^s with a dummy variable indicating entry to the labour market in the last ten years); second variable *m_unsy1t10* — capturing the additional impact of current macro conditions on immigrants who entered the labour market recently (*migrant dummy* × *unsy1t10*). As discussed previously, new immigrants may be more adversely affected by an economic downturn. However, for those natives who entered the labour market recently they may have acquired the skills rising in demand in the labour market, may be able to adapt to changing conditions more easily than older workers, and firms may invest more in them given young workers' longer expected work-lives. Therefore, they may be more insulated from the adverse impacts of business cycles.

Columns (6) to (8) check sensitivity of results to the specification in column (5), especially to the inclusion of controls for U^s. These results will be discussed in the next section.

The important result that emerges from Tables 4a and 5a — which is consistent across both models of LFP and employment outcomes — is that cohort effects are very sensitive to the inclusion of controls for macro-economic conditions. For both outcomes the specification that does not control for macro conditions (column 1) shows significant cohort effects which suggests that controlling for years since migration, latter immigrants cohorts are doing worse than earlier immigrants cohorts. Controlling for common effects of macro conditions on immigrants and native-born in the next specification causes the cohort effects to become smaller, however, there still remain significant cohort effects. Adding (*ysm* × *unemployment at entry*) the interaction term in the next specification (column 3) does not result in any significant changes in other coefficient estimates and the estimated coefficient for this interaction term is insignificant. This suggests that effect of entry macro conditions does not vary with years of residence in the host country. The next two specifications control for macro conditions while allowing the effects to vary between immigrants and the native-born. However, the two specifications give drastically different results. In column (4), where cohort dummies are interacted with U^x, almost all cohort effects become insignificant. In column (5), however, which includes controls for recent labour market entrants the results show that estimated cohorts effects become smaller (especially so for the LFP outcome) but not all cohort effects become insignificant.

In column (4) estimated coefficients for the added interaction terms lie in the same direction as the estimated cohort effects in previous specifications (for example, in Table 4a, column (4), the coefficient estimates of the interaction term for the earliest cohort — those that arrived in 1960s and 1970s — is positive and significant while the coefficient for the latest cohort — those that arrived in 1990s — is negative and significant). However, as discussed before, those interaction terms may be confounding the cohort effects with the effects of current macro conditions on immigrants. The next specification tries to overcome this problem. If as hypothesized in the previous literature it is the new immigrants that may be more cyclically sensitive, then it is sensible to allow for an interaction term to allow for this possibility. The interaction term used for this is current macro conditions interacted with a dummy indicating whether an individual entered the labour market in the last ten years (*unsy1t10* variable) and a second interaction term which further allows a different impact on recent immigrants (*m_unsy1t10*). For survey year 1979, this last term would be capturing immigrants who arrived between 1969–78, for survey year 1985 those who arrived between 1975–84, for survey year 1996 those who arrived between 1986–95, etc. By construction, this interaction term, while controlling for recent labour market entry, is not related to any specific arrival cohort contrary to the previous specification in column (4). This latter specification is the *preferred* specification in this paper and discussions in the remainder of this section will be addressing the results emerging from this specification.

The decline in cohort effects between column (1) and column (5) suggests that without controlling for macro conditions the cohort effects capture differences in performance of immigrants resulting from different macroeconomic conditions along their assimilation path as well as the other unobserved characteristics. Especially for the LFP outcome an important part of the deterioration as portrayed by cohort effects in column (1) disappears once one controls for macro conditions. For example, for the 1993–96 cohort, Table 4b shows that without controls for macro conditions this cohort had 7.6 percentage points lower labour force participation. Controlling for macro conditions this differential drops to 3.3 percentage points. Unfavourable macro conditions may be resulting in withdrawal of many immigrants from the labour market who may be investing in human capital skills or may simply be discouraged by their prospects in the labour market.

For the employment outcome, after controlling for macro conditions, there still remain strong cohort effects for immigrants who landed after 1986 which suggests a declining quality among labour force participants. The impact of controlling for macro conditions on estimated cohort effects is less in this case. For example, Table 5b shows that without controlling for macro conditions 1993–96 cohort had 8.6 percentage points higher unemployment probability and this falls to 6.7 percentage points when effects of macro conditions are controlled for.

Both macro conditions at entry and current macro conditions have an adverse impact on LFP and employment with the effects of the latter being much greater. The effects of entry macro conditions, however, are small for both LFP and employment outcomes. One percentage point increase in unemployment rate at the time of entry leads to a 0.1 percentage point decline in LFP and employment rates. The marginal effects for employment outcome in Table 5b suggest that four percentage point increase in unemployment rate at the time of entry is equal to gains from one more year of residence.[16] However, this result should not be interpreted as overall impact of business cycles being small since the effects of survey year macro conditions are much larger. For both the LFP and employment outcome a one-percentage point increase in survey year unemployment rate leads to 0.5 percentage points decline in LFP and employment rates for a new immigrant. If a recession is long-lived with high unemployment rates

---

[16]The unemployment rate increased by about four percentage points in the two recessions from 1979 to 1983, and from 1989 to 1993.

for a number of consecutive years, then an immigrant landing at the beginning of this period could be significantly more disadvantaged than one who lands during an expansionary period.

Interaction terms for the effects of current macro conditions on recent entrants (given by *unsy1t10* and *m_unsy1t10*) provides evidence that new immigrants are more sensitive to the business-cycle conditions and native-born are more insulated from these conditions. There is no evidence that effects of macro conditions at entry (scarring effect) disappear with increasing years of residence given the insignificant coefficient on *ysm* × U^e interaction term.

While this paper finds small but significant negative effects of entry macro conditions on LFP and employment, Chiswick, Cohen and Zach (1997) find poor macro conditions at the time of entry to have no adverse effect on the incidence of unemployment among immigrants in the United States. The results for the effects of survey year macro conditions and greater sensitivity of new immigrants to business cycles are, however, in line with previous studies in the literature.

The coefficient on *ysm* for the LFP outcome is positive but insignificant, whereas for the employment outcome it is positive and significant, providing evidence of assimilation. With the inclusion of controls for macro conditions for the employment model the size of the coefficient for years since migration increases twofold. A similar result is obtained by McDonald and Worswick (1998) where they show that neglecting the impact of macro conditions at the survey year leads to a significant understatement in the rate of assimilation. Therefore, not only the estimated cohort effects but also the assimilation profiles are sensitive to the inclusion of controls for business cycles.

Sensitivity of results to controls for unemployment rate at entry. Figure 4 plots the annual unemployment rate over 1946–98 which shows an upward trend over much of the sample period. Given the entry macro conditions are captured by the unemployment rate at the time of entry, one may be concerned that a higher unemployment rate may be a proxy for a more recent immigrant cohort. This may cause some spurious correlations by capturing any change in the unobserved components of immigrant quality over this period. To check the sensitivity of results, the paper first tests for different specifications using all sample years 1979–97. Secondly, the sample is restricted to immigrants who arrived during a period over which there was no upward trend in unemployment rate and the results are replicated for this subsample.

Figure 4: Annual Unemployment Rate, Canada, 1946–1998

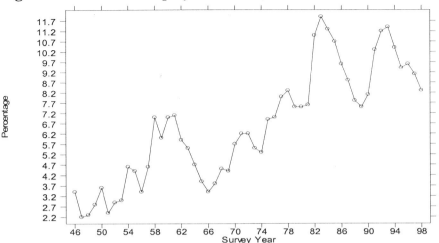

First, using the entire sample the paper estimates the following specifications: Column (6) of the Tables 4a and 5a omit the variables related to unemployment rate at entry. This causes a slight increase in the estimated cohort effects while the remaining coefficient estimates are mostly robust to this change in specification. Column (8), on the other hand, controls for entry macro conditions in an alternative way by dividing the range of values for unemployment at entry into five equal intervals and creating a dummy variable for each. The variable *unen5* is equal to 1 if unemployment at entry is in the interval (9.8, 11.7]; 0 o.w. The variable *unen4* is equal to 1 if entry unemployment rate is in the interval (7.9, 9.8]; 0 o.w. etc. The resulting coefficient estimates for the common variables are very similar in columns (5) and (8).[17]

---

[17]To further check the sensitivity of results in column (5) for additional controls, a variable is added to the model in column (7) that is employed in the previous literature. The variable *M_unempent* interacts a migrant dummy with the unemployment at entry to test whether immigrants are more sensitive to entry macro conditions than natives are. If immigrants are more sensitive as hypothesized, this estimated coefficient would be expected to have a negative sign and the cohort effects are expected to decline. However, for LFP the coefficient estimate is positive while cohort effects become much stronger for the last three cohorts, both contrary to the expectation. For employment outcome the coefficient estimate for *M_unempent* is almost zero, yet, it causes the cohort effects to disappear. Given these anomalous results this variable is likely causing some spurious correlations.

Second, the sample of immigrants is restricted to those who arrived between 1977 and 1996. The unemployment rate at entry during this period fluctuated a lot; however, it does not have an upward trend. In other words, a higher unemployment rate is not associated with a more recent immigrant cohort. The results in Tables 4a and 5a are replicated with this subsample and the coefficient estimates for LFP and employment outcomes are presented in Tables 6a and 7a, and the marginal effects in Tables 6b and 7b correspondingly. The conclusions drawn from Tables 6a and 7a are the same as conclusions from Tables 4a and 5a, showing that results are not an artifact of a spurious correlation between unemployment rate at entry and cohort dummies.

Conclusions

This paper studies the effects of macroeconomic conditions on labour market outcomes of immigrants. Allowing for cohort effects, both effects of macro conditions at the time of arrival and at the time of survey year are explored. Previous studies in the literature, however, study either the effects of macro conditions at arrival by assuming away the cohort effects or the effects of macro conditions at the time of the survey allowing for cohort effects. Also, for the first time in literature this paper explores the impacts at the labour force participation (LFP) margin. Using 19 annual cross-sections of Survey of Consumer Finances covering the period 1979 to 1997 it is shown that estimates of cohort effects are very sensitive to the inclusion of controls for macroeconomic conditions. Without controls for macroeconomic conditions there are significant negative cohort effects for the latter immigrant cohorts suggesting that they are doing worse than the earlier immigrant cohorts. Controlling for macro conditions and allowing the effects to vary between immigrants and native-born results in cohort effects to become significantly smaller. This result suggests that the deterioration in assimilation of recent immigrants documented in the previous literature is partly due to the adverse economic conditions. Macro conditions at the time of entry to the labour market have adverse impacts on LFP and employment probability. A higher unemployment rate at the survey year has a stronger negative effect on both. With the inclusion of controls for macro conditions the significance and magnitude of the coefficient measuring assimilation (coefficient on *years since migration*)

Abdurrahman Aydemir

Table 6a: Labour Force Participation Outcome — Coefficient Estimates (probit models using fixed effects specification, 1979–97 SCF sample, immigrant year of arrival >=1977)

Variable	(1)	(2)	(3)	(4)	(5)	(6)	(7)	(8)
Coh6670	--	--	--	--	--	--	--	--
Coh7175	--	--	--	--	--	--	--	--
Coh7679	-0.004 (0.13)	-0.009 (0.14)	-0.027 (0.14)	-0.144 (0.29)	0.243 (0.19)	0.227 (0.19)	-0.395 (0.38)	0.241 (0.19)
Coh8082	-0.108 (0.12)	-0.088 (0.12)	-0.097 (0.13)	0.038 (0.21)*	0.170 (0.17)	0.127 (0.17)	-0.478 (0.37)	0.107 (0.17)
Coh8385	-0.236 (0.13)*	-0.170 (0.14)	-0.151 (0.14)	0.033 (0.21)	0.149 (0.19)	0.0002 (0.18)	-0.573 (0.42)	0.077 (0.19)
Coh8689	-0.369 (0.12)***	-0.336 (0.12)***	-0.346 (0.13)***	0.013 (0.22)	-0.074 (0.18)	-0.115 (0.18)	-0.709 (0.38)*	-0.095 (0.18)
Coh9092	-0.501 (0.12)***	-0.433 (0.12)***	-0.436 (0.12)***	0.018 (0.29)	-0.163 (0.18)	-0.245 (0.17)	-0.856 (0.39)**	-0.177 (0.18)
Coh9396	-0.715 (0.11)***	-0.651 (0.11)***	-0.650 (0.11)***	-0.081 (0.28)	-0.397 (0.16)**	-0.514 (0.16)***	-1.150 (0.42)***	-0.440 (0.17)***
Ysm	0.003 (0.02)	0.006 (0.02)	0.022 (0.04)	0.019 (0.04)	0.024 (0.04)	0.001 (0.02)	0.086 (0.05)	0.031 (0.05)
Ysmsq	-0.0004 (0.001)	-0.0004 (0.001)	-0.0005 (0.001)	-0.0004 (0.001)	-0.001 (0.001)	-0.001 (0.001)	-0.001 (0.001)	-0.001 (0.001)
Unempt	--	-0.018 (0.009)**	-0.017 (0.009)*	-0.018 (0.009)**	-0.024 (0.009)**	--	-0.025 (0.009)***	--
Unempsy	--	-0.042 (0.009)***	-0.042 (0.009)***	-0.040 (0.009)***	-0.045 (0.01)***	-0.049 (0.009)***	-0.045 (0.009)***	-0.043 (0.01)***
Ysm*unempt	--	--	-0.002 (0.004)	-0.002 (0.004)	-0.002 (0.004)	--	-0.009 (0.005)*	-0.003 (0.004)
M_unempent	--	--	--	--	--	--	0.074 (0.04)*	--
M_unsy70	--	--	--	0.017 (0.03)	--	--	--	--
M_unsy80	--	--	--	-0.055 (0.02)***	--	--	--	--
M_unsy90	--	--	--	-0.069 (0.03)**	--	--	--	--
Unsy1t10	--	--	--	--	0.039 (0.009)***	0.036 (0.01)***	0.039 (0.009)***	0.037 (0.009)***
M_unsy1t10	--	--	--	--	-0.057 (0.02)***	-0.053 (0.02)***	-0.058 (0.02)***	-0.055 (0.02)***
Unen5	--	--	--	--	--	--	--	-0.189 (0.09)**
Unen4	--	--	--	--	--	--	--	-0.241 (0.07)***
Unen3	--	--	--	--	--	--	--	-0.132 (0.05)***
Unen2	--	--	--	--	--	--	--	-0.194 (0.04)***
Wald Chi2	1195.16	1253.37	1253.87	1284.03	1278.05	1262.40	1280.21	1287.71
No. of obs.	60472	60472	60472	60472	60472	60472	60472	60472

Notes: 1. * indicates significance at the 10% level, ** and *** at the 5% and 1% levels respectively.
2. Other control variables are used in estimation but not presented in these tables for conciseness. Those include controls for region of residence, size of the centre of residence, education, age, marital status, and mother tongue.

Table 6b: Labour Force Participation Outcome — Marginal Effects (probit models using fixed effects specification, 1979–97 SCF sample, immigrant year of arrival >=1977)

Variable	(1)	(2)	(3)	(4)	(5)	(6)	(7)	(8)
Coh6670	--	--	--	--	--	--	--	--
Coh7175	--	--	--	--	--	--	--	--
Coh7679	-0.0003 (0.01)	-0.0007 (0.01)	-0.002 (0.01)	-0.012 (0.03)	0.014 (0.009)	0.013 (0.009)	-0.036 (0.05)	0.014 (0.009)
Coh8082	-0.009 (0.01)	-0.007 (0.01)	-0.008 (0.01)	0.023 (0.01)	0.010 (0.009)	0.008 (0.01)	-0.045 (0.05)	0.007 (0.01)
Coh8385	-0.020 (0.01)	-0.014 (0.01)	-0.013 (0.01)	0.020 (0.01)	0.0009 (0.01)	0.0001 (0.01)	-0.058 (0.06)	0.005 (0.01)
Coh8689	-0.030 (0.01)	-0.029 (0.01)	-0.029 (0.01)	0.009 (0.01)	-0.005 (0.01)	-0.008 (0.01)	-0.066 (0.05)	-0.007 (0.01)
Coh9092	-0.060 (0.02)	-0.045 (0.02)	-0.045 (0.02)	0.012 (0.02)	-0.012 (0.02)	-0.020 (0.02)	-0.110 (0.08)	-0.014 (0.02)
Coh9396	-0.090 (0.02)	-0.080 (0.02)	-0.080 (0.02)	-0.006 (0.02)	-0.036 (0.02)	-0.053 (0.02)	-0.182 (0.11)	-0.042 (0.02)
Ysm	0.0002 (0.002)	0.0005 (0.002)	0.002 (0.003)	0.001 (0.003)	0.002 (0.003)	0.0001 (0.002)	0.006 (0.004)	0.002 (0.003)
Ysmsq	-0.0001 (0.0001)	-0.0001 (0.0001)	-0.0001 (0.0001)	-0.0001 (0.0001)	-0.0001 (0.0001)	-0.0001 (0.0001)	-0.0001 (0.0001)	-0.0001 (0.0001)
Unempent	--	-0.001 (0.0007)	-0.001 (0.0007)	-0.001 (0.0007)	-0.002 (0.0006)	--	-0.002 (0.0007)	--
Unempsy	-0.003 (0.0008)	-0.003 (0.0008)	-0.003 (0.0008)	-0.003 (0.0008)	-0.003 (0.0007)	-0.003 (0.0007)	-0.003 (0.0008)	-0.003 (0.0007)
Ysm*unempent	--	--	-0.0001 (0.0003)	-0.0001 (0.0003)	-0.0001 (0.0002)	--	-0.0006 (0.0003)	-0.0002 (0.0003)
M_unempent	--	--	--	--			0.005 (0.003)	
M_unsy70	--	--	--	0.001 (0.003)			--	
M_unsy80	--	--	--	-0.004 (0.001)			--	
M_unsy90	--	--	--	-0.005 (0.002)			--	
Unsy1t10	--	--	--		0.003 (0.0006)	0.003 (0.0006)	0.003 (0.0006)	0.003 (0.0006)
M_unsy1t10	--	--	--		-0.004 (0.001)	-0.004 (0.001)	-0.004 (0.001)	-0.004 (0.001)
Unen5	--	--	--					-0.014 (0.007)
Unen4	--	--	--					-0.018 (0.006)
Unen3	--	--	--					-0.009 (0.004)
Unen2	--	--	--					-0.016 (0.005)

Notes: Average marginal effects for the following reference person: migrant, living in Ontario, size of centre of residence>500K, married, has some secondary education or postsecondary education but no postsecondary certificate or diploma, age between 30 and 34, mother tongue is neither French nor English. Average marginal effects are calculated using the estimated coefficients from Table 6a. Standard errors are calculated by delta method and presented in parenthesis.

Abdurrahman Aydemir

Table 7a: Employment Outcome (conditional on labour force participation) — Coefficient Estimates (probit models using fixed effects specification, 1979–97 SCF sample, immigrant year of arrival >=1977)

Variable	(1)	(2)	(3)	(4)	(5)	(6)	(7)	(8)
Coh6670	--						--	--
Coh7175	--						--	--
Coh7679	-0.262 (0.11)**	-0.277 (0.11)**	-0.304 (0.12)***	0.024 (0.26)	-0.160 (0.16)	-0.163 (0.16)	-0.215 (0.32)	-0.167 (0.16)
Coh8082	-0.261 (0.11)**	-0.243 (0.11)**	-0.256 (0.11)**	-0.003 (0.21)	-0.113 (0.15)	-0.144 (0.15)	-0.169 (0.33)	-0.130 (0.15)
Coh8385	-0.310 (0.12)***	-0.254 (0.13)**	-0.226 (0.13)*	0.035 (0.21)	-0.069 (0.17)	-0.198 (0.16)	-0.131 (0.37)	-0.087 (0.17)
Coh8689	-0.455 (0.11)***	-0.418 (0.11)***	-0.433 (0.11)***	-0.179 (0.19)	-0.288 (0.16)**	-0.314 (0.16)**	-0.343 (0.33)	-0.308 (0.16)**
Coh9092	-0.588 (0.11)***	-0.509 (0.11)***	-0.514 (0.11)***	0.007 (0.29)	-0.366 (0.15)**	-0.431 (0.15)***	-0.426 (0.35)	-0.371 (0.16)**
Coh9396	-0.763 (0.11)***	-0.718 (0.11)***	-0.716 (0.11)***	-0.243 (0.28)	-0.579 (0.15)***	-0.671 (0.15)***	-0.643 (0.38)*	-0.596 (0.15)***
Ysm	0.053 (0.02)**	0.056 (0.02)**	0.080 (0.04)**	0.081 (0.04)**	0.081 (0.04)**	0.053 (0.02)**	0.087 (0.05)*	0.082 (0.04)**
Ysmsq	-0.003 (0.001)**	-0.003 (0.001)**	-0.003 (0.001)**	-0.003 (0.001)**	-0.003 (0.001)**	-0.003 (0.001)**	-0.003 (0.001)**	-0.003 (0.001)**
Unempent	--	-0.016 (0.01)	-0.015 (0.01)	-0.016 (0.01)	-0.019 (0.01)*		-0.019 (0.01)*	
Unempsy	--	-0.075 (0.01)***	-0.075 (0.01)***	-0.072 (0.01)***	-0.077 (0.01)***	-0.080 (0.01)***	-0.077 (0.01)***	-0.078 (0.01)***
Ysm*unempent	--		-0.002 (0.003)	-0.003 (0.003)	-0.003 (0.003)		-0.003 (0.004)	-0.003 (0.004)
M_unempent	--			--	--	--	0.006 (0.04)	--
M_unsy70	--			-0.039 (0.03)	--	--	--	--
M_unsy80	--			-0.029 (0.02)	--	--	--	--
M_unsy90	--			-0.058 (0.03)*	--	--	--	--
Unsy1t10	--			--	0.017 (0.008)**	0.016 (0.008)*	0.018 (0.008)**	0.017 (0.008)**
M_unsy1t10	--			--	-0.0274 (0.014)*	-0.024 (0.01)*	-0.028 (0.01)*	-0.027 (0.01)*
Unen5	--			--	--	--	--	-0.111 (0.08)
Unen4	--			--	--	--	--	-0.073 (0.07)
Unen3	--			--	--	--	--	-0.041 (0.05)
Unen2	--			--	--	--	--	-0.012 (0.05)
Wald Chi2	425.17	464.61	465.44	500.99	484.89	478.45	484.85	482.40
No. of obs.	57898	57898	57898	57898	57898	57898	57898	57898

Notes: 1. * indicates significance at the 10% level, ** and *** at the 5% and 1% levels respectively.
2. Other control variables are used in estimation but not presented in these tables for conciseness. Those include controls for region of residence, size of the centre of residence, education, age, marital status, and mother tongue.

Table 7b: Employment Outcome (conditional on labour force participation) — Marginal Effects (probit models using fixed effects specification, 1979–97 SCF sample, immigrant year of arrival >=1977)

Variable	(1)	(2)	(3)	(4)	(5)	(6)	(7)	(8)
Coh6670	--	--	--	--	--	--	--	--
Coh7175	--	--	--	--	--	--	--	--
Coh7679	-0.023 (0.01)	-0.024 (0.01)	-0.027 (0.01)	0.002 (0.02)	-0.012 (0.01)	-0.013 (0.01)	-0.017 (0.03)	-0.013 (0.01)
Coh8082	-0.023 (0.01)	-0.021 (0.01)	-0.022 (0.01)	-0.0002 (0.01)	-0.008 (0.01)	-0.011 (0.01)	-0.013 (0.03)	-0.010 (0.01)
Coh8385	-0.028 (0.01)	-0.022 (0.01)	-0.019 (0.01)	0.002 (0.01)	-0.005 (0.01)	-0.016 (0.01)	-0.010 (0.03)	-0.006 (0.01)
Coh8689	-0.040 (0.01)	-0.036 (0.01)	-0.037 (0.01)	-0.013 (0.02)	-0.022 (0.01)	-0.025 (0.01)	-0.027 (0.03)	-0.023 (0.01)
Coh9092	-0.067 (0.02)	-0.053 (0.02)	-0.054 (0.02)	0.001 (0.02)	-0.033 (0.02)	-0.041 (0.02)	-0.040 (0.04)	-0.033 (0.02)
Coh9396	-0.100 (0.02)	-0.089 (0.02)	-0.089 (0.02)	-0.020 (0.03)	-0.061 (0.03)	-0.078 (0.03)	-0.072 (0.06)	-0.064 (0.03)
Ysm	0.004 (0.002)	0.004 (0.002)	0.006 (0.003)	0.006 (0.003)	0.006 (0.003)	0.004 (0.002)	0.006 (0.003)	0.006 (0.003)
Ysmsq	-0.0002 (0.0001)	-0.0002 (0.0001)	-0.0002 (0.0001)	-0.0002 (0.0001)	-0.0002 (0.0001)	-0.0002 (0.0001)	-0.0002 (0.0001)	-0.0002 (0.0001)
Unempent	--	-0.001 (0.0007)	-0.001 (0.0007)	-0.001 (0.0007)	-0.001 (0.0007)	--	-0.001 (0.0007)	--
Unempsy	--	-0.005 (0.001)	-0.005 (0.001)	-0.005 (0.001)	-0.005 (0.001)	-0.006 (0.001)	-0.005 (0.001)	-0.005 (0.001)
Ysm*unempent	--	--	-0.0002 (0.0002)	-0.0002 (0.0002)	-0.0002 (0.0002)	--	-0.0002 (0.0003)	-0.0002 (0.0002)
M_unempent	--	--	--	-0.003 (0.002)	--	--	0.0004 (0.002)	--
M_unsy70	--	--	--	-0.002 (0.001)	--	--	--	--
M_unsy80	--	--	--	-0.004 (0.002)	--	--	--	--
M_unsy90	--	--	--	--	--	--	--	--
Unsy1t10	--	--	--	--	0.001 (0.0005)	0.001 (0.0006)	0.001 (0.0005)	0.001 (0.0006)
M_unsy1t10	--	--	--	--	-0.002 (0.0009)	-0.002 (0.0009)	-0.002 (0.0009)	-0.002 (0.0009)
Unen5	--	--	--	--	--	--	--	-0.008 (0.006)
Unen4	--	--	--	--	--	--	--	-0.005 (0.005)
Unen3	--	--	--	--	--	--	--	-0.003 (0.004)
Unen2	--	--	--	--	--	--	--	-0.001 (0.004)

Notes: Average marginal effects for the following reference person: migrant, living in Ontario, size of centre of residence>500K, married, has some secondary education or postsecondary education but no postsecondary certificate or diploma, age between 30 and 34, mother tongue is neither French nor English. Average marginal effects are calculated using the estimated coefficients from Table 7a. Standard errors are calculated by delta method and presented in parenthesis.

Abdurrahman Aydemir

increases. Therefore, not only the estimated cohort effects but also the assimilation profiles are sensitive to the inclusion of controls for business cycles.

In this paper the adverse impacts of the entry macro conditions are shown to be permanent but small. Therefore, long-term consideration may outweigh concerns resulting from the short-term macro conditions in the labour market while deciding on whether to tie the level of immigration to the business cycle. Also, the results showing that there is a decline in the LFP rate without any evidence of catching up suggests that there may be a discouraged worker effect. New immigrants, therefore, may be supported with policies that encourage job search, especially if they arrived during a downturn, to keep their attachment to the labour force.

References

Bodman, P. and M. Crosby (2000), "Phases of the Canadian Business Cycle", *Canadian Journal of Economics* 33(3), 618–633.

Chiswick, B.R., Y. Cohen and T. Zach (1997), "The Labour Market Status of Immigrants: Effects of the Unemployment Rate at Arrival and Duration of Residence", *Industrial and Labour Relations Review* 50(2), 289–303.

Chiswick, B. and P. Miller (1999), "Immigrant Earnings: Language Skills, Linguistic Concentrations and the Business Cycle", Working Paper No. 152 (Chicago: Center for the Study of the Economy, University of Chicago, published in *Journal of Population Economics*, October 2001).

Hashmi, A. (1987), "Post-migration Investments in Education by Immigrants in the US" (Chicago: Department of Economics, University of Illinois at Chicago).

McDonald, T. and C. Worswick (1997), "Unemployment Incidence of Immigrant Men in Canada", *Canadian Public Policy/Analyse de Politiques* 23(4), 353–373.

_____ (1998), "The Earnings of Immigrant Men in Canada: Job Tenure, Cohort, and Macroeconomic Conditions", *Industrial and Labour Relations Review* 51(3), 465–482.

Nakamura, A. and M. Nakamura (1992), "Wage Rates of Immigrant and Native Men in Canada and the United States", in B.R. Chiswick (ed.), *Immigration, Language and Ethnicity: Canada and the United States* (Washington, DC: American Enterprise Institute), 145–166.

Statistics Canada (1980–1998), *Survey of Consumer Finances, Individuals Age 15 and Over, With or Without Income* (Ottawa: Statistics Canada).

Stewart, J. and T. Hyclak (1984), "An Analyses of Earnings Profiles of Immigrants", *Review of Economics and Statistics* 66(2), 292–303.

Appendix: Variable Definitions

Table A1: Variable Definitions

Variable	Definition
LFP	Dummy variable equal to 1 if individual participated in the labour market in the reference year; 0 otherwise
Employed	Dummy variable equal to 1 if individual was employed in the reference year and reported positive earnings; 0 otherwise
Coh6670	Dummy variable equal to 1 if individual is a migrant who arrived during 1966–1970; 0 otherwise
Coh7175	Dummy variable equal to 1 if individual is a migrant who arrived during 1971–1975; 0 otherwise
Coh7679	Dummy variable equal to 1 if individual is a migrant who arrived during 1976–1979; 0 otherwise
Coh8082	Dummy variable equal to 1 if individual is a migrant who arrived during 1980–1982; 0 otherwise
Coh8385	Dummy variable equal to 1 if individual is a migrant who arrived during 1983–1985; 0 otherwise
Coh8689	Dummy variable equal to 1 if individual is a migrant who arrived during 1986–1989; 0 otherwise
Coh9092	Dummy variable equal to 1 if individual is a migrant who arrived during 1990–1992; 0 otherwise
Coh9396	Dummy variable equal to 1 if individual is a migrant who arrived during 1993–1996; 0 otherwise
	(Control group is natives for the cohort variables)
Ysm	Years Since Migration (0 for native-born)
Ysmsq	Years Since Migration Squared (0 for native-born)
Unempent	Unemployment rate at entry
Unempsy	Regional unemployment rate at the survey year
M_unempent	Unemployment rate at entry interacted with migrant dummy
Ysmunen	Unempent interacted with Ysm variable
M_unsy70	Unempsy interacted with a dummy variable that is equal to 1 if an individual is a migrant who arrived before 1980 and 0 otherwise
M_unsy80	Unempsy interacted with a dummy variable that is equal to 1 if an individual is a migrant who arrived between 1980 and 1989, and 0 otherwise
M_unsy90	Unempsy interacted with a dummy variable that is equal to 1 if an individual is a migrant who arrived after 1989, and 0 otherwise
Unen5	Dummy variable equal to 1 if unemployment rate at entry is between (9.8, 11.7]; 0 o.w.
Unen4	Dummy variable equal to 1 if unemployment rate at entry is between (7.9, 9.8]; 0 o.w.
Unen3	Dummy variable equal to 1 if unemployment rate at entry is between (6.0, 7.9]; 0 o.w.
Unen2	Dummy variable equal to 1 if unemployment rate at entry is between (4.1, 6.0]; 0 o.w.
Unen1	Dummy variable equal to 1 if unemployment rate at entry is between (2.2, 4.1]; 0 o.w. — excluded category
Unsy1t10	Unemployment rate at the survey year interacted with the dummy variable indicating whether the individual entered to the labour market in the last ten years
M_unsy1t10	Unsyt1t10 variable interacted with a migrant dummy

Abdurrahman Aydemir

Immigrant and Non-Immigrant Earnings by Postsecondary Field of Study

Stephan McBride and Arthur Sweetman

Introduction

Canada's federal system for economic (skilled) class immigrants assigns points to immigrant candidates for, among other characteristics, the level of education attained. Education, however, is treated as if it is homogeneous; applicants may have different quantities, but no consideration is given to how education might vary along other dimensions. This might be an appropriate approach for several reasons. For example, if those other dimensions are hard to quantify, if they have few economic implications, or if selecting immigrants on these criteria might have other adverse impacts (perhaps it would affect outcomes for the pre-existing population, both the Canadian-born and earlier cohorts of immigrants). Nevertheless, outside the immigration system, education is considered to vary along several dimensions. It might, for example, be of a particular "quality", where quality can be defined according to various metrics such as academic

This research has been supported by Human Resources Development Canada's Applied Research Branch (HRDC – ARB). Statistics Canada generously provided access to the census data used in the analysis. The paper is, of course, solely the responsibility of the authors and all opinions are theirs alone.

marks (e.g., grade point average), standardized test scores, or school or program reputation or ranking. For some purposes education might be differentiated according to the language of instruction. This paper focuses on one particular distinguishing feature of postsecondary education that is both easy to quantify, and will be seen to have important economic implications: it normally involves specialization. That is, students usually focus on a particular field of study.[1]

It is plausible that taking postsecondary field of study into account in the points system is a policy that might want to be considered. Moreover, although the federal government does not currently consider field of study, Quebec's point system does take it into account in a limited way by assigning bonus points for fields that are considered to be valuable in the labour market and in short supply. That is, Quebec's "liste des formations privilégiées" contains a relatively short and very specific list of both college, and university undergraduate and graduate, fields of study that are of value in its economy.[2] A related, but broader approach has recently been put forward by the province of British Columbia. The Ministry of Community, Aboriginal and Women's Services, which oversees the provincial immigrant nominee program, announced that employers will be allowed to nominate individuals in pure and applied sciences, computer sciences, and computer, electronic, electrical and mechanical engineering for that program. Part of the focus of this program is to facilitate the immigration of international students who have taken Canadian programs in these subjects.[3] These initiatives suggest that understanding the impact of field of study on Canadian labour market outcomes is increasingly important.

Even if such a federal policy direction is not desirable, the impact of postsecondary field of study is a subject worth understanding since it impacts the labour market outcomes and integration of immigrants to Canada. It is noteworthy that field of study and occupation are quite different measures. While graduates from some fields of study largely work in particular occupations (or industries), many fields produce students who

---

[1] While many of the dimensions along which education varies may interact, exploring these interactions is beyond the scope of this study.

[2] This is broadly similar to the Australian model.

[3] BC Ministry of Community, Aboriginal and Women's Services *Backgrounder* and *News Release* (December 10, 2002).

Arthur Sweetman and Stephan McBride

work in a very wide range of occupations, and even the mostly highly occupation-specific fields have a large fraction of graduates working in fields other than the most common one. This study, therefore, explores and documents the Canadian labour market outcomes of immigrants as a function of their postsecondary field of study without regard for their current, and perhaps transitory, occupation.

Current work by Ferrer and Riddell (2002) looks at how immigrants integrate into the Canadian labour market as a function of their detailed level of education, but it does not look at field of study. There is also research looking at selected labour market outcomes by field of study (e.g., Finnie, 2001; Côté and Sweetman, 2000), but this literature does not look at immigrant status, or focus exclusively on the Canadian educated. Li (2001) explores the economic value of educational certifications/degrees (e.g., a bachelor's degree), not fields, but does use field of study as a statistical control (presented in his Appendix Table 1). However, he uses very coarse measures of field (e.g., social science including law is treated as a single field) and confounds their impact with current occupation and industry, which is appropriate given his objective, but does not allow one to focus on field of study in its own right.

Using census data, this study takes a highly disaggregated approach, looking at field of study by sex, level of education, and whether the education was completed in Canada or elsewhere. Unfortunately, we cannot distinguish between immigrant classes (e.g., economic, family and refugee) in these data, and this prevents us from focusing on the economic class that is assessed according to the points system for its labour market attributes. Nevertheless, we do observe important differences in earnings by field of study. Our most important findings include the following. First, all of the groups examined, and most importantly, immigrants and the Canadian-born of the same sex and level of education, have quite different distributions of field of study. Immigrants are much less likely to have an education degree, and more likely to be in engineering and sciences. Second, while immigrants have substantial earnings differences across fields of study, they are observed to, for the most part, have smaller differences between the high and low earnings fields of study than the Canadian-born. Third, field of study explains some of the immigrant-Canadian-born earnings gap, but is only one factor among many and is no more important, and is much less important for the females, than other criteria such as age and language knowledge. This is not surprising given that field of study has not been a selection criteria to date. If it were made a selection criteria, then undoubtedly it would, by design, play a larger role in differentiating foreign-educated immigrants from the Canadian-born.

The format of this paper is as follows. In the next section, data employed will be described. Then, in the third section, descriptive statistics are used to position the postsecondary group under study in a broader set of educational categories and descriptive statistics by detailed field of study are presented. Subsequently, in the following section, regressions are employed to explore the field of study impact controlling for the obvious and substantial differences across the subpopulations under study, and predictions are generated based on these regressions. Then, in section five, decompositions are utilized to gage the overall impact of field of study and put it in perspective compared to other variables such as age. The final section concludes.

Data

For this project the only feasible data are the national censuses, and we use 1986, 1991, and 1996, 20% files. The questions addressed in this study, however, are cross-sectional in nature and for those we present only the results from the 1996 census. Despite focusing on the 1996 results, we generated the same results for each census year in almost all cases. For the most part there are few substantive differences across census years. There is, for example, no clear trend in the premium to computer science across the three censuses. One important difference, however, was that the 1991 census reports earnings from 1990, which was the peak of the business cycle and immigrant workers fared relatively well, but this tended to affect the entire distribution and not the gaps between disciplines. Large samples are required to permit analysis of the detailed subpopulations of interest. Along with the common demographics, each census provides information on earnings and detailed major fields of study for the highest level of postsecondary education.

The sample for analysis, unless otherwise stated in reference to a particular portion of the analysis, includes all individuals between the ages of 25 and 65 with no missing responses, not residing in the Territories, not attending school (though this is not available for the 1986 census), and who are permanent residents (only in 1996). Further, we drop those immigrants who landed in the first six months of the census year since we are not interested in the very strong short-run entry effect. In most analyses we take a random 33% subsample of the Canadian-born comparison group to facilitate estimation given the very large sample size. In the earnings portion of the analysis the sample is further restricted to those with positive wage and salary income, and positive weeks worked. Some previous analyses have made tighter restrictions, such as those with at least 40 weeks of work (e.g., Baker and Benjamin, 1994), however, for policy purposes the larger sample is more appropriate since it better reflects the relevant population. In the econometric regressions we further focus on individuals with exactly one of three educational attainments: college or trades certificate, bachelor's degree, or master's degree.

Looking at detailed fields is important since, as will be seen, there is substantial heterogeneity among the broad classifications frequently employed. For example, all of the social sciences, including law and business, is one grouping in the file most commonly employed. In contrast, postsecondary fields such as political science or economics need to be independently observed. Still, there are limits to disaggregation, and the 440 different fields of study available are collapsed into 54 primary fields, which are employed in our analysis. Of course, for those with Canadian education the field reported in the census data need not reflect an immigrant's field at the time of entry, since the census only collects the field of the highest level of postsecondary at the census date.

Earnings are defined to be the sum of wage and salary income and non-negative self-employment income. All values exceeding $250,000 are top-coded to this value; less than 1% of individuals are constrained by this. The log-earnings variable is the natural logarithm of earnings. An immigrant is simply defined as someone not born in Canada. Total years of schooling is derived from three census questions: years of elementary and secondary schooling, years of university, and years of other postsecondary. Individuals with less than a complete year of postsecondary are coded to have obtained one-half year of added schooling. Schooling is top-coded at 24.[4]

Immigrants are separated into those with, and without, Canadian education. To be classified as Canadian-educated, the individual's years of schooling plus five is at least as great as his or her age-at-arrival. All those with years of schooling greater than age at immigration clearly have some

---

[4]No college recipients are affected by this restriction; one bachelor recipient is affected, and less than 1% of all master's degree recipients are influenced.

Canadian education. But, those with fewer years than their age at immigration may have had discontinuous schooling and have obtained some of their education in Canada. The classification algorithm is, therefore, conservative in that individuals who do not attend school continuously may be included in the foreign-educated category despite having some Canadian education, and choosing age five is similarly conservative. Since the Canadian education likely results in more favourable outcomes in the Canadian labour market, coefficient estimates for the foreign-educated will probably be somewhat better than they would be if we had better measures of where the education was obtained.

Descriptive Statistics

Descriptive Statistics Across Levels of Education

Before looking at field of study, an initial set of descriptive statistics comparing levels of education is provided to place the study into context. Tables 1 and 2 are for females and males respectively. Panels A, B, and C present an overview of, in sequence, the Canadian-born, and the foreign- and Canadian-educated immigrant populations. These tables provide basic descriptive statistics by highest level of education. The upper portion of each panel comprises both those who work and those with zero earnings and weeks of work, while the working subsample at the bottom of each panel includes only those with positive earnings and weeks of work in the relevant year. Focusing first on the females, it is clear that many more immigrants are foreign, rather than Canadian, educated and that this group is older than the other two. The size differences between the two groups are greatest at the lower levels of education since Canadian-educated immigrants tend to have higher educational credentials. In looking at the sample sizes, recall that the Canadian-born sample is a 33% random sub-sample of the file, whereas the two immigrant samples are 100% samples of the file or 20% of the population. Some substantial differences are visible among the three groups. The foreign-educated are, on average, over four years older than the Canadian-born, and six and a half years older than the Canadian-educated immigrants. There are also important differences by

Table 1: Descriptive Statistics by Highest Level of Education — 1996 Females

				Canadian-Born Females						
	<HS	HS	Col	BA -	BA	BA +	MD	MA	PHD	Total
Age	46.17	41.55	40.52	45.93	38.62	41.55	37.91	42.15	44.65	42.59
Years school	9.48	12.24	13.50	15.22	17.09	17.62	20.19	19.05	22.05	12.48
Urban (%)	41.44	55.48	52.14	56.57	67.04	69.52	70.62	75.82	80.69	51.84
Visminority (%)	0.60	0.84	0.97	0.87	2.09	1.28	2.46	1.52	2.11	0.94
No Work in Yr (%)	46.24	24.00	16.75	18.19	9.83	9.89	2.66	7.28	5.88	27.03
English (%)	65.48	61.98	68.65	53.67	59.24	60.30	51.35	53.45	46.28	64.23
French (%)	23.11	18.97	13.18	18.10	9.23	6.10	5.49	6.07	2.48	17.27
Bilingual (%)	10.70	19.03	18.14	28.22	31.51	33.59	43.16	40.48	51.09	18.25
Neither (%)	0.71	0.01	0.02	0.01	0.02	0.02	0.00	0.00	0.15	0.24
Earnings ($)	7,884	15,211	18,063	22,911	29,672	34,069	71,229	40,009	46,604	16,137
Working subsample										
Hours	26.96	29.60	29.90	30.61	32.46	34.20	39.73	35.06	38.45	29.75
Weeks	41.17	44.17	43.96	44.80	45.05	45.54	46.52	46.05	47.40	43.65
Earnings	16,413	21,078	22,940	29,246	33,653	38,518	73,361	44,360	49,846	23,508
Frequency (%)	31.96%	24.77%	27.53%	2.62%	9.41%	1.52%	0.25%	1.78%	0.17%	100%
Number	124,906	96,806	107,623	10,234	36,771	5,926	977	6,953	663	390,859

				Foreign-Educated Immigrant Females						
	<HS	HS	Col	BA -	BA	BA +	MD	MA	PHD	Total
Age	49.58	44.84	45.99	45.36	42.91	44.66	44.40	44.17	46.83	46.81
Years school	8.34	12.44	13.76	15.87	16.69	17.35	18.72	18.32	20.67	11.90
Urban (%)	87.87	87.15	83.99	86.84	88.75	88.24	86.27	88.85	87.87	86.92
Visminority (%)	47.99	54.85	44.94	58.70	66.66	50.59	49.44	42.10	31.35	50.53
No Work in Yr (%)	49.59	34.24	24.78	24.70	22.31	21.02	22.85	18.08	12.44	36.05
English (%)	68.87	82.51	85.76	79.60	82.59	71.62	77.06	75.85	65.16	77.30
French (%)	5.99	4.20	3.48	3.50	2.02	3.81	2.17	1.61	2.06	4.44
Bilingual (%)	4.02	7.22	8.84	14.10	13.70	22.83	17.90	21.64	32.58	7.90
Neither (%)	21.12	6.07	1.92	2.80	1.69	1.75	2.87	0.89	0.21	10.36
Earnings ($)	7,792	11,662	15,482	16,519	18,675	21,033	39,170	24,805	38,955	12,518
Working subsample										
Hours	28.59	29.79	29.99	29.77	30.65	31.27	33.25	32.16	35.65	29.73
Weeks	42.54	43.23	43.79	43.39	43.31	42.59	43.02	43.55	45.28	43.19
Earnings	16,663	19,168	22,117	23,636	25,967	29,002	55,482	32,950	46,580	21,153
Frequency (%)	39.59%	20.84%	22.36%	3.37%	8.67%	1.47%	0.53%	2.72%	0.45%	100%
Number	86,492	45,542	48,863	7,363	18,946	3,206	1,151	5,946	973	218,482

				Canadian-Educated Immigrant Females						
	<HS	HS	Col	BA -	BA	BA +	MD	MA	PHD	Total
Age	42.96	40.03	39.85	42.44	38.08	41.39	38.80	42.59	45.30	40.46
Years school	10.50	12.66	14.11	16.29	17.33	17.97	20.39	19.43	22.05	14.10
Urban (%)	73.52	79.84	78.44	82.31	85.21	84.56	82.76	85.65	86.32	79.63
Visminority (%)	14.06	21.21	27.92	36.25	41.52	25.61	47.20	29.55	21.25	26.23
No Work in Yr (%)	32.43	19.89	15.30	14.76	10.07	8.97	4.50	7.96	4.66	18.09
English (%)	89.27	85.65	85.56	77.01	72.35	64.21	68.79	62.29	53.28	81.99
French (%)	1.88	1.29	1.31	1.09	1.03	1.03	1.09	0.89	0.73	1.32
Bilingual (%)	7.80	12.87	13.02	21.75	26.59	34.67	30.12	36.76	45.85	16.40
Neither (%)	1.06	0.20	0.12	0.15	0.04	0.09	0.00	0.06	0.15	0.29
Earnings ($)	12,589	17,776	19,779	24,439	29,255	34,340	72,221	40,131	47,879	21,468
Working subsample										
Hours	29.63	30.50	30.59	32.51	32.99	34.24	40.17	34.65	38.83	31.39
Weeks	44.04	45.01	44.62	45.30	45.35	45.40	47.29	45.64	47.12	44.90
Earnings	19,930	23,309	24,569	30,001	33,708	38,824	76,939	44,671	51,726	27,522
Frequency (%)	18.41%	24.50%	29.80%	3.12%	15.76%	2.63%	0.75%	4.22%	0.81%	100%
Number	15,709	20,909	25,428	2,662	13,449	2,241	644	3,604	687	85,333

Source: 1996 Canadian census. Note that the frequency and number of observations are for the entire sample, not the subsample.

Postsecondary Field of Study

years of school: overall, it is just over 1.5 years greater for the Canadian-educated immigrants, but over half a year less for those educated outside Canada, compared to those born in the country. This is an interesting distinction since previous work, such as Borjas (1993), has combined the two immigrant groups and noted that immigrants, overall, have more years of schooling than the Canadian-born. The gap he observes seems to be attributable to the Canadian-educated subgroup.

There are several other striking differences across the three panels. Urbanization is dramatically greater among the immigrant population, especially the foreign-educated subsample. From almost 52% for the Canadian-born, urbanization rises to just under 80% for the Canadian-educated, and to about 87% for immigrants educated outside Canada. Further, visible-minority status exhibits even larger gaps. Less than 1% of the Canadian-born women describe themselves as visible minorities, while 26% of the Canadian-educated immigrants do, and this compares to 50% for those immigrants educated outside Canada. The fraction of each group that worked zero weeks in the year preceding the census, a measure of labour force participation, has an interesting pattern across the three groups. Overall, in the right-most column, it is seen to be 27% for the Canadian-born, but lower, at 18% for Canadian-educated immigrants, and higher, at 36% for foreign-educated immigrants. These differences are non-trivial. The ranking is the same across all levels of education, but is much higher for those with lower levels of schooling. At the lowest level of schooling, less than a high school degree, the percentage not working is very similar for the Canadian-born and foreign-educated immigrant groups.

Language currently spoken also has an interesting pattern. Immigrants, especially those educated in Canada, are much more likely to speak English, and much less likely to speak French, than the Canadian-born. Those educated elsewhere are much (about 40 times) more likely to speak neither language. Foreign-educated immigrants with less than a high school degree are a notable group. They are massively more likely than any other subgroup to speak neither of Canada's official languages. Over 21% of this group fall into this category and it may hinder their labour market integration. Overall, almost all those who speak neither official language are in the foreign-educated immigrant group. Undoubtedly, part of the reason that the foreign-educated remain in this group, that is they do not pursue a Canadian education, is related to their official language abilities (along with age and other characteristics).

Arthur Sweetman and Stephan McBride

Before turning to the subsample of those who worked in the previous year, which is equal to the total sample less the fraction who did not work in the previous year as indicated in the upper portion of each panel, it is worth looking at the earnings for the entire population. This number is an average of the earnings for those who work, and zeros for those without any earnings in the year. The number for those who work is of greater interest and is usually the focus of attention and policy, but, for immigration purposes, including the zeros is also of some interest. Canadian-educated immigrants clearly have the highest earnings of the three groups for this sample. This arises both because they are more likely to work, and because (as will be seen below) they have higher earnings when they do work. Looking at the working subpopulations, there are again some clear differences across the groups and levels of education. These differences are somewhat similar to those observed for the "no work in the previous year" variable. Canadian-educated immigrants work more hours per week, more weeks per year, and have higher annual earnings than either of the other groups. In contrast, foreign-educated immigrants and the Canadian-born have very similar hours per week, and weeks per year, but the Canadian-born earned, on average, about $2,350 more in 1995. Interestingly, there is a clear gradient in all three variables with education, and the differences across groups are most pronounced at the lower levels of education.

Scanning across educational levels for the three panels in Table 1, it is clear that Canadian-educated immigrants have higher levels of educational certification than either of the other two female groups. Further, conditional on a particular level of education (each distinct column), the Canadian-educated immigrants and the Canadian-born have generally similar outcomes, however, the foreign-educated immigrant females do worse in terms of earnings in each education category, especially at the higher levels of education.

Table 2 provides similar information for men as was provided above for women. There is, as has been observed previously (see, e.g., Benjamin, Gunderson and Riddell, 1998, for a textbook discussion of male-female earnings gaps), a difference in levels between men and women, with the former having greater weeks and hours of work, and greater annual earnings. Also, the males, especially the immigrant groups, are more likely to have a higher level of education. Comparing the frequency numbers on the bottom of Tables 2 and 3, the foreign-educated immigrants have higher percentages of people in the highest three categories recorded, and somewhat fewer people at the high school and college levels. In contrast, the Canadian-educated immigrants, perhaps because they are younger, are

Table 2: Descriptive Statistics by Highest Level of Education — 1996 Males

	Canadian-Born Males									
	<HS	HS	Col	BA -	BA	BA +	MD	MA	PHD	Total
Age	44.77	40.52	41.14	44.39	40.31	44.30	44.62	44.71	47.88	42.41
Years school	9.38	12.41	13.31	15.61	17.27	17.88	20.23	19.19	21.65	12.51
Urban (%)	39.88	55.79	50.29	62.64	69.95	68.74	64.49	73.07	75.95	51.00
Visminority (%)	0.71	1.03	0.85	1.08	1.94	1.28	2.40	1.22	1.18	0.97
No Work in Yr (%)	23.90	9.74	7.95	8.83	4.55	6.07	2.44	4.81	3.84	13.26
English (%)	66.58	62.26	68.40	53.37	61.86	59.78	59.30	56.35	51.91	65.09
French (%)	19.73	14.78	11.93	10.72	5.86	5.80	3.23	4.39	1.32	14.18
Bilingual (%)	13.19	22.94	19.63	35.92	32.28	34.40	37.47	39.24	46.77	20.54
Neither (%)	0.50	0.02	0.04	0.00	0.01	0.02	0.00	0.02	0.00	0.19
Earnings ($)	19,157	29,826	32,247	38,646	48,854	54,194	110,334	61,541	65,823	30,661
Working subsample										
Hours	34.44	38.82	38.71	40.28	41.36	41.35	47.16	41.80	42.92	38.06
Weeks	41.56	45.90	45.54	47.20	48.13	48.28	48.91	48.50	49.06	44.98
Earnings	27,993	34,918	36,617	45,045	53,022	59,225	116,127	65,161	71,635	37,704
Frequency (%)	33.89%	20.55%	29.43%	1.68%	9.39%	1.42%	0.58%	2.57%	0.49%	100%
Number	134,380	81,489	116,701	6,648	37,212	5,621	2,292	10,202	1,954	396,499

	Foreign-Educated Immigrant Males									
	<HS	HS	Col	BA -	BA	BA +	MD	MA	PHD	Total
Age	48.93	44.35	48.08	46.54	45.09	46.68	48.72	46.23	49.24	47.33
Years school	8.64	12.58	13.66	16.27	16.99	17.75	19.33	18.66	20.80	12.73
Urban (%)	87.67	89.66	82.36	90.37	90.59	90.09	78.59	89.14	85.29	86.86
Visminority (%)	46.37	60.63	36.71	60.93	67.17	51.49	53.97	49.79	41.65	48.76
No Work in Yr (%)	25.30	15.92	13.41	14.14	11.61	11.49	10.52	9.05	7.07	17.24
English (%)	73.19	80.92	85.35	78.28	83.33	70.79	77.87	76.60	70.09	79.09
French (%)	5.56	3.91	3.31	3.04	1.65	2.72	1.40	1.42	1.36	3.83
Bilingual (%)	7.13	10.01	9.95	16.11	13.48	25.04	19.33	21.40	28.24	10.83
Neither (%)	14.12	5.16	1.40	2.57	1.55	1.45	1.40	0.59	0.31	6.25
Earnings ($)	18,349	21,451	28,192	27,284	32,703	34,978	85,287	41,472	54,913	26,100
Working subsample										
Hours	35.23	37.09	38.11	37.80	38.27	38.38	46.11	39.92	41.47	37.36
Weeks	43.68	44.52	45.36	45.04	45.63	45.22	46.93	46.16	47.73	44.85
Earnings	26,739	27,865	35,131	34,798	40,413	43,466	100,996	49,544	63,070	34,304
Frequency (%)	33.39%	16.31%	27.80%	3.09%	9.90%	1.94%	1.07%	4.51%	2.00%	100%
Number	69,015	33,700	57,452	6,386	20,451	4,005	2,214	9,315	4,132	206,670

	Canadian-Educated Immigrant Males									
	<HS	HS	Col	BA -	BA	BA +	MD	MA	PHD	Total
Age	41.42	38.86	41.73	42.99	40.07	43.72	42.73	44.67	48.65	41.30
Years school	10.52	12.95	14.30	16.65	17.52	18.34	20.66	19.58	21.87	14.65
Urban (%)	73.54	80.57	76.26	84.35	85.79	82.48	79.59	83.57	83.30	79.18
Visminority (%)	17.36	26.02	22.37	33.78	37.98	26.94	42.79	29.13	26.10	25.94
No Work in Yr (%)	23.90	9.74	7.95	8.83	4.55	6.07	2.44	4.81	3.28	13.26
English (%)	88.79	84.27	86.69	77.73	75.43	69.79	72.35	67.45	61.29	82.15
French (%)	1.53	0.93	0.90	0.95	0.60	0.85	0.51	1.00	0.36	0.95
Bilingual (%)	8.94	14.62	12.32	21.21	23.92	29.23	27.14	31.51	38.31	16.69
Neither (%)	0.74	0.18	0.09	0.11	0.05	0.13	0.00	0.04	0.04	0.21
Earnings ($)	25,488	30,949	35,057	37,671	46,169	50,926	112,084	58,271	67,592	38,131
Working subsample										
Hours	38.12	39.21	39.71	40.44	41.22	41.54	49.06	41.90	42.94	40.06
Weeks	45.09	46.63	46.76	46.95	47.85	48.16	48.64	48.34	49.25	46.89
Earnings	31,835	35,463	39,211	43,763	50,163	56,427	117,319	63,137	71,760	43,303
Frequency (%)	17.25%	19.37%	32.26%	2.94%	15.94%	2.54%	1.47%	5.82%	2.42%	100%
Number	16,027	17,999	29,975	2,735	14,812	2,357	1,367	5,404	2,245	92,921

Source: 1996 Canadian census. Note that the frequency and number of observations are for the entire sample, not the subsample.

Arthur Sweetman and Stephan McBride

much less likely to have incomplete high school and more likely to have a university bachelor's or advanced degree. However, the broad patterns of demographics are similar, even if not exactly the same for the two sexes. The foreign-educated are older than their Canadian-born counterparts, and the Canadian-educated are younger. Both immigrant groups are more urbanized, and much more likely to be a visible minority. Once again, almost only the foreign-educated speak neither official language, but the gap is not as large as it is for the women, because foreign-educated males are more likely to speak an official language.

Descriptive Statistics by Field of Study

The remainder of the analysis focuses mostly on field of study within three postsecondary educational categories; those whose highest level of education is a college degree or certificate, a bachelor's degree, or a master's degree. We attempted to look at those with PhDs, but the sample sizes were too small to permit individual fields to be studied reliably. We do include them in some portions of the analysis, but their inclusion is limited. Some of the descriptive statistics that follow also include an "other post-secondary" group, but we do not explore it in detail.

Descriptive statistics by field of study are presented in Tables 3 through 6. Tables 3 and 4 look at, respectively, the distribution of individuals across fields and mean earnings by field for females in each of the three groups. Tables 5 and 6 do the same for males. All of the tables in this section are based on the sample of all individuals regardless of weeks of work or earnings in the previous year. Thus there are a number of individuals with zero earnings in each cell. This looks at a different question than that answered by looking only at workers (i.e., those with strictly positive earnings); in thinking about immigration policy, the entire population, regardless of work status, is relevant for thinking about issues such as poverty and tax payments. We focus on workers exclusively in the earnings regressions below, but on the entire sample in subsequently looking at unemployment insurance and other government transfers. Further, Tables 1 and 2 contain very slightly larger samples than 3 through 6 since there is some non-response to the field of study question in the census. Also, the columns do not always sum to 100% since some cells contained too few individuals for reliable estimates to be provided and those cells are left blank.

Table 3: Frequency for Females (Column %) — 1996 Canadian Census

Field	Canadian-Born				Foreign-Educated Immigrants				Canadian-Educated Immigrants			
	College	Bachelor	Master's	Other PS	College	Bachelor	Master's	Other PS	College	Bachelor	Master's	Other PS
Education												
Education	8.35	30.65	27.09	38.74	7.81	15.19	17.70	19.16	7.51	16.73	21.13	26.69
Fine & AppliedArts												
FineArt	10.55	3.69	3.32	2.76	10.73	4.32	3.94	3.78	12.70	3.89	3.33	3.43
Literature & Humanities												
History	1.05	1.91	1.45	0.90	-	2.28	2.54	0.92	-	2.14	2.55	0.99
Media	0.09	1.94	6.82	1.59	0.59	1.75	3.38	1.63	0.96	1.71	5.83	1.37
English	0.05	3.78	2.40	1.37	0.37	3.47	3.84	1.86	0.20	4.73	4.14	2.26
French	-	1.03	1.01	0.71	-	0.86	0.79	0.65	0.06	1.39	1.08	0.90
Other Literature	0.21	1.33	1.61	0.88	0.45	3.31	5.22	2.73	0.36	2.76	4.83	1.97
Philosophy Theology	0.97	2.09	3.32	1.48	0.53	3.11	1.87	1.98	0.71	2.64	2.22	1.64
Other Humanities	0.41	2.09	3.16	1.19	0.67	0.87	1.65	0.94	0.44	2.05	2.83	1.32
Social Science												
Economics	0.03	1.34	1.34	0.34	0.57	3.86	3.94	1.95	0.17	3.24	2.22	1.14
Geography	0.04	1.14	0.75	0.39	-	0.69	0.81	0.32	-	0.95	-	-
Political Science	-	1.41	1.17	0.39	-	1.23	1.63	0.45	-	1.97	1.67	0.83
Psychology	0.44	5.97	6.50	2.07	0.19	2.82	3.36	1.39	0.40	6.14	4.25	2.44
Sociology Criminology	0.13	3.67	1.71	1.26	0.08	1.91	1.70	0.61	0.17	3.69	1.86	1.59
Specialized Admin.	2.42	2.42	3.94	5.09	2.01	1.02	1.53	1.81	2.32	1.57	2.64	2.20
Commerce	4.63	3.69	6.16	3.11	5.32	7.65	4.09	6.09	6.85	5.88	7.02	5.87
Finance	5.87	3.64	1.57	5.10	7.00	9.11	3.05	8.11	9.22	5.84	2.61	7.98
Secretarial Studies	23.97			1.91	20.86			3.73	19.89			1.82
Marketing	2.14	1.11	0.60	1.22	1.95	1.00	-	0.92	2.99	0.97	-	1.52
Law	0.21	2.57	1.91	1.76	0.13	1.30	1.72	1.54	0.30	2.11	1.64	1.59
Other Social Science	3.87	4.17	7.34	2.84	2.20	3.30	3.75	1.76	3.30	2.90	6.19	1.68
Agricultural & BioScience												
Agriculture	1.04	0.63	0.45	0.38	0.95	0.91	1.08	0.61	0.80	0.51	-	-
Biology		2.03	1.91	0.59	-	1.95	2.76	0.92	-	3.28	2.69	1.10
Other Life Science	0.14	2.09	1.35	-	0.14	2.63	2.17	-	0.20	2.00	1.28	-
Household Science	2.65			0.90	5.60			1.54	2.14			0.85
Fish Wildlife Manage	0.17			-	0.19			-	0.12			-

Field	Canadian-Born				Foreign-Educated Immigrants				Canadian-Educated Immigrants			
	College	Bachelor	Master's	Other PS	College	Bachelor	Master's	Other PS	College	Bachelor	Master's	Other PS
Engineer&Applied Science												
Architecture	-	0.34	-	-	-	0.84	1.26	0.74		0.48	-	-
Other Engineering		0.49	0.66	0.21		1.50	2.74	1.33		0.78	-	-
Chemical Engineering		0.19	-	-		0.71	0.72	0.29		0.30	-	-
Civil Engineering		0.20	-	-		0.88	1.40	0.61		0.29	-	-
Electrical Engineering		0.11	-	-		0.90	1.56	0.70		0.55	-	-
Mechanical Engineer		0.15	-	-		0.51	1.31	0.54		-	-	-
Forestry	0.06	0.13	-	-		-	-	-		-	-	-
Landscape Architect	0.25	-	-	-	0.24	-	-	-	0.26	-	-	-
Health Professions												
Medicine		1.50	1.84	5.88		2.56	3.43	10.78		2.33	2.89	12.03
Other Health		6.24	7.16	10.77		6.41	4.09	11.07		5.17	5.11	6.70
Nursing	10.84				11.17				8.88			
Medical Assistant	7.12				7.14				4.56			
Public Health	0.90	0.14		1.32	0.86	-		0.32	0.87	-		0.79
Rehab Medicine	0.23	1.82		1.14	0.47	1.16		1.57	0.16	1.46		1.28
Medical Technician	4.70	0.48		1.52	3.10	1.46		1.73	4.75	0.78		1.26
Math & Physical Sciences												
Mathematics		1.10	0.50	0.30		1.76	2.39	0.66		2.16	1.11	0.78
Computer Science		1.15	-	0.72		2.41	2.71	1.47		3.04	1.33	1.79
Chemistry	0.07	0.41	-	-	0.25	1.57	2.52	0.97	0.18	0.96	1.03	-
Physics	-	-	-	-		0.50	0.86	0.29		-	-	-
Earth Science	0.06	0.19	0.49	-		0.32	0.93	-		0.27	-	-
Other Science	0.54	0.89	0.46	0.45	0.68	1.59	0.84	0.80	0.73	1.61	0.89	0.96
Other												
Trades	0.97	-			1.62	0.17		0.29	1.11	-		
Electronic Technology	3.65				4.29				5.58			
Environment Tech	0.13				-				-			
Mechanic	0.52				0.63				0.39			
Transport Technology	0.50				0.87				0.45			
Observations	107,434	36,715	6,952	17,127	48,755	18,918	5,944	11,694	25,382	13,432	3,602	5,537

Source: 1996 Canadian Census. Dashes imply that the cell contents are suppressed for reasons of confidentiality.

Table 4: Earnings for Females — 1996 Canadian Census

Field	Canadian-Born				Foreign-Educated Immigrants				Canadian-Educated Immigrants			
	College	Bachelor	Master's	Other PS	College	Bachelor	Master's	Other PS	College	Bachelor	Master's	Other PS
Education												
Education	16,356	28,871	42,543	26,227	13,275	18,477	25,918	17,896	18,759	29,426	44,567	31,241
Fine & Applied Arts												
FineArt	12,126	21,335	25,591	20,168	11,356	14,468	17,800	13,784	13,563	18,477	22,317	20,813
Literature & Humanities												
History		26,222	34,982	28,462		16,272	15,764	13,997		29,054	29,105	27,157
Media	21,410	28,916	35,430	28,472	15,616	16,847	28,859	15,030	20,640	27,197	36,410	23,478
English	17,212	27,133	30,230	30,885	12,991	18,335	26,804	16,496	20,020	27,514	33,039	31,373
French	18,418	28,369	31,528	27,932		17,283	36,027	13,603		31,164	31,139	30,839
Other Literature	19,593	27,475	31,339	22,438	15,971	13,593	21,654	14,243	18,828	27,361	35,452	27,764
Philosophy Theology	15,054	21,676	25,628	18,518	10,941	13,885	16,581	12,851	14,015	22,980	29,054	18,046
Other Humanities	16,912	24,944	35,302	23,580	13,432	20,119	22,631	19,277	18,162	25,837	28,039	26,182
Social Science												
Economics	17,908	31,318	61,272	35,448	13,345	16,259	20,733	18,938	22,994	26,687	32,145	28,487
Geography	16,027	28,442	37,018	30,828		18,351	17,810	12,572		29,964		
Political Science		28,602	40,077	27,186	17,511	17,051	18,155	15,182	16,584	26,949	30,440	29,718
Psychology	15,382	25,597	33,466	25,499	15,014	17,547	22,769	17,287	23,056	27,009	32,720	26,602
Sociology Criminology	20,208	27,023	37,826	26,554	17,558	19,802	26,201	17,930	21,841	26,042	32,822	26,696
Specialized Admin.	21,707	30,681	48,383	30,304	17,057	20,024	27,951	19,532	22,526	27,528	49,696	31,498
Commerce	20,213	34,158	55,186	30,638	17,626	17,671	30,677	17,756	22,608	29,279	50,428	27,930
Finance	20,596	37,174	46,350	32,662	15,456	19,078	27,938	18,455	18,314	32,197	46,563	31,905
Secretarial Studies	16,273			19,070	15,759	18,040		15,214	23,820	29,050		23,541
Marketing	22,964	34,394	51,175	30,266	19,286	16,221	26,143	17,053	23,499	42,695		29,307
Law	21,337	50,659	51,231	43,237	13,832	19,341	31,096	16,814	19,543	28,151	70,115	40,965
Other Social Science	18,034	26,837	37,333	22,142				17,687			41,317	25,878
Agricultural & BioScience												
Agriculture	14,324	23,436	31,231	15,882	9,668	12,556	15,009	13,223	13,238	25,717		
Biology		25,298	32,544	26,293		18,472	19,192	15,563		25,560	32,983	29,581
Other Life Science	21,417	24,366	32,440		18,789	14,926	17,406		22,989	25,054	24,232	
Household Science	11,932			24,455	10,825			15,132	15,069			27,977
Fish Wildlife Manage	13,562				10,486				16,535			

Field	Canadian-Born				Foreign-Educated Immigrants				Canadian-Educated Immigrants			
	College	Bachelor	Master's	Other PS	College	Bachelor	Master's	Other PS	College	Bachelor	Master's	Other PS
Engineer&Applied Science												
Architecture	-	25,623	-	-		14,108	20,368	14,440		24,500		
Other Engineering		35,606	43,404	25,197		18,087	25,808	17,079		37,682		
Chemical Engineering		36,818	-	-		17,582	23,222	19,574		41,842		
Civil Engineering		34,949	-	-		16,098	16,899	15,353		31,635		
Electrical Engineering		46,977	-	-		16,886	25,511	15,268		40,288		
Mechanical Engineer		42,168	-	-		15,919	23,893	14,248				
Forestry	17,769	29,583	-	-	-	-	-	-				
Landscape Architect	18,689				14,396				21,087			
Health Professions												
Medicine		39,605	57,384	69,849		22,933	29,931	36,984		39,039	64,274	70,055
Other Health			39,973				29,787			33,390	50,158	
Nursing	24,803	32,535		25,889	20,950	27,571		23,511	25,443			28,558
Medical Assistant	16,401				16,054				17,017			
Public Health	24,386	34,913		30,361	17,079			27,738	26,851			35,932
Rehab Medicine	18,115	32,940		34,104	25,379	30,117		29,045	17,377	34,539		32,440
Medical Technician	21,672	27,536		27,170	15,859	22,595		18,354	22,129	28,400		30,810
Math & Physical Sciences												
Mathematics		35,259	42,055	35,245		20,423	28,391	13,957		31,326	35,843	22,532
Computer Science		41,954		31,357		26,993	33,451	20,333		38,776	40,096	33,361
Chemistry	27,695	30,272			14,399	18,538	26,156	18,496	23,920	29,157	40,621	
Physics			44,996			16,833	29,499	12,609		30,161		
Earth Science	19,748	30,714				20,021	20,596	-	-			
Other Science	22,439	32,595	42,383	29,312	15,637	17,462	20,618	15,887	20,342	26,514	29,458	19,688
Other												
Trades	18,069	-			14,131	13,434	-	10,465	20,517			
Electronic Technology	20,575				16,984				22,679			
Environment Tech	16,222				-				-			
Mechanic	18,781				16,534				17,956			
Transport Technology	18,585				14,163				21,049			
Average	18,070	29,683	40,000	29,527	15,493	18,676	24,807	19,994	19,788	29,247	40,146	34,032

Source: 1996 Canadian Census. Dashes imply that the cell contents are suppressed for reasons of confidentiality.

Table 5: Frequency for Males (Column %) — 1996 Canadian Census

Field	Canadian-Born				Foreign-Educated Immigrants				Canadian-Educated Immigrants			
	College	Bachelor	Master's	Other PS	College	Bachelor	Master's	Other PS	College	Bachelor	Master's	Other PS
Education												
Education	1.57	13.93	19.03	16.47	1.52	4.80	7.57	5.99	1.39	7.26	12.98	10.07
Fine & AppliedArts												
FineArt	3.96	1.95	1.62	1.80	5.90	1.94	1.95	2.26	5.94	2.14	1.63	1.97
Literature & Humanities												
History	-	2.87	2.09	1.40	-	1.48	1.63	0.85	-	2.28	2.41	1.13
Media	0.92	1.65	1.80	1.42	0.36	0.99	1.18	1.20	0.84	1.36	1.55	1.16
English	0.05	1.76	1.58	0.87	0.13	1.61	1.23	0.73	-	1.94	1.68	0.70
French	-	-	-	-	-	-	-	-	-	-	-	-
Other Literature	0.07	0.50	0.66	0.54	0.13	1.04	1.31	0.98	-	0.73	1.67	0.65
Philosophy Theology	0.82	2.87	6.53	2.30	0.50	2.62	4.31	1.87	0.54	2.37	4.59	1.57
Other Humanities	0.49	1.28	2.77	0.85	0.48	0.54	1.21	0.40	0.45	1.12	2.07	0.78
Social Science												
Economics	0.07	4.31	3.55	1.48	0.21	4.96	4.39	2.53	0.12	5.10	3.33	2.08
Geography	0.10	2.33	1.10	0.96	0.07	0.65	0.60	0.48	-	1.72	0.81	0.82
Political Science	0.04	2.51	1.70	0.96	-	1.51	1.29	0.69	-	2.51	1.87	0.92
Psychology	0.11	2.56	2.70	1.19	-	0.84	0.99	0.39	0.10	2.55	2.04	0.98
Sociology Criminology	0.13	1.78	1.27	1.29	0.06	0.89	0.65	0.67	0.20	1.72	1.04	0.96
Specialized Admin.	2.04	3.55	5.19	6.00	1.84	1.10	1.55	2.06	1.98	1.20	2.04	2.53
Commerce	3.46	8.26	14.21	7.38	2.76	8.50	8.69	6.65	4.59	7.64	13.18	7.60
Finance	3.41	7.11	3.85	12.13	4.20	8.90	4.54	9.25	4.79	7.19	3.67	11.43
Secretarial Studies	1.27			-	1.60				0.86			-
Marketing	2.01	1.58	0.89	2.18	1.44	1.04	0.69	1.35	2.20	1.04	0.80	1.74
Law	0.14	4.76	3.14	4.65	0.11	2.24	1.77	2.17	0.13	3.20	2.57	2.67
Other Social Science	3.62	1.22	2.41	1.09	1.13	0.90	1.33	0.60	2.36	0.72	1.87	0.70
Agricultural & BioScience												
Agriculture	1.61	1.53	0.89	3.50	2.20	1.64	1.44	1.61	1.43	0.73	0.61	1.38
Biology		2.13	1.91	0.91		1.34	1.03	0.60		2.58	1.55	0.99
Other Life Science	0.11	0.49	0.61		0.10	0.57	0.83		0.11	0.58	0.63	
Household Science	2.03			-	3.66			-	2.28			-
Fish Wildlife Manage	1.04			-	0.92			-	0.56			-

Arthur Sweetman and Stephan McBride

Field	Canadian-Born				Foreign-Educated Immigrants				Canadian-Educated Immigrants			
	College	Bachelor	Master's	Other PS	College	Bachelor	Master's	Other PS	College	Bachelor	Master's	Other PS
Engineer & Applied Science												
Architecture		1.10	0.87	0.68	-	2.25	2.25	2.47		1.53	1.20	1.55
Other Engineering	0.05	5.05	3.87	2.51		8.95	9.30	8.45		7.44	8.07	5.24
Chemical Engineering		1.05	0.64	0.25		1.50	1.87	0.67		1.37	1.35	0.48
Civil Engineering		2.67	1.76	1.15		5.49	5.77	4.22		2.93	2.70	1.94
Electrical Engineering		2.84	1.61	1.47		7.60	6.83	5.43		5.71	4.11	3.09
Mechanical Engineer		3.02	1.22	0.85		6.31	5.82	5.42		3.83	2.59	2.45
Forestry	0.52	0.96	0.41	0.67	0.11	0.37	0.43	0.30	0.32	0.53	-	-
Landscape Architect	0.91			-	0.63			-	1.55			-
Health Professions												
Medicine		1.18	2.44	14.99		1.79	2.99	17.92		1.76	3.44	20.55
Other Health			0.68				0.87				0.67	
Nursing	0.44	0.34		0.46	0.46	0.42		0.71	0.42	0.30		-
Medical Assistant	0.56			0.00	0.51				0.46			
Public Health	3.47			0.36	3.50				3.30			
Rehab Medicine	0.03	0.26		-	0.06	0.23		0.42	-	-		-
Medical Technician	1.50	0.20		1.31	1.26	0.64		1.30	1.52	0.33		1.21
Math & Physical Sciences												
Mathematics		2.02	1.30	0.76		2.20	2.05	0.92		2.74	2.13	1.57
Computer Science		3.23	1.58	1.95		4.68	4.83	2.91		6.55	3.11	3.46
Chemistry	0.17	1.12	0.80	0.52	0.26	2.15	1.87	1.17	0.26	1.87	1.22	0.99
Physics	-	0.80	0.92	0.23	0.07	1.46	1.71	0.64	-	1.30	1.46	-
Earth Science	0.22	1.25	1.62	0.48	0.18	1.02	1.86	0.50	0.17	1.20	1.76	-
Other Science	0.40	1.51	0.54	0.76	0.41	1.93	0.71	0.85	0.54	2.33	0.78	1.43
Other												
Trades	26.22	0.12	-	0.49	27.37	0.55	-	1.25	23.50	-	-	0.73
Electronic Technology	13.05				12.54				16.85			
Environment Tech	0.81				0.38				0.45			
Mechanic	18.28				16.95				14.59			
Transport Technology	4.25				5.91				4.75			
Observations	116,472	37,163	10,200	14,543	57,358	20,429	9,313	12,591	29,933	14,795	5,402	6,448

Source: 1996 Canadian Census. Dashes imply that the cell contents are suppressed for reasons of confidentiality.

Postsecondary Field of Study

429

Table 6: Earnings for Males — 1996 Canadian Census

Field	Canadian-Born				Foreign-Educated Immigrants				Canadian-Educated Immigrants			
	College	Bachelor	Master's	Other PS	College	Bachelor	Master's	Other PS	College	Bachelor	Master's	Other PS
Education												
Education	26,235	38,373	50,960	41,436	20,407	30,401	35,294	25,707	26,868	41,750	54,758	41,817
Fine & Applied Arts												
FineArt	25,767	27,839	43,646	28,870	22,971	22,708	28,649	23,133	27,528	28,957	33,128	32,145
Literature & Humanities												
History		41,448	54,125	39,981		28,406	34,667	18,675		37,667	47,840	45,004
Media	30,751	36,319	40,180	34,072	26,775	23,200	35,517	20,996	32,586	38,512	41,752	36,130
English	23,642	35,389	46,184	40,445	25,019	30,046	34,751	23,705	-	35,103	38,381	37,621
French	-	-	-	-	-	-	-	-	-			
Other Literature	26,013	36,372	36,463	31,870	23,892	18,331	30,291	23,215	-	38,485	43,821	31,800
Philosophy Theology	26,649	32,051	34,158	28,013	21,869	26,845	30,028	25,126	27,073	34,629	33,031	34,758
Other Humanities	26,573	39,441	46,273	31,534	20,020	30,532	35,199	27,239	29,882	35,192	49,788	32,648
Social Science												
Economics	31,093	52,009	63,522	50,758	28,042	35,146	35,435	26,229	53,351	43,765	62,587	46,934
Geography	34,383	40,282	47,888	39,565	27,162	30,137	36,554	26,072	-	43,701	45,874	36,217
Political Science	34,785	42,815	50,503	43,556	-	27,883	33,121	24,563	-	41,239	42,188	32,108
Psychology	26,078	40,775	45,613	35,769	-	30,203	46,671	27,378	38,457	40,124	46,477	41,663
Sociology Criminology	37,945	40,231	45,496	40,613	20,154	27,494	27,965	20,884	34,664	34,454	42,031	37,582
Specialized Admin.	32,939	47,294	65,215	44,287	26,365	30,025	34,755	29,011	32,703	41,028	62,590	42,462
Commerce	38,558	57,232	91,664	52,823	30,622	29,472	51,760	27,887	36,980	48,259	76,390	47,247
Finance	39,480	58,630	73,415	57,700	31,082	34,676	45,524	38,166	40,630	54,054	68,206	53,392
Secretarial Studies	27,131				22,473				33,753			-
Marketing	39,105	47,833	64,502	44,786	31,957	28,097	47,661	38,730	40,967	46,217	53,803	41,911
Law	37,749	79,892	97,403	76,977	33,121	34,961	36,910	32,770	34,931	69,433	79,791	71,710
Other Social Science	34,801	38,463	51,991	31,908	25,266	23,908	35,565	25,081	35,867	36,761	48,817	27,466
Agricultural & BioScience												
Agriculture	23,480	38,869	50,637	26,675	19,729	23,349	29,530	24,042	24,990	36,165	44,948	27,386
Biology		40,419	46,096	42,972		28,847	39,876	28,878		39,092	47,045	42,539
Other Life Science	32,625	38,249	47,300	-	23,400	28,160	30,291	-	31,403	35,183	54,007	-
Household Science	22,976			-	22,916			22,674	26,866			
Fish Wildlife Manage	25,508			-	25,706				-			

Arthur Sweetman and Stephan McBride

Table: Earnings by Postsecondary Field of Study

Field	Canadian-Born				Foreign-Educated Immigrants				Canadian-Educated Immigrants			
	College	Bachelor	Master's	Other PS	College	Bachelor	Master's	Other PS	College	Bachelor	Master's	Other PS
Engineer&Applied Science												
Architecture		41,290	39,043	36,943		27,044	35,329	27,348		39,333	41,650	39,177
Other Engineering	21,048	57,959	68,002	46,365	–	39,556	48,383	32,854	–	52,752	58,105	50,273
Chemical Engineering		64,871	70,182	47,505		41,863	49,932	45,736		58,980	63,266	40,689
Civil Engineering		54,159	62,832	42,886		31,868	38,658	28,501		51,980	58,494	37,150
Electrical Engineering		58,445	67,963	46,603		36,298	45,087	32,174		48,649	59,856	43,014
Mechanical Engineer		55,987	65,977	61,773		34,726	43,951	34,694		56,115	63,404	41,112
Forestry	31,727	52,581	68,890	41,235	25,496	34,586	23,908	24,855	39,294	42,206		–
Landscape Architect	31,683			–	27,239			–	32,300			
Health Professions												
Medicine		54,367	106,756	111,348		36,058	70,036	84,065		50,249	104,611	110,982
Other Health			57,263				56,105				57,183	
Nursing	33,199	35,937		33,978	30,047	29,809		28,862	29,284	33,011		
Medical Assistant	23,548				23,246				25,870			
Public Health	33,188			39,434	27,208	–		–	38,373			
Rehab Medicine	28,244	44,718			31,471	48,833		53,407				
Medical Technician	32,859	59,824		60,595	27,474	27,788		33,995	36,429	35,004		64,395
Math & Physical Sciences												
Mathematics		56,053	62,013	49,527		35,283	43,519	26,960		50,313	53,186	53,085
Computer Science		51,866	59,237	43,220		36,079	40,206	30,133		44,512	58,040	36,144
Chemistry	39,952	51,405	50,429	47,643	29,793	36,269	35,662	31,398	42,325	50,617	50,358	45,481
Physics		46,831	55,204	36,379	29,839	34,497	40,819	28,133	–	45,810	53,343	–
Earth Science	37,815	50,517	54,768	49,407	33,769	39,672	39,179	30,747	42,265	49,317	54,350	
Other Science	34,806	50,153	50,564	45,704	27,339	29,252	39,141	26,951	33,472	43,421	50,521	43,315
Other												
Trades	31,025	45,303	–	33,791	29,128	28,006	–	28,841	35,650	–	–	44,575
Electronic Technology	36,259				29,812				36,344			
Environment Tech	33,838				31,452				34,671			
Mechanic	31,689				29,378				34,812			
Transport Technology	34,042				32,180				38,921			
Average	32,262	48,864	61,553	55,967	28,205	32,716	41,479	39,930	35,066	46,155	58,275	58,292

Source: 1996 Canadian Census. Dashes imply that the cell contents are suppressed for reasons of confidentiality.

Table 3 presents the frequency of observed fields for females by level of education for the Canadian-born, the foreign-educated, and Canadian-educated immigrants. An immediate difference is obvious on the first line; immigrants, regardless of where they are educated, are much less likely to have education degrees. A few other important differences are worth emphasizing. For example, immigrants are more likely to study non-English, and non-French, literature, more likely to study economics, commerce and finance, and less likely to study specialized administration. Immigrant women are also more likely to study engineering and to pursue medicine and science-oriented fields such as mathematical science, and pure and applied sciences, including computer science and chemistry. Some of these differences are quite large, for example, foreign-educated immigrant females are about 85% more likely to have a bachelor's degree in medicine than are the Canadian-born.[5] Immigrants who obtain at least some of their education in Canada are just over 25% likely to have a bachelor's degree in medicine. Immigrant and Canadian-born women have very different distributions of fields of study.

Men, in Table 5, are seen to have a broadly similar pattern of differences in the distribution of fields of study, although there are also differences associated with gender. Men in each of the three groups are much less likely to study education or fine arts than women. Further, some of the differences observed between the Canadian-born and immigrants among females are not observable among males. In particular, immigrant males are no more likely, and perhaps slightly less likely, to pursue commerce and finance than the Canadian-born. Immigrant males are, however, less likely to pursue law. As is the case among women, immigrant men are much more likely to choose disciplines in the sciences and engineering than the Canadian-born.

Earnings among females, in Table 4, are seen to vary substantially across disciplines, with science and engineering graduates earning somewhat more than those with a social science and humanities background (of course, this is the combined result of the number of hours and weeks worked, and the hourly wage). There are, however, some notable excep-

---

[5]Note that the census questions include a special category for those who have a degree in "medicine, dentistry, veterinary medicine and optometry" and these are included in the bachelor's level unless the respondent indicates the presence of a master's degree. These categories are combined and labelled as medicine. This contrasts to Tables 1 and 2, where they are isolated into the MD column.

Arthur Sweetman and Stephan McBride

tions. For example, among the Canadian-born with a master's degree those in economics had the highest earnings. More importantly, a pattern appears to exist such that immigrants educated in Canada have earnings comparable to the Canadian-born, while foreign-educated immigrants have much lower earnings across most disciplines.

Turning to male earnings in Table 6, education, fine arts, humanities and agricultural and biological sciences are seen, in general, to have lower annual earnings for all three population subgroups. Social sciences are extremely diverse, while engineering, health, and math and physical sciences tend to be somewhat more uniformly higher. Once again, foreign-educated immigrants earn less than the other two, which are broadly similar though the estimates do vary. Some fields, such as law, seem to have a particularly large difference depending upon where the education was obtained. Immigrants educated in law outside Canada receive massively less, for example, about $35,000 less per year at the bachelor's level, than those educated in Canada.

Regression Analysis of Earnings by Field of Study

The descriptive statistics in Tables 3 through 6 do not control for issues of relevance to the labour market such as differences in age, or place of residence, which clearly affect earnings and differ substantially across the subpopulations of interest. Further, many questions of interest focus on those who participate in the workforce. Therefore, in accord with the previous literature, this section focuses on those with positive earnings and weeks of work. If the distribution of fields of study is changed by policy, then, in terms of earnings, this is the relevant group to study (though the proportion of each group that works may also be an issue). These regressions control for observable characteristics to get a better picture of field of study effects for similar individuals. The dependent variable is the natural logarithm of annual earnings. In addition to the independent variables observed in the tables, these regressions also contain nine province of residence indicators (that is, variables where each equals one if the case is true, and zero otherwise; sometimes they are called dummy variables), 23 census metropolitan area indicators, along with three census area indicators for British Columbia, Ontario, and Québec that capture a set of smaller urban centres (i.e., each is set to one if the person lives in a small urban centre) and a quartic (fourth order polynomial) in age. Note that the regressions do not control for occupation. This is appropriate in this context since occupation is endogenous. By omitting occupation, these regressions provide a better measure of a "pure" field of study effect. This also allows the value that follows from some fields having graduates that are more flexible than others and being able to be employed across a variety of occupations to be observed. Baker and Benjamin (1994) omit occupation for a similar reason, though they are not looking at field of study.

Tables 7 through 10 each contain selected results from two distinct regressions, one for each sex. Each regression includes the Canadian-born, and the two immigrant groups, thus allowing comparisons. Separate regressions are run for each of: bachelor's degree (Tables 7 and 8), college certificate or diploma (Table 9), and master's degree (Table 10). The tables are formatted to make the output as parsimonious as possible given the need to display results for a large number of fields of study. Tables 7 and 8 display two distinct parts of the same two regressions: Table 7 presents selected background coefficients, and Table 8 shows those for field of study. For the regressions in Tables 9 and 10 the background coefficients are suppressed since they have a similar pattern to those in Table 7 and they are not the focus of this study. Each regression has the following format:

$$
(1) \quad \begin{aligned} \ln(earnings) &= b_0 + b_{FI} FI + b_{CI} CI + b_{CB} X + b_{FI} FI * X + b_{CI} CI * X + \\ & f_{CB} Field + f_{FI} FI * Field + f_{CI} CI * Field + \varepsilon \end{aligned}
$$

where the b's and f's are coefficients to be estimated, FI and CI are indicator (zero or one) variables indicating whether the observation is a foreign-educated, or Canadian-educated, immigrant. The vector X contains the background (non-field of study) variables including: age, place of residence, visible minority, age at immigration and language. Some of these background variables, the set of arrival cohort, age at immigration, and source region indicators, are unique to immigrants, in which case they are set to zero for the Canadian-born. This set-up implies that, for each variable that is common to the three groups, both sets of immigrant coefficients estimate differences from the "base case" Canadian-born one. However, those coefficients, such as age at immigration, that are unique to immigrants, do not have an interpretation that involves deviations. Note that, similarly to the other variables that are in common, the immigrant *Field* coefficients are also defined as deviations, or differences, from the

Canadian-born average. The total effect for immigrants is the sum of the two coefficients.[6]

Bachelor's Degree Holders

The first two regressions compare each immigrant group (Canadian- and foreign-educated) to the Canadian-born, where all those included in the regressions have exactly a bachelor's degree. Table 7 presents the interesting background variables' coefficients. Regression results for females are on the left, and those for males are on the right. Only the Canadian-educated immigrant females' indicator variable is statistically significantly different from the overall regression intercept (which is effectively the intercept for the Canadian-born), as seen in the first row. Note that this indicator variable reflects the (ln)*earnings* for the combination of the omitted groups: that is, those who are not visible minorities, speak English, arrived between 1961 and 1965 at age 16 to 20, from the region of origin that includes the United States, the United Kingdom, Australia, New Zealand, and other English-speaking countries, and the like. This suggests that controlling for the observables in the regression, the male and foreign-educated immigrant's earnings are comparable. Of course, controlling for other factors is not innocuous, as will be seen in the predictions in Tables 11 and 12. Strikingly, the visible-minority indicator is effectively zero for the Canadian-born females, but large, statistically significant, and negative for the Canadian-born males. Neither Canadian-educated immigrant visible-minority coefficients differs from that for the Canadian-born. However, both foreign-educated visible-minority coefficients are negative and statistically significant. Like the visible-minority indicators, the language variables appear to differ across the sexes. Relative to those who speak only English, the omitted group, Canadian-born females who speak French have a premium, whereas the equivalent males have a deficit. Further, immigrant males have an even larger deficit, while there is no additional gain (or loss) for the females. Females also have a premium for being bilingual, while

---

[6]We explored a variety of related specifications, for example, forcing the Canadian-born and each immigrant group to have common field of study coefficients, or suppressing the field of study coefficients altogether, but there were no important changes from the current findings that resulted. In particular, the age at immigration, cohort, and source country coefficients were relatively stable.

Table 7: 1996 Bachelor's Degree: Earnings

Variables	Females			Males		
	Cdn Born	Foreign Educ	Cdn Educ	Cdn Born	Foreign Educ	Cdn Educ
Immigrant/Intercept	9.783***	-0.039	-0.112**	9.814***	0.077	0.007
	[0.017]	[0.153]	[0.046]	[0.016]	[0.173]	[0.042]
Vismin	0.007	-0.083*	-0.021	-0.152***	-0.119***	0.043
	[0.022]	[0.047]	[0.043]	[0.019]	[0.035]	[0.036]
Language Knowledge						
French	0.045***	-0.014	0.082	-0.063***	-0.151**	-0.195*
	[0.015]	[0.069]	[0.092]	[0.015]	[0.062]	[0.101]
Bilingual	0.061***	0.097***	0.010	0.004	0.021	-0.004
	[0.009]	[0.028]	[0.023]	[0.008]	[0.022]	[0.019]
Neither	0.313	-0.594**	-0.737	-0.282	0.060	0.010
	[0.277]	[0.299]	[0.555]	[0.380]	[0.387]	[0.572]
Arrival Cohort						
i9195		-0.606***	-0.399***		-0.610***	-0.138*
		[0.063]	[0.080]		[0.050]	[0.080]
i8690		-0.242***	-0.220***		-0.293***	-0.192***
		[0.064]	[0.055]		[0.050]	[0.048]
i8185		-0.160**	-0.135***		-0.195***	-0.046
		[0.065]	[0.048]		[0.051]	[0.041]
i7680		-0.082	-0.039		-0.086*	-0.028
		[0.064]	[0.042]		[0.051]	[0.035]
i7175		-0.053	0.003		-0.113**	-0.061**
		[0.063]	[0.038]		[0.050]	[0.031]
i6670		0.038	0.023		-0.069	-0.010
		[0.065]	[0.037]		[0.051]	[0.030]
i5660		0.100	-0.014		-0.144*	-0.001
		[0.120]	[0.044]		[0.087]	[0.033]
i2555		-0.038	0.062		-0.559***	-0.001
		[0.274]	[0.043]		[0.192]	[0.032]
Age-at-Immigration						
ia05		-	0.047		-	0.067***
		-	[0.031]		-	[0.025]
ia610		-	0.035		-	0.069***
		-	[0.031]		-	[0.025]
ia1115		-	0.034		-	0.040
		-	[0.031]		-	[0.025]
ia2125		-0.129	-0.044		0.275*	-0.052**
		[0.140]	[0.031]		[0.165]	[0.026]
ia2630		-0.176	-0.137		0.213	-0.136
		[0.140]	[0.148]		[0.165]	[0.101]
ia3135		-0.278**	-		0.141	-
		[0.140]	-		[0.165]	-
ia3640		-0.368***	-		0.081	-
		[0.142]	-		[0.165]	-
ia4145		-0.435***	-		-0.037	-
		[0.144]	-		[0.166]	-
ia4650		-0.537***	-		-0.010	-
		[0.152]	-		[0.169]	-
ia5165		-0.461***	-		-0.037	-
		[0.167]	-		[0.172]	-

Region of Origin				
Western Europe	-0.009	0.013	-0.187***	-0.056**
	[0.051]	[0.033]	[0.042]	[0.025]
Southern Europe	-0.104	0.087**	-0.409***	-0.055*
	[0.099]	[0.039]	[0.068]	[0.028]
Other Europe	-0.188***	-0.049	-0.479***	-0.076**
	[0.039]	[0.041]	[0.030]	[0.032]
India & Pakistan	-0.242***	-0.173***	-0.297***	-0.106**
	[0.051]	[0.050]	[0.038]	[0.043]
China	0.066	0.080*	-0.202***	-0.095**
	[0.051]	[0.047]	[0.038]	[0.039]
Japan & Korea	-0.158**	-0.160**	-0.207***	-0.205***
	[0.066]	[0.080]	[0.049]	[0.071]
South East Asia	0.014	0.006	-0.311***	-0.094**
	[0.048]	[0.049]	[0.038]	[0.043]
Africa	-0.025	0.014	-0.251***	-0.013
	[0.050]	[0.046]	[0.036]	[0.037]
Mexico & S. America	-0.031	-0.011	-0.214***	-0.107***
	[0.052]	[0.043]	[0.039]	[0.037]
Other	-0.163***	-0.138**	-0.419***	-0.142***
	[0.054]	[0.060]	[0.038]	[0.045]
Field of Study Controls				
Fields		Yes		Yes
Fields*Immig		Yes		Yes
Observations		120672		132974
R-squared		0.099		0.167

Source: 1996 Canadian Census.
Notes: Heteroskedastic consistent standard errors in brackets. Significance Level: * 10%; ** 5%;
*** 1%. Also included in the regression are nine province of residence indicators, 23 census
metropolitan area indicators, three census area indicators for BC, ON, and PQ, and a fourth
order polynomial in age.

males who are bilingual do not have earnings that differ, on average, from those who speak only English. Most strikingly, males who speak neither language appear to have no earnings penalty, whereas the foreign-educated females have a large one. Of course, as seen in the descriptive statistics, there are very few observations in this group; for example, Canadian-born workers with bachelor's degrees who speak neither official language.

The arrival cohort coefficients have a similar pattern to that seen in previous work starting with Chiswick's (1978) seminal article. That is, the more recent entry cohorts have lower earnings. Of course, this is a mixture of time in the country and any changes in cohort composition, or labour market opportunities, that may have occurred.[7] Interestingly, the profile is

---

[7]Since this is cross-sectional data, the arrival cohort, and age at immigration, coefficients measure changes in the unobserved characteristics and differing labour market environments that affect the earnings of immigrants inasmuch as they

Postsecondary Field of Study

steeper for the foreign-educated, suggesting that Canadian education may alleviate some of the cohort effects. Since the omitted group is those who immigrated between 1961 and 1965, there is evidence that males who immigrated prior to that (and remain in the labour market in 1996) have poorer outcomes. Age at immigration has a profile such that those who immigrate at a young age have better labour market outcomes. Note that the omitted category for both immigrant groups is those who arrive between the ages of 16 and 20. Region of origin is also correlated with earnings. The omitted category is those who immigrate from the industrialized, English speaking countries: the United Kingdom, United States, Australia, New Zealand, and related countries. The females, on the other hand, are for the most part much less affected by region of origin. In contrast, it has an important impact on males. For both sexes though, the coefficients are much smaller for those educated in Canada.

Some results from regressions that are not presented are quite interesting. Consider the same control variables presented in Table 7. Across the various immigrant groups, there appears to be no appreciable correlation between field of study and these variables that is also correlated with earnings. That is, when the set of field indicator variables is removed, there is no substantial change in any of the other coefficients presented other than immigrant status. This lack of a correlation is remarkable. Further, when field of study is removed completely from the regression there is neither an increase, nor a decline, across arrival cohort coefficients as a result. If the immigrant admission system were increasingly selecting individuals because of their having valuable (or less valuable) fields of study, then these coefficients would alter when the field of study variables are added to the regression. But this does not occur. Rather, field of study appears to be completely neutral in relation to arrival cohort effects. It is also neutral with respect to age at immigration. Further, and perhaps most surprisingly, it is not correlated with region of origin.

Turning to the field of study coefficients in Table 8, however, it is clear that while field may not be correlated with the other regressors, it clearly captures an important source of earnings variation across individuals. The

---

are correlated with earnings as well as economic integration effects or those related to age at immigration itself. Also, these have the interpretation of differences from what would be expected for a Canadian-born person of the same age. For a discussion of the identification issues see Schaafsma and Sweetman (2001). See also Borjas (1985, 1995), Baker and Benjamin (1994), and Bloom, Grenier and Gunderson (1995).

Arthur Sweetman and Stephan McBride

Table 8: 1996 Bachelor's Degree: Earnings

Variable	Female			Male		
	Cdn Born	Foreign Educ	Cdn Educ	Cdn Born	Foreign Educ	Cdn Educ
Immigrant/Intercept	9.783***	-0.039	-0.112**	9.814***	0.077	0.007
	[0.017]	[0.153]	[0.046]	[0.016]	[0.173]	[0.042]
Fine & Applied Arts						
Fine Arts	-0.480***	0.251***	0.017	-0.515***	0.141**	0.004
	[0.018]	[0.051]	[0.055]	[0.021]	[0.061]	[0.061]
Lit. & Humanities						
History	-0.162***	0.084	0.123*	-0.139***	-0.039	-0.048
	[0.024]	[0.066]	[0.071]	[0.017]	[0.066]	[0.059]
Media Studies	-0.088***	0.099	-0.015	-0.205***	-0.004	0.024
	[0.023]	[0.071]	[0.075]	[0.022]	[0.079]	[0.073]
English	-0.201***	0.211***	0.018	-0.246***	0.036	-0.128**
	[0.017]	[0.054]	[0.049]	[0.021]	[0.063]	[0.063]
French	-0.104***	-0.043	0.175**	-0.165***	0.013	0.086
	[0.031]	[0.102]	[0.086]	[0.051]	[0.156]	[0.191]
Other Literature	-0.224***	0.097	0.005	-0.210***	-0.107	0.087
	[0.028]	[0.062]	[0.066]	[0.040]	[0.086]	[0.098]
Philosophy	-0.264***	0.255***	0.113*	-0.325***	0.160***	0.051
	[0.024]	[0.060]	[0.067]	[0.018]	[0.053]	[0.058]
Other Humanities	-0.161***	0.204**	0.011	-0.324***	0.069	-0.078
	[0.025]	[0.099]	[0.077]	[0.032]	[0.119]	[0.108]
Social Science						
Economics	0.054**	0.093*	-0.093	0.101***	-0.117***	-0.062
	[0.028]	[0.057]	[0.062]	[0.015]	[0.044]	[0.044]
Geography	-0.148***	0.125	-0.023	-0.044***	0.089	0.037
	[0.025]	[0.099]	[0.085]	[0.017]	[0.080]	[0.057]
Political Science	-0.068***	0.066	0.004	-0.028	-0.093	-0.043
	[0.027]	[0.085]	[0.071]	[0.018]	[0.065]	[0.056]
Psychology	-0.167***	0.150***	0.042	-0.118***	-0.056	-0.036
	[0.014]	[0.056]	[0.045]	[0.018]	[0.078]	[0.056]
Sociology	-0.126***	0.130**	0.030	-0.069***	-0.110	-0.025
	[0.017]	[0.066]	[0.055]	[0.021]	[0.080]	[0.066]
Public Admin.	0.128***	0.026	-0.079	0.161***	-0.087	-0.080
	[0.021]	[0.085]	[0.078]	[0.016]	[0.072]	[0.074]
Commerce	0.158***	-0.043	-0.019	0.199***	-0.217***	-0.156***
	[0.017]		[0.047]	[0.012]	[0.039]	[0.039]
Finance	0.226***	-0.087**	-0.063	0.253***	-0.161***	-0.073*
	[0.017]	[0.039]	[0.047]	[0.012]	[0.038]	[0.040]
Marketing	0.134***	0.173*	-0.053	0.150***	-0.090	-0.086
	[0.029]	[0.093]	[0.096]	[0.022]	[0.075]	[0.078]
Law	0.359***	-0.296***	-0.109	0.439***	-0.364***	-0.130***
	[0.020]	[0.083]	[0.067]	[0.014]	[0.056]	[0.050]
Other Soc Sci	-0.007	0.132**	-0.003	-0.036	-0.055	-0.100
	[0.016]	[0.052]	[0.058]	[0.025]	[0.080]	[0.091]

Agri. & Bio Science						
Agriculture Sci	-0.221***	0.124	0.298**	-0.037	-0.121*	-0.169*
	[0.041]	[0.101]	[0.139]	[0.024]	[0.065]	[0.095]
Biological Sci	-0.112***	0.231***	0.108*	-0.014	-0.236***	-0.055
	[0.023]	[0.068]	[0.060]	[0.019]	[0.066]	[0.055]
Other Life Sci	-0.138***	0.105*	-0.037	-0.065	-0.008	-0.077
	[0.023]	[0.061]	[0.071]	[0.040]	[0.102]	[0.108]
Eng. & Applied Sci						
Architecture	-0.290***	0.202*	0.157	-0.094***	-0.095	-0.157**
	[0.052]	[0.110]	[0.146]	[0.026]	[0.059]	[0.069]
Other Engineering	0.112**	0.152*	0.319***	0.299***	-0.106***	-0.037
	[0.046]	[0.086]	[0.113]	[0.014]	[0.037]	[0.039]
Chemical Eng.	0.400***	-0.227*	0.315*	0.465***	-0.190***	-0.150**
	[0.070]	[0.123]	[0.181]	[0.027]	[0.066]	[0.072]
Civil Engineering	0.158**	-0.060	0.144	0.276***	-0.213***	-0.043
	[0.067]	[0.113]	[0.177]	[0.018]	[0.044]	[0.053]
Electrical Eng.	0.520***	-0.155	0.115	0.408***	-0.199***	-0.148***
	[0.084]	[0.127]	[0.146]	[0.017]	[0.041]	[0.044]
Mechanical Eng.	0.307***	-0.108	-0.201	0.329***	-0.223***	-0.052
	[0.068]	[0.120]	[0.177]	[0.016]	[0.039]	[0.044]
Forestry	0.051	-0.043	0.020	0.288***	-0.486***	-0.091
	[0.091]	[0.282]	[0.293]	[0.028]	[0.118]	[0.112]
Health Science						
Medicine	0.372***	-0.069	-0.028	0.327***	-0.105*	0.056
	[0.026]	[0.063]	[0.067]	[0.025]	[0.063]	[0.066]
Nursing	0.157***	0.177***	0.098**	0.054	0.089	-0.176
	[0.014]	[0.040]	[0.047]	[0.051]	[0.117]	[0.146]
Public Health	0.014	0.654**	-0.191	0.271**	-0.151	0.116
	[0.089]	[0.282]	[0.239]	[0.131]	[0.348]	[0.329]
Medical Techn.	-0.029	0.170**	0.007	0.018	0.010	-0.089
	[0.045]	[0.082]	[0.112]	[0.063]	[0.110]	[0.142]
Natural Science						
Mathematics	0.191***	-0.054	-0.116	0.212***	-0.128**	-0.048
	[0.031]	[0.074]	[0.072]	[0.020]	[0.057]	[0.055]
Computer Sci	0.333***	0.148**	0.079	0.257***	0.051	-0.023
	[0.029]	[0.064]	[0.064]	[0.016]	[0.045]	[0.043]
Chemistry	-0.003	0.066	0.146	0.140***	-0.087	-0.089
	[0.050]	[0.085]	[0.107]	[0.027]	[0.060]	[0.065]
Physics	0.178	-0.029	0.211	0.096***	-0.091	-0.006
	[0.114]	[0.171]	[0.221]	[0.031]	[0.069]	[0.077]
Earth Sci	0.079	0.132	0.000	0.134***	-0.030	-0.120
	[0.067]	[0.161]	[0.192]	[0.025]	[0.078]	[0.076]
Other Science	0.042	0.055	-0.030	0.077***	-0.148**	-0.049
	[0.035]	[0.077]	[0.084]	[0.023]	[0.060]	[0.059]
Trades & Technology						
Trades	-0.016	-0.363	0.242	0.323**	-0.314	-0.455
	[0.362]	[0.457]	[0.770]	[0.150]	[0.199]	[0.309]
Observations			120672			132974
R-squared			0.099			0.167

Source: 1996 Canadian Census.

Notes: Heteroskedastic consistent standard errors in brackets. Significance Level: * 10%; ** 5%; *** 1%.

Arthur Sweetman and Stephan McBride

first column for each sex contains the coefficients for the Canadian-born, and the subsequent two columns' coefficients are deviations from that Canadian-born coefficient for each immigrant group. Thus, on average, immigrants in a particular field of study obtain earnings commensurate with the coefficient for the Canadian-born, plus the relevant for their difference from the Canadian-born. Note that a degree from an educational faculty is the omitted field of study, so it shifts the immigrant indicator variable. That indicator, and the overall intercept, are presented in the first row of the table; this row replicates a row in Table 7. The coefficients suggest a strong pattern of earnings differences across fields of study, with those in fine and applied arts, humanities, the traditional social sciences (except economics), and agriculture and biological sciences earning less than those with education degrees.[8] In contrast, those with administration, business and law degrees earn more, on average, as do those with engineering and applied science, health science and natural science degrees.

For immigrant females the differences from the Canadian-born are quite varied. There are relatively few statistically significant differences between the Canadian-born and Canadian-educated immigrants, but where there are differences the immigrants tend to have higher earnings. In contrast, foreign-educated immigrants have earnings that are sometimes above, and sometimes below, those of the Canadian-born in the same field. Interestingly, the differences tend to offset the low earnings of the Canadian-born in fine and applied arts, and literature and humanities (though this is not universal), but be more mixed in the high-paying engineering and applied sciences, health professions, and natural sciences. Overall, there appears to be less variance across fields for the foreign-educated immigrants than for the Canadian-born females. Recall that each immigrant is also affected by the relevant immigrant coefficients seen in Table 7. For the males the pattern is somewhat different. The coefficients for the Canadian-educated immigrants are, like those for the females, not different from zero, which suggests that the field premium is the same as that for the Canadian-born, but all the differences are negative, not positive. Coefficients for the male foreign-born fields also tend to be negative, when

---

[8]The term "traditional social sciences" is used to refer to those disciplines usually in social science faculties in universities: for example, economics, geography, political science and the like. This contrasts with the broader census definition, which includes professional fields within business, law and administration. We observe that the findings for these two sets of fields are quite different.

statistically significant, but are occasionally positive. In general, the coefficients tend to offset the extremes of the Canadian-born distribution, being negative for high earning fields, and positive for low earning ones, though the number of negative coefficients is larger. Overall, for both sexes, the Canadian-educated immigrants have returns to field of study that are more similar to the Canadian-born than to the foreign-educated. However, for all except the Canadian-educated immigrant females, the premiums of the highest paying fields tend to be muted relative to the Canadian-born. Conversely, immigrants in many of the lowest paying fields have higher earnings than their Canadian-born counterparts. It is worth noting that medicine shows very small differences across the groups, despite the much higher likelihood of immigrants having medical degrees, while there is a very substantial deficit for immigrants with law degrees.

College Degree Certificate and Diploma Holders

Unlike the set of regressions for those with a bachelor's degree, we only present the field of study and immigrant/intercept coefficients for those with college certification, and these are in Table 9. Among the Canadian-educated immigrants with a college degree, most of the immigrant field of study coefficients are not statistically different from zero, although there are a few notable exceptions, such as psychology and earth sciences, which have substantial premia for the female immigrants. Thus the Canadian-educated immigrants have quite similar earnings premia across field of study as the Canadian-born. The foreign-educated have greater differences from the Canadian-born, but most coefficients are still not different from zero. Unlike the females, for the males almost none of the statistically significant immigrant coefficients are positive. Perhaps somewhat more strongly than that seen at the bachelor's level, there is a broad pattern (though there are exceptions) whereby those fields that are higher earning among the Canadian-born have a negative coefficient for both immigrant groups when the coefficient is different from zero. Thus, while the ranking of fields according to earnings is not substantially altered, the difference between the lowest and highest earning fields tends to be less extreme among the immigrant population.

Arthur Sweetman and Stephan McBride

Table 9: 1996 College: Earnings

Variable	Female			Male		
	Cdn Born	Foreign Educ	Cdn Educ	Cdn Born	Foreign Educ	Cdn Educ
Immigrant/Intercept	9.410***	0.017	-0.032	9.601***	0.250***	-0.014
	[0.014]	[0.051]	[0.045]	[0.019]	[0.067]	[0.065]
Fine & Applied Arts						
Fine Arts	-0.203***	0.069*	0.080*	-0.112***	-0.046	-0.046
	[0.014]	[0.040]	[0.046]	[0.020]	[0.057]	[0.068]
Humanities						
Media Studies	0.141***	-0.138*	0.070	0.073***	-0.004	-0.010
	[0.022]	[0.081]	[0.084]	[0.023]	[0.091]	[0.086]
Literature	-0.002	0.118	0.191*	-0.067	0.097	-0.047
	[0.035]	[0.074]	[0.103]	[0.048]	[0.107]	[0.152]
Philosophy	-0.164***	-0.082	-0.041	0.000	-0.069	-0.061
	[0.022]	[0.087]	[0.095]	[0.024]	[0.077]	[0.097]
Othr. Humanities	-0.048	0.099	0.102	-0.076	-0.159	0.003
	[0.051]	[0.122]	[0.152]	[0.048]	[0.135]	[0.186]
Social Science						
Economics	0.109	0.069	0.106	0.162***	-0.026	0.050
	[0.110]	[0.137]	[0.208]	[0.062]	[0.119]	[0.176]
Geography	0.148**	-0.403	0.117	0.184***	0.076	-0.082
	[0.065]	[0.279]	[0.232]	[0.041]	[0.153]	[0.151]
Political Science	0.205	-0.026	-0.067	0.052	0.205	-0.437*
	[0.127]	[0.248]	[0.405]	[0.078]	[0.250]	[0.260]
Psychology	-0.160***	0.385***	0.206*	-0.079	0.122	0.229
	[0.032]	[0.127]	[0.124]	[0.050]	[0.224]	[0.184]
Socology Crim	0.152***	0.058	0.123	0.319***	-0.443**	0.028
	[0.054]	[0.200]	[0.177]	[0.047]	[0.192]	[0.141]
Public Admin	0.219***	0.008	0.037	0.172***	-0.105*	0.000
	[0.016]	[0.054]	[0.062]	[0.020]	[0.063]	[0.074]
Commerce	0.196***	-0.007	0.053	0.271***	-0.110**	-0.109*
	[0.013]	[0.037]	[0.043]	[0.018]	[0.055]	[0.064]
Finance	0.172***	-0.016	0.053	0.274***	-0.063	-0.055
	[0.012]	[0.033]	[0.039]	[0.018]	[0.052]	[0.064]
Secretary Stud.	0.070***	0.073**	0.039	0.103***	-0.058	0.169*
	[0.009]	[0.029]	[0.035]	[0.026]	[0.076]	[0.100]
Law	0.245***	0.140	-0.059	0.294***	-0.158	-0.128
	[0.044]	[0.164]	[0.135]	[0.046]	[0.139]	[0.175]
Other Social Sci	0.096***	-0.092*	0.021	0.335***	-0.243***	-0.006
	[0.014]	[0.054]	[0.053]	[0.018]	[0.073]	[0.072]
Agricultural & Bio Sci						
Agriculture Sci	-0.136***	-0.076	-0.077	-0.039*	-0.022	-0.030
	[0.026]	[0.091]	[0.108]	[0.023]	[0.065]	[0.085]
Other Life Sci	0.174***	0.055	-0.096	0.219***	-0.042	0.053
	[0.055]	[0.155]	[0.166]	[0.052]	[0.165]	[0.190]
Home Ec.	-0.097***	0.000	0.057	-0.065**	0.104	0.161*
	[0.023]	[0.056]	[0.084]	[0.027]	[0.070]	[0.092]
Fisheries	-0.001	-0.139	0.105	0.125***	-0.048	0.169
	[0.080]	[0.219]	[0.294]	[0.036]	[0.100]	[0.145]

Eng. & Applied Science						
Forestry	0.077	0.637	-0.298	0.242***	-0.345**	0.005
	[0.075]	[0.460]	[0.391]	[0.027]	[0.138]	[0.117]
Landscape Arch	0.026	0.143	0.155	0.181***	-0.065	-0.040
	[0.045]	[0.137]	[0.163]	[0.024]	[0.082]	[0.077]
Health Science						
Nursing	0.447***	-0.095***	-0.037	0.288***	0.048	-0.197*
	[0.010]	[0.030]	[0.038]	[0.029]	[0.081]	[0.106]
Medical Assist.	0.055***	0.061	0.053	0.028	0.049	-0.062
	[0.014]	[0.042]	[0.057]	[0.035]	[0.102]	[0.128]
Public Health	0.463***	-0.086	0.100	0.377***	0.074	-0.047
	[0.027]	[0.137]	[0.120]	[0.051]	[0.204]	[0.193]
Medical Techn.	0.278***	-0.091*	-0.134***	0.283***	-0.098	0.099
	[0.013]	[0.046]	[0.048]	[0.022]	[0.070]	[0.080]
Natural Science						
Chemistry	0.463***	-0.337**	-0.177	0.438***	-0.219**	0.065
	[0.078]	[0.139]	[0.183]	[0.043]	[0.107]	[0.130]
Physics	0.144	0.447	0.423	0.257***	0.068	-0.059
	[0.232]	[0.397]	[1.040]	[0.099]	[0.200]	[0.285]
Earth Science	0.213**	-0.211	0.690**	0.282***	-0.115	0.031
	[0.092]	[0.251]	[0.351]	[0.039]	[0.114]	[0.148]
Other Science	0.326***	-0.328***	-0.276***	0.198***	-0.088	-0.084
	[0.030]	[0.085]	[0.104]	[0.032]	[0.094]	[0.102]
Trades & Technology						
Building Tech.	0.266***	-0.028	0.027	0.311***	-0.135**	-0.039
	[0.043]	[0.099]	[0.122]	[0.019]	[0.057]	[0.070]
Trades	0.074**	-0.026	0.045	0.198***	0.003	0.012
	[0.035]	[0.089]	[0.112]	[0.017]	[0.050]	[0.062]
Electronics Tech	0.187***	-0.074*	0.110**	0.332***	-0.100**	-0.029
	[0.015]	[0.044]	[0.047]	[0.016]	[0.049]	[0.060]
Environ. Tech	0.081	0.324	0.305	0.358***	0.021	0.007
	[0.068]	[0.328]	[0.272]	[0.028]	[0.102]	[0.117]
Mechanic	0.181***	0.016	-0.132	0.320***	-0.080	-0.045
	[0.045]	[0.116]	[0.164]	[0.017]	[0.049]	[0.062]
Transport Tech	0.169***	0.145	0.044	0.359***	-0.097*	0.015
	[0.043]	[0.106]	[0.154]	[0.020]	[0.053]	[0.068]
Observations		212061			169539	
R-squared		0.066			0.083	

Source: 1996 Canadian Census.
Notes: Heteroskedastic consistent standard errors in brackets. Significance Level: * 10%; ** 5%; *** 1%
Also included in the regression are nine province of residence indicators,
23 census metropolitan area indicators, three census area indicators for BC, ON, and PQ, a fourth order
polynomial in age, and all the regressors listed in Table 7.

Master's Degree Holders

Table 10 presents coefficient estimates for those with a master's degree. The pattern is somewhat different from that observed at the bachelor's and college levels. Here, for both sexes and many of the fields, foreign-educated immigrants are seen to do remarkably well relative to the Canadian-born, while the Canadian-educated immigrants do less well.[9] However, despite the change in the ranking of Canadian- and foreign-educated immigrants relative to the Canadian-born, the general pattern of the Canadian-born coefficients remains quite similar to the coefficients for those with a bachelor's degree. That is, those with degrees in fine and applied arts, literature and humanities, traditional social sciences, and agricultural and biological sciences have lower earnings than the omitted (comparison) education field, while those in economics, and administration and commerce related fields tend to do better, as do those in engineering, health and natural sciences. However, especially for the females, the earnings advantage in engineering and particularly natural sciences is not found in as many fields as it was for those with a bachelor's degree. In terms of the ranking of broad fields of study, as seen in the combination of immigrant and Canadian-born coefficients, the pattern is similar to that for those with a bachelor's degree. Individuals with an arts or humanities degree, and to a lesser extent traditional social sciences, and agricultural or biological sciences, earn less, while those on the administrative and business side do better, as do those in engineering and health. Natural sciences is now more similar to the omitted group, except for mathematics and computer sciences. This pattern of the graduates from the sciences, business, administration and law having higher earnings than other graduates is common to all three levels of education, though it is somewhat less pronounced for the college group.

Overall, field of study is seen to be an important predictor of earnings at all three levels of education, with the more science and business-related fields obtaining higher earnings, and humanities, agricultural and biological fields obtaining less, although each level has its own distinguishing features. Relative to bachelor's degrees, immigrants with master's degrees appear to have superior outcomes compared to their Canadian-born counterparts.

---

[9]Note that Canadian-educated immigrants with a master's degree may have had all of their education in Canada, or only that last degree.

Table 10: 1996 Master's Degree: Earnings

	Female			Male		
Variable	Cdn Born	Foreign Educ	Cdn Educ	Cdn Born	Foreign Educ	Cdn Educ
Immigrant/Intercept	9.782***	-1.000	-0.079	9.747***	0.702	0.143**
	[0.046]	[0.922]	[0.077]	[0.040]	[0.447]	[0.061]
Fine & Applied Arts						
Fine Arts	-0.629***	0.135	-0.036	-0.506***	0.302***	-0.246**
	[0.040]	[0.086]	[0.108]	[0.039]	[0.087]	[0.110]
Lit. & Humanities						
History	-0.299***	-0.092	0.075	-0.218***	0.266***	-0.001
	[0.057]	[0.114]	[0.128]	[0.037]	[0.092]	[0.094]
Media Studies	-0.136***	-0.024	0.050	-0.283***	0.466***	-0.107
	[0.029]	[0.085]	[0.081]	[0.039]	[0.104]	[0.109]
English	-0.329***	0.377***	-0.030	-0.230***	0.241**	-0.426***
	[0.046]	[0.091]	[0.100]	[0.045]	[0.106]	[0.108]
French	-0.205***	0.444***	-0.172	-0.177*	0.344	-0.427*
	[0.072]	[0.167]	[0.178]	[0.096]	[0.212]	[0.256]
Other Literature	-0.275***	0.264***	0.076	-0.237***	0.255**	-0.074
	[0.055]	[0.091]	[0.102]	[0.063]	[0.113]	[0.118]
Philosophy	-0.514***	0.047	0.085	-0.445***	0.337***	-0.038
	[0.040]	[0.116]	[0.123]	[0.023]	[0.062]	[0.069]
Other Humanities	-0.346***	0.194	0.010	-0.324***	0.138	-0.228
	[0.054]	[0.143]	[0.146]	[0.058]	[0.150]	[0.150]
Social Science						
Economics	0.210***	-0.310***	-0.217	0.141***	0.034	-0.215***
	[0.058]	[0.098]	[0.134]	[0.030]	[0.066]	[0.080]
Geography	-0.123***	-0.043	-0.289**	-0.048	0.117	-0.019
	[0.047]	[0.137]	[0.131]	[0.032]	[0.095]	[0.096]
Political Science	-0.058	-0.232*	-0.084	-0.074*	0.063	-0.253**
	[0.061]	[0.131]	[0.150]	[0.040]	[0.100]	[0.103]
Psychology	-0.178***	0.072	-0.028	-0.134***	0.290***	-0.107
	[0.031]	[0.090]	[0.093]	[0.033]	[0.108]	[0.096]
Sociology Crim	-0.066	0.158	-0.004	-0.075	-0.097	-0.311**
	[0.053]	[0.121]	[0.137]	[0.046]	[0.130]	[0.131]
Public Admin	0.196***	-0.126	0.055	0.165***	-0.132	-0.051
	[0.036]	[0.117]	[0.109]	[0.026]	[0.090]	[0.094]
Commerce	0.258***	0.105	0.018	0.268***	0.059	-0.152***
	[0.030]	[0.083]	[0.078]	[0.019]	[0.052]	[0.051]
Finance	0.239***	-0.076	0.012	0.268***	0.052	-0.133*
	[0.055]	[0.102]	[0.121]	[0.028]	[0.064]	[0.077]
Marketing	0.173**	-0.118	-0.554***	0.193***	0.156	-0.353**
	[0.081]	[0.228]	[0.201]	[0.053]	[0.136]	[0.148]
Law	0.147***	0.000	0.167	0.369***	-0.246***	-0.258***
	[0.051]	[0.121]	[0.138]	[0.030]	[0.087]	[0.087]
Other Soc Sci	-0.128***	0.199**	0.126	-0.044	0.063	-0.092
	[0.028]	[0.081]	[0.078]	[0.034]	[0.095]	[0.098]

Arthur Sweetman and Stephan McBride

Agri. & Bio Science						
Agricultural Sci	-0.099	-0.171	-0.056	-0.127**	0.040	0.045
	[0.104]	[0.176]	[0.240]	[0.055]	[0.103]	[0.165]
Biological Sci	-0.230***	0.194*	0.013	-0.080**	0.295***	-0.039
	[0.051]	[0.106]	[0.116]	[0.040]	[0.108]	[0.110]
Other Life Sci	-0.228***	0.193	-0.137	-0.004	0.165	-0.035
	[0.065]	[0.122]	[0.166]	[0.063]	[0.131]	[0.168]
Eng. & Applied Sci						
Architecture	-0.356***	0.301*	-0.798***	-0.263***	0.416***	-0.158
	[0.100]	[0.163]	[0.277]	[0.053]	[0.091]	[0.126]
Other Engineering	-0.078	0.328***	0.494**	0.224***	0.182***	-0.130**
	[0.080]	[0.120]	[0.212]	[0.028]	[0.053]	[0.062]
Chemical Eng	0.316*	-0.074	-0.064	0.352***	0.084	-0.182
	[0.174]	[0.246]	[0.330]	[0.062]	[0.099]	[0.126]
Civil Engineering	0.111	-0.395**	0.031	0.276***	-0.010	-0.202**
	[0.139]	[0.183]	[0.256]	[0.038]	[0.066]	[0.089]
Electrical Eng	0.229	-0.101	0.318	0.222***	0.336***	0.011
	[0.184]	[0.218]	[0.327]	[0.040]	[0.066]	[0.081]
Mechanical Eng	0.134	0.045	0.438	0.289***	0.136**	-0.175*
	[0.162]	[0.198]	[0.411]	[0.047]	[0.068]	[0.090]
Forestry	-0.143	-0.624	0.426	0.179**	-0.300*	-0.228
	[0.196]	[0.500]	[0.567]	[0.076]	[0.173]	[0.211]
Health Science						
Medicine	0.271***	0.102	0.196*	0.583***	0.217***	-0.078
	[0.050]	[0.097]	[0.112]	[0.034]	[0.074]	[0.080]
Other Health	0.046	0.071	0.069	0.098	0.174	-0.145
	[0.028]	[0.079]	[0.084]	[0.065]	[0.132]	[0.162]
Natural Science						
Mathematics	0.081	0.252*	-0.062	0.124***	0.106	-0.152
	[0.087]	[0.131]	[0.184]	[0.044]	[0.086]	[0.101]
Computer Science	0.151	0.294**	0.052	0.188***	0.338***	0.026
	[0.101]	[0.133]	[0.177]	[0.043]	[0.071]	[0.088]
Chemistry	0.094	0.208	-0.004	0.017	0.202**	-0.137
	[0.102]	[0.139]	[0.195]	[0.057]	[0.098]	[0.127]
Physical Science	0.139	0.148	0.232	0.040	0.219**	-0.124
	[0.205]	[0.254]	[0.358]	[0.055]	[0.097]	[0.119]
Earth Science	-0.027	-0.002	0.340	0.041	0.095	-0.091
	[0.094]	[0.175]	[0.266]	[0.044]	[0.090]	[0.106]
Other Science	-0.076	-0.002	0.013	-0.084	0.468***	-0.095
	[0.100]	[0.185]	[0.210]	[0.066]	[0.137]	[0.151]
Observations		26439			40865	
R-squared		0.163			0.186	

Source: 1996 Canadian Census.
Notes: Heteroskedastic consistent standard errors in brackets. Significance Level: * 10%; ** 5%; *** 1%
Also included in the regression are nine province of residence indicators, 23 census metropolitan area
indicators, three census area indicators for BC, ON, and PQ, a fourth order polynomial in age, and all the
regressors listed in Table 7.

Postsecondary Field of Study   447

Predicted Annual Earnings by Field

To facilitate comparisons across fields, sex, and the location where immigrants received their education, predicted annual earnings for each group is presented in Table 11 for females, and Table 12 for males. These predictions are generated from the regressions presented in Tables 7 through 10, with the transformation to dollars from the log-earnings regressions made using Duan's (1983) smearing approach. The predictions are for a person who is 40-years old (and hence on the flat portion of the age-earnings profile), and all other relevant characteristics that do not define the prediction (e.g., excluding the field variables), and are not specific to immigrants (e.g., place of residence or language knowledge), set at the mean for the sample containing all three groups. Of those characteristics that are specific to immigrants, the arrival cohort and place of origin are set at the combined sample mean of the two immigrant groups, while the age at immigration variable is set to the 16 to 20 age group. The age at immigration variable is treated differently because it does not entirely overlap for each immigrant group.

Note that, for both immigrant groups, the average earnings predicted for those with a bachelor's degree in education are lower than the mean for the Canadian-born, despite the immigrant coefficients in Table 7 not being statistically significant. This also differs, especially for the Canadian-educated, from that seen in Tables 4 and 6. (Of course, the samples are not directly comparable since the predictions are for those who work, whereas the descriptive statistics include those who do not.) This is in part because the immigrant-specific variables (cohort, age at immigration, and place of origin) imply an earnings deficit relative to the Canadian-born. But, more importantly, this counterfactual forces the immigrants and Canadian-born to have the same set of characteristics, whereas, as seen in the descriptive statistics, immigrants tend to have characteristics associated with higher earnings (they tend to live in cities and high-wage provinces, the foreign-educated are older). The same effect is present in all predictions in each column; any changes within a column are due to the field of study co-efficients exclusively, while movements across columns also follow from the "background" coefficients in the regressions, some of which are presented in Table 7. These predictions, therefore, reflect the expected (or average) nominal annual earnings in 1995 for a 40-year old with "average" characteristics.

Table 11: Predicted Earnings for Female Workers — 1996 Canadian Census

Field	Canadian-Born			Foreign-Educated Immigrants			Canadian-Educated Immigrants		
	College	Bachelor	Master's	College	Bachelor	Master's	College	Bachelor	Master's
Education									
Education	23179	36769	49501	18940	25669	37062	20714	28130	41082
Fine & AppliedArts									
FineArt	18928	22759	26397	16570	20417	22625	18321	17712	21124
Literature & Humanities									
History		31267	36724		23750	25073		27054	32854
Media	26683	33676	43187	18993	25947	31574	25586	25377	37675
English	-	30083	35622	-	25923	38877	-	23423	28704
French	-	33142	40327	-	22167	47049	-	30199	28186
Other Literature	23130	29387	37585	21276	22614	36637	25018	22594	33671
Philosophy Theology	19683	28224	29596	14824	25422	23219	16884	24181	26734
Other Humanities	22088	31307	35034	19917	26796	31846	21849	24206	29369
Social Science									
Economics	25855	38819	61066	22641	29750	33531	25693	27056	40813
Geography	26867	31717	43759	-	25095	31369	-	23703	-
Political Science	-	34337	46699	-	25605	27717	-	26363	35633
Psychology	19761	31129	41444	23720	25256	33343	21689	24838	33460
Sociology Criminology	26992	32418	46351	23369	25785	40644	27277	25569	38328
Specialized Admin	28856	41807	60241	23779	29942	39772	26747	29548	52803
Commerce	28185	43081	64044	22862	28798	53261	26568	32345	54099
Finance	27530	46098	62874	22147	29506	43642	25947	33110	52786
Secretarial Studies	24854			21838			23106		
Marketing	-	42057	58864	-	34902	-	-	-	28087
Law	29627	52634	57318	27851	27333	42922	24966	36119	56203
Other Social Science	25507	36496	43541	19016	29066	39777	23279	27837	40993
Agricultural & BioScience									
Agriculture	20235	29487	44813	15328	23295	28291	16747	30390	-
Biology		32883	39342		28918	35745		28018	33065
Other Life Science	27587	32028	39391	23824	24839	35778	22402	23606	28501
Household Science	21037			17189			19893		
Fish Wildlife Manage	23163			16465			22990		
Engineer&Applied Science									
Architecture		27507	-		23506	35056		24633	-
Other Engineering	-	41116	45802	-	33422	47588		43283	-
Chemical Engineering		54866	-		30527	47235		57536	-
Civil Engineering		43071	-		28319	27890		38049	-
Electrical Engineering		61865	-		36983	42103		53107	-
Mechanical Engineer		49957	-		31295	44358		-	-
Forestry	25024	38706	-	-	-	-	-	-	-
Landscape Architect	23793			22424			24820		
Health Professions									
Medicine		53350	64900		34773	53803		39690	65521
Other Health			51832			41661			46082
Nursing	36240	43039		26928	35857		31197	36310	
Medical Assistant	24485			21272			23078		
Public Health	36845	37277		27628	-		36372	-	
Rehab Medicine	-	-	-	-	-		-	-	
Medical Technician	30596	35724		22836	29567		23923	27517	
Math & Physical Sciences									
Mathematics		44525	53694		29441	51730		30326	41896
Computer Science		51288	57544		41523	57828		42458	50316
Chemistry	36810	36671	-	21465	27337	50108	27569	32457	44927
Physics	-	-	-	-	29766	49420	-	-	-
Earth Science	28667	39793	-	-	31696	36003	-	30446	-
Other Science	32104	38345	45899	18905	28291	34299	21781	28473	38581
Other									
Trades	24950	-		19871	17578	-	23326	-	
Electronic Technology	27945			21208			27886		
Environment Tech	25142			28394			-		
Mechanic	27787			23082			21759		
Transport Technology	27434			25915			25631		

Source: 1996 Canadian Census. Dashes imply that the cell contents are suppressed for reasons of confidentiality.

Postsecondary Field of Study

Focusing first on the predictions for females in Table 11, three patterns are apparent. First, there is a clear trend to higher earnings with increasing education, from college to bachelor's to master's degrees. However, note that many of the health, physical science and trades fields at the college (bachelor's level) have earnings that are comparable or higher than the lower earning humanities and fine arts university (master's) fields. Second, earnings among the Canadian-born typically exceed those of both immigrant groups when comparing the same field and level of education. However, no strong statements can be made regarding the two immigrant groups' earnings rankings. Usually they are quite close, but which has higher earnings varies across field of study. It is important to recall that these are predictions for annual earnings, and can vary because of the hourly wage, hours per week, and weeks per year. Third, in general, while the same fields that are high earning in one column are also in another, as observed for the regression output, there appears to be less variance across fields for the immigrant groups than for the Canadian-born.

Looking next at the predictions for the males in Table 12, the same three patterns observed for the females are obvious. As is commonly observed, mean earnings for males exceed those for females. Note that in some cases, especially at the master's level, immigrants in particular fields have the same or greater earnings than their Canadian-born counterparts. Examples of this include the foreign-educated with master's degrees in medicine and architecture. In other fields, notably law, immigrants have substantial earnings deficits relative to the Canadian-born.

Oaxaca-Blinder Decompositions

While it is useful to look at the variation across fields, it is also useful to formalize the impact of the different returns to, and the distribution of, field of study on the immigrant-Canadian-born earnings gap. This is done in a series of Oaxaca-Blinder decompositions. This approach can only compare across two groups, and it can only deal with variables that are common to the immigrants and Canadian-born. Hence, it does not look at the determinants of the distribution of earnings within the immigrant sample (e.g., it does not look at source region). Each variable in the regressions is allowed to have immigrant and Canadian-born coefficients, and earnings differences are attributed either to differences in the distribution of the

Arthur Sweetman and Stephan McBride

Table 12: Predicted Earnings for Male Workers — 1996 Canadian Census

Field	Canadian-Born			Foreign-Educated Immigrants			Canadian-Educated Immigrants		
	College	Bachelor	Master's	College	Bachelor	Master's	College	Bachelor	Master's
Education									
Education	34508	51728	61029	32361	45492	49786	33566	42901	62006
Fine & AppliedArts									
FineArt	30857	30916	36812	27623	31298	40601	28657	25737	29238
Literature & Humanities									
History		45035	49052		38091	52211		35595	49805
Media	37124	42134	45995	34688	36890	59792	35745	35800	42006
English	-	40430	48475	-	36857	50340	-	29499	32162
French	-	-	-	-	-	-	-	-	-
Other Literature	32274	41943	48131	33363	33155	50668	-	37939	45406
Philosophy Theology	34515	37359	39093	30214	38573	44664	31586	32604	38251
Other Humanities	31978	37413	44153	25578	35247	41363	31193	28698	35717
Social Science									
Economics	40559	57224	70300	37047	44783	59314	41494	44595	57582
Geography	41470	49510	58197	41951	47569	53381	-	42588	57991
Political Science	36353	50312	56698	-	40335	49261	-	39978	44728
Psychology	31894	45992	53392	-	38249	58201	39017	36782	48760
Sociology Criminology	47468	48288	56598	28596	38042	41889	47464	39066	42133
Specialized Admin	40987	60764	71972	34596	48993	51438	39855	46523	69496
Commerce	45270	63118	79803	38021	44671	69032	39468	44796	69656
Finance	45391	66606	79757	39969	49888	68509	41796	51328	70938
Secretarial Studies	38258			33852			44084		
Marketing		60123	74037		48342	70588		45773	52854
Law	46291	80270	88305	37058	49036	56317	39625	58433	69282
Other Social Science	48220	49914	58378	35456	41540	50721	46606	37475	54092
Agricultural & BioScience									
Agriculture	33194	49861	53747	30463	38852	45657	31332	34937	57102
Biology		50992	56310		35415	61688		40013	55016
Other Life Science	42950	48493	60765	38635	42309	58474	44059	37226	59605
Household Science	32351			33664			36968		
Fish Wildlife Manage	39097			34945			45024		
Engineer&Applied Science									
Architecture		47085	46908		37653	58003		33371	40712
Other Engineering		69742	76387	-	55152	74788	-	55764	68119
Chemical Engineering		82317	86761		59892	76956		58776	73507
Civil Engineering		68164	80441		48463	64948		54139	66762
Electrical Engineering		77789	76228		56088	86981		55651	78278
Mechanical Engineer		71907	81460		50599	76136		56611	69454
Forestry	43935	69000	73024	29181	37323	44126	42933	52257	-
Landscape Architect	41357			36337			38653		
Health Professions									
Medicine		71740	109318		56821	110843		62913	102741
Other Health			67339			65371			59175
Nursing	46017	54595		45268	52501		36768	37971	
Medical Assistant	35495			34973			32436		
Public Health	50301	-		50820	-		46703	-	
Rehab. Medicine	-	-	-						
Medical Technician	45790	52685		38932	46808		49182	39980	
Math & Physical Sciences									
Mathematics		63949	69094		49473	62676		50527	60292
Computer Science		66870	73660		61901	84216		54171	76782
Chemistry	53466	59507	62099	40274	47987	61983	55475	45154	55013
Physics	-	56918	63514	44791	45694	64487	-	46944	57009
Earth Science	45769	59168	63560	38258	50516	57030	45905	43501	58983
Other Science	42063	55874	56101	36122	42399	73087	37635	44120	51824
Other									
Trades	42071	71466	-	39584	45908	-	41399	-	-
Electronic Technology	48113			40837			45484		
Environment Tech	49349			47246			48322		
Mechanic	47526			41150			44176		
Building Technology	47112			38596			44068		
Transport Technology	49394			42020			48787		
Other Fields	42277	53517	50285	36508	52038	61306	38828	51308	58533

Source: 1996 Canadian Census. Dashes imply that the cell contents are suppressed for reasons of confidentiality.

underlying characteristics, or differences in the return to (i.e., the co-efficient for) each characteristic, which reflect how the same characteristic (as measured by the census) is valued in the labour market on average for each group.

$$\ln(earnings) = X_{CB}\beta_{CB} + \varepsilon_{CB}$$
(2) *and*
$$\ln(earnings) = X_{imm}\beta_{imm} + \varepsilon_{imm}$$

where "*CB*" indicates "Canadian-Born", "*imm*" immigrant (either Canadian- or foreign-educated since each is compared to the Canadian-born in turn), X is the data, β a vector of coefficients, and ε an error term. The first regression is estimated using only the Canadian-born data, and the second only the immigrant data for whichever group is of interest. Predictions are then made for each regression at its own mean values of the X's, and at the other groups' mean values. Differences between various sets of these predictions are the focus of attention. In particular, one can ask questions such as: What would average immigrant wages be if they had the Canadian-born's set of fields of study (endowments) but their own returns (coefficients)? What if they had their own field endowments, but the Canadian-born coefficients? These types of counterfactuals are the subject of Tables 13 and 14. In these tables, three sets of numbers are presented for each set of variables of interest. For each, a positive value indicates that the Canadian-born have an earnings advantage (a positive gap) relative to the relevant immigrant group (either Canadian- or foreign-educated), whereas a negative number implies the reverse. All such earnings gap estimates are in percentages, and are from regressions that control for the observable characteristics. The first number is the difference in earnings attributable to the set of variables indicated. For example, in Table 13, the age coefficients for foreign-educated females with a college certificate (upper left-hand corner of the table) are associated with 32.7% larger earnings for the immigrant group relative to the Canadian-born (i.e., the negative sign implies the immigrant group has an earnings premium). The second number, −1.5, suggests that differences in the age variable itself play only a small part in generating this difference.

Most of the earnings gap comes from differences in the return to age, with all female subgroups of immigrants having much higher returns, that is, for female immigrants earnings increase with age much more quickly than they do for the Canadian-born. This likely results from age reflecting

Arthur Sweetman and Stephan McBride

both the earnings effects of increasing age (and relatedly potential labour market experience) and years since migration. Recall that the regressions underlying these decompositions cannot contain variables such as years since migration variables since they are not available for the Canadian-born. Thus, this makes sense since we are not controlling for the immigrant integration effect, and integration is correlated with age — immigrants appear to have a much steeper age-earnings profile because, in this context, age is measuring both its own effect and that associated with economic integration.

Table 13 examines female earnings in 1996, and has eight columns. The first four present results for the foreign-educated immigrants, and the next for the Canadian-educated ones. Results are presented for six sets, or groups, of coefficients. The way that these are set up, a positive number indicates the percentage earnings advantage for the Canadian-born, while a negative number indicates the advantage for the immigrant group in question. For the first column, immigrants are seen to have an advantage in every category except visible-minority status.

The effect for the language coefficients is worth discussing. Across all of the regressions in Table 13, the effects are large and negative. That in column (1) implies a 50% earnings advantage for foreign-educated immigrants — recalling the descriptive statistics in Tables 1 and 2, college graduate immigrant women are more likely to speak neither official language, and less likely to speak French. Also, their return to speaking English, or both official languages, is very substantial, and the return to speaking French is modest for both groups. The overall effect of the endowments is close to zero, but the remarkable earnings advantage obtained by those who speak English or are bilingual provides them with an overall earnings advantage in terms of language. Therefore, it appears that, holding the other characteristics constant, those females who report speaking neither English nor French have earnings comparable to similar Canadian-born workers, but those who do speak one or both of the official languages have a substantial earnings premium. Although the magnitude varies, this effect is obvious for all the columns in the table, except the Canadian-educated PhDs. Of course, these are correlations, not causal impacts.

Despite having an earnings advantage in almost every category, we saw earlier in the descriptive statistics that the foreign-educated immigrant group on average earns less, not more, than their Canadian-born counter-parts. For reasons that are not related to the observed factors in these regressions, the immigrants have a very large earnings disadvantage, as

Table 13: Female Earnings Decompositions — 1996 Canadian Census

	Foreign-Educated Immigrants				Canadian-Educated Immigrants			
	College	Bachelor	Master's	PhD	College	Bachelor	Master's	PhD
AGE	-32.7	-17.7	-22.3	-129.3	-17.8	-9.1	-21.8	-44.4
Endowments	-1.5	-6.9	-3.8	-2.1	-0.4	-0.5	-2.3	-1.6
Coefficients	-31.2	-10.8	-18.7	-127.1	-17.4	-8.6	-19.6	-42.6
PROVINCE	-4.5	-0.9	0.3	14.5	-1.8	.2	1.9	17.6
Endowments	-2.7	-1.9	-0.4	-1.2	-3.1	-2.5	-0.2	-1.9
Coefficients	-1.9	1	0.6	15.9	1.3	4.4	2.1	19.7
CMAs	-5.5	-13.3	-7.5	-11.1	-8.5	-7.2	10.8	6.4
Endowments	-11.4	-7.3	-3.9	0.5	-8.7	-5.9	-3.6	1.9
Coefficients	5.9	-6	-3.6	-11.6	0.2	-1.3	14.4	4.5
FIELD	-2.3	-9.3	-4.7	18.3	-2	-1.5	0	7.3
Endowments	-0.3	-3	-0.8	-0.9	0.6	-0.9	-0.3	1.2
Coefficients	-2	-6.3	-3.9	19.2	-2.6	-0.6	0.3	6.1
VISMIN	0.8	7.8	3.3	7.1	1.1	3.6	3.5	2.6
Endowments	1.1	-0.9	0.7	1.1	0.7	-0.5	0.5	0.7
Coefficients	-0.3	8.7	2.6	6	0.4	4.1	3	1.9
LANGUAGE	-50.3	-67.2	-53.2	-116.1	-153.4	-53	-155.9	4
Endowments	0.4	4.8	-0.9	4.4	0.1	1.3	-0.2	1.9
Coefficients	-50.7	-72	-52.3	-120.5	-153.5	-54.3	-155.7	2.1
TOTAL	7.2	35.9	46	24.6	-5.3	1.2	5.7	-1
Endowments	-14.4	-19.6	-8.5	-2.4	-10.7	-10.1	-6.2	0.8
Coefficients	-80.3	-108.4	-97.3	-296.7	-171.6	-83.2	-248.9	-19
Shift Paramtr.	101.9	163.9	151.7	323.8	177	94.5	260.8	17.2

Source: 1996 Canadian Census.
Notes: Positive values denote Canadian-born earnings advantages (%); negative values denote immigrant earnings advantages (%).

Arthur Sweetman and Stephan McBride

reflected in the shift, or intercept, term. Since only common factors are included in the decompositions, the shift parameter includes the average effects of age at immigration, place of origin, economic integration and other unobserved factors. Thus, overall, the college graduate foreign-educated female immigrants in column (1) earn 7.2% less (or the Canadian-born earn 7.2% more); the immigrants have an advantage on the observable characteristics, but start from a much lower base. Most of the other educational categories in this table have a broadly similar result: the Canadian-born have a large earnings advantage for unobserved reasons that might include factors such as the quality of language knowledge, Canada-specific skills, lack of credential recognition, discrimination or other issues.

Focusing on field of study, in Table 13 for females and Table 14 for males, differences in the current distributions of field are not seen to have consistently large impacts on earnings differences between the Canadian-born and the various immigrant groups (as opposed to across fields within groups where large differences were seen earlier). For females, the magnitude of the impact of field of study is not large compared to that of other variables, while for men it is of a comparable influence to the other sets of characteristics under study. Nevertheless, in most columns the immigrants have a small earnings advantage because of their being somewhat more likely to be in higher valued fields of study. Although, as seen earlier, there is great heterogeneity among fields of study, it appears that the differences between the Canadian-born and each immigrant group never explain more than a 14% earnings difference, and for some groups close to none of the difference is explained. In all cases for the males, and most of those for the females, the field endowments have a negative sign, suggesting that the various immigrant groups have, compared to the Canadian-born, a distribution of fields that is associated with higher earnings. However, the magnitude of the effect is always small, never more than 5.6%. The coefficients (the relative economic return to fields) provide more mixed results, sometimes being associated with relatively higher earnings for immigrants, but frequently the reverse is true (especially for the males). Thus, if immigrants had the same distribution of fields of study as the Canadian-born, most subgroups would suffer an earnings loss relative to the Canadian-born. This is consistent with the results observed in the regressions and the tables showing the distribution of immigrants across fields. Of course, policy could be used to change the distribution of field of study among immigrants and increase the fraction in high-paying fields. Note, that this analysis measures the importance of the current distribution of field of study in explaining existing differences in earnings;

Table 14: Male Earnings Decompositions — 1996 Canadian Census

	Foreign-Educated Immigrants				Canadian-Educated Immigrants			
	College	Bachelor	Master's	PhD	College	Bachelor	Master's	PhD
AGE	-11.6	-6.6	17.4	-45.1	-0.7	-3.8	0.9	51.2
Endowments	-3.9	-8	-1.2	-1.5	-0.4	-0.7	-1	-3.8
Coefficients	-7.7	1.4	18.5	-43.7	-0.3	-3.1	2	5.5
PROVINCE	0.2	5.3	-0.1	0.9	-6.4	-3.8	6	9.8
Endowments	-3.5	-3.3	-1.4	1.4	-3.7	-3.1	-1.4	0.4
Coefficients	3.4	8.5	1.2	-0.5	-2.7	-0.8	7.5	9.2
CMAs	8	14.4	9.7	7.4	0	-3.4	0	3.3
Endowments	-5	-4.1	-3.6	-2.7	-3.9	-3	-2.2	-1.6
Coefficients	13	18.5	13.3	10.1	3.9	-0.4	2.2	4.9
FIELD	0	7	-13.7	-17.4	1.8	3.7	9.3	-0.4
Endowments	-0.6	-5.6	-5.2	-3.7	-0.4	-2.7	-3.2	-1.6
Coefficients	0.6	12.6	-8.5	-13.7	2.2	6.4	12.5	1.2
VISMIN	12.8	23.5	12.2	10.4	6.1	7.8	4.7	3
Endowments	3.9	9.7	7.8	10.4	2.4	5.4	4.7	6.6
Coefficients	8.9	13.8	4.4	0	3.7	2.4	0	-3.6
LANGUAGE	-2.5	-3.6	-27.8	-23.7	3.3	-2.4	19.4	7.3
Endowments	0.6	4.5	0.7	10.9	-0.1	2.7	1.2	6.8
Coefficients	-3.1	-8.1	-28.5	-34.6	3.4	-5.1	18.2	0.5
TOTAL	15.4	38.1	38.2	16.5	-3.7	5.7	2.5	-4.8
Endowments	-8.5	-11.1	-3.6	4.4	0.4	-4.2	-3.4	0.2
Coefficients	15.1	28.7	-14.8	-97.6	-6.1	-4.6	50.8	73
Shift Paramtr.	8.8	20.5	56.6	109.7	10.2	14.5	-44.9	-78

Source: 1996 Canadian Census.

Notes: Positive values denote Canadian-born earnings advantages (%); negative values denote immigrant earnings advantages (%).

Arthur Sweetman and Stephan McBride

it says nothing about what might occur if field of study were added to the points system.

The pattern of decompositions across census years was conducted for the 1986 and 1991 censuses, but is not presented since it is broadly similar, though the shift parameter is not as empirically important in 1991 for the females and the PhD column varies for both sexes (as seen in Tables 1 and 2, the PhD sample size is the smallest of the education groups and, therefore, the results for that level should be viewed as having less precision). As has been seen in much previous research (e.g., Schaafsma and Sweetman, 2001), the 1996 census reported worse outcomes for recent immigrants than had earlier censuses. These tables suggest that the origin of this phenomenon does not rest in any of the observed characteristics that are common to immigrants and the Canadian-born, including field of study. It is plausible that the business cycle played an important role, but there is no evidence other than the dating of the censuses to substantiate this hypothesis in the data employed in this study.

Conclusion

Overall, the analysis finds that postsecondary field of study is an important determinant of earnings for both the Canadian-born and immigrant populations. However, while immigrants are more likely to be in a higher paying field, the difference is relatively small. Although we only present results from the 1996 census, a similar analysis was conducted for the 1986 and 1991 censuses, and the pattern of results was consistent.

Turning to the details of the analysis, first, to facilitate the study conceptually, the working age population under study was initially divided into 18 subpopulations identified by: sex (female and male), immigrant classification (those born in Canada, Canadian-educated immigrants, and foreign-educated), and highest postsecondary degree (college, bachelor's and master's). Since there are 54 fields of study, although not all apply to each level of education, these subpopulations reduce the parsimony of the study, but are required to facilitate a meaningful analysis of a heterogeneous issue. Further, to provide the context for the exploration of postsecondary field of study, initial descriptive statistics looking across levels of education are provided for each of the six sex-immigrant/Canadian-born groups. The most striking general observation across all levels of education is that, for both sexes, Canadian-educated immigrants have extremely good labour market outcomes, in terms of earnings, hours per week, and weeks per year. They are better than those for the Canadian-born, and far better than those for foreign-educated immigrants. In part, this is because Canadian-educated immigrants have high levels of education. In contrast, immigrants without a Canadian education have fewer years of education, are less likely to have had work in the year, and have lower earnings.

There are also very sizable differences in demographic characteristics across the six sex-immigrant/Canadian-born groups. For both sexes, the foreign-educated are the oldest of the groups, and they are almost alone in having a sizable fraction of individuals who speak neither of Canada's official languages. A high fraction of those who speak neither language have less than a high school education. On other dimensions, both immigrant groups (Canadian- and foreign-educated) are dramatically more likely to be a visible minority and live in an urban area.

Initial descriptive statistics by field of study for the three selected levels of education show all three groups to have quite different distributions across field of study. Especially for females, but also for males, the Canadian-born group is much more likely, two to three times, to have a teaching degree. Immigrants, especially immigrant females compared to Canadian-born females, are much more likely to be in engineering and applied science, or in math, physical sciences and medicine. In general, female immigrants are more likely to enter "traditionally male", and higher paying, disciplines that are science or math related than are Canadian-born females (for example, economics comprises 1.34% of female Canadian-born bachelor's degrees, but 3.86 and 3.24 of the foreign- and Canadian-educated immigrant ones).

Simple descriptive statistics of mean salaries by group and field show many differences across fields within levels of education that are on the order of 30 to 50% for the Canadian-born. For example, in 1996 Canadian-born male graduates with a bachelor's degree in English received, on average, $35,389 per year, whereas mechanical engineers received $55,987. Females, on average, had lower earnings, but the gaps across fields were similar: fine art graduates earned $21,335, whereas those in mathematics received $35,259 (mechanical engineering was $42,168). Canadian-educated immigrants have comparable, or higher, earnings to the Canadian-born, but the foreign-educated immigrants have lower ones. Further, the field of study differentials within the foreign-educated subgroup are not as large.

At the bachelor's level, the statistical regressions reinforce the observation that the differences between fields is not as large for immigrants, especially for the foreign-educated, as it is for the Canadian-born. This is not to say that no field differences exist, or that the pattern is perfectly "smooth", but that there is a general tendency for fields with positive premia for the Canadian-born to have a reduction in that premium observed for the immigrant subsample (although the premia remain substantial).

For college graduates there are far fewer differences in field of study premia between the Canadian-born and immigrant populations. The premia by field are, however, broadly similar with the more science and technology oriented fields having greater earnings along with those in business, law and related fields. At the master's level the pattern is quite different. Field of study premia are still observed, but foreign-educated immigrants with a master's degree generally have positive premia relative to the Canadian-born, especially in the lower paying arts, and literature and humanities fields. This, once again, serves to reduce the differential between the high- and low-paying fields for the immigrant population relative to the Canadian-born one.

Predictions based on the regressions above reinforce the earnings differences observed previously across both levels of education and fields of study in terms that are readily interpretable. On average, those with higher levels of education, and in fields in sciences (though not agricultural and biological sciences) and many of the non-traditional social sciences (e.g., business), tend to have higher earnings. These two factors trade off against each other and, on average, those with college level degrees in physical sciences and trades have earnings that are comparable, and for the males frequently higher, than those with bachelor's degrees in fine and applied arts, and humanities. In comparing both immigrant groups to the Canadian-born, it is important to recall that the predictions are for the average source region and birth cohort, and for those who arrive between the ages of 15 and 20. For most fields, immigrants are observed to have earnings that are below those of Canadian-born individuals in the same field and that the gaps are sometimes substantive. For example, Canadian-born females with a bachelor's degree in psychology earn $31,229, on average, compared to $25,256 for foreign-educated immigrants, and $24,838 for those with at least some education in Canada. For high-paying fields, the dollar gaps can be much larger. Many of these gaps across the Canadian-born and immigrant groups are accentuated in the predictions relative to the descriptive statistics. This arises from differences in the samples and the procedure employed; the counterfactual sets characteristics to be the same across the three groups (except for those defining the cell for the prediction, and the immigrant-specific variables). However, immigrants tend to have characteristics that are associated with higher earnings (e.g., they tend to be more urbanized), and when the effect of these characteristics is removed, the earnings gap between immigrants and the Canadian-born increases.

A set of (Oaxaca-Blinder type) decompositions are used to compare each immigrant group to its Canadian-born counterpart within each degree level. This analysis allows any differences to be decomposed into differences in endowments, and the return on those endowments. Field of study is treated as one type of endowment and it is found to explain at most about 14% of the difference in earnings between the two groups. Age, associated within the range of a 20 to 30% premium for the various immigrant female groups, though somewhat less for the males, and language, associated with an over 50% premium for the females, but again less for the males, appear to be much more important characteristics economically for the females and equally important for the males. Thus, field of study is a relatively more important predictor of earnings differences with the Canadian-born for males than females. However, for the females none of the observed characteristics explain as much as is left unexplained. For males, the observed characteristics explain a much higher fraction of the variance in earnings, but the "shift parameter" — a measure of differences that are not associated with the observed characteristics — remains quite large. Immigrants almost always have economic advantages in terms of their characteristics, and they frequently have returns to those characteristics that are greater than those of the Canadian-born, but they almost always have an even larger deficit in terms of characteristics associated with their immigrant status (such as time in Canada).

Overall, there are sizeable earnings differences across fields of study, and these differences are observed for both immigrant groups and the Canadian-born. However, the magnitude of the differences are, in general, slightly smaller for the immigrant groups, especially the foreign-educated, compared to the Canadian-born. Thus, British Columbia's approach to finding high-earning immigrants, described in the introduction, receives support from this study. That is, Canadian-educated immigrants have extremely good labour market outcomes, and the fields that British Columbia's government identified also tend to have higher than average earnings.

This study does not look at the impact that this type of focused immigration policy, were it expanded in scale, might have on those already working in the Canadian labour market (both Canadian-born and previous entry cohorts of immigrants). This is an area that should be explored in

Arthur Sweetman and Stephan McBride

future research should the policy of targeting immigrants by field of study be pursued, especially if the fraction of immigrants in such fields grows substantially. Relatedly, it would be worth considering the social impacts of an immigrant pool comprised largely of individuals from a narrow set of fields of study.

If field of study were to be used in the points system, it would also be advantageous to collect data on field of study at landing — that is, the field that would be employed by the points system. For the foreign-educated, the field observed in the census is that at landing, but this need not be the case for those with Canadian education since the field of their highest level of postsecondary may have changed, or been established for the first time, following their arrival in Canada. While some of the Canadian-educated arrived in Canada at a sufficiently young age that they would not have entered postsecondary before landing, there is a substantial group of the Canadian-educated for whom the field recorded in the census may not reflect the one that would have been observed at landing. In a similar vein, for policy purposes with respect to the points system, field of study is only relevant for those who are assessed under that system. The census data employed in this study do not allow immigrant class to be observed; collecting information that allowed field to be identified along with immigrant category would be valuable.

Beyond the points system this study gives insight into the economic integration and labour market performance of immigrants to Canada. It suggests that the economic premia associated with field is quite important, but it appears not to be as important for immigrants as for the Canadian-born since the differences between the high- and low-earnings fields of study are usually smaller for the immigrant groups. It also shows that there is great economic value in Canadian education.

References

Baker, M. and D. Benjamin (1994), "The Performance of Immigrants in the Canadian Labor Market", *Journal of Labor Economics* 12(3), 369–405.

Benjamin, D., M. Gunderson and W.C. Riddell (1998), *Labour Market Economics: Theory, Evidence and Policy in Canada,* 4th ed. (Toronto: McGraw-Hill, Ryerson).

Bloom, D.E., G. Grenier and M. Gunderson (1995), "The Changing Labor Market Position of Canadian Immigrants", *Canadian Journal of Economics* 28(4), 987–1005.

Borjas, G.J. (1985), "Assimilation, Change in Cohort Quality, and the Earnings of Immigrants", *Journal of Labor Economics* 3(4), 463–489.

_____ (1993), "Immigration Policy, National Origin and Immigrant Skills: A Comparison of Canada and the United States", in D. Card and R. Freeman (eds.), *Small Differences that Matter: Labor Markets and Income Maintenance in Canada and the United States* (Chicago: University of Chicago Press).

_____ (1995), "Assimilation and Changes in Cohort Quality Revisited: What Happened to Immigrant Earnings in the 1980s?" *Journal of Labor Economics* 13(2), 201–245.

Chiswick, B.R. (1978), "The Effect of Americanization on the Earnings of Foreign-Born Men", *Journal of Political Economy* 86(5), 897–921.

Côté, S. and A. Sweetman (2000), "Does It Matter What I Study? Post-Secondary Field of Study and Labour Market Outcomes in Canada", WRNET Working Paper (Vancouver: UBC).

Duan, N. (1983), "Smearing Estimate: A Nonparametric Retransformation Method", *Journal of the American Statistical Association* 78, 605–610.

Ferrer, A.M. and W.C. Riddell (2002), "Educational Credential and Immigrant Assimilation" (Vancouver: Department of Economics, University of British Columbia). Unpublished paper.

Finnie, R. (2001), "Fields of Plenty, Fields of Lean: The Early Labour Market Outcomes of Canadian University Graduates by Discipline", *The Canadian Journal of Higher Education* 21(1),141–176.

Li, P.S. (2001), "The Market Worth of Immigrants' Educational Credentials", *Canadian Public Policy/Analyse de Politiques* 27(1), 23–38.

Schaafsma, J. and A. Sweetman (2001), "Immigrant Earnings: Age at Immigration Matters", *Canadian Journal of Economics* 34(4), 1066–1099.

Comments

Louis Grignon

I am happy to be discussing the papers by Bert Waslander and by Abdurrahman Aydemir. These are two good papers. They focus on a similar topic, but they take different approaches and I learned something from both.

Let me start by talking a bit about Bert Waslander's paper. The paper tries to explain the falling earnings of new immigrant men in the 1990s. It underlines that the decline was substantial: a decline of $12,000 constant dollars to a level of $13,000 between 1980 and 1995. It uses a human capital model and census data from 1981, 1986, 1991, and 1996 and concentrates on eight large Canadian cities. The human capital model is a basic model with eight variables, including visible minority status and education, and is augmented with a moving average of three years of the unemployment rate. New immigrants are defined as those who came in the two to four-year period prior to the survey year.

The results are a bit tentative and the author is careful about that. He says that unemployment may have played a role but the results are not that robust. There is no way to tell whether earnings of immigrants have become more sensitive to the unemployment rate or not. Still, the paper concludes that unemployment cannot be the only factor behind the decline in earnings of immigrants over the last ten years. It states that ethnic composition and greater discounting of the education and experience of recent immigrants are also important factors. The paper contains a very large period effect that accounts for almost half of the decline, and I think it is fair to say that this is a measure of our ignorance about what really caused the decline.

What I liked about the paper is the focus on earnings of all individuals including those who did not work to capture both wage and employment effects. I like the use of four censuses instead of one or two. I like the good, catchy introduction that explains well the rationale of the study. What I especially like is the effort at making the results tangible, providing a few key figures that would translate the technical results into results that are tangible for policymakers or lay persons. This is very important and I encourage researchers to try to do this, to go that one step further and to translate their results into the tangible numbers to which the average person can relate.

What are my suggestions and comments for improvement? I would suggest exploiting the city dimension of the study. You should explain why only eight cities are included in the paper. The human capital model used is a bit basic, and some variables could be added — language, country of origin, occupation, and other personal characteristics. Some of the discussion I found a bit cryptic and it would benefit from some further discussion. I would encourage that the Figures 2 and 3 show Canada minus the eight cities instead of Canada as a whole. It would then be a more interesting chart.

Now, let me turn to Abdurrahman Aydemir's paper. I really liked the paper; it is an impressive effort. I encourage people to read it. The author is trying to disentangle cyclical from non-cyclical effects on the labour market outcomes of immigrants. He looks at both the impact on employment and labour force participation. He evaluates separately the entry effect and the contemporaneous effect of the labour market condition. The main hypothesis or the main question the paper is trying to address is: Does the timing of immigration have a permanent scarring effect on future labour market performance?

The data — again its very innovative aspect — are 19 annual cross-sections of the Survey of Consumer Finances (SCF). This gets around the problem of small sample in the SCF. The analysis is restricted to males 25–55; that is an aspect I like less. Why always study only men? Women are working in the labour market. They are an important group and we should do more to study them.

The model again is a human capital model with a lot more variables though — education, age, mother tongue — augmented with the region of residence, size of region, marital status, etc., years since migration both in level and quadratic and a cohort dummy and unemployment rate at both entry and survey years.

The results can be summarized in one sentence — it is the economy stupid! The author finds that macro conditions at entry have small permanent effects and that the economic condition in later years has a more important effect. The inclusion of macro controls reduces significantly the size of the cohort effect and that is what I am not too sure about. The inclusion of the macro controls looks a lot like a set of cohort dummies and I think there may be a problem of multi-colinearity in the results as well. When you see parameters becoming insignificant it just means we do not know exactly what the size of the impact is. That does not mean there is no impact. So, I am not fully convinced by the interpretation of the results given by the author. Maybe I am tough to convince, but I am not fully convinced.

What I like about the paper is that it is a very original, thorough piece of research, a massive undertaking, and an innovative way of exploiting the SCF. A few suggestions: there is a need to spell out the implications further. What do the results mean? Work on the conclusion a bit. Make results more tangible, and there you could borrow a page from Bert Waslander's paper in trying to pick up a few numbers and make them sing, make them tell the story. It is useful for policymakers. When you say the results are "significant", or "large", or "small" it means something to you, but the policymaker does not have a way to see if it is important for him or her. I would also present the results for the control variables, the X matrix. I was looking all over for them and they are not in the paper. I agree that the focus of the presentation should not be on these results but they should be somewhere in the paper.

In summary, this is a very nice piece of work, but I am not sure I buy the main conclusions. I think the main policy implications could be stated as: the labour market at entry has some scarring effects, and we need to give serious consideration to adjusting the level of immigration over the business cycle, otherwise there are costs both contemporaneously and in the long term with a potentially permanent impact on the labour market performance of immigrants in the economy.

Section VII

Social Inclusion and Immigrant Integration

Occupational Dimensions of Immigrant Credential Assessment: Trends in Professional, Managerial and Other Occupations, 1970–1996

Jeffrey G. Reitz

The potential for proper assessment and recognition of immigrants' foreign-acquired credentials may vary among occupational fields for several reasons. Occupations vary in the importance attached to specific education-based skills, and they vary in the nature of the procedures used for assessing such skills. They also vary in the importance attached to other types of skills. And finally, they vary in the skills profiles of applicant pools available at any one time. All these variations may have significant implications for immigrants, because they may carry implications for how employers are likely to respond to qualifications with which they are unfamiliar, such as those that immigrants bring with them from their respective countries of origin. Hence an examination of immigrant credential assessment on an occupation-specific basis may be very helpful in understanding the transferability of immigrant qualifications.

Over time, these occupation-specific processes may be changing with the emergence of the knowledge economy, and these changes also may

This research has been supported by a grant from the Social Sciences and Humanities Research Council of Canada. The technical assistance of Michelle Maneck and Stephanie Choquette is gratefully acknowledged.

carry implications for trends in immigrant employment success. An increasingly knowledge-based economy produces changes in the occupational structure, in processes for skills assessment within occupations, and in the supply of highly-educated native-born workers. Hence skill-assessment processes encountered by successive cohorts of newly-arriving immigrants also may be changing.

Occupational variations in immigrant credential assessment also may have important policy implications. Although labour force studies of immigrants rarely have included analyses of occupational differences, most discussions of remedial measures assume that occupation-specific procedures must be addressed (e.g., Conger, 1994; Conger and Bezanson, 1996; Cumming, Lee and Oreopoulos, 1989; Mata, 1994; McDade, 1988; Ontario Ministry of Training, Colleges and Universities, 2002; Skills for Change, 1995; Training and Development Associates, 1999). For example, the policy focus on the regulated professions might seem to suggest a prevailing belief that those occupations are most significant in the under-utilization of immigrant skills, but evidence on this point is lacking.

The following analysis focuses on variations among professional and managerial occupations in the immigrant skill validation process, and on ways in which institutional changes associated with the emergence of a knowledge economy may be affecting immigrant employment success. After a review of theoretical considerations and possibilities, an analysis will be presented focusing on immigrants arriving in Canada between 1970 and 1995, based on public-use sample data from four successive censuses between 1981 and 1996.

Immigrant Credential Assessment in the Knowledge Economy

Immigrants in Canada today are being recruited on the basis of skills potentially enabling their employment in occupations and professions of the emerging knowledge economy — and this has raised important new questions about processes of immigrant integration and adjustment.

In the past, prior to the introduction of points-based selection criteria in the late 1960s, most immigrants tended to possess few credentialed skills. The expectation was that they would assume relatively low-level positions in unskilled or semi-skilled occupations, or at best among the skilled trades.

In that situation, the process of immigrant settlement and adjustment hinged largely upon such matters as labour demand in particular industries; access to appropriate job-related information, to networks of contact, and to unionized sectors; and the additional possibility of discrimination based on immigrant status or origins. Employer recognition of education-based skills was a relatively minor part of the process.

However, with the advent of the knowledge economy — producing growth of professional and managerial occupations requiring high levels of education, and rapid increases in native-born university and other educational credentials — the importance of educational credentials for immigrants has increased substantially. It became expected that immigrants should compete directly with native-born workers in highly-skilled occupations.

Since the 1960s this objective has been served by means of skills-based immigrant selection criteria (the points system). Initially, skills-based selection worked fairly well, in the sense that the new immigrants — from more diverse origins around the world — on average had higher levels of education than native-born Canadians, and were fairly successful in gaining access to skilled employment. This was true despite the fact that their credentials were often significantly discounted by Canadian employers (Baker and Benjamin, 1994; Li, 2001; Reitz, 2001a; see also Watt and Bloom, 2001). Immigrants received substantially lower earnings premiums for qualifications such as education and experience, compared to native-born workers. Earnings disadvantages are particularly large for immigrants from non-European backgrounds most distant from the mainstream population in terms of racial or cultural characteristics (Reitz and Sklar, 1997). At the same time, because of their substantial educational lead over native-born Canadians, many of these immigrants achieved considerable employment success and relatively few fell into poverty.

The reasons for the discounting of immigrant credentials are poorly understood. No doubt employers often lack familiarity with standards of education or professional practice in many other countries. An important issue is whether — or the extent to which — immigrant qualifications are truly transferable and equivalent to those of the native-born. If they are not equivalent, then the discounting of those qualifications by employers would represent entirely appropriate labour market behaviour: hiring on the basis of capacity to do the job. However, to the extent they are equivalent, then the discounting of those qualifications would amount to a form of employment discrimination, and would represent a significant waste of valuable human capital.

Over time, the employment situation of newly-arriving immigrants has become much more difficult. The earnings of newly-arriving immigrants has fallen substantially over the period since the 1970s, and reached particularly low levels during the early 1990s. Although some of this most recent experience undoubtedly was affected by the severe recession, analysis of longer term trends points to institutional change as a more enduring basis for the downward trend (Reitz, 2001b). There are indications as well that the discounting of immigrant educational qualifications may be increasing in Canada (Reitz, 2001b, 2003a), a trend which also suggests the potential significance of institutional change.

One aspect of institutional change concerns the trend towards increased levels of education. Average educational levels in the native-born Canadian workforce have risen very rapidly, more rapidly in fact than those of immigrants during most of the 1970s and 1980s, and the result has been that the immigrant advantage in education credentials has been substantially eroded (Reitz, 2001b, pp. 596–601). The impact on immigrants of the rapid increase in native-born education is compounded, of course, by discounting of immigrants' education. The significance of the impact of educational expansion in Canada on immigrants is reflected in comparative trends in the United States. Educational expansion in the United States has slowed, and the advantage that immigrants in Canada previously enjoyed relative to their American counterparts has been reduced (Reitz, 1998, 2001c, 2003b).

Criteria applied to educational qualifications in the labour market also appear to be changing. It is clear that over time in most industrial societies, there has been a general increase in the importance of higher education for access to employment opportunities across a wide range of occupations (Hunter, 1988; Hunter and Leiper, 1993; Baer, 1999). Most often, this change is attributed primarily to the increased impact of education on worker productivity in a technologically advanced post-industrial economy (Bell, 1973; Bell and Graubard, 1997). Possibly-related tendencies such as credentialism, the prestige value of education, and managerial cloning (Arrow, Bowles and Durlauf, 2000; Bowles and Gintis, 2000) also may be important. The changing role of education in labour markets is reflected in a range of institutional developments, including change in the organizational role of "personnel" and its professionalization in the form of "human resource management", changing relations between corporations and educational institutions in employee recruitment for certain critical occupations, rapid expansion of educational institutions themselves, and the development of professional schools oriented towards the needs of local labour markets.

In many respects, these economic and institutional changes may promote meritocracy and hence create pressures towards a more functionally-appropriate assessment of all credentials, including the foreign-acquired credentials of immigrants. At the economic level, human capital theory emphasizes that where education-based skills affect productivity, employers are under competitive pressure to seek the most highly educated and skilled workers, and to disregard personal characteristics irrelevant to productivity, such as gender, birthplace, ethnic origin, and race. The impact of any prejudices against immigrants, and in particular racial minority immigrants, would not necessarily be eliminated by such competitive pressures, but it would be expected to diminish. At the institutional level, codification of hiring and promotion procedures focusing on objective knowledge-based criteria could guard against arbitrary and potentially discriminatory practices. This would militate against undue and arbitrary dismissal of the relevance of foreign qualifications.

However, other aspects of these trends may work at cross-purposes, and undermine credential recognition for immigrants. At the economic level, transferability of foreign-acquired skills may be a problem, in terms of their functional relevance. There may be differences in occupational or educational standards in the immigrants' place of origin, or institutional differences which affect the nature of the skills required for work in particular occupations.

But even where transferability is not at issue, traditional prejudices may operate, and the institutional development of the knowledge economy itself may present barriers. Education may be valued for reasons other than its purely functional relevance, such as its prestige or authority-enhancing capacity, attributes which foreign credentials, and foreigners themselves, may lack. Some employers may tend to distrust the relevance of foreign qualifications because they lack familiarity with them, and because of a fear of the risks involved in "taking a chance" on what may be seen as an unknown quantity. Bureaucratic procedures in hiring may be tailored to local educational institutions, disadvantaging the foreign-trained. All these skill-recognition difficulties would compound other obstacles faced by immigrants, such as those based on language, ethnic or cultural background, or race.

Therefore, even in a labour market in which education-based skills are significant, and in which employers attempt to ensure compliance with meritocratic practice, immigrants may experience difficulty. Their inability to gain recognition for their foreign-acquired qualifications may become an important handicap in their settlement and adjustment. Which of these processes may predominate is difficult to predict, and the processes of change over time also are elusive.

Occupations, Credential Assessment and Immigrants

Occupational change, particularly in the most highly-skilled professional and managerial fields, is also a key part of the emerging knowledge economy. Occupations vary in the procedures that employers use to assess job qualifications. These differences could have impacts on immigrant credential assessment, and hence may provide important clues to the general nature of immigrant credential assessment.

Skill Assessment in Professional and Managerial Occupations

In this research, the focus is on analysis of specific occupational fields that differ by knowledge content, and on change over time in these occupations. Employment practices may be expected to vary according to the knowledge-content of the occupational field, the priority given to credential assessment, and the organizational processes involved. Hence, occupations may vary in how immigrant qualifications are likely to be assessed. As knowledge occupations grow in importance, and as institutional arrangements for the assessment of qualifications change, the employment experiences of immigrants may be expected to change.

Professional occupations have developed elaborate and often highly bureaucratized procedures for credential assessment, and the prevalence of these occupations has grown as a component of the workforce. Management occupations also often have very high educational requirements — and even higher earnings — but less codified entry procedures. At the same time, educational levels have increased across a wide range of occupations not normally considered as part of the knowledge economy.

Professional occupations in science and engineering, health sciences, education and social science-related fields have been given considerable attention in discussions of the emerging "knowledge class" (Bell, 1973, pp. 212 ff.). Presumably, these are the professions where there is a particularly strong connection between education and effective performance, so market pressures may be expected to offset any tendency to discount immigrant skills — certainly among immigrants from culturally similar groups, and to some extent even among racial minority immigrants. Institutional arrangements in professional occupations provide for the most careful evaluation of the credentials of job candidates, with detailed procedures to ensure the selection of the best possible candidate. In certain professional fields, the codification of standards in general is quite high relative to other occupations.

Within the professions, science-based fields such as the natural sciences and engineering, or medicine and health sciences (Cole, 1986), may have more stringently codified hiring criteria than professions with a stronger social component, such as education or social work. Professions also vary in the significance of their licensing bodies, particularly where the professional field involves direct relations with clients. The social dimension of some professional fields may thus involve serious difficulties for immigrants. Social criteria inevitably have a strong local component, and it is precisely the transferability from foreign to local that is at issue in the case of immigrants with foreign qualifications. Hence, there may be few opportunities for immigrants to demonstrate their capacity to operate in a local environment. This may lead to more discounting of foreign credentials in the very professions in which local criteria may be more likely to have weight relative to purely objective professional standards.

There is also significant variation in levels of educational qualification involved — bachelor's degree as opposed to higher post-graduate qualification — which might affect the competitive position of immigrants. The higher the level of qualification, presumably the greater the specificity of credentials, and the greater the potential to enforce meritocratic practice. Nevertheless, it may be difficult to predict the relative salience of the benefits that result from careful and intensive deliberation as opposed to the disadvantages that could result from possibly arbitrary bureaucratic procedures.

Certain managerial occupations, particularly in knowledge-intensive industries, also form part of the knowledge class, because effective management in these fields is more complex and demands an understanding of technical issues. Management positions include the highest levels within the most knowledge-intensive industries, such as many manufacturing enterprises, business services and finance, government, and the health and education sectors. This stands in contrast to management in retail or wholesale trade, for example, or in the personal service sector. Managers in knowledge-intensive industries often are recruited from the ranks of professionals. As will be seen, educational levels in these managerial occupations are quite high.

To the extent that hiring in knowledge-based managerial positions is parallel to that in the professions, the implications for immigrants might be similar. However, in managerial occupations, job candidates will be selected on the basis of criteria that are less strongly related to purely educational qualifications, criteria such as responsibility, leadership, and "perspective". Even managerial training may not ensure that the candidate possesses these qualities, so educational credentials may weigh less heavily in the final selection of candidates. Management is often regarded as being as much an "art" as a science, and so the required skills among these managers are less codified, and selection processes less bureaucratized, compared to the professions. Even in sectors such as health and education, where managers often are recruited from the ranks of the related professions, promotion may be based on a perception of managerial ability which is not measured exclusively in terms of professional advancement, and perhaps not even primarily in such terms.

The requirement for managers to exercise authority over other workers may lead to the use of social criteria not necessarily related to managerial know-how itself. Perceptions of the potential effectiveness of candidates for managerial positions may also be shaped by social characteristics seen as affecting their credibility as authority figures. Immigrants, particularly racial minority immigrants, may be seen as unlikely to command managerial authority in the workplace. As a result they may encounter a "glass ceiling" parallel to what has been experienced by women.

Based on a consideration of these professional/managerial differences in the specificity of skill assessment, it would be expected that skill discounting for immigrants would be less prominent in professional occupations, and more prominent in managerial occupations.

Many of the same considerations suggest that skill discounting may be greatest outside the "knowledge class" occupations altogether, in clerical and sales occupations, for example, and in factory work. Educational criteria are applied in many of these occupations, yet without the detailed focus on credential assessment more common in the knowledge occupations. Social criteria here also may override such technical assessments of educational backgrounds.

Institutional Change in the Knowledge Economy

There are three aspects of change over time which might carry implications for immigrants. One is the increase in the proportion of the workforce employed in knowledge occupations — the size of the "knowledge class".

To the extent that skill validation processes differ in these occupations, with consequences for immigrants, their growth in size over time would imply an increased impact on immigrants.

A second aspect is the possibility of change in the role of education in the occupational recruitment processes. Professionalization implies, among other changes, that educational criteria may become more highly specific, and organizational procedures for determining the qualifications of job candidates more formalized. These changes may take place relatively quickly in occupations within the knowledge economy, though they may also occur in other occupations with lower educational requirements. Changes in the role of education may affect the opportunities for immigrants to demonstrate the equivalence of their foreign-acquired qualifications.

Finally, a third aspect of change over time is the increase in the supply of highly educated native-born workers. If the increase is very rapid, employers may feel less pressure to consider foreign qualifications seriously. An ample supply of native-born competitors ensures that requirements can be met without taking whatever risks may be thought to be associated with hiring or promoting foreign-educated applicants.

In this context, it deserves mention that the impact of the changing educational profile of the workforce may vary by occupational sector. It is well-known that although educational standards have been increasing in professional and managerial occupations, they have increased even more rapidly in the less-skilled occupations. Moreover, educational levels have a significant impact on employment and employment earnings outside the knowledge occupations as well as within. Hence the negative impact on immigrants of an increased supply of highly educated native-born workers may be greater precisely in the occupations in which there are fewer organizational procedures to ensure adequate consideration of foreign qualifications. This suggests that highly-skilled immigrants may feel the impact of the non-recognition of their skills not only in their failure to gain access to professional or managerial occupations, but also in the even greater earnings disparities in their employment *outside* the knowledge occupations.

Data and Measures

The analysis will compare immigrant and native-born occupational attainment in knowledge occupations in various professional and managerial fields, and earnings differences both within and across occupations, by gender. In Canadian census data for 1981, 1986, 1991, and 1996, immigrants arriving in the most recent ten-year period are compared with the native-born population.[1] This enables us to consider how the entry of immigrants into the workforce is affected by changing labour market conditions. It also means that the entire analysis addresses characteristics of immigrants arriving since 1970, after skill-based selection was introduced.

Knowledge-based occupations were identified based on educational levels for persons classified by occupation, with consideration given also to industry of employment. The 1980 Standard Industrial Classification (SIC) is available for all four censuses. Occupation codes for 1981, 1986, and 1991 were based on the 1980 Standard Occupational Classification (1980 SOC). However, the 1980 SOC was not available in 1996. Instead,

---

[1]Sample sizes for the analysis, based on the population aged 20–64 with positive earnings, for each census year, are as follows:

	1981	1986	1991	1996
Men				
Born in Canada	102,895	107,323	172,889	159,548
Immigrants, last ten years	6,602	4,938	9,707	11,826
Other immigrants	18,445	20,376	31,358	27,378
Missing	170	232	2,456	1,445
Total	128,112	132,869	216,410	200,197
Women				
Born in Canada	72,973	83,395	147,322	140,779
Immigrants, last ten years	5,224	4,198	8,652	10,348
Other immigrants	12,532	15,318	25,466	23,343
Missing	117	175	2,070	1,148
Total	90,846	103,086	183,510	175,618
Grand Total	218,958	235,955	399,920	375,815

Jeffrey G. Reitz

in 1991 a new Standard Occupational Classification (1991 SOC) was introduced, which distinguished occupations specifically on the basis of four skill levels from low to high: I , II, III, and IV; this was continued for 1996. Hence the time-series is divided into two segments: 1981–1986–1991, and 1991–1996, with the latter based on the more skill-based coding.

Knowledge occupations include two main groups: professions and management. In the 1980 SOC classification for 1981, 1986, and 1991, the professional categories include natural sciences and engineering, social sciences and related occupations, health occupations and occupations in education. In each case, levels of education are quite high and do not vary greatly by industry of employment. Therefore, anyone employed in these occupations was considered as working in a knowledge occupation. In the 1991 classification (1991 SOC) the classification of professionals includes only those at skill level IV, a somewhat higher standard than for the 1980 SOC. Specific professional fields such as science and engineering also can be identified.

In management occupations, average levels of education vary widely by industry. Levels of education are highest for managers in education, health, government, and business services; somewhat lower but still fairly high in finance, communication, manufacturing, and primary industries; and lowest in construction, transportation and storage, trade, and accommodation, food and beverage services. For the 1980 SOC-based classification, managers in the first two groups of industries were included as working in knowledge-based occupations. For the 1991 SOC-based classification, it was stipulated that only "senior managers" and "middle and other managers" were included, both at the highest skill level IV (hence supervisors and foremen/women at skill level III were not included).[2]

Level of education is measured as a categorical variable distinguishing those with no postsecondary education from: (i) those with at least some postsecondary education, (ii) those with a bachelor's degree or equivalent, and (iii) those with post-graduate degrees. In some analyses, a measure of total years of education is also used. However, the primary interest is in the market valuation of immigrant credentials such as bachelor's degree and post-graduate degree. Although most immigrants completed their education

---

[2]Further details on these measures are available upon request.

in their country of origin (or elsewhere outside Canada), a small proportion[3] likely would have completed their education in Canada. In such cases the highest qualification would be Canadian rather than foreign. Since the analysis estimates the recognition of foreign-acquired qualifications based on data from all immigrants, it may therefore lead to a corresponding degree of overestimation of what would be found if those with Canadian-acquired education were to be excluded.

Five categories of racial minorities are included as dummy variables: Black, Chinese, South Asian, Filipino, and Other Non-European (for 1981, only Black and Chinese categories are available). This measure is based primarily[4] on ethnic origins; in 1996 the measure was validated using a new variable more clearly intended to tap into racial groups (see Reitz, 2001b).

Occupational attainment is analyzed using logistic regression, separately for men and women, with independent variables including immigrant status, the three levels of postsecondary education introduced as dummy variables, minority origins, language knowledge (French, English, both, and, for immigrants, neither), and residence in a major urban area (Toronto, Montreal, or Vancouver, vs. the rest of Canada).[5] The analysis also includes interaction terms for immigrant status and educational levels. These interaction terms reflect the distinctive impact that each level of education has for immigrants compared to the native-born. Negative coefficients therefore represent the extent of discounting of immigrant credentials.

The earnings analysis is an OLS regression based on unlogged annual earnings, separately for native-born and immigrant men and women, with coefficients converted to proportions of native-born earnings.[6] The control variables are the same as for the occupational analysis, with the addition of years of work experience, and, for immigrants, years since immigration (to

---

[3]In a sample of immigrants aged 20–64, who arrived in the ten-year period prior to the census, those completing their education in Canada would most often be those in their 20s, who arrived in the early part of the decade.

[4]In the case of immigrants, persons of European origin not born in Europe or the United States were classified as Other Non-European.

[5]Some analyses also include work experience as a control variable.

[6]An explanation of the difference between this procedure and analysis based on logged earnings is provided in Reitz and Sklar (1997); see also Hodson (1985) and Tienda and Lii (1987, p. 148).

Jeffrey G. Reitz

capture the impact of variations across the ten years since arrival). Squared terms are included for both measures of years. In the earnings analysis, skills discounting is reflected in immigrant/native-born differences in the coefficients for levels of education.

In both sets of regressions, coefficients for racial origins (net of other variables) reflect differences in the employment experience of immigrants of minority origins compared to immigrants of European origins. These coefficients may be interpreted as reflecting differences in the recognition of skills among origins groups. Certain analyses also include terms for interactions between origins and educational levels, to capture variations among origins groups in the extent of discounting of specific skill levels.

Trends in Knowledge Occupations in Canada

The proportion of Canadian workers employed in any knowledge occupation increased slowly but steadily over the period between 1981 and 1996. Table 1 presents data on the percentages of men and women in knowledge occupations during each time period, and also (for reference) describes persons in those occupations in terms of mean years of education, percentages with university degrees, and mean earnings.

Among men, the percentage working in knowledge occupations expanded from 19.6% in 1981 to 20.6% in 1986 and 22.5% in 1991 based on the 1980 codes; based on the 1991 codes the knowledge occupations among men expanded only slightly if at all between 1991 and 1996, from 18.9% to 19.0%. Gender differences in overall knowledge-occupation employment are not large, although women have a different occupational profile within the category than men. Men have greater concentration in the managerial occupations than women, a difference that is reduced somewhat over time. Overall, women have a somewhat higher representation in knowledge occupations than men. Women's percentages in knowledge occupations increased from 23.7% in 1981 to 26.1% in 1986 and 29.0% in 1991 based on the 1980 codes; based on the 1991 codes the percentages of women in knowledge occupations increased from 19.3% in 1991 to 20.5% in 1996. The gender difference is smaller when the more explicitly skill-based 1991 codes are used. Increases over time are somewhat greater for women.

Workers in the professions outnumber those in managerial positions by about two or three to one, depending on which measure is used (the 1991 scale shows a larger proportion of professionals compared to managers, at

Table 1: Trends in Knowledge Occupations, Canada, 1981–1996

	1980 Codes			1991 Codes	
	1981	*1986*	*1991*	*1991*	*1996*
Men					
Knowledge-based professions	**11.8%**	**12.0%**	**13.1%**	**12.4%**	**13.4%**
Years of education (mean)	16.01	16.18	16.24	16.80	16.90
University degree (%)	56.1%	56.6%	55.1%	67.0%	69.0%
Earnings (ratio to mean for men)	1.33	1.36	1.34	1.43	1.45
Management of knowledge-based industries	**7.9%**	**8.6%**	**9.3%**	**6.5%**	**5.6%**
Years of education (mean)	14.47	14.76	14.91	15.02	15.33
University degree (%)	34.3%	37.9%	38.6%	40.0%	44.5%
Earnings (ratio to mean for men)	1.56	1.62	1.55	1.71	1.81
Total, knowledge occupations	**19.6%**	**20.6%**	**22.5%**	**18.9%**	**19.0%**
Years of education (mean)	15.39	15.59	15.69	16.19	16.44
University degree (%)	47.4%	48.8%	48.2%	57.8%	61.8%
Earnings (ratio to mean for men)	1.42	1.47	1.43	1.53	1.56
Not in the knowledge occupation	**80.4%**	**79.4%**	**77.5%**	**81.1%**	**81.0%**
Years of education (mean)	11.28	11.75	12.21	12.24	12.63
University degree (%)	4.6%	5.6%	6.9%	6.5%	8.2%
Earnings (ratio to mean for men)	0.90	0.88	0.88	0.88	0.87
Women					
Knowledge-based professions	**10.3%**	**20.6%**	**21.5%**	**16.1%**	**17.5%**
Years of education (mean)	14.78	15.02	15.25	16.12	16.35
University degree (%)	31.1%	35.5%	38.0%	51.8%	57.2%
Earnings (ratio to mean for women)	1.36	1.36	1.33	1.52	1.55
Management of knowledge-based industries	**2.1%**	**5.5%**	**7.4%**	**3.1%**	**3.1%**
Years of education (mean)	13.77	14.02	14.29	14.68	15.13
University degree (%)	23.3%	25.0%	27.5%	33.3%	61.1%
Earnings (ratio to mean for women)	1.69	1.71	1.60	1.87	1.95
Total, knowledge occupations	**23.7%**	**26.1%**	**29.0%**	**19.3%**	**20.5%**
Years of education (mean)	14.61	14.81	15.00	15.89	16.16
University degree (%)	29.8%	33.3%	35.3%	48.8%	54.6%
Earnings (ratio to mean for women)	1.42	1.43	1.40	1.57	1.61
Not in the knowledge occupation	**39.8%**	**73.9%**	**71.0%**	**80.7%**	**79.5%**
Years of education (mean)	11.52	11.94	12.37	12.47	12.90
University degree (%)	4.1%	5.4%	6.8%	7.0%	9.6%
Earnings (ratio to mean for women)	0.87	0.85	0.84	0.86	0.84

Jeffrey G. Reitz

least at the high skill levels of concern here). Both categories grew over the 1981–1996 period. However, although management in knowledge-based industries expanded strongly during the 1980s, in the 1990s there appears to have been a significant retrenchment. On the other hand, each of the major professional fields expanded: science and engineering, social science and related fields, health and related fields, and education.

As the knowledge occupations have expanded, levels of education of incumbents within those occupations also have risen. This has been possible because the supply of educated workers has expanded more rapidly than the size of the knowledge class itself. Educational levels tend to be somewhat higher in the professional fields compared to management, although earnings are substantially higher on the management side. Average years of education attained by workers in the knowledge occupations increased by about 0.3 years between 1981 and 1991, and about 0.3 years between 1991 and 1996; proportions of these workers with degrees increased by 4% in each time period. These increases apply roughly both to professional and to managerial occupations.

Outside knowledge occupations, increases in educational levels in some ways were actually greater than they were inside knowledge occupations. Mean years of education attained increased by 0.9 years between 1981 and 1991, and by 0.4 years between 1991 and 1996. Proportions of workers with university degrees increased by only 2.5% and 0.6%, respectively, although in proportional terms the increases were also quite large. These data may perhaps point to the conclusion that the growth in supply of educated workers has outstripped the demand in knowledge occupations. Whether or not that is the case, the market for highly educated workers has been changing in both sectors.

The increasing earnings premium paid for higher education, found in many studies, may vary across occupations and have a specific pattern in relation to occupational change. Earnings analyses show that the increased value of education exists across the entire workforce (e.g., Reitz, 2001b). Some of the increase in value arises because of the rising relative earnings of professional and managerial occupations for which education is a prerequisite; some arises because of the increased importance of education in attaining the best-paid jobs within the knowledge occupations; and some arises because of an increased impact on earnings in occupations outside the knowledge economy. The organizational processes by which these changes occur may differ across occupational categories.

Gender differences in specific occupational concentrations are reflected in gender inequality in earnings. Such gender inequality in earnings is about the same magnitude, and shows the same trends, both inside and outside the knowledge occupations. In 1981, the mean earnings of women in knowledge occupations were about 65% of the mean earnings of men in knowledge occupations, rising to 72% in 1991. Based on the 1991 code, the relative earnings figure rose from 76 to 79% between 1991 and 1996.

Representation of Immigrants in Knowledge Occupations

Although newly-arrived immigrant men and women are substantially represented in knowledge occupations, the trend over the period 1981 to 1996 was negative. Table 2 presents the differences in terms of the ratio of percentages of immigrant and native-born men and women in professions and management, and in knowledge occupations overall.

In 1981, among men, immigrant representation in knowledge occupations was actually higher than for the native-born (ratios greater than one), but this advantage eroded over the period to 1996. This earlier advantage was based on even greater representation in professional fields, and less in management. In both areas there has been an erosion of the position of newly-arrived immigrants over time.

Among women, immigrant representation has been substantially less both in professional and in managerial occupations, and the large increases in representation for native-born women are not reflected in the patterns among immigrants. In other words, immigrant women are falling behind the progress made by native-born women in knowledge occupations. Among recent immigrant women in 1996, representation in knowledge occupations stood at only about two-thirds of the levels observed for native-born women.

Immigrant Access and Earnings in Knowledge Occupations, 1996

The actual effect of immigrant status, educational qualifications, and origins on access to knowledge occupations, and the implications of immigrant earnings, can best be addressed by means of regression analyses. "Access"

Table 2: Participation by Recent Immigrants and Native-Born in Knowledge Occupations, by Gender, 1981–1996

	1980 Codes			1991 Codes	
	1981	1986	1991	1991	1996
Men					
Knowledge-based professions					
Native-born	11.0	11.3	12.5	11.8	12.6
Recent immigrant	16.1	14.9	14.6	13.7	13.6
Ratio	1.5	1.3	1.2	1.2	1.1
Management of knowledge-based industries					
Native-born	7.9	8.6	9.4	6.5	5.6
Recent immigrant	5.7	5.9	6.3	4.2	3.2
Ratio	0.7	0.7	0.7	0.6	0.6
<u>**Total, knowledge occupations**</u>					
Native-born	18.9	19.9	21.9	18.2	18.2
Recent immigrant	21.8	20.8	20.9	17.9	16.8
Ratio	1.2	1.0	1.0	1.0	0.9
Women					
Knowledge-based professions					
Native-born	20.4	21.2	22.1	16.6	17.8
Recent immigrant	16.4	15.1	16.4	11.2	12.1
Ratio	0.8	0.7	0.7	0.7	0.7
Management of knowledge-based industries					
Native-born	4.0	5.6	7.6	3.1	3.2
Recent immigrant	2.7	3.0	4.2	1.6	1.6
Ratio	0.7	0.5	0.6	0.5	0.5
<u>**Total, knowledge occupations**</u>					
Native-born	24.4	26.8	29.7	19.7	21.0
Recent immigrant	19.1	18.2	20.6	12.8	13.7
Ratio	0.8	0.7	0.7	0.6	0.7

to knowledge occupations here refers to the likelihood of entry into such occupations for persons with given levels of qualification, so the effects of specific characteristics on entry into knowledge occupations may reflect preferences as well as constraints. The primary variables of interest are immigrant status, interaction of levels of education with immigrant status, and racial minority group membership, with each analysis conducted separately by gender; other variables are included as controls for confounding characteristics. The analysis begins with a focus on data from 1996.

Access to Professional and Managerial Occupations

Regarding access to knowledge occupations, logistic regression procedures reported in Table 3 enable us to examine the impact of the primary variables with controls for language knowledge and also local labour market conditions in particular urban areas of settlement.

Net of education, immigrant status reduces representation in knowledge occupations for both men and women, and somewhat more for women than for men (−0.86 and −0.53 respectively; see Equation 1). With both levels of education and education/immigrant-status interactions included in the equations, these figures represent the size of the recency-of-immigration barrier to employment in the knowledge occupations for those with no post-secondary education. The negative coefficients for the interaction terms indicate how the size of this barrier increases at higher levels of qualification. These data confirm that it is not only immigrant status, but the additional discounting of immigrants' postsecondary degree qualifications as well, which produces the underrepresentation of immigrants in knowledge occupations. There are substantial barriers to employment in knowledge occupations for immigrants possessing higher degrees, both at the bachelor's degree level and at the post-graduate level.

Most racial minorities experience greater barriers to employment in knowledge occupations than do immigrants of European origins, among both men and women (see Equation 2). This suggests that additional discounting of the qualifications of racial minorities occurs at all levels of education within these occupations. There is an important exception, the case of Chinese men. Chinese men have *greater* representation in knowledge occupations, relative to their educational levels. However, Blacks, South Asians, and Filipinos all experience substantial additional barriers to employment in knowledge occupations, both men and women. The co-efficients for these groups are all in the range between −0.4 and −1.5. Other non-European men experience smaller barriers, and Chinese and other non-

European women experience no significant differences from immigrants of European origins.

The earlier theoretical or speculative discussion suggesting that barriers to immigrant access in managerial occupations in knowledge-based industries would be greater than the barriers to access in professional occupations is confirmed by the data in Table 3 (compare Equations 3 and 4). Educational qualifications are required for entering all these occupations, but not only are managerial occupations less open to recent immigrants, in several respects the credential discounting process appears to be more extreme. First, among men, for immigrants with post-graduate degrees the barriers to access in managerial employment are greater than they are in the professions. Second, the barriers experienced by immigrant women are greater for all levels of education in management jobs than in the professions. And finally, racial minorities encounter much greater barriers to access in managerial occupations than in the professional occupations. This is true even for the Chinese men for whom accessibility overall is higher. Chinese men experience increased access on the professional side rather than the managerial.

Immigrants find greater opportunities in the professions, where one expects greater emphasis on formal credentials as the means of access. Questions about the quality of foreign credentials are more often resolved in favour of immigrants in the professional fields. By the same token, on the managerial side other, non-credential-related, criteria are invoked which work against immigrants. For men, the barriers are greatest in competitions among those with post-graduate degrees; the data suggest that these barriers are generally even higher for women and for racial minorities.

Earnings Implications

In the earnings determination process, the occupational location of immigrants has an important bearing on the way in which their educational credentials are discounted. There is discounted monetary valuation of immigrant educational credentials in three distinct processes: access to knowledge occupations, earnings determination within knowledge occupations, and interestingly, also in earnings determination outside the knowledge sector. Figures in Table 4 are metric regression coefficients expressed as proportions of mean native-born earnings within gender groups, separately for the native-born and recent immigrants. Numbers specifically reflecting educational discounting for immigrants — namely the immigrant/native-born difference in the proportional impact of specific educational credentials on earnings — are shown in the bottom three lines in the table

Table 3: Relative Access to Knowledge Economy Occupations for Recent Immigrants, Logistic Regression, 1996

Dependent Variable:	All Knowledge Occupations				Professions Only		Management Only	
	Eq. 1		Eq. 2		Eq. 3		Eq. 4	
	B	Sig.	B	Sig.	B	Sig.	B	Sig.
Men (N=171374)								
Immigrant, 1986–1995	-0.53	0.0000	-0.47	0.0000	-0.35	0.0317	-0.55	0.0003
Education								
Some postsecondary	1.20	0.0000	1.16	0.0000	1.54	0.0000	0.67	0.0000
Bachelor's degree	3.51	0.0000	3.42	0.0000	3.87	0.0000	1.62	0.0000
Post-bachelor's degree	4.49	0.0000	4.39	0.0000	4.42	0.0000	2.09	0.0000
Education-immigrant interactions								
Imm*some postsecondary	0.15	0.1871	0.18	0.1402	0.24	0.1530	-0.02	0.8951
Imm*bach. deg.	-0.46	0.0001	-0.37	0.0018	-0.27	0.1144	-0.16	0.3627
Imm*post-bach. deg.	-0.44	0.0003	-0.44	0.0005	0.09	0.6006	-0.60	0.0013
Other characteristics								
Black			-0.52	0.0000	-0.25	0.0342	-1.04	0.0000
Chinese			0.35	0.0000	0.35	0.0000	0.14	0.1522
South Asian			-0.53	0.0000	-0.45	0.0000	-0.45	0.0032
Filipino			-1.47	0.0000	-1.21	0.0000	-1.96	0.0001
Other Non-European			-0.12	0.0122	-0.08	0.1450	-0.14	0.0597
Knowledge of French			-0.28	0.0000	-0.13	0.0002	-0.47	0.0000
French and English			0.26	0.0000	0.13	0.0000	0.30	0.0000
Neither French nor English			-0.46	0.0178	-1.01	0.0005	0.22	0.3568
Toronto			0.21	0.0000	0.07	0.0070	0.30	0.0000
Montreal			0.06	0.0218	0.10	0.0013	-0.02	0.5548
Vancouver			0.01	0.6728	-0.01	0.7196	0.05	0.3112
Constant	-3.15	0.0000	-3.17	0.0000	-4.07	0.0000	-3.70	0.0000

Table 3: continued

Women (N=151127)

	B	Sig.	B	Sig.	B	Sig.	B	Sig.
Immigrant, 1986–1995	−0.86	0.000	−0.66	0.000	−0.44	0.010	−1.19	0.000
Education								
Some postsecondary	1.61	0.000	1.62	0.000	1.97	0.000	0.49	0.000
Bachelor's degree	3.46	0.000	3.45	0.000	3.81	0.000	1.17	0.000
Post-bachelor's degree	4.45	0.000	4.43	0.000	4.54	0.000	1.69	0.000
Education-immigrant interactions								
Imm*some postsecondary	0.26	0.066	0.25	0.092	0.12	0.485	0.48	0.072
Imm*bach. deg.	−0.34	0.019	−0.27	0.074	−0.31	0.083	0.15	0.599
Imm*post-bach. deg.	−0.43	0.006	−0.49	0.002	−0.35	0.061	0.25	0.396
Other characteristics								
Black			−0.43	0.000	−0.29	0.012	−1.13	0.002
Chinese			0.07	0.275	0.06	0.414	0.14	0.319
South Asian			−0.59	0.000	−0.57	0.000	−0.35	0.123
Filipino			−1.38	0.000	−1.39	0.000	−0.91	0.009
Other Non-European			−0.04	0.396	−0.09	0.067	0.20	0.039
Knowledge of French			0.10	0.000	0.18	0.000	−0.27	0.000
French and English			0.08	0.000	0.02	0.349	0.24	0.000
Neither French nor English			−0.35	0.107	−0.47	0.067	0.01	0.975
Toronto			0.08	0.000	−0.06	0.009	0.51	0.000
Montreal			0.03	0.263	0.00	0.945	0.12	0.019
Vancouver			0.01	0.860	−0.08	0.017	0.31	0.000
Constant	−3.19	0.000	−3.24	0.000	−3.78	0.000	−4.17	0.000

Note: In equations with only immigrant status, for men, B = −0.11 for women, B = −0.53.

Table 4: Proportional Effect of Levels of Education and Race on Earnings of Native-Born and Recent Immigrants, by Gender, 1996
OLS Regression (for full equations see Appendix)

	Equation 1	Equation 2	Equation 3	Equation 4
	All Occupations		Knowledge Occupations	Other Occupations
		(Eq. w/ Know Occ.)		
Men				
Native-born				
Some postsecondary	0.19	0.15	0.08	0.16
Bachelor's degree	0.69	0.49	0.52	0.38
Post-graduate degree	0.79	0.52	0.44	0.54
Black	−0.21	−0.20	−0.24	−0.18
Chinese	−0.10	−0.10	−0.04	−0.14
South Asian	−0.12	−0.13	0.03	−0.16
Filipino	−0.27	−0.25	−0.30	−0.25
Other nationality	−0.27	−0.27	−0.32	−0.27
Recent immigrants				
Some postsecondary	0.10	0.08	0.05	0.08
Bachelor's degree	0.32	0.18	0.35	0.13
Post-graduate degree	0.47	0.24	0.33	0.20
Black	−0.25	−0.22	−0.31	−0.22
Chinese	−0.21	−0.23	−0.32	−0.20
South Asian	−0.21	−0.18	−0.14	−0.19
Filipino	−0.27	−0.20	−0.33	−0.19
Other nationality	−0.20	−0.18	−0.19	−0.18
Immigrant/native-born difference				
Some postsecondary	−0.09	−0.08	−0.03	−0.08
Bachelor's degree	−0.37	−0.30	−0.16	−0.25
Post-graduate degree	−0.33	−0.28	−0.12	−0.34

Table 4: continued

Women

Native-born				
Some postsecondary	0.23	0.16	0.17	0.14
Bachelor's degree	0.74	0.46	0.56	0.37
Post-graduate degree	0.98	0.59	0.66	0.46
Black	-0.19	-0.15	-0.40	-0.13
Chinese	0.06	0.05	0.09	0.05
South Asian	-0.12	-0.11	-0.03	-0.12
Filipino	-0.29	-0.26	-0.15	-0.29
Other nationality	-0.12	-0.14	-0.19	-0.12
Recent immigrants				
Some postsecondary	0.10	0.07	0.15	0.07
Bachelor's degree	0.32	0.21	0.39	0.17
Post-graduate degree	0.44	0.25	0.39	0.22
Black	-0.03	-0.02	0.18	-0.04
Chinese	0.02	0.01	-0.01	0.02
South Asian	-0.10	-0.08	-0.06	-0.08
Filipino	-0.08	-0.03	-0.11	-0.02
Other nationality	-0.06	-0.05	-0.08	-0.04
Immigrant/native-born difference				
Some postsecondary	-0.13	-0.09	-0.02	-0.07
Bachelor's degree	-0.42	-0.25	-0.17	-0.19
Post-graduate degree	-0.54	-0.35	-0.27	-0.24

for men and women, respectively. (For the metric coefficients themselves, see Appendix).

As background to the occupational analysis, Equation 1 in Table 4 shows that across all occupations for both men and women in 1996, the earnings boost for postsecondary education was substantially less for immigrants than for the native-born. Immigrant men received 9% less additional earnings for some postsecondary education compared to their native-born counterparts, 37% less additional earnings for a Bachelor of Arts degree, and 33% less additional earnings for a post-graduate degree. Among women the discounting is even more substantial: 13%, 42%, and 54%, respectively.

As is well-known from many other studies, racial minorities including immigrants and also the native-born experience earnings disadvantages beyond what would be expected based on levels of education, work experience, and language knowledge, with the specific dollar amounts varying among specific minorities, by immigrant status and by gender. The only real exception to this general trend is for Chinese women, among whom the earnings coefficients are positive (for black immigrant women the coefficient is negative but not statistically significant). Chinese men, on the other hand, still experience overall earnings disadvantages.

In a separate analysis not presented here, it was found that the discounting of immigrant qualifications at the Bachelor of Arts level seems to be particularly marked for racial minorities. The impact of race on educational discounting at particular levels of education was examined in more detailed regression models which include interaction terms for minority group and educational level. Among immigrants, the direct effect of race remains the most powerful effect, particularly for men, but in addition, there are significant (or near significant) interaction terms specifically at the Bachelor of Arts level for each of the minority groups. There is also a significant interaction effect for South Asian native-born men and women at the Bachelor of Arts level.[7] Speculatively, it may be that

---

[7]For immigrants, in a modified Equation 1 with 15 terms added for interactions between three educational levels and five racial categories, there are BA-race interactions which are negative (between −3,500 and −7,800 in 1996 dollars) and significant (at or very near the 0.05 level) for Black, Chinese and South Asian men and women, and for Filipino men. Most of the other education/race interactions are also negative, but none are near significance. (One coefficient, for the interaction between BA degree and Other Non-European origins, is positive and significant.) In almost every case, the size of the coefficient is much less when knowledge occupation is added to the equation, and statistical significance disappears.

Jeffrey G. Reitz

increased discounting occurs at the Bachelor of Arts level because for immigrants, that degree lacks specificity in terms of professional relevance (so that, among other things, less rigorous consideration may be given to formal qualifications where the bachelor's degree is pertinent to employment). Post-graduate degrees provide that greater specificity, thus reducing the extent of discounting.

Equations 2 to 4 in Table 4 add information about the three distinct processes related to participation in knowledge occupations referred to above. Equation 2 provides two important new insights into the value of qualifications for immigrants, and to the process of qualification recognition and discounting. First, some of the earnings disadvantage of immigrants, including racial minority immigrants, is due to their failure to access knowledge occupations, which in turn is partly related to the discounting of immigrant qualifications. This can be seen in the fact that the numbers reflecting educational discounting are all somewhat smaller after work in a knowledge occupation has been included in the regression. Second, barriers in access to knowledge occupations are only a small part of the overall process by which immigrant credentials are discounted in earnings determination. This is shown by the fact that although controls for work in professional and managerial occupations reduce the extent of credential discounting, much or most of it remains.

Equations 3 and 4 enable us to examine and compare the extent of discounting of immigrant qualifications inside knowledge occupations and outside such occupations, respectively. Within knowledge occupations, the discounting of qualifications in determining earnings levels — reflecting in part access to higher-level occupations within the broader category — is very much reduced. *Outside* knowledge occupations there is very significant credential discounting, particularly for men. In fact, among men the most substantial discounting of immigrant qualifications occurs outside knowledge occupations. At the Bachelor of Arts and post-graduate levels among men, the discounting in knowledge occupations is 12 to 16%, compared to 25 to 34% in other occupations. Particularly relative to the lower earnings levels within these other occupations, the discounting appears large. Among women, discounting appears to be fairly large both inside and outside the knowledge occupations.

What this means is that for immigrants, exclusion from knowledge occupations has a double impact on earnings. Not only are their skills discounted in their being denied access to knowledge occupations, and to the best-paid occupations within that category, but also the value of their skills is very substantially reduced elsewhere in the labour market. Whereas for the native-born, possession of a Bachelor of Arts degree or higher credential has considerable value even for those working outside professional or managerial fields, for immigrants those qualifications are far less useful in gaining positions with solid earnings potential.

For racial minorities, there is a consistently negative component in all analyses, and negative interactions (for example, education-race) in many of them. This implies further reductions in earnings, magnifying the impact of educational discounting in all three aspects: in access to knowledge occupations, in access to earnings within those occupations, and in access to earnings outside the knowledge occupations.

Trends Affecting Immigrants and Knowledge Occupations, 1981–1996

Now consider how the trends over the period 1981–1996 have altered circumstances for newly arriving immigrants. Among both men and women, recent immigrant access to knowledge occupations has declined not only overall (as was seen above in Table 2), but also relative to qualifications. Table 5 shows the percentage of recent immigrants with university and other qualifications who have successfully gained employment in knowledge occupations compared to their native-born counterparts. Among men, between 1981 and 1991 the relative disadvantage of recent immigrants grew for those with some university, for those with bachelor's degrees, and for those with post-graduate degrees. Between 1991 and 1996, the disadvantage grew for those with some university and those with bachelor's degrees, but fell slightly for those with post-graduate degrees. Among women, the immigrant disadvantages tended to be greater, and to remain so for the entire period 1981–1996. The most significant change was for women with post-graduate degrees. In that group, the disadvantage for immigrants grew from −16.8% in 1981 to −28.8% in 1991.

For university graduates only, the logistic regression analysis in Table 6 shows that barriers restricting immigrant access to knowledge occupations increased over time. For university-graduate men, the coefficients representing immigrant access to knowledge occupations declined from −0.52 in 1981 to −0.66 in 1991 (1980 codes) and from −0.74 in 1991 to −0.81 in 1996 (1991 codes). For university-graduate women, the coefficients are more negative across the entire period. With controls for the indicated variables, the trends are similar (except for 1981 when the origins controls

Table 5: Participation by Recent Immigrants and Native-Born in Knowledge Occupations By Level of Education and Gender, 1981–1996

| | | 1980 Codes | | | | | | 1991 Codes | | | |
| | | 1981 | | 1986 | | 1991 | | 1991 | | 1996 | |
		%	Diff.[1]	%	Diff.[1]	%	Diff.[1]	%	Diff.[1]	%	Diff.[1]
Men											
Secondary or less	Native-born	6.5		6.6		7.7		4.8		4.1	
	Recent immigrant	3.2	−3.4	3.8	−2.8	5.1	−2.5	3.5	−1.4	2.5	−1.6
Some university	Native-born	18.2		18.5		19.7		13.7		12.5	
	Recent immigrant	17.9	−0.3	16.8	−1.7	16.4	−3.3	11.1	−2.7	8.9	−3.5
Bachelor's degree	Native-born	66.1		63.6		63.2		63.0		59.0	
	Recent immigrant	51.3	−14.8	46.0	−17.6	45.4	−17.8	43.8	−19.2	35.0	−24.0
Post-graduate degree	Native-born	82.5		81.7		77.8		81.6		79.3	
	Recent immigrant	70.6	−11.9	69.2	−12.5	60.9	−16.9	60.6	−21.0	59.4	−19.9
Women											
Secondary or less	Native-born	7.9		9.2		11.4		3.9		3.9	
	Recent immigrant	5.0	−2.9	5.3	−3.9	5.7	−5.8	2.1	−1.7	1.7	−2.2
Some university	Native-born	32.7		32.1		32.1		18.7		17.1	
	Recent immigrant	22.7	−10.0	20.2	−11.9	22.1	−10.0	10.8	−8.0	10.2	−6.9
Bachelor's degree	Native-born	67.3		66.4		66.3		60.2		56.6	
	Recent immigrant	40.7	−26.6	38.2	−28.2	39.8	−26.5	31.4	−28.8	28.2	−28.3
Post-graduate degree	Native-born	82.7		81.0		82.4		79.9		77.8	
	Recent immigrant	65.9	−16.8	66.5	−14.4	53.6	−28.8	47.5	−32.4	49.2	−28.5

Note: [1]Difference is the arithmetic difference between the percentage of immigrants in knowledge occupations, and the percentage of the native-born in knowledge occupations.

Table 6: Participation by Immigrants and Native-Born in Knowledge Occupations Logistic Regression, University Graduates Only, by Gender, 1981–1996

| | | 1980 Codes | | | | | | 1990 Codes | | | |
| | 1981 | | 1986 | | 1991 | | 1991 | | 1996 | |
	B	Sig.	B	Sig.	B	Sig.	B	Sig.	B	Sig.
Men										
Eq. 1 Immigrant	−0.52	0.000	−0.56	0.000	−0.66	0.000	−0.74	0.000	−0.81	0.000
Eq. 2 Immigrant	−0.61	0.000	−0.42	0.000	−0.58	0.000	−0.77	0.000	−0.63	0.000
Eq. 3 Immigrant	−0.59	0.000	−0.43	0.000	−0.55	0.000	−0.67	0.000	−0.61	0.000
Immigrant * post-grad degree	−0.04	0.741	0.02	0.914	−0.07	0.483	−0.22	0.020	−0.04	0.638
N	13777		15466		27976		27976		29732	
Women										
Eq. 1 Immigrant	−0.96	0.000	−0.88	0.000	−1.09	0.000	−1.16	0.000	−1.12	0.000
Eq. 2 Immigrant	−0.94	0.000	−0.69	0.000	−0.90	0.000	−0.92	0.000	−0.89	0.000
Eq. 3 Immigrant	−0.98	0.000	−0.82	0.000	−0.72	0.000	−0.73	0.000	−0.81	0.000
Immigrant * post-grad degree	0.11	0.510	0.31	0.095	−0.46	0.000	−0.45	0.000	−0.19	0.050
N	7920		10853		22754		22754		27621	

Note: Equation 1 includes no control variables; Equation 2 includes possession of a post-graduate degree, origins (Black, Chinese, South Asian, Filipino and Other; for 1981 only Black and Chinese), language knowledge, residence in Toronto, Vancouver, and Montreal, and years of work experience; Equation 3 adds an interaction term for immigrants with post-graduate degrees.

Jeffrey G. Reitz

were more limited). The equation with the interaction term for the distinctive impact of post-graduate degrees held by immigrants shows that most often the effect was negative, but not statistically significant.

If higher professional standards in knowledge occupations increase immigrant access, then trends towards reduced immigrant access to those knowledge occupations require explanation. The trends do not necessarily imply that such professional standards have declined. Instead, it may be that other factors affecting the immigrants' fate have come into play. Two possibilities were mentioned earlier. One was that increased bureaucratization could erect artificial barriers affecting immigrants. The other was that an increased supply of highly educated, native-born workers could reduce the organizational need to review and research immigrant qualifications carefully. In the case of women, it may be that the trend towards increased entry by native-born women into many of these occupations has reduced opportunities for immigrant women.

The overall impact of trends in credential recognition on immigrant earnings, and the impact of differences among occupational groups, can be examined in OLS regression with annual earnings as a dependent variable. The analyses have been repeated across all four censuses (including controls for work experience, origins, language, and urban residence, and time since arrival for immigrants), and key results are summarized in Table 7. Table 7 presents the native-born/immigrant differences in earnings premiums for specific educational qualifications, expressed as a proportion of mean earnings for the native-born, separately by gender. There are four sets of results, representing differences across all occupations, differences arising from reduced access to knowledge occupations (the change introduced by controls for professional and managerial occupations), differences within knowledge occupations, and differences within other occupations.

The first set of results show that the earnings impact of the discounting of immigrant qualifications increased significantly over the period 1981–1996, for both men and women, and particularly for those with higher qualifications. These trends point towards a growing pattern of immigrant skill underutilization. Overall, this trend is more negative for immigrant women than for immigrant men.

The second and third set of results together show that declining access to the best-paid knowledge occupations is a significant component of the decline in skill recognition. The earnings impact of reduced access to knowledge occupations is reinforced by the increasing relative earnings levels in knowledge occupations. Within knowledge occupations, the earnings impact of skill underutilization increased initially, but then declined in the later period, particularly for women.

Table 7: Relative Immigrant Earnings Premiums for Specific Levels of Education, Overall and by Work in Knowledge Occupations, by Gender, 1981–1996

	1980 Codes			1991 Codes	
Proportion by which immigrant earnings premiums are different than for native-born, metric coefficients expressed as proportion of mean native-born earnings	1981	1986	1991	1991	1996
Men					
Overall					
Some postsecondary education	0.02	−0.01	−0.09	−0.09	−0.09
Bachelor's degree	−0.20	−0.23	−0.27	−0.27	−0.37
Post-graduate degree	−0.20	−0.30	−0.29	−0.29	−0.33
Due to reduced access to knowledge occupations					
Some postsecondary education	0.02	0.01	0.00	−0.01	−0.01
Bachelor's degree	0.01	−0.01	−0.02	−0.04	−0.06
Post-graduate degree	0.04	0.03	−0.01	−0.03	−0.05
Due to relative earnings premiums within knowledge occupations					
Some postsecondary education	−0.06	0.02	−0.16	0.00	−0.03
Bachelor's degree	−0.24	−0.19	−0.24	−0.09	−0.16
Post-graduate degree	−0.25	−0.27	−0.32	−0.16	−0.12
Due to relative earnings premiums outside knowledge occupations					
Some postsecondary education	0.01	−0.01	−0.07	−0.08	−0.08
Bachelor's degree	−0.14	−0.17	−0.20	−0.19	−0.25
Post-graduate degree	−0.09	−0.22	−0.17	−0.24	−0.34

Table 7: continued

Women

Overall

Some postsecondary education	-0.08	-0.13	-0.12	-0.12	-0.13
Bachelor's degree	-0.30	-0.42	-0.40	-0.40	-0.42
Post-graduate degree	-0.25	-0.54	-0.54	-0.54	-0.54

Due to reduced access to knowledge occupations

Some postsecondary education	-0.05	-0.05	-0.03	-0.04	-0.04
Bachelor's degree	-0.13	-0.13	-0.10	-0.13	-0.17
Post-graduate degree	-0.12	-0.09	-0.11	-0.16	-0.19

Due to relative earnings premiums within knowledge occupations

Some postsecondary education	-0.03	-0.11	-0.20	-0.32	-0.02
Bachelor's degree	-0.29	-0.32	-0.31	-0.41	-0.17
Post-graduate degree	-0.06	-0.39	-0.53	-0.56	-0.27

Due to relative earnings premiums outside knowledge occupations

Some postsecondary education	0.00	-0.04	-0.05	-0.06	-0.07
Bachelor's degree	0.10	-0.13	-0.20	-0.19	-0.19
Post-graduate degree	0.00	-0.33	-0.18	-0.25	-0.24

And finally, there is also a trend during the period towards reduced value of immigrant qualifications in the less-skilled occupations outside the professions and management.

Conclusions: Theory and Policy

The results of this study clarify processes of qualification-assessment in knowledge-based occupations and how these affect immigrants. Although immigrant skills are frequently discounted in professional fields, the extent of such discounting is actually greater in the management of knowledge-based industries, and greater still in occupations at lower skill levels. This confirms the theoretical expectation that skill validation in the most professionalized settings promotes more effective consideration of the foreign-acquired credentials of immigrants.

On the basis of such patterns, it might have been expected that an increased predominance of knowledge-based occupations would have led to an improvement in the recognition of immigrant qualifications. The trend, however, has been in the opposite direction. Despite differences in credential assessment between knowledge-based occupations and others, both sectors contribute to the overall trend towards reduced credential recognition for immigrants.

Among the reasons for the trend, one factor affecting all skill levels in the occupational structure is the significant increase in the supply of highly educated native-born workers. Whatever the adequacy of this supply in objective terms, the relative increase would affect the competitive position of immigrants. An increased supply of workers with familiar qualifications reduces the pressure on employers to probe the relevance of the unfamiliar qualifications of immigrants. The increased supply might have an equal impact on professional occupations, where credential assessment procedures are elaborate and detailed, and on a wide range of less-skilled occupations, where assessment is more casual and informal.

Specific aspects of these trends require further analysis. Clearly, university training for immigrants is useful in overcoming employment handicaps. Still, the lack of recognition of Bachelor of Arts-level qualifications, particularly for racial minorities, is of interest. It may be that foreign qualifications acquire the greatest credibility when they reflect the most specific professional skills, and that a general bachelor's degree lacks that credibility, particularly when granted in Asia, Africa or Latin America.

Jeffrey G. Reitz

The slower pace of entry of immigrant women into knowledge-based occupations also requires further analysis. One might have expected the increased access to knowledge occupations among native-born women to carry over and assist immigrant women, but such a trend is quite limited in these data. Whether gender interacts with immigrant status and race in affecting the thoroughness of credential validation processes, and resulting skill recognition for immigrants, is a question worth pursuing.

The extensive discounting of immigrant qualifications outside the knowledge occupations is a phenomenon that deserves more attention than it has received. Education is having an increased impact on employment across many occupations, including those at relatively lower skill levels. It is in these sectors that qualifications may be considered in a less rigorous manner, which allows bias against the unfamiliar to have a more decisive impact on decision-making. It appears that immigrants are particularly vulnerable in such settings. In a sense, this magnifies the problem of non-recognition of immigrant skills in the professions and management. Highly-skilled immigrants who fail to gain access to occupations in these sectors face a very uncertain alternative in the wider occupational labour market, and find that their skills are even less relevant and useful in that context.

There are certain policy implications to be pursued as well. The emphasis in much contemporary discussion is on qualification recognition within highly-skilled occupations. The analysis here suggests that such occupations already provide increased access for immigrants. But the analysis may also help account for the emphasis placed on the problems faced by the highly skilled. When highly-qualified immigrants fail to gain access to the knowledge-based occupations for which they were trained, they find a particularly difficult situation elsewhere in the labour market. Whereas native-born workers with university training are able to use that training to certain advantage across a wide range of occupations, such is much less true for immigrants. To put it in the colloquial, the stereotype of immigrant PhD's driving taxis may reflect the extreme consequences of skill discounting for that group. When university-trained immigrants do not do professional work, they are more often consigned to very low-skill occupations. Thus, the consequences of non-recognition of qualifications are magnified.

Efforts to address non-recognition of immigrant qualifications have focused on professional fields such as licensed professions, but achieving institutional change in other areas may actually prove more difficult. Licensing of professionals may involve bureaucracies that are hard to move, but at least the organizational requirements are fairly clear. In contrast, there may be no such clear organizational strategy for addressing non-recognition of immigrant qualifications outside the professions or management, in a less formally structured labour market lacking institutional regulation of employment. In fact, the earnings impact of formal qualifications in many occupational sectors may not arise from a formal organizational procedure at all; it may reflect informal processes and activities as yet not well understood.

References

Arrow, K., S. Bowles and S. Durlauf, eds. (2000), *Meritocracy and Economic Inequality* (Princeton, NJ: Princeton University Press).

Baer, D. (1999), "Educational Credentials and the Changing Occupational Structure", in J. Curtis, E. Grabb and N. Guppy (eds.), *Social Inequality in Canada: Patterns, Problems and Policies*, 3d ed. (Scarborough: Prentice Hall Allyn and Bacon Canada), 92–106.

Baker, M. and D. Benjamin (1994), "The Performance of Immigrants in the Canadian Labour Market", *Journal of Labour Economics* 12, 369–405.

Bell, D. (1973), *The Coming of Post-industrial Society: A Venture in Social Forecasting* (New York: Basic Books).

Bell, D. and S.R. Graubard, eds. (1997), *Toward the Year 2000: Work in Progress*, with a new preface by D. Bell and S.R. Graubard (Cambridge, MA: The MIT Press).

Bowles, S. and H. Gintis (2000), "Does Schooling Raise Earnings by Making People Smarter?" in K. Arrow, S. Bowles and S. Durlauf (eds.), *Meritocracy and Economic Inequality* (Princeton, NJ: Princeton University Press), 118–136.

Cole, S. (1986), "Sex Discrimination and Admission to Medical School, 1929–1984", *American Journal of Sociology* 92, 549–567.

Conger, S. (1994), *The Assessment and Recognition of the Occupational Qualifications of Foreign-Trained Workers* (Ottawa: Heritage Canada).

Conger, S. and L. Bezanson (1996), *Review of Credential Assessment Services in Canada*, report prepared for the Departments of Canadian Heritage, Citizenship and Immigration, and Human Resources Development (Ottawa: The Canadian Guidance and Counselling Foundation).

Cumming, P.A., E.L.D. Lee and D.G. Oreopoulos (1989), *Access! Task Force on Access to Professional and Trades in Ontario* (Toronto: Ministry of Citizenship).

Hodson, R. (1985), "Some Considerations Concerning the Functional Form of Earnings", *Social Science Research* 14 (December), 374–394.

Hunter, A.A. (1988), "Formal Education and Initial Employment: Unravelling the Relationships Between Schooling and Skills over Time", *American Sociological Review* 53, 753–765.

Hunter, A.A. and J.M. Leiper (1993), "On Formal Education, Skills, and Earnings: The Role of Educational Certificates in Earnings Determination", *Canadian Journal of Sociology* 18(1), 21–42.

Li, P.S. (2001), "The Market Worth of Immigrants' Educational Credentials", *Canadian Public Policy/Analyse de Politiques* 27(1), 23–38.

Mata, F. (1994), *The Non-accreditation of Immigrant Professionals in Canada: Societal Impacts, Barriers and Present Policy Initiatives* (Ottawa: Citizenship and Immigration Canada).

McDade, K. (1988), *Barriers to Recognition of the Credentials of Immigrants in Canada*, Studies in Social Policy (Ottawa: Institute for Research on Public Policy).

Ontario Ministry of Training, Colleges and Universities (2002), *The Facts Are in! A Study of the Characteristics and Experiences of Immigrants Seeking Employment in the Regulated Professions in Ontario* (Toronto: Ontario Ministry of Training, Colleges and Universities).

Reitz, J.G. (1998), *Warmth of the Welcome: The Social Causes of Economic Success for Immigrants in Different Nations and Cities* (Boulder, CO: Westview Press).

_____ (2001a), "Immigrant Skill Utilization in the Canadian Labour Market: Implications of Human Capital Research", *Journal of International Migration and Integration* 2(3), 347–378.

_____ (2001b), "Immigrant Success in the Knowledge Economy: Institutional Change and the Immigrant Experience in Canada, 1970–1995", *Journal of Social Issues* 57(3), 579–613.

_____ (2001c), "Terms of Entry: Social Institutions and Immigrant Earnings in American, Canadian and Australian Cities", in M. Cross and R. Moore (eds.), *Globalization and the New City: Migrants, Minorities and Urban Transformations in Comparative Perspective* (Houndmills, Basingstoke, Hampshire, UK: Palgrave Macmillan), 50–81.

_____ (2003a), "Immigration and Canadian Nation-Building in the Transition to a Knowledge Economy", in W.A. Cornelius, P.L. Martin, J.F. Hollifield and T. Tsuda (eds.), *Controlling Immigration: A Global Perspective*, 2d ed. (Stanford, CA: Stanford University Press), forthcoming.

_____ (2003b), "Immigrant Success and the Expansion of Education in American and Canadian Cities, 1770–1990", in J.G. Reitz (ed.), *Host Societies and the Reception of Immigrants: Institutions, Markets and Policies* (San Diego, CA: Center for Comparative Immigration Research, University of California), forthcoming; condensed version in R. Breton and J.G. Reitz (eds.), *Globalization and Society: Processes of Differentiation Examined* (New York: Greenwood Press).

Reitz, J.G. and S.M. Sklar (1997), "Culture, Race, and the Economic Assimilation of Immigrants", *Sociological Forum* 12(2), 233–277.

Skills for Change (1995), *Identifying Opportunities and Overcoming Barriers to Employment for Foreign-Trained Engineers in Ontario* (Toronto: Skills for Change).

Training and Development Associates (1999), *Reaching our Full Potential: Prior Learning Assessment and Recognition for Foreign-Trained Canadians* (Ottawa: Canadian Labour Force Development Board).

Tienda, M. and D.-T. Lii (1987), "Minority Concentration and Earnings Inequality: Blacks, Hispanics, and Asians Compared", *American Journal of Sociology* 93(July), 141–165.

Watt, D. and M. Bloom (2001), *Exploring the Learning Recognition Gap in Canada*, Phase 1 Report. "Recognizing Learning: The Economic Cost of Not Recognizing Learning and Learning Credentials in Canada" (Ottawa: Conference Board of Canada).

Jeffrey G. Reitz

Appendix
Earnings of Native-Born and Recent Immigrants, by Gender, 1996 Overall, and within Knowledge Occupations and Other Occupations, OLS Regression

	Occupational Group							
	All Occupations		Knowledge Occ.		Other Occup.			
	B	Sig.	B	Sig.	B	Sig.	B	Sig.
	Eq. 1		Eq. 2		Eq. 3		Eq. 4	
Men								
Native-Born								
Some postsecondary	**6460**	0.000	**5196**	0.000	**2807**	0.000	**5296**	0.000
Bachelor's degree	**23292**	0.000	**16518**	0.000	**17466**	0.000	**12991**	0.000
Post-graduate degree	**26932**	0.000	**17717**	0.000	**15016**	0.000	**18152**	0.000
Work experience	2388	0.000	2237	0.000	3458	0.000	2031	0.000
Exp. squared	−42	0.000	−39	0.000	−62	0.000	−36	0.000
French	−5075	0.000	−4696	0.000	−9812	0.000	−4342	0.000
French and English	−537	0.001	−1103	0.000	−259	0.580	−1172	0.000
Toronto	7416	0.000	6743	0.000	12280	0.000	5109	0.000
Montreal	2103	0.000	2034	0.000	2687	0.000	1936	0.000
Vancouver	5105	0.000	5007	0.000	4815	0.000	5122	0.000
Black	−7065	0.000	−6800	0.000	−8212	0.072	−6218	0.000
Chinese	−3250	0.001	−3552	0.000	−1199	0.608	−4831	0.000
South Asian	−4127	0.004	−4537	0.001	928	0.833	−5588	0.000
Filipino	−9161	0.001	−8343	0.003	−10168	0.399	−8632	0.001
Other nationality	−9126	0.000	−9289	0.000	−10789	0.000	−9068	0.000
Professional			9793	0.000				
Manager			21783	0.000				
Constant	2029	0.000	3250	0.000	4431	0.000	5563	0.000
Recent Immigrants								
Some postsecondary	**3534**	0.000	**2569**	0.000	**1794**	0.609	**2739**	0.000
Bachelor's degree	**10915**	0.000	**6263**	0.000	**11997**	0.001	**4359**	0.000
Post-graduate degree	**15799**	0.000	**8158**	0.000	**11104**	0.001	**6649**	0.000
Work experience	1127	0.000	1112	0.000	2037	0.000	980	0.000
Exp. squared	−23	0.000	−23	0.000	−42	0.000	−20	0.000
French	−2134	0.082	−1584	0.183	−6288	0.305	−1220	0.258
French and English	1146	0.109	291	0.675	−2392	0.246	995	0.153
Not French nor English	−1621	0.047	−958	0.227	222	0.970	−1254	0.071
Toronto	1463	0.001	1480	0.001	270	0.868	2001	0.000
Montreal	−2847	0.000	−2748	0.000	−1641	0.517	−2697	0.000
Vancouver	290	0.629	593	0.307	−3417	0.116	1698	0.002
Years since arrival	1543	0.000	1877	0.000	2721	0.007	1667	0.000
Years squared	−31	0.233	−64	0.011	−62	0.499	−64	0.008
Black	−8461	0.000	−7556	0.000	−10363	0.004	−7487	0.000
Chinese	−6980	0.000	−7823	0.000	−10752	0.000	−6775	0.000
South Asian	−7044	0.000	−6193	0.000	−4819	0.055	−6439	0.000
Filipino	−9000	0.000	−6874	0.000	−11096	0.027	−6478	0.000
Other nationality	−6740	0.000	−6176	0.000	−6477	0.000	−6204	0.000
Professional			13326	0.000				
Manager			21420	0.000				
Constant	6475	0.000	5262	0.000	7226	0.117	7184	0.000

Earnings of Native-Born and Recent Immigrants, OLS Regression, 1996

Women

Native-born

Some postsecondary	**5048**	0.000	**3351**	0.000	**3629**	0.000	**3101**	0.000
Bachelor's degree	**15982**	0.000	**9852**	0.000	**12098**	0.000	**7892**	0.000
Post-graduate degree	**21073**	0.000	**12784**	0.000	**14216**	0.000	**9850**	0.000
Work experience	1390	0.000	1220	0.000	2054	0.000	1056	0.000
Exp. squared	−26	0.000	−23	0.000	−41	0.000	−20	0.000
French	−1950	0.000	−2023	0.000	−1207	0.002	−2310	0.000
French and English	941	0.000	613	0.000	1205	0.000	551	0.000
Toronto	7085	0.000	6684	0.000	7761	0.000	6554	0.000
Montreal	2524	0.000	2471	0.000	1439	0.000	2865	0.000
Vancouver	4869	0.000	4758	0.000	3363	0.000	5262	0.000
Black	−4074	0.000	−3173	0.000	−8512	0.009	−2847	0.000
Chinese	1191	0.072	1073	0.092	1837	0.223	1084	0.117
South Asian	−2490	0.009	−2436	0.007	−714	0.793	−2680	0.004
Filipino	−6288	0.001	−5684	0.002	−3295	0.668	−6342	0.000
Other nationality	−2540	0.000	−2907	0.000	−4084	0.000	−2550	0.000
Professional			10046	0.000				
Manager			18959	0.000				
Constant	1697	0.000	3144	0.000	6159	0.000	4874	0.000

Recent Immigrants

Some postsecondary	**2237**	0.000	**1489**	0.000	**3156**	0.262	**1511**	0.000
Bachelor's degree	**6841**	0.000	**4411**	0.000	**8344**	0.003	**3734**	0.000
Post-graduate degree	**9424**	0.000	**5300**	0.000	**8327**	0.004	**4713**	0.000
Work experience	622	0.000	609	0.000	1563	0.000	550	0.000
Exp. squared	−12	0.000	−12	0.000	−44	0.000	−11	0.000
French	−2594	0.003	−2290	0.007	−3741	0.475	−2306	0.004
French and English	1510	0.004	872	0.085	398	0.805	1169	0.024
Not French nor English	−2095	0.000	−1854	0.000	−2575	0.619	−2095	0.000
Toronto	2672	0.000	2534	0.000	77	0.953	2925	0.000
Montreal	−752	0.181	−677	0.218	−3888	0.072	−253	0.633
Vancouver	1832	0.000	1740	0.000	1356	0.426	1853	0.000
Years since arrival	1621	0.000	1611	0.000	2411	0.005	1482	0.000
Years squared	−70	0.000	−72	0.000	−104	0.164	−68	0.000
Black	−612	0.260	−437	0.410	3937	0.102	−895	0.075
Chinese	455	0.273	312	0.441	−296	0.845	533	0.178
South Asian	−2225	0.000	−1751	0.000	−1204	0.570	−1807	0.000
Filipino	−1745	0.001	−611	0.215	−2345	0.380	−433	0.347
Other nationality	−1395	0.000	−1049	0.004	−1640	0.263	−924	0.009
Professional			8838	0.000				
Manager			12439	0.000				
Constant	787	0.273	687	0.326	612	0.868	1412	0.035

Jeffrey G. Reitz

Public Attitudes Towards Immigrants and Immigration: Determinants and Policy Implications

Victoria M. Esses, Gordon Hodson and
John F. Dovidio

Examining arguments made about immigration in Canada and the beliefs
that underlie them is important for understanding attitudes towards immigrants and immigration and for devising strategies for attitude change. In
this paper, we focus on four beliefs about immigration to Canada, present
some of our research examining the role of these beliefs in determining
attitudes towards immigrants and immigration, and describe some potential
strategies for counteracting these effects. The four beliefs we focus on here
are: (i) immigrants compete with Canadians already living here for
economic resources, such as jobs, (ii) immigrants compete with Canadians
already living here for value and cultural dominance, (iii) immigrants from
specific parts of the world pose threats to Canadians, and (iv) immigrants
are different from Canadians in fundamental ways and are not part of the
Canadian in-group. We also discuss and present data suggesting that certain
types of people are especially likely to hold these beliefs, and thus to hold
negative attitudes towards immigrants and immigration.

Evidence of these Beliefs in the Media

Arguments against current levels of immigration to Canada and negative beliefs about immigrants are prevalent on anti-immigration Web sites and, to some extent, in news stories about immigration. For example, a perusal of the Canada First Web site (www.canadafirst.net) provides many examples of the different types of beliefs that exist about immigrants and immigration. High rates of immigration are equated with high unemployment, and immigrants are described as taking jobs away from Canadians.[1] Immigrants are described as bringing in non-European cultural values and customs, and pictures are used to demonstrate the "unpleasant", changing nature of Canadian society as a result of high levels of immigration.[2] The claim that Canada is a nation of immigrants is refuted by suggesting that, in fact, current immigrants to Canada are very different from the (predominantly European) immigrants of previous generations who created Canada.[3] Finally, since September 11, 2001, immigrants from the Middle East have been targeted as a particular threat to Canadians, in terms of safety, security, and basic cultural incompatibility.[4]

These claims are not limited to anti-immigration Web sites, however. They are also evident in news stories and editorials about immigration, and in recent papers and books (see Corcoran, 2002). For example, Diane Francis of the *National Post* has spoken out against Canada's immigration policy on numerous occasions, citing security risks and the economic costs of immigration (e.g., Francis, 2001, 2002a), and has recently published a book, *Immigration: The Economic Case* (2002b) which makes similar arguments. Daniel Stoffman's (2002) book, *Who Gets In: What's Wrong With Canada's Immigration Program, and How to Fix it,* discusses job and economic losses to immigrants, and national security risks. Finally, a Fraser Institute paper by Michael Collacott, "Canada's Immigration Policy: The Need for Major Reform" (2002), focuses on the economic costs of

---

[1]See <http://www.canadafirst.net/immi_jobs/index.html>.

[2]See <http://www.canadafirst.net/pictures/index.html>.

[3]See <http://www.canadafirst.net/myths/myth1.html>.

[4]For example, <http://www.canadafirst.net>.

immigration, and possible cultural and value clashes between immigrants and non-immigrants. Thus, the four beliefs about immigration that we have chosen to focus on here are derived from arguments against immigration currently available to the Canadian public.

Theoretical Perspectives Relating to these Beliefs

Theories of intergroup relations and group conflict suggest that each of these beliefs about competition, group identity, and threat may have a role to play in promoting negative relations between non-immigrants and immigrants. First, in terms of the belief that immigrants compete with Canadians already living here for economic resources such as jobs, Realistic Group Conflict Theory (e.g., Bobo, 1988; LeVine and Campbell, 1972; Sherif, 1966) and the more recent Instrument Model of Group Conflict (see also Esses *et al.*, 2001; Esses, Jackson and Armstrong, 1998) propose that intergroup attitudes and behaviour reflect group interests and are based, at least in part, on the nature of and the compatibility of group goals. When group goals are compatible, positive relations are likely to result, but when group goals are incompatible and groups are seen as competing for resources, conflict and negative intergroup relations will result. Inter-group conflict in turn promotes hostility towards the competitive out-group. It is important to note that actual competition for resources does not need to exist in order for this hostility to be induced. Rather, it is the *perception* of competition that leads to conflict and intergroup hostility. This hostility may be manifested in the expression of negative attitudes towards members of the other group and in attempts to avoid contact with members of the group. Thus, the belief that immigrants compete with Canadians already living here for economic resources would be expected to promote negative attitudes towards immigrants and opposition to immigration.

Second, in addition to the perception that immigrants compete with Canadians already living here for economic resources, immigrants may be seen as competing with Canadians for value and cultural dominance. That is, immigrants may be seen as competing with Canadians for establishing which group's culture and values are most "important" or most "correct" (see also Esses, Haddock and Zanna, 1993; and Greenberg, Solomon and Pyszczynksi, 1997). This relates to theorizing about the role of value threat in intergroup relations (e.g., Sears, 1988; Stephan and Stephan, 2000). For example, Symbolic Racism Theory (Sears, 1988) suggests that perceptions of value threat, in particular with respect to threats to Whites from Blacks in the United States, lead to opposition to policies and programs that benefit Blacks. Similarly, Stephan and Stephan's Integrated Threat Theory of Prejudice proposes that threats to the worldview of the in-group have a causal role to play in prejudice towards out-groups. Thus, the belief that immigrants compete for value and cultural dominance with Canadians would be expected to cause opposition to immigration and negative attitudes towards immigrants.

Relatedly, and third, immigrants from specific regions of the world may be perceived to pose a variety of additional threats to Canadians. The Integrated Threat Theory of Prejudice (Stephan and Stephan, 2000) hypothesizes that these threats may include any threat to the welfare of the group or its members. In addition, the extent and nature of these threats might differ depending on the specific out-group in question. In turn, these perceived threats are proposed to lead to negative attitudes towards the source of threat and lack of support for relevant policies. Thus, at present, immigrants from the Middle East may be especially likely to be perceived as posing a threat to Canadians, leading to negative attitudes towards Middle Eastern immigrants and possible support for national-origin restrictions on immigration.

Fourth, another key belief is that immigrants are different from Canadians in fundamental ways and are not part of the Canadian in-group. According to Social Identity Theory (Tajfel and Turner, 1979; see also Self-Categorization Theory: Turner et al., 1987), the categorization of people into out-groups and an in-group stimulates a motivation to maintain or achieve a sense of positive group distinctiveness. Strategies for doing so include denigrating out-groups and limiting the opportunities of other groups and their members. Thus, the belief that immigrants are not part of the Canadian in-group may lead to denigration of immigrants and opposition to immigration.

In sum, there is a reason to expect that each of these four beliefs — resource competition, value competition, threat to welfare, and group identity — may be related to negative attitudes towards immigrants and immigration. In addition, these four types of beliefs may be interrelated, and may be endorsed more strongly by certain types of individuals than by others. That is, there may be systematic differences between individuals in the likelihood of holding these beliefs. We turn next to two individual difference variables related to prejudice that may relate to the extent to

Victoria M. Esses, Gordon Hodson and John F. Dovidio

which people hold these different beliefs, and perhaps consequently to their attitudes about immigrants and immigration.

The Role of Individual Differences

Social Dominance Orientation is a personality measure designed to assess individual differences in the belief in equality and preference for hierarchically structured social systems (Pratto, 1999; Sidanius and Pratto, 1999). Individuals who are high in social dominance orientation believe that unequal social outcomes and social hierarchies are appropriate and typically express negative attitudes towards minority groups. We would expect that individuals who desire a hierarchical structure in society believe that groups must continually compete for their place in society. Thus, they may be especially likely to believe in the existence of zero-sum competition between groups for resources that can be used to obtain status and power. This may even extend beyond perceived competition for resources and be a general tendency to see the world as involving competition for dominance in all domains of life (see also Sidanius, Pratto and Bobo, 1994). We would expect, then, that high social dominance oriented individuals would be especially likely to endorse both of the first two key beliefs — immigrants compete with Canadians already living here for resources, and immigrants compete with Canadians already living here for value and cultural dominance (see also Esses et al., 2001; Esses, Jackson and Armstrong, 1998). Because of their desire for a hierarchy of groups in society, high social dominance oriented individuals may also be particularly sensitive to group boundaries, and thus to differences between groups. As a result, they may be unlikely to see immigrants as part of the Canadian in-group and instead may be especially likely to endorse the belief that immigrants are different from Canadians in fundamental ways. To the extent that high social dominance oriented individuals endorse these three beliefs, they would be expected to be particularly likely to hold negative attitudes towards immigrants and immigration.

In contrast to Social Dominance Orientation, Right-Wing Authoritarianism may be more related to the belief in more general threats from immigrants from particular regions of the world. Whereas high social dominance orientation may involve a view of the world as a competitive place, high right-wing authoritarianism may involve a view of the world as a dangerous place (see Duckitt *et al.*, 2002). Right-wing authoritarianism involves submission to authority, conventionalism, and willingness to aggress against those who do not follow conventional ways (Altemeyer, 1988, 1996). High right-wing authoritarians tend to be threatened by a variety of out-groups and to hold negative attitudes towards these groups. We might expect, then, that high right-wing authoritarians would also be especially likely to be threatened by and to hold negative attitudes towards immigrants and immigration.

The Relation Between these Beliefs and Immigration Attitudes

To highlight the role of these four key beliefs in determining negative attitudes towards immigrants and immigration, we describe here a study conducted at the University of Western Ontario in the fall and winter of 2001. We examined the relation between these beliefs and three important variables: attitudes towards immigration to Canada, attitudes towards immigrants in Canada, and support for origin-based immigration policies. It is sometimes claimed by groups and individuals that although they oppose current levels of immigration, this has no bearing on their attitudes towards or treatment of immigrants.[5] Thus, we examined separately attitudes towards immigration versus attitudes towards immigrants. In addition, we included the assessment of support for origin-based restrictions on immigration because of an increased concern about Middle Eastern immigration to Canada since the September 11, 2001 terrorist attacks on the United States. For example, a recent poll found that 43% of respondents believe that Canada accepts too many immigrants from Arab countries, compared to 16% who believe that Canada accepts too many immigrants from Europe (Baxter, 2002; see also Walton and Kennedy, 2002).

Participants were 102 undergraduate students (37 men, 65 women) at the University of Western Ontario, whose age ranged from 17 to 47 years old. All were Canadian citizens, with 88 born in Canada and 14 born

---

[5]See <http://www.fraserinstitute.ca/shared/readmore.asp?sNav=nr&id=480>; <http://www.canadafirst.net/myths/myth8.html>.

outside Canada. They were asked to complete a variety of measures, in which our key variables of interest were embedded.

The assessment of attitudes towards immigration included items routinely used in national surveys (e.g., "If it were your job to plan Canada's immigration policy, would you decrease or increase the level of immigration?"). The assessment of attitudes towards immigrants focused on overall attitudes towards immigrants (e.g., What is your overall attitude towards immigrants?"). The assessment of support for origin-based immigration policies asked respondents to indicate their degree of support for immigration policies that take into account the applicant's country of origin. The descriptive statistics for these variables are presented in Table 1. As is evident, overall attitudes are relatively neutral, though there was considerable variability in participants on these measures. The relations among the measures are shown in Table 2. As in our previous research (e.g., Esses, Jackson and Armstrong, 1998), attitudes towards immigration and attitudes towards immigrants are highly correlated though not completely redundant. Support for origin-based immigration policies is also significantly correlated with attitudes towards immigration and attitudes towards immigrants, but these relations are much less substantial. For example, negative attitudes towards immigrants and support for origin-based immigration policies share only about 10% of their variance.

Beliefs about Immigration to Canada

To assess the beliefs about immigration that formed the focus of our study, we utilized four separate measures (see Table 3). The measure of zero-sum resources is a balanced measure of zero-sum beliefs about economic and power relations between immigrants and non-immigrants (e.g., "The more business opportunities are made available for immigrants, the fewer business opportunities are available for Canadians already living here.") (Esses *et al.*, 2001; Esses, Jackson and Armstrong, 1998). The measure of zero-sum values/culture is a balanced measure of zero-sum beliefs about values and culture that we developed for this research (e.g., "Allowing immigrant cultures to thrive means that Canadian culture is weakened."). The measure of one group representation assesses the extent to which individuals see immigrants and non-immigrants as part of one group (e.g., "The distinction between immigrants and non-immigrants is artificial. We are all Canadians."). Finally, the measure of threat by immigrants from specific regions of the world asks about threats to Canadians in a variety of

Table 1: Descriptive Statistics for Attitudes Towards Immigration, Attitudes Towards Immigrants, and Support for Origin-Based Immigration Policies

	Mean	S.D.	Minimum	Maximum
Attitude towards immigration (−4 to +4)	1.19	1.70	−3.00	4.00
Attitude towards immigrants (−4 to +4)	2.01	1.60	−3.00	4.00
Support for origin-based immigration policies (1 to 9)	4.20	2.89	1.00	9.00

Note: N = 101–102.

Table 2: Correlations Between Attitudes Towards Immigration, Attitudes Towards Immigrants, and Support for Origin-Based Immigration Policies

	1	2	3
1. Attitude towards immigration			
2. Attitude towards immigrants		0.80**	−0.26**
3. Support for origin-based immigration policies			−0.33***

Note: N = 101–102. * $p < .05$, ** $p < .01$, *** $p < .001$ (two-tailed).

Table 3: Measures of Beliefs about Immigration to Canada

Zero-Sum Resources

1. Canadians already living here lose out when immigrants make political and economic gains.
2. As immigrants gain political power, Canadians already living here lose out.
3. The more business opportunities are made available for immigrants, the fewer business opportunities are available for Canadians already living here.
4. More tax dollars spent on immigrants means fewer tax dollars spent on Canadians already living here.
5. The more educational opportunities are available for immigrants, the fewer educational opportunities are available for Canadians already living here.
6. The more power immigrants obtain, the more difficult it is for Canadians already living here.
7. More good jobs for immigrants does not mean fewer good jobs for Canadians already living here. (R)
8. Educational opportunities for immigrants means fewer spots and opportunities for Canadians already living here.
9. Allowing immigrants to decide on political issues means that Canadians already living here have less say in how the country is run.
10. Canadians already living here may no longer have a say in how this country is run because immigrants are trying to take control.
11. Money spent on social services for immigrants means less money for services for Canadians already living here.
12. Progress for immigrants does not mean that it will be harder for Canadians already living here to get ahead. (R)
13. More immigrants in positions of power does not mean fewer good jobs for Canadians already living here. (R)
14. When immigrants make economic gains, Canadians already living here do not lose out economically. (R)
15. When immigrants make economic gains, it is not at the expense of Canadians already living here. (R)

... continued

Table 3 continued

Zero-Sum Values/Culture

1. Allowing immigrant cultures to thrive means that Canadian culture is weakened.
2. It is difficult for Canadian culture to thrive when immigrant cultures are practised here.
3. The more immigrants promote their own culture, the less opportunity there is for Canadian culture to thrive.
4. When immigrants promote their own values, it is at the expense of Canadian values.
5. When immigrants are encouraged to maintain their cultural practices, Canadian culture is weakened.
6. Immigrants are trying to promote their own culture at the expense of Canadian culture.
7. Allowing immigrants to follow their traditions does not weaken the practice of Canadian traditions. (R)
8. When immigrant values are accepted in this country, fewer Canadian values are upheld.
9. Canadian religions are suffering because of the variety of religions practised by immigrants.
10. The religious beliefs held by immigrants cannot co-exist with Canadian religious beliefs.
11. The variety of languages spoken by immigrants detracts from the teaching of English in our schools.
12. Immigrant and Canadian cultures can co-exist in this country and each remain strong. (R)
13. It is not difficult for Canadians to promote their culture when so many immigrants are doing the same. (R)
14. The Canadian way of life is not incompatible with that of immigrants. (R)
15. The values held by immigrants are not incompatible with Canadian values. (R)

... **continued**

Victoria M. Esses, Gordon Hodson and John F. Dovidio

Table 3 continued

One-Group Representation

1. I don't think of people in terms of being immigrants or non-immigrants, only as people who are now part of one group — Canadians.
2. The distinction between immigrants and non-immigrants is artificial. We are all Canadians.

Threat

1. To what extent is Canadian *safety/security* threatened by people from the following geographic regions? (United States, Europe, Asia, Middle East, Africa)
2. To what extent is Canadian *psychological well-being* threatened by people from the following geographic regions? (United States, Europe, Asia, Middle East, Africa)
3. To what extent is Canadian *identity* threatened by people from the following geographic regions? (United States, Europe, Asia, Middle East, Africa)
4. To what extent is Canadian *religious life* threatened by people from the following geographic regions? (United States, Europe, Asia, Middle East, Africa)
5. To what extent are Canadian *values* threatened by people from the following geographic regions? (United States, Europe, Asia, Middle East, Africa)

Note: R = reverse coded; for all measures, alpha > 0.76.

domains (e.g., safety/security, psychological well-being) and assesses separately perceived threats by people from the United States, Europe, Asia, Middle East, and Africa. It is important to note that this measure assesses perceived threats from people from different regions of the world, without specifically focusing on immigrants per se. In this way, it is clearly distinguishable from the zero-sum resources and values/culture measures. In all cases, average scores were computed across items within a measure, and the reliabilities of all four measures were quite high (>0.76).

The descriptive statistics for these measures are presented in Table 4. Participants provided a large range of responses to these measures, with mean perceptions suggesting overall mild to moderate endorsement of these beliefs. The relations among the measures are shown in Table 5. The zero-sum resources and zero-sum values/culture measures are quite highly correlated, suggesting the possibility that the degree of one's belief in group competition may be a generalized tendency, transcending domains of relevance. In contrast, the zero-sum belief measures are only mildly to moderately correlated with the one-group representation measure and the measure of threat by people from specific regions of the world.

Individual Difference Variables

The two individual difference variables included in this study were Social Dominance Orientation (Pratto *et al.*, 1994) and Right-Wing Authoritarianism (Altemeyer, 1996). As mentioned earlier, Social Dominance Orientation is a personality measure designed to assess individual differences in belief in inequality and preference for hierarchically structured social systems (e.g., "Some groups of people are just more worthy than others; All groups should be given an equal chance in life (R)"), (Pratto *et al.*, 1994; Pratto, 1999; Sidanius and Pratto, 1999). It is a 16-item balanced scale, with good reliability (alpha = 0.87 in the current study).

Right-Wing Authoritarianism (Altemeyer, 1996) is a personality measure designed to assess belief in traditional values, submission to authority, and willingness to aggress against individuals who are seen as threatening traditional ways (e.g., "Once our government leaders and the authorities condemn the dangerous elements in our society, it will be the duty of every patriotic citizen to help stomp out the rot that is poisoning our country from within; Obedience and respect for authority are the most important virtues children should learn"). It is a 30-item balanced scale, with good reliability (alpha = 0.92 in the current study). Individuals who

Table 4: Descriptive Statistics for Zero-Sum Resources, Zero-Sum Values/Culture, One-Group Representation, and Threat by Immigrants from Specific Regions

	Mean	S.D.	Minimum	Maximum
Zero-sum resources (1 to 7)	3.03	1.09	1.00	5.73
Zero-sum values (1 to 7)	2.69	1.06	1.00	5.20
One-group representation (1 to 7)	5.13	1.52	1.50	7.00
Middle East threat (1 to 9)	3.97	1.80	1.00	7.80
Asia threat (1 to 9	3.07	1.49	1.00	6.80
Africa threat (1 to 9)	2.43	1.26	1.00	6.40
US threat (1 to 9)	3.86	2.08	1.00	9.00
Europe threat (1 to 9)	2.71	1.47	1.00	7.40

Note: N = 101–102.

Table 5: Correlations Between Zero-Sum Resources, Zero-Sum Values/Culture, One-Group Representation, and Threat by Immigrants from Specific Regions

	1.	2.	3.	4.	5.	6.	7.	8.
1. Zero-sum resources		0.74***	–0.38***	0.29**	0.19	0.20	–0.04	0.10
2. Zero-sum values			–0.39***	0.39***	0.33***	0.27**	0.03	0.19
3. One-group representation				–0.40***	–0.28**	–0.07	0.02	–0.08
4. Middle East threat					0.69***	0.49***	0.24*	0.29**
5. Asia threat						0.65***	0.48***	0.67***
6. Africa threat							0.18	0.41**
7. US threat								0.75**
8. Europe threat								

Note: N = 101–102. * p < .05, ** p < .01, *** p < .001 (two-tailed).

are high in right-wing authoritarianism have been described as self-righteous individuals who feel threatened by members of other groups (see Altemeyer, 1988).

As in previous research (Esses, Jackson and Armstrong, 1998; Pratto *et al.*, 1994), Social Dominance Orientation and Right-Wing Authoritarianism were only weakly related, r (100) = 0.19, p < 0.06. In addition, they showed rather different relations to a measure of participants' political orientations included in this study. The political orientation item asked participants to indicate their political leaning on a scale from very liberal to very conservative. As expected, we found that Social Dominance Orientation was not significantly correlated with political leaning, r (100) = 0.08, ns, whereas Right-Wing Authoritarianism showed a significant positive correlation with political leaning, r (100) = 0.37, p < .001. Thus, high right-wing authoritarians tended to also rate themselves as politically conservative.

Correlational Findings

To examine the relation between the four key beliefs that formed the basis of our research and immigration attitudes, we first examined the correlations between the beliefs and immigration attitudes. We also examined the correlations between Social Dominance Orientation, Right-Wing Authoritarianism, and immigration attitudes. As shown in Table 6, zero-sum beliefs about resources and zero-sum beliefs about values strongly predict attitudes towards immigration and immigrants, and support for origin-based immigration policies. One-group representation also predicts these attitudes. In terms of perceived threats by people from specific

Table 6: Correlations Between Beliefs about Immigration, Personality Measures, and Immigration-Related Attitudes

	Attitude Towards Immigration	Attitude Towards Immigrants	Support for Origin-Based Immigration Policies
Zero-sum resources	−0.57***	−0.57***	0.41***
Zero-sum values	−0.53***	−0.51***	0.30**
One-group representation	0.35***	0.47***	−0.39***
Middle East threat	−0.25*	−0.21*	0.36***
Asia threat	−0.22*	−0.14	0.19
Africa threat	−0.38***	−0.18	0.13
US threat	0.03	0.00	0.05
Europe threat	−0.07	0.00	0.10
Social Dominance Orientation	−0.23*	−0.26**	0.26**
Right-Wing Authoritarianism	−0.04	0.01	0.18

Note: N = 101–102. * p < .05, ** p < .01, *** p < .001 (two-tailed).

regions of the world, it is clear that perceived threat from Middle Eastern immigrants most consistently predicts attitudes, though perceived threats from Asian and African immigrants also predict attitudes towards immigration. As is also evident from Table 6, Social Dominance Orientation consistently predicts the immigration attitudes, whereas Right-Wing Authoritarianism does not.

Mediational Analyses

To determine whether high social dominance oriented individuals are less favourable towards immigration and immigrants, and are more supportive of origin-based restrictions on immigration, *because of* the four types of beliefs about immigration, we first looked at the relations between Social Dominance Orientation and these beliefs. For the purpose of these analyses, in examining perceived threat we focused specifically on threat from Middle Eastern immigrants. As shown on the left of Figure 1, Social Dominance Orientation is significantly related to the four types of beliefs. Thus, high social dominance oriented individuals are especially likely to endorse zero-sum beliefs about resources, zero-sum beliefs about values and culture, beliefs about threat from Middle Eastern people, and are especially likely to reject the idea that immigrants and non-immigrants are part of one group.

Following the procedure outlined by Baron and Kenny (1986), we then used a series of multiple regression analyses to determine whether these beliefs mediate the relation between Social Dominance Orientation and immigration attitudes. Figure 1 shows the results of the mediational analyses for attitudes towards immigration. As shown at the top of Figure 1, when Social Dominance Orientation and zero-sum resources are used together to predict attitudes towards immigration, the effect of Social Dominance Orientation on attitudes towards immigration is reduced to non-significance, whereas the effect of zero-sum resources remains significant. Thus, the relation between Social Dominance Orientation and attitudes towards immigration is due to high social dominance oriented people holding zero-sum beliefs about resources. Similar results are obtained for zero-sum values, one-group representation, and Middle Eastern threat as mediators of the relation between Social Dominance Orientation and attitudes towards immigration. Thus, high social dominance oriented individuals hold unfavourable attitudes towards *immigration* because they hold these different types of beliefs.

Victoria M. Esses, Gordon Hodson and John F. Dovidio

Figure 1: Tests of Mediation Between Social Dominance Orientation and Attitudes Towards Immigration

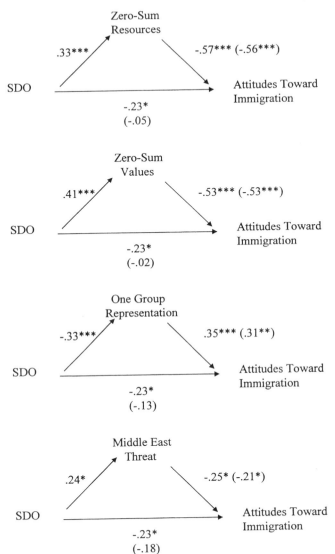

Note: Pearson correlations are indicated on figure paths. Numbers in parentheses indicate partial correlations from multiple regression analyses where Social Dominance Orientation and the potential mediator are entered together to predict attitudes towards immigration. *** p < .001, ** p < .01, * p < .05.

Figure 2 shows the mediational analyses for attitudes towards immigrants. In this case, zero-sum beliefs about resources, zero-sum beliefs about values and culture, and one-group representation play a mediational role, whereas beliefs about threat from Middle Eastern people do not. Thus, high social dominance oriented individuals hold unfavourable attitudes towards *immigrants* because they hold zero-sum beliefs about the relationship between immigrants and non-immigrants (both in terms of resources and values), and because they do not see immigrants as part of their national group.

Finally, Figure 3 shows the mediational analyses for support for origin-based immigration policies. Once again, all four types of beliefs have a mediational role to play. That is, high social dominance oriented individuals support *origin-based immigration policies* because they hold the four different types of beliefs.

Summary

The four types of beliefs we have focused on — zero-sum beliefs about resources, zero-sum beliefs about values, one-group representation, and threat from Middle Eastern people — significantly predict attitudes towards immigration, attitudes towards immigrants, and support for origin-based immigration policies. In addition, these beliefs, particularly the zero-sum beliefs and one-group representation, tend to mediate the significant relation between Social Dominance Orientation and immigration attitudes. It seems, then, that these beliefs have a role to play in promoting opposition to immigration. In addition, contrary to popular claims that one can oppose immigration without implications for attitudes towards immigrants,[6] the arguments against current immigration levels also seem to have a role to play in promoting unfavourable attitudes towards *immigrants*. Finally, amid growing support among the Canadian public for origin-based immigration policies (Baxter, 2002), it seems that support for such policies is promoted by these types of beliefs.

Whereas Social Dominance Orientation systematically predicted the immigration attitudes, Right-Wing Authoritarianism did not. This is consistent with our previous research (see Esses *et al.*, 2001; Esses, Jackson

---

[6]See <http://www.fraserinstitute.ca/shared/readmore.asp?sNav=nr&id=480>; <http://www.canadafirst.net/myths/myth8.html>.

Victoria M. Esses, Gordon Hodson and John F. Dovidio

Figure 2: Tests of Mediation Between Social Dominance Orientation and Attitudes Towards Immigrants

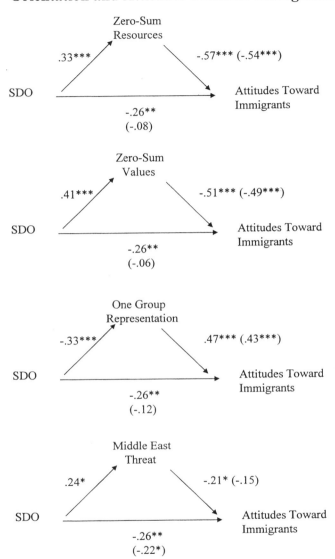

Note: Pearson correlations are indicated on figure paths. Numbers in parentheses indicate partial correlations from multiple regression analyses where Social Dominance Orientation and the potential mediator are entered together to predict attitudes towards immigrants. *** $p < .001$, ** $p < .01$, * $p < .05$.

Figure 3: Tests of Mediation Between Social Dominance Orientation and Support for Origin-Based Immigration Policies

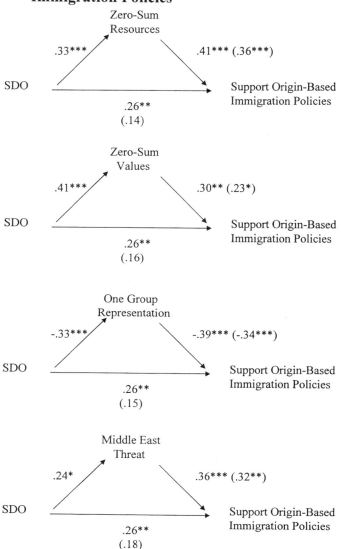

Note: Pearson correlations are indicated on figure paths. Numbers in parentheses indicate partial correlations from multiple regression analyses where Social Dominance Orientation and the potential mediator are entered together to predict support for origin-based immigration policies. *** $p < .001$, ** $p < .01$, * $p < .05$.

Victoria M. Esses, Gordon Hodson and John F. Dovidio

and Armstrong, 1998) and suggests that belief in group hierarchies and competition between groups may be crucial for determining immigration attitudes. Conventionalism and submission to authority, as assessed in terms of Right-Wing Authoritarianism, seem to have less of a role to play.

In addition, although perceived threat from Middle Eastern people was significantly related to attitudes towards immigrants and immigration, these relations tended to be weaker than those evident for the three other types of beliefs. Also, in contrast to the other three types of beliefs, perceived threat from Middle Eastern people did not mediate the relation between Social Dominance Orientation and attitudes towards immigrants. These findings are potentially attributable to our strategy for assessing perceived threat, which did not focus on immigrants per se. Perceived threat from Middle Eastern people did, however, show a strong relation to support for origin-based immigration policies, and significantly mediated the relation between Social Dominance Orientation and this support. In this case, the immigration attitude being assessed specifically focuses on the potential national origins of immigrants so that threat from people of a particular origin would be expected to have more of a role to play.

Strategies for Counteracting these Effects

Given that we have gained some knowledge of the bases of negative attitudes towards immigrants and immigration, and support for origin-based policies, what strategies might we implement to counteract these effects? To be effective, these strategies would have to be particularly targeted at high social dominance oriented individuals, who are especially likely to hold negative immigration attitudes and hold beliefs that bolster these attitudes. Two possibilities that we have explored to date are to provide information that contradicts zero-sum beliefs about economic and power relations between immigrants and non-immigrants, and to provide arguments in favour of seeing immigrants and non-immigrants as part of one common group (see Esses et al., 2001). Both strategies target key beliefs held by high social dominance oriented individuals.

Targeting Zero-Sum Beliefs

The first strategy seemed quite straightforward. We reasoned that because perceptions of zero-sum competition between immigrants and non-immigrants for resources lead to unfavourable immigration attitudes, targeting and challenging these beliefs directly might serve to improve immigration attitudes. This approach would be particularly relevant to people who are high in Social Dominance Orientation, who are especially likely to see immigrants as competing with their group for resources. To evaluate this strategy, we conducted a study in which 150 University of Western Ontario undergraduate students were presented with one of three editorials about immigration to Canada which we developed specifically for this purpose: neutral, positive, or targeting zero-sum beliefs. Following some filler tasks, we assessed their attitudes towards immigrants and immigration (see Esses *et al.*, 2001). The neutral editorial discussed general and benign immigration issues. The positive editorial discussed the economic benefits of immigration, in terms of employment and more general financial prosperity for the country. The crucial editorial targeting zero-sum beliefs went one step further. In the context of discussing the economic benefits of immigration, this editorial directly contradicted the type of zero-sum beliefs found to be related to immigration attitudes. For example, it stated, "It is not the case that when immigrants make gains in employment, it is at the expense of Canadians already living here."

The editorials had the predicted effect, but only for people low in Social Dominance Orientation (see Table 7). The editorial containing positive information about immigration and the editorial targeting zero-sum beliefs led to more favourable attitudes towards immigrants and immigration for individuals low in Social Dominance Orientation. Contrary to our expectations, however, for individuals high in Social Dominance Orientation, whereas the positive information editorial had no effect on attitudes, the editorial targeting zero-sum beliefs seemed to have a rebound effect. Compared to the control condition, participants in this condition had more *negative* attitudes towards immigrants. A trend in the same direction was evident for attitudes towards immigration.

One interpretation of these results might be that the message targeting zero-sum beliefs was not credible in general. However, this seems unlikely because the message was effective in improving the attitudes of people low in Social Dominance Orientation. Instead, we suggest that people high in Social Dominance Orientation, who chronically hold zero-sum beliefs, may have attempted to counter-argue this message that challenges such a central

Table 7: Attitudes Towards Immigrants as a Function of Social Dominance Orientation and Manipulation of Zero-Sum Beliefs about Resources

	Message		
Social Dominance	*Neutral*	*Positive*	*Not Zero-Sum*
Low	1.70	2.90	2.58
High	1.36	1.44	0.67

Note: N = 150. Possible range = –4 to +4.

aspect of their worldview, reinforcing their zero-sum beliefs and negative attitudes towards immigrants. Thus, directly targeting zero-sum beliefs may not be a generally effective strategy for improving negative attitudes towards immigrants and immigration because of the reactance it can create in people high in Social Dominance Orientation.

One-Group Representation

The second strategy we utilized focused on one-group representation and attempted to promote the perception that immigrants and non-immigrants are all part of one common Canadian in-group. This builds on research on the Common Ingroup Identity Model (Gaertner and Dovidio, 2000; Gaertner et al., 1993; Gaertner et al., 1999), which has demonstrated the benefits of recategorizing in-group and out-group members as members of a more inclusive, superordinate group. In particular, Gaertner, Dovidio, and their colleagues propose that increasing the salience of a common in-group identity (for example, by emphasizing membership in shared social categories or interdependence between groups) produces more positive attitudes towards former out-group members through processes involving pro-ingroup bias. Of importance, Gaertner et al. (1999) note that it is not the case that the development of a common in-group requires that each group give up its former identity completely. Rather, it is possible (and sometimes beneficial) for group members to maintain hyphenated, or dual, identities (Hornsey and Hogg, 2000).

To examine the effects of the one-group representation strategy, we conducted a study in which 160 University of Western Ontario undergraduates were presented with one of four editorials about immigration to Canada which we had developed specifically for this purpose: neutral, common ethnic roots, common Canadian identity, or both common ethnic roots and common Canadian identity (Esses *et al.*, 2001; Esses *et al.*, in press). Following some filler tasks, we assessed their attitudes towards immigrants and immigration. The neutral editorial presented general and benign information about immigrants. The remaining three editorials all focused on a common in-group including immigrants and non-immigrants, though in different ways. The editorial emphasizing common ethnic roots was intended to form a connection between participants and immigrants through a common history of immigration. To do so, it reminded participants that immigrants of different ethnic backgrounds have a long history in Canada, and that they themselves could likely trace their own ethnic roots (though not the *same* ethnic roots for all people). In other words, this editorial suggested that most Canadians are "ethnics" of some sort. For example, it stated, "Many ethnic groups in Canada today are descended from people who immigrated to Canada within the past century." The editorial emphasizing common national identity similarly was intended to form a connection between immigrants and non-immigrants, but through a common present and future, rather than past. To do so, it emphasized a united national identity that includes both native-born individuals and immigrants in what it means to be Canadian. For example, it stated, "Whether we immigrated to Canada yesterday or several generations ago, we are all united today in our common Canadian identity." The final editorial included both common ethnic roots and common national identity passages.

No significant effects were found on attitudes towards immigration. In terms of attitudes towards immigrants, however, we found that across individuals low *and* high in social dominance orientation, the three editorials designed to induce a common, inclusive national identity produced more positive attitudes than did the neutral editorial (Table 8). For high social dominance oriented individuals, the editorials that focused on a common Canadian identity or on both common ethnic roots and a common Canadian identity were most effective.

Table 8: Attitudes Towards Immigrants as a Function of Social Dominance Orientation and Manipulation of Common Ethnic Roots and Common National Identity

	Message			
Social Dominance	*Neutral*	*Common Ethnic Roots*	*Common National Identity*	*Common Roots and Identity*
Low	1.77	2.65	2.28	2.59
High	1.28	1.85	2.12	2.47

Note: N = 160. Possible range = –4 to +4.

It is of interest that no significant effects of the messages were evident in attitudes towards immigration. In the present case, the common in-group messages were more specifically directed at recategorizing current immigrants as part of the in-group than at promoting increased immigration in general. Over time, however, more favourable attitudes towards immigrants might translate into more open immigration policies via contact and familiarity with immigrants (see Gaertner *et al.*, 1999).

Conclusions

In this paper, we explored the hypothesis that beliefs about immigration are critical factors in opposition to current immigration levels, support for origin-based immigration policies, and negative attitudes towards immigrants. In particular, we found that four basic beliefs — beliefs about resource competition, value competition, threats to well-being, and different group membership — systematically predicted more negative attitudes about immigration and immigrants. Our research has further demonstrated that people higher in Social Dominance Orientation hold more negative attitudes about immigration and immigrants, and that these negative attitudes are mediated by perceptions of resource and value competition and by perceptions that immigrants do not belong to their Canadian in-group.

Understanding the nature of the beliefs and the individual differences that underlie attitudes towards immigrants and immigration can critically inform strategies designed to promote more positive attitudes. In particular, if we wish to garner support for our current immigration policies and acceptance of immigrants in Canada, we will have to work to counteract these beliefs.

However, these principles need to be applied cautiously. As we initially expected, presenting information that was designed to undermine zero-sum beliefs about competition between Canadians and immigrants produced more positive attitudes among people low in Social Dominance Orientation. However, perhaps because this intervention aroused reactions and defensiveness among people for whom zero-sum beliefs are an important aspect of their worldview, this information exacerbated negative attitudes towards immigrants for people high in Social Dominance Orientation. Instead, for those high in Social Dominance Orientation, an intervention that led them to view immigrants as part of the Canadian in-group, which capitalized on their strong tendency to view the world in terms of hier-archically structured social categories, effectively improved their attitudes towards immigrants.

Taken together, our results demonstrate how psychological factors, such as Social Dominance Orientation, and psychological processes, such as perceptions of zero-sum relations and social categorization, can jointly shape attitudes towards immigrants and immigration. Understanding the nature of these relationships can determine the most influential bases of negative attitudes, identify the actual sources of resistance to immigration to Canada, and guide interventions aimed at improving attitudes towards immigrants and immigration. This perspective also illustrates the valuable, complementary roles that theory and application can play to address contemporary social issues and problems. By understanding why negative attitudes exist, who is likely to hold these attitudes, and how negative attitudes can be effectively combated, it may be possible to benefit from the diverse talents, resources, and cultures of immigrant groups in Canada and forge productive relations that will benefit all groups and our society as a whole.

Victoria M. Esses, Gordon Hodson and John F. Dovidio

References

Altemeyer, B. (1988), *Enemies of Freedom: Understanding Right-wing Authoritarianism* (San Francisco: Jossey-Bass).

_____ (1996), *The Authoritarian Specter* (Cambridge, MA: Harvard University Press).

Baron, R.M. and D.A. Kenny (1986), "The Moderator-Mediator Variable Distinction in Social Psychological Research: Conceptual, Strategic, and Statistical Considerations", *Journal of Personality and Social Psychology* 51, 1173–1182.

Baxter, J. (2002), "Asian, Arab Immigrants Least Favoured: Canadians are more Open to Accepting Newcomers from Europe, Latin America, and Africa", *Ottawa Citizen*, September 12.

Bobo, L. (1988), "Group Conflict, Prejudice, and the Paradox of Contemporary Racial Attitudes", in P.A. Katz and D.A. Taylor (eds.), *Eliminating Racism: Profiles in Controversy* (New York: Plenum), 85–114.

Canada First Immigration Reform Committee (2002), <http://www.canadafirst.net>.

Collacott, M. (2002), "Canada's Immigration Policy: The Need for Major Reform". At <http://www.fraserinstitute.ca/admin/books/files/immigration.pdf>.

Corcoran, T. (2002), "Red Flags Over Immigration", *National Post*. At <http://www.nationalpost.com/financialpost/story.html?id=%7B3DDC42A8-7734-468D-8606-758DA5C07F4F%7D>, October 3.

Duckitt, J., C. Wagner, I. du Plessis and I. Birum (2002), "The Psychological Bases of Ideology and Prejudice: Testing a Dual Process Model", *Journal of Personality and Social Psychology* 83, 75–93.

Esses, V.M., G. Haddock and M.P. Zanna (1993), "Values, Stereotypes, and Emotions as Determinants of Intergroup Attitudes", in D.M. Mackie and D.L. Hamilton (eds.), *Affect, Cognition and Stereotyping: Interactive Processes in Group Perception* (San Diego: Academic Press), 137–166.

Esses, V.M., L.M. Jackson and T.L. Armstrong (1998), "Intergroup Competition and Attitudes Toward Immigrants and Immigration: An Instrumental Model of Group Conflict", *Journal of Social Issues* 54, 699–724.

Esses, V.M., J.F. Dovidio, L.M. Jackson and A.H. Semenya (in press), "Attitudes Toward Immigrants and Immigration: The Role of National and International Identities", in D. Abrams, J.M. Marques and M.A. Hogg (eds.), *The Social Psychology of Inclusion and Exclusion* (Philadelphia: Psychology Press).

Esses, V.M., J.F. Dovidio, L.M. Jackson and T.L. Armstrong (2001), "The Immigration Dilemma: The Role of Perceived Group Competition, Ethnic Prejudice, and National Identity", in V.M. Esses, J.F. Dovidio and K.L. Dion (eds.), *Immigrants and Immigration, Journal of Social Issues* 57 (Special issue), 389–412.

Francis, D. (2001), "Federal Policy Alarms Reader: Annual Immigration Target Makes Matters Worse", *National Post*, June 12.

_____ (2002a), "No Improvement in Woes: Little Coordination Between Police and 'Refugee' Practices", *National Post*. At <http://www.nationalpost.com/financialpost/story.html?id=%7BB55238DC-E400-4140-8EA3-6A66B478C7A9%7D>, October 8.

_____ (2002b), *Immigration: The Economic Case* (Toronto: Key Porter Books).

Gaertner, S. L. and J.F. Dovidio (2000), *Reducing Intergroup Bias: The Common Ingroup Identity Model* (Philadelphia, PA: Psychology Press).

Gaertner, S., J.F. Dovidio, J.A. Nier, C.M. Ward and B.S. Banker (1999), "Across Cultural Divides: The Value of a Superordinate Identity", in D.A. Prentice and D.T. Miller (eds.), *Cultural Divides: Understanding and Overcoming Group Conflict* (New York: Russell Sage), 173–212.

Gaertner, S., J.F. Dovidio, P.A. Anastasio, B.A. Bachman and M.C. Rust (1993), "The Common Ingroup Identity Model: Recategorization and the Reduction of Intergroup Bias", in W. Stroebe and M. Hewstone (eds.), *European Review of Social Psychology* 4 (Chichester, England: John Wiley), 1–26.

Greenberg, J., S. Solomon and T. Pyszczynski (1997), "Terror Management Theory of Self-Esteem and Cultural Worldviews: Empirical Assessments and Cultural Refinements", in M.P. Zanna (ed.), *Advances in Experimental Social Psychology*, Vol. 29 (Orlando, FL: Academic Press), 61–139.

Hornsey, M.J. and M.A. Hogg (2000), "Intergroup Similarity and Subgroup Relations: Some Implications for Assimilation", *Personality and Social Psychology Bulletin* 26, 948–958.

LeVine, R.A. and D.T. Campbell (1972), *Ethnocentrism: Theories of Conflict, Ethnic Attitudes, and Group Behavior* (New York: Wiley).

McFarland, S.G. and S. Adelson (1996), "An Omnibus Study of Personality, Values, and Prejudice". Paper presented at the annual meeting of the International Society for Political Psychology, Vancouver, July.

Pratto, F. (1999), "The Puzzle of Continuing Group Inequality: Piecing Together Psychological, Social, and Cultural Forces in Social Dominance Theory", in M.P. Zanna (ed.), *Advances in Experimental Social Psychology*, Vol. 31 (San Diego: Academic Press), 191–263.

Pratto, F., J. Sidanius, L.M. Stallworth and B.F. Malle (1994), "Social Dominance Orientation: A Personality Variable Predicting Social and Political Attitudes", *Journal of Personality and Social Psychology* 67, 741–763.

Sears, D.O. (1988), "Symbolic Racism", in P.A Katz and D.A. Taylor (eds.), *Eliminating Racism: Profiles in Controversy* (New York: Plenum), 53–84.

Sherif, M. (1966), *Group Conflict and Cooperation: Their Social Psychology* (London: Routledge and Kegan Paul).

Sidanius, J. and F. Pratto (1999), *Social Dominance: An Intergroup Theory of Social Hierarchy and Oppression* (New York: Cambridge University Press).

Sidanius, J., F. Pratto and L. Bobo (1994), "Social Dominance Orientation and Political Psychology of Gender: A Case of Invariance?" *Journal of Personality and Social Psychology* 67, 998–1011.

Stephan, W.G. and C.W. Stephan (2000), "An Integrated Threat Theory of Prejudice", in S. Oskamp (ed.), *Claremont Symposium on Applied Social Psychology* (Hillsdale, NJ: Erlbaum), 23–46.

Stoffman, D. (2002), *Who Gets In: What's Wrong with Canada's Immigration Program, and How to Fix it* (Toronto: Macfarlane, Walter and Ross).

Tajfel, H. and J.C. Turner (1979), "An Integrative Theory of Intergroup Conflict", in W.G. Austin and S. Worchel (eds.), *The Social Psychology of Intergroup Relations* (Monterey, CA: Brooks/Cole), 33–48.

Turner, J.C., M.A. Hogg,, P.J. Oakes, S.D. Reicher and M.S. Wetherell (1987), *Rediscovering the Social Group: A Self-Categorization Theory* (Oxford, UK: Basil Blackwell).

Walton, D. and P. Kennedy (2002), "Muslims Feel Doubts Linger: More Canadians are Suspicious of Other Groups than a Year Ago, New Poll Reveals", *Globe and Mail*, September 7, p. A5.

Visible-Minority Neighbourhood Enclaves and Labour Market Outcomes of Immigrants

Feng Hou and Garnett Picot

Since the 1970s, the major source countries for immigrants to Canada have steadily shifted from Europe to Asia, Africa, the Caribbean, and South America. The majority of recent immigrants are from visible-minority populations: Blacks, Chinese, South Asians, and other smaller groups. Most settled in Canada's three largest metropolitan areas. As a consequence, during the 1980s and 1990s, Toronto, Montreal, and Vancouver experienced large changes in the racial composition of their populations. Between 1981 and 1996, visible minorities as a share of the total population increased from 13.6% to 31.6% in Toronto, from 5.2% to 12.2% in Montreal, and from 13.9% to 31.1% in Vancouver.[1] In 1996, Toronto alone accounted

---

[1]Calculated from the 1981, 1986, 1991, and 1996 census 20% macro-data files. Visible minorities are defined by the Employment Equity Act as "persons, other than Aboriginal peoples, who are non-Caucasian in race or non-white in color". The regulations that accompany the Act identify the following visible-minority groups: Chinese, South Asians (e.g., East Indian, Pakistani, Punjabi, Sri Lankan), Blacks (e.g., African, Haitian, Jamaican, Somali), Arab/West Asians (e.g., Armenian, Egyptian, Iranian, Lebanese, Moroccan), Filipinos, Southeast Asians (e.g., Cambodian, Indonesian, Laotian, Vietnamese), Latin Americans, Japanese, Koreans, and others (Kelly, 1995). Prior to the 1996 census, the visible-minority status was derived from responses to questions on ethnic origin, mother tongue, place of birth, and religion. In the 1996 census, the visible-minority status was

for 42% of the nation's visible-minority population; Montreal and Vancouver combined, accounted for another 30%.

Increases in visible-minority populations through immigration profoundly affect the racial/ethnic make-up of urban neighbourhoods. The existence and expansion of ethnic enclaves — neighbourhoods with a substantial presence of minority populations — involves not just changes in ethnic composition, but also creates a "social and symbolic centrality" of a minority group for its members as well as for the dominant society (Buzzelli, 2000). The emergence of ethnic enclaves often transforms the physical and social characteristics of neighbourhoods, challenges the "way of life" established among long-term residents, and may generate tensions within local space (Ray, Halseth and Johnson, 1997). Social and economic interaction, both within a minority group and between the group and the rest of society, can be influenced by the existence of ethnic enclaves, and affect residents' lives on a daily basis.

Although ethnic enclaves are "neither a new phenomenon nor one occurring exclusively with any particular group" (Taeuber and Taeuber, 1965), they are on the increase among visible-minority populations as a result of immigration patterns of the past 20 years. Visible-minority immigrants arriving during the 1980s and 1990s face different socio-economic environments than earlier immigrants did. Socially, Canada's multiculturalism policies encourage minority communities to preserve and enhance their cultural heritages. Economically, immigrant assimilation outcomes have deteriorated, affecting members of minority communities during the past 20 years. These socio-economic forces may affect various immigrant groups differently for various reasons.

Ethnic enclaves may have positive and/or negative economic effects for the ethnic minority group. In particular, the question of whether ethnic enclaves facilitate or impede the integration of immigrants into Canadian society has significant implications for immigrant-settlement policies.

---

based on respondents' self-identification. If using the 1991 approach, the derived counts for 1996 would be 6% higher than the counts from the direct method for total visible-minority population in Canada, 3.6% higher for Blacks, 1.6% for Chinese, 2.9% for South Asians, 61.9% higher for Arab/West Asians, and 3.4% lower for Filipinos. Thus the 1996 counts for most groups are comparable with those derived from the earlier approach. The large discrepancy for Arab/West Asians is primarily due to the exclusion of most Arab/West Asian multiple responses to the question on visible-minority status, and requires cautions in making cross-census comparison (Renaud and Costa, 1999).

Feng Hou and Garnett Picot

Using census data from 1981, 1986, 1991, and 1996, this study first documents the emergence of highly concentrated visible-minority neighbourhoods and their socio-economic conditions in Canada's three largest metropolitan areas. The focus is on the three largest visible-minority groups in Toronto, Montreal, and Vancouver, most often the Chinese, South Asians (e.g., East Indian, Pakistani, Punjabi, Sri Lankan), and Blacks (e.g., African, Haitian, Jamaican, Somali). This study further examines the association between living in a visible-minority neighbourhood and an immigrant's labour market outcomes.

The Consequences of Living in Ethnic Enclaves: A Literature Review

Ethnic enclaves, such as Toronto's Jewish neighbourhoods, "Little Italies" and "Chinatowns" in the first half of the twentieth century represented a refuge where new immigrants could escape from the foreign environment. More importantly, within ethnic enclaves were located economic opportunities that some new immigrants had difficulties finding elsewhere (Murdie and Teixeira, 2000). Thus, the economic and social significance of ethnic enclaves was apparent at a time when immigrants primarily consisted of manual labourers and the places of residence and places of work were closely located. However, much has changed in the economic structure and characteristics of immigrant populations. There has been no consensus in the literature regarding the association between living in ethnic neighbourhoods and immigrants' labour market performance in contemporary societies.

One line of reasoning argues that there is a diminishing role of neighbourhoods in people's daily life, as contemporary society witnesses an ever-expanding spatial scale of social relations (Bolt, Burgers and van Kempen, 1998). People now can function in different social networks that are not strongly limited by physical barriers and spatial obstacles. Social ties and economic opportunities are no longer attached or confined to the neighbourhood. Applying this line of reasoning would suggest that ethnic enclaves have a reduced influence on the social and economic integration of immigrants.

However, a large body of literature in the United States, based mostly on the experience of Blacks, suggests that racial enclaves exert strong negative impacts on their residents. Many Black ghettos in the United States are associated with limited economic opportunities, a concentration of poverty, and substandard social and environmental conditions. Ghetto residents are often isolated from the outside world and develop attitudes and behaviours against the basic ideals and values of the mainstream society (Massey and Denton, 1993). The existence of racial/ethnic enclaves may also increase the visibility of racial group differences and intensify racial antagonism and preferences.

Contrary to the prevailing view in the United States, which emphasizes the negative aspects of residential segregation, some Canadian studies have focused on the positive roles of neighbourhood segregation in sustaining cultural pluralism (Driedger, 1978). More recent studies have explored residential concentration as bases for the establishment of ethnic business and entrepreneurships (Teixeira, 2000; Lo *et al.*, 2000).

Specific to the economic adjustment of immigrants, both positive and negative effects of living in ethnic/racial enclaves may originate from ethnic economies and ethnic networks. The ethnic economy — businesses primarily operating in ethnic neighbourhoods and relying on own-group members for their employees and clientele — can facilitate immigrants' settlement by providing easily accessible jobs. This may be particularly true for the newly-arrived and less well-educated. In a review of the literature on this topic, Galster, Metzger and Waite (1999) note that positive features might include the encouragement of: (a) social capital formation; (b) informal on-the-job training and business apprenticeship with ethnically based companies; (c) higher productivity in these companies by clustering same-language workers; (d) denser network of job-sharing information; and (e) acknowledgement and valuation by ethnic employers of foreign educational credentials.

However, some potentially negative effects may be associated with working within an ethnic economy (Galster, Metzger and Waite, 1999). Employment in an ethnic economy is often associated with poor working conditions and low wages (Reitz, 1990). Workers in the ethnic economy may be more likely to accept exploitive situations. Exclusive participation in the ethnic economy and closed within-group networks may also hamper immigrants' employment in the wider economy, thereby reducing incentives to acquire the host-country language(s), or to gain working experience and educational qualifications (Fong and Ooka, 1999). Social isolation was shown to be particularly harmful for groups with low socio-economic status. Ooka and Wellman (2000) found that in Toronto, members of low-status ethnic groups tended to achieve higher income when they established ties outside their own ethnic group.

Naturally, the impact of the ethnic economy and ethnic networks may vary among groups, depending on their group cohesion and the nature of the ethnic economy. For instance, in Toronto, the Chinese ethnic economy developed from a traditional Chinese economy that was primarily small scale, located in Chinese neighbourhoods, and focused on consumer goods and services, to one that is rapidly diversifying in size, location, and industrial structure. Chinese businesses in finance, real estate, insurance, and high technology are also emerging (Lo *et al.*, 2000). A 1998 count showed that one-third of computer wholesale and manufacturing firms in Toronto were owned and operated by Chinese (cited in Lo *et al.*, 2000). In contrast to the Chinese population, which is relatively homogenous in their traditional culture and language, Blacks in Toronto are fragmented by language, country of origin, and religion. Blacks' neighbourhood concentration is lower than other major visible-minority groups. Compared with other groups, Black businesses rely less on their community resources, are more dispersed, and tend to be smaller in size (Teixeira, 2000).

Along a different line, Borjas (1995) develops the notion of "ethnic capital" which refers to the average amount of human capital in the preceding generation of the ethnic group. According to this view, ethnic capital can influence the income levels of the children in the ethnic population, beyond the effects of the immediate families' human capital. That is, the characteristics of the ethnic group to which children belong can influence intergenerational income mobility. Belonging to a particular group can retard intergenerational improvements for relatively disadvantaged ethnic groups, as well as delay the deterioration of skills and economic outcomes (i.e., the regression towards the mean) for the more advantaged groups. Borjas finds that one of the mechanisms by which this process is promoted is through ethnic neighbourhoods or enclaves. He finds that residential segregation and the influence of ethnic capital on the process of intergenerational income mobility are intimately linked.

While there are many empirical studies on the general effects of living in racial/ethnic enclaves, only a few have empirically examined the relationship between residential segregation and immigrants' labour market outcomes, and most of them are US-based studies. Galster, Metzger and Waite (1999) examined the effects of own-group concentration on immigrant's economic advancement in the 1980s. Using data from the 1980 and 1990 US censuses and focusing on 14 immigrant groups in five metropolitan areas, they found that rising residential exposure to other members of one's immigrant group increased a group's poverty rate and decreased its employment rate. They interpreted this result to mean that the negative effects of ethnic economy might offset any other possible advantages. Furthermore, they found that a group's exposure to other neighbourhood characteristics, such as non-employment, low education, and dependence on public assistance, was associated with lower educational, occupational, and employment achievements.

With a similar approach, but using more sophisticated analytical methods (by controlling the fixed effects of year of immigration, national origin, and metropolitan area of residence), Borjas (2000) examined the association between residential concentration and assimilation for 90 immigrant groups in the United States. He found that an immigrant group's rate of wage growth and improvement in educational attainment and English-language proficiency between 1980 and 1990 were negatively associated with the group's share in a metropolitan area's adult-age population.

The above two studies both measured ethnic enclaves or residential segregation at the metropolitan level and compared the economic assimilation of an immigrant group across metropolitan areas with various degrees of ethnic concentration. However, it is problematic to interpret the association between ethnic concentration at the metropolitan area level and immigrants' labour market performance. First, ethnic concentration does not necessarily lead to ethnic economy. As discussed above, the Chinese and Blacks have similar shares in Toronto's total population, yet ethnic economy is much stronger among the Chinese. Second, an observed negative association between ethnic concentration and labour market performance could result from the disadvantages of working in an ethnic economy (such as exploitive working conditions and isolation from the mainstream labour market) or simply reflect an equilibrium situation arising from geographic differences in the cost of ethnic goods. The cost of ethnic goods, such as ethnic foods, ethnic institutions and organizations that provide group-specific services, tends to be low in areas where an ethnic group concentrates. An ethnic immigrant would move to a low-concentration area only if higher earnings compensate for the higher cost of ethnic goods (Chiswick and Miller, 2002).

Furthermore, the above two US studies were unable to account for the impacts of differential exposure to own-group members within a metropolitan area where members of an immigrant group face similar conditions in the mainstream labour market, ethnic economy, and cost of ethnic goods. However, they have different levels of exposure to residential segregation; some live in ethnic enclaves, others do not. The degree of exposure to own-group neighbours may reflect differences among immigrants in economic success, cultural assimilation, as well as preferences to living close to own-group members and discrimination that may reduce the likelihood of a visible-minority group living close to other groups. On the other hand, exposure to their own-group neighbours may have impacts on their performance in the labour market. Given the same observable individual characteristics that affect immigrants' economic success and cultural assimilation, do immigrants of a minority group who live in their enclaves have poorer or better labour market outcomes than those who have few own-group neighbours? Furthermore, is the association between exposure to own-group neighbours and labour market performance particularly strong among those who have more difficulties in adjusting to the Canadian labour market (such as recent arrivals, immigrants with low educational level, and immigrants who do not speak one of the official languages)? In this paper, we examine these questions for the three largest visible-minority groups in Toronto, Montreal, and Vancouver.

Data and Methods

Data and Measures

This study uses micro-data from the 1981, 1986, 1991, and 1996 Canadian census 20% sample files. The analyses are focused on the three largest visible-minority groups in each of the three largest metropolitan areas in Canada, including the Chinese, South Asians, and Blacks in Toronto, Blacks, Arab/West Asians, and the Chinese in Montreal, and the Chinese, South Asians, and Filipinos in Vancouver.

The census tract is used in this paper as the basic unit of neighbourhood. Census tracts have carefully designed attributes, contain a wide range of demographic and socio-economic information, and allow for national and historical statistical comparisons. A few tracts with populations less than 500 (based on about 100 sample population) are excluded from analyses in order to obtain a reliable estimate of neighbourhood ethnic compositions and economic conditions. In 1996, there were 802 census tracts with a population over 500 in Toronto, 749 in Montreal, and 297 in Vancouver. The population within census tracts ranged from 550 to 25,000 with a mean of 5,200 in Toronto, from 550 to 21,000 with a mean of 4,320 in Montreal, and from 700 to 196,200 with a mean of 6,010 in Vancouver.

In the analysis, we examine the association between immigrants' residential segregation and labour market performance. In particular, we ask whether the exposure to one's own ethnic group results in an employment effect, and for those employed, an earnings effect, or an occupational segregation effect. Hence, we focus on three labour market outcomes for immigrants: the probability of having employment, the degree of occupational segregation, and annual employment earnings (wages and salaries) levels. For the employment outcome, we examine whether exposure to own-group neighbours is associated with the probability of active participation in the labour market, independent of individual characteristics and neighbourhood economic conditions. The study population includes immigrants who are between 25 and 64 years of age, not disabled, and not attending school full-time. For those who are employed, we have a measure of occupation and hence examine whether exposure to own-group neighbours is associated with occupational segregation, that is, the probability of working in an occupation in which the share of a group is at least twice as large as the group's share in the city's workforce. Four-digit classification of occupations (approximately 500) is used to define occupational segregation. For those who are employed, we further ask whether exposure to own-group neighbours is associated with their level of annual earnings.

Our focal explanatory variable is residential exposure to own-group members. We create a composite "exposure" variable that consists of the exposure to own-group members in the individual's census tract, plus the exposure to own-group members in nearby neighbourhoods, weighted by the distance of the other neighbourhoods to the individual's neighbourhood. As distance increases, the value added to the exposure variable declines. The composite exposure variable is created to deal with the potential effect of neighbourhood clustering. The effect on labour market outcomes may be quite different if one lives in an isolated neighbourhood, as opposed to one that is spatially adjacent to many other neighbourhoods with high concentrations of the same minority group. Being part of a very large minority community (many adjacent neighbourhoods) may result in a greater "treatment" effect than if one is in a single, isolated neighbourhood. The availability of ethnic businesses and networks that affect labour market outcomes could be quite different in the two cases.

More specifically, for neighbourhood i, the original exposure measure is p_i (% of population of the same group). The alternative composite exposure measure is

$$Px_i = (p_i + \Sigma\, c_{ij}{}^*p_j)/(1 + \Sigma c_{ij})$$

where $j=1\ldots n-1$, n is the total number of neighbourhoods in the city. The distance function $c_{ij} = \exp(-d_{ij})$, d_{ij} is the distance in kilometers between neighbourhood i and j, p_i and p_j are the proportions of a visible-minority group in neighbourhood i and j. The distance function assumes that the influence of surrounding areas diminishes rapidly with distance from the target neighbourhood i (Massey and Denton, 1988).

To provide a sense of the values obtained for this composite variable, assume that an individual lives in a census tract with a minor presence of his/her own-group members ($pi= 5\%$). Assume further that there are two immediately adjacent tracts with a strong presence of the minority group (35% of the population are from this group), with the centres of the tracts being 2 kilometers apart. Assume that all other neighbourhoods with a concentration of same minority group members are too distant to have any effect on the value of the variable. In this case, the original "exposure" index would be 5, and the value for the expanded composite measure would be 11.4. Thus, the individual's situation, originally described as living in a neighbourhood with a "minor" presence of own-group members, has moved to one that is now described as a "moderate" presence, using the classifications described in Table 2.

In multivariate analyses, we also include neighbourhood low-income rate as a control for neighbourhood economic conditions since neighbourhoods with a large presence of visible-minority populations may also have poor economic conditions. Controlling for other neighbourhood contextual variables will help us to determine whether it is the exposure to own-group members or exposure to other neighbourhood conditions that is associated with labour market outcomes. Although more indicators of neighbourhood socio-economic conditions are available, such as unemployment rate, occupational structure, educational level, and family structure, these aggregated variables are highly correlated with one another. The addition of these variables may result in a small gain in correcting model mis-specification but serious multicollinearity (Pickett and Pearl, 2000). In this study, we use low-income rate rather than other neighbourhood contextual conditions as the control variable because the low-income rate is more uniformly associated with the presence of visible minorities in the neighbourhoods across groups than are other variables (see Table 3).

We also include individual level variables commonly used to predict labour market outcomes of immigrants, such as education, age as a proxy for experience, language, years since immigration, and family structure. Appendix Table A1 contains the definitions of outcome variables and individual-level and neighbourhood-level explanatory variables.

Methodological Issues

The study addresses a number of technical issues. One important concern is the difficulty of making causal inferences with cross-sectional data. For instance, if exposure to own-group neighbours is observed to be *associated* with poor labour market outcomes, this may be the result of one of two possible causal paths (or both). It may be that those who are less successful economically are more likely to move to visible-minority neighbourhoods, or, alternatively, living in visible-minority neighbourhoods may exert a negative effect on labour market outcomes. In the present study, we attempt to address this issue by placing some temporal ordering of the outcomes. More specifically, we restrict the sample to immigrants who lived in their "current" (at time of measurement of labour market outcomes) neighbourhood for one year or more. That is, we measure neighbourhood of residence in one year, and labour market outcomes the next (with the exception of employment earnings which cover the calendar year prior to the census, although only those who are currently employed are included in the analysis. Restriction to residents who had stayed in the same neighbourhood for at least five years yields similar results). Statistically, current labour market outcomes will not affect past choices of neighbourhoods. Thus, we have reason to believe that in the model any observed association is more likely to be related to the effect of living in a minority enclave (or not) on labour market outcomes, simply because of the timing. However, we are not willing to make a definitive statement on the causal direction, because current labour market outcomes could be highly correlated with past outcomes, (although they could not "cause" past choices) which in turn could affect past choices of neighbourhoods. Hence, the issue of the direction of causality remains uncertain. Our first task is to determine if there is any association between exposure to own-minority group and labour market outcomes.

Feng Hou and Garnett Picot

A second technical issue confronted in this study is the possibility of non-linear associations between neighbourhood context and labour market outcomes, or a threshold effect of neighbourhood context (Buck, 2001). We tested the possibility of non-linear effects by treating exposure to own-group neighbours as both a continuous (linear) and categorical (possibly non-linear) variable, and comparing the results. We found no particular threshold points and a larger effect when the variable was treated as continuous.

One issue that this study could not fully address is selection bias. People do not necessarily randomly choose neighbourhoods. Some unobserved variables, such as the motivation to assimilate, may affect both people's neighbourhood choices and their labour market outcomes. For example, immigrants with a strong motivation to assimilate may both choose not to live in a visible-minority neighbourhood and achieve better labour market outcomes. In this case, the selection bias would lead to an overestimate of the neighbourhood effect. In the absence of valid instrumental variables, randomized mobility experiments are an appropriate approach to avoid the selection issue (Oreopoulos, 2002). However, such "natural" experiments are rare, and the data are often limited to particular population groups (e.g., low-income people).

The fourth technical issue addressed in the paper relates to the use of multi-level data. In our analyses, individuals' labour market outcomes are predicted by both individual level and neighbourhood level variables. There is a problem of independence (or lack of it) of observations within a neighbourhood; all people in the neighbourhood have the same value of the neighbourhood variable. To address this issue, we used hierarchical linear (random-coefficient regression) models (HLM). The HLM5 software is employed (Raudenbush *et al.*, 2000). Basically, one can think of HLM as estimating two simultaneous equations, one at the individual level, and one at the neighbourhood level, as indicated below.

For each outcome (employment, working in segregated occupations, and earnings), we estimate three different model specifications. The first model specification includes both an individual-level model and a neighbourhood-level model. In the individual-level model, all individual-level variables are included, and all the slopes are fixed across neighbour-hoods (i.e., Bs associated with Xs in the individual-level model take on the same value across all neighbourhoods), but the individual-level model treats the intercept as random across neighbourhoods. That is, the effect of a change in X on the outcome variable is the same for all individuals in all neighbourhoods, but the level of the outcome is allowed to vary across neighbourhoods. The neighbourhood-level model then predicts the variation in outcomes among neighbourhoods (as indicated by a varying intercept term) as a function of exposure to own-group members. The coefficient of interest is then γ_{01}, on the exposure variable (P_{xi}). The regressions in the first specification are described below.

Individual level: $Y_{ij} = \beta_{0j} + \beta_{1j}X_{1ij} + \ldots \beta_{nij}X_{nij} + r_{ij}$;

Neighbourhood level: $\beta_{0j} = \gamma_{00} + \gamma_{01} \text{Exposure} + \mu_{0j}$.

The second model specification is the same as that described above, but it simply adds neighbourhood low-income rate to the neighbourhood-level β_{0j} model. Now the neighbourhood level model becomes: $\beta_{0j} = \gamma_{00} + \gamma_{01} \text{Exposure} + \gamma_{02} \text{LowIncomeRate} + \mu_{0j}$. This is done to test whether the effect of exposure to own-group members is mediated by neighbourhood economic conditions.

In the third model specification, we focus on three population groups of particular interest: recent immigrants (living in Canada less than five years), immigrants with less than high school graduation, and immigrants with neither English nor French as their home language. These groups are viewed to be the most susceptible to poor labour market outcomes. Being part of a minority enclave may have stronger effects on their labour market outcomes, either positive or negative, than for other groups. On the positive side, the enclave may be more important in providing employment and support to these immigrants than to others who can more readily adapt to labour markets associated with the majority population. On the negative side, the enclave may also serve to isolate these individuals more than others who have more experience in Canada, better mainstream language skills and higher levels of education.

To proceed with the third model, we first test, among each of the three selected groups, whether the slopes for the individual-level variables vary across neighbourhoods. If they do not, we keep them fixed in the model. If any of these three slopes is random (i.e., varies across neighbourhoods), we further test to determine whether the variation of the slope among neighbourhoods is associated with exposure to own-group neighbours and neighbourhood low-income rate. For instance, for the slope of recent immigrants, we would add an equation: $\beta_{1j} = \gamma_{10} + \gamma_{11} \text{Exposure} + \gamma_{12} \text{LowIncomeRate} + \mu_{1j}$ at the neighbourhood level. If no significant associations are found, the slope is fixed as in specifications 1 and 2 so that the model remains parsimonious. The purpose of specification 3 is to

Feng Hou and Garnett Picot

examine whether exposure to own-group neighbours has different or more apparent effects on those who are least likely to succeed in the mainstream labour market. This approach is conceptually similar to introducing interaction terms in order to differentiate effects for the three most vulnerable groups from those of the rest of the population.

All the models are estimated for immigrant men and women separately. In most cases, the results for immigrant men and women are very similar. In the following section on regression analyses, we only present results for men, but discuss results for women when differences emerge between men and women in the association between exposure to own-group neighbours and labour market outcomes.

Results

The Emergence of Chinese, Black, and South Asian Neighbourhoods in Canadian Cities

Increasing exposure to own-group members in the same neighbourhood. Among the three largest visible-minority groups, in virtually all cities, there was a dramatic rise in the extent to which visible-minority group members are exposed to own-group neighbours in their neighbourhoods. In Toronto, on average,[2] the percent of the population in neighbourhoods[3] that is Chinese rose from 9.6% in 1981 to 24.9% in 1996 (Table 1). In Vancouver, this proportion rose from 18.1% to 30.3%. Similar increases, although to lower levels, are observed for other major visible-minority groups in Toronto and Vancouver. Montreal generally has the lowest level of "visible-minority enclaves", as only among Blacks is there a significant

---

[2]Only neighbourhoods that have at least one member of a particular ethnic group (e.g., Chinese) are included in the calculation of the mean. The average percentage of group X in neighbourhoods where group X members live is calculated as $P_x = \Sigma(x_i/X)(x_i/t_i)$. It gives the probability for members of group X that the next person sampled from the same neighbourhood will be an X group member.

[3]That is, neighbourhoods with at least one Chinese person.

Table 1: Average Percentage of Same Group Members in the Neighbourhood for the Three Largest Visible-Minority Groups in Toronto, Montreal, and Vancouver, 1981 and 1996

| | | | By Length of Stay in Canada | | | | | Gini Index of Group |
		Total	5 years or less	6 to 10 years	11 to 15 years	16 to 20 years	long-term and Canadian-born	Concentration in Neighbourhoods
Toronto								
Chinese	1981	9.6%	10.6%	8.8%	8.8%	9.9%	3.0%	0.60
	1996	24.9%	29.0%	26.8%	22.8%	22.0%	6.8%	0.65
South Asian	1981	5.8%	6.3%	6.0%	5.0%	3.5%	1.2%	0.59
	1996	16.4%	18.2%	17.0%	17.1%	15.3%	6.1%	0.60
Black	1981	7.6%	8.2%	8.1%	7.3%	6.2%	1.4%	0.55
	1996	12.6%	15.1%	13.9%	12.8%	11.6%	6.6%	0.54
Montreal								
Black	1981	4.7%	5.1%	5.0%	4.2%	4.1%	1.0%	0.61
	1996	10.1%	11.5%	11.7%	11.5%	9.7%	5.2%	0.59
Arab/	1981	6.4%	6.9%	5.8%	6.8%	7.6%	1.8%	0.71
West Asian	1996	9.0%	10.0%	9.2%	7.8%	8.2%	2.7%	0.68
Chinese	1981	3.0%	3.0%	3.0%	3.2%	3.0%	1.4%	0.75
	1996	6.2%	7.3%	7.0%	5.5%	5.7%	2.1%	0.66
Vancouver								
Chinese	1981	18.1%	20.3%	17.4%	17.6%	17.8%	6.6%	0.62
	1996	30.3%	29.8%	30.9%	32.9%	31.9%	11.1%	0.53
South Asian	1981	6.8%	7.5%	6.6%	6.7%	6.4%	2.2%	0.51
	1996	20.3%	24.4%	23.9%	21.2%	19.3%	9.1%	0.63
Filipino	1981	2.1%	2.3%	2.1%	1.9%	1.5%	0.5%	0.64
	1996	4.1%	4.5%	4.2%	4.3%	3.7%	1.5%	0.50

proportion (10.1%) of the neighbourhood population who are Blacks. These smaller values in Montreal are a result of the smaller visible-minority population in that city.

At any point in time, say 1996, immigrants who are new to Canada are more likely to live in a visible-minority neighbourhood than are immigrants who have been in Canada for many years. Therefore, the effect of being in a visible-minority enclave, whether positive or negative, is more of an issue among recent immigrants than among longer term immigrants or the Canadian-born (Table 1).

Visible-minority immigrants, regardless of how long they have been in Canada, have increasingly through the 1980s and 1990s found themselves living in neighbourhoods with larger numbers of people from their own minority group. In particular, each wave of recent arrivals (those in Canada for five years or less) has found itself living in neighbourhoods that increasingly resemble visible-minority enclaves.[4] Among the Chinese in Toronto, in 1981, on average recent arrivals lived in neighbourhoods where 10.6% of the population was Chinese; by 1996 this had increased to 29%, an almost threefold increase. Other cases where recent arrivals tend to live in neighbourhoods with large own-group populations are the Chinese (29.8% in 1996) and South Asians in Vancouver (24.4%), and South Asians (18.2%) and Blacks (15.1%) in Toronto (Table 1).

Not only did recent immigrants increasingly find themselves in neighbourhoods populated by their own-group members at time of entry, but as their number of years in Canada increased, so too did their tendency to be in own-group neighbourhoods (Figure 1). For instance, among the 1976–80 cohort of Chinese immigrants to Toronto, upon arrival an average 10% of the people in their neighbourhoods were Chinese. Among this same quasi-cohort after 16–20 years in Canada and residing in Toronto, 22% of the people in their neighbourhoods were Chinese. The same general pattern is observed for all recent immigrant cohorts in all cities.[5] Increasing spatial assimilation of a visible-minority group, in the sense of increasing probability to live side by side with majority group members, is unlikely to happen if large in-flows of new immigrants of the group continues.

---

[4]The only exception is Arabs/West Arabs in Montreal. This group had a decrease in average percent of population of same ethnic background living in the same neighbourhood between 1991 and 1996. This is most likely due to the problem of changes in defining the Arab/West Asian group. See note 1 for details.

[5]Again, the Arab/West Arab group is an exception. See the note 4.

Figure 1: Proportion of Same Visible-Minority Group Members in the Neighbourhood by Immigrant Cohort and Year Since Immigration

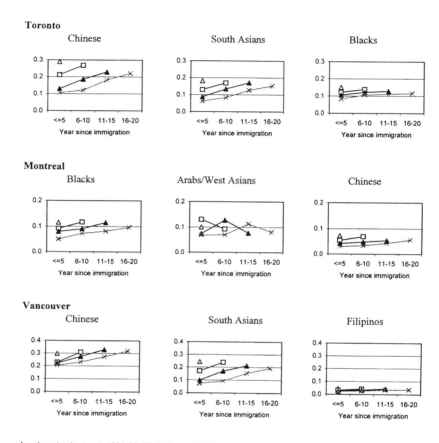

Immigrant cohorts: △ 1991-95, 80-1976 × 85-1981 ▲ , 90-1986 □

Feng Hou and Garnett Picot

Note that overall this increase in the tendency towards "visible-minority enclaves" is not due to a significant rise in the concentration of the Chinese (or other visible-minority groups) in particular neighbourhoods. As shown by the Gini index that reflects the tendency for a particular group to concentrate in a small number of neighbourhoods (Table 1, right end column), visible-minority groups are distributing themselves among neighbourhoods in much the same way in 1996 as they did in 1981. While the Gini is quite large in some cases, displaying substantial concentration, there has not been an overall increase. Of the nine visible-minority group-city combinations, neighbourhood concentration fell in six cases, and rose in three. Rather, the large increase in visible-minority enclaves is simply due to the fact that a larger share of the population of these cities is now from these minority groups; and the population of a particular minority group has been proportionately rising in most neighbourhoods.

A large increase in the number of visible-minority neighbourhoods. In the three largest Canadian cities, the number of neighbourhoods (census tracts) with a strong presence of a visible-minority group population increased dramatically since 1981. In Table 2, census tracts are classified according to the presence of a visible-minority group in the neighbourhood: no presence, minor presence (up to 10% of the population in the neighbour-hood is from the same visible-minority group), moderate presence (10% to 30%), strong presence (30% to 50%), and dominant presence (over 50%).

In 1981, among the three largest visible-minority groups in the three cities, there were only two neighbourhoods with a dominant ethnic presence: two Chinese neighbourhoods in Vancouver. By 1996, there were 24 such neighbourhoods, virtually all (except two) Chinese communities; 12 in Toronto, nine in Vancouver and one in Montreal. If one combines the "strong presence" and the "dominant presence" neighbourhoods (i.e., those where the minority group has more than a 30% share of the population), the number of such neighbourhoods increased from 6 in 1981 to 142 in 1996. Three-quarters of these visible-minority enclaves were Chinese (103 out of 142), and they were primarily in Toronto and Vancouver. There were relatively few Black enclaves in Canadian cities: ten in 1996. Montreal had relatively few visible-minority enclaves (five in 1996) compared to Toronto (73) and Vancouver (64).

The significance of the rise in visible-minority neighbourhoods depends in part upon the extent to which a visible-minority group locates in these neighbourhoods. Certainly not all of visible-minority group

Table 2: Distribution of Census Tracts by the Presence of the Three Largest Visible-Minority Group Population in Toronto, Montreal, and Vancouver, 1981 and 1996

Toronto

	Chinese				South Asian				Black			
	1981		1996		1981		1996		1981		1996	
	No.	%	No.	%	No.	%	No.	%	No.	%	No.	%
No presence	53	8.9	25	3.1	55	9.2	24	3.0	27	4.5	17	2.1
Minor presence	510	85.4	614	76.6	529	88.6	602	75.1	531	88.9	655	81.7
Moderate presence	31	5.2	117	14.6	13	2.2	156	19.5	39	6.5	123	15.3
Strong presence	3	0.5	34	4.2			20	2.5			7	0.9
Dominant presence			12	1.5								

Montreal

	Black				Arab/West Asian				Chinese			
	1981		1996		1981		1996		1981		1996	
	No.	%	No.	%	No.	%	No.	%	No.	%	No.	%
No presence	106	16.4	48	6.4	174	26.9	115	15.4	314	48.5	152	20.3
Minor presence	532	82.2	630	84.1	465	71.9	614	82.0	329	50.9	584	78.0
Moderate presence	9	1.4	68	9.1	8	1.2	19	2.5	4	0.6	12	1.6
Strong presence			2	0.3								
Dominant presence			1	0.1			1	0.1			1	0.1

Vancouver

	Chinese				South Asian				Filipino			
	1981		1996		1981		1996		1981		1996	
	No.	%	No.	%	No.	%	No.	%	No.	%	No.	%
No presence	10	4.1	1	0.3	12	4.9	9	3.0	72	29.6	11	3.7
Minor presence	183	75.3	159	53.5	222	91.4	243	81.8	171	70.4	284	95.6
Moderate presence	47	19.3	81	27.3	9	3.7	37	12.5			2	0.7
Strong presence	1	0.4	47	15.8			7	2.4				
Dominant presence	2	0.8	9	3.0			1	0.3				

Note: no presence — without any member of the visible-minority group; minor presence —with > 0 –10% of the visible-minority group population; moderate presence — > 10–30%; strong presence > 30–50%; dominant presence — over 50%.

Feng Hou and Garnett Picot

members live in visible-minority neighbourhoods. Generally speaking, Blacks tend not to live in "Black" neighbourhoods (because there are fewer of them), while among the Chinese a significant proportion live in Chinese neighbourhoods. Continuing with the "more than 30%" definition of a minority neighbourhood, in Toronto, 7% of Blacks, 23% of South Asians, and 41% of Chinese lived in their respective minority neighbourhoods. In Vancouver, 52% of Chinese and 29% of South Asians lived in their minority neighbourhoods. Few minority group members in Montreal lived in such neighbourhoods — 3% for Blacks, 7% for Arabs/West Asians, and 1% for the Chinese.

Approximately one-half of Chinese *recent* immigrants (arrived in Canada within ten years) lived in their minority enclaves in 1996 in Toronto and Vancouver, but only 2% in Montreal. Among South Asians the value ranged from 23% in Toronto and 39% in Vancouver. In contrast, Black recent immigrants were far less likely to be in their communities than were other groups; only 4% (Montreal) to 10% (Toronto) found themselves in such an environment.

In summary, there has been a dramatic increase in the number of visible-minority neighbourhoods, particularly in Toronto and Vancouver. Forty to 50% of the Chinese population lived in such neighbourhoods, as did one-quarter to one-third of the South Asian population. Issues associated with residence in visible-minority enclaves will become increasingly important, as the prevalence of such communities rises.

Socio-economic conditions in visible-minority neighbourhoods. A growing body of literature in the United States and Europe has provided evidence of the negative consequences of living in deprived neighbourhoods on individuals' socio-economic mobility, health status, and criminal activity (Massey and Denton, 1993; Pickett and Pearl, 2001). There continues to be a debate regarding the extent of "neighbourhood effects" for economic outcomes (Oreopoulos, 2002), but for educational, criminal, and health outcomes, effects of neighbourhood socio-economic conditions appear to be real. Thus, the socio-economic conditions in minority neighbourhoods would impinge on the benefits or disadvantages for those who choose or have to live in these areas.

In this study, visible-minority neighbourhoods tend to have higher unemployment rates and low-income rates than other census tracts. As the presence of a minority group increases, so too does the unemployment rate and low-income rate (Table 3). For example, in Toronto, even though the proportion of the neighbourhood population with university degrees is quite

Table 3: Socio-Economic Conditions of Tracts by the Presence of Visible-Minority Groups in Toronto, Montreal, and Vancouver, 1996 (in percent)

Toronto

	Chinese				South Asian				Black			
	% with University Education	Unemployed Rate	Low-Income Rate	% Lone-Parent Family	% with University Education	Unemployed Rate	Low-Income Rate	% Lone-Parent Family	% with University Education	Unemployed Rate	Low-Income Rate	% Lone-Parent Family
No presence	12.1	7.1	13.2	11.1	22.1	6.4	13.7	11.5	20.7	7.2	12.5	11.0
Minor presence	19.1	8.9	19.6	15.7	20.9	8.4	19.1	15.1	20.8	8.1	17.9	14.0
Moderate presence	22.0	9.9	24.8	16.9	14.1	11.8	26.4	18.2	12.1	13.9	34.2	24.3
Strong presence	20.3	10.2	26.3	15.5	11.8	13.1	28.3	17.6	8.7	18.3	48.5	33.7
Dominant presence	21.2	11.2	28.4	11.7								

Montreal

	Black				Arab/West Asian				Chinese			
	% with University Education	Unemployed Rate	Low-Income Rate	% Lone-Parent Family	% with University Education	Unemployed Rate	Low-Income Rate	% Lone-Parent Family	% with University Education	Unemployed Rate	Low-Income Rate	% Lone-Parent Family
No presence	13.7	10.2	19.9	15.7	11.0	11.4	23.7	20.1	11.7	11.9	22.8	18.9
Minor presence	17.1	11.6	23.7	19.0	16.9	12.3	24.8	19.5	17.3	12.2	25.0	19.7
Moderate presence	10.5	18.4	37.1	25.4	27.0	14.2	30.3	13.9	22.8	15.1	37.6	15.8
Strong presence	10.6	19.0	40.5	31.6	18.1	21.8	42.7	19.5				
Dominant presence	6.9	35.8	76.4	56.2					16.9	13.2	36.8	15.1

Vancouver

	Chinese				South Asian				Filipino			
	% with University Education	Unemployed Rate	Low-Income Rate	% Lone-Parent Family	% with University Education	Unemployed Rate	Low-Income Rate	% Lone-Parent Family	% with University Education	Unemployed Rate	Low-Income Rate	% Lone-Parent Family
No presence	10.0	7.9	11.1	9.3	19.0	8.0	22.9	14.0	23.8	5.2	14.4	10.4
Minor presence	16.0	7.7	19.7	13.5	11.4	10.6	26.5	14.6	17.3	8.5	23.5	14.1
Moderate presence	21.4	8.9	26.1	14.7	8.8	15.4	29.6	15.8	16.3	16.8	47.5	28.2
Strong presence	16.8	9.8	29.0	14.6	10.2	14.6	29.1	11.9				
Dominant presence	16.3	10.5	34.7	15.3								

Feng Hou and Garnett Picot

constant across neighbourhoods, as one moves from those with a minor presence of Chinese to those with a dominant presence, the unemployment rate rises from 8.9% to 11.2% (as of June 1996), and the low-income rate increases from 19.6% to 28.4%. Similar trends are observed among Chinese communities in Vancouver. The Black neighbourhoods in Montreal display a particularly high low-income and unemployment rate in 1996; the one census tract with a "dominant" Black presence registers unemployment of 36%, and a low-income rate of 76%. It is also populated with less-educated people and a much larger percentage of single-parent families (56%) than other tracts. The story for Black neighbourhoods is similar in Toronto, although less extreme.

There are, of course, many reasons for these results. The social and human capital of members of the minority communities may be substantially lower than average, as is the case for Blacks and South Asians in particular. Even among those visible-minority immigrants with university degrees, the extent to which they can convert their education to economic resources may be inhibited by "credentialism". It is often difficult for Canadian employers to evaluate the degrees and other forms of higher education held by immigrants from developing countries, resulting in a decrease in the economic value of such education. And it is well-known that economic outcomes for successive waves of immigrants to Canada have been declining through the 1980s and 1990s (Reitz, 2001), and their low-income rate has been rising, often to very high levels (Picot and Hou, 2002). Since recent immigrants tend to cluster in minority communities more than other immigrants, and their economic outcomes are inferior, this too will affect the socio-economic conditions in minority neighbourhoods.

However, beyond the direct effects such as individual immigrants' human capital and length of stay in Canada, does residential exposure to visible-minority enclaves influence the labour market outcomes of the residents? And is the effect of living in minority enclaves independent of neighbourhood economic conditions? It is to these questions that we now turn.

The Associations Between Living in Minority Enclaves and Labour Market Outcomes

Employment. To summarize the rather detailed findings that follow, we note that for men in general the association between exposure to own-group members and the probability of being employed is usually negative in sign, but often weak and/or insignificant. The exception to the weak association is the instance of Blacks in Toronto, and Black recent immigrants in Montreal, where the negative association is both statistically significant and quite large. However, as noted earlier, among the major visible-minority groups the exposure to own-group members is the smallest among Black immigrants.

Now the detail. Table 4 presents the results of hierarchical logistic regression models for immigrant men. To save space, the coefficients associated with the individual level variables in each model are not presented in the tables. The B coefficients in the tables are directly from the logistic model estimation, and as such cannot be interpreted in an intuitive manner. However, one can easily derive the probability of being employed for an individual with particular characteristics using $P = \exp(B_x)/(1 + \exp(B_x))$. For example, in the model for the Chinese in Toronto, a reference individual (arrived in Canada 20 years ago, uses English or French as home language, has a university degree, is the male adult in a two-adult family with kids, has the group mean in years of experience, and has 0% of own-group members in his neighbourhood, see Appendix), the probability of being employed $= e^{2.941}/(1 + e^{2.941}) = 0.95$.

The significant γ_{01} in model 1 for Chinese immigrants suggests that increased exposure to own-group members is significantly associated with reduced probability of being employed. However, the coefficient is very small, so the association is considered as weak. For instance, the probability of being employed for the above-mentioned reference person would only be reduced from 0.95 to 0.947 if he lives in a neighbourhood with 10% Chinese residents, rather than in one with no Chinese residents, and to 0.937 if he lives in a neighbourhood with 50% Chinese residents. For a recent arrival (≤ 5 years) ($b = -1.419$) who uses Chinese as home language ($b = -0.408$) and has a less than high-school education ($b = -0.379$), the probability of being employed would be reduced from 0.665 if he lives in a neighbourhood with 10% Chinese residents to 0.619 if he lives in a neighbourhood with 50% Chinese residents.[6]

In model 2 for the Chinese in Toronto, the addition of neighbourhood low-income rate does not mediate the effect of exposure to own-group

---

[6]Probability for a Chinese immigrant living a neighbourhood with 10% Chinese is $(e^{2.941-1.420-.408-.379-10*.005}/(1 + e^{2.941-1.420-.408-.379-10*.005}) = .665$. Probability for the individual living in a neighbourhood with 50% Chinese is $(e^{2.941-1.420-.408-.379-50*.005}/(1 + e^{2.941-1.420-.408-.379-50*.005}) = .619$.

Feng Hou and Garnett Picot

Table 4: Results of Hierarchical Generalized Linear Models for Immigrants' Probability of Being Employed, Men Aged 25 to 64

Toronto

	Chinese (n=12348)						South Asians (n=11759)						Blacks (n=7166)					
	Model 1		Model 2		Model 3		Model 1		Model 2		Model 3		Model 1		Model 2		Model 3	
	B	se	B	se	B	se	B	se	B	se	B	se	B	se	B	se	B	se
Variation in Intercept B0 (neighbourhood means)																		
Intercept γ00	2.941	.098 *	3.017	.106 *	3.017	.106 *	2.762	.094 *	3.058	.105 *	3.058	.105 *	2.528	.131 *	2.746	.135 *	2.746	.135 *
Exposure to own group members γ01	-0.005	.002 *	-0.005	.002 *	-0.005	.002 *	-0.006	.004	-0.006	.004	-0.006	.004	-0.039	.008 *	-0.022	.008 *	-0.022	.008 *
Neighbourhood low-income rate γ02			-0.004	.002 *	-0.004	.002 *			-0.015	.002 *	-0.015	.002 *			-0.017	.003 *	-0.017	.003 *
Variation in Slope for recent immigrants					ns						ns						ns	
Variation in slope for non official language					ns						ns						ns	
Variation in slope for < highschool					ns						ns						ns	

Montreal

	Blacks (n=2828)						Arab/West Asians (n=2788)						Chinese (n=1581)					
	Model 1		Model 2		Model 3		Model 1		Model 2		Model 3		Model 1		Model 2		Model 3	
	B	se	B	se	B	se	B	se	B	se	B	se	B	se	B	se	B	se
Variation in Intercept B0 (neighbourhood means)																		
Intercept γ00	2.106	.161 *	2.483	.175 *	2.688	.196 *	2.278	.158 *	2.745	.165 *	2.7448	.165 *	2.034	.246 *	2.125	.267 *	2.125	.267 *
Exposure to own group members γ01	-0.028	.014 *	-0.012	.014	-0.040	.018 *	0.003	.016	0.014	.012	0.014	.012	-0.008	.027	-0.007	.027	-0.007	.027
Neighbourhood low-income rate γ02			-0.021	.004 *	-0.023	.005 *			-0.026	.004 *	-0.026	.004 *			-0.005	.005	-0.005	.005
Variation in Slope for recent immigrants											ns						ns	
Intercept					-0.143	.383												
Exposure to own group members					-0.084	.034 *												
Neighbourhood low-income rate					0.005	.008												
Variation in slope for non official language											ns						ns	
Intercept					-0.853	.298 *												
Exposure to own group members					0.057	.027 *												
Neighbourhood low-income rate					0.010	.007												
Variation in slope for < highschool											ns						ns	
Intercept					-0.631	.318 *												
Exposure to own group members					0.077	.027 *												
Neighbourhood low-income rate					-0.005	.007												

Vancouver

	Chinese (n=9284)						South Asians (n=3908)						Filipinos (n=1089)					
	Model 1		Model 2		Model 3		Model 1		Model 2		Model 3		Model 1		Model 2		Model 3	
	B	se	B	se	B	se	B	se	B	se	B	se	B	se	B	se	B	se
Variation in Intercept B0 (neighbourhood means)																		
Intercept γ00	2.579	.122 *	2.723	.134 *	3.429	.283 *	2.932	.197 *	3.151	.242 *	3.151	.242 *	2.558	.315 *	2.779	.381 *	2.779	.381 *
Exposure to own group members γ01	0.001	.003	0.004	.003	-0.014	.007 *	-0.009	.003 *	-0.008	.004 *	-0.008	.004 *	-0.091	.066	-0.049	.077	-0.049	.077
Neighbourhood low-income rate γ02			-0.009	.003 *	-0.018	.010			-0.009	.008	-0.009	.008			-0.013	.012	-0.013	.012
Variation in Slope for recent immigrants					ns						ns						ns	
Variation in slope for non official language											ns						ns	
Intercept					-1.204	.293 *												
Exposure to own group members					0.021	.008 *												
Neighbourhood low-income rate					0.010	.010												
Variation in slope for < highschool					ns						ns						ns	

Note: all models included fixed effects for the following control variables: years since immigration, education, experience, family structure. see Apendix for the definitions of these variables. Full model tables are available upon request.

members, although the low-income rate is significantly associated with reduced probability of being employed. In model 3, the variation in the slopes (Bs) among neighbourhoods is not statistically significant for the three most vulnerable groups where this test is conducted: recent immigrants, those with non-official home language, and the less-educated. Thus, the effects of these individual level variables do not vary among neighbourhoods, and it is not necessary to test whether such possible variation in the slopes is associated with the "exposure" variable in the second-level neighbourhood model. The association between the variation in the intercept term (β_{0j}) and the exposure variable is identical in model 3 to that observed in specifications 1 and 2.

In *Toronto*, exposure to own-group members seems to have no significant association with the probability of having employment among South Asian immigrants, although the effect of neighbourhood low-income rate is significant.

By comparison, exposure to own-group members has a strong negative association with the probability of being employed among Black immigrants. Based on the coefficients in model 1, the probability of being employed would fall from 0.895 if a Black male immigrant with the reference characteristics (who arrived in Canada 20 years ago, uses English or French as home language, has a university degree, is the male adult in a two-adult family with kids) lives in a neighbourhood with 10% Black residents to 0.795 if he lives in a neighbourhood with 30% Black residents. With the addition of the neighbourhood low-income rate, in model 2, the coefficient associated with exposure to own-group members is reduced by 40% but remains statistically significant and substantial. The negative effect of the neighbourhood low-income rate is also significant.

In *Montreal*, exposure to own-group members also has a strong negative association with employment among Black immigrants (model 1). However, this association becomes statistically insignificant when the neighbourhood low-income rate is controlled for (model 2). Moving to model 3, there are significant variations in the slopes (i.e., association between individual effects and employment) among neighbourhoods, so it is necessary to determine if this variation can be explained by differences in "exposure". Among these three populations, the significant coefficients in the bottom half of the table (i.e., 0.057 and 0.077) in model 3 suggests that the employment disadvantage of exposure to own-group members is re-duced for those speaking neither English nor French as the home language, and the less-educated, as compared to other groups. However, living near more own-group members increases the disadvantage of recent immigrants relative to long-term immigrants. Thus, for the overall Black population, in model 3 there is a significantly negative association between exposure and employment. Among recent immigrants, this negative effect is greatly enhanced (the coefficient is $-0.040 + (-0.084) = -0.124$). For the other two populations of interest, the effect is, if anything, small and positive. Exposure to own-group members is not significantly associated with the probability of being employed for Arab/West Asian and Chinese immigrants.

In *Vancouver*, exposure to own-group members is negatively associated with the probability of being employed for South Asian immigrants, but the effect is small. For Chinese and Filipino immigrants, the coefficient of exposure to own-group members is not significant.

Overall, the results are similar for immigrant women, but if anything, the negative associations between "exposure" and employment are even weaker, and in some specific cases, weakly positive. Of the nine visible-minority group-city combinations, there is a negative and significant association in three cases among men and in two cases among women (tables available upon request). In the following cases, the results are different for women. Among South Asians in Toronto and Arab/West Asians in Montreal, the association between exposure to own-group neigh-bours and the probability of being employed is positive and significant among immigrant women who speak neither official language. This association is also positive and significant among recent Chinese immigrant women in Toronto.

Occupational segregation. Previous studies have investigated ethnic con-centration in labour markets and its implications for group inequality (Reitz, 1990). Our concern here is whether living in minority neighbour-hoods is associated with immigrants' concentration in labour markets either through ethnic networks or social isolation. To summarize the findings that follow, the association between exposure to own-group members and working in a segregated occupation among immigrant men is generally positive in sign (except for the Chinese in Montreal), but is statistically significant in only four of the nine cases. However, the positive association is rather strong for South Asians in Toronto, Blacks in Montreal, and among the less-educated Chinese in Vancouver.

A segregated occupation is one in which a group's share of employ-ment in the occupation, for the group of interest (say, the Chinese), is at least twice that of the group's share of the city workforce. A binary variable is created and defined as segregated occupations (1) and all others (0). The same econometric approach as described in the above employment section is used.

In *Toronto*, exposure to own-group members is positively associated with working in a highly segregated occupation for the three visible-minority groups (Table 5). The association is particularly strong for South Asian immigrants. Based on model 2 for South Asian immigrants, for a reference person as defined above, the probability of working in a segregated occupation increases from 0.048 if he lives in a neighbourhood with 10% same-group residents to 0.079 if the neighbourhood has 30% South Asian residents, assuming both neighbourhoods have a low-income rate of 15%. In similar situations, the probability increases from 0.240 to 0.262 for Chinese immigrants. For Black immigrants, the association between exposure to own-group members and working in a segregated occupation becomes statistically insignificant once neighbourhood low-income rate is controlled for.

In *Montreal*, exposure to own-group members has a rather strong association with working in highly segregated occupations among Black immigrants. Based on model 2 for Black immigrants, the probability of working in a segregated occupation for a reference person increases from 0.094 if he lives in a neighbourhood with 10% Black residents to 0.255 if the neighbourhood has 30% Black residents, assuming both neighbour-hoods have a low-income rate of 15%. For Arab/West Asian and Chinese immigrants, exposure to own-group members is not significantly associated with working in a segregated occupation.

In *Vancouver*, exposure to own-group members is strongly associated with working in a segregated occupation among South Asian immigrants even after controlling for the neighbourhood low-income rate (model 2). The probability of working in a segregated occupation for a reference immigrant increases from 0.091 if he lives in a neighbourhood with 10% South Asian residents to 0.191 in a neighbourhood with 30% South Asian residents, assuming both neighbourhoods have a low-income rate of 15%. For Chinese immigrants, only among those with less than high school education is exposure to own-group members significantly associated with

Table 5: Results of Hierarchical Generalized Linear Models for Immigrants' Probability of Working in a Segregated Occupation, Men Aged 25 to 64

Toronto

	Chinese (n=9828)						South Asians (n=10736)						Blacks (n=6308)					
	Model 1		Model 2		Model 3		Model 1		Model 2		Model 3		Model 1		Model 2		Model 3	
	B	se	B	se	B	se	B	se	B	se	B	se	B	se	B	se	B	se
Variation in Intercept B_0 (neighbourhood means)																		
Intercept γ_{00}	-1.355	.082 *	-1.500	.093 *	-1.447	.093 *	-3.373	.102 *	-3.506	.115 *	-3.506	.115 *	-3.250	.176 *	-3.397	.179 *	-3.397	.179 *
Exposure to own group members γ_{01}	0.007	.002 *	0.006	.002 *	0.004	.002	0.028	.005 *	0.027	.005 *	0.027	.005 *	0.025	.009 *	0.010	.008	0.010	.008
Neighbourhood low-income rate γ_{02}			0.008	.002 *	0.008	.003 *			0.007	.003 *	0.007	.003 *			0.013	.003 *	0.013	.003 *
Variation in Slope for recent immigrants					ns						ns						ns	
Variation in slope for non official language					ns						ns						ns	
Variation in slope for < highschool											ns						ns	
Intercept					-0.549	.206 *												
Exposure to own group members					0.011	.004 *												
Neighbourhood low-income rate					0.005	.006												

Montreal

	Blacks (n=2221)						Arab/West Asians (n=2143)						Chinese (n=1219)					
	Model 1		Model 2		Model 3		Model 1		Model 2		Model 3		Model 1		Model 2		Model 3	
	B	se	B	se	B	se	B	se	B	se	B	se	B	se	B	se	B	se
Variation in Intercept B_0 (neighbourhood means)																		
Intercept γ_{00}	-2.904	.195 *	-2.941	.203 *	-2.941	.203 *	-0.807	.142 *	-0.703	.155 *	-0.703	.155 *	-1.123	.241 *	-1.331	.249 *	-1.331	.249 *
Exposure to own group members γ_{01}	0.063	.012 *	0.061	.013 *	0.061	.013 *	0.006	.018	0.011	.018	0.011	.018	-0.011	.014	-0.004	.014	-0.004	.014
Neighbourhood low-income rate γ_{02}			0.002	.003	0.002	.003			-0.007	.005	-0.007	.005			0.011	.004 *	0.011	.004 *
Variation in Slope for recent immigrants					ns						ns						ns	
Variation in slope for non official language					ns						ns						ns	
Variation in slope for < highschool					ns						ns						ns	

Vancouver

	Chinese (n=7055)						South Asians (n=3535)						Filipinos (n=993)					
	Model 1		Model 2		Model 3		Model 1		Model 2		Model 3		Model 1		Model 2		Model 3	
	B	se	B	se	B	se	B	se	B	se	B	se	B	se	B	se	B	se
Variation in Intercept B_0 (neighbourhood means)																		
Intercept γ_{00}	-2.925	.164 *	-3.3	.189 *	-3.061	.200 *	-2.645	.146 *	-2.672	.205 *	-2.832	.234 *	-1.758	.250 *	-1.893	.294 *	-1.893	.294 *
Exposure to own group members γ_{01}	0.007	.004	0.001	.004	-0.004	.005	0.036	.006 *	0.036	.006 *	0.049	.006 *	0.065	.052	0.048	.059	0.048	.059
Neighbourhood low-income rate γ_{02}			0.021	.005 *	0.016	.006 *			0.001	.006	0.000	.008			0.007	.010	0.007	.010
Variation in Slope for recent immigrants					ns						ns						ns	
Variation in slope for non official language					ns						ns						ns	
Variation in slope for < highschool																	ns	
Intercept					0.065	.301					1.693	.326 *						
Exposure to own group members					0.017	.007 *					-0.034	.007 *						
Neighbourhood low-income rate					0.013	.008					0.002	.011						

Note: all models included fixed effects for the following control variables: years since immigration, education, experience, family structure. Full model tables are available upon request.
see Appendix for the definitions of these variables.

an increased probability of working in segregated occupations.[7] For Filipino immigrants, the association between exposure to own-group members and occupational segregation is not significant.

The results for immigrant women are very similar to those for immigrant men. The positive association is rather strong for South Asians in Toronto and Blacks in Montreal. The major difference from the pattern for immigrant men is that the association between exposure to own-group neighbours and occupational segregation among Chinese women is not significant in Toronto, but is significant in Vancouver.

Employment earnings. A summary of the findings suggests that in the majority of cases (seven out of nine), there is no statistically significant association between exposure to own-group members and employment earnings among immigrant men. Negative associations are found among Blacks in Montreal and South Asians in Vancouver.

The dependent variable in these regression models is the log of annual earnings, and the same econometric approach as described above is employed.

In *Toronto*, a negative and fairly large association between exposure to own-group neighbours and earnings is observed in model 1 for Blacks and South Asians (Table 6). However, once other possible neighbourhood effects are controlled for through the low-income rate (such as the exposure to a large low-income population that might affect motivation, for example, and hence labour market outcomes), the association becomes insignificant. Exposure to own-group members has no significant association with earnings among Chinese immigrant men.

In *Montreal*, exposure to own-group members is significantly associated with reduced earnings among Black immigrants even after controlling for neighbourhood low-income (model 2). With similar characteristics, a Black immigrant living in a neighbourhood with 10% Blacks earns 40% more than one living in a neighbourhood with 30% Blacks [(−0.020*(10−30)]. Among Arab/West Asian immigrants, the main effect of exposure to own-group members is not significant, but exposure

---

[7]For instance, the probability of working in a segregated occupation for a recent Chinese immigrant (b= −0.078) who speaks Chinese at home (b=0.509) and with less than high school education would increase from 0.119 when his neighbourhood has 10% Chinese residents to 0.149 when the neighbourhood has 30% Chinese.

Feng Hou and Garnett Picot

Table 6: Results of Hierarchical Linear Models for Immigrants' Log Earnings, Working Men Aged 25 to 64

Toronto

	Chinese (n=8320)						South Asians (n=9450)						Blacks (n=5567)					
	Model 1		Model 2		Model 3		Model 1		Model 2		Model 3		Model 1		Model 2		Model 3	
	B	se	B	se	B	se	B	se	B	se	B	se	B	se	B	se	B	se
Variation in Intercept B₀ (neighbourhood means)																		
Intercept γ_{00}	10.140	.019 *	10.302	.028 *	10.302	.028 *	10.130	.022 *	10.279	.031 *	10.276	.032 *	10.104	.031 *	10.209	.037 *	10.209	.037 *
Exposure to own group members γ_{01}	-0.001	.001	0.000	.001	0.000	.001	-0.004	.002 *	-0.003	.002	-0.003	.002	-0.011	.003 *	-0.005	.003	-0.005	.003
Neighbourhood low-income rate γ_{02}			-0.007	.001 *	-0.007	.001 *			-0.006	.001 *	-0.006	.001 *			-0.006	.001 *	-0.006	.001 *
Variation in Slope for recent immigrants					ns						ns						ns	
Variation in slope for non official language					ns						ns						ns	
Variation in slope for < highschool					ns						ns						ns	
Intercept											-0.485	.071 *						
Exposure to own group members											0.009	.003 *						
Neighbourhood low-income rate											0.000	.002						

Montreal

	Blacks (n=1908)						Arab\West Asians (n=1631)						Chinese (n=998)					
	Model 1		Model 2		Model 3		Model 1		Model 2		Model 3		Model 1		Model 2		Model 3	
	B	se	B	se	B	se	B	se	B	se	B	se	B	se	B	se	B	se
Variation in Intercept B₀ (neighbourhood means)																		
Intercept γ_{00}	9.984	.047 *	10.107	.060 *	10.107	.060 *	9.955	.043 *	10.033	.060 *	10.031	.061 *	9.613	.073 *	9.778	.107 *	9.778	.107 *
Exposure to own group members γ_{01}	-0.025	.007 *	-0.020	.007 *	-0.020	.007 *	-0.005	.008	-0.001	.008	0.000	.008	-0.011	.020	-0.005	.020	-0.005	.020
Neighbourhood low-income rate γ_{02}			-0.006	.002 *	-0.006	.002 *			-0.004	.002 *	-0.005	.002 *			-0.007	.003 *	-0.007	.003 *
Variation in Slope for recent immigrants					ns												ns	
Intercept											-0.352	.151 *						
Exposure to own group members											-0.035	.014 *						
Neighbourhood low-income rate											0.006	.005						
Variation in slope for non official language					ns						ns							
Variation in slope for < highschool					ns						ns							

Vancouver

	Chinese (n=5779)						South Asians (n=3037)						Filipinos (n=880)					
	Model 1		Model 2		Model 3		Model 1		Model 2		Model 3		Model 1		Model 2		Model 3	
	B	se	B	se	B	se	B	se	B	se	B	se	B	se	B	se	B	se
Variation in Intercept B₀ (neighbourhood means)																		
Intercept γ_{00}	10.03	.032 *	10.105	.044 *	10.083	.045 *	10.130	.035 *	10.290	.069 *	10.290	.069 *	10.117	.074 *	10.158	.095 *	10.158	.095 *
Exposure to own group members γ_{01}	-0.002	.001	0.000	.001	0.000	.001	-0.007	.002 *	-0.006	.002 *	-0.006	.002 *	-0.035	.022	-0.019	.023	-0.019	.023
Neighbourhood low-income rate γ_{02}			-0.004	.002 *	-0.004	.002 *			-0.007	.002 *	-0.007	.002 *			-0.003	.004	-0.003	.004
Variation in Slope for recent immigrants					ns						ns						ns	
Variation in slope for non official language					ns						ns						ns	
Variation in slope for < highschool											ns						ns	
Intercept					-0.514	.108 *												
Exposure to own group members					0.009	.003 *												
Neighbourhood low-income rate					0.000	.003												

Note: all models included fixed effects for the following control variables: years since immigration, education, experience, weeks worked in 1995, hours worked per week, occupation, family structure. see Appendix   for the definitions of these variables. Full model tables are available upon request.

to own-group members tends to increase the earnings difference between recent and long-term immigrants. Among the Chinese, exposure to own-group members is not significantly associated with employment earnings.

In *Vancouver*, the main effect of "exposure" on earnings is insignificant for the Chinese and Filipinos; it is negative, significant, and substantial for South Asians. The earnings difference is 12% between two persons with similar characteristics when one is in a neighbourhood that has 10% South Asians and the other 30% [as in model 2, $-0.006*(10-30)=0.12$].

In almost all the cases, the results for immigrant women are similar to those for immigrant men. The only noticeable difference from the pattern for men is that the negative association between exposure to own-group neighbours and employment earnings is significant among black women in Toronto even after controlling for neighbourhood low-income rate.

Conclusion and Discussion

The mass in-flows of visible-minority immigrants since the early 1980s has made the ethnocultural mosaic in Canada's large cities more diverse and visible. Between 1981 and 1996, the number of visible-minority enclaves, defined as census tracts with at least 30% of the population from the same visible-minority group (Chinese, South Asian or Black) increased from 6 to 137 in Toronto and Vancouver. Three-quarters of these enclaves were Chinese (102). Montreal only had five such enclaves in 1996, three of which were Black.

The rapid emergence of these visible-minority enclaves is not due to visible-minority immigrants becoming more concentrated in a small number of neighbourhoods. Rather, it is simply that a larger share of the population of these cities is now from these visible-minority groups; the proportion of the population from a particular visible-minority group has been rising in most urban neighbourhoods. Consequently, visible-minority immigrants, regardless of how long they have lived in Canada, have increasingly found themselves living in neighbourhoods with larger numbers of people from their own group.

In particular, among recent visible-minority immigrants, neighbourhood "exposure" to own-group members at time of entry rose dramatically through the 1980s and 1990s. Furthermore, as years in Canada increased for these immigrants, so too did their neighbourhood exposure to own-group members. This trend is at odds with the predictions of the traditional spatial assimilation model. According to that model, as immigrants become adjusted culturally and economically in the receiving society, they would move away from ethnic enclaves to neighbourhoods with better socio-economic conditions and reside primarily with majority group members. However, given the increased presence of visible-minority immigrants in most urban neighbourhoods, the likelihood of living with majority group members did not increase through time.

If the observed trend continues, the number of visible-minority en-claves will further increase and new visible-minority immigrants will have less potential contact with the white population in the same neighbourhood. Given this context, the possible effects of living in visible-minority enclaves on the integration of immigrants into Canadian society become an increasingly important question. In terms of labour market outcomes, overall we found a quite weak effect of exposure to own-group neighbours. Generally speaking, the association between exposure and employment was negative, but often not significant. The association between exposure and working in a segregated occupation was positive, but also often not significant, and there appeared to be generally little association between exposure and employment earnings. However, there were some important group differences. Among Chinese immigrants, who were the most segregated and most likely to live in visible-minority enclaves, and hence for whom the effects could be most important, the associations between exposure to own-group members and labour market outcomes were usually very weak. In contrast, among Black immigrants, who were the least segregated and least likely to live in their enclaves, the associations between exposure to own-group neighbours and labour market outcomes were often negative and strong.

Given the cross-sectional nature of data and potential selection bias, one must treat these results with caution. However, most often the potential selection biases tend to overestimate the neighbourhood effects. Hence, to the extent that there is a selection bias (unknown), the negative effects reported were likely overestimated, if anything.

Although visible-minority immigrants may not gain economically by living near their own-group members, they may benefit in many other ways. Even if they experience small potential negative economic effects, they may be willing to pay the small price and prefer neighbourhoods where they can live among people who share a common language and culture (Borjas, 2000). In this sense, it is encouraging to find that exposure to own-group members was at the most only weakly associated with negative labour market outcomes, and in a few cases, living in minority enclaves tends to moderate the employment difficulties among immigrants who spoke neither official language or had low levels of education, particularly among immigrant women. These results imply that in Canada's urban settings visible-minority immigrants' residential segregation is not strongly related to their economic segregation and disadvantages.

References

Bolt, G., J. Burgers and R. van Kempen (1998), "On the Social Significance of Spatial Location, Spatial Segregation and Social Inclusion", *Netherlands Journal of Housing and the Built Environment* 13, 83–95.

Borjas, G.J. (1995), "Ethnicity, Neighbourhoods and Human-capital Externalities", *The American Economic Review* 85(3), 365–390.

_____ (2000), "Ethnic Enclaves and Assimilation", *Swedish Economic Policy Review* 7, 89–122.

Buck, N. (2001), "Identifying Neighbourhood Effects on Social Exclusion", *Urban Studies* 38, 2251–2275.

Buzzelli, M. (2000), "Toronto's Postwar Little Italy: Landscape Change and Ethnic Relations", *The Canadian Geographer* 44(3), 298–305.

Chiswick, B. and P. Miller (2002), "Do Enclaves Matter in Immigrant Adjustment?" Paper presented at the annual meeting of the American Economic Association, Atlanta.

Driedger, L. (1978), "Ethnic Boundaries: A Comparison of Two Urban Neighbourhoods", *Sociology and Social Research* 62, 193–211.

Fong, E. and E. Ooka (1999), "Paying the Price for Economic Succession: The Social Cost of Ethnic Economy Participation", Research Summary for the Toronto Joint Center of Excellence for Research on Immigration and Settlement.

Galster, G., K. Metzger and R. Waite (1999), "Neighbourhood Opportunity Structure and Immigrants' Socioeconomic Advancement", *Journal of Housing Research* 10, 95–127.

Kelly, K. (1995), "Collecting Census Data on Canada's Visible Minority Population: A Historical Perspective", Cat. No: 89F0031MPE (Ottawa: Statistics Canada).

Lo, L., V. Preston, S. Wang, K. Reil, E. Havery and B. Siu (2000), "Immigrants' Economic Status in Toronto: Rethinking Settlement and Integration Strategies", Research Report to the Toronto Joint Center of Excellence for Research on Immigration and Settlement.

Massey, D.S. and N.A. Denton (1988), "The Dimensions of Residential Segregation", *Social Forces* 67(2), 281–315.

_____ (1993), *American Apartheid: Segregation and the Making of the Underclass* (Cambridge, MA: Harvard University Press).

Murdie, R.A. and C. Teixeira (2000), "Towards a Comfortable Neighbourhood and Appropriate Housing: Immigrant Experiences in Toronto", Working Paper No. 10 (Montreal: CERIS).

Ooka, E. and B. Wellman (2000), "Does Social Capital Pay Off More Within or Between Ethnic Groups — Analyzing Job Searchers in Five Toronto Ethnic Groups", Research Report to the Toronto Joint Center of Excellence for Research on Immigration and Settlement.

Oreopoulos, P. (2002), "Do Neighbourhoods Influence Long-term Labour Market Success? A Comparison of Adults Who Grew Up in Different Public Housing Projects", Analytical Studies Research Paper Series, Cat. No. 11F0019 No 185 (Ottawa: Statistics Canada).

Pickett, K.E. and M. Pearl (2001), "Multilevel Analyses of Neighbourhood Socio-economic Context and Health Outcomes: A Critical Review", *Journal of Epidemiology and Community Health* 55(2), 111–122.

Picot, G. and F. Hou (2002), "Rising Low-Income among Recent Immigrants in Canada". Paper presented at the Canadian Employment Research Forum Conference and annual meetings of Canada Economics Association, Calgary.

Ray, B., G. Halseth and B. Johnson (1997), "The Changing 'Face' of the Suburbs: Issues of Ethnicity and Residential Change in Suburban Vancouver", *International Journal of Urban and Regional Research* 21, 75–99.

Raudenbush, S., A. Bryk, Y.F. Cheong, R. Congdon (2000), *HLM^{TM} 5: Hierarchical Linear and Nonlinear Modeling* (Lincolnwood, IL: Scientific Software International, Inc.).

Renaud, V. and R. Costa (1999), "1996 Census of Population: Certification Report" (Ottawa: Population Group. Housing, Family and Social Statistics Division, Statistics Canada).

Reitz, J. (1990), "Ethnic Concentrations in Labour Markets and their Implications for Ethnic Inequality", in R. Breton *et al.* (eds.), *Ethnic Identity and Equality: Varieties of Experiences in a Canadian City* (Toronto: University of Toronto Press).

_____ (2001), "Immigrant Success in the Knowledge Economy: Institutional Changes and the Immigrant Experience in Canada, 1970–1995", *Journal of Social Issues* 57, 579–613.

Taeuber, K.E. and A.F. Taeuber (1965), *Negroes in Cities* (New York: Atheneum).

Teixeira, C. (2000), "Community Resources and Opportunities in Ethnic Economies: A Case Study of Portuguese and Black Entrepreneurs in Toronto", *Urban Studies* 38, 2055–2078.

Appendix
Table A1: Variables Used in Multivariate Analyses

Variable Name	Categories or Definitions
1. Labour market outcomes	
Employment	(1) Employed, (0) unemployed or not in the labour force. For population age 25 to 64 not disabled and not attending full-time school
Occupation segregation	(1) Working in an occupation in which the share of the group is twice as large as the group's share in the city's workforce, (0) others. For employed peopled aged 25 to 64
Log wages	Log wages and salaries for population aged 25 to 64 with positive wages and salaries in the year prior to the census date
2. Individual level variables	
Years since immigration	$<=5$ years 6–10 years 11–15 years 16–20 years > 20 years (reference)
Home language	Non-official language English or French (reference)
Education	Less than high school High school Some postsecondary With university degree (reference)
Experience Experience squared	(Age-years of schooling – 6) – group mean Experience squared
Family Structure	Unattached individual Lone-parent family Two adults without kids Two adults with kids (reference)

Feng Hou and Garnett Picot

Appendix Table A1 continued

Occupation*	Managerial
	Business services
	Professional
	Arts, cultural, recreation, and sports
	Sales and services
	Trades, transportation and equipment
	Processing, manufacturing, utilities
	(reference)
Weeks worked*	Weeks worked in 1995
Hours worked*	Hours worked in reference week

3. Neighbourhood level variables

Within group exposure	Weighted percent of population that is of same ethnic group in neighbourhoods, see text for details
Neighbourhood low-income	Percent of low-income population

Note: * variables on occupation, weeks worked and hours worked are used only in models for earnings.

Mental Health of Immigrant and Non-Immigrant Children in Canada: Results of the National Longitudinal Study of Children and Youth

Violet Kaspar

For about two decades, more than 200,000 immigrants arrive in Canada each year. Demographic trends indicate increasingly rising rates of foreign-born and visible-minority Canadians in the population. Based on 2001 Canada census data, the population contained the highest proportion of foreign-born Canadians (18.4%) observed in 70 years, and the four million visible minorities in Canada represented a three-fold increase in the number of visible minorities observed in the Canadian population over two decades (Statistics Canada, 2003). The population of immigrant children in Canada increased by 26% during the five years between 1991 and 1996 (CIC, 1999); one in five children living in Canada is an immigrant, or child of immigrant parents (Kelly, 1995).

Preparation of this article was supported by operating grants from the Canadian Institutes of Health Research (# FRN–MOP–53250) and the Social Sciences and Humanities Research Council of Canada (#410–98–1342), and by a Canadian Institutes of Health Research, Health Career Award (#C1C–42726).

According to a deficit perspective, immigrant children and youth are considered at risk for psychiatric distress or disorders due to accumulating adversities related to socio-economic circumstances, excessive role strains, racial and ethnic discrimination, as well as pre-migration trauma. Reports based on clinical and small community studies showed increased rates of depression, alcohol and substance abuse, delinquent behaviour, suicidal ideation, and psychopathology among foreign-born youth (Caplan, Choy and Whitmore, 1992; Hovey and King, 1996; Robert and Sobhan, 1992).

However, emerging epidemiological research evidence presents a contradiction, demonstrating comparable or lower rates of childhood psychiatric distress or disorders in newcomer compared to non-immigrant youth (Escobar, 1998; Hernandez and Charney, 1998; Klimidis, Stuart and Minas, 1994; Vega et al., 1998; Zhou, 1997). The robustness of the effect across social and political systems, and economic and ethnic structures of the receiving countries has been attributed to selection factors operating to ensure that the most healthy individuals and families are screened and admitted, as well as psychosocial resources, including family and ethnic community support.

Accumulating evidence supports the view that, on most criteria, immigrant children are at least as well adjusted as non-immigrant children, or they often surpass the national health status, despite increased rates of most major risk factors, including poverty, functional illiteracy, living in a high-risk neighbourhood, and lower socio-economic status. Notwithstanding, it is premature to draw definitive conclusions. One concern is the comparability of immigrant health studies conducted in different countries distinguished on the basis of racial and ethnic origins of immigrants admitted into the country, as well as social and political systems, and economic structures, including poverty rates. Second, it is not clear whether the initial health advantages of immigrant children sustain over a longitudinal period.

A task force report compiled by Hernandez and Charney highlighted the importance of length of stay and generational effects for understanding immigrant child health. They reported how "over time and across generations, as immigrant children become part of American society, many of these advantages [in health and well-being] do not appear to be sustained" (1998, p.1). Similar results have been reported based on studies conducted in Canada and Australia (Noh, Beiser and Kaspar, 1999). However, relatively little research has focused on determining explanations of why immigrants may lose their initial health advantages. Implicit in many studies is the influence of stress on the deterioration of immigrant

Violet Kaspar

children's health. However, the issue has not been examined systematically, operationalizing stressors as measured constructs, and assessing whether transitions into or out of stressful conditions influence changes in immigrant children's health and adjustment outcomes.

A confluence of pre- and post-migration stressful experiences may operate, either independently or in combination with displacement, to place immigrant children and youth at increased risk for poor mental health outcomes (Kaspar, 2002). Some immigrant youth may be at increased risk due to experiences of extraordinary stress prior to migration. According to a recent Canadian study, the rate of psychopathology among adolescent members of refugee families in Quebec was 21% (Tousignant *et al.*, 1999). The comparative provincewide rate for adolescents was 11%. Studies conducted in the United States demonstrated that at least 50% of Cambodian teenagers who arrived as refugees suffer persistent and severe symptoms of posttraumatic stress disorder (Kinzie and Sack, 1991).

Research also highlights the significance of post-migration stress as a determinant of the health and developmental adjustments of immigrant children. The experience of poverty represents an important aspect of the post-migration experience of immigrant children. Recent immigrant children are nearly three times as likely to be living in poverty than their non-immigrant counterparts (HRDC, 1999; National Council of Welfare, 1998; US. Department of Health and Human Services, 1998). More than one-third (36.4%) of immigrant children in Canada, aged 4 to 11 years old, were living in poverty in 1994–95; the rate for non-immigrant children was 13.3% (Beiser, Hou, Hyman and Tousignant, 2002). Detrimental effects of poverty on children's physical and mental health, academic achievement, and other developmental outcomes have been documented consistently in the literature. In addition, research highlights the importance of distinguishing the effects of *chronic and transient poverty*. In one study, poor children tended to have lower IQs and more internalizing difficulties than never-poor children; however, *persistent poverty* had a stronger negative effect than intermittent experiences of poverty (Duncan, Brooks-Gunn and Klebanov, 1994). McLeod and Shanahan (1996) observed more detrimental mental health outcomes among children with histories of persistent poverty than among transiently poor or non-poor children.

Relatively few studies addressed the impact of poverty on the health and adjustment of immigrant children. Although immigrant families are more likely to be poor than their non-immigrant counterparts, immigrant children appear at least as healthy as non-immigrant children, and often out-perform them in school (Hernandez, 1999; Klimidis, Stuart and Minas,

1994; Chang, Morrisey and Koplewicz, 1995; Zhou, 1997; Zhou and Bankston, 1998). Research shows that relative health status tends to decrease from foreign-born children, to native-born children of immigrant parents, to children of non-immigrant parents, even though poverty rates also decrease in the same direction (Hernandez, 1999; Hernandez and Charney, 1998; Beiser, Hou, Hyman and Tousignant, 2002). The findings suggest that immigrant status may protect children, at least temporarily, from negative health consequences of poverty.

Finally, developmental psychopathology and clinical literatures emphasize the etiological significance of negative environmental conditions, particularly in family domains, for the development of emotional and behavioural maladjustments in children (Noshpitz, Adams and Bleiberg, 1998). In contemporary developmental and cross-cultural research, family, as a primary socialization agent, represents an important determinant of children's social, emotional, and cognitive functioning (Chen and Kaspar, in press). Empirical evidence demonstrates compromises in children's mental health associated with negative home environments, including parenting and family functioning related factors, socio-economic strain, parental distress, and family dissolution (Biederman *et al.*, 1995; Green *et al.*, 1991; HRDC, 1999; Rutter, 1990).

Family functioning, parenting behaviours, and family structure stability also constitute important influences on children's adjustment outcomes (Bornstein, 1991; Chen and Kaspar, in press; Parke and Buriel, 1998). Empirical studies demonstrated significant associations between *family dysfunction*, as well as *family breakdown*, and children's mental distress (Amato and Keith, 1991; Grych and Fincham, 1990; Hetherington and Stanley-Hagan, 1999). Among other stressful conditions thought to compromise children's successful adjustments are *ineffective parenting practices*, with research demonstrating negative effects of ineffective parenting across cultures and diverse socio-economic conditions (Bornstein, 1991; Chen and Kaspar, in press). *Parental psychopathology* is another important factor adversely affecting the mental health of children (Downey and Coyne, 1990; Gotlib and Lee, 1990). The salience of these family context variables, and how they operate to influence developmental pathways and children's health and adjustment, has rarely been examined in cross-cultural research, or research on immigrants.

Violet Kaspar

The Study

Using two waves (cycles 2 and 3) of data collected through the Statistics Canada and Human Resources Development Canada National Longitudinal Study of Children and Youth, this study compares children from immigrant and non-immigrant families on indexes of emotional and behavioural adjustment, including internalizing and externalizing problems, and pro-social behaviour. Consistent with the view that emotional and behavioural maladjustments in children represent responses to negative environmental conditions, particularly in family domains (Noshpitz, Adams and Bleiberg, 1998), this study examines the psychological impact, across a two-year longitudinal period, of family structure stability, poverty status, parenting behaviours, parental distress, and family dysfunction.

The analysis of psychological outcomes focused on children's emotional and conduct problems, representing two of the most prevalent domains of symptoms and disorders of childhood (ibid.). Also, a positive dimension of children's behavioural outcomes, prosocial behaviour, was analyzed for this study. Very few studies address positive outcomes. Emphasis on maladaptive outcomes suggests that lack of psychopathology is equivalent to successful adaptation. However, this approach does not provide an adequate depiction of children's adjustment. Many youth exposed to high levels of stress develop into well-adjusted, competent, and high functioning adults, an observation that has prompted the view that lack of experience in dealing with stress places youth at risk later in the lifespan (Rutter, 1990). Theory and empirical evidence have pointed to the emerging significance of positive outcomes in the assessment of psychological functioning in children (Taylor and Brown, 1988).

Theoretical Approach. The conceptual framework guiding this research is based on aspects of the developmental psychopathology (Sroufe and Rutter, 1984) and stress-process (Pearlin *et al.*, 1981) theories. Models based on these major theoretical and conceptual frameworks have been adapted and applied successfully in epidemiological, population health studies examining determinants of minority and immigrant health, including stressful life conditions affecting the health and adjustment of adults and youth (Kaspar and Noh, 2001). The proposed framework includes multiple domains of stress (e.g., poverty, family structure and instability factors, and family environmental stress), and emotional and behavioural outcomes.

Study Objectives and Hypotheses

Using data from two waves of the NLSCY, the present analysis was designed to address the following specific objectives among immigrant and non-immigrant children.

1. To examine rates of emotional problems, conduct problems, and prosocial behaviours in children of immigrant and non-immigrant families across time. Consistent with *the healthy immigrant effect*, it is hypothesized that immigrant children would show better psychological and behavioural adjustments than non-immigrant children. Based on previous literatures, it is hypothesized that initial health advantages of immigrant children would reduce over time.

2. To examine changes in immigrant and non-immigrant children's adjustment outcomes as predicted by family stability conditions (e.g., living in a single-parent family, and transitions into single-parent and two-parent families). Family breakdown represents a stressor that may place children at risk for emotional and behavioural maladjustment. The literature also supports the view that transitions into single-parent situations are contemporaneous with endings of negative quality marital relationships, and may be associated with improvements in children's adjustment. This may be particularly relevant for non-immigrant children; family stability may represent a primary provision of family life that is more supportive of immigrant children's well-being than quality of the marital relationship of their parents.

3. To compare the effects of changes in poverty status on the adjustment of children from immigrant and non-immigrant families. It is hypothesized that exposure to persistent poverty and transitions into poverty will predict deteriorating emotional and behavioural adjustment outcomes in children. Movement out of poverty will predict improvements in children's adjustment outcomes, particularly for immigrants. Research shows that immigrant families experience temporary poverty that can be gradually overcome with adjustment to the labour market in the receiving country. This hypothesis is supported by research to show that poverty affects immigrant children primarily through material deprivation; poverty in non-immigrants is often associated with material deprivation accompanied by persistent cycles of disadvantage in family and social environments.

Violet Kaspar

4. To examine changes in immigrant and non-immigrant children's adjustment outcomes as predicted by family environment stressors, including ineffective parenting, parental depression, and family dysfunction. It was hypothesized that family environment stressors would predict poor adjustment outcomes in both immigrant and non-immigrant children. Consistent with literature citing the protective effects of familial conditions as most salient for young children whose psychological needs may be met mostly within the family system, it may be expected that the negative effects of stressful family conditions may impact similarly on the adjustment of immigrant and non-immigrant children.

Data and Methods

Sample

Data for this study were derived from cycles 2 and 3 of the NLSCY, a nationwide study of approximately 23,000 children, followed up every two years, and ranging in age from newborn to 11 years at the time of the cycle 1 survey in 1994–95. The present study focused on a subsample of 6,760 children who were between 6 and 11 years old at the time of the cycle 3 survey (in 1998–99), since behavioural measures for this age group were different from those for younger children in the cycle 2 survey and for older children in the cycle 3 survey. Mental health ratings obtained at cycle 2 were based on parental ratings for younger children (four to nine years old). Cycle 3 data only for children in the sample who participated at cycle 2 were included for analysis in this study.

The original NLSCY sampling strategy relied on household selection through a multi-stage stratified cluster probability sampling procedure. Population weights were assigned to compensate for the differential representation of population groups. Following Statistics Canada's recommendations, in performing multivariate analysis, population weights were rescaled to an average weight of 1, so the sum of the rescaled weights equalled the sample size. However, these population weights do not reflect the survey design effect, and tend to underestimate standard errors. Statistical techniques, such as the bootstrap procedure, can take into account both issues of sample weights and survey design. However, sample stratum information is needed for such procedures, but were not available to this study.

Children of immigrant families were identified for comparison against the remaining children constituting the national comparison sample. Children of immigrant families consisted of those entering Canada as immigrants and those born in Canada to at least one immigrant parent. There were 757 children of immigrant families in the sample. Among them, 69 were born in foreign countries.

Sample Size Limitations. It was not possible to conduct separate analyses for foreign-born and Canadian-born children of immigrant parents, since the sample size was not large enough to meet Statistics Canada's guidelines for reliable estimation.[1] The small sample size also precluded finer-grained analyses to investigate whether the mental health advantages applied to immigrant children from different immigrant classes (such as refugees vs. immigrants) and from various cultural and ethnic backgrounds. Similarly, sample constraints did not permit examining the roles of protective factors, such as parental social support and coping, which might further explain or mitigate the effects of stress on the mental health of immigrant and non-immigrant children.

Selection and Operational Definitions of Variables

Children's Emotional and Behavioural Outcomes. Three measures of developmental behaviours constituted the study outcomes: (i) emotional problems, (ii) conduct problems, and (iii) prosocial behaviours. These scales showed high reliability, with the Cronbach alpha ranging from 0.77 to 0.84. For each measure of developmental behaviours, respondents were asked to answer several questions, endorsing each as either "never or not true", "sometimes or somewhat true", or "often or very true".

---

[1]According to Statistics Canada's guidelines for statistical analysis and release, acceptable estimates should have a sample size of 30 or more, and a coefficient of variation less than 16.5%. Although the sample size of foreign-born children was larger than 30, the breakdowns by changes in poverty status, family structure or other variables contained sample sizes much less than 30.

The *prosocial behaviours* scale contained ten items: "sympathy to someone who has made a mistake", "will try to help someone who has been hurt", "volunteers to help clear a mess someone else has made", "if there is a quarrel or dispute, will try to stop it", "offers to help other children who are having difficulty with a task", "comforts a child who is crying or upset", "spontaneously helps to pick up objects which another child has dropped", "will invite bystanders to join in a game", "helps other children who are feeling sick", "takes the opportunity to praise the work of less able children". The scale score ranged from 0 to 20.

Emotional problems, characterized by feelings of anxiety and depression, were measured with an eight-item scale. Sample items included: "seems to be unhappy, sad, or depressed", "not as happy as other children", "too fearful or anxious", "worried", "cries a lot", and "appears miserable, unhappy, tearful, or distressed". Scores on the scale ranged from 0 to 16, a higher score indicating a higher level of emotional disorder.

Conduct problems, characterized by aggression, physical or indirect, or violation of social norms were assessed using a six-item scale: "gets into many fights", "physically attacks people", "threatens people", and "cruel, bullies or mean to others". Scale scores ranged from 0 to 12.

Emotional and behavioural outcomes ratings were based on parental reports, and though reliance on proxy informants (usually the mother) for assessments of children's mental health is typical in research, variations in perceptions and evaluations of psychological distress symptoms across informants raise concerns about biased ratings. The literature reports poor correspondence between children's self-reports and parental ratings of child mental health, with parents tending towards appraising their children's mental health more positively and reporting significantly fewer pathological symptoms. The discrepancy may be exaggerated in immigrant and refugee populations (Rousseau and Drapeau, 1998). While this discordance issue represents a potential source of bias that raises concern about the underestimation of mental distress among immigrant children in this study, the longitudinal nature of the study, and controlling for previous mental health, served to minimize or "control" biases due to reliance on parental reports.

Poverty and Changes in Poverty Status. Poverty status in the present study was a relative indicator of low income based on Statistics Canada's low-income cut-offs (LICOs). LICOs take into account income versus expenditure patterns in seven family-size categories and in five community-size groups. Compared with the average household, a family at or below the

LICO spends 20% more of its income on food, clothing, and shelter. In 1998, a family of four living in large cities and with a before-tax income below $33,000 would be classified as low-income status (Paquet, 2001). The method of creating groupings to indicate changes in poverty status for this study classified families into four categories: *Persistently Poor* (poor at both cycles), *Newly Poor* (from non-poor at cycle 2 to poor at cycle 3), *Newly Non-poor* (from poor at cycle 2 to non-poor at cycle 3), and *Non-poor* (non-poor at both cycles).

Family Stability. A four-category variable was created to capture changes in family structure: *Family Formation* — single, divorced, or widowed parents at the time of the cycle 2 survey were married or common law at cycle 3; *Family Breakdown* — married or common law parents at cycle 2, and divorced or widowed at cycle 3; *Both Parents at both cycles*; and *Single Parents at both cycles*.

Parent and Family Environment Factors. The NLSCY measure of *parenting behaviours* relied on the Parenting Practices Scale developed by Strayhorn and Weidman (1988), with additional questions developed by Dr. M. Boyle at Chedoke-McMaster Hospital. Previous NLSCY analyses of this inventory of items identified three factors: positive interactions, ineffective interactions, and consistency of parenting practices (HRDC, 1996). Only the ineffective interactions scale was used in the current analysis since it was found to have consistent effects on various developmental outcomes.

The measure of *parental depression* drew upon the Centre for Epidemiological Studies Depression Scale (CES-D), a widely-used survey instrument originally developed by the National Institute of Mental Health (Radloff, 1977). To ease respondent burden, the NLSCY employed a 12-question, abbreviated version of the CES-D.

Family functioning was measured using the Family Assessment Device, a 12-item questionnaire developed by the Chedoke-McMaster Hospital group (Epstein, Baldwin and Bishop, 1983). The scale assesses communication, problem-solving, affective responsiveness (i.e., readiness of family members to show feelings), affective involvement (i.e., readiness of family members to help and support each other), and family roles. In the analysis, this variable was coded so that a higher score reflected a higher level of family dysfunction.

Violet Kaspar

Control Variables. Control variables included *age* and *education* of the PMK (parent most knowledgeable about the child), as well as *age, gender, length-of-stay (in years) in Canada,* and *previous mental health* of the child. A dummy variable, non-white (1=non-white, 0=white), was created as a crude measure to control for racial/ethnic heterogeneity in the population. This variable is not included in the multivariate regression models for non-immigrant children, since this group contained only about 1% non-white children. Among immigrant children, 29.1% were non-white.

Statistical Analyses

The present study took advantage of the longitudinal design of the NLSCY. Cross-sectional studies are subject to the ambiguity of causal order: for example, do harsh parenting practices impair children's behavioural adjustments, or do children's behavioural problems contribute to parents resorting to harsh parenting practices? Analyses based on cross-sectional data also are subject to specification bias due to the omission of un-measured factors, for example, are children's behavioural problems and impaired parenting behaviours both influenced by some unmeasured characteristics of parents, such as social adjustment, skills, enthusiasm, and dependability, that will also affect children's outcomes? Analyses of, for example, changes in economic status and children's behavioural problems mitigate problems of causal ordering and specification bias.

Descriptive Statistics. The present study first examined differences, at a descriptive level, in family structure, economic situations, and family environment and parenting conditions of children of immigrant and non-immigrant families at the cycle 2 and cycle 3 NLSCY surveys. Similarly, emotional and behavioural outcomes of immigrant and non-immigrant children are described.

Multivariate Analyses. The conditional change or static-score model (Finkel, 1995) was used to examine the effect of selected mental health determinants on changes in children's developmental outcomes. The basic form of this model was:

$$Y_2 = b_0 + b_1 Y_1 + b_1 X_1 + \dots bn X_n + e$$

In this model, Y_2 represents time 2 (e.g., cycle 3 NLSCY) developmental behaviours, and Y_1, time 1 (e.g., cycle 2 NLSCY) developmental behaviours. Inclusion of the prior level of the dependent variable can take into account the possible negative correlation between initial scores on a variable and subsequent change. The prior level of the dependent variable in the model can also serve to control, at least partially, for omitted variables that influence the change in the dependent variable (Finkel, 1995). Previous studies showed that the level of initial symptomatology was a much better predictor of psychological distress than the stressors to which the individual had been exposed (Schaufeli and Van Yperen, 1992).

In the model, b_1 indicates the stability of children's developmental behaviours, and b_1-1, the effect of Y_1 on the changes of Y over time. Separate models were constructed for each of the three selected indicators of developmental behaviours in this study.

X_1 to X_n in the model are all the variables representing basic socio-demographic characteristics, changes in family structure, income status, and parental characteristics. It can be demonstrated that b_n indicates the causal effect of X_n on the *change* of Y, controlling for Y's prior levels and other variables in the model; "e" is the error term.

Using the conditional change panel model, this study first examined whether immigrant and non-immigrant children changed differently in the selected adjustment outcomes after controlling for their changes in family environment and poverty. Then, for each selected outcome, models were constructed for immigrant and non-immigrant children separately in order to examine whether effects of family environment and poverty variables varied by immigrant status. This approach is similar to models with interaction terms between immigrant status and all other variables. However, the inclusion of too many interaction terms would cause multicollinearity. This longitudinal analysis was about changes. In the conditional change panel models, the previous level of the developmental outcome was controlled, thus previously existing connections among developmental outcome, poverty, and parental characteristics were taken into account.

Violet Kaspar

Results

Emotional and Behavioural Outcomes

Descriptive results on family environment and economic conditions for immigrant and non-immigrant children are presented in Table 1. Results showed that immigrant children were significantly more likely than non-immigrant children to be living in two-parent households at the time of the cycle 2 survey (87.4% vs. 81.9%, $p < 0.0001$). At the cycle 3 survey, this difference disappeared (82.5% vs. 81.4%, $p = 0.357$), with immigrant and non-immigrant children just as likely to be living with two-parents at the

Table 1: Children's Family Environment by Immigration Status, Based on Parental Reports for Children Aged 6 to 11 in 1998–1999

		Immigrants		Non-Immigrants		P-Value of Difference
		(%)		(%)		
Living with two parents	1996/97	87.4		81.9		<0.0001
	1998/99	82.5		81.4		0.357
Living in poor families	1996/97	32.7		22.6		<0.0001
	1998/99	24.8		16.7		<0.0001
		mean	std	mean	std	
Ineffective parenting	1996/97	8.73	5.25	9.02	3.57	0.010
	1998/99	8.57	5.12	8.81	3.40	0.031
Parental depression	1996/97	5.22	8.18	4.38	4.99	<0.0001
	1998/99	4.94	7.38	4.56	5.16	0.021
Family dysfunction	1996/97	8.86	7.33	7.95	4.72	<0.0001
	1998/99	9.12	7.06	8.37	4.66	<0.0001

time of the cycle 3 survey. The diminished difference was associated with a reduced percentage of immigrant children living in two-parent families at cycle 3 relative to cycle 2.

Table 1 also shows that immigrant children were more likely to be exposed to negative economic circumstances at both cycles 2 and 3 surveys of the NLSCY. At cycle 2 (1996–97), nearly one-third (32.7%) of immigrant children lived in poverty; 22.6% of non-immigrant children lived in poverty at cycle 2. The difference was statistically significant ($p < 0.0001$). At cycle 3, immigrant children again were significantly more likely to be living in poverty than non-immigrant children (24.8% vs. 16.7%, $p < 0.0001$).

Mean scores on ineffective parenting, parental depression, and family dysfunction are presented in the lower panel of Table 1. Results showed that non-immigrant parents had higher scores on ineffective parenting relative to immigrant parents at cycle 2 (8.73 vs. 9.02, $p = 0.010$). The difference, in the same direction, remained statistically significant at cycle 3 (8.57 vs. 8.81, $p = 0.031$). However, immigrant parents did not show advantages over non-immigrants on parental depression and family dysfunction. Immigrant parents exhibited significantly more depressive symptoms than non-immigrant parents at both the cycles 2 and 3 survey (5.22 vs. 4.38, $p < 0.0001$ at cycle 2, and 4.94 vs. 4.56, $p = 0.021$ at cycle 3). Similarly for family dysfunction, immigrant parents rated higher on family dysfunction than non-immigrant parents at both cycles 2 and 3 of the survey (8.86 vs. 7.95, $p < 0.0001$ at cycle 2, and 9.12 vs. 8.37, $p < 0.0001$ at cycle 3).

Therefore, immigrant children appeared to be exposed to more stressful living contexts with respect to poverty and family environment. As reported in Table 1, at both cycles 2 and 3 of the survey, immigrant children experienced significantly more negative economic circumstances, as well as negative family environments, including higher rates of parental depression and family dysfunction, than did non-immigrant children. Also, although immigrant children were less likely to live in single-parent families at cycle 2 than were non-immigrant children, the effect diminished to non-significance by the time of the cycle 3 survey.

Mean scores of emotional problems, conduct problems, and prosocial behaviours of immigrant and non-immigrant children between 6 and 11 years old at cycles 2 and 3 are shown in Table 2. At cycle 2, on all three indicators of emotional and behavioural outcomes, immigrant children showed better adjustments than their non-immigrant counterparts. Results presented in Table 2 also demonstrated that, while the healthy immigrant

Violet Kaspar

Table 2: Children's Mental Health Outcomes by Immigration Status, Based on Parental Reports for Children Aged 6 to 11 in 1998–1999

		Immigrants		Non-Immigrants		P-Value of Difference
		mean	std	mean	std	
Emotional problems	1996/97	2.32	3.16	2.51	2.43	0.011
	1998/99	2.55	3.44	2.71	2.48	0.052
Conduct problems	1996/97	1.21	2.17	1.50	1.81	<0.0001
	1998/99	1.14	2.03	1.39	1.74	<0.0001
Prosocial behaviours	1996/97	12.69	5.19	12.42	3.65	0.025
	1998/99	13.32	5.17	13.26	3.48	0.580

effect was sustained at cycle 3 for conduct problems, immigrant children did not show significant advantages over non-immigrant children in emotional problems and prosocial behaviours across the two years to cycle 3. The results are suggestive of immigrant children losing their initial adjustment advantages exhibited two years prior.

Based on the descriptive results presented in Tables 1 and 2, immigrant children exhibited significantly better emotional and behavioural adjustment than their non-immigrant counterparts. Across the two-year study period, however, immigrant children tended to lose their health advantages. At the same time, immigrant children faced higher exposures to poverty, family dysfunction, and parental depression across both cycles of the survey. These data were further examined in a multivariate model, where a regression analysis was conducted for emotional and behavioural outcomes, regressed simultaneously on immigrant status, previous mental health and other control variables, and poverty, family stability, and parental variables. Results presented in Table 3 demonstrated no differences in the selected outcomes between immigrant and non-immigrant children, after controlling for previous mental health, socio-demographic variables, and changes in family stability status, parenting factors, and economic situations. Further multivariate analyses showed, however, that some adverse life circumstances had different effects on changes in adjustment

Table 3: Unstandardized Regression Coefficients for Mental Health Outcomes of Children Aged 6–11 in 1998–1999

Independent variables	Emotional Problems		Conduct Problems		Prosocial Behaviours	
	B	se	B	se	B	se
Constant	1.582	0.253**	0.788	0.174**	6.171	0.405**
Previous mental health, 1996–97	0.565	0.012**	0.559	0.011**	0.464	0.012**
Immigrant children	−0.008	0.073	−0.070	0.050	−0.011	0.114
Child's age	0.046	0.018**	0.018	0.012	0.032	0.028
Girl	0.006	0.057	−0.162	0.039**	0.984	0.089**
PMK's age	−0.009	0.006	−0.006	0.004	0.011	0.009
PMK finished high-school	0.266	0.063**	0.099	0.043*	−0.148	0.099
Living with a single parent	−0.100	0.167	−0.055	0.114	0.533	0.261*
Moved from two to one parent	−0.528	0.145**	−0.172	0.099	0.421	0.227
Moved into step/blended family	−0.735	0.214**	−0.619	0.145**	0.861	0.336**
Newly poor	0.092	0.152	0.224	0.103*	−0.091	0.233*
Newly non-poor	0.230	0.098*	0.374	0.067**	−0.377	0.149*
Persistently poor	0.010	0.100	0.119	0.068	−0.100	0.154*
Increases in ineffective parenting	0.137	0.008**	0.082	0.006**	−0.041	0.013**
Increases in PMK depression	0.035	0.005**	0.021	0.004**	−0.001	0.008**
Increases in family dysfunction	0.009	0.005	−0.008	0.004*	−0.014	0.008
Sample size	5,758		5,779		5,240	
R-squared	0.320		0.343		0.270	

Note: * p<.05, ** p<.01

outcomes for immigrants and non-immigrants. Regression models to examine effects on adjustment outcomes, conducted separately for immigrant and non-immigrant children, are presented in Table 4.

Changes in family composition and breakdown, poverty status and transitions, parental characteristics, and family dysfunction tended to show numerous associations with children's emotional and behavioural adjustments. However, patterns were not clear, and sometimes inconsistent. Results for each emotional and behavioural outcome are discussed in turn below.

Emotional Problems. Results showed that transitions from single-parent families to step- or blended families predicted reductions in emotional problems in immigrant ($\beta = -2.337$, $p < 0.05$) and non-immigrant ($\beta = -0.622$, $p < 0.01$) children, and this was over and above the effects of control variables (including child's previous mental health, age and gender, white/non-white status, and parental age and education, and length-of-stay in Canada), and economic and family/parent environment variables in the model. Moreover, this effect was stronger among immigrant than non-immigrant children. Transitions from two-parent to single-parent families also significantly predicted reductions in emotional problems, but this effect was observed only for non-immigrant children; changes in emotional problems in immigrant children were not associated with this transition in family structure.

Few statistically significant findings emerged with respect to the effects of economic transitions on changes in immigrant and non-immigrant children's emotional problems. For immigrant children, being "newly non-poor" was associated with escalation in emotional problems. No other transition in poverty status demonstrated significant associations with changes in emotional problems for immigrant children. For non-immigrant children, no economic transition category was significantly associated with changes in emotional problems.

Finally, parent-related factors appeared important for the emotional well-being of children. Increases in ineffective parenting significantly predicted increases in emotional problems for both immigrant and non-immigrant children. Similarly, increases in parental (PMK) depression significantly predicted the escalation of emotional problems in immigrant and non-immigrant children. Increases in family dysfunction were not significantly associated with changes in emotional problems for either immigrant or non-immigrant children.

Table 4: Unstandardized Regression Coefficients for Mental Health Outcomes of Children Aged 6–11 in 1998–99, for Immigrant and Non-immigrant Children

| | Emotional Problems | | | | Conduct Problems | | | | Prosocial Behaviours | | | |
| | Non-immigrants | | Immigrants | | Non-immigrants | | Immigrants | | Non-immigrants | | Immigrants | |
Independent variables	B	se	B	se	B	se	B	se	B	se	B	se
Constant	1.797	.267**	1.106	.867	0.910	.190**	0.688	.503	5.656	.428**	8.311	1.390**
Previous mental health, 1996–97	0.579	.012**	0.531	.042**	0.574	.011**	0.490	.035**	0.475	.012**	0.423	.041**
Years in Canada	-	-	-0.011	.009	-	-	-0.002	.005	-	-	0.030	.015*
Non-white	-	-	-0.802	.194**	-	-	-0.252	.116*	-	-	0.256	.331
Child's age	0.024	.018	0.094	.056	0.005	.013	0.076	.033*	-0.019	.028	0.251	.097**
Girl	0.046	.059	-0.134	.180	-0.191	.042**	0.006	.108	0.983	.092**	1.051	.305**
PMK's age	-0.009	.006	-0.008	.016	-0.006	.004	-0.014	.010	0.023	.009*	-0.018	.028
PMK finished high-school	0.345	.065**	0.032	.215	0.132	.046**	0.009	.131	-0.149	.100	-0.301	.379
Living with a single parent	-0.193	.171	0.283	.625	-0.101	.120	-0.067	.370	0.635	.265*	-0.769	1.022
Moved from two to one parent	-0.677	.148**	0.181	.552	-0.203	.104	-0.092	.323	0.735	.232**	-1.767	.880*
Moved into step/blended family	-0.622	.213**	-2.337	.939*	-0.588	.148**	-1.333	.555*	0.960	.331**	1.392	1.716
Newly poor	0.166	.165	-0.178	.429	0.268	.115*	0.079	.254	-0.185	.247	0.718	.728
Newly non-poor	0.030	.107	0.816	.278**	0.170	.075*	0.979	.168**	-0.161	.160	-0.816	.460
Persistently poor	-0.076	.111	0.198	.273	0.177	.078*	-0.115	.162	-0.148	.169	-0.050	.453
Increases in ineffective parenting	0.136	.009**	0.126	.025**	0.084	.006**	0.068	.015**	-0.035	.013**	-0.039	.041
Increases in PMK depression	0.030	.005**	0.063	.016**	0.025	.004**	0.002	.010	0.011	.008	-0.032	.027
Increases in family dysfunction	0.008	.006	0.006	.016	-0.012	.004**	0.004	.010	-0.025	.009**	0.034	.027
Sample size	5,176		602		5,157		602		4,687		538	
R-squared	0.341		0.296		0.362		0.314		0.290		0.246	

Note: * p<.05, ** p<.01

Violet Kaspar

Conduct Problems. Living in single-parent headed families, and transitions from two-parent to single-parent families were not significantly associated with changes in conduct problems, and this held for both immigrant and non-immigrant children. Transitions from single-parent families into step-blended families were significantly associated with reduced conduct problems in immigrant ($\beta = -1.333$, $p < 0.05$) and non-immigrant ($\beta = -0.588$, $p < 0.01$) children, over and above the effects of other variables in the model. This effect was stronger in immigrant than in non-immigrant children.

After controlling for other variables in the model, results showed that persistent poverty and economic transitions predicted increases in levels of conduct problems in non-immigrant children. The escalation of conduct problems in non-immigrant children was predicted by living in persistent poverty, becoming newly poor, and becoming newly non-poor. For immigrant children, changes in conduct problems were not significantly associated with persistent poverty or transitions into poverty. However, becoming newly non-poor was significantly associated with escalations in conduct problems in immigrant children ($\beta = 0.979$, $p < 0.01$), and this effect was stronger than the observed effect for non-immigrant children becoming newly non-poor.

Increases in ineffective parenting were associated with elevating levels of conduct disorder in immigrant and non-immigrant children. Increases in parental depression significantly predicted increased conduct problems in non-immigrants; parental depression was not significantly related to changes in conduct problems in immigrant children. Finally, increases in family dysfunction were significantly associated with reductions in non-immigrant children's conduct problems. Changes in conduct problems in immigrant children were not related to family dysfunction.

Prosocial Behaviours. Results on children's prosocial behaviours appeared most related to family stability factors, particularly for non-immigrant children. For non-immigrant children, increases in levels of prosocial behaviour were significantly associated with living in single-parent families. Also, among non-immigrant children, transitions from single-parent families to step- or blended families, as well as the reverse transition, from two-parent to single-parent families, were significantly associated with increases in prosocial behaviour scores.

Non-immigrant children's poverty circumstances were not significantly related to increases in prosocial behaviours. Transitions into newly poor circumstances were, however, significantly related to reductions in prosocial behaviours among immigrant children. Changes in immigrant children's prosocial behaviours were not significantly associated with any other category of poverty circumstances, including persistent poverty and transitions into poverty.

Reductions in prosocial behaviours among non-immigrant children were significantly associated with increases in ineffective parenting and family dysfunction. These family environment stressors were not significantly related to changes in prosocial behaviours among immigrant children. Increases in parental depression were not related to changes in children's prosocial behaviours, both among immigrant and non-immigrant children.

Discussion

The primary objectives of this study aimed to examine health disparities in immigrant versus non-immigrant children across a two-year period, as well the effects of multiple domains of adverse life circumstances on changes in the psychological and behavioural adjustments of immigrant and non-immigrant children. The initial advantages in adjustment outcomes of immigrant children over their non-immigrant counterparts appeared to diminish over the two-year period to follow-up, at least at a descriptive level. This deterioration of immigrant children's health status was contemporaneous with their persistently higher exposures to poverty, family dysfunction and parental depression over the two-year study period. At a more substantive level, however, no significant differences in the emotional and behavioural adjustments of immigrant and non-immigrant children were observed after controlling for the effects of socio-demographic variables in a multivariate model. Notwithstanding, the duration to follow-up may not have been sufficiently long to establish a basis for more definitive conclusions. Nor were assimilation-related constructs assessed. As immigrant children acculturate within a new socio-cultural milieu, they may increasingly adopt North American values and life-styles, clash in values with parents and peer groups, participate in unhealthy behaviours, including smoking and drinking, as well as experience exposure to such negative forces as social exclusion or discrimination (Rumbaut, 1994). The mental health effects of assimilation on youth remain understudied aspects of research on immigrant child health.

Consistent with the view that children's adjustment may be best understood as a response to negative environmental conditions, particularly in family domains (Noshpitz, Adams and Bleiberg, 1998), effects of family environment conditions, including family structure stability, economic situations, and parenting behaviours, parental distress and family dysfunction were highlighted in this study. The contributions of these factors to children's health and adjustments were a focus of this study, and will be discussed in turn.

Family Structure Transitions and Children's Adjustment

For immigrant and non-immigrant children, changes in adjustment outcomes generally were not significantly related to invariably *living in a single-parent family*. However, transitions in family structure appeared to have some relevance for the well-being of children. Generally, *transitions into step-blended families* were most significantly related to improvements in psychological and behavioural adjustments of both immigrant and non-immigrant children, though reductions in emotional and conduct problems among children moving into step-blended families were much stronger for immigrant than for non-immigrant children. A possible explanation is that the addition of a new adult family member might provide an improved environment for children. However, family structure stability may be particularly relevant for the psychological and behavioural adjustments of immigrant children. Whether immigrant children remained in their original family, or moved into a step-blended family, they experienced improvements in adjustment outcomes related to emotional and conduct problems. Among non-immigrant children, some improvements in adjustment were accompanied by marital breakdowns, or transitions from two-parent to single-parent families; however, transitions in family structure related to marital breakdowns had no bearing on changes in the adjustment outcomes of immigrant children. While family breakdown represents a stressor that may place children at risk for emotional and behavioural maladjustment, transitions into single-parent situations may be contemporaneous with endings of negative quality marital relationships, and may be associated with improvements in children's adjustment. This study found that improvements associated with transitions from two-parent to single-parent families were observed among immigrant children, but not non-immigrant children. The pattern of results is consistent with a view that a two-parent family situation may be more critical for the adjustment of immigrant children. Immigrant children may function better in two-parent families, perhaps because family structure stability represents a potentially more primary provision of the family system, supporting immigrant children's well-being more than quality of the marital relationship of their parents. Non-immigrant children might be better off living with a single parent than with two parents with a dysfunctional relationship (Hetherington and Stanley-Hagan, 1999).

Poverty and Children's Adjustment

Rather weak effects of economic changes in the family were observed for outcomes related to emotional problems and prosocial behaviours, and significant effects seemed to show few consistent directions in their influences on children's adjustment outcomes. Overall, children's adjustment problems did not deteriorate among persistently poor families.

Among immigrant children, being persistently poor or newly poor was not associated with further escalations in emotional and behavioural problems, or decreases in positive behaviours (prosocialness). Similarly, changes in emotional problems and prosocial behaviours were generally non-responsive to situations of persistent poverty among non-immigrant children.

The overall pattern of results is consistent with research to show that net of the effects of individual child and parental characteristics, poverty exerts a relatively small impact on children's adjustment (Duncan, Brooks-Gunn and Klebanov, 1994; Smith, Brooks-Gunn and Klebanov, 1997). These study findings may be accounted for, to a certain degree by government interventions. In Canada and the United States, most poor families can meet basic material needs for food, housing, and health care through governmental transfers and programs. Although homelessness and hunger still affect some Canadian children, relatively few poor children in Canada suffer the extremes of material deprivation that cause severe physical or social disadvantages (Canadian Council on Social Development, 1999).

However, some of the current study findings related to the impact of transitions into and out of poverty for immigrant and non-immigrant children provide some important insights, highlighting the significance of economic transitions for children's adjustment. Among immigrant children, transitions out of poverty, from poor (at cycle 2) to non-poor (at cycle 3), predicted increases in emotional and conduct problems, and reductions in prosocial behaviours. However, transitions into poverty did not predict significant changes in immigrant children's adjustment outcomes. In contrast, changes in non-immigrant children's emotional problems and prosocial behaviours were not associated with transitions out of poverty. Similar to immigrant children, non-immigrant children showed increases in conduct problems with transitions out of poverty, but clear disadvantages with respect to increasing conduct disorder across time were observed for non-immigrant children making transitions into poverty. Immigrant children in newly poor families did not face the disadvantages of non-immigrant children with respect to conduct disorder. Although prolonged exposure to poverty, or becoming newly poor, may not further escalate immigrant children's emotion or conduct problems, non-immigrant children living in persistent poverty, or making transitions into and out of poverty experienced increases in conduct disorder across the two-year study period.

Therefore, all categories of economic disadvantage and transitions tended to be more strongly associated with changes in adjustment outcomes related to conduct disorder among non-immigrant children. In sharp contrast to the results among non-immigrant children, changes in adjustment outcomes could not be predicted by exposure to persistent poverty or movement into poverty among immigrant children. Only increases in conduct problems were observed among immigrant children becoming newly non-poor, and this effect was much stronger than the similar effect observed for non-immigrant children.

Probably because poor immigrant children suffered a higher extent of material deprivation, enduring across the two-year period between cycles 2 and 3 of the NLSCY surveys, their responses to increases in family income were more complex. A possible explanation is that poverty in immigrant families may be due primarily to unemployment and under-employment in the first few years of resettlement (Beiser, Hou, Kaspar and Noh, 2002). After an initial period of high unemployment, immigrants in Canada eventually achieve higher rates of labour force participation and higher employment income than native-borns (Beaujot, 1991; DeVoretz, 1995). Thus, poverty may be a transient feature of the early stages of resettlement. For non-immigrant families, however, poverty is probably not part of a transition process, but an enduring feature of a matrix of social and economic disadvantage. Among non-immigrants, the concomitants of poverty include not only financial burden, but also social isolation and compromised self-esteem (Beiser, Johnson and Turner, 1993).

Other underlying dynamics regarding the importance of transitions out of poverty for children's adjustment outcomes were suggested in the study by Beiser, Hou, Kaspar and Noh (2002). Based on cycle 1 data of the

NLSCY, bivariate correlation results indicated that, among families in persistent poverty, absolute income increases were significantly associated with new employment of parents and reduced dependence on social welfare. It is possible that the new employment of parents did not bring enough income into the household to pull the family significantly beyond the poverty line. At the same time, low-paying jobs may have represented a new source of stress for parents. Furthermore, working parents were no longer able to spend as much time with the child relative to when they were not employed. Thus, small economic gains resulting from new employment may not contribute to improvements in the health and adjustment of children moving out of poverty.

Parental Characteristics, Family Dysfunction, and Children's Adjustment

Consistent with developmental research and theory, the study results supported the importance of effective parenting for children's adjustment (Bornstein, 1991; Chen and Kaspar, in press; Parke and Buriel, 1998). Increases in *ineffective parenting* tended to be associated most clearly with poor adjustment outcomes in children. Immigrant and non-immigrant children's maladjustment related to deteriorating emotional well-being and increasing conduct problems were significantly predicted by increases in ineffective parenting. Reductions in prosocialness were observed only among non-immigrant children exposed to ineffective parenting.

A somewhat similar pattern was observed for *parental depression*. Increases in parental depression predicted increased emotional problems for both immigrant and non-immigrant children. Only non-immigrant children showed increases in conduct problems associated with increasing parental depression. Among non-immigrant and immigrant children, prosocialness remained unchanged with increases in parental depression. Results on emotional problems were consistent with the view that parental psychopathology is an important factor adversely affecting the mental health of children (Downey and Coyne, 1990; Gotlib and Lee, 1990). Generally, the significance of ineffective parenting and parental psychopathology for the well-being of children is consistent with the view that the family represents a primary socialization influence that operates similarly for immigrant and non-immigrant children.

596   *Violet Kaspar*

Further support for the salience of family factors for children's adjustment was observed with respect to increases in *family dysfunction* demonstrating significant associations with children's maladjustment. However, the negative influences of family dysfunction on children's adjustment outcomes in this study were more prominent for non-immigrant children. The lack of a similar pattern of results for immigrant children suggests a potentially low salience of family dysfunction for their good adjustment. This is consistent with the implication that family stability may be more critical to the adjustment of immigrant children than quality of familial relationships. However, an alternative explanation is possible in that the index of family functioning used in this study may not have captured relevant aspects of functional family life for cultural minorities. The measure of family functioning focused heavily on communication, and affective expression and involvement. These represent factors that may be less indicative of optimal family functioning in some cultures where emphasis is placed on respecting role hierarchies, and exhibiting reduced affective expression as more appropriate qualities of positive family functioning.

Conclusions

The findings of this study emphasized the significance of the family system for understanding the long-term effects of adversity on children's health and developmental adjustments. Developmental and clinical literatures implicate the etiological significance of negative family context conditions for the development of emotional and behavioural maladjustments in children (Chen and Kaspar, in press; Noshpitz, Adams and Bleiberg, 1998). Some notable complexities in understanding the role of family socialization influences on children's adjustment were demonstrated through the present study. First, the relevance of *transitions* in family structure, including transitions due to marital dissolution or moving from a single-parent to a two-parent family, appeared to hold the greatest significance for children's adjustment. Furthermore, different types of transitions in family structure appeared to have different influences on immigrant and non-immigrant children. Family structure stability appeared more important to the healthy adjustments of all children, but effects were stronger for immigrant compared to non-immigrant children, while transitions into single-parent families were related to deteriorating adjustments of immigrant children, but improvements in the adjustments of non-immigrant children. Collectively, the findings are consistent with the view that family structure stability may represent a more primary provision of the family system than relationship quality for immigrants than for non-immigrants.

The importance of the family system for the health adjustment of children was also supported through results of this study demonstrating how increases in *ineffective parenting* were associated with poor adjustment outcomes in children. Effects of ineffective parenting operated similarly to produce deteriorations in the adjustments of immigrant and non-immigrant children, suggesting that the impact of poor parenting may transcend immigrant status. The consistent effect of parenting may be due to the relatively young age of children in this study, since protective effects of familial conditions may be most salient for young children whose psychological needs may be met mostly within the family system.

The impact of poverty on children's adjustment was complex, but also pointed to the importance of *transitions* for understanding children's developmental adjustments. Escalations in emotional and behavioural problems, and reductions in prosocialness in children were non-responsive to exposure to persistent poverty. The overall pattern of results is consistent with research to show that net of the effects of individual child and parental characteristics, poverty exerts a relatively small impact on children's adjustment. However, there appeared to be detrimental effects on the adjustments of immigrant children whose families made transitions out of poverty; the effect was not observed in non-immigrant children. This finding requires further investigation to identify what factors help to explain why immigrant children moving out of poverty do not benefit to the extent that non-immigrant children benefit from moving out of poverty. Possible explanations may be related to the absolute amounts of monetary gains associated with transitions out of poverty, as well as sources of economic gain, including underemployment among immigrants.

Deteriorations in the developmental adjustments of children appeared to be less responsive to the influences of transitions into poverty for immigrant than non-immigrant children. Probably because poor immigrant children suffered a higher extent of material deprivation, enduring across the two-year study period, their responses to increases in family income were more complex. In addition, it is possible that poverty in immigrant families represents a transient feature of the resettlement process that may be overcome, but for non-immigrant families, poverty is an enduring feature related to unyielding social and economic disadvantages.

With hopes of a better life for their children being a primary motivation for immigrating (Hernandez and Charney, 1998; Zhou and Bankston, 1998), the success of the second generation may be the true indicator of the effectiveness of resettlement policies and processes in Canada. Understanding factors that may hamper or promote the health and developmental adjustments of immigrant children would serve the promotion of children's well-being by providing information to guide the formulation of health promotion programs and interventions.

References

Amato, P.R. and B. Keith (1991), "Parental Divorce and Well-being of Children: A Meta-analysis", *Psychological Bulletin* 110, 26–46.

Beaujot, R. (1991), *Population Change in Canada: The Challenges of Policy Adaptation* (Toronto: McClelland & Stewart).

Beiser, M., F. Hou, I. Hyman and M. Tousignant (2002), "Poverty, Family Process, and the Mental Health of Immigrant Children in Canada", *American Journal of Public Health* 92(2), 220–227.

Beiser, M., F. Hou, V. Kaspar and S. Noh (2002), "Changes in Poverty Status and Developmental Behaviours: A Comparison of Immigrant and Non-immigrant Children in Canada". Paper presented at HRDC conference, Ottawa, January.

Beiser, M., P.J. Johnson and R.J. Turner (1993), "Unemployment, Under-Employment and Depressive Effect among Southeast Asian Refugees", *Psychological Medicine* 23, 731–743.

Biederman, J., S. Milberger, S. Faraone, K. Kiely, *et al.* (1995), "Family-Environment Risk Factors for Attention-Deficit Hyperactivity Disorder: A Test of Rutter's Indicators of Adversity", *Archives of General Psychiatry* 52(6), 464–470.

Bornstein, M.H. (1991), *Cultural Approaches to Parenting* (Hillsdale, NJ: Lawrence Erlbaum Associates).

Canada. Citizenship and Immigration Canada (CIC) (1999), *Facts and Figures: Immigration Overview*, Cat. No. I–291–06–99E (Ottawa: Citizenship and Immigration Canada).

Canada. Human Resources Development Canada (HRDC) (1996), *Special Surveys: National Longitudinal Survey of Children and Youth, User's Handbook and Microdata Guide* (Ottawa: Supply and Services Canada).

_____ (1999), *Applied Research Bulletin: Special Edition on Child Development* (Ottawa: HRDC).

Canadian Council on Social Development (1999), *CCSD Response to Recent Development of Welfare-to-work Programs* (Ottawa), downloaded from <www.ccsd.ca>, July 2000.

Caplan, N., M.H. Choy and J.K. Whitmore (1992), "Indochinese Refugee Families and Academic Achievement", *Scientific American* 266(2), 36–42.

Chang L., R.F. Morrisey and H.S. Koplewicz (1995), "Prevalence of Psychiatric Symptoms and their Relation to Adjustment among Chinese-American Youth", *Journal of the American Academy of Child and Adolescent Psychiatry* 34, 91–99.

Chen, X. and V. Kaspar (in press), "Cross-Cultural Research in Childhood", to appear in U.P. Gielen and J. Roopnarine (eds.), *Childhood and Adolescence in Cross-Cultural Perspective* (New York: Greenwood Press/Ablex).

DeVoretz, D. (1995), *Diminishing Returns: The Economics of Immigration Policy* (Toronto: University of Toronto Press).

Downey, G. and J. Coyne (1990), "Children of Depressed Parents: An Integrative Review", *Psychological Bulletin* 108, 50–76.

Duncan, G.J., J. Brooks-Gunn and P. Klebanov (1994), "Economic Deprivation and Early Child Development", *Child Development* 65, 296–318.

Epstein, N.B., L.M. Baldwin and D.S. Bishop (1983), "The McMaster Family Assessment Device", *Journal of Marital and Family Therapy* 9, 171–180.

Escobar, J.I. (1998), "Immigration and Mental Health: Why are Immigrants Better Off?" *Archives of General Psychiatry* 55, 781–782.

Finkel, S. (1995), *Causal Analysis with Panel Data*, Sage University Paper series on Quantitative Applications in the Social Sciences, No. 07–105 (Thousand Oaks, CA: Sage).

Gotlib, I.H. and C.M. Lee (1990), "Children of Depressed Mothers: A Review and Directions for Future Research", in C.D. McCann and N.S. Endler (eds.), *Depression: New Directions in Theory, Research, and Practice* (Toronto: Wall and Thompson), 187–208.

Green, B., M. Karol, M. Grace, G. Vary, H. Leonard, G. Glesser and S. Smitson-Cohen (1991), "Children and Disaster: Age, Gender, Parental Effects on PTSD Symptoms", *Journal of the American Academy of Child and Adolescent Psychiatry* 30, 945–951.

Grych, J.H. and F.D. Fincham (1990), "Marital Conflict and Children's Adjustment: A Cognitive-Contextual Framework", *Psychological Bulletin* 108, 267–290.

Hernandez, D.J., ed. (1999), *Children of Immigrants: Health, Adjustment, and Public Assistance* (Washington, DC: National Academy Press).

Hernandez, D. and E. Charney (1998), *From Generation to Generation: The Health and Well-Being of Children in Immigrant Families* (Washington, DC: National Academy Press).

Hetherington, M.E. and M. Stanley-Hagan (1999), "The Adjustment of Children with Divorced Parents: A Risk and Resiliency Perspective", *Journal of Child Psychology and Psychiatry and Allied Disciplines* 40(1), 129–140.

Hovey, J.D. and C.A. King (1996), "Acculturative Stress, Depression, and Suicidal Ideation among Immigrant and Second Generation Latino Adolescents", *Journal of the American Academy of Child and Adolescent Psychiatry* 35, 1183–1192.

Kaspar, V. (2002), "Posttraumatic Stress Disorder: Diagnosis, Prevalence, and Research Advances", *Sociological Focus* 35(1), 97–108.

Kaspar, V. and S. Noh (2001), "Discrimination and Identity: An Overview of Theoretical and Empirical Research". Paper presented at meeting of the Canadian Ethnic Studies Association (Halifax), November.

Kelly, K. (1995), "Visible Minorities: A Diverse Group", *Canadian Social Trends*, 37, 2–8.

Kinzie, J.D. and W.H. Sack (1991), "Severely Traumatized Cambodian Children: Research Findings and Clinical Investigations", in F.L. Ahearn and J.L. Athey (eds.), *Refugee Children: Theory, Research, and Services* (Baltimore: Johns Hopkins University), 92–105.

Klimidis, S., G. Stuart and I.H. Minas (1994), "Immigrant Status and Gender Effects on Psychopathology and Self-Concept in Adolescents: A Test of the Migration-Morbidity Hypothesis", *Comparative Psychiatry* 35, 393–404.

McLeod, J.D. and M.J. Shanahan (1996), "Trajectories of Poverty and Children's Mental Health", *Journal of Health and Social Behavior* 37, 207–220.

National Council of Welfare (1998), *Poverty Profile 1996*, Cat. No. H67–1/4–1996E (Ottawa: Minister of Public Works and Government Services Canada).

Noh, S., M. Beiser and V. Kaspar (1999), "Developing a Research Program in the Mental Health of Children and Youth of Immigrant Families". Paper presented at the Third National Metropolis Conference, Vancouver, BC, January.

Noshpitz, J.D., P.L. Adams and E. Bleiberg, eds. (1998), *Handbook of Child and Adolescent Psychiatry*, Volume 7, *Advances and New Directions* (San Francisco: Jossey-Bass).

Paquet, B. (2001), "Low Income Cutoffs from 1991 to 2000 and Low Income Measures from 1990 to 1999", *Income Research Paper Series*, Cat. No. 75F0002MIE2001007 (Ottawa: Statistics Canada).

Parke, R.D. and R. Buriel (1998), "Socialization in the Family: Ethnic and Ecological Perspectives", in N. Eisenberg (ed.), *Handbook of Child Psychology*, Volume 3, *Social, Emotional, and Personality Development* (New York: Wiley), 463–552.

Pearlin, L.I., E.G. Menaghan, M.A. Lieberman and J.T. Mullan (1981), "The Stress Process", *Journal of Health and Social Behavior* 22, 337–356.

Radloff, L. (1977), "The CES-D Scale: A Self-Report Depression Scale for Research in the General Population", *Applied Psychological Measurement* 1, 385–401.

Robert, R.E. and M. Sobhan (1992), "Symptoms of Depression in Adolescence: A Comparison of Anglo, African, and Hispanic Americans", *Journal of Youth Adolescence* 21, 639–651.

Rousseau C. and A. Drapeau (1998), "Parent-Child Agreement on Refugee Children's Psychiatric Symptoms: A Transcultural Perspective", *Journal of the American Academy of Child and Adolescent Psychiatry* 37(6), 629–636.

Rumbaut, R.G. (1994), "The Crucible Within: Ethnic Identity, Self-esteem, and Segmented Assimilation among Children of Immigrants", *International Migration Review* 28, 748–794.

Rutter, M. (1990), "Psychosocial Resilience and Protective Mechanisms", in J. Rolf, A.S. Masten, D. Cicchetti, H.H. Neuchterlein and S. Weintraub (eds.), *Risk and Protective Factors in the Development of Psychopathology* (Cambridge: Cambridge University Press), 181–214.

Schaufeli, W.B. and N.W. Van Yperen (1992), "Unemployment and Psychological Distress among Graduates: A Longitudinal Study", *Journal of Occupational and Organizational Psychology* 65, 291–305.

Smith, J., J. Brooks-Gunn and P. Klebanov (1997), "Consequences of Living in Poverty for Young Children's Cognitive and Verbal Ability and Early School Achievement", in G. Duncan and J. Brooks-Gunn (eds.), *Consequences of Growing Up Poor* (New York: Russell Sage Foundation), 131–189.

Sroufe, A.L. and M. Rutter (1984), "The Domain of Developmental Psychopathology", *Child Development* 55, 17–29.

Statistics Canada (1998), "National Longitudinal Survey of Children and Youth: Cycle 2, 1996", *The Daily*, October 28.

_____ (2003), *Canada's Ethnocultural Portrait: The Changing Mosaic, 2001 Census (2001 Census: Analysis Series)*, Cat. No. 96F0030XIE2001008 (Ottawa: Supply and Services Canada).

Strayhorn, J.M. and C.S. Weidman (1988), "A Parent Practices Scale and its Relation to Parent and Child Mental Health", *Journal of the American Academy of Child and Adolescent Psychiatry* 27, 613–618.

Taylor, S. and J.D. Brown (1988), "Illusion and Well-Being: A Social Psychological Perspective on Mental Health", *Psychological Bulletin* 103, 193–210.

Tousignant, M., E. Habimana, C. Biron, C. Malo, E. Sidoli-Leblanc and N. Bendris (1999), "The Quebec Adolescent Refugee Project: A Psychopathology and Family Variables in a Sample from 35 Nations", *Journal of the American Academy of Child and Adolescent Psychiatry* 38(11), 1426–1432.

United States. Department of Health and Human Services (1998), *Trends in the Well-being of American's Children and Youth* (Washington, DC: GPO).

Vega, W.A., B. Kolody, S. Aguilar Gaxiola, E. Alderete, R. Catalano and J. Caraveo-Anduaga (1998), "Lifetime Prevalence of DSM-III-R Psychiatric Disorders among Urban and Rural Mexican Americans in California", *Archives of General Psychiatry* 55, 771–778.

Zhou, M. (1997), "Growing Up American: The Challenge Confronting Immigrant Children and Children of Immigrants", *Annual Review of Sociology* 23, 63–95.

Zhou, M. and C.L. Bankston (1998), *Growing Up American: How Vietnamese Children Adapt to Life in the United States* (New York: Russell Sage Foundation).

Comments

Eric Fong

Voluminous studies on the topic of social inclusion of immigrants are published every year. The topic has received so much attention because the social inclusion of immigrants indicates whether or not these newcomers are able to enjoy their entitlement of full rights and privileges in the new country. At the same time, the findings can be viewed as the barometer measuring social cohesion in society. The four papers in this session represent major aspects of the vast literature on the social integration of immigrants. The following comments are drawn from material in these papers and they discuss three issues related to research on the social inclusion of immigrants.

First, these papers all touch on a core topic of immigrant research. They all discuss obstacles facing immigrants with respect to economic and social integration. Reitz shows that there has been a decline in accessing best-paid positions among recently arrived immigrants. Hou and Picot show that immigrants residing in neighbourhoods of ethnic concentrations, a process natural to most recent immigrants, can hamper their labour market performance. The study by Esses and her colleagues explores negative attitudes towards groups. Finally, Kaspar's paper documents that immigrant children tend to lose their mental-health advantages over time.

The reason that research on the economic and social integration of immigrants emphasizes the obstacles facing immigrants is partly the commonality of the phenomenon across a wide range of receiving countries and immigrant groups. As well, identifying these obstacles can have significant policy implications. To understand the obstacles facing immigrants, most studies explore the role of human capital and demographic factors. They usually show that the human capital of immigrants has a lower rate of return than that of non-immigrants, controlling for other factors. However, interpretation of the differences in estimated coefficients varies. For example, one of these papers suggests that the difference reflects the discount effects of foreign credentials on earnings. However, we can equally well suggest that the limited social networks of immigrants or other factors contribute to the differences. These different interpretations of results illustrate a need to further delineate the causes of the lower return of human capital in order to improve the economic and social integration of immigrants. However, to explore some of the proposed causes may require further analysis, and some of the analyses require more detailed data beyond the commonly used census data.

Second, as reflected in most of these papers, the research on immigrant social integration has been focused on the role of human capital. In recent years, many studies have extended their perspective to explore the role of social capital. This approach is strongly affected by the traditional understanding that, when immigrants stay in a country longer and acquire the necessary human and social capital, their economic and social well-being improve. Therefore, when we study performance in the labour market or the social well-being of immigrants, we focus on the role of individual characteristics. However, recent studies also suggest that most activities do not occur in a vacuum. They are embedded in a unique spatial context. The paper by Hou and Picot nicely demonstrates the importance of this view. Similarly, the paper by Reitz has carefully controlled for possible census metropolitan area effects. In fact, since the mid-1980s with the publication of *The Truly Disadvantaged* by William Wilson and a series of papers by Douglas Massey and his colleagues in the 1980s and 1990s, research has clearly documented the importance of place in understanding the economic performance and social integration of groups.

The role of place is critical to our study of immigration in Canada and has considerable policy implications. Immigrants do not settle evenly in Canadian cities and each Canadian city has its own unique economic specializations. These urban contexts can have a strong impact on the adaptation of immigrants. For example, the economic performance of immigrants who settle in cities with a large number of ethnic members who can support an elaborate ethnic economy may be different from the economic performance of immigrants in cities with only a small number of their own ethnic group, controlling for their human capital. Similarly, the

Eric Fong

labour force participation of immigrants who settle in a city with a stronger economy will be different from that of immigrants who settle in a city with a weak economy. Therefore, the effect of urban context should be considered in our analysis.

Finally, this set of papers demonstrates that the integration of immigrants is multidimensional. It involves economic, spatial, and psychological dimensions as well as group reactions. These dimensions are interrelated. For example, Hou and Picot suggest that spatial integration is related to economic integration. Kaspar shows that economic integration, that is, poverty, is related to mental well-being. At the same time, Esses *et al.* imply that public belief can affect economic and spatial integration. Given these complexities, I think we need to develop a more comprehensive model to explain integration of immigrants. The model should not be set up to explain one single dimension of integration (such as earnings), but should be able to delineate the complicated relationships among all these dimensions of integration while considering multi-level explanations of individual and family characteristics and urban contexts.

In short, these papers address a number of interesting issues related to immigrant integration. At the same time, they also suggest some issues that research on immigrants should explore further.

Section VIII

Wrap-Up Panel on Broad Labour Market Issues and Future Directions for Canadian Immigration Policy

Panel Comments

Naomi Alboim

First of all, in the same way that people have said over and over again during the past two days that immigration is not the silver bullet to deal with Canada's economic issues, dare I say to a group of economists that I do not think that our immigration policy should be assessed purely on economic terms. We have to bear in mind the other reasons why we are in the immigration business and we must not forget the social and humanitarian objectives of our nation-building project.

Although not the focus of this conference, I would like to go back for a moment to what Alan Green said in his opening talk, which I think is really important. We need to talk more about what kind of society we want to build and what role immigration plays in that project. The whole question of who is "us" is something that I think we have to deal with, along the lines of Yvan's suggestions for developing a national consensus, and building on Vicki Esses' talk, we have to look at how we feel about "they" becoming "us". And I think we do have to explore the "r" word and talk about race and racialization and racism and some of the attitudinal issues that have to be dealt with in that context.

But we are focussing on skilled workers at this conference, so that will be the focus of my comments. One of the things that has been interesting for me over the past two days is that we have looked almost exclusively at the human capital of the immigrant as the major predictor of the economic success of, and economic contribution by, the immigrant. My concern is that that is only, at best, one-half of the equation. We have not spent much time at all talking about what kind of institutional change might be necessary on the part of the receivers, users, or beneficiaries of this human capital, in order to maximize it. We have not really talked about the role of employers very much. We have not talked very much about the educational institutions, the professional regulatory bodies, etc.

We can ask for higher and higher education levels as part of our immigrant selection criteria but it is going to be useless if those years of education are not recognized. We can ask for more and more years of experience and that will be useless unless the experience achieved overseas is valued by people here in Canada. We can ask for higher and higher skill levels and that will be useless unless we determine some method for assessing competencies in a non-culturally biased way and in a way that is relevant to the occupation that people want to practice.

So, that is to say that I think we need to deal with some of these institutional change issues and we have to put the onus not just on the immigrant, but on Canadian society. Not just governments, but all the various stakeholders and labour market partners have a role to play, and we have to deal with some of the attitudinal issues that Vicki was talking about.

The next thing I want to talk about is the regionalization of immigration and that raises the whole issue of the role of cities which we really have not spoken very much about either in the past two days. So, first of all I agree with Alan Green and Tom Jensen who said that they were not really sure that there was a problem in terms of the numbers of immigrants that were going to Toronto, Montreal, and Vancouver. I tend to agree with them. I am not sure that there is a problem. Those cities are thriving. They are all doing quite well. Those three cities are not complaining at all about the numbers of immigrants coming in. They do not want to reduce the numbers coming in. All they are saying is: first, they want a seat at the table so that they can play a role in terms of the policy decisions that impact on them; and second, they want recognition that they are absorbing some of the initial costs and need support in that regard. Some of those initial costs we did talk about during the conference. For example, the social assistance costs paid by cities when sponsorship breakdowns occur. Some might say that the federal government should assume some responsibility for those costs given that it approves the sponsorship agreements for family reunification. They should perhaps also support the social assistance costs and shelter costs paid by cities for refugee claimants even though the federal government holds all the policy levers for the refugee determination process, as well as the public health costs that cities pay for, often due to the lack of proper notification for medical surveillance or inadequate overseas screening. So, the cities say to the federal government: "Compensate us appropriately for the roles that we have to play. Let us be at the table. Let us influence policy but don't stop immigrants from coming to our areas."

Nevertheless, there may be some good public policy reasons for Canadians to have concerns about most immigrants going to just those three cities in the sense of a growing divide between three metropolitan, cosmopolitan, racially diverse, culturally diverse, growing, competitive cities benefiting from immigration on the one hand, and the rest of Canada on the other. So there may be other reasons why we want to look at a regionalization policy.

I think we can learn from the Manitoba experience in this regard, which has been very interesting. I agree with Sam Laryea, though, who indicated that seeing immigration as an answer to depopulation in certain areas or an answer to economic development in depressed areas is wrong-headed. It is not going to work. Why should immigrants go where Canadians won't go? Why should they stay there?

However, there are a number of second-tier cities which are growing and need human capital. Those cities have real opportunities and are interested in having immigrants come and stay. Maybe we should focus on those second-tier cities for any regionalization strategies but let us make sure that the immigrants are given all the information they need to make an informed choice regarding where to live and that they are the ones who make the decision.

I agree with Tom Jensen that it should be a bottom-up process where the cities should be driving the initiative to attract and retain immigrants and I think the biggest factor (there are a whole range of others), that skilled immigrants will take into account when deciding where to go, will be: will they be able to work in the occupation for which they have been trained? Can they enter or re-enter that occupation as quickly as possible, going through as few hoops as possible? I think that there are real opportunities at the local level for some of the stakeholder networks to be brought together to develop processes that allow for as quick a transition as possible for skilled immigrants into those labour markets. That will be the competitive edge that cities have in attracting immigrants.

This will require institutional change at the local level. Some things will have to be done, as Jeffrey Reitz has indicated, on a sector- or occupation-specific basis. But it requires a systemic and systematic approach: starting overseas by providing as much information as possible to prospective immigrants before they even come; determining an assessment of the immigrant's education, skills, and experience that is fair and competency-based and in relation to what they need to practice; identifying the gaps that need to be filled; and then focusing all energies on how to fill those gaps as quickly as possible with *bridging programs* so that people can re-enter their occupations. More about this approach can be found in a paper I wrote for the Maytree Foundation called "Fulfilling the Promise".

Both Jeffrey Reitz' and Arthur Sweetman's work demonstrate that those who have some Canadian educational experience do better than those with only education achieved abroad. We also know that employers are more comfortable with Canadian credentials and look to Canadian educational institutions for their potential pool of entrants. Now, if the bridging programs were housed in universities and community colleges, the immigrants would get the upgrading they need, access to a network of fellow students and faculty, a Canadian credit for the little bridging that they need, and access to the employer market.

Don DeVoretz and Alan Green both talked about their strong reservations about Denis Coderre's proposed regionalization strategy that would bring in skilled workers as temporary workers who would be provided with permanent resident status after three to five years only if they stayed in communities other than Toronto, Vancouver, and Montreal for that period. Aside from the moral issues, the potential Charter issues, and the notion of indentured servitude, their status as temporary workers itself is problematic. It means that they would not be eligible for any language training or for those bridging programs that I have just mentioned. Their families would not be eligible for any kind of programs or services because they are officially only here temporarily. Their spouses and children would not be allowed to work and would not be eligible for student loans. They would have to pay higher tuition fees as international students. All this means the skilled workers would either not bring their families with them for the three to five years, or their families would not be able to begin their integration process on an equal footing with other immigrants. Neither is a good alternative. Neither would be an incentive for skilled workers to choose to come to Canada.

Let me suggest an alternative. Those second-tier cities that are interested in attracting highly skilled immigrants could promote themselves overseas by "selling" what they have to offer in their communities. These "settlement packages" put together by all the local stakeholders working together, could offer everything we have heard about — the opportunity to enter the workforce in their occupations as quickly as possible; educational opportunities for their kids; bridging opportunities for themselves; language

Naomi Alboim

training for themselves and their families; ethnic networks in those communities; affordable housing; cultural and recreation opportunities for their families; and very importantly, receptive communities that are welcoming to immigrants. If that information from a variety of cities about their "settlement packages" is provided to prospective immigrants overseas before they even come, the skilled immigrants will make informed choices. My bet is these folks are pretty smart people and they will go where they think they will be able to enter the labour market in their occupations most quickly and have the best opportunities for themselves and their families. If those "settlement packages" are in place, their settlement will be successful and chances are, people will stay of their own free will.

Panel Comments

Barry Chiswick

I wish to share with you some thoughts generated by this conference. On the issue that came up on the aging of the population, this is of interest in a lot of countries that might see immigrants as a solution to a falling population. Whenever demographers do the calculations for the low-fertility, high-income countries, they conclude that you would need more immigrants than would be politically feasible to bring about a stable age distribution of the population. But what I do not see among the demographers and economists who study this issue is serious attention given to modelling and analyzing what is the optimal size of the population. Does it really matter if the population is 20% lower or 20% higher? If it does matter, for whom does it matter? There is the issue of not just the size of the population but also the rate of change, the rate of population growth. The rate of population growth may be a more important factor in terms of economic welfare than the absolute size of the population.

We talk about the aged relative to the population as a whole. What may be relevant, however, is the dependency ratio, that is, children plus aged divided by the total population. A lower fertility rate, other things being the same, actually means a lower dependency ratio because there are fewer children. The work that most people do today is really much easier physically than the work that people did 50 years ago. People 65 years old today are much healthier than 65-year-olds were 50 years ago. When Bismarck picked age 65 as the pension age in Germany it was a good age to pick because hardly anybody lived that long. There was not much of a pension burden. But now most people live beyond 65 and are very healthy. I think we have to give much more thought, not only in Canada but in the United States as well, to raising the age at which people start getting retirement benefits. In the United States the age for the onset of social security benefits is now creeping up, but the rate of creep in the age at which full benefits start, is really trivial. There are no silver bullets, but the primary solution to the problem of the rising dependency ratio is to change whom we define as dependent by raising the age at retirement.

Another thing I want to mention is that we are in a situation in which we have a lot of "footloose people". We used to talk about footloose industries, industries that can hop around from country to country. I think we are also seeing a lot of footloose people. There is now an international labour market for high-skilled manpower. All the developed countries want to grab high-skilled workers. Even Japan, until the recent downturn, was talking about creating special programs for high-skilled manpower. This is going to have profound effects. It means that wages across countries for high-skilled labour are going to become more equal. The inequality in earnings across countries among high-skilled workers is going to shrink, but the inequality in earnings across countries for low-skilled labour, is going to increase. The inequality of earnings within countries is going to increase. There are going to be increased social tensions as a consequence of what I see as a widening gap between the wages of high-skilled and low-skilled workers.

What we have seen over the last 25 years in the United States is a phenomenon that is likely to continue. And in this regard, Canada, in particular, has to give serious thought to whether it wants to be a way station or a training ground for people on the move to the United States. What kinds of immigration and other policies can Canada adopt to reduce the extent to which it makes investments in people who then go elsewhere? The distinction between permanent and temporary visas may not be a really meaningful distinction because temporary visas can be converted to permanent visas quite easily, and just because somebody has a permanent visa does not mean the person is going to stay where they are.

The high rate of mobility between the United States and Canada is actually not a new phenomenon. Marcus Lee Hanson published a book called *The Mingling of the Canadian and American Peoples* which emphasized the substantial cross-border migration between the United States and Canada in the 80 years prior to its publication in 1940.

Usually at immigration conferences people say: "We need low-skilled workers." This frequently comes up in the context of caring for the aging population and this is a phenomenon that has been going on in all of the developed countries. Nursing homes in the United States are staffed heavily by women from the Philippines. And actually in Israel, they do not have a term "home health-care worker", it does not exist; the term that they use is "Philippina" meaning a woman from the Philippines. A friend of mine was telling me that his mother just hired a "Rumanian Philippina". Unfortunately, at least in the United States and I suspect in Canada as well, there is a large pool of relatively low-skilled native-born workers. When low-skilled people are brought in they may provide us with cheaper health care for our parents and grandparents, but they also provide greater competition in the labour market for the low-skilled native-born in the United States, Canada, Israel, and other countries. This only exacerbates the inequality in income in the host country. There really is no particular "need" for low-skilled immigration. The United States has programs to bring in low-skilled workers who benefit the high-income people who are influential in making the policy. Their presence harms the low-income native-born Americans who would compete with them.

We can think in terms of how visas are rationed and essentially now we have visas rationed on the basis of skill, on the basis of family ties, humanitarian (refugee) visas, and so-called temporary work-related visas. But the primary visa mechanism in the United States is through family ties.

Let me mention something about the family visas, leaving aside spouses and minor children. When my grandparents went from Europe to the United States, they had the very real expectation that they would never see the people they left behind, that they would never speak with them. There would be an occasional letter, perhaps, but that would be all. Today, people fly around the world casually. It is pretty easy to go from one place to another and airfares are relatively cheap compared to incomes in the developed countries. International telephone service is also very cheap. Increasingly people are not even using the telephone, they are using the Internet. When family events occur in the United States or Mexico or other sunny countries, these events are typically videotaped and the videotape is sent to the other place. Family events in the United States are videotaped and sent to the origin and videos done at the origin are sent to the destination. I believe that the compelling argument for family reunion as an aspect of immigration policy has decreased. I think it has been oversold. What drives the family-based visa policy is ethnic politics rather than humanitarian concerns.

Finally, I want to suggest a reformulation of immigration policy. When somebody from an LDC, in particular, gets a visa they are the winner of a very valuable lottery. They are having a huge increase in their permanent wealth. Why do we give it away? Why don't we sell it? Why don't we capture some of the economic rent that the immigrants from poorer countries receive when they get a visa? The income tax system could be used as the collection mechanism. This would increase the number of visas issued by the American and Canadian authorities, and would have many beneficial consequences, including helping to compensate the host population for taking in immigrants.

Panel Comments

Don DeVoretz

I'd like to discuss briefly the research I am doing and address three issues that were the subject of this panel's discussion: Canada's future needs for unskilled immigrants, whether these immigrants should have temporary or permanent status, and how Canadian and United States border issues will affect future Canadian immigration policies.

Let us look at these issues in more detail and project outcomes into the twenty-first century. The first trend I see is a growth in Canadian non-permanent immigrants. This temporary movement will appear in two parts. First, temporary immigrants will arrive via traditional avenues such as student visas, NAFTA visas, and possibly as natural persons under DOA-II. Given this projected growth, we must address one major point in any temporary program, namely the conversion rights of temporary immigrants to a permanent status in Canada. We must evaluate what have we done right and done wrong in existing programs, such as the "nanny program" or our agricultural temporary workers visa program to search for a set of equitable conversion principles.

Future temporary immigration to Canada also appears in a new dimension. Canada will see triangular movement of highly skilled Canadian immigrants. Canada is at the apex of this triangle and will act as an *entrepôt* country with China at the base of the triangle sending highly skilled immigrants to Canada. These highly skilled immigrants from the PRC enter Canada and Canada equips them (unlike the United States) with additional subsidized specific human capital and a passport, which some use to leave to complete the triangular movement.

The research institute I am involved with in Vancouver, RIIM, is constructing a series of studies to look at various triangles in order to define the economic profiles of the stayers and leavers. We want to know who comes to Canada and stays, and who leaves. Borjas and Bratsberg argued that this phenomenon is a sorting problem with either the best or the weakest leaving. RIIM's access to the Chinese census has allowed us to match up people who came to Canada from China/Hong Kong and were resident in Canada in 1996 and obtained Canadian citizenship, but were residents of Hong Kong in 2001. In sum, we want to know how the returnees are performing in Hong Kong relative to the Chinese stayers in Canada to see whether the strongest or weakest performers have left Canada. Finally, we want to know how this triangular movement has undermined the traditional tenets of Canada's permanent admissions program as the triangle grows in size.

My final point asks, how will Canadian immigration policies and issues be affected by events in the United States? There are two schools of thought. One school says September 11, 2001 is a transitory phenomenon while others argue it is a watershed or major shift in the North American immigration environment. I happen to believe it is a major watershed and I think it will affect many of Canada's immigration policies in the twenty-first century. For example, China would like to negotiate a tourist visa with Canada to allow Chinese tourists to enter Canada. What is the biggest stumbling block in this tourist visa? It is the United States' concerns with border security with the possible increased Chinese visitor presence in Canada. In a similar fashion, if Canada signs an agreement with China or other Third World countries to accept "natural", that is, unskilled persons, under the proposed GATTS agreement (DOA-II) there would be additional concerns.

The second focal point for the Canada-United States immigration harmonization is at the US border. Several questions emerge. What Canadians will be admitted? Will the TN visa still exist in the future? One thing we know for certain, there will be pressure from the United States to conform to their concepts of a secure border and narrow definitions of citizenship.

In sum, I see many new challenges to Canada using immigration as a component of future economic development in an increasingly insecure world.

Don DeVoretz

Panel Comments

W. Craig Riddell

As the papers presented at this conference have illustrated, immigration is a major research and policy issue in Canada at the present time. My comments will focus on two dimensions of this subject. First, I offer some general observations about immigration research and policy. These observations are principally directed at achieving a more informed public debate on immigration issues. Second, I discuss some questions relating to the interface between immigration and education and skill formation — another subject that is currently high on the research and policy agenda, and for some of the same underlying reasons. These comments draw heavily on recent research with UBC colleagues Ana Ferrer and David Green that examines how the education and skills of workers are valued in the Canadian labour market. In this ongoing work we are investigating these questions for immigrants as well as for the native-born. The results, although preliminary, are pertinent to a number of the issues that were raised at the conference.

My general observations deal with immigration research and immigration policy, and how research could contribute to a more informed policy debate. I make these comments as someone who has largely been an outsider to the debates on immigration policy — more of a consumer than a producer of research on immigration. The first observation is to register some concern that as a society we seem to be putting too many of our eggs in the immigration basket, at least in terms of *economic* policy objectives. Canadians are frequently being told that high levels of immigration are needed to help prevent looming skill shortages, to help offset problems associated with an aging population, and to maintain population growth and high living standards. Those who make such claims are asserting that immigration can make an important contribution to achieving these policy goals. In fact there is considerable reason to be sceptical about these claims. This is not to say that immigration policy can't help economic performance. However, those who contribute to the policy debate in this area should be more cautious than they often are about claims such as: (i) that immigration will lead to significantly higher living standards for Canadians; (ii) that high levels of immigration can have a significant effect on the demographic dynamics that will be taking place over the longer term; and (iii) that immigration will significantly reduce possible skill shortages. In this respect I am echoing the point stated so clearly by Alan Green in his opening remarks that immigration should not be viewed at the present time as a silver bullet for economic policy. If there is a strong case for high levels of immigration it is more likely to be as a component of *social* policy rather than economic policy. We may advocate high rates of immigration as a means of providing opportunities to those who seek better lives for themselves and their families. We may also favour immigration as a means of achieving a more diverse and culturally heterogeneous society. But we should be circumspect regarding claims that high rates of immigration will bring major economic benefits.

A second observation is that despite the evident importance of immigration in Canada there are a number of major gaps in our knowledge about how immigrants fare in Canadian society. We are unlikely to fill these gaps without improvements to the data available to researchers. It is worthwhile considering the limitations of existing data and how these might be ameliorated. Several of my suggestions deal with data.

At the conference we heard a good deal about the poor labour market performance of immigrants in the last couple of decades.[1] This is quite appropriate — the relatively poor earnings of recent immigrant cohorts is a serious issue and one we need to understand better than we do. It is important, however, to remember that researchers are a bit like the drunk who is looking for his lost keys under the lamp post because that is where the light is, not where the keys were dropped. Researchers look where the

---

[1]Studies by Baker and Benjamin (1994), Bloom, Grenier and Gunderson (1995), McDonald and Worswick (1998), Grant (1999), and Green and Worswick (2002) document the changing relative economic status of immigrants to Canada.

data are, and there are often important issues that are not being addressed because we do not have suitable data available to examine them. One that was not raised at the conference is how do second-generation immigrants fare. The research that is being discussed about the labour market performance of immigrants relates to new arrivals, and an important issue for economic performance generally, and as well as many social policy issues, is how do the children of immigrants fare in terms of economic success. Here there is at least some reason to be a bit more optimistic than we might be on the basis of the recent earnings behaviour of first-generation immigrants, at least from the US evidence. In the United States, as in Canada, shifts in immigrant source countries have been associated with a decline in the relative economic status of immigrants in recent decades (see, e.g., Chiswick, 1978; and Borjas, 1985, 1995). In an interesting contribution, Card, DiNardo and Estes (2000) analyze the comparative performance of US immigrants and their children from the 1940s to the 1990s. Over this extended period there has been little relative change in the economic status of the second generation of immigrant families. There is some relative decline in the second generation among lower income groups, but among middle and upper income groups there is little indication of a shift — despite the changes in the economic status of the immigrant parents. Furthermore, the degree of intergenerational assimilation (measured by intergenerational correlations in education or in earnings, or by inter-ethnic marriage patterns) did not decline systematically between the cohort of second-generation children raised in the 1940s and 1950s and those raised in the 1960s and 1970s. As in the past, second-generation children tend to have higher education and higher earnings than the children of native-born Americans. Indeed, they tend to do better in the labour market than do the children of the native-born even after you control for their higher education. Unfortunately, because of data limitations — the absence of large-scale datasets that identify the Canadian-born children of immigrants — little is known about the performance of second-generation immigrants in Canada. Here is a case where the addition of a single question – Where were your parents born? – to the Labour Force Survey (LFS) or the census can open up a wide range of research possibilities. This question was included on the 2001 census, and this will enable researchers to address some important issues relating to second-generation immigrants. As discussed below, consideration should also be given to including this question (and others relating to immigration) in the Labour Force Survey.

There is also a strong case for including some questions relating to immigrant status in the LFS, either in the regular monthly survey or in a periodic supplement. The census has been the workhorse for immigration research for a long time. Although this may continue to be the case, the census has many limitations for this purpose. Census data are not available to researchers on a timely basis, the labour market information is quite limited, the five-year intervals between censuses make it difficult to take into account cyclical conditions, and the public use files impose limitations on the research questions that can be addressed. The LFS has many advantages that the census lacks: high quality labour market information, including variables not available in the census such as hourly wages, union status and establishment or firm size, and data that are available on a timely basis and at frequent intervals. Since the substantial revisions to the survey implemented in 1997, the LFS is much more useful for addressing a variety of research questions. This research potential could be significantly enhanced by the addition of a few questions relating to immigrant status. For example, simply asking the respondent whether he or she was born in Canada, and if not, the year of arrival and country of origin would substantially expand the potential for high quality research on Canadian immigration issues.

The third general observation relates to an important point made in the paper by Green and Worswick (2002), and that is, what is the relevant counterfactual for assessing the labour market performance of immigrants. Previous studies on the earnings and assimilation of immigrants treat the counterfactual as the native-born population as a whole. But immigrants are trying to work their way into a new labour market, and the point made by Green and Worswick is that the appropriate group to compare their labour market outcomes to may be others who are also trying to establish themselves. So the relevant counterfactual may be the outcomes experienced by new entrants, re-entrants, and those who have been displaced from their previous employment and are trying to re-establish themselves in the job market. Green and Worswick use new entrants to the labour market. It may be possible to develop a somewhat broader counterfactual group that includes workers who are re-entering the labour market or who have been displaced. Empirical evidence suggests that these groups experienced difficulties in the 1980s and 1990s. These were dismal decades not just for immigrants, but also for young people trying to enter the labour market, those who were permanently displaced from their job, and for individuals who left the labour market for a while and re-entered. Adopting the Green and Worswick approach may result in a significant change in how we view the relative economic status of recent immigrants. For example, Green and Worswick (2002) conclude that approximately 60% of the cross-cohort

W. Craig Riddell

decline in immigrant earnings in the 1980s can be attributed to general declines across cohorts of new entrants of all kinds into the Canadian labour market.

Let me now turn to a brief discussion of two current projects relating to the education and skills of immigrants, and how their human capital is rewarded in the Canadian labour market. The first, a project with Ana Ferrer (Ferrer and Riddell, 2003), is investigating the economic returns to education experienced by immigrant and native-born Canadians.

The extent to which the education and skills of immigrants are utilized and rewarded in the labour market is a major policy issue. Indeed, some analysts claim that the unrecognized skills and credentials of the foreign-born represent a substantial loss to the Canadian economy and a significant burden on new arrivals.[2] Because of these concerns, several recent government reports have identified the recognition of immigrants' credentials as a priority for Canadian immigration and labour market policy.[3]

Our study examines how the human capital of immigrants is rewarded in the Canadian labour market. In order to focus on the recognition of immigrants' credentials, we take advantage of the richness of the education information in the Canadian census, and distinguish between two dimensions of educational attainment: years of completed schooling and degrees, diplomas or certificates received. Doing so allows us to estimate "sheepskin effects" — the gain in earnings associated with receipt of a degree or diploma, controlling for years of completed schooling.[4] Using data from the 1981, 1986, 1991, and 1996 censuses, we study the evolution of the returns to the human capital of immigrant and native-born workers in Canada. Like earlier studies, we find that the labour market experience

---

[2]The Conference Board of Canada estimates the loss of income associated with unrecognized skills/credentials of the foreign-born to be approximately $3.2 billion, and identifies immigrants as one of the groups most disadvantaged in the labour market because of unrecognized learning (Conference Board of Canada, 2001). Reitz (2001) estimates that the annual loss due to underutilization of immigrants' skills is $2.4 billion.

[3]See, for example, Advisory Council on Science and Technology (2000) and Human Resources Development Canada (2002).

[4]These effects can be interpreted as the difference in earnings between program completers and dropouts with the same years of schooling. See Ferrer and Riddell (2002) for an analysis of sheepskin effects among native-born Canadians.

of immigrants in their country of origin is valued much less than the experience of comparable native-born workers. A similar result holds for the years of schooling of immigrants. However, the estimated sheepskin effects for immigrants are generally as large as or larger than the earnings gains received by native-born Canadians for equivalent degrees, certificates or diplomas. This finding suggests that — despite much belief to the contrary — immigrant credentials do appear to be valued in the Canadian labour market. In particular, relative to immigrants without a degree or diploma, immigrants who have completed an educational program experience substantial earnings gains associated with these educational credentials.

In the case of high school diplomas and university bachelor's degrees, we generally find that the associated earnings gain is approximately the same for immigrants as for the native-born. Native-born Canadians who graduate from high school earn about 6% more than their counterparts with the same years of schooling but without having completed secondary school. Immigrants with a high school diploma experience a similar earnings premium. Similarly, both native-born Canadians and immigrants with a university bachelor's degree receive substantially higher — typically in the range of 15–20% higher — earnings than otherwise comparable secondary school graduates without a university degree. For college diplomas and trade certificates (with or without high school graduation) and university postgraduate degrees, the earnings gains for immigrants exceed those of the native-born. The largest difference in the estimated sheepskin effects between immigrants and native-born Canadians is that associated with university postgraduate degrees.

The fact that immigrant sheepskin effects are equal to or greater than those of the native-born does not, of course, imply that average earnings of immigrants with a given level of educational attainment are on a par with those of similarly educated Canadians. The magnitudes of the immigrant credential effects we estimate are relative to immigrants without the degree or diploma but with otherwise similar characteristics. In addition, as noted earlier, the returns to years of schooling are also systematically lower for immigrants compared to the native-born. What these results do imply is that the gap in earnings between immigrants and the native-born is narrowed (or at least not widened) by completion of educational programs. The result is analogous to the impact of education on the gender earnings differential. In Canada, the returns to education are substantially higher for women than for men (Ferrer and Riddell, 2002). This does not imply that well-educated women earn more, on average, than well-educated men. However, it does imply that the gender earnings gap is smaller among well-educated individuals than among those with low levels of education.

Our paper also offers additional insights into the decline in the earnings of recent immigrants, in particular into the extent to which the decline is associated with lower valuation of credentials. To explore this avenue, we analyze the dynamics of the valuation of years of schooling and credentials between 1980 and 1995. In order to account for changes in the distribution of the immigrant population, we also examine the relationship between country of origin and the value placed by employers on the human capital of immigrants. Although we find important differences regarding how the market rewards the credentials of immigrants from the US/UK, Europe, Asia, Africa, and South America, there is little evidence that there have been downward trends in the valuation of immigrant credentials between 1980 and 1995. The most substantial change over the sample period is that for postgraduate degrees, the incremental value of which has been decreasing for native-born Canadians but increasing for immigrants.

These findings suggest that the frequently heard claim that the credentials of immigrants are not recognized needs to be treated with some caution. For immigrants, the increase in earnings associated with a degree or diploma (for given years of education and experience) is as large as or larger than that of a comparable Canadian worker. Do these results imply that we should not be concerned about immigrant credential recognition? At this point, I believe the answer is "no". A variety of evidence suggests that this issue should continue to receive policy attention. At the same time, we should be cautious in predicting that major earnings gains are likely to result from improvements in recognizing immigrants' credentials. The largest earnings gaps appear to be associated with those with relatively low levels of education, not with individuals with high levels of educational attainment.

The second project, a joint work with Ana Ferrer and David Green (Ferrer, Green and Riddell, 2003), examines the role played by literacy skills in the labour market earnings of immigrants in the province of Ontario. This project builds on earlier research on the impact of literacy skills on earnings using a sample consisting of native-born Canadians (Green and Riddell, 2003).

Our starting point is the general finding in immigration research that immigrants earn less than native-born Canadians with the same measured education and labour market experience. This earnings differential diminishes with time spent in Canada. That is, there is a negative "entry effect" followed by a process of earnings "assimilation" as immigrant earnings catch up to (and perhaps exceed) those of otherwise comparable native-born workers. Understanding the source of the entry effect and the rate at which immigrant earnings catch up to those of the native-born is a central issue in immigration research. As noted previously, another important question is why recent immigrant cohorts have experienced larger negative entry effects and slower earnings assimilation than their predecessors.

The low initial earnings are often attributed to immigrant human capital being specific to the country of origin. Skills generated by education and/or work experience in the source country may not be easily transferable to the new labour market. If this is the case, immigration policy might attempt to identify skills that are more readily transferred or implement programs that improve the process of skill transfer after arrival. However, an alternative explanation for the lower earnings of immigrants is that domestic employers discriminate against immigrants — that is, pay immigrant workers less than equally productive native-born workers. The policy implications of this hypothesis are quite different.

Investigating these issues is difficult without direct measures of skills. In this study we take advantage of a rich dataset of immigrants from Ontario — the Ontario Immigrant Literacy Survey (OILS) — which includes standard demographic and labour market information and results from literacy tests. These literacy skills are assessed in English or French, and thus are those applicable to the Canadian labour market. In addition, the OILS data contain more precise information than is generally available on where education was obtained and age at immigration. The latter allows us to identify separately work experience in the country of origin and in Canada. For a comparison group of native-born workers we use the Canadian component of the International Adult Literacy Survey (IALS).

Our analysis suggests a number of potentially important results. One that builds on a series of recent papers is the need to account carefully for where education and experience were acquired when examining immigrant earnings. As Friedberg (2000) finds for Israel and Green and Worswick (2002) conclude for Canada, we also find that lower immigrant earnings compared to native-born workers can be largely attributed to substantially lower returns to foreign work experience. These studies point to the importance of understanding the source of the "discounting" of work experience in the source country by employers in the new country.

In this context, it is worth noting that immigration researchers — indeed, labour market researchers more generally — typically do not have access to high quality information on labour market experience. The vast majority of studies use Mincer "potential experience" — defined as Age - Years of schooling - 6. This measure assumes that individuals begin school at age 6, enter the labour market immediately following school completion, and remain in the labour market continuously until the date of the survey. This measure overstates the actual experience of individuals who exit the workforce for a period of time, which is the reason that many labour market studies exclude women for whom the Mincer measure is likely to be particularly inaccurate. Potential experience may also substantially overstate actual work experience among immigrants from some source countries. For example, long periods of non-employment are common among workers from some countries, especially among well-educated workers who queue for extended periods to obtain high-paying public sector jobs. The Mincer measure may also be biased by measurement error in years of completed schooling. For these reasons, improved data on actual work experience may be needed to better understand the reasons why foreign "potential experience" receives so little value in the Canadian labour market.

The OILS data also allow us to separate those who completed their education in the source country from those who completed their education after arriving in Canada. We find that there are important differences between these two groups. In particular, after controlling for language ability, immigrants who completed their education after arrival in Canada experience returns to human capital equivalent to those of native-born Canadians.[5]

Another finding is that the returns to literacy skills in terms of higher earnings are as large as (or even larger) than are those for the native-born. As in previous research with a sample of native-born workers using the IALS data (Green and Riddell, 2003), literacy skills have a substantial payoff in the job market. The fact that the impact of literacy skills on the earnings of immigrants is as large as that on the earnings of native-born Canadians indicates that there is no "discounting" of this dimension of immigrant human capital by Canadian employers. That is, when we measure the skills of immigrants and the native-born using the same metric, additional skills have the same payoff for both groups.

---

[5]There are also large differences in school quality across countries. Sweetman (2003) finds that such differences, as measured by cross-country variation in international student achievement tests in mathematics and science, help explain earnings differences among immigrants who completed their education prior to arrival in Canada.

Together, these two ongoing projects suggest that the sources of the lower return to the measured human capital of immigrants are more complex than simple discrimination stories would imply. The credentials of immigrants are indeed rewarded in the Canadian labour market, at least relative to immigrants without these credentials. Furthermore, when we have access to data on directly observed skills, we find that additional skills enhance the earnings of immigrants to the same extent (or even to a greater extent) as they enhance the earnings of native-born Canadians.

References

Advisory Council on Science and Technology (2000), *Stepping Up: Skills and Opportunities in the Knowledge Economy*. Report of the Expert Panel on Skills (Ottawa: Industry Canada).

Baker, M. and D. Benjamin (1994), "The Performance of Immigrants in the Canadian Labor Market", *Journal of Labor Economics* 12 (July), 369–405.

Bloom, D.E., G. Grenier and M. Gunderson (1995), "The Changing Labour Market Position of Canadian Immigrants", *Canadian Journal of Economics* 28, 987–1005.

Borjas, G.J. (1985), "Assimilation and Changes in Cohort Quality Revisited: What Happened to Immigrant Earnings in the 1980s", *Journal of Labor Economics* 3 (October), 463–489.

_____ (1995), "Assimilation, Changes in Cohort Quality Revisited and the Earnings of Immigrants", *Journal of Labor Economics* 13 (April), 201–245.

Card, D., J. DiNardo and E. Estes (2000), "The More Things Change: Immigrants and the Children of Immigrants in the 1940s, the 1970s and the 1990s", in G.J. Borjas (ed.), *Issues in the Economics of Immigration* (Chicago: University of Chicago Press and NBER), 227–269.

Chiswick, B.R. (1978), "The Effect of Americanization on the Earnings of Foreign-Born Men", *Journal of Political Economy* 86(5), 897–921.

Conference Board of Canada (2001), *Brain Gain: The Economic Benefits of Recognizing Learning and Learning Credentials in Canada* (Ottawa: The Conference Board of Canada).

Ferrer, A.M. and W.C. Riddell (2002), "The Role of Credentials in the Canadian Labour Market", *Canadian Journal of Economics* 35 (November), 879–905.

_____ (2003), "Education, Credentials and Immigrant Earnings" (Vancouver: Department of Economics, University of British Columbia). Unpublished paper.

Ferrer, A.M., D.A. Green and W.C. Riddell (2003), "Literacy Skills and Immigrant Earnings", mimeo, Department of Economics, University of British Columbia (June).

Friedberg, R.M. (2000), "You Can't Take it With You? Immigrant Assimilation and the Portability of Human Capital", *Journal of Labor Economics* 18 (April), 221–251.

Grant, M.L. (1999), "Evidence of New Immigrant Assimilation in Canada", *Canadian Journal of Economics* 32 (August), 930–955.

Green, D.A. and W.C. Riddell (2003), "Literacy and Earnings: An Investigation of the Interaction of Cognitive and Unobserved Skills in Earnings Generation", *Labour Economics* 10, 165–184.

Green, D.A. and C. Worswick (2002), "Earnings of Immigrant Men in Canada: The Roles of Labour Market Entry Effects and Returns to Foreign Experience". Study prepared for Citizenship and Immigration Canada.

Human Resources Development Canada (2002), *Knowledge Matters: Skills and Learning for Canadians* (Ottawa: Human Resources Development Canada).

McDonald, T. and C. Worswick (1998), "The Earnings of Immigrant Men in Canada: Job Tenure, Cohort and Macroeconomic Conditions", *Industrial and Labor Relations Review* 51 (April), 465–482.

Reitz, J.G. (2001), "Immigrant Skill Utilization in the Canadian Labour Market: Implications of Human Capital Research", *Journal of International Migration and Integration* 2(3), 347–378.

Sweetman, A. (2003), "Immigrant Source Country School Quality and Canadian Labour Market Outcomes" (Kingston: School of Policy Studies, Queen's University). Unpublished paper.

Panel Comments

Yvan Turcotte

I am not an economist, but a plain public servant. I have learned much at the conference, but I still have a number of questions. I will raise three of them here.

My first question or set of questions deals with what we call the education criterion in the selection grid, with the fact that some immigrants who were selected on the basis of their human capital, including their education level, become underemployed, not being able to find a job that is the kind of job their level of education should command for them. We view the situation as a waste of human capital, and we may blame it often on the difficulties these immigrants have in getting their diplomas recognized, or on the rigidity of the rules of admittance to the professional associations, or on the fact that these immigrants do not have a network of friends and relatives to help them to find the most appropriate job, or on the possibility that some employers are discriminating against immigrants from some origins. Probably all of these reasons have some basis, but I wonder if there is not another reason for this situation. Maybe it has something to do with the fact that the diplomas that are issued by various universities do not have the same weight, the same market value. The diploma that a person gets from Harvard or from the Sorbonne or from Queen's University might have a higher value on the market than the diploma that someone gets from a Third World university. After all, all universities and colleges do not have the same level of means, the same amount of resources coming from the state or from private sources to pay the best teachers, to help them to conduct their research, to buy the best equipment, or to organize conferences on immigration. I am fully aware that this question is a tricky one, a very sensitive question. I do not want to suggest in any way that the difference of value of diplomas should be related to the difference of value on the people bearing these diplomas. For instance, if someone from the Third World studies in a rich country's university, he or she should not have any more difficulty to find a job than a native who studied at the same university. If he or she does have more difficulty it means that there are other factors such as those that I have referred to before. But still it is a worthwhile question. Indeed, I will add a related question. If such a market value of diplomas exist, should it be reflected or taken into account in the selection grids? Should we decide on the number of points we give to the "quality" of education, not only to the level or the field of the study but also to the institution that delivered the diploma?

The second question I want to raise has to do with demography. This conference is about immigration policy needed for the twenty-first century. To address this question, most of the presentations during the conference focused on economic questions and issues. Except for Roderic Beaujot's paper, we did not hear a lot about demographic issues, even if, as we all know, the current demographic dynamics in Canada and in Quebec obviously provide a reason to look at the role immigrants might play in shaping the demographic future of the country. The purpose of the policy of immigration and of its selection tools is to achieve a balance between different considerations — humanitarian, family, and economic issues are mirrored in the grids and the planning we do. For example, besides the points we are giving now for education, occupation, linguistic ability, should we not give more points for demographic criteria like the age of the principal applicant as well as the age of the spouse or even the fact that there is a spouse and the fact that there are children, and the age of the children? My question is, within the trade-off that the selection grid is made of, should we increase the weight of demographic factors in the final decision even if the result of doing so is that we end up with principal applicants who have lower levels of education or lower language ability but who would be younger, would have more children. I know that other categories like the humanitarian class may already provide us with younger people. But still, is the current balance we achieve the optimal balance regarding the demographic objectives we may have in immigration?

Finally, the last question I wish to raise. Except for some of the opening remarks delivered by Alfred MacLeod at the beginning of the conference, we did not talk about what I would call the social consciousness or, should

I say, the national consciousness that is needed to continue or carry on with an open immigration policy. This kind of consciousness should be the very basis of such a policy. Now I know this is difficult to achieve or even to measure. Immigration has a tremendous consequence at the economic level, but also at the social, cultural, and demographic levels. It shapes over decades the very fabric of a society or a community. Is the population involved enough in the decision-making process regarding immigration? Is this process that leads to decision-making open enough to allow, say, a policy to admit up to 1% of the Canadian population year after year? In Quebec's Immigration Department we take pride in the fact that polls show that the Quebec population supports immigration. The polls show that a clear majority of Quebecers thinks that we should maintain or increase the intake of immigrants. For example, a recent survey, I think it was in the year 2000, conducted all over the country showed that 70% of Quebecers thought at that time that immigration was not too high. When you add those who said it was just enough and those who said we should have room for some more, you get to 70%. The same survey showed that this proportion was 57% in the rest of Canada. For a community where efforts to maintain itself are sometimes described as tribal by some commentators, this is a very refreshing result. I think that it is a manifestation of a certain openness or opening towards immigration. It perhaps also reflects the fact that, in Quebec for the last 20 years, we have been conducting a general consultation every three years with the population on immigration objectives and maybe has helped sustain such an attitude of ongoing immigration.

Summary of Discussion

Michael Baker made several points. First, if Canada charges new immigrants a processing fee (in effect a "head tax"), one of the options that might be considered is to pay the funds so-raised back to the country that sent them for their education and other contributions that they have put into that person up to that point in time.

Second, the "dependency ratio" should not be viewed as a single number, but should be broken down between young and elderly because of the different costs associated with each. In Canada, for example, there are substantial income transfers that go to the elderly. Indeed, for many elderly, the term "dependency" does not seem appropriate nowadays because of their financial security.

Third, if Canada is going to foster second-tier cities selling their packages to prospective immigrants abroad, it would be an idea for these communities to first try them out in Canada, perhaps in Atlantic Canada and elsewhere where unemployment rates are currently high. Alice Nakamura reinforces this point. How people and jobs get matched up in the labour market is not straightforward. Employers in Alberta outside the big cities may have job openings that job-seekers in Atlantic Canada, say, know nothing about. Fostering information on job openings more widely across regions within Canada is important. But also surveys of immigrants and of locals in the labour market should make a point of asking people how they found their jobs so that more research can be done in this whole area of job-worker matching for both immigrants and native-born.

Barry Chiswick briefly noted that, beyond analyzing why people move from one country to another, there is a further question posed by Paul Miller in Australia of looking at why people choose to stay. The biggest single reason he and others can find for why people stay is that they have children when they come here and they are looking at the quality of life — security, stability, democracy — provided for the next generation.

Summary of Discussion

Contributors

Michael G. Abbott is Associate Professor in the Department of Economics at Queen's University.

Naomi Alboim is a Fellow in the School of Policy Studies at Queen's University.

Abdurrahman Aydemir is a Senior Research Economist in the Family and Labour Studies Division at Statistics Canada and in the Department of Economics at the University of Western Ontario.

Charles M. Beach is Professor in the Department of Economics and Director of the John Deutsch Institute at Queen's University.

Roderic Beaujot is Professor in the Population Studies Centre within the Department of Sociology at the University of Western Ontario.

David Card is Professor in the Department of Economics at the University of California at Berkeley.

Barry Chiswick is Research Professor and Head of the Department of Economics at the University of Illinois at Chicago.

Gerald L. Clément is the Assistant Deputy Minister in the Immigration and Multiculturalism Division at Manitoba Labour and Immigration.

Don DeVoretz is Professor in the Department of Economics at Simon Fraser University and is Co-Director of RIIM, and IZA Research Fellow.

W. Erwin Diewert is Professor in the Department of Economics at the University of British Columbia.

John F. Dovidio is Professor in the Department of Psychology at Colgate University.

Victoria M. Esses is in the Department of Psychology at the University of Western Ontario.

Eric Fong is Associate Professor in the Department of Sociology at the University of Toronto.

Marc Frenette is in the Business and Labour Market Analysis Division of Statistics Canada.

Alan G. Green is Professor Emeritus in the Department of Economics at Queen's University.

Gilles Grenier, Professeur titulaire, Département de science économique, Université d'Ottawa.

Louis Grignon is the Director of Income Security and Labour Market Studies at Human Resources Development Canada.

Vincent Hildebrand is Assistant Professor in the Department of Economics at Glendon College, York University.

Gordon Hodson is in the Department of Psychology at the University of Wales, Swansea.

Feng Hou is in the Business and Labour Market Analysis Division at Statistics Canada.

Martha Justus is a Manager in the Strategic Research and Data Division, Priorities, Planning and Research Branch at Citizenship and Immigration Canada.

Violet Kaspar is Assistant Professor in the Department of Psychiatry at the University of Toronto and Scientist at the Centre for Addiction and Mental Health-Clark Site in Toronto.

Samuel Laryea is in the Applied Research Branch, Strategic Policy, at Human Resources Development Canada.

Jessie-Lynn MacDonald is a Project Manager in the Special Survey Division at Statistics Canada.

Alfred MacLeod is Assistant Deputy Minister of Strategic Directions and Communications at Citizenship and Immigration Canada.

Stephan McBride is a doctoral student in the Department of Economics at Stanford University.

James Ted McDonald is Associate Professor in the Department of Economics at the University of New Brunswick.

John McHale is Associate Professor in the School of Business at Queen's University.

Alice Nakamura is Professor of Management Science in the School of Business at the University of Alberta.

Masao Nakamura is in the Commerce Faculty and is Director of the Centre for Japanese Research at the University of British Columbia.

Doug Norris is Director General with the Census and Demographic Statistics Branch at Statistics Canada.

Garnett Picot is Director General with the Socio-Economic Analysis Branch in the Business and Labour Market Analysis Division at Statistics Canada.

Jeffrey G. Reitz is Professor of Sociology, and the R.F. Harney Professor of Ethnic, Immigration and Pluralism Studies in the Munk Centre for International Studies at the University of Toronto.

W. Craig Riddell is Professor in the Department of Economics at the University of British Columbia.

Janice Gross Stein is the Belzberg Professor of Conflict Management and the Director of the Munk Centre for International Studies at the University of Toronto.

Arthur Sweetman is Associate Professor in the School of Policy Studies at Queen's University.

Yvan Turcotte, sous-ministre adjoint, Ministère des Relations avec les citoyens et de l'Immigration.

Bert Waslander is a Senior Research Associate at Informetrica Limited.

Stuart J. Wilson is Assistant Professor in the Department of Economics at the University of Regina.

Christopher Worswick is Associate Professor in the Department of Economics at Carleton University.

Queen's Policy Studies
Recent Publications

The Queen's Policy Studies Series is dedicated to the exploration of major policy issues that confront governments in Canada and other western nations. McGill-Queen's University Press is the exclusive world representative and distributor of books in the series.

John Deutsch Institute for the Study of Economic Policy

Framing Financial Structure in an Information Environment, Thomas J. Courchene and Edwin H. Neave (eds.), Policy Forum Series no. 38, 2003
Paper ISBN 0-88911-950-3 Cloth ISBN 0-88911-948-1

Towards Evidence-Based Policy for Canadian Education/Vers des politiques canadiennes d'éducation fondées sur la recherche, Patrice de Broucker and/et Arthur Sweetman (eds./dirs.), 2002   Paper ISBN 0-88911-946-5
Cloth ISBN 0-88911-944-9

Money, Markets and Mobility: Celebrating the Ideas of Robert A. Mundell, Nobel Laureate in Economic Sciences, Thomas J. Courchene (ed.), 2002
Paper ISBN 0-88911-820-5 Cloth ISBN 0-88911-818-3

The State of Economics in Canada: Festschrift in Honour of David Slater, Patrick Grady and Andrew Sharpe (eds.), 2001   Paper ISBN 0-88911-942-2
Cloth ISBN 0-88911-940-6

The 2000 Federal Budget: Retrospect and Prospect, Paul A.R. Hobson and Thomas A. Wilson (eds.), Policy Forum Series no. 37, 2001   Paper ISBN 0-88911-816-7
Cloth ISBN 0-88911-814-0

School of Policy Studies

Delicate Dances: Public Policy and the Nonprofit Sector, Kathy L. Brock (ed.), 2003   Paper ISBN 0-88911-953-8 Cloth ISBN 0-88911-955-4

Beyond the National Divide: Regional Dimensions of Industrial Relations, Mark Thompson, Joseph B. Rose and Anthony E. Smith (eds.), 2003
Paper ISBN 0-88911-963-5 Cloth ISBN 0-88911-965-1

The Nonprofit Sector in Interesting Times: Case Studies in a Changing Sector, Kathy L. Brock and Keith G. Banting (eds.), 2003
Paper ISBN 0-88911-941-4 Cloth ISBN 0-88911-943-0

Clusters Old and New: The Transition to a Knowledge Economy in Canada's Regions, David A. Wolfe (ed.), 2003 Paper ISBN 0-88911-959-7
Cloth ISBN 0-88911-961-9

Knowledge, Clusters and Regional Innovation: Economic Development in Canada, J. Adam Holbrook and David A. Wolfe (eds.), 2002
Paper ISBN 0-88911-919-8 Cloth ISBN 0-88911-917-1

Lessons of Everyday Law/Ledroit du quotidien, Roderick Alexander Macdonald, 2002   Paper ISBN 0-88911-915-5 Cloth ISBN 0-88911-913-9

Improving Connections Between Governments and Nonprofit and Voluntary Organizations: Public Policy and the Third Sector, Kathy L. Brock (ed.), 2002 Paper ISBN 0-88911-899-X Cloth ISBN 0-88911-907-4

Governing Food: Science, Safety and Trade, Peter W.B. Phillips and Robert Wolfe (eds.), 2001   Paper ISBN 0-88911-897-3 Cloth ISBN 0-88911-903-1

The Nonprofit Sector and Government in a New Century, Kathy L. Brock and Keith G. Banting (eds.), 2001   Paper ISBN 0-88911-901-5 Cloth ISBN 0-88911-905-8

The Dynamics of Decentralization: Canadian Federalism and British Devolution, Trevor C. Salmon and Michael Keating (eds.), 2001   ISBN 0-88911-895-7

Institute of Intergovernmental Relations

Canada: The State of the Federation 2001, vol. 15, *Canadian Political Culture(s) in Transition,* Hamish Telford and Harvey Lazar (eds.), 2002 Paper ISBN 0-88911-863-9 Cloth ISBN 0-88911-851-5

Federalism, Democracy and Disability Policy in Canada, Alan Puttee (ed.), 2002 Paper ISBN 0-88911-855-8 Cloth ISBN 1-55339-001-6, ISBN 0-88911-845-0 (set)

Comparaison des régimes fédéraux, 2ᵉéd., Ronald L. Watts, 2002 ISBN 1-55339-005-9

Health Policy and Federalism: A Comparative Perspective on Multi-Level Governance, Keith G. Banting and Stan Corbett (eds.), 2001 Paper ISBN 0-88911-859-0 Cloth ISBN 1-55339-000-8, ISBN 0-88911-845-0 (set)

Disability and Federalism: Comparing Different Approaches to Full Participation, David Cameron and Fraser Valentine (eds.), 2001   Paper ISBN 0-88911-857-4 Cloth ISBN 0-88911-867-1, ISBN 0-88911-845-0 (set)

Federalism, Democracy and Health Policy in Canada, Duane Adams (ed.), 2001 Paper ISBN 0-88911-853-1 Cloth ISBN 0-88911-865-5, ISBN 0-88911-845-0 (set)

Available from: McGill-Queen's University Press
c/o Georgetown Terminal Warehouses
34 Armstrong Avenue
Georgetown, Ontario L7G 4R9
Tel: (877) 864-8477
Fax: (877) 864-4272
E-mail: orders@gtwcanada.com